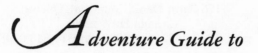
*A*dventure Guide to

Ireland

Tina Neylon

HUNTER

HUNTER PUBLISHING, INC,
130 Campus Drive, Edison, NJ 08818
☎ 732-225-1900; 800-255-0343; fax 732-417-1744
www.hunterpublishing.com

Ulysses Travel Publications
4176 Saint-Denis, Montréal, Québec
Canada H2W 2M5
☎ 514-843-9882, ext. 2232; fax 514-843-9448

Windsor Books
The Boundary, Wheatley Road, Garsington
Oxford, OX44 9EJ England
☎ 01865-361122; fax 01865-361133

ISBN 1-58843-367-6
© 2004 Hunter Publishing, Inc.

*This and other Hunter travel guides are also available as e-books
through Amazon.com, NetLibrary.com and other digital partners. For
more information, e-mail us at comments@hunterpublishing.com.*

Cover photo: *Co. Clare, Cliffs of Moher* (see page 307).
All photos courtesy Failte Ireland unless otherwise indicated.
Back cover photo: *Co. Roscommon, Roscommon Abbey* (see page 373),
Ireland West Tourism.

Maps by Toni Wheeler, © 2004 Hunter Publishing, Inc.
Index by Nancy Wolff

2   3   4

Contents

Maps

Introduction

Ireland has a lot to offer – unforgetta-ble scenery, friendly people, and op-portunities to enjoy a huge range of sports, entertainment of all kinds, and historic sites to explore.

Whether it's attending the theater, lis-tening to talented musicians, or discov-ering our history in the countryside or in the many museums all over the is-land, there is much to make a stay truly unforgettable. With about 100 million people worldwide claiming some Irish ancestry, you may be inter-ested in coming here to discover your roots.

Outside our cities are areas where you can spend hours away from the hustle and bustle of modern life, where there is hardly any traffic and the only sounds you hear are birds singing or waves crashing against the shore. Although a small island, Ireland has a surprisingly varied land-scape, even within each county.

One of its greatest assets is its people, who are generally friendly and talkative. Many of the Irish are creative, and our writers, dramatists, composers and musicians have an international reputation that is stag-gering, considering the size of the country. Irish visual artists, film-makers, craftspeople and fashion designers are renowned throughout the world.

Whether you come to Ireland to fish, play golf, or walk its hills, to attend an artistic event, to visit our heritage sites, to discover your roots, or just because you want to relax and do nothing in attractive surroundings, there really is something for you here.

The island is made up of the Republic of Ireland and Northern Ireland, the latter being part of the UK (the United Kingdom of Great Britain and Northern Ireland). Northern Ireland is called Ulster, "the Six Counties," or just the North. To avoid confusion, I use the Republic or the North to distinguish between the two parts of the island. Where material refers to the entire island, it is called Ireland. Those of us who live in the Republic call our country Ireland, and not Éire – its name in Irish and used only on our postage stamps.

The People & Their Culture

■ Population

The population of the Republic is 3.9 million (Census 2002) and of Northern Ireland 1.6 million (Census 2001). The majority live in urban centers, with the counties along the western seaboard sparsely populated. Some 40% of the entire population of the Republic lives within 60 miles (97 km) of Dublin; only 9% live in its northwest region, made up of counties Cavan, Donegal, Leitrim, Monaghan and Sligo.

Northern Ireland is the second most sparsely populated part of the UK, after Scotland, with 317 people per square mile (122 per square km), and with a predominantly young population – 25% under 16 and 37% under 25.

■ Religion

The Republic's Constitution guarantees freedom of conscience and the free profession and practice of religion to all citizens. According to a recent census, the population's religions were: Roman Catholic, 91%; Church of Ireland (Anglican), 2.5%; Presbyterian, 0.4%; Methodist, 0.1%; Jewish, less than 0.1%; and about 3% belonging to other religious groupings or with no specific beliefs.

While the majority of the population in the Republic still marries in church and have their children christened, few attend church regularly, especially in urban centers.

Northern Ireland's Two Communities

Protestants outnumber Catholics, although there has been significant inter-marriage. In the 2001 census, 40.3% stated their religion as Catholic, an increase of 3% in 10 years, and 20.7% as Presbyterian, 15.3% as Church of Ireland and 3.5% as Methodist. A further 6.1% belonged to other Protestant, Christian or Christian-related denominations, and 0.3% stated they belonged to other religions, while 13.8% indicated they had no religion or didn't answer the question. Protestants are overwhelmingly Presbyterian and have religious, cultural and familial links with Scotland.

Catholics are in the majority in some parts of Ulster – Derry city, Co. Fermanagh, Co. Armagh and parts of Belfast – while making up less than 10% of the population in other areas: Larne and the Co. Antrim coast, Bangor and North Down, east Belfast.

■ Social Change

There have been huge changes in attitude towards sexuality over the last 20 years or so, although conservative groups continue to be a force. Note that divorce became legal in the Republic only in the 90s. The Irish have what could be called an "ostrich attitude" – stick your head in the sand, pretend there isn't a problem and it will go away!

Some of the changes have come about through the influence of television, which arrived in 1962, and among the most popular programs are British soaps and American comedies like *Friends* and *The Simpsons*.

Now, at last, there's an acceptance of couples living together out of wedlock and of children born to single mothers or co-habiting couples, although you do still hear some criticism. Attitudes towards homosexuality have been slower to change, and there's very much of an urban-rural divide. Some of this is caused by ignorance and a confusion about pedophilia within the Catholic Church in the 90s, so gays unfortunately are seen as dangerous to children.

Cities have gay pubs and clubs, publications, help lines and a general acceptance, but in quieter areas of the Republic there is still prejudice, or at least what is perceived as such, and gays are often reluctant to "come out"

Gay visitors should not worry, as tourists are accepted and not expected to have the same mores as residents. However, whatever your sexuality, be sensible about how you behave in public, especially in villages and rural areas.

■ The Outside World

The Irish have always traveled overseas, from the days when missionaries went out with their Christian message throughout Europe. Conditions at home meant that millions emigrated over the centuries, and it was only in the 1990s that more Irish returned than left the country. That happened because of the economic success of the Republic, which brought other changes, not all good.

You will be surprised, even shocked, at the ugliness of some of the houses and hotels built over the last 20 years or so – even in scenic areas of the Republic.

Overseas, we are thought of as a nation of talkers and to some extent that is still true, especially in rural areas. In the Republic, our cities, especially Dublin, are choked with traffic, and house prices are astronomical, so people are under more pressure than they used to be. That means we are more inclined to keep our distance from each other and from visitors.

In most rural towns and villages there is still a more relaxed attitude; you'll be greeted on the street, and conversation will be initiated in the pub or shop. Sadly, though, *céad míle fáilte* (a hundred thousand welcomes) is no longer true everywhere.

In shops, restaurants and hotels in the cities of the Republic these days you will often be served by non-nationals, which is a new experience. Up to 20 years ago most Irish met non-Caucasians only overseas, and some in the Republic have reacted with racist attitudes towards those who come here as refugees or economic migrants – seeing them as a threat. The situation wasn't helped by the Irish government, which was very slow to develop fair policies, although they have improved. You do still see patently unjust treatment – especially toward blacks – as when they are singled out on the Enterprise train between Belfast and Dublin and asked for identification.

In Northern Ireland, the people are generally very welcoming. With unrest for so many years, the tourism industry was adversely affected and now that the Peace Process has brought new investment there are lots of new buildings in the cities.

Of course, it is not advisable to go to areas where there is sectarian tension, but such places are few these days. The rural areas of the North are absolutely beautiful, the towns and villages very attractive and the people charming.

■ Political Discussions

While most of us are proud of our heritage and quick to react to criticism from outsiders, many have become far more self-critical than we used to be. Perhaps that's a sign of a new self-confidence.

In the Republic, the majority are bored or frustrated with political problems in the North and it may come as a surprise to visitors that it is difficult to engage them in conversation on the subject. The opposite is true in the North, where it is much more a live issue, and people there seem happy to discuss the political and social scene in the Republic as well as in their own part of the country.

■ Fun & Pride

The Irish have a huge appetite for fun (or *craic*, pronounced "crack"), and great pride in their achievements worldwide in such areas as sports, music, and literature. Sports are a passion with most of us – especially GAA (Gaelic Athletic Association) or the games of hurling and Gaelic football. Soccer is equally popular, particularly since the Republic qualified for the

World Cup in the 90s. English soccer teams have thousands of supporters in Ireland.

■ Music

All types of music are popular, from classical to hard rock. The main classical performing groups are the **National Symphony Orchestra of Ireland** and the **Ulster Orchestra**. Among well-known classical performers are flautist James Galway and pianist John O'Conor. Opera always attracts big audiences, and the annual festival in Wexford is internationally renowned. Unfortunately, classically trained singers have to work overseas much of their time as there is no state-supported opera company.

Traditional & Popular

Traditional music experienced a massive revival from the 1960s on, helped by the genius of composer Sean Ó Riada. Groups such as The Dubliners and The Chieftains appeared, who are still popular today. In the 70s, Horslips merged the traditional with hard rock, and the Boomtown Rats, led by Bob Geldof, brought punk to Ireland.

Some of the big names in music worldwide are Irish, including U2, Van Morrison, Enya, and the late Rory Gallagher. Solo singers like Christy Moore, Brian Kennedy, Sinead O'Connor, Mary Black, and Dolores Keane, are very popular. In recent years The Corrs, a family from Dundalk, have become very successful, and their music, while belonging in the pop genre, has a distinctly Irish sound. The boy band Westlife and singer Samantha Mumba are successful overseas and at home.

The most successful of all Irish musicians on the contemporary scene is the rock group U2, with their lead singer Bono. He's known worldwide for his work on world debt with Bob Geldof, organizer of Live Aid, which raised money for famine relief. Knighted in Britain, he is now Sir Bob.

TRADITIONAL MUSIC

Traditional music is played in many pubs. Sometimes they're organized sessions, others are impromptu and anyone who can play is welcome to join in. Instruments include the bodhrán, (a hand-held drum made from goatskin), the fiddle, tin whistle, accordion, the mandolin, and the spoons. (Yes, they are ordinary spoons, but, in the hands of someone who can play them, they give a great sound.) Sessions often include unaccompanied singing. Go to at least one session.

■ Dance

Irish dancing has also experienced a renaissance since the eruption of Riverdance on the scene in 1994. Conceived as an interval act for the Eurovision Song Contest, the combination of music by Limerick-born Bill Whelan and the performance of a troupe of dancers led by Irish-Americans Jean Butler and Michael Flatley, it was the most exciting performance most of us had ever seen of Irish dancing. Riverdance became a full-length show, with three separate troupes touring the world – such was its success.

From being judged by many as rather antiquated and stiff, the toe-tapping rhythms of traditional Irish dance became, literally overnight, something we want to watch, take part in and export.

■ Film

The Irish love the cinema, and attendance grows year after year. There are art-house cinemas in cities on both sides of the border, and there are also annual festivals. The **Cork Film Festival** is one of the oldest anywhere – celebrating 50 years in 2005.

With the wonderful locations it offers, and many trained crew and talented actors, it's no wonder that Ireland is often used by film-makers from overseas. *Braveheart* and *Saving Private Ryan* were among recent feature films that used Irish locations. Many of the biggest names in cinema have worked here, including Alfred Hitchcock, John Ford, David Lean and John Huston, who made his home here. The John Huston School of Film was established at University College, Galway, in 2003.

There's also a thriving film industry in the country, with film-makers going on to success working overseas; others have achieved international attention while staying here. Directors Jim Sheridan and Neil Jordan won Oscars for their feature films, *My Left Foot* and *The Crying Game*, and Irish actors, such as Gabriel Byrne, Liam Neeson, Pierce Brosnan, and Colin Farrell, have become international stars of the screen.

■ A Nation of Writers

The Irish are renowned for writing – from the early Christian period when we were known as "the island of saints and scholars" there's been a fascination with the written word, in both Irish and English. The Celtic Revival or Irish Literary Renaissance of the late 19th and early 20th century was a reminder of how the country has a culture distinct from Britain. The leading writers of that period included WB Yeats, playwright John Millington Synge (*The Playboy of the Western World*) and George Moore.

Ulysses by James Joyce (1882-1941) is considered one of the most innovative novels of the 20th century. Leading poets include the late Louis MacNeice and Patrick Kavanagh, and Seamus Heaney, John Montague and Thomas Kinsella. Leading prose writers include Flann O'Brien, Elizabeth Bowen, Frank O'Connor, John McGahern and Roddy Doyle (who won the Booker Prize), and William Trevor.

∎ Theater

 The Abbey was founded during the Celtic Revival and is the **National Theatre of Ireland**. There's a huge amateur drama movement all over the island, and a number of small professional companies tour the many venues. Talented contemporary dramatists, including Brian Friel, Conor McPherson, Marie Jones, and Martin McDonagh, are following in the footsteps of Oliver Goldsmith, Richard Brinsley Sheridan, Oscar Wilde, George Bernard Shaw and Sean O'Casey. Samuel Beckett, both novelist and dramatist, was one of the most influential writers anywhere in the 20th century.

Nobel Prize Winners
George Bernard Shaw, Samuel Beckett, and poets WB Yeats and Seamus Heaney were all awarded the Nobel Prize for Literature.

∎ Visual Arts

 There are hundreds of galleries, most of which can be visited for free, and a network of arts centers where you'll see works by contemporary artists. Pay a visit to the **Ulster Museum** in Belfast and the **National Gallery** in Dublin to see art produced in previous centuries. Also look out for public sculptures as you travel around the country.

∎ Language

 English is the spoken language of Ireland. Irish is also used all over the island, though spoken with varying degrees of proficiency. In the Republic it was made a compulsory subject at school – which was counter-productive. It is only in recent years that most people have developed an enthusiasm for the language and its distinct culture, and in the Republic there are now many all-Irish schools. A lot of people in the Republic use some Irish words in conversation, and there is an Irish language radio station and television station, TG4, its programs subtitled in English.

> *I've never heard anyone ever say "Begorrah" or "Top of the morning to you" except on screen or as a joke!*

Native Irish-Speaking Areas

Gaeltachts are areas where the Irish language is still spoken and where residents are given financial incentives by the government for its promotion and for the preservation of our cultural heritage. Every summer thousands of Irish teenagers stay in Gaeltachts for three-week vacations to learn the language – they are sent home if caught speaking English!

There are sizeable *Gaeltacht* areas in Co. Donegal; Connemara, Co. Galway, Ring, Co. Waterford, and in Co. Meath. Also, Ballyvourney and Cuil Aodh (Coolea) and Cape Clear Island, which you can reach from Baltimore, all in West Cork, and Dingle, Ballyferriter and Dunchaoin (Dunquin) in Kerry. If you're interested, contact them at: ☎ (66) 915-2423 from overseas; info@gaelsaoire.ie; www.gaelsaoire.ie.

Road signs and the names on shops are in Irish in *Gaeltacht* areas. You'll hear the language spoken, but residents don't expect tourists to be able to answer! They also have pubs with traditional music sessions and *céilís* (literally translated as "dance gatherings"), especially during the summer season.

> *A céilí is great fun and visitors are encouraged to get up and dance. Often someone calls out directions for the dances, or you'll be helped by partners. The dances have titles, such as the Siege of Limerick or The Walls of Ennis. If you get the chance, go to one. The best are those attended by locals, which you'll find all over the country, rather than those organized with overseas visitors in mind.*

Ulster-Scots

Many, even among the Irish themselves, see the island as having only two languages and traditions, but this is incorrect. Northern Ireland has another distinct heritage, which is experiencing a huge revival of interest since the signing of the Good Friday Agreement in 1998. The agreement established the Ulster-Scots Agency as part of the North-South Language Body.

In the 1600s tens of thousands of Scots crossed the very narrow channel of the Irish Sea, which separates the two countries, and settled in Antrim and further afield. The majority of them spoke not Gaelic or English, but Scots, a Germanic language closely related to English. Its descendant is Ulster-Scots, also known as Ullans.

The Good Friday Agreement was the first official document to mention Ulster Scots and states that it represents "part of the cultural wealth of the island of Ireland" and is now "a recognized regional language" under the European Charter for Regional and Minority Languages.

The **Ulster-Scots Agency** has produced a fascinating series of free leaflets and other publications that include details of its legacy in the United States. It can be contacted at: 10-12 Brunswick Street, Belfast, ☎ (028) 9023 1113; fax 9023 1898; info@ulsterscotsagency.org.uk; www. ulsterscotsagency.com.

IRISH WORDS IN PLACE NAMES

Togher	track
Clon or cloon, from cluain	meadow
Curragh	grassy plain
Charraig	rock
Creagan	rocky place
Coill	woodland
Doire	oak wood
Tubber	sacred well
Inis	island
Clar	plain
Cnoc	hill
Dun	fort
Ri	king
Ard	high
Cil	church
Beg	little
Mor	big

■ Myths & Legends

 Two significant Irish legends are the Children of Lir and the Táin. You'll enjoy visiting sites associated with them if you know the stories.

The Children of Lir

Lir, a chieftain of the Tuatha de Danann tribe, married the beautiful Eva, daughter of King Bov the Red, and they were very happy. When Eva died young, Lir survived his broken heart only because of his love for their four children. He eventually married again, but his new wife Aoife (the Irish for Eve, pronounced "eefa") became insanely jealous of her stepchildren.

One day, when Lir was out hunting, she took the children to the shores of Lough (Lake) Derravaragh, where she cast a spell on them, turning them into swans, and condemning them to stay there for 300 years. After the 300 years passed, they spent another 300 years on the Sea of Moyle and a further 300 on Inis Glora in the Atlantic.

By then Saint Patrick had arrived in Ireland and was preaching about Christ. One of his followers, Kemoc, prayed with the children of Lir. As he did so, their white feathers fell away and he saw a very old woman and three ancient men. He baptised them. When they died they were buried in one grave as they wished. As Kemoc knelt to pray at their graveside, four beautiful white swans took flight for the heavens.

The Táin

Its full title is Táin Bó Cuailgne – the Cattle Raid of Cooley. This tale is at the center of the Ulster Cycle of heroic tales, parts of which date from the eighth century, with some passages probably composed 200 years later, and considered Ireland's greatest epic. It tells the story of a cattle raid, the invasion of Ulster by the armies of Queen Maeve and King Ailill of Connacht and their allies, as they try to carry off the great Brown Bull of Cuailnge (Cooley).

One night Queen Maeve and her husband compare possessions; he owns a great white bull called Finnbennach, which only the great Brown Bull can equal, so she sets off with her armies determined to return with the Brown Bull. Only Cúchulainn, the greatest of all Celtic heroes, who guards the Bull and the lands of Ulster, stands in her way, but his warriors have fallen asleep under a spell. There are many battles before Maeve eventually captures the Bull and sets off home, but the Ulster warriors wake and defeat her armies. The white and brown bulls fight, and both are killed.

The Táin Trail

The Táin Trail, a cycling or driving route, takes in a number of sites, some associated with events in The Táin. It covers approximately 365 miles/585 km from Rathcroghan, Co. Roscommon, in the west, where the Royal Palace of Queen Maeve stood, across the middle of the country to the Cooley peninsula, and back again. There's a trail map guide available from Tourist Offices that lists recommended accommodations. See pages 114, 115 and 190 for trail details.

Introduction

There's a marvelous translation of the epic from Irish by Thomas Kinsella, with brush drawings by Louis le Brocquy, published by Oxford University Press – look for a copy.

History

■ Prehistory

There are traces of food-gatherers and hunters dating back to the Mesolithic period, around 8000 BC, but the first inhabitants who left signs of buildings and boundary walls were Neolithic peoples, who arrived 6,000 years ago from Britain or Europe to grow crops and breed livestock. They are responsible for the many megalithic monuments, including dolmens, court-cairns and passage-tombs, dotting the landscape today.

The Bronze Age, from about 2500 to 600 BC, saw the exploitation of Ireland's rich deposits of copper and left a legacy of bronze axe and spearheads, shields, cauldrons and tools. The most beautiful are those made for personal ornament, often in gold and a half-moon shape, including earrings, dress fasteners, and jewelry for the neck or hair. Stone circles and wedge tombs were built in this period.

The first Celtic people appeared during the Iron Age after 600 BC. Large enclosures on hills, such as the one at Tara, Co. Meath, and some cliff-top promontory forts date from this time. You will also see many ring-forts, which were established by wealthy farmers. They were called "raths" if they had earthen banks, or "cashels" if they had stone walls.

■ The Arrival of Christianity

The first written records are documents ascribed to the missionary Saint Patrick in the fifth century. A substantial body of literature survives from that time in both Latin and Irish – including annals, genealogies, and king lists. By the middle of the sixth century, monasteries had become centers of learning and art, where the Bible was studied, and manuscripts were copied, many of them beautifully illuminated. This was the time that Ireland became known as "the island of saints and scholars," when missionaries and teachers traveled to Britain and throughout Europe.

Law tracts from the seventh and eighth centuries give a good idea of society at that time, a hierarchy of kings, clerics and poets, the free and enslaved. The country was never united politically, although 150 or so minor kingdoms shared a common culture. Kings ruled locally, there were over-kings who ruled a number of areas, and then others ruling a province. The Uí Néill (O'Neills), the leading dynasty for much of the period, were based in the northern half of Ireland, with their capital at Tara. They lost power in the early 11th century and then a number kings jostled for the position of High King.

■ The Vikings

Viking invaders started making incursions from the ninth century on and looked likely to take over the country. They founded towns at Dublin, Cork, Limerick, Waterford and Wexford, and developed trading networks overseas. Brian Boru is famous for his victory over them at the Battle of Clontarf in 1014, but his main importance is that he ended the monopoly of the Uí Néills as High Kings. Eventually, the Viking enclaves were assimilated and Irish kings who dominated them gained an advantage over their rivals.

■ The Anglo-Norman Invasion

 The first attempts to unite the island politically began with the Anglo-Norman invasion of 1170, which happened because they had been invited! Over the next 700 years, the island was ruled with varying degrees of success by the English (later the British) Crown.

Leading those first arrivals was the Earl of Pembroke, Richard de Clare, known as Strongbow. He landed in Co. Wexford with his army, invited into the country by Dermot MacMurrough, the King of Leinster, who had lost his throne to his rival high-king Rory O'Connor. Later, Strongbow married Aoife (Eve), daughter of MacMurrough, and became King of Leinster.

There's a famous painting by Daniel Maclise depicting the marriage of Aoife and Strongbow in the National Gallery, Dublin, which is huge and well worth a look.

In late 1171 King Henry II arrived with a large force and colonization increased. The invaders would build a large mound of raised earth surrounded by a fence, with a wooden tower on top. This primitive castle, known as a motte, was easy to defend and was used as a base for raiding the lands of the local Irish king. When the king was beaten, his land was shared among the invader's supporters. Military conquest was followed by the introduction of the agricultural system used in England, based on the manor, and peasants and artisans were encouraged to come to Ireland. Impressive castles replaced the wooden towers.

New towns sprang up all over the island, and today what remains of their walls and castles are a reminder of that period of economic boom in the 13th century. They include Kilkenny (left), Clonmel, Carrick, Carlow and New Ross in the southeast, Kinsale and Youghal in Co. Cork, Tralee in Kerry, Drogheda, Dundalk, Ardee, and Trim, all north of Dublin, and Carrickfergus in Co. Antrim. Sligo, Galway, Athenry, Nenagh, Athlone, Roscommon and Mullingar were also founded by the English during this period.

■ Beyond the Pale

Resistance to the invader continued and, by the late 15th century, the power of the English monarch was restricted to a small area around Dublin. In order to protect it, a line of fortifications called the Pale was built and the Irish outside it were regarded as savages. The expression "beyond the pale," still used today, survives from that period.

In 1541 Henry VIII changed his title from Lord of Ireland to King of Ireland, the first English monarch to claim the whole island. When his daughter, the Protestant Elizabeth I, succeeded him in 1558 there was a huge increase in religious differences with the Catholic Irish, leading to a number of rebellions during her reign. The greatest of them was led by Hugh O'Neill, the Earl of Tyrone, who defeated the English at the Yellow Ford in 1598. Yellow Ford is 15 miles (24 km) from Drumcree, the center of intense inter-communal conflict every July to this day.

In 1601 Spanish troops landed at Kinsale, Co. Cork, and O'Neill marched to support them. The Battle of Kinsale marked the end of Gaelic Ireland, when O'Neill's men were decisively beaten by the English forces under Lord Mountjoy. O'Neill surrendered after Elizabeth offered him a pardon.

■ The Flight of the Earls

Faced with growing English influence, O'Neill and the Earl of Tyrconnell, Rory O'Donnell, and their families (a total of 99 men, women and children) left Ireland in 1607. Their destination was Spain, but storms drove them ashore in France and, eventually reaching Spanish Flanders, they discovered that Philip of Spain had made peace with King James and wouldn't help them recover their lands. The departure of the Gaelic nobles marked the end of an era and was a cultural disaster.

WHAT YOU CAN SEE NOW

There are six interpretative/heritage centers where you can learn about this period. The **Flight of the Earls Heritage Center** at Rathmullan, from where the Earls embarked, and the **Donegal Ancestry, Heritage Exhibition and Genealogy Center**, is not far away in Ramelton, both in Co. Donegal (see pages 392-93).

Over the border in Northern Ireland, visit the award-winning **Tower Museum** to learn all about the Siege of Derry. Travel on from there to the **Ulster Plantation Center** in Draperstown, see the miniature villages and **Manor Lodge at Moneymore** and **Bellaghy Bawn** a few miles away. For full details, see pages 15 and 485 or contact The Ulster Plantation Center, 50 High Street, Draperstown, ☎ (028) 7962-7800; fax 7962-7732; info@theflightoftheearls.com; www.theflightoftheearls.com.

■ The Plantation of Ulster

In 1609 began the systematic colonization, known as the Plantation of Ulster, at the time the most ambitious ever undertaken. Confiscated land in the counties of Donegal, Tyrone, Derry, Armagh, Cavan and Fermanagh were divided into precincts and then subdivided. They were given to the following: "servitors" – army commanders and the King's servants; "undertakers" – men of property who undertook to bring over Protestants from England and Scotland; and "deserving Irish" – those who had changed sides before the Earl's rebellion.

The town of Virginia in Cavan and the state of Virginia in America were founded at this time.

The first plantations of Irish lands had taken place earlier in the 1550s, mainly to seize the estates of the rebellious O'Mores and O'Connors on the borders of the Pale. Soldier-farmers were settled in Laois and Offaly, now in the Republic, which were renamed Queen's and King's counties.

The native Irish rebelled in 1641-42, killing a reported 12,000 settlers, and reprisals were carried out by an army of Scots led by General Robert Monro.

■ Cromwell

King Charles I was executed in 1649 and England was then ruled by Parliament. In Ireland, opposition to this was brutally suppressed by an army led by Oliver Cromwell. His name still evokes expressions of disgust, even hatred, in many parts of the country. He carried out massacres at Drogheda and Wexford, and thousands of Catholics were resettled or transported abroad, some sent to the island of Monserrat, where Saint Patrick's Day is still celebrated. Their land was seized – 41% of Antrim, 26% of Down, 34% of Armagh, 38% of Monaghan. Although Charles II was restored to the English throne in 1660, the land seizures were left largely untouched.

■ The Siege of Derry

In 1688, three years after being crowned, the Catholic King James II fled when William of Orange, later William III, landed in England. In Derry, 13 apprentice boys closed the gates of the city on December 7 in the face of Catholic soldiers.

The following year, James landed in Ireland with French troops and marched on Derry, to be met on April 18 with cries of "No surrender!" – a cry echoed in our own time by Ian Paisley and others who resist power-sharing with Catholics or nationalists.

King James laid siege to the city but failed to take it. Then, on July 1, 1690, William defeated him at the Battle of the Boyne and James fled back to France. The supremacy of the Protestants was assured by victory at the Battle of Aughrim in 1691. The Treaty of Limerick in the same year allowed 15,000 Irish soldiers to leave in order to serve France's Louis XIV and promised Catholic toleration, which was not fulfilled. In fact, the Penal Laws excluded them from political life and hindered their economic advancement.

WHAT YOU CAN SEE NOW

The Siege of Derry and the Battle of the Boyne were seminal events in Irish history, which have influenced our people ever since. If you're interested in learning about them, visit the following:

The Tower Museum, Derry, ☎ (028) 7137-2411, is open daily July-August, Tues.-Sat. rest of year.

The **Battle of the Boyne** site near Drogheda, ☎ (041) 984-1644, is open daily in summer.

Aughrim, on the main N6 Dublin-Galway road, four miles (6.4 km) west of Ballinasloe, ☎ (090) 9673939, is open Tues.-Sun., June-September.

■ A Peaceful Period

Next came a period of relative peace. During this time, colonists from England and Huguenots from France established the linen industry in Ulster, which grew to be the largest in the world. The great forests that had covered much of the country were cut down, which opened up more land for farming. Ulster, formerly the poorest of the four provinces, became the most prosperous.

Huguenots also settled in other parts of the country, including Cork and Dublin. They are now remembered in an area of Cork City Center and in the Huguenot graveyard at St. Stephen's Green in Dublin.

■ Political Unrest

The memories of dispossession, massacre and persecution etched into the consciousness of both Protestants and Catholic swas to lead to political and social unrest over the following centuries, right up to the present.

■ The Penal Laws

Reports in the 1690s that Irish who had fled abroad were encouraging a French invasion, added to an exaggeration of the 1641 "massacres," led to the introduction of anti-Catholic legislation. These measures restricted the freedom to educate their children, to carry arms, to inherit, own, lease or work land, to employ or trade, to enter the main professions, and in 1728 they were denied the vote.

Bear in mind that in 1732 Irish households were 73% Catholic.

■ The Georgian Period

The years from 1728 to 1793 mark the high point of Protestant Ascendancy – when many Palladian and neo-classical houses and beautifully landscaped demesnes were created. Estate villages were also laid out at this time. The ruling class was committed to the island's economic development and built a road network, constructed canals, and drained rivers. Limerick, Cork and Waterford grew substantially and the Wide Streets Commissioners transformed Dublin, sweeping away the crowded medieval streets. Fine new public buildings and wide thoroughfares linking elegant Georgian squares made it one of the most attractive cities of the period. Between 1692 and 1785 the Irish Parliament raised revenue and made laws.

■ The 1798 Rebellion

The 18th century was a period of prosperity for some, but sectarian unrest continued. In the 1780s, a group called the Catholic Defenders was formed in Co. Armagh to resist raids by Protestants, and in 1791, when the United Irishmen was founded in Belfast and Dublin, they joined them. The United Irishmen brought together Protestants, Dissenters and Catholics, initially in the hope of bringing about reforms, including Catholic emancipation. At first the British government reformed some of the Penal Laws, but that ended when in 1793 war broke out between revolutionary France and Britain. The National Assembly in Paris promised the assistance of France to all nations seeking freedom, and Theobald Wolf Tone went there to seek help for the Irish cause.

In December, 1796, French troops arrived off Bantry Bay, Co. Cork; only bad weather prevented the landing and saved Britain from defeat. After that, Irish society was polarized as many joined the British army and the United Irishmen's numbers swelled. By the Spring of 1798 a campaign of British terror was destroying the United Irishmen and many of its leaders had been arrested, including Theobald Wolf Tone and Robert Emmet. Those still free called an immediate rising before French aid could arrive. There were major rebellions in Wexford in the southeast and Antrim and Down in the north. Tens of thousands took part. There were minor skirmishes elsewhere, especially around Dublin.

After the defeat of the main risings, a small French Army landed on the west coast at Killala, Co. Mayo, in August. Thousands joined them and they succeeded in inflicting one major defeat on the British. By autumn, the rebellion had been brutally defeated, and many thousands killed.

The Lambeg Drum

The first time the giant drum was seen in Ireland was with the Dutch Guards Regiment accompanying King William on his way to the Boyne in 1690. Between then and 1795 the tradition of the drum survived in individual families and various Williamite societies. When the Orange Order was founded the drums provided a link with King William, and ever since have been used in marches. The drum got its name from the village where they were made for many years. Over the last 20 years regular drumming matches have taken place, the largest in Markethill, Co. Armagh, on the last Saturday in July, when 50-60 drummers take part. The Grand Orange Lodge of Ireland, Schomberg House, 368 Cregagh Road, Belfast, BT6 9YE, ☎ (028) 9070-1122, fax 9040-3700.

■ Catholic Emancipation & Daniel O'Connell

Although 1778-92 had seen the repeal of much anti-Catholic legislation, Catholics still could not sit in Parliament. The successful barrister Daniel O'Connell, born in Derrynane, Co. Kerry, founded the Catholic Association in 1823 and in the general election of 1826 Catholics voted for Members of Parliament sympathetic to their cause. In 1828 O'Connell won a by-election in Co. Clare but couldn't take his seat in Parliament until two years later when Catholics were emancipated.

O'Connell, known as the Liberator, then launched a campaign to repeal the Act of Union, supported by the Young Irelanders and the Church, and in 1843 organized huge meetings around the country. He was imprisoned when the one planned for Clontarf in Dublin was declared illegal.

THE ORANGE ORDER

The Loyal Orange Institution, usually known as the Orange Order, was founded in 1795 in Loughgall, a village in Co. Armagh, after the Battle of the Diamond between the Roman Catholic Defenders and the Protestants of the area. When it ended, the Protestants formed a circle, joined hands and declared their brotherhood in loyalty to the Crown, the country and the Reformed religion.

Although seen as bigoted and anti-Catholic by many, the Order argues that it is a positive rather than a negative force, that it does not foster intolerance, and that its condemnation of religious ideology is directed against church doctrine and not against individual members. Take a look at its website: www.grandorange.org.uk.

■ Emigration Before the Great Famine

In the 18th century most emigrants to America were Ulster-Scots from what is now Northern Ireland, who saw opportunities in the colonies. Starting small, their numbers rose to about 50,000 a year in the 1770s. Some were affluent, others went there as indentured servants. The American War of Independence interrupted the process, but by 1827 they were up to 20,000 a year again, reaching 65,000 in 1831-32 and averaging that number until 1845. Most of them landed first on Canadian soil.

Others were attracted to Britain, where the industrial revolution of the early 19th century meant more work opportunities. There were already significant numbers of Irish in most British cities by 1800, and they quickly increased. Between the 1780s and 1845, 50-65,000 Irish felons were transported to Australia, a minority of them political prisoners.

■ The Great Famine

Most people have only heard of the Great Famine of 1845, but in fact there were 16 crises about food, most often caused by bad weather, starting in the period from 1800.

When an incurable fungal disease attacked the potato crop in 1845, and recurred three times over the next four years, it was a disaster for the rural poor, who depended on the potato as their staple. Relief from official and private sources was woefully inadequate. Between 1845-49, roughly one million died, 40% from Connacht, 30% from Munster, 21% from Ulster and 9% from Leinster. Another million emigrated, and the population dropped to 6.5 million.

The Great Famine left a memory in the Irish psyche of a tragedy that could have been avoided. The country was still exporting grain while its people literally died on the roadsides as wagons passed them on their way to the ports.

Relief was sometimes given only if the starving peasantry would "earn" it by working – which is why there are famine walls and roads in some parts, including those in Mourne and in Fermoy, Co. Cork. Many others were taken into workhouses, where families were split up, and the meanest landlords evicted tenants who couldn't pay their rents. It's a period that still evokes shudders of horror from most Irish people. In 1999, the centenary of the Famine, Prime Minister of Britain Tony Blair apologized for British mishandling of the situation.

The Famine Walk

In Co. Mayo in March 1849, several hundred starving people set out on a desperate walk from Louisburgh to Doolough, struggling across 10 miles (16 km) of windswept boggy moors and treacherous mountain slopes. They were heading for a mansion where dinner was being served to the Board of Guardians, who had the powers to release food or issue certificates of destitution so the poor could enter the workhouse. The Louisburgh people were denied both. So they turned and headed home. On the way back about 100 men, women and children died.

You can still see the ridges and hollows of the potato beds and the ruins of many tiny stone dwellings in the Louisbourgh area and elsewhere, including on Achill Island.

In 1841 the Choctaw Indians in Mississippi were forced from their homelands to journey hundreds of miles to Oklahoma, many of them dying on the way in what became the Trail of Tears. In April 1847 the Choctaw Indians sent money to a famine relief fund in Ireland, reported in *The Arkansas Intelligencer.*

Every May there's a Famine Walk from Doolough to Louisburgh, often joined by one of the Choctaw Nation, and well-known campaigners for human rights. On the monument erected by AFRI (Aid from Ireland) in 1994 an inscription reads: "In 1991 we walked AFRI's great famine walk at Doolough and soon afterwards we walked the road to freedom in South Africa." (Archbishop Desmond Tutu)

■ Late 19th Century

A number of individuals and groups continued to contribute to the growth of political and cultural nationalism, while among Protestants the desire to maintain the Union (with Britain) gained in popularity. In the 1840s the Young Ireland movement, whose Thomas Davis edited the newspaper *The Nation*, agitated for reform. The Irish Parliamentary Party in London, led first by Isaac Butt and then by Charles Stewart Parnell, made some gains. A revolutionary wing to the nationalist movement, the Irish Republican Brotherhood, known as the Fenians, emerged.

The government introduced some reforms, including the Land Acts, transferring ownership from landlord to tenant, disestablished the Church of Ireland, and set up agencies to develop poor areas. These were not enough and agitation for independence continued. The Liberal Prime Minister Gladstone twice tried to introduce a Home Rule bill, which was defeated by the Conservatives and Unionists.

■ A Nation Once Again

Culturally, the Irish were developing their own identity. The **Gaelic Athletic Association** was founded in 1884, dedicated to traditional Irish sports, and in 1893 the **Gaelic League** was established with the aim of halting the decline of the language. It was the time too of the Irish Literary Renaissance, when a new pride was discovered in a culture distinct from Britain. In 1905, Sinn Féin (We Ourselves) was founded.

Captain Boycott

The word "boycott" comes from an incident during agitation about land in the 1880s, when Irish farmers rebelled against the cruelty of a landlord called Captain Boycott, and adopted the strategy which has been used around the world since then. A film called *Captain Boycott* was made in 1947 starring Stewart Granger.

■ The Ulster Question

A campaign of opposition to Home Rule was led by Edward Carson and James Craig from 1912-14, and included the signing of the Solemn League and Covenant, the formation of the Ulster Volunteer Force, and gun-running into Larne. It was concentrated in Ulster, where there was the greatest number of Protestants. The National Volunteers were formed to oppose them.

The outbreak of war in Europe in 1914 halted developments, as the Home Rule bill was suspended until its end. Ulster receiving special treatment, and its nine counties excluded from the bill, was opposed by nationalists.

■ The 1916 Rising

Led by inspirational figures, including Padraig Pearse and James Connolly, the Easter Rising was poorly planned, and a disaster for the Volunteers, with high casualties and the survivors interned. The insurrection lasted only six days, but its effects were far-reaching. The British, by executing its leaders, created martyrs who inspired others to follow them.

■ The War of Independence

In 1918 Sinn Féin had a huge victory in the General Election, except in Ulster. Dáil Eireann, a republican assembly, was founded the following year and a guerilla war started by the IRA. The British government reacted by recruiting ruthlessly aggressive units, called the Black and Tans because of their uniforms, to fight against them. It was another tactical mistake, as it lessened the government's moral authority in the eyes of the world.

There was a truce in 1921, following the formal partitioning of the country and the establishment of Northern Ireland, and a negotiating team went to London, led by Michael Collins and Arthur Griffith.

■ The Civil War

The Treaty they signed in December 1921 was unacceptable to many republicans – Collins remarked afterwards that he'd signed his own death warrant, which proved sadly true – as they felt it did not fully recognize the country's independence. Éamon de Valera, leader of the underground government during the War of Independence, was prominent among the dissenters. Civil War erupted in June 1922 and there was unrest for a year, with leading figures on both sides killed.

Treaty supporters under WT Cosgrave formed the first Cumann na nGaedheal (Fine Gael) government in 1923. In 1926 De Valera founded his own party, Fianna Fail, which came to power for the first time in 1932.

The Land

The island is strategically located on major air and sea routes between North America and northern Europe. It has been divided into four provinces for centuries: Ulster, Connaught, Leinster and Munster. Part of Ulster is in the Republic – which can be confusing for visitors, as many think it refers only to the political entity of Northern Ireland.

The Republic is slightly larger than West Virginia, with a total area of 26,706 square miles (70,280 sq km), of which 26,178 square miles (68,890 sq km) is land and 528 square miles (1,390 sq km) is water.

Northern Ireland is about the size of Connecticut and is part of the United Kingdom (UK) of Great Britain and Northern Ireland. It covers 5,500 square miles (14,300 square km), is about 85 miles (137 km) from north to south and 110 miles (177 km) wide. In the middle is Lough Neagh, the largest lake in the British Isles.

■ Climate

Ireland's climate is temperate maritime, moderated by the Gulf Stream, which brings warm waters to Western Europe from the Caribbean, and prevailing southwesterly winds.

Summer	57-61°F (14-16°C)
Winter	39-45°F (4-7°C)

Temperatures below 25°F (-4°C) are rare. The weather can be unpredict-able, with wonderful warm or sunny days at the most unexpected times and sudden heavy rain showers when the sky had appeared cloudless just minutes before.

The mean annual temperature is around 50°F (10°C). In winter only oc-casionally does the temperature drop to below 32°F (0°C) and snow is in-frequent. January and February are generally the coldest months of the year when average daily temperatures are 37-39°F (4°C-8°C). The warm-est months are July and August, with daytime temperatures ranging from 59 to 68°F (15°C-20°C). A hot day in summertime could produce temperatures of 72-75°F (22°C-24°C) and, on rare occasions, as high as 86°F (30°C).

Rainfall

Annual rainfall is about 43 inches (1,100 mm) and is well distributed throughout the year. It varies from 30 inches (750 mm) in parts of the east to between 40 and 50 inches (1,000-1,250 mm) in the west, with mountainous districts exceeding 80 inches (2,000 mm). Almost every-where the wettest months are December and January, and the driest is April, except in southern parts where it is June. There is little hail or snow. Ireland really is the Emerald Isle – with grass that shade of green because of the consistent humidity. Clouds drift in from the Atlantic all year round and often give the landscape, especially along the west, a misty dream-like appearance – what is referred to by residents as a "soft day."

■ Terrain

Most of the island is level, with a rolling interior plain surrounded by rug-ged hills and low mountains. There are sea cliffs along the west coast, in-cluding Slieve League in Co. Donegal, which are the highest in Europe, and the spectacular Cliffs of Moher in Co. Clare. The highest points on the island are Carrauntoohil in Co. Kerry (3,414 feet/1,041 m) and Slieve Donard, in the Mourne Mountains of Co. Down in the North (2,795 feet/852 m).

Flora & Fauna

 The island was separated from mainland Europe after the last great Ice Age, so it has a narrow range of flora and fauna. Native flora is temperate zone, with over 900 species of flowering plants, conifers and ferns. Most of the island is covered by grassland or peatland. Large areas of Clare, Galway and Mayo are limestone outcrops, and elsewhere there are ridges of limestone gravel, with scrubby woodland dominated by hazel, and sometimes ash and yew. Alder is another common tree, and there is a lot of holly, ivy and gorse. Of particular interest because of unusual geographic distribution are tropical species in the southwest, and Arctic Alpine reminders of the Ice Age as well as Mediterranean species in the unique Burren in Co. Clare.

 There's a lot of fascinating detail about flora on www.habitas.org.uk/flora.

In the countryside you are likely to see rabbits and hares, squirrels, sometimes hedgehogs, foxes, badgers, and the non-native mink, which causes a lot of destruction.

■ Boglands

There are three main kinds of bogland – raised, blanket and mountain – each with a distinctive flora. Raised bogs vary in size from a few acres to miles and most are in the country's central plain. The largest are harvested by Bórd na Móna (the peat development authority) for fuel. These areas have a range of bog-moss species, as well as heathers and sedges.

Most blanket bogs are near the west coast, covering large areas. They have developed on gentle slopes with high rainfall, and vegetation includes moor grass and sedge. Mountain bogs resemble blanket bogs.

ORGANIZING FOR NATURE

Irish Seal Sanctuary, An Clochan, Tobergregan, Garretstown, Co. Dublin, ☎ (01) 835-4370.

Tree Council of Ireland, The Park, Cabinteely, Dublin 18. ☎ (01) 284-9211; fax 284-9197. www.treecouncil.ie and for the North, www.treecouncil.org.uk.

Coillte, The Irish Forestry Board, Leeson Lane, Dublin 2. ☎ (01) 661-5666, fax 678-9527, www.coillte.ie.

Bird Watch Ireland – www.birdwatch.ie.

Birdwatch Northern Ireland, www.birdwatch-ni.co.uk.

■ Natural Resources

There's natural gas off the coast and base-metal exploration over the past 40 years has led to discoveries, particularly of zinc-lead, of which the Republic is the largest European producer. Zinc-lead is mined at Navan, Galmoy and Lisheen. Recent exploration work has also confirmed the country's potential for gold deposits, adding to significant quantities of a variety of industrial minerals, including gypsum, talc, calcite, dolomite, rooting slate, limestone aggregate, building stone, sand and gravel.

Turf/Peat

There are limited resources of coal, but significant reserves of peat in bogs. Peat, usually known as turf, is used both for electricity generation and for domestic heating. It has a distinctive smell, which you'll either love or hate. Bord na Móna, a State company, was established in 1946, and supplies about 10% of the Republic's energy, most of it used to generate electricity. It also produces compressed turf in manageable blocks called peat briquettes, used by families for heating. Its moss peat is extensively used by the horticulture sector and a large export market has been developed.

Renewable Energy Sources

Only about 2% of the Republic's energy requirement is provided by renewable energy technologies. The largest contributors are the Electricity Supply Board's hydroelectric schemes and Biomass, particularly wood. The Republic's first wind farms are on blanket bog at Bellacorrick, Co. Mayo, and at Carnsore Point, Co. Wexford. In 1996 the Irish government launched a €126.97 million renewable energy initiative, supported by the European Regional Development Fund. Among its objectives is a wave energy plant.

Agriculture

Although there's been a gradual decline in the relative importance of agriculture over the last few decades, it remains one of the most important sectors in the Irish economy, on both sides of the border.

The vast majority of farms are owned and operated by farming families, but what has changed is the increase in part-time farming as, in order to survive, farmers have had to find other sources of income. Many have found work in agriculture-related industries, such as food processing. The reduction in the agricultural workforce has also seen an increase in the average size of farm business and much more specialization.

FARMS YOU CAN VISIT

All over Ireland there are working farms open to the public, and they are well worth visiting. Look out for signs as you travel around, or ask at Tourist Information offices.

Introduction

In the Republic, farms tend to be larger on the better land in the east and south of the country. With mild temperatures and relatively high rainfall, conditions are ideal for stock raising, so livestock husbandry dominates production. Land use in the Republic in the 1990s was: arable, 13%; pastures, 68%; forests and woodland, 5%; other, 14%.

FARM SHOWS

In rural areas agricultural shows are held annually during the summer, and you really should see if there is one happening when you visit. They're usually on Sundays, when farmers can relax a little, and they give you some idea of life in the country. Animals are paraded and judged, often there are jumping events for horses, as well as displays of produce – from cakes to plants, flowers, fruit and vegetables. There are lots of competitions you can watch or join in – from tug of war to sheaf throwing, and other entertainment, including displays of Irish dancing. The shows are great fun and friendly.

Forestry

From being densely forested, the country lost most of its trees during the 17th century and it's only since the 1950s that efforts have been made to redress this in the Republic, through a program of reforestation sponsored by the State, with about 70% of forests in public ownership. There's an "open forest" policy that provides public access, ranging from picnic stops to nature trails to forest parks with camping facilities.

Planting by the private sector has increased dramatically in recent years, encouraged by grants. While the proportion of land area covered by forests is low, the planting rate is the highest per capita forest-planting program of any developed country.

With its combination of soils and a moist mild climate, Ireland is particularly suited to conifers. Because it is an island, the country enjoys relative isolation from pests and disease and this makes it a healthy environment for growing trees. Ancient native forests were mainly of oak, mixed with some ash and elm. Scots pine and birch grew on poorer soils and there were scrub woodlands of alder and willow on marshy ground near lakes and rivers.

The emphasis has changed from predominantly European trees to coniferous species since new planting intensified starting in the 1950s, which is why most are Sitka spruce and lodgepole pine from the western part of North America. These species today comprise nearly 84% of total planting, which has been criticized by many people interested in the countryside, but the proportion of broadleaves being planted is thankfully increasing.

For information about forests in the Republic, check www.coillte.ie and, in Northern Ireland, the **Royal Forestry Society** at www.rfs.org.uk.

Government

 The island is divided politically, with the Republic occupying five sixths of it, split into 26 counties. Northern Ireland is made up of six counties – Antrim, Armagh, Down, Fermanagh, Londonderry/Derry and Tyrone.

What is now the Republic became the **Irish Free State** in 1922, while the six counties in the north remained under the jurisdiction of the UK, ratified by the Boundary Commission in 1929.

With nationalists forming a substantial minority within the borders of the six counties, there were tensions that have developed into violence now and then over the years. They came to a head in 1969 when peaceful Civil Rights marches, inspired by contemporary events in the United States, were attacked by the police. This led to what became known as The Troubles.

The Republic

In 1937 the Irish Free State adopted a written constitution. It declared itself a Republic in 1948. It is a parliamentary democracy governed by the Oireachtas, which consists of the President and the Legislature. The Legislature has two houses – Dáil Éireann (a house of representatives) and Seanad Éireann (a senate or upper house). The Head of State is the President, elected by the people every seven years, and whose role is non-executive.

The head of government is the Taoiseach (Chieftain in Irish) or Prime Minister, and general elections, organized under a proportional representative system, have to be held at least every five years.

The main political parties in the Republic are: Fianna Fail, Fine Gael, Labour, Progressive Democrats, Sinn Féin, The Green Party, and The Socialist Party.

Northern Ireland

In the North the political situation is more complicated. Voters return Members of Parliament to Westminster, London, although Sinn Féin MPs do not take up their seats. The British government appoints a Secretary of State for Northern Ireland and runs the Northern Ireland Office in Belfast.

Under the Good Friday (or Belfast) Agreement of 1998 voters also elect MLAs, Members of the Legislative Assembly, which sits at Stormont.

In May, 1998, there were referenda on both sides of the border in order to ratify the Agreement, which was supported by over 90% in the Republic and over 70% in the North. The subtleties of its text left some areas ambiguous or unresolved, which have caused difficulties in its full implementation.

Life has however improved dramatically for most in Northern Ireland, with an almost total end to violence. Also under the Agreement, North-South bodies and a British-Irish Council were set up, which have increased co-operation between the two parts of the island, and between Ireland and Britain.

The main political parties in Northern Ireland are: the Ulster Unionist Party, the Social Democratic and Labour Party (SDLP), Sinn Féin, Democratic Unionist Party, Alliance Party, Progressive Unionist Party, and Women's Coalition.

David Trimble of the Ulster Unionist Party, and John Hume of the nationalist SDLP, were jointly awarded the Nobel Peace Prize in 1998 "for their efforts to find a peaceful solution to the conflict in Northern Ireland."

The Economy

Both Ireland and Britain joined the European Economic Community (now the **European Union**) in 1973. As a result, substantial grants speeded up the modernization in both parts of the island, but especially the Republic. While agriculture is still important in both jurisdictions, tourism and high-tech industries are making substantial inroads.

■ The Republic's Success in the 1990s

Electronic, chemical and pharmaceutical multinationals are the main industrial employers in the Republic, attracted by substantial State aid. During the 1990s the Republic emerged as Europe's high-growth economy due to a number of factors. These included a young and educated workforce, State policies encouraging overseas investment and a commitment to open markets, and a partnership approach between government, employers and trade unions. Also, a large number of Irish who had emigrated during previous decades returned home with experience gained abroad, many with capital to invest. Although the UK is still its largest trading partner, the EU accounts for almost half of all of its exports.

■ Industrial Development in the Republic

When the Irish State was founded in 1922, industry was made up of a small number of manufacturers – most involved in food, drink and textiles, and focused on the home market. Protectionist measures introduced in the 1930s to encourage expansion didn't work and the country's industrial breakthrough did not come for another two decades. In 1952 **Córas Tráchtála**, the Irish Export Board, was founded, and capital incentive schemes encouraged new industries. The IDA (**Industrial Development Authority**) was set up to promote the indigenous sector and also to attract foreign companies. It has been particularly successful in electronics, engineering and pharmaceuticals.

TO DEVELOP IRELAND

Enterprise Ireland is responsible for developing indigenous industry; **Shannon Development** (or SFADCO – the Shannon Free Airport Development Company) and the authority for Irish-speaking areas – **Udarás na Gaeltachta** – promotes investment in their specific regions. **Forfás** (the policy and advisory board for industrial development, science and technology) coordinates activities among these and other agencies.

■ Companies from Overseas

There are over 1,100 overseas-owned manufacturing/international services companies in the Republic, including over 450 from the US, 175 from Germany and 160 from the UK. There are also about 100 State-sponsored bodies working in transport, telecommunications and the promotion of tourism, trade and industrial development.

■ The Republic's Fishing Industry

Commercial sea fishing and fish farming are very important to the economy. The main varieties of sea fish landed are herring, cod, whiting, mackerel, plaice, ray, skate and haddock. Among shellfish, the main varieties are lobsters, crab and prawns. Bord Iascaigh Mhara (BIM - Sea Fisheries Board) is the State body with primary responsibility for the development of the sea fishing and aquaculture industries.

Aquaculture now provides employment in remote and disadvantaged areas, having grown from a negligible level in the mid-1980s. There are jobs too in feed and equipment manufacture and in processing. Farmed salmon accounts for about 75% of the value of aquaculture output. BIM's development program is geared towards the expansion of both finfish and shellfish farming.

■ The Economy of Northern Ireland

Due to its political problems, from the late 1960s, investment levels were poor, which led to high levels of unemployment, with a large number of those employed working in unskilled or skilled manual occupations. Outside Belfast and Derry, Northern Ireland is mainly rural and has a strong agricultural economy, with dairy products and beef most important.

What is encouraging is that, since the 90s, millions of pounds have been invested in the economy by companies convinced that the Peace Process will work. In fact, throughout the 1990s Northern Ireland enjoyed the fastest economic growth of any region of the UK.

Between 1990 and 2000, manufacturing output increased by a staggering 47.7%. Over 90% of new jobs created were in electronics, telecoms and international traded services, including software. The strong growth of these and related sectors indicates a move towards a knowledge-based economy, aided in particular by substantial investments from North American and Japanese companies.

Unemployment is currently running at its lowest level since records began and has fallen steadily from a peak of 17.2% in 1986 to 5.2% in August 2003.

The Good Friday Agreement has led to the transformation of many towns and cities in the North, and there are lots of new hotels and places to eat, drink, and enjoy a vibrant nightlife.

Investing in Northern Ireland

The body which assists overseas companies interested in locating in the North is **Invest Northern Ireland**. The number of overseas companies setting up has increased, attracted by a well-motivated and highly educated English-speaking workforce. The North has the fastest growing economy in the UK, with a competitive business environment, and an infrastructure that is absolutely top class.

Generous assistance is available through Invest Northern Ireland, including financial incentives and recruitment and training support tailored to each company's needs. Invest NI continues to give support throughout the lifetime of a commercial venture. Find out more at www.investni.com.

Jerpoint Abbey carvings, Kilkenny (see page 209)

Little Skellig Island from Skellig Michael, Co. Kerry (see page 280)

Travel Information

Just the Facts

Electrical Current

The standard electricity supply is 220 volts AC in the Republic and 240 volts AC in Northern Ireland (50 cycles), so you'll need a transformer and a plug adapter. Travel adapters, to convert two-pin plugs to the standard three-pin, can be bought at the airport or many electrical suppliers.

Passport

Required.

Travel Insurance

Strongly advised.

Emergency Number

Dial 999 and ask for police, fire or ambulance service.

Telephones

When in Dublin, dial phone numbers without the prefix (for example, ☎ 123-4567). For calls to Dublin from anywhere else in the Republic, the prefix (01) is needed. Other prefixes apply in other regions, as detailed in the chapters below, and similar rules apply. Note that the more heavily populated regions have seven-digit phone numbers, while the others have only six digits. To call Ireland from overseas, dial 011 353 (the country code for Ireland), then the local prefix and the number.

Callsave: Sometimes called **Lo-call**, this is the term for numbers that begin with 1850 and that are charged at a local rate, wherever you call from in Ireland – much cheaper than the long-distance rate. Numbers prefixed by 1800 are free.

Time Zone

Greenwich Mean Time – five hours ahead of New York or EST.

Language

English.

What to Pack

Comfortable clothing and sensible shoes for exploring, plus specialized gear if taking part in sports. Bring one smart outfit for dining out. Always pack one warm sweater and rainwear; in summer a light waterproof jacket, which will roll up for carrying, is ideal.

Water Supply

Water is drinkable everywhere. Bottled water, available everywhere, is cheapest if bought in supermarkets.

Taxes

Usually included in bills.

Valued Added Tax can be reclaimed by tourists when leaving the country. Look out for signs in shops – you need your passport and a form needs to be completed in the shop.

Tipping

Give 10% of the bill if a service charge is not included, assuming you are happy with the service. Service is charged only as part of the bill in larger hotels and upmarket restaurants.

Taxi drivers and hotel porters expect a small tip.

Unless drinks are served at your table, a tip is not expected in a pub.

Embassies

American Embassy: 42 Elgin Road, Ballsbridge, Dublin 4. ☎ (01) 668-8777; fax 668-8056; www.usembassy.ie.

American Consulate General, Queen House, Queen Street, Belfast. ☎ (028) 9032-8239.

Canadian Embassy, 65 St. Stephen's Green, Dublin 2. ☎ (01) 417-4100; emergency number ☎ (01) 478-1476; fax 417-4101; dublin@dfait-maeci.gc.ca; www.canadaeuropa.gc.ca/ireland.

Consulate of Canada - Belfast, Mrs JM Rankin, Honorary Consul, PO Box 405, Belfast. ☎ (28) 9066-0212; fax 9068-7798.

Useful Addresses in the US & Canada

Tourism Ireland markets both parts of Ireland overseas.

- 345 Park Avenue, New York, NY 10154, ☎ 800-223-6470; fax 00-1-212-371-9059; www.tourismireland.com.
- 2 Bloor Street West, Suite 1501, Toronto, Canada M4W 3E2. ☎ 800-223-6470; www.tourismireland/com.

Tourist Board for the Republic – Fáilte Ireland, Baggot Street Bridge, Dublin 2. ☎ 1850-23-03-30; www.ireland.ie.

Northern Ireland Tourist Board, 59 North Street, Belfast, BT1 1NB and 16 Nassau Street, Dublin 2. ☎ 1850-230-230 and 353 (01) 1-679-1977 (Dublin office dialed from the North); info@nitb.com; www. discovernorthernireland.com.

Orientation

■ When to Visit

Ireland makes a great holiday destination at any time of the year, but the countryside is at its most attractive from April to the end of September when there are leaves on deciduous trees, the fields are at their greenest, and there are lots of wildflowers.

If you're attracted by outdoor activities, choose that period too, as the weather is at its best in spring there's yellow gorse on the hills and fuschia in the hedges, and in autumn the changing colors of the leaves brighten every landscape.

If you are particularly interested in history and heritage, visiting Ireland from spring to autumn is also the best time, as you have access to all sites, although some of them stay open all year round.

The cities are at their busiest with overseas visitors in July and August, so if you prefer a quiet time, aim to come outside those months. A winter holiday here, between October and early March, has the advantage of some lower prices for accommodation and people generally have more time to welcome you.

■ Getting Here

By Air

There are scheduled direct flights from the US to Shannon, Dublin and Belfast International Airport in Northern Ireland via Shannon, London and Glasgow. You can also fly from New York to Belfast City Airport via other UK cities. There are charter flights available as well.

AIR TRAVEL FROM USA/CANADA		
From	**To**	**Airline**
Atlanta	Shannon/Dublin	Delta Airlines
Baltimore	Shannon/Dublin	Aer Lingus
Boston	Shannon/Dublin	Aer Lingus
Chicago	Shannon	Royal Jordanian
Chicago	Shannon/Dublin	Aer Lingus
Los Angeles	Shannon/Dublin	Aer Lingus
Newark	Dublin/Shannon	Continental Airlines
Newark	Belfast City (via other UK city)	British European (Flybe)
New York	Shannon	Aer Lingus
New York	Dublin	Aer Lingus

AIRLINE CONTACT DETAILS		
Delta	**www.delta.com**	In US, ☎ 800-241-4141; in Canada, ☎ 800-221-1212; in Ireland (Dublin), ☎ (01) 407-3165; elsewhere in Republic, ☎ 1800-768-080; in Northern Ireland, ☎ 0800-414-767
Aer Lingus	**www.aerlingus.com**	In US, ☎ 1-800-IRISH AIR or 474-7424; in Ireland, ☎ 0818-365-000
Royal Jordanian Airlines	**www.rja.com.jo**	In US, ☎ 800-223-0470
Continental Airlines	**www.continental.com**	In US, ☎ 800-231-0856
British European	**www.flybe.com**	From outside UK, ☎ (44) 870-889-0908; from the Republic, ☎ 1890-925-532.
Air Canada (with many flights to the UK)	**www.aircanada.com**	In Canada/US, ☎ 1-888-247-2262; in Irish Republic; ☎ (01) 679-3958; from Northern Ireland, ☎ 00353-1-679-3958

Major Airports in the Republic

Dublin, ☎ (01) 814-1111; www.dublinairport.ie.

Shannon, ☎ (061) 712-400; local in Republic, ☎ 1890-742-6666; www.shannonairport.ie.

Cork, ☎ (021) 432-9602; www.corkairport.ie.

Major Airports in Northern Ireland

Belfast International Airport, ☎ (028) 9442-2888; www.belfastairport.com.

Belfast City Airport, ☎ (028) 9093-9093; www.belfastcityairport.com.

City of Derry Airport, ☎ (028) 7181-0784; www.derry.net/airport.

You can use other airports in Ireland, including Cork, Waterford, Kerry, Sligo, Galway, Donegal and Derry, by flying through Britain or Europe. For example, fly across the Atlantic with American Airways, Virgin Atlantic, British Airways to the UK, then use one of the budget or smaller airlines. Internal flights are also available.

For Flights from the UK & Europe or Within Ireland

- **Ryanair**, www.ryanair.com.
- **Jetmagic**, www.jetmagic.com.
- **AerAaran**, www.aerarannexpress.com.
- **easyJet**, www.easyjet.com.
- **bmi**, www.flybmi.com.
- **British European**, www.flybe.com.

By Sea

 You can travel to Ireland by sea from the UK, France or Spain.

There are services from Pembroke in Wales to Cork and Rosslare; from Hollyhead in Wales and from Liverpool in England to Dublin and Dun Laoghaire.

There are also services from Stranraer, Cairnryan and Troon, all in Scotland; and Liverpool and Fleetwood in England to Larne and Belfast in Northern Ireland.

Contacts for Travel by Sea

- **P&O Irish Sea**, www.poirishsea.com.
- **Stena Line**, www.stenaline.co.uk.
- **SeaCat**, www.seacat.co.uk.
- **NorseMerchant Ferries**, www.norsemerchant.com.

Travel Information

- **IrishFerries**, www.irishferries.com.
- **Swansea Cork Ferries**, www.swansea-cork.ie.
- **Brittany Ferries**, www.brittanyferries.com.

■ Immigration & Customs

Documents

You need a passport and, if you plan to rent a car, a driving license. You should take out travel insurance before leaving home so you can relax and enjoy your stay. Shop around for good value when buying, and check that it gives you medical cover and that all your personal belongings are included.

In Ireland you will receive free medical attention only in an emergency. You'll have to pay for any other treatment and if you need to stay overnight in a hospital.

If you need special medicines, remember to bring them with you; they will be available in Ireland, but probably under a different name. For minor ailments, chemists or pharmacies can give you useful advice and supply remedies.

Customs Procedures

Customs operate green and red channels at ports and airports. Go through the green channel if you have nothing to declare over the duty and tax-free allowances for overseas visitors. Go through the red channel if you have goods to declare or if you are unsure about import restrictions. Remember, you must hand in your form to claim back VAT on purchases before leaving Ireland.

You should not bring food with you, as there are import restrictions on meat products and other foodstuffs. The import of pets is also strictly controlled.

You are entitled to certain duty- and tax-free allowances. Check at the airport's duty-free shop before departure. Tourists under 17 are not entitled to tobacco or drinks allowances in the North, under 18 in the Republic.

Reclaiming VAT

Value Added Tax (VAT) is charged at 17½% on most goods bought in the North and at 13½% in the Republic. It is included in the price of the item, and not always listed separately on your receipt. If you buy items or souvenirs, check whether the store operates the Retail Export Scheme (Northern Ireland) or the Tax Back Scheme (Republic), which allows you to reclaim VAT on goods for export. The shop assistant will need your passport to complete the Tax-Free Shopping form, which you present at Customs prior to departure.

■ Money

The Republic of Ireland was one of the EU Member States that adopted the single currency of the European Economic and Monetary Union (EMU) in 1999. The United Kingdom did not, so Northern Ireland, which is part of the UK, remains a Sterling area. Don't forget to change some of your money if crossing the border.

■ Currency

 The currency of the Republic is the euro (€), so if you arrive from one of the other EU States (apart from the UK) you can use their currency. There are 100 cents to €1 and coins are in denominations of 1, 2, 5, 10, 20 and 50 cents, as well as €1 and 2. Notes are in denominations of €5, 10, 20, 50, 100, 200 and 500.

In Northern Ireland there are 100 pennies to £1, and coins come in denominations of 1p, 2p, 5p, 10p, 20p, 50p, £1 and £2. Notes are in denominations of £5, £10, £20, £50 and £100.

The currencies of the Republic and Northern Ireland are not interchangeable, although many of the larger city shops in the North accept euros.

Banks, ATMs & Currency Exchange

All banks have Automatic Teller Machines (ATMs). Any bank will exchange your money, as will most building societies and post offices.

Generally, banks are open Monday-Wednesday, 10 am-4 pm, Thursday and Friday, 10 am-5 pm. None is open on Saturday or Sunday.

Travelers' Checks

For safety reasons, travelers' checks are a good idea. Remember that you must present your passport when cashing them. Also, if planning to visit both parts of Ireland you will need them in both currencies (sterling and euros).

Credit Cards

Most businesses accept American Express (Amex), MasterCard (MC) and Visa (V). A few accept Diners Club (DC). If your credit card is lost or stolen, you can report its loss in any bank, and should do so immediately. You should also call the 800 number provided by your credit card company. Remember to report it to the police too, for insurance purposes.

■ Post Offices

 Post offices are open Monday-Friday, 9 am-5:30 pm, and Saturday until 1 pm. Almost every town and village has one, and you are also able to buy stamps in many shops.

■ Staying Safe

Visitor Safety

 Ireland is not a dangerous country, and its people are generally friendly and helpful, particularly away from the cities. Northern Ireland has the second-lowest crime rate in Europe. Even during the years of civil unrest, tourists were rarely directly affected. However, it is foolish to go into areas where there are tensions, especially around July 12, so take advice locally.

Just as they are anywhere in the world, tourists can be targets for thieves in Irish towns and cities, because they often carry expensive cameras and other equipment and are vulnerable as they check maps or ask for directions.

Sadly, these days it is not a good idea to wander around on foot late at night, as there has been an increase in unprovoked violent attacks in large towns and cities when pubs and nightclubs close. Groups of young people gather, often close to take-out restaurants and fast food outlets, then set upon others. Ask locals if you aren't sure about an area, or arrange to be picked up by taxi after an event.

While many of these recent attacks have nothing to do with robbery, there are thieves around. Don't carry a lot of cash and, if challenged, hand it over, rather than risk injury. Be wary of pickpockets in crowded streets, or when withdrawing money from cash machines. Always carry your credit card separately so that if your wallet is snatched you are not left totally without money. If you have a room safe in your hotel, use it. You don't need to carry your passport with you as you explore.

Report Any Loss

If the worst happens, report your loss immediately to the nearest **Garda Station** (Garda Siochana – literally "the Guardians of the Peace" – is the Republic's Police Service) or in the North to the **PSNI** (Police Service of Northern Ireland). You must do this in order to be able to claim from your insurance.

If travelling by car, put your luggage in the trunk out of sight when parking. If you are involved in a road accident, you must call the police to the scene, as otherwise your insurance company will not cover you.

Victim Support

The police will put you in touch with the charitable organization Victim Support, which does its best to sort out any problems you may have if robbed, injured or traumatized. There are branches all over the island.

- **Dublin Head Office.** ☎ (01) 478-5295; fax 478-5187; www.touristvictimsupport.ie.
- **Belfast Head Office.** ☎ (028) 9022-2181;www.victimsupport. org.

Sickness or Injury

If you are taken ill, or are injured while in Ireland, you should call a local doctor, known as a GP (General Practitioner). Ask at your accommodation, or check the phone book. You may be referred to the nearest hospital but, unless it is a serious injury, it is not a good idea to call there first, as the Accident and Emergency departments at all Irish hospitals are very busy and you could spend many hours waiting to be seen.

■ Getting Around

Car Rentals

The advantage of using a car is that you can wander away from the main roads and discover the real Ireland, and stop and go where you wish. I can't recommend this strongly enough.

Relax & Enjoy It

Many of our roads are narrow and winding, and you are likely to meet agricultural equipment on them during the summer months – it's part of the charm of Ireland, so don't get impatient. Just relax.

In many parts of the country you only have to turn off a main route to be immediately in another world, with roads winding between hedges and the only sound birdsong. Some minor roads are so little used that there is grass growing down the middle of them! Allow yourself plenty of time to explore, rather than dashing between destinations.

Unfortunately, renting cars is more expensive in the Republic than in most other destinations in Europe, so check for rates and special deals. Alternatively, you could rent a car for part of your trip and use public transport for the remainder. Most cars have manual gearshift, so ask in advance if you want an automatic. Some airlines offer reduced car rental rates if you book at the time you make your flight reservations.

Be sure that your rental insurance covers you if planning to cross the border. Make sure when quoted a price that it is the total cost, as insurance and VAT may be added.

CAR RENTAL COMPANIES	
Most of the following have desks at the main airports.	
In Northern Ireland	
Avis	www.avisworld.com, ☎ (028) 9045-2017
Hertz	www.hertz.co.uk or www.hertz.com, ☎ (028) 9073-2451
National	☎ (028) 9073-9400
Europcar	www.europcar.com, ☎ (028) 9045-0904
Budget	www.budget.com, ☎ (028) 9045-1111
In the Republic	
Avis	☎ 1890-405-060
Murrays	www.europcar.ie, Dublin Airport, ☎ (01) 812-0410, Shannon Airport, ☎ (061) 701-200, Cork Airport, ☎ (021) 491-7300
Enterprise	☎ (021) 497-5133
National	☎ (021) 432-0755
Sixt Irish	www.irishcarrentals.com, ☎ 1890-206-088

Maps

An excellent map, covering the whole island, is Michelin No 405, scale 1:400,000 or 1 inch to 6.3 miles, which I use all the time. It shows nature reserves, forest walks, historic sites, as well as other useful information.

If you want to concentrate on part of Ireland, there are very useful maps called *Ireland West, East, North* and *South* – their scale is 1: 250,000, about 1 inch to 4 miles, and they also list things to see and do.

There are detailed Ordnance Survey maps available for all areas, which you can buy in main bookstores and tourist information offices. If you are coming here to hillwalk or climb, you would be advised to invest in detailed maps.

In the Republic national routes are marked on maps and on the roads with the letter N, and minor roads have the prefix R and a number.

In Northern Ireland the main routes are marked with A and the minor with a B.

Road Rules

We drive on the left and pass on the right. Traffic on a roundabout (rotary) has priority. Until you become accustomed to it, be especially careful when joining or leaving roundabouts, and when setting off again after a break from driving.

Speed limits are 30 mph (48 kmh) in towns, 60 (97 kmh) on most roads, 70 (113 kmh) on dual carriageways and motorways. The limits are indicated on signs.

Seat belts are compulsory for all drivers and passengers and motorcyclists must wear helmets.

The State of the Roads

In Northern Ireland you will notice that there are plenty of well signposted pullouts where you can check your map, picnic or, often, enjoy a spectacular view. Some of these areas even have public toilets. The road surfaces are good everywhere.

There are far fewer pullouts, and fewer signposts in the Republic, and many roads, even major ones, are in a dreadful condition, with potholes.

Road Signs

Road signs on minor roads are often noticeable by their absence in the Republic and, even where you see them frequently, they do not give distances, which can be irritating. If you stop to ask distances, the Irish may give them as shorter than they are, as though they want to please you.

> *Traditionally, the Irish mile was 480 yards longer than the English mile. On old stone milestones both in the North and the Republic you'll still see distances measured in Irish miles.*

In the Republic, note that speed limit signs are in miles, while road signs are in kilometers. All part of the charm of Ireland, perhaps.

Note that the most important warning signs, such as yield to traffic on a major road ahead and speed limits, have red edges.

Other warning signs of some danger or hazard, such as roundabout ahead or road narrows ahead, have a yellow background with markings in black.

Information signs, such as Bray 2 km, are white with the road number in yellow letters on a green panel within a larger sign, such as N17.

Signs for tourist attractions have cream letters on a brown background and use pictorial symbols for the attraction.

Parking

"Disc parking" is in operation in cities, including Galway, Limerick and Cork. Buy discs in garages on approach roads or in shops and follow the simple directions. In Dublin there are parking meters that take coins in some areas.

Shopping centers often have parking. You usually have to pay at a machine before returning to your car.

Clamping of cars has been introduced in Irish cities, so don't risk it by parking illegally, as it is costly and time-consuming getting your car unclamped or having to retrieve it from the pound where it has been transported.

Ask locals for help – they will know where you can park and where to buy discs if necessary.

By Rail

The Republic

 Irish Rail or Iarnród Éireann, ("iron road of Ireland" in Irish; www.irishrail.ie) runs the railway service.

There are two main rail stations in Dublin: **Connolly** serving the north and northwest, and **Heuston** serving the south and west. The main routes from Heuston are to: Cork, Limerick, Tralee, Galway, Westport, Ballina, Waterford. From Connolly they are to: Sligo, Belfast (Enterprise Service jointly run with Northern Ireland Railways), Wexford, Rosslare Europort.

Other intercity routes are: Cork to Tralee, Cork to Limerick, and Limerick to Rosslare Europort.

A suburban service also operates between Cork and Cobh.

GOOD VALUE. There are cheap inter-city day round-trips available at certain times.

Useful Phone Numbers

- **Irish Rail Enquiries and Sales**, 35 Lower Abbey Street, Dublin, ☎ (01) 703-1888.
- **Irish Rail Travel Center**, 65 Patrick Street, Cork, ☎ (021) 450-4888.
- **Heuston Station**, Dublin, ☎ (01) 836-8222.
- **Connolly Station**, Dublin, ☎ (01) 703-1843.
- **Limerick Station**, ☎ (061) 418-666.
- **Galway Station**, ☎ (091) 564-222.
- **Waterford Station**, ☎ (051) 873-401.
- **Sligo Station**, ☎ (071) 91916-9888.

■ Timetable Information

Schedules can be obtained by phoning the Éareann Information line at ☎ 1850 366222, or from one of the following talking timetable numbers:

Route	Phone Number
Dublin/Cork	01 8054200 or 021 4504544
Dublin/Limerick	01 8054211 or 061 413355
Dublin/Galway	01 8054222
Dublin/Waterford	01 8054233
Dublin/Westport	01 8054244
Dublin/Sligo	01 8054255
Dublin/Tralee	01 8054266
Dublin/Belfast	01 8054277
Dublin/Rosslare	01 8054288
Dublin/Ballina	01 8054299

Northern Ireland

The rail service operator is **Northern Ireland Railways**. For both rail and bus inquiries, contact Translink at ☎ (028) 9066-6630, www.translink.co.uk.

Travel Information

You do not need a passport to travel between Northern Ireland and the Republic, as there are no border controls.

There are four main rail routes from Belfast Central Station, ☎ (028) 9089-9411: north to Derry City via Ballymena and Coleraine, northeast to the port of Larne, east to Bangor along the shores of Belfast Lough or Lake, and south to Dublin via Newry.

The Belfast-Dublin Enterprise Express takes just over two hours, with eight trains daily in both directions (five on Sundays).

GOOD VALUE. Cheap day returns are available for the **Enterprise Express**. There is a free bus service into the city center for passengers arriving at Belfast Central. **Rail runabout tickets** (seven days unlimited travel) are available from main Northern Ireland Railway (NIR) stations. Irish Rail-Iarnród Éireann has great value **Explorer Rail** tickets (Republic only) valid on Intercity, DART and Suburban rail. There's also the **Irish Explorer Rail and Bus** ticket – for use in the Republic only. For travel all over the island there's the **Irish Rover Rail**, and the **Emerald Card** for rail and bus. These can be picked up at major train stations throughout Ireland.

RAIL & BUS PASSES				
Pass Name	**Version**	**Area**	**Duration**	**Price**
Emerald Card	Rail & Bus	Republic & North	Any 8 days in 15 Any 15 days in 30	€168 €290
Irish Explorer	Rail & Bus	Republic only	Any 8 days in 15	€145
Irish Rover	Rail only	Republic & North	Any 5 days in 15	€122
Irish Explorer	Rail only	Republic only	Any 5 days in 15	€98
Irish Rover	Rail only	Republic & North	Any 3 days in 8 Any 8 days in 15 Any 15 days in 30	€60 €135 €195
Irish Rambler	Rail only	Republic only	Any 3 days in 8 Any 8 days in 15 Any 15 days in 30	€45 €100 €145

By Bus

The island has a good network connecting cities and towns, including many places not served by rail.

Busárus is the main bus station in Dublin. It's close to Connolly rail station.

There's a **Stationlink** bus (fare less than one euro) that connects Heuston Station, Busárus, Connolly Station, stopping near O'Connell Street en route.

Belfast has two bus stations – one on Laganside, the other behind the Europa Hotel, so don't get confused.

Express coaches run between cities and larger towns. They are a great way of seeing the country, as you are higher than in a train or car, and they're cheaper than rail travel.

> **GREAT VALUE. Rambler** tickets are available for unlimited travel by bus within the Republic for three, eight and 15 days. **Irish Rover** tickets allow unlimited travel throughout the island for the same periods.

Useful Phone Numbers

For all inquiries about bus or rail travel in Northern Ireland, call **Translink,** ☎ (028) 9066-6630, www.translink.com. For bus information, e-mail info@buseireann.ie, visit their website at www.buseireann.ie, or call one of the numbers below.

■ Bus Stations

- Central Bus Station (Busárus) Dublin, ☎ (01) 836-6111.
- Cork, ☎ (021) 450-8188.
- Killarney, ☎ (064) 30011.
- Limerick, ☎ (061) 313-333.
- Galway, ☎ (091) 562-000.
- Waterford, ☎ (051) 879-000.
- Tralee, ☎ (066) 712-3566, info@buseireann.ie, www.buseireann.ie.

■ Telephones

The international code for the Republic is 353 and for Northern Ireland 44. The international code if calling the USA or Canada from Ireland is 1.

Buy a prepaid callcard, sold in shops all over the country, to make phone calls, or look for a phone that takes your credit card. You can be charged a ridiculous amount to phone from your hotel room.

Travel Information

Within the Republic, use the complete number listed, including prefix, if phoning outside your immediate area. For example, ☎ 01-679-1977 for the Northern Ireland Tourist Office in Dublin. If you are in Dublin, drop the 01 prefix. From Northern Ireland, that same number becomes ☎ 00353 1-679-1977, as if you were calling from overseas.

Within Northern Ireland use numbers as listed with prefix 028. If you are calling the North from the Republic, the prefix changes to 048.

From the rest of the world, use the international access code followed by country code, omitting 0. So ☎ (028) 9066-6630, the Translink (rail and bus) enquiry number within Northern Ireland, becomes ☎ 0044-28-9066-6630.

■ Newspapers & Magazines

 In the Republic there are three daily broadsheets – *The Irish Times, The Irish Independent*, both published in Dublin, and *The Irish Examiner,* which is published in Cork. In addition, there are two evening tabloids, *The Evening Herald* and *The Evening Echo* – the latter published by *The Examiner.*

In Northern Ireland the main daily papers are *The Irish News, The Belfast Telegraph, The Newsletter* and *The Derry Journal.*

On Sundays you can buy: *The Sunday Independent, Ireland on Sunday, Sunday Tribune* and *Sunday Business Post*, plus in the North, *Sunday Life*.

All the British daily and Sunday papers are available in Ireland, with parts of them produced specifically for the Irish market. In cities, you can buy American and other papers from overseas.

All over the country there are also weekly papers produced locally which give visitors a great insight into life in the area and are useful for checking on entertainment that's available. The *In Dublin* magazine is excellent for listings, as is *Magpie*, which covers arts and entertainment in the Galway/Mayo area. There's also a free monthly publication called art, which covers the North. You'll find it in Tourist Information offices and other centers.

 Arts Websites: The all-Ireland arts and entertainment websites are **www.art.ie** and **www.art.co.ni**.

■ TV & Radio

Multi-channel television is available almost everywhere, which means you can watch British as well as Irish channels, plus CNN, Sky and some European channels.

The national broadcaster in the Republic is **RTÉ** – Radio Telefis Eireann – which has three TV channels – RTÉ One and Network Two, and the Irish language TG4. There's also an independent channel, **TV3**. The national radio stations run by RTÉ are Radio One, 2FM, Lyric FM, and the Irish language Radio na Gaeltachta. There are also many independent and local radio stations all over the island.

In Northern Ireland, the **BBC** and **Ulster Television** are the main channels, and BBC has radio stations in Belfast and Derry.

■ Food & Drink

Irish food has improved dramatically in recent decades, encouraged by leading hoteliers, including the Allen family of Ballymaloe House Hotel, Co. Cork, who were among the first to show us that, using fresh and locally produced ingredients, our cuisine couldn't be bettered anywhere.

We've always eaten a lot of meat, especially beef and lamb, but the growing interest in good food in Ireland itself has also seen an increase in the use of fish and shellfish.

BORD BIA

Bord Bia is the Irish Food board. It runs the Féile Bia program (a celebration of quality food) with the Restaurants Association of Ireland, the Irish Hotels Federation, and the support of the farming community. Participants show a commitment to use high quality and local produce. See www. bordbia.ie for a list. Pick up a copy of **A Taste of Ulster**, a free brochure listing hotels, restaurants, pubs, guesthouses and coffee shops that make the best use of local produce, published by the Northern Ireland Tourist Board.

Typical Fare

A full Irish breakfast consists of cereal, sometimes porridge, followed by sausages, rashers of bacon, with white or black pudding, and fried egg (you may be offered a choice of poached or scrambled). Pudding is made from animal blood – which may sound revolting, but isn't. In Northern Ireland, breakfast usually includes a wonderful choice of breads, including soda farls (miniature white soda breads) and scones.

Continental breakfast has become very popular with the health-conscious – in Ireland it usually includes soda or wholemeal bread.

If you want to sample a typically Irish meal at lunchtime or in the evening, have bacon and cabbage, or Irish stew, made with mutton and vegetables. Potatoes boiled in their jackets used to be served with most meals, but sadly they are usually replaced with chips (French fries). Ask if potatoes are available – they are far more nutritious and delicious with a dab of butter.

French fries are called chips in Ireland; what North Americans call chips are called crisps here.

Smoked salmon served on soda bread makes a substantial snack, which is also very Irish, at any time of the day.

European and international cuisine has become very popular and menus often include dishes such as pasta, pizza and tacos. Vegetarians are better looked after than they used to be, when their only option was an omelet, and are now offered a range of dishes.

In recent decades a number of small **cheese producers** have appeared and there is a huge selection of what are often called "farm cheeses." Do try them. They are absolutely delicious and so much better than the over-processed variety.

Drink

All over the world everyone has heard of **Guinness**, but other Irish stouts are produced in Cork called **Murphys** and **Beamish**. Most pubs have one or more of them on draught, which is considered much better than in bottles. Stout is good for you, in moderation.

In pubs and hotel bars you'll find a huge variety of beers and lagers – some "on tap," which is the same as "on draught."

Wine is all imported and, in the Republic, expensive because of Government taxes. If you want only a glass, ask for a miniature bottle (which should cost the same), as otherwise you may be served from a bottle that may have been open for some time. Also, unless you are a connoisseur, if ordering a bottle ask for the "house wine" from a menu, as they are usually perfectly acceptable and much cheaper.

You don't have to drink alcohol to go to a bar or pub. There are plenty of other drinks available, including tea and coffee. Never drink when driving.

A recent development found around the country are microbreweries producing their own beers, often using pure ingredients and old recipes. You'll find them in Carlow, Cork, Inagh in Co. Clare, Dublin and elsewhere.

Where to Eat

You can find plenty of fast food outlets throughout the country, including McDonalds, Burger King and Supermacs, an Irish company. There are also lots of places selling take-out food, where you can buy deep-fried fish, chicken, sausages and chips, or pizzas. Garage forecourts often have sandwiches for sale or a hot food counter.

In villages and towns there are small cafés and coffee shops where snacks and meals are available during the main trading hours of 9 am to 5:30 or 6 pm. If you can't find one, see if there is a hotel nearby or a pub. Many pubs serve food, sandwiches, soup, and full meals, often only at lunchtime. Look for signs outside them giving details of their menus and hours.

You can dine in the evenings in almost all hotels, even if not resident. Note that you may need to book in advance, particularly during the main tourist season.

At lunchtime, many hotels and pubs have a carvery, serving a substantial meal at reasonable cost. The choice usually includes roast meat, served with vegetables, a fish dish and a vegetarian option. Soup and dessert is available too. Be wary about the soup – which is often made from a packet.

Even if the weather isn't great, you can enjoy a picnic, especially if you've got a car. If you can, buy the food in a supermarket. Most hotel rooms have a tea and coffee tray, so you can have a hot drink. Unless money is no problem, avoid hotel mini-bars; all items in them are exorbitantly priced.

Pubs

The pub (public house) is at the center of every village, town and city. In the cities there's a recent development – maxi-pubs, which are very big and noisy and attractive mainly to the young. Many pubs have televisions (sometimes more than one set) blaring these days, which is a shame. They also screen important soccer and rugby matches on huge screens – so avoid them at that time, unless that's what you enjoy.

Travel Information

Generally, if you want to experience the real Irish pub, look for smaller, traditional premises even in cities. There are thousands of them all over the island. Especially in rural towns and villages, they have a regular clientele, who usually enjoy chatting to visitors and will answer your questions about local sights and history. Many of them also have regular music sessions. Shannon Development produces a free leaflet listing them all in that region; otherwise, ask locally.

Tipping & Service Charges

Check your restaurant bill and, if service is not included (it usually is) and you are satisfied with your experience, give a tip of 10-15%. You should also tip taxi drivers and hotel porters if happy with their service. In larger pubs, where you receive table service, you are expected to give a small tip, but not if you order at the counter.

■ Shopping

 Ireland is becoming multi-cultural at last and even small towns have a huge variety of food shops catering to different cultures. As well as chainstores and shopping centers, there are many smaller shops, which often make the experience more enjoyable since they give you more of an opportunity to talk with the locals.

Although they are vanishing these days, in towns and villages you still find shops selling everything from milk to sweeping brushes, sometimes with half the premises occupied by a pub. Also there are some businesses that are a combination of a real estate service, a funeral service, and an off-licence (which sells alcohol for consumption off the premises and is therefore not a pub) – looking after their clients almost from cradle to grave!

If you are picnicking or staying in an apartment, go to a country market to buy vegetables, cheeses, and eggs straight from the farm. Markets usually have stalls selling delicious homemade cakes, breads, jams, chutneys, and so on.

There are craft shops all over the country, and you can visit many artists and craftspeople where they work and buy directly from them. It makes your purchase much more memorable and cuts out the middleman – plus you are supporting our talented people. Look out for signs on the roads or ask locally.

LITTER

In an effort to do something about the dreadful litter problem in the Republic, a tax on plastic carrier bags was introduced in 2002. It reduced the use of them by 1.2 billion bags per year. It costs only a few cents to buy a plastic bag, but most Irish people now use more durable shopping bags instead, and it has made a noticeable difference everywhere.

Fines have also been introduced for on-the-spot littering.

■ Restrooms

You will find automated public restrooms in some town car parks.

Shopping centers have public restrooms, which you usually have to pay to use. Alternatively, stop into one of the larger department stores, or have a drink in a pub or coffee bar and use their facilities.

Public Holidays

In both parts of Ireland the following are public holidays when banks and most shops are closed, public transport has a limited service, and some museums and heritage centers change opening times.

- January 1.
- March 17 – St. Patrick's Day.
- Easter Monday – first Monday in May.
- December 25 – Christmas Day.
- December 26 – St. Stephen's Day or Boxing Day.

In the Republic, the first Monday in June and August, and the last Monday in October are also public holidays. In Northern Ireland, the last Monday in May, July 12 (Orangeman's Day), and the last Monday in August are public holidays.

■ Major Festivals

There are more than 350 annual festivals, so it would be impossible to list them all here. To find out, contact the tourist boards (see details in each county chapter), or look at the website of **The Association of Irish Festival Events** (AOIFE): www.aoifeonline.com; ☎ (090) 9643779; aoifeonline@eircom.net.

Note that festivals are sometimes called Fleadh (from the Irish "festive occasion") or Féile ("welcome").

There are also special weekends or longer with lectures, seminars, lots of entertainment, usually organized in memory of a notable figure – for example WB Yeats in Sligo – and some are included here. Contact the tourist boards for further information.

Calendar of Events

January

Waterford New Music Week

February

Irish Masters Snooker, Dublin

Yeats Winter Weekend, Sligo

March

West Cork Rally (auto driving competition)

St. Patrick's Festival, Dublin, leading up to the 17th, St. Patrick's Day, when there's a huge parade and celebrations in every city and town in the Republic, in Belfast, Derry and at the St. Patrick Centre, Downpatrick, Co. Down.

April

World Irish Dancing Championships – venue varies

Circuit of Ireland Motor Rally

Kerry Arts Festival

Cuírt International Literature Festival, Galway

May

Cork International Choral Festival

Cathedral Quarter Arts Festival, Belfast

Fishing Festival, Lough Erne, Co. Fermanagh

Wicklow Gardens Festival

Bray Jazz Festival

Open Shore Fishing Competitions, Limavady and Roe Estuary, Co. Londonderry

Vogler Spring Festival, Sligo – chamber music by the Vogler String Quartet and guest artists

Balmoral Show, Belfast – Ulster's premier agricultural show, with everything from sheep shearing and sheepdog trials to show jumping and dog shows

Ballyclare Horse Fair, Antrim

Rugby Sevens by the Sea, Kinsale

Feile na Bealtaine, Dingle – arts and politics

All Ireland Amateur Drama Festival, Athlone

Larne Music Festival

Bantry Mussel Festival

Galway Early Music Festival

Fleadh Nua, Ennis – traditional music, dance

Kenmare Walking Festival

Listowel Writers' Week

West Cork Chamber Music Festival, Bantry

June

Inishowen Agricultural Vintage Show

Cat Laughs Comedy Festival, Kilkenny

Edenderry Angling Festival

Women's Mini Marathon, Dublin

Causeway Coast Golf Tournament

Clonakilty Agricultural Show

Ballyjamesduff Pork Festival

Walled City Festival, Derry

Music Weekend, Youghal

Irish Derby, Kildare

Castleward Opera, Co. Down

Killarney Summerfest

Holywood International Jazz Festival, Co. Down

Kells Heritage Festival

July

Castlebar International 4 Day Walks

European Open Golf

Yeats Summer School, Sligo

Dances at Lunasa, Derry

Ballybunion Bachelor Festival
Salthill Air Show, Galway
Dublin Jazz Week
Ballina Street Festival and Arts Week
Eagle Wing Community Festival, Bangor, Co. Down
Wexford Hooves and Grooves (horses and music!)
Willie Clancy School of Traditional Music, Milltown Malbay, Co. Clare
Achill Island Seafood Festival
Galway Arts Festival
Irish Coffee Festival, Foynes
Killaloe Music Festival
Boyle Arts Festival
Castlerea International Rose Festival

August
Mitchelstown Music Festival
Galway Race Week
Dublin Horse Show
West Belfast Festival
Kilkenny Arts Festival
Puck Fair, Killorglin
Birr Vintage Week
Connemara Pony Show
Rose of Tralee Festival
Merriman Summer School, Co. Clare
Rose of Glasson Festival (near Athlone)

September
International Deep Sea Angling Festival, Cobh
Clarinbridge Oyster Festival
Lisdoonvarna Matchmaking Festival
Heritage Week – all counties
Swords Heritage Festival
All-Ireland Hurling Final, Dublin
Cork Folk Festival

National Ploughing Championships

Waterford International Festival of Light Opera

Galway International Oyster Festival

Ballinasloe Horse Fair

All-Ireland GAA Football Final, Dublin

Dublin Theatre and Fringe Festival

October

Cork International Film Festival

Wexford Festival Opera

Donegal International Walking Festival

Belfast Festival

Kerry Film Festival

Cork Jazz Festival & Kinsale Fringe Jazz Festival

Dublin City Marathon

November

Cork Arts Festival

Ennis Trad Festival

Patrick Kavanagh weekend, Inniskeen, Monaghan

Accommodations

 All types of accommodations are available, from five-star hotels to hostels, castles to camping parks, apartments and houses for rent, or you can spend all or part of your holiday cruising the waterways, or in a horse-drawn caravan, gently meandering along backroads. You can book almost all of them online.

The Star System

Hotels and guesthouses are classified by Bord Fáilte in the Republic and by the Northern Irish Tourist Board, working with the Irish Hotels Federation.

They use a star system:

☆☆☆☆☆ An international standard of comfort and service with luxurious and spacious guest accommodations, including suites; high-quality restaurants with table d'hôte and à la carte menus.

☆☆☆☆ Large hotels with a high standard of comfort and service in well-appointed premises; all bedrooms ensuite; cuisine meets exacting standards; comprehensive room service.

☆☆☆ Good facilities with a wide range of services; all bedrooms ensuite; food available all day.

☆☆ Good facilities with reasonable accommodations and most bedrooms ensuite.

☆ Hotels with acceptable standards of accommodations and food. Some bedrooms have ensuite facilities.

■ Rates

HOTEL PRICE CHART	
Price per person, per night, with two sharing, including breakfast.	
$	Under US $50
$$	US $50-$100
$$$	US $101-$175
$$$$	US $176-$200
$$$$$	Over US $200

Rates are based on two people sharing a room, and the rate given is per person. In almost all hotels, a supplement is charged when only one person occupies a room. Where a hotel charges by the room, rather than per person sharing, it will be specified. This usually applies with large chains such as Jurys Inns and Travel Inns, though others may do so as well when guest numbers are down. There are special reductions at some hotels for over 55s.

■ Options

Where you stay depends on your budget and personal taste. If you want the best – including room service, on-site leisure facilities, perhaps a golf course – then go for a four- or five-star hotel. If you prefer something special and uniquely Irish, look at castles and private homes, such as Hidden Ireland (see page 60). Many international and UK chains now have hotels here, including Radisson, Hilton, Holiday Inn, Ibis, Travelodge, and Posthouse, so you may already be familiar with them and what they offer.

■ How to Book

Both tourist boards have a booking service on their websites. You can also book accommodations at any of the tourist information offices in Ireland.

- ■ Republic: **www.ireland.travel.ie/accommodation**.
- ■ The North: **www.discovernorthernireland.com**.

Alternatively, contact the Gulliver Call Center from the US and Canada at ☎ 001-800-668-668-66; or reservations@gulliver.ie.

Another useful website is **www.irelandhotels.com**, run by the Irish Hotels Federation, which produces a very useful annual guide to member hotels and guesthouses all over Ireland. You can book online, and also find special packages for those interested in angling or golf.

■ Hotel Chains

There are a number of chains and some groups of independently owned and operated hotels that get together for marketing purposes. Special low rates are often available online, and at times there are reduced rates for staying more than one night.

THE AUTHOR RECOMMENDS

Irish Country Hotels ☆☆☆, family-owned and -run, with highest standards of attention, in idyllic settings. $$. ☎ (01) 295-8900; fax 295-8940; info@irishcountryhotels.com; www. irishcountryhotels.com.

Manor House Hotels ☆☆☆ and ☆☆☆☆, luxury and boutique hotels, with country-house atmosphere, period features and furnishings. $$$. info@manorhousehotels.com; www. manorhousehotels.com.

Choice Hotels Ireland (part of Choice Hotels International) has hotels all over Ireland, under three brands: **Clarion**, usually in city centers, are ☆☆☆☆ and have excellent facilities. $$$$. **Quality Inns** are mostly ☆☆☆, in tourist areas, some with leisure centers. $$$. **Comfort Inns and Hotels** are for the budget traveler and have comfortable accommodations with minimal facilities. $-$$. Single and room-only rates and special deals are offerred. From overseas ☎ 1-800-500-600; in Republic 1850-605-705; from North 353-21-490-8282; fax 427-1489; info@choicehotelsireland.ie; www.choicehotelsireland.ie.

Great Southern Hotels, at Cork, Dublin and Shannon airports, plus the four-star Parknasilla in Co. Kerry; the newest is in Derry. ☎ (01) 214-4800; fax 214-4805; res@ho-gsh.com; www.gshotels.com. Prices start at $ per person, room only.

Jurys Hotels have a number of properties in Dublin, including the Berkeley Court (see Dublin chapter, page 103) and other cities. They are members of The Leading Hotels of the World. $$$, lower rates available online, from $$ room only. Jurys Inns in main cities are for the budget market; rooms sleep at least two; from $. www.jurysdoyle.com.

Best Western are independently owned all over Ireland. Getaway breaks start at $$ midweek for two nights; $$$ for five nights, including breakfast. International ☎ 1-800-WESTERN; in Republic (01) 676-6776; mail@bestwestern.com; www.bestwestern.com.

 Callsave: Sometimes called **Lo-call**, these are numbers that begin with 1850 and that are charged at a local rate, whereever you call from in Ireland – much cheaper than the long-distance rate. Numbers prefixed by 1800 or 0800 are free.

Brian McEnniff includes hotels in counties Sligo, Mayo and Donegal. Callsave in Republic ☎ 1850-468-357; Freephone from North ☎ 0800-039-0035; centralreservations@brianmceniffhotels.com; www.brianmceniffhotels.com.

Tower Hotel Group includes the only hotel within the medieval city walls of Derry. Others in Killarney, Co. Kerry, and Faithlegg, near Waterford City, have golf courses. ☎ (01) 873-0199 or Callsave in Republic ☎ 1850-252-252; fax 873-0194; reservations@thg.ie; www.towerhotelgroup.com.

Stay Somewhere Special

Hidden Ireland is a network of private houses offering visitors the chance to experience country life in a way not usually available to tourists. All buildings are of historic interest, some in their own estates. Part of the enjoyment of staying in any of them is that their owners are interesting, and none is large, so you have the chance to meet your fellow guests, sometimes dining with them and your hosts. Prices start at $$. ☎ (01) 662-7166; fax 662-7144; info@hidden-ireland.com; www.hidden-ireland.com. Some of its member properties are also available for rent.

Ireland's Blue Book is an association of country manor houses, castles and restaurants, all offering wonderfully high standards of personal attention with traditional hospitality, accommodation and fine cuisine in beautiful surroundings. Among them are **Moy House** near Lahinch, Co. Clare, (one of my favorite buildings in the entire country) and the multi-award-winning five-star **Park Hotel**, Kenmare, Co. Kerry. ☎ (01) 676-9914; fax 631-4990; enquiry@irelandsbluebook.com; www.irelands-blue-book.ie.

Note that properties belonging to these groups are usually not classified under the hotel star system.

Budget Option

Some hotel chains, including Jurys Inns and Travelodge, offer the budget option of paying per room, rather than per person, with breakfast and other meals usually available either on the premises or close by. Most have a choice of rooms – doubles, twins or family rooms (which sleep four). They can be excellent value if at least two are traveling together.

GOING SOLO

The Irish are welcoming to visitors traveling alone and Ireland is safe for women. I often travel alone, but am careful about returning to my accommodation unaccompanied late at night when staying in a city or large town. The only disadvantage of going solo is having to pay a single-person supplement in many hotels.

■ Non-Chain Hotels

Hotels that are not part of a chain, a marketing group or an association are often included in www.irelandhotels.com, appear on tourist board lists and are in *Be Our Guest: Hotels & Guesthouses Guide*, published by the Irish Hotels Federation. They vary in quality and facilities offered.

■ Castles

Some castles are now hotels and I have profiled them under the relevant county section in this guide. The following is a selection of others, with price range starting at $$.

Cabra Castle, Kingscourt, Co. Cavan. Cromwell and King James are said to have stayed here. The castle is set in 100 acres with a nine-hole golf course, and in Dun a Rí National Park. There are rooms in the castle, and others in the former granary. ☎ (042) 966-7030, www.cabracastle.com.

Leslie Castle, Glaslough, Co. Monaghan. This is where ex-Beatle Paul McCartney remarried. It has only 14 rooms and marvelous grounds, with ancient forests and lakes. ☎ (047) 88109, www.castleleslie.com.

Kilkea Castle, Castledermot, Co. Kildare. Ireland's oldest inhabited castle, built in 1180, is now one of its most luxurious hotels. It has an indoor pool, gym and 18-hole golf course. ☎ (059) 9145156, www.kilkeacastle.com.

Rent a Castle

Luttrellstown Castle dates from the 15th century and has a beautiful and peaceful setting in its own 560-acre estate, yet is only 20 minutes from the center of Dublin or the airport. It has the feeling of a very gracious and historic private home. It also has excellent sporting facilities, including golf, fishing, horseback riding, clay pigeon shooting, and bikes available for rent. There are also tennis courts, an outdoor swimming pool and a croquet lawn. You can have exclusive use of the castle; it accommodates 28 in 14 wonderful rooms, which cost from €8,000 per night, including breakfast, or from €56,000 per week. ☎ (01) 808-9900; enquiries@luttrellstown.ie; www.luttrellstown.ie.

■ Bed & Breakfasts

 If you like a home-away-from-home experience, choose a family-run guesthouse or B&B. You meet Irish people, who can advise you about the locality, and generally two can stay overnight for half the cost of a hotel.

If the B&B or guesthouse displays a shamrock symbol it means it's been approved by the tourist board. However, those without a shamrock are not dreadful. It costs money to be registered and some owners decide not to bother. There are advantages to choosing an approved establishment, as many accept prepaid vouchers and take credit cards, and if you do have a serious complaint afterwards you can take it up with Bord Fáilte/ Northern Ireland Tourist Board. Both tourist boards produce guides to bed and breakfasts, and there are others, including the following.

THE TOWN & COUNTRY HOMES ASSOCIATION

The Association has over 1,700 members, all over the island, and publishes an annual guide. About 70% of the homes can be booked by e-mail. An example is Altamont House, Westport, Co. Mayo, a pre-Famine house, tastefully modernized. Contact Mrs Rita Sheridan, ☎ (098) 25226.

Another, very different property is St. Jude's, Fortfield Terrace, Upper Rathmines, Dublin City. Contact Mrs Aida Boyle, ☎ (01) 497-2517.

The Association's head office is Belleek Road, Ballyshannon, Co. Donegal, ☎ (071) 9822-222; fax 22-207; admin@ townandcountry.ie; www.townandcountry.ie.

Farmhouse B&Bs are another option. Almost all listed in brochures are in the Republic and in rural areas, many on working farms. An example is one of the oldest houses in Ireland, built in 1611, on a working beef and sheep farm on the River Foyle – **The McKeans**, The Hall Greene, near Lifford, Co. Donegal, ☎/fax (074) 9141318. Another is the comfortable modern home of the Fitzpatrick family, **Coolmore Agri Farmhouse**, Knocktopher, Co. Kilkenny, ☎ (056) 7768727.

VEGETARIANS

If you're a vegetarian, hotels and guesthouses will do their best to cater for you. Some specialize in this market, among them the following:

Cussens Cottage, Ballygrennan, Bulgaden, Kilmallock, Co. Limerick, a guesthouse serving vegetarian, vegan and macrobiotic food, uses their own organic vegetables and has pure water from a well on-site. ☎ (063) 98926; cussenscottage@eircom.net; http://homepage.eircom.net/-cussenscottage.

At **Shiplake Mountain Hostel**, near Dunmanway, West Cork, accommodations range from a traditional farmhouse to gypsy caravans. Organic vegetarian meals are served. ☎ (023) 45750; www.shiplakemountainhostel.com.

Temple Country House and Spa, Horseleap, Moate, Co. Westmeath, a 250-year-old house on 100 acres, offers contemporary pampering. It caters to vegetarian, vegan and special diets. ☎ (0506) 35118; fax 35008; info@templespa.ie; www.templespa.ie.

Temple Country House is a member of the Health Farms of Ireland Association, www.healthfarmsofireland.com.

The award-winning **Pheasant's Hill Bed and Breakfast**, Downpatrick, Co. Down, serves vegetarian breakfasts on request and sells free-range and organic foods in its farm shop. ☎ (028) 4461 7246; info@pheasantshill.com; www.pheasantshill.com.

■ Hostels

The **IHH (Independent Holiday Hostels of Ireland)** is a cooperative of more than 100 hostels all over the island, each unique, and most run by their owners. All are approved by the tourist boards, offering friendly and very reasonably priced accommodation. Most are open all year and you'll find hostels in almost every county and in the main cities. Overnight charges start at around £6 or €10 per person for dormitories, and aver-

Travel Information

age £10 or €14 for the more limited number of private rooms. Facilities vary; some include breakfast, in others you cook for yourself. Staying in a hostel is a great way of meeting others, including Irish people. Many of these properties host music sessions or other events, or you can hire bikes, go horseback riding or canoeing locally. ☎ (01) 836-4700; fax 836-4710; info@hostels-ireland.com; www.hostels-ireland.com.

Non-members can stay in hostels run by An Óige, the branch of the **International Youth Hostel Association** in the Republic. It has 32 hostels in a variety of locations, including city centers and seaside resorts. Despite its name, you don't have to be young to join. You need an International Guest Card. You buy six Welcome Stamps (costing less than €2 each) from one of the hostels and attach them to a Guest Card; this makes you a full member of Hostelling International. ☎ (01) 830-4555; fax 830-5808; mailbox@anoige.ie; www.irelandyha.org.

■ Rental Properties

 There is a huge selection of flats and houses with kitchens where you can cook for yourself. Some are listed on tourist board websites, and many are available for breaks shorter than a week. The majority can be rented all year round, and they're cheaper outside the main tourist season.

Among the more unusual are the chalets in **Killykeen Forest Park** in Co. Cavan, run by Coillte, the Forestry Service. They sleep four-six and all are within 100 yards of Lough, or Lake, Oughter, with boats and bikes for rent on site. Within the 600-acre forest park there are walks and trails, and the area attracts anglers. Open all year, chalets available for two nights or more. ☎ (048) 433-2541; killykeen@coillte.ie; www.coillte. ie. If this type of vacation appeals to you, contact the following organizations:

Self Catering Ireland has a range of properties on its books, ranging from penthouses to traditional thatched cottages, many of them on the coast and near leisure facilities. ☎ (053) 33999, fax 33808. Callsave in Ireland, ☎ 1850-200-236; info@selfcatering-ireland.com; www. selfcatering-ireland.com.

Some of the same properties belong to **Active Ireland**, a company specialising in rentals of upmarket properties and four- and five-star holiday homes, including renovated 18th-century courtyard houses, mills, cottages, golf lodges, country houses and estates. They also organize golfing packages. Among the properties they list are The Harbour Mill, Westport, Co. Mayo, which also offers special romantic breaks, and the luxury houses at Roney Beach, Gorey, Co. Wexford. The Music Hall Apartments in Temple Bar are among the city center apartments and mews houses available in Dublin. ☎ (01) 478-2045; fax 478-4327; info@ activeireland.ie; www.activeireland.ie.

Irish Cottage Holiday Homes has clusters of eight-20 cottages in 35 locations. ☎ (01) 475-1932; fax 475-5321; info@irishcottageholidays.com; www.irishcottageholidays.com.

Home from Home Holidays has three- and four-star properties all near beaches, golf courses or other outdoor facilities. ☎ (023) 33110; fax 33873; info@homefromhomeholidays.com; www.homefromhome.ie.

Other Useful Websites

■ For **rural cottages**: www.cottagesinireland.com.

■ For **Donegal and Londonderry properties**: www.ruraltourismireland.com.

SOMETHING SPECIAL

The **Irish Landmark Trust** is a charity that rescues buildings of character and architectural merit from neglect. Once restored, they are available for rent. They're all over the country and range from quirky water towers to garden follies, lighthouses to castles. The smallest of them sleep two.

They are: Salterbridge Lodge, Cappoquin, Co. Waterford, in the marvelous Blackwater Valley, and the miniature medieval castle at Annesgrove, Castletownroche, Co. Cork, with its historic and wonderful gardens. ☎ (01) 670-4733; fax 670-4887; info@irishlandmark.com; www.irishlandmark.com.

Also, see under Co. Antrim, page 480, for a scheme involving the restoration of cottages for holiday rentals.

■ Cruising

 You don't have to know anything about boats to enjoy a cruising vacation. Full instruction is given before you head off. Some of the operators are listed in the relevant chapter and others include the following:

Carrickcraft, Kinnego Marina, Oxford Island, Lurgan, Co. Armagh, Northern Ireland, has two marinas on the Shannon and one on the Erne. A two-berth boat in July costs about €700 per week, €400 for a weekend. ☎ (028) 3834-4993; fax 3834-4904; sales@carrickcraft.com; www.cruise-ireland.com.

Prices are about the same on **Silver Line Cruisers**, based at The Marina, Banagher, Co. Offaly, between the lakes called Lough Ree and

Travel Information

Lough Derg. ☎ (0509) 51112; fax 51632; silverline@eircom.net; www. silverlinecruisers.com.

■ Camping & RV Parks

 There are campsites all over Ireland with sites available for touring caravans, motorhomes and tents, many in scenic areas. It's a good choice for a relaxing budget holiday, as you save a lot on your accommodation.

The most useful website is **www.camping-ireland.ie**, which lists over 100 sites, some in the North. It has an online booking facility. Sites are inspected and graded by the tourist boards.

The Northern Ireland Tourist Board publishes a free *Guide to Caravanning and Camping*, which is well worth getting. All the sites included have been inspected and given a rating under the UK Star Quality Scheme. Some examples from the guide:

☆☆☆☆ **Gortin Glen**, seven miles (11.3 km) north of Omagh, Co. Tyrone, which is opposite the forest park, near the Ulster History Park and only six miles from the Ulster American Folk Park. Open all year, bikes for hire, excellent service, cleanliness, maintenance. ☎ (028) 8164-8108; gortinholidaypark@omagh.gov.uk.

☆☆☆☆ **Cushendun Caravan Park**, Co. Antrim, close to beach and a half-mile from the village. Open Easter-September 30. ☎ (028) 2176-1254.

In the Republic, among the most attractive is the **Curragh Chase Caravan and Camping Park**, in a forest park run by Coillte, the State Forestry. It's on the N69, about 15 miles (25 km) southwest of Limerick City. The forest park has walks, nature trails, gardens and the ruins of the 18th-century Curragh Chase House. Open May-mid-Sept. ☎ (061) 396-349; fax 338-271; okeefe_e@coillte.ie; www.coillte.ie.

Europe's most westerly campsite is ☆☆ **Oratory House Camping** (Teach Campail an Aragail) at Gallurus, Dingle, Co. Kerry. This is one of the most beautiful and quiet parts of the country, and the campground is on the coast and surrounded by scenic walks and archaeological sites, including the Oratory, hence its name. Open May 1 to Sept 24. ☎ (066) 915-5143; fax 915-5504; tp@iol.ie; www.camping-ireland.ie.

At the other end of the Republic is the ☆☆☆☆ **Táin Holiday Village** in Co. Louth, at the foot of the Cooley Mountains and on the shore of Carlingford Lough. It has indoor leisure facilities, including a pool, and a licensed bar and restaurant. Open March 1-end October. ☎ (042) 937-5385; 937-5417; tainhol@eircom.net; www.tainvillage.com.

Surfers come from all over the world to Strandhill Beach, Co. Sligo. It's also a great area for walkers, with its miles of sandy beach backed by dunes. ☆☆☆ **Strandhill Caravan and Camping Park** is open April 17-end September. ☎ (071) 91916-8111, www.camping-ireland.ie.

> **PRICE GUIDE**
>
> Charges differ, depending on facilities and time of year. One- to two-person tents are charged from €9-15 per tent per night (£6-10); motorhomes or caravans, from €14-30.

Renting an RV or Tent

Among the companies you can rent from are:

- **O'Meara Camping**, 4-6 Bridgefoot Street, (off Thomas St.) Dublin. ☎ (01) 670-8639.
- **Carra Caravans Ltd**, Castlebar, Co. Mayo. ☎ (094) 9032054; fax 32351.
- **Inny Camping**, Ballymahon, Co. Longford. ☎ (090) 6432123; innycamp@iol.ie.

Renting a Motorhome

- **Motorhome Depot Ltd**, Kilbride, Co. Meath. ☎ /fax (01) 822-0563; depot@motorhome.ie.
- **Motorhome Ireland Ltd**, 8 Station Road, Saintfield, Co. Down, Northern Ireland. ☎ (028) 519-519; fax 519509; rental@motorhome-irl.co.uk; www.motorhome-irl.co.uk.

Horse-Drawn Caravans

 For a relaxing time, take a holiday in a horse-drawn caravan. You don't have to know about handling a horse, as you're given instructions. You will see a small area, and get to know it intimately as you move at walking pace. The following are members of the Irish Horse Drawn Caravan Federation, www.horsecaravanholidays.ireland.ie:

- **Mayo Horsedrawn Caravan Holidays**, Belcarra. Castlebar. ☎ (094) 9032054 or 32351; post@mayoholidays. com.
- **Kilvahan Horse Drawn Caravans**, Portlaoise, Co. Laois. ☎ (0502) 27048; fax 27225; kilvahan@eircom.net.
- **Into the West Horse Drawn Caravans**, Cartron House Farm, Ballinakill, Kylebrack, Loughrea, Co. Galway. ☎ (090) 9745211; fax 45987; cartronhouse@hotmail.com.

Travel Information

■ **Slattery's Horse Drawn Caravans**, 1 Russell Street, Tralee, Co. Kerry. ☎ (066) 718-6240; fax 718-6270; caravans@slatterys.com.

Special Interest Trips

Trips devoted to a particular activity, including writing, painting and cooking, are available. You'll find some of them on the tourist board websites. Or contact one of the following.

Contact **The Irish Writers' Centre** about writing holidays. ☎ (01) 872-1302; www.writerscentre.ie. Or you might enjoy the workshops and other events at **Listowel Writers' Week**, Co. Kerry, in late May. ☎ (068) 21074; writersweek@eircom.net; www.writersweek.ie.

Holly Farm Painting Holidays, Rathdrum, Co. Wicklow. ☎ (0404) 46912; ayvoca@iolfree.ie.

The Jazz Whistler Studio Painting Holiday Center, Mount Eagle, Brosna, Co. Kerry. ☎ (066) 44494; info@jazzwhistler.com; www.jazzwhistler.com.

Courses are available at the wonderful **Ballymaloe Cookery School** in East Cork, run by TV chef and author of a number of cookery books, Darina Allen. ☎ (021) 464-6785; fax 464-6909; enquiries@ballymaloe-cookery-school.ie; www.cookingisfun.ie.

There are many hotels and guesthouses offering fishing vacations. Among them are **Riverside Fishing Holidays**, Swinford, Co. Mayo. ☎ (094) 9252729; fax 52729; info@riversidefishing.com; www.riversidefishing.com.

Mornington House, Multyfarnham, Co. Westmeath. ☎ (044) 72191; fax 72338; info@mornington.ie; www.morningtonhouse.com.

The Great Fishing Houses of Ireland is a co-operative including 21 of the best game fishing establishments in the country. Accommodation ranges from comfortable guesthouses to hotels or country mansions, all run by people with a keen interest in the sport or who have enthusiastic fishing specialists on their staff. Contact Peter Mantle, Chairman, who runs the beautiful Delphi Lodge at Leenane, Co. Galway. ☎ (095) 42222; delfish@iol.ie; www.irelandfishing.com or www.irelandflyfishing.com.

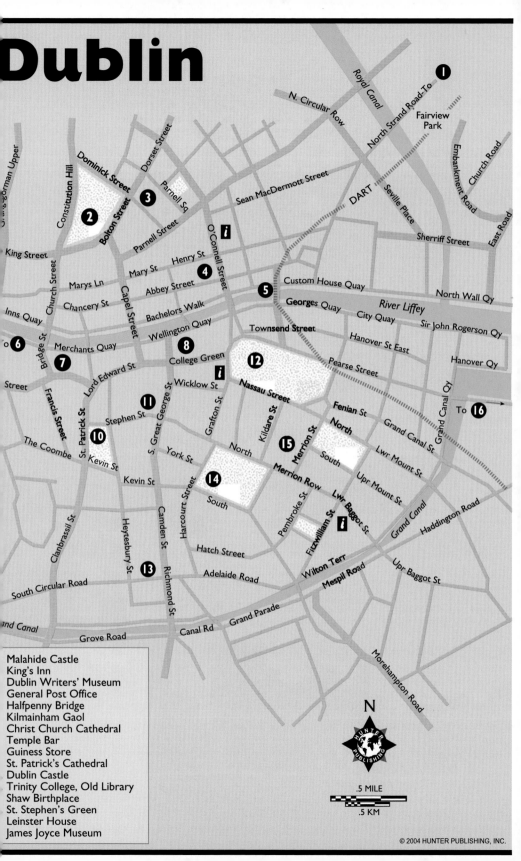

Dublin

1. Malahide Castle
2. King's Inn
3. Dublin Writers' Museum
4. General Post Office
5. Halfpenny Bridge
6. Kilmainham Gaol
7. Christ Church Cathedral
8. Temple Bar
9. Guiness Store
10. St. Patrick's Cathedral
11. Dublin Castle
12. Trinity College, Old Library
13. Shaw Birthplace
14. St. Stephen's Green
15. Leinster House
16. James Joyce Museum

© 2004 HUNTER PUBLISHING, INC.

Above: Radisson Hotel, Dublin (see page 104)

Below: Ardgillan Castle, Balbriggan, Dublin (see page 98)

Above: Drimnagh Castle and Gardens, Long Mile Road, Dublin (see page 88)

Below: Heather, Wicklow Mountains (see page 124-25)

Above: Kilruddery House Gardens, Bray, Wicklow

Below: Bective Abbey, Navan, Meath (see page 138)

Above: Tara, Meath (Meath Tourism - see pages 134, 137, 138)

Below: Trim Castle, Meath (Meath Tourism - see page 138)

Adventures

■ Cycling

Cycling routes are mentioned throughout this text and often driving routes are suitable for bikes.

The **Sustrans National Cycle Network** in the North (www. sustrans.org.uk; its name comes from "sustainable transport") is a UK charity. Its flagship project is the National Cycle Network, with routes traversing the North.

Useful Contacts

■ **National Cycle Network** – www.nationalcyclenetwork. org.uk.

■ **Ulster Cycling Federation** – www.nireland.com/ulster-cyclingfederation.

■ In the Republic the official body is **Cycling Ireland**, ☎ (01) 855-1522, fax 855-1771, which organizes a number of annual events.

■ Golf

There are golf courses all over Ireland, from championship 18-hole courses to nine-hole facilities, and many are listed under their location.

Ireland hosts a number of international competitions each year, and you'll find details on the tourist board websites. Many hotels have their own courses, or can arrange tee times for you nearby.

A number of specialist operators arrange inclusive golfing vacations. Among them are:

■ **The Carr Golf Group.** ☎ US toll-free 800-882-2656, (01) 822-6662; fax 822-6668; info@carrgolf.com; www.carrgolf. com.

■ **Irish Golf Tours Ltd.** ☎ (051) 381728; info@irishgolftours. com; www.irishgolftours.com.

■ **Online Golf Travel.** ☎ US toll-free 877-227-1481, (01) 824-6210; fax 890-0689; info@onlinegolftravel.com; www.golfingireland. com.

■ **Swing** specializes in playing the most renowned courses in the southwest, and arranges tee times for you. ☎ (066) 712-

5733; fax 7123-651; swing@iol.ie; www.swinggolfireland. com.

■ To play golf on the links courses in the *Gaeltacht* areas of Donegal, Mayo and Galway, contact **Gael Saoire**, ☎ (066) 915-2423; fax 915-2429; info@gaelsaoire.ie.

Check out the tourism websites for the area of Ireland you plan to visit and you'll find further information. Tourist boards also publish brochures, including North West Tourism's *Ireland's Great Atlantic Links*.

Useful Contacts for Golfing in Ireland

■ www.golf.travel.ie.

■ www.globalgolf.com.

■ www.irishgolfexperience.com.

■ For general queries about amateur golf, contact the **Golfing Union of Ireland**. ☎ (01) 269-4111; fax 269-5368; gui@iol. ie, www.gui.ie.

■ Horseback Riding

The Irish love horses. They are renowned for breeding and for some of the best jockeys in the world. Some of the many equestrian centers and other facilities are listed under each location in this guide.

You can visit the **Irish National Stud** in Kildare Town. Open daily, February-November, 9:30 am-6 pm. ☎ (0450) 521617; fax 522964; stud@ irish-national-stud.ie; www.irish-national-stud.ie. See page 354 for details about the Irish Horse Museum in Co. Galway.

■ Walking

There are lots of town trails, and walks along towpaths beside canals, rivers or in forests. Many are mentioned throughout this book.

Way-marked trails have been developed all over Ireland over the last 20 years, and are designed so that a reasonably fit person can follow them. The trails don't usually rise above 300 m or 1,000 ft, they take you through magnificent scenery, and are divided into stages, or offer a circular route. There's a free booklet that gives details of all the ways, and includes lists of recommended maps and guides, how to access the ways and provides route contacts. Consult the website at www. irishwaymarkedways.ie.

While you can follow them just using the waymarks (the symbol of a walking man), you should take a map or map-guide with you so you don't miss the archaeological and historical sites along the way. Maps are available from bookshops, tourist offices and from **EastWest Mapping**, ☎ (054) 77835.

If climbing or hill walking, never head off alone and always leave details of your route and your estimated time of return with someone. Every year mountain rescue teams are called out, often to come to assist overseas visitors. These brave people risk their lives to save others – and do so on a voluntary basis.

WALKING VACATIONS

If you want to have a walking vacation without having to organize it yourself, there are a number of operators.

Go Ireland organizes a choice of walks in different areas, including Antrim and Fermanagh. ☎ (066) 976-2094; goireland@goactivities.com; www.goactivities.com.

South-West Walks Ireland has guided and self-guided vacations in the North and the Republic. ☎ (066) 712-8733; swwi@iol.ie.

Walking and Talking in Ireland offers eight-day vacations in Antrim and Donegal. During the walks you hear about the culture, history, geography and politics of both areas. ☎/fax (074) 9159366; info@walktalkireland.com; www.walktalkireland.com.

Other useful sites are **www.walkingkerry.com** and **www. gateway-to-the-burren.com**.

■ Watersports

With such a wonderful coastline, and so many inland waterways and loughs, the country offers numerous watersports.

Angling

Ireland is a paradise for anyone interested in fishing. Its coastline, over 3,000 miles long (4,800 km), is washed by some of the cleanest seas in Europe and it has many inland waterways, plus some of the most lightly fished freshwaters.

The landscape, with small fields and wild bogs, is littered with loughs (lakes) of all sizes and drained by many rivers, and there are over 7,000 miles (11,300 km) of riverbank for the coarse angler.

Visiting anglers are welcome to fish by becoming a member of the local controlling club or by purchasing a day, week, or season permit. Permits, also called tickets, are available from fishing tackle shops and some hotels and guesthouses.

Angling Options

Game angling is defined as the pursuit of native fish in wild places. Salmon, trout and sea trout are native species. Grilse are salmon that have spent a winter at sea. Sea trout, despite their name, can be found in rivers and loughs (lakes) around the Irish coast. Brown trout are found in most river and lough systems and, although a single species, are of many different colors and sizes as they change according to their environment.

Open Season for Game Angling

The salmon and sea trout season opens on January 1st in some fisheries. Most fisheries open at various later dates up to March 20th. Most brown trout fisheries open between February 15th and March 1st. Most fisheries close on September 30th, with some exceptions that close on various dates between September 15th and October 12th. Most brown trout fisheries close on September 30th, with some exceptions closing on dates between September 15th and October 12th

A State licence is required for salmon and sea trout angling. Buy one from the local Fisheries Board, or from tackle and sports shops in the area.

Coarse angling refers to bream, tench, roach, rudd, perch, eels, dace, carp, and hybrids; and, because wherever in Ireland you find good shoals of coarse fish, you will find some pike as well, they are also included.

There is no close season for coarse fishing in Ireland, and fish that feed throughout the year, such as pike, roach and perch, can be fished for in every month. Species such as tench, bream and rudd, which are most active in the warmer months, have a natural season extending from April to about October.

WHEN TO FISH

Information on the best times to fish is available on the website of the Central Fisheries Board at **www.cfb.ie**.

Fisheries Regions

In the Republic there are seven Regional Fisheries Boards.

The **Western Fisheries Region** takes in all the inland river systems on the Atlantic Coast from Pigeon Point near Westport, Co. Mayo, through Co. Galway, to Hags Head, just south of the Cliffs of Moher in Co. Clare. ☎ (091) 563118; fax 566335; info@wrfb.ie; www.wrfb.ie.

Shannon Regional Fisheries Board covers the inland fisheries of the Shannon catchment, the River Feale catchment in north Co. Kerry and the rivers of Co. Clare flowing westwards to the Atlantic. ☎ (061) 300238; fax 300308; info@shannon-fishery-board.ie; www.shannon-fishery-board-ie.

The **South Western Regional Fisheries Board** looks after counties Cork and Kerry, from Knockadoon Head to Kerry Head. ☎ (026) 41221; fax 41223; swrfb@swrfb.ie; www.swrfb.ie

The **Southern Regional Fisheries Board** extends along the coast from Kileen Point in the east to Knockadoon Head in the west and inland as far as the head waters of the Suir in Offaly to the north and of the Blackwater in Kerry to the west. ☎ (052) 23624; fax 23971; enquiries@srfb.ie; www.srfb.ie.

The area covered by the **Eastern Regional Fisheries Board** extends the full length of the east coast from Carlingford Lough in Co. Louth to Killen Point just east of Bannow Bay, Co. Wexford. The inland extent of the region follows the river catchments to Emyvale and Scotstown in Co. Monaghan, Virginia and Bailieboro in Co. Cavan and Tyrrellspass, Co. Westmeath. ☎ (01) 278-7022; fax 278-7025; info@erfb.ie; www.fishingireland.net.

The **North Western Fisheries Region** stretches from Mullaghmore Head, Co. Sligo to Pigeon Point, Clew Bay, Co. Mayo. It includes the catchments of all rivers and lakes that flow into the sea between these two points as well as the coastal areas. ☎ (096) 22623; fax 70543; nwrfb@iol.ie; www.northwestfisheries.ie.

The **Northern Regional Fisheries Board** extends from Mullaghmore Head to Malin Head, taking in some of the most dramatic scenery and productive fisheries in the country. It's also home to a significant stretch of the Shannon-Erne Canal, which links the Shannon navigation to the Enniskillen in Northern Ireland. ☎ (071) 9851435; fax 51816; hllyoyd@nrfb.ie; www.nrfb.ie.

Northern Ireland

The **Fisheries Conservancy Board** is the public body looking after the salmon and inland fisheries of the North, except the fisheries of the Foyle, Carlingford and the Irish Lights Commission. ☎ (028) 3833-4666; www.fcbni.com.

The **Department of Culture, Arts and Leisure** is responsible for the conservation, protection and development of inland wild fish stocks, and the development of angling and aquaculture undertakings in inland waters in Northern Ireland (excluding Lough Foyle and Carlingford Lough). ☎ (028) 9025-8861.

The **Foyle, Carlingford and Irish Lights Commission** is one of the six North/South Implementation Bodies established by the British and Irish Governments under the Good Friday Agreement. It's responsible for, among other things, the licensing and development of salmon and inland fisheries in the Foyle and Carlingford areas and is usually known as the Loughs Agency. ☎ (028) 7134-2100.

Websites for Fishing

Fishing in Northern Ireland – www.discovernorthernireland.com/angling, info@nitb.com.

Angling in Ireland – www.angling-in-ireland.com.

The Foyle System (see pages 512-13) – www.foylefishing.net.

The Bann System (see page 513) – www.bannsystem.infm.ulst.ac.uk.

Diving

 Recreational diving is possible all year round in Northern Ireland, except in severe weather, as there are so many sheltered bays and sea-loughs. There's great visibility, more than 2,000 marine species to enjoy, as well as lots of historic wrecks. Lessons are available and there are excellent support facilities.

DV Diving arranges packages for individuals and groups, with various travel and accommodation choices. Their qualified advanced instructors have extensive knowledge of local waters, especially the inland sea of Strangford Lough and the wreck-strewn Irish Sea coast of Co. Down. All equipment and instruction can be provided. Contact Dave or Tony Vincent, DV Diving. ☎ /fax (028) 9146-4671; info@dvdiving.co.uk; www.dvdiving.co.uk.

Norsemaid Sea Enterprises run diving cruise vacations, from Bangor Marina in Co. Down. Contact Alan or Iris Wright. ☎ (028) 9181-2081; fax 9182-0194; salutay@btinternet.com; www.salutay.com.

DIVE ACCOMMODATION SUGGESTION

North Irish Lodge, Islandmagee, Co. Antrim is the first PADI (Professional Association of Diving Instructors) Dive Resort in the North, with luxury cottages where you cook for yourself. It offers a choice of dives, including wreck diving, drift dives, shore dives and scenic dives, with drop-offs ranging from 49 feet (15 m) to over 140 feet (60 m). Contact Caroline Steele. ☎ /fax (028) 9338-2246; caroline@activityholsni.co.uk; www.activityholsni.co.uk.

Sailing

 The Killary Adventure Company, based on Killary Fjord in Leenane, Co. Galway, offers a huge range of all-inclusive weekend and longer stays with activities that include watersports like skiing, kayaking, Hobie cat sailing and speed boat trips. There are also loads of land-based experiences to enjoy. You stay in the Lodge on Killary Harbor (€43 per person B&B; €71-€81 for dinner & B&B) or at K2 - The Killary Centre (from €14 per person B&B; double and twin room from €28 per person). ☎ (095) 43411; fax 43414; adventure@killary.com; www.killary.com.

You can learn to sail and take lessons in watersports at a number of other centers. The following is a partial listing. Check tourist board websites for more.

International Sailing and Powerboating Centre, Cobh, Co. Cork, provides accommodation if required. ☎ (021) 481-1237; info@sailcork. com; www.sailcork.com.

South East Cruising School. Wicklow Town, ☎ (0404) 69970; sailsoutheast@eircom.net.

Glenans Irish Sailing Club, Collanmore Island, Co. Mayo and Baltimore, Co. Cork. Hostel-style accommodation available. ☎ (01) 661-1481; fax 676-4249; info@glenans-ireland.com; www.glenans-ireland.com.

Kilrush Creek Adventure Centre, Co. Clare. Lodge on site, also land activities. Located on Kilrush Creek Marina, they provide certified kayaking, sailing and powerboat courses, as well as windsurfing, archery and land games. ☎ (065) 905-2855; fax 905-2597; kcac@eircom.net; www. kcac.nav.to.

Surfing

Among locations popular with surfers are **Portrush**, Co. Antrim, and sites along the west coast, including **Strandhill** near Sligo Town and **Spanish Point**, Co. Clare. **The Irish Surfing Association** is worth contacting at ☎ (096) 49428; www.isasurf.ie.

Sporting Websites

Inland Waterways Association of Ireland, www.iwai.ie.

Mountaineering Council of Ireland, www.mountaineering.ie.

Irish Amateur Rowing Union (IARU), www.ul.ie/~rowing/iaru.html.

Irish Sailing Association (ISA), www.sailing.ie.

Irish Canoe Union, www.irishcanoeunion.ie.

Blue Flags are awarded to beaches and marinas that satisfy a number of criteria, including water quality, environmental education, information and management, safety and services. They are highly prized awards, given only for one season at a time by a non-governmental organization, the Foundation for Environmental Education operating in Europe, Africa and America. Check out www.blueflag.org.

SAFETY FIRST

Lifeguards are on duty during the summer season (June to the end of August), but only on the most frequented beaches, so do check locally about safety before swimming or taking part in other watersports. If taking to the water in a boat, wear a lifejacket at all times and make sure you know the weather forecast. Listen to local advice regarding conditions. Every year the volunteers of the Royal National Lifeboat Service of Ireland risk their lives to save others, many of them visitors from overseas.

■ Spectator Sports

The GAA

The **Gaelic Athletic Association**, usually called the GAA, was founded in 1884 and is more than a sporting organization. Dedicated to supporting hurling, football, camogie, handball and rounders, it also actively promotes Irish culture – including the language, traditional music and dance. You'll see GAA grounds in every town all over the Republic and quite a few in nationalist areas of the North.

Hurling is a bit like hockey, played with a small ball (sliothar in Irish) and a curved stick or hurley (camán). It's mentioned in Irish folklore dating back 2,000 years, and is played by teams of 15. It's a fast and exciting game to watch. **Camogie** is similar, played by females.

Gaelic football is a mixture of soccer and rugby, and older than either of them. The ball is round, slightly smaller than a soccer ball, and goalposts are the same shape as on a rugby pitch, with the crossbar lower than in rugby and higher than soccer. It's played by teams of 15 and is very popular. **Handball** is played in pairs or doubles, by striking a ball against a forecourt wall. You'll see courts on the outskirts of towns or villages.

Croke Park, on the north side of Dublin, is where All-Ireland Finals and other important games are played and it houses the GAA (Gaelic Athletic Association) Museum. Open May-September, Monday-Saturday, 9:30 am-5 pm, Sunday, noon-5 pm, October-April, Monday-Saturday, open 10 am, Sundays all year, noon-5pm except on match days. ☎ (01) 855-8176; fax 855-8104; gaamuseum@crokepark.ie; www.gaa.ie.

Horseracing

Point-to-point races are held all over the country on farmland during the first six months of the year. You'll see signs advertising them, they're advertised in local papers, or you could ask at your hotel. They're very exciting and always attract large crowds, as do races at Irish courses.

Take a look at the website of **Horse Racing Ireland** (www.hri.ie), where you can learn a lot about horses, including how to bet. There are several racecourses you might want to visit.

- **Cork Racecourse** is at Mallow, 20 miles (32 km) north of the city. www.corkracecourse.ie.
- **The Curragh** is in Co. Kildare and is the home of the Irish Derby. www.curragh.ie.

- **Down Royal** is the leading racecourse in the North. www.downroyal.com.
- **Fairyhouse** has hosted the Irish Grand National since 1870. www.fairyhouseracecourse.ie.
- **Galway** has a Racing Festival in summer. www.galwayraces.com.
- **Kilbeggan** is in the middle of the country. www.kilbegganraces.com.
- **Leopardstown** is the course nearest to Dublin city. www.leopardstown.com.
- **Limerick** is the country's newest course. www.limerick-racecourse.com.
- **Naas** is in Co. Kildare, the county most associated with horse breeding. www.naasracecourse.com.
- **Punchestown** is near Dublin. www.punchestown.com.
- **Tipperary** is another county where horses are bred. www.tipperaryraces.ie.
- **Tramore** on the Waterford coast has held races for over 200 years. www.tramore-racecourse.com.
- **Wexford** is another coastal course. www.wexfordraces.ie.

Watching the races is lots of fun, and everyone is very friendly. All the courses have great facilities for eating and drinking, and you can have a really good time.

Greyhound Racing

The popularity of greyhound racing in Ireland has soared in the last few years, with over a million attending in 2002. This is mainly because the venues have improved enormously, and now offer fine dining as well as all the excitement of betting on the races (you can also bet on races taking place at other tracks on the tote).

You can enjoy the experience in Derry and Dungannon in the North, and in the Republic at Shelbourne Park, Dublin; in Dundalk, Longford, Mullingar, Galway, in Newbridge, Co. Kildare; Limerick, Thurles, Kilkenny, Enniscorthy, Waterford, Tralee, Youghal and Cork. Check www.igb.ie.

Tracing Your Ancestors

There is a very useful free booklet published jointly by Bord Fáilte and the Northern Ireland Tourist Board. It's full of advice and contact details, and also tells you about clan gatherings. ☎ 1-850-230-330 in Ireland or 1-800-223-6470 in

North America for information. You can do research yourself or pay professionals, and there are Genealogy Centres all over the island, listed under the relevant counties below.

■ Heritage Organizations

In the Republic, the **State Heritage Service** runs many sites, including castles and historic houses. Its counterpart in the North is the **National Trust**, a UK charity, which looks after a variety of sites, including the Giant's Causeway, nature reserves, gardens, and stately homes.

Save Some Money

If you're planning to visit more than two sites, it's well worth buying a Heritage Card in the Republic or becoming a member of the National Trust. You can do so at the first site visited or contact the following:

Heritage Card. ☎ (01) 647-2461; heritagecard@ealga.ie; www.heritageireland.ie.

The National Trust. ☎ (028) 9751-072; fax 9751-1242; www.nationaltrust.org.uk.

You can also save money with a **Heritage Island Explorer** card, which you get when you buy the *Heritage Island Touring Guide*. It lists the many top tourist attractions included under their 2-for-1 discount plan and the card also offers discounted admission at all Heritage Ireland Centers. You can get it from tourist offices or contact heritage.island@indigo.ie; www.heritageisland.com.

WORLD HERITAGE SITES

World Heritage Sites are those deemed by UNESCO (United Nations Educational, Scientific and Cultural Organisation) to be of "outstanding universal value to humanity, based on their merits as best examples of cultural or natural heritage."

There are three on the island of Ireland: **Brú na Bóinne** – the Boyne Valley, which includes Newgrange and Knowth, **Skellig Michael**, off the coast of Co. Kerry, and the **Giant's Causeway**, Co. Antrim, in Northern Ireland.

Heritage Towns

You'll notice travelling around, that some places announce themselves as a "Heritage Town." The designation means that the town or village has a unique character because of its architecture and the way it has been preserved, giving visitors a special feeling about its history. Some of these communities have a Visitor Centre, while others offer signposted trails or guided tours. There's a map-leaflet listing them, available through www.heritagetowns.com.

Four Courts, River Liffey, Dublin

Dublin

Dublin is the Republic of Ireland's capital and largest city, named from the Irish "dubh linn" meaning black pool. The name comes from the fact that the site of the city was formerly a black, slimy expanse of mud, through which the River Liffey flowed sluggishly to the sea. It now has a pleasant setting on the east coast of the Irish Sea, looking out over Dublin Bay, with a long sandy shoreline to its north. Granite

mountains form the southern boundary of the county, and the city is bisected by the River Liffey.

It's a cultural city with theaters, including the famous Abbey, cinemas, galleries and museums, as well as many historic sites worth seeing. It also has an excellent range of shops, restaurants, pubs, clubs, plus all types of accommodation.

Dublin City

■ History

Dublin appeared as **Eblana** on Ptolemy's map of 140 AD. The **Vikings** arrived around 841, set up a trading post on the south bank of the Liffey, around Islandbridge and Kilmainham, and were defeated by Brian Boru at Clontarf in 1014. After the **Anglo-Norman** conquest of 1169 the city became their seat of power, with a castle near where Dublin Castle stands today.

In the 18th century the city was one of the most elegant anywhere, with its Georgian squares and architecture. Ireland's Parliament met in Dublin in the elegant building opposite Trinity College, now the Bank of Ireland (you had to be a Protestant and male to be elected to Parliament). Handel performed *The Messiah* for the first time in Dublin in 1742.

All changed with the **Act of Union** (1800) when the city, as a reaction to the French Revolution and the United Irishmen rising, lost its political power to London. Agitation for Home Rule increased over the next 100 years or so, leading to the **Easter Rising** (1916), when the Irish Republic was proclaimed at the General Post Office on O'Connell Street.

Recent Times

Dublin has become a very cosmopolitan city, the economy has greatly improved, and there's been a huge increase in immigrants. These developments have not all had a positive effect. Traffic has become a major problem, house prices are very high, and the city now sprawls in all directions. A third of the Republic's population lives in the greater Dublin area.

Although planning decisions in less prosperous times led to the destruction of many fine buildings and ugly replacements, Dublin is still an attractive city, particularly along the river. There are many wonderful examples of Georgian architecture, along with some good examples of more contemporary design.

TOURIST INFORMATION

Dublin Tourism Center is in a lovely old church on Suffolk Street, off Dame Street. It has information on the entire island, and there's a 24-hour touch screen outside. Open July-August, Monday-Saturday, 9 am-7 pm, Sunday 10:30 am-3 pm; September-June, Monday-Saturday, 9 am-5:30 pm, Bank Holidays 10:30 am-3 pm. For other Tourism offices, see end of chapter, page 106.

■ Getting Here

Dublin Airport is 10 km north of the city center (via N1/M1/E01). The main **railway stations** are Connolly and Heuston.

By Bus

Busárus is the bus station. The **Stationlink** bus connects the railway stations and Busárus, stopping in the city center. There are also frequent buses from Heuston into the center; one-way tickets cost less than one euro.

Airlink Express Bus links O'Connell Street, Busáras, Connolly Station, Temple Bar and Heuston Station.

Dublin Bus operates other services to the airport. Reach them at 59 Upper O'Connell Street. ☎ (01) 873-4222; info@dublinbus.ie; www.dublinbus.ie.

Aircoach runs every 15 minutes from the airport with 15 stops near main hotels. ☎ (01) 844-7118; fax 844-7119; www.aircoach.ie.

By Taxi

Traveling from the airport to the city takes 20-50 minutes, depending on traffic, and costs at least €20. (Traffic into Dublin is busiest from 7-11 am; outwards from the city, 3-7 pm is the busiest time.) A taxi stand is outside the Arrivals Hall on the right; rates are displayed in the taxis.

■ Getting Around

Seeing the city is best done on foot or bus. The county is best explored by bus, DART or car.

Dublin Bus Office, 59 Upper O'Connell Street. ☎ (01) 873-4222; www.dublinbus.ie.

DART (Dublin Area Rapid Transit), an electrified train service, runs parallel to the coast from Howth, north of the city, to Bray in Co. Wicklow to the south, with plenty of stops and connections with bus routes. There are three DART stops in the city center – Tara Street, Pearse Street and Connolly Station. It's a cheap and pleasant way of getting around, but avoid peak times when trains are crammed.

Suburban Rail – Arrow Services connect satellite towns in the surrounding counties of Kildare, Louth and Wicklow with the city, from Connolly or Heuston stations.

The Luas is the latest development in Dublin transportation – Luas is Irish for speed – an on-street light rail/tram system. For more information, see www.luas.ie.

Bus tours are the easiest way to explore, especially if time is limited. You can hop on and off, and your ticket gives you reduced entry to some sites. Tickets can be purchased on board, from office or online, from the Tourism Centre and offices, or major hotels. Tours are run by Dublin Bus (see above) and by Irish City Tours, 33 Batchelor's Walk. ☎ (01) 872-9010; www.irishcitytours.com.

*Take a breather in one of the city's open spaces. **Phoenix Park**, founded in 1662, is the largest city park in Europe, and **St. Stephen's Green**, laid out as a public park in 1890 by Sir Arthur Edward Guinness, of the drink family, is very close to the center.*

■ Sightseeing

O'Connell Street

 The city's main thoroughfare is wide, flanked by interesting buildings, as well as some unattractive ones. Efforts are being made to improve it, but unfortunately it has ugly plastic signs, litter and a number of fast food outlets.

Despite negative aspects, it is worth seeing the **General Post Office** (GPO), where on Easter Monday, 1916, a group of rebels led by Pádraig Pearse, proclaimed the Irish Republic. British forces shelled it and most of the street from a gunboat in the Liffey. The rebels held out for five days and 16 of their leaders were executed and 200 imprisoned. You can still see bullet holes in the building and inside there's a sculpture by Oliver Sheppard of the mythical Celtic warrior Cúchullain in memory of the Easter Rising heroes.

Dominating the skyline is the **Spire**, seven times the height of the GPO, erected in 2003 to mark the Millennium, standing on the site of Nelson's Column which was blown up by the IRA in 1965. The Spire's tip sways when the wind is strong, but don't worry – that's part of its design.

College Green

Cross O'Connell Bridge, and on the right is the pedestrian **Halfpenny Bridge**, named after the toll charged from 1821 until the early 1900s. Pass the **Bank of Ireland** on College Green, opposite Trinity College, the home of the Irish Parliament from 1783 to 1801, a marvelous building in neo-classical style. The **Arts Center** in Foster Place next to it houses an interactive museum, also a venue for recitals, exhibitions, and theater. Open Tuesday-Friday, 10 am-4 pm. ☎ (01) 671-1488.

Trinity College

This is the oldest university in Ireland, founded in 1591 by Queen Elizabeth of England. Its cobbled quadrangles are surrounded by cream-colored stone buildings. Famous students include Oliver Goldsmith, Edmund Burke, Dean Swift, J.M. Synge, Samuel Beckett, and the author of *Dracula*, Bram Stoker.

The Book of Kells, an illuminated manuscript of the gospels, dating from about 806, was in the Long Room of the Old Library, but because of visitor numbers it is now the center of an exhibition on the third floor of the Main Library. There are 860 pages, and each day one is turned. Open Monday-Saturday, 9:30 am-5 pm; Sunday, October-May, noon to 4:30 pm; Sunday, June-September, 9:30 am-4:30 pm. A combined ticket is available with *The Dublin Experience*, multimedia audio-visual show telling the city's story. Open May-September, 10 am-5 pm.

The **Douglas Hyde Gallery**, at the Nassau Street entrance to Trinity College, hosts exhibitions of contemporary art. They are open Monday-Friday, 11-6; Thursday, 11-7; Saturday, 11-4:45. ☎ (01) 608-1116.

> *Greene's Bookshop at 16 Clare Street, behind Trinity and close to the entrance to the Millennium Wing of the National Gallery, is worth a stop. Downstairs are new books, some at bargain prices; upstairs is a treasure trove for anyone seeking rare and out-of-print titles at low prices. Browse the shelves at your leisure. It's especially good for books by Irish authors, and you may even bump into a writer or two. ☎ (01) 676-2554; www.greenesbookshop.com.*

St. Stephen's Green

Sadly, many of the buildings around the Green were demolished to make way for ugly ones in the 1960s, but some older ones remain. **Newman House** on the south side of the green is actually two houses built around 1738 and now named after the cardinal who was the first Rector of the Catholic University of Ireland when it was founded in 1853. Gerald Manley Hopkins, the Jesuit priest and poet, was Professor of Classics here from 1884-89 and his room has been restored. James Joyce was the university's most famous student from 1899-1902.

Dublin

A PAUSE IN ELEGANT SURROUNDINGS

On the north side of the green, **The Shelbourne Hotel** looks out over it and retains the elegance and atmosphere of times past. It's an institution, a wonderful place to stay, with charming staff, but if your budget isn't up to it you can still enjoy its hospitality by taking morning coffee in the Lord Mayor's parlor. Afternoon tea is also memorable; they serve bite-size sandwiches and delicious pastries, and you're entertained by a pianist.

The Horseshoe Bar is popular with locals, including politicians and business people. You can also dine in the hotel's fine restaurant No 27 The Green (booking is recommended), or have lunch in the Shelbourne Bar, surrounded by the political cartoons of Martyn Turner.

Room Reservations, toll-free US/Canada ☎ 800-543-4300; in Ireland, ☎ 800-409-090. $$$-$$$$ room or suite. www.shelbourne.ie.

Kildare Street

Around the corner, is **Leinster House**, built as the home of the Duke of Leinster in 1745, which today houses the Oireachtas (the two houses of government), as well as the National Library and Natural History Museum.

There are three branches of the **National Museum** – Archaeology and History on Kildare Street, Natural History behind it on Merrion Street, and Decorative Arts and History in the former Collins Barracks away from the center, off Ellis Quay across the river from Heuston Station. Admission is free to all, except special exhibitions, and they have free lunchtime and evening lectures too. Open Tuesday-Saturday, 10 am-5 pm, Sunday, 2-5 pm. Guided tours available. ☎ (01) 677-7444; fax 677-7459, marketing@museum.ie. Admission free.

You can travel between the three branches on the Museumlink bus, for a small charge. Tickets are sold in the museums. Service hourly, Monday-Saturday, 8 am-5:30 pm, Sundays, 1-5 pm.

The National Museum

Learn about the country's history and see examples of artifacts, including gold ornaments from the Bronze Age, hoards dating from the Celtic Iron Age, as well as some of the most famous Christian treasures – among them the Ardagh Chalice, the Tara Brooch and the Clonmacnoise Crozier. A favorite display of mine is called Ten Years Collecting, in which a selection of items discovered by the public are shown in labeled boxes – you lift the lid to take a look. There's a café as well as a book and gift shop.

A visit to the National Museum on Kildare Street will save you a lot of reading, as the displays cleverly tell you enough about the country and its people to aid your enjoyment as you venture farther afield.

The Natural History Museum

Quaint and delightful, founded in 1857, the NHM houses a collection of animals from all over the world, some now extinct. The building itself, faced in granite, is designed to harmonize with the National Gallery on the other side of Leinster House. Personal favorites are the rabbits and hares, the grizzly bear, the basking shark and the giant Irish elk. Anyone interested in fishing will love these exhibits. There's a book and gift shop.

The Museum of Decorative Arts & History

Displays cover everything from folklife to silver ceramics and glassware to weapons and costume. It's housed in the beautifully restored Collins

Barracks and will entertain and enthrall you for hours. There are special events and temporary exhibitions, plus a café and book and gift shop.

The National Gallery of Ireland

The gallery is on Merrion Square with a recently built extension, the Millennium Wing, and a second entrance on Clare Street. Admission is free, except for special exhibitions. It has 54 galleries and more than 11,000 works of art, including many examples of Western European art and the most important collection of Irish art.

Free public tours are offered on Saturday at 3 pm and Sunday at 2, 3 and 4 pm; there's also a series of events, and a free brochure gives details.

> **TIME SAVER**
>
> If your time is limited, concentrate on the Irish art – from the 18th and 19th centuries in the Milltown Wing; modern in the Millennium Wing and the Yeats Museum and Shaw Room, both in the Dargan Wing. The Gallery has a café, a restaurant, and two shops.

Open Monday-Saturday, 9:30 am-5:30 pm, Thursday, to 8:30 pm; Sunday, noon-5:30 pm. ☎ (01) 661-5372; fax (01) 661-5372; artgall@eircom.ie; www.nationalgallery.ie.

The Cultural Quarter

Close to the city's center, the area has been developed as a cultural quarter, with the **Irish Film Center**, the **National Photographic Archive**, **Arthouse Multimedia Center**, **Temple Bar Galleries**, plus lots of bars, restaurants, shops. It can be very busy, especially in the evening and on weekends. It attracts young people from all over the country and the UK, who spill out onto the streets with drinks in their hands.

> **FREE ENTERTAINMENT**
>
> During the summer a free outdoor festival called **Diversions** is held in Meeting House Square. It has films, music and other live performances. Pick up a copy of the free guide locally or check the website: www.templebar.ie; info@temple-bar.ie, ☎ (01) 677 2255.
>
> Every Saturday from 10 am to 5 pm enjoy all sorts of delicious things to eat at the **Food Market**, and browse the old and new titles at the small **Book Market**.

Dublin

More City Sights

You'll probably need to take a taxi or bus to do more sightseeing, although some of the following are within walking distance of the center.

Drimnagh Castle was, until 1954, one of the oldest continually inhabited Castles in Ireland, and is an outstanding example of an old feudal stronghold. It is the only Irish castle still to be surrounded by a flooded moat, a very picturesque feature, described in 1780 as a "very deep ditch of water supplied from the Green Hills." It is now stocked with fish. The castle, built of local grey limestone, consists of a restored Great Hall and medieval undercroft, a tall battlement tower with lookout posts, and other separate buildings, including stables, old coach, dairy and folly tower. One of the most attractive aspects of Drimnagh is the garden – a formal 17th-century layout with box hedges, yews, mop head laurels and an allée of hornbeam. Open April-October, Wednesday, Saturday, Sunday, 12-5 pm. Open only on Wednesdays the rest of the year. Long Mile Road, Drimnagh, Dublin 12, ☎ (0)1 450-2530.

Christ Church Cathedral is Dublin's oldest building, erected in 1038 by the Danish King Sitric, although most of what remains is Norman. Services take place at least three times a day, and visitors of all denominations or none are welcome to attend. Open daily (except December 26), Monday-Friday, 9:45-5 pm; Saturday and Sunday, 10 am-5 pm. Small donation requested. Guided tours and leaflets available.

The cathedral's unique crypt is almost as big as the church above. It features an exhibition, Treasures of Christ Church, that includes gilt plate given by King William in 1697 to celebrate winning the Battle of the Boyne; the tomb of Strongbow; and a medieval reliquary that holds the heart of St. Laurence O'Toole, the city's patron. Admission charge. ☎ (01) 677-8099; welcome@cccdub.ie; www.cccdub.ie.

Marsh's Library, close to Christ Church, was founded in 1701 by Archbishop Narcissus Marsh. It's the oldest public library in the country and holds about 250,000 books, most from the 16th to 18th centuries. See the tiny reading cubicles, beautiful oak bookcases and the cages where those consulting rare volumes were locked in.

 *If literary Dublin attracts you, visit the **Dublin Writers' Museum** on Parnell Square at the top of O'Connell Street, and find out about places associated with writers. Next door is the **Irish Writers' Centre**, which holds readings and other events. ☎ (01) 872-1302; www.writerscentre.ie.*

The **James Joyce Center** is nearby on North Great George's Street, and the birthplace of **George Bernard Shaw** is on Synge Street.

The Guinness Storehouse, St. James' Gate, is where you learn all about how the "dark stuff" is made and the history of the brewery spanning more than 250 years. Visits end in the Sky Bar with a glass of Guinness and a wonderful view of the city. Open daily, 9:30 am-5 pm. ☎ (01) 453-8364; www.guinness.com.

IMMA – the Irish Museum of Modern Art – is housed in part of what used to be the Royal Hospital Kilmainham where wounded soldiers were looked after. The magnificent neoclassical building, dating from 1680, was modeled on Les Invalides in Paris, and is used for special events.

My Favorite & It's Free

The **Chester Beatty Library** is in the Clock Tower building in the grounds of Dublin Castle, (where you can visit the State Apartments), and is a very attractive and stimulating place to visit. The library's collection was given to Ireland by the American Chester Beatty, who had made his fortune in mining and retired to live here in 1950.

If you are not an avid reader, don't be put off by its name, as you see far more than books. Displayed are manuscripts, prints, miniature paintings, icons, objets d'art as well as early printed books from Asia, the Middle East, North Africa and Europe. One floor is devoted to Beatty and his collection and the other to the great religions of the world. There's a peaceful Roof Garden, a gift shop and café plus special events and temporary exhibitions.

Free tours of the library's highlights are offered on Wednesday at 1 pm and Sunday at 3 pm and 4 pm. Admission is free. Opening hours: May-September, Monday-Friday, 10 am-5 pm; Saturday, 11 am-5 pm, Sunday, 1-5 pm; October-April, closed Mondays. ☎ (01) 407-0750; fax 407-0760; info@cbl.ie; www.cbl.ie.

Kilmainham Gaol opened in 1796 and two years later the leaders of the rebellion were imprisoned there. Robert Emmet, Charles Stewart Parnell, Eamon De Valera are just some of the well-known people incarcerated here until the gaol closed in 1924. The leaders of the 1916 Rising were executed by firing squad in the stone-breaking yard; their names are listed on a plaque. You can see the grim conditions in the tiny cells in the restored building and there's a guided tour and an audio-visual presentation and exhibition.

St. Patrick's Cathedral is the national cathedral of the Church of Ireland and the largest church in the country. There's been a church on the site since 450 and there's a legend that St. Patrick baptized converts at a well nearby. The present building dates from 1191. Jonathan Swift, author of *Gulliver's Travels*, was Dean here from 1713-45 and there are lots

Dublin

of reminders of him. Open daily, 9 am-6 pm, except November-February when it closes at 5 pm on Saturdays and 3 pm on Sundays. Visitors of all faiths are welcome. Small admission charge. ☎ (01) 453-9472 (office), 475-4817 (Cathedral); www.stpatrickscathedral.ie.

My Favorite Dublin Pubs

McDaids, 3 Harry Street, off Grafton Street, is a famous literary pub, where writer Brendan Behan was among regulars. It was once the city morgue and later a chapel, which is why its décor is Gothic. It has jazz and blues sessions. ☎ (01) 679-4395.

O'Neills, 2 Suffolk Street, just across street from Tourist Center, is a traditional pub, popular with residents. It serves a good, reasonably priced, lunch. There's been a pub here for 300 years. ☎ (01) 679-3656.

The Brazen Head, 20 Lower Bridge Street, down the hill from Christ Church Cathedral. The oldest pub in Dublin, it has rooms connected by low passages, with live music nightly. This spot can get crowded in tourist season. ☎ (01) 679-5186.

The Dawson Lounge, 25 Dawson Street, off St. Stephen's Green. You could easily walk past its entrance, as this must be the smallest pub in the city, at the bottom of a corkscrew staircase. It opened in the 1940s, and has a great atmosphere. ☎ (01) 677 5909.

■ Adventures on Foot

Walking Tours

 Historical Walking Tour: Led by history graduates of Trinity College, this two-hour walk starts at front gate of Trinity College. It's run May-September, Monday-Friday, 11 am and 3 pm; Saturday and Sunday, 11 am, 12 and 3 pm; October-April, Friday-Saturday-Sunday at noon. ☎ (01) 878-0227; fax 878-3787; tours@historicalinsights.ie; www.historicalinsights.ie.

Literary Pub Crawl: Two actors perform humorous extracts from city's best-known writers, there are visits to four pubs, and a quiz with prizes. Meet upstairs at The Duke, 9 Duke Street for this two-hour jaunt. April-October, nightly at 7:30 pm, Sundays at noon and 7:30 pm all year, November-March, Thursday, Friday and Saturday at 7:30 pm. Book at Tourist Center, Suffolk Street, ☎ (01) 670-5602; fax 670-5603/454-5680; info@dublinpubcrawl.com; www.dublinpubcrawl.ie.

Musical Pub Crawl: Two professional musicians tell the story of Irish music in 2½ hours. Meet upstairs at Oliver St. John Gogarty's on corner of Fleet Street and Angelsea Street, Temple Bar, 7:30 pm. May-October, nightly; November, February, March, April, Friday and Saturday only. Book at Tourist Center or call on the night you plan to attend. ☎ (01) 478-0193; fax 475-1324; info@musicalpubcrawl.com; www.musicalpubcrawl.com.

The Zozimus Ghostly Experience: Named after a real character, this 1½-hour tour visits scenes of murders, great escapes, and mythical happenings in the medieval city. Meet at the pedestrian entrance to Dublin Castle on Dame Street. Tour times vary, but usually are 9 pm in summer and 7 pm winter. You must book at Dublin Tourism Center or by phone, ☎ (01) 661-8646; fax 676-0504; info@zozimus.com; www.zozimus.com.

Other Walking Tours: There is a choice of heritage trails as well, dealing with culture, Georgian buildings, the Old City. They start at the Tourism Center in the church on Suffolk Street, off Dame Street, and can be reserved there.

There are marked trails along the towpaths of both the **Royal Canal**, north of the city center, and the **Grand Canal**, to its south, a pleasant way of exploring Dublin City. For information, phone the Waterways Service of Dúchas, the Heritage Service, ☎ (01) 647-6000.

■ Adventures on Water
Boating

 An unusual way of seeing the city is with **Viking Splash Tours**, in which you travel on a reconditioned Duck – a World War II amphibious vehicle. Starting in Bull Alley Street, beside St. Patrick's Cathedral, the tours take you by some of the sights and then you splash into the Grand Canal Harbor and continue from there. You don't get wet and it's fun.

Ducks run from February to November, with 10 tours a day. Check times and book by credit card, ☎ (01) 855-3000. You can also book at Dublin Tourism centers, or at the departure point, 64-5 Patrick Street. Also viking@esatclear.ie; www.vikingsplashtours.com.

With its location on Dublin Bay and the River Liffey, the city and county offer many opportunities for water-based activities. If you're a sailor, make contact with the local clubs to find out about upcoming events.

Sailing, kayaking, and canoeing are some of the activities available in the coastal towns, but you don't have to leave the city since **The Surfdock Centre** runs courses and rents equipment. It's at Grand Canal Yard, Ringsend, where it has 42 acres (17 hectares) of enclosed freshwater for its courses in kayaking, sailing, and windsurfing. ☎ (01) 668-3945; fax 668-1215; www.surfdock.ie.

The **Clontarf Yacht and Boat Club** is on the coast just two miles (3.2 km) north of Dublin city center, on the bus and DART routes. ☎ (01) 833-2691; info@cybc.ie.

Fishing

Dublin's waters are managed by the Eastern Regional Fishery Board, and there's loads of information on its website at www.fishingireland.net or at info@erfb.ie.

The **Royal Canal** north of the city center and the **Grand Canal** to the south are popular with local anglers, and visitors should contact the local club concerned (listed below).

At Ballybough near Croke Park, the Royal Canal, between locks 1-2, has recently been developed. For **Belcamp Coarse Angling Club**, contact Paul McDonnell. ☎ (01) 847-6120.

There have been good catches of roach, bream and perch along the Royal at Ashtown, where 45 permanent pegs have been installed and stocks have been improved. The stretch is between locks 9-10 on Scribblestown Road. Contact the **Dublin and District Angling Club**, Secretary David McNiece. ☎ (01) 821-0834.

Members of the local angling club fish the stretch of the Grand Canal from the Lough and Quay pub in Clondalkin to the M50 bridge. Fishing stands have been installed along it by the Waterways Service, and roach and tench are the main catch. Contact John Travers of the **Clondalkin and District Angling Club**, ☎ (01) 457-3793.

The **Portobello Angling Club** runs regular matches during the summer along the Grand Canal between Dolphin's Barn and Portobello, and welcomes visitors. There are good stocks of tench, as well as pike and roach. ☎ (01) 453-0430.

For the **Dublin Angling Club**, contact Paul Kelly, 39 Verschoyle Avenue, Saggart Abbey, Saggart, Co. Dublin. ☎ (01) 451 8518.

Outside the city center, among the best places for coarse fishing is the **Pollaphuca Reservoir** at Blessington Lake. You can buy permits from Charles Camping, ☎ (045) 865-351, and Gyves Shop, ☎ (045) 865-153, both in Blessington.

Another popular area is the **Leixlip Reservoir**. It's above the hydroelectric station and dam on the River Liffey, with access next to the Salmon Leap Inn. The reservoir is owned by the ESB (Electricity Supply Board) and a small section is leased to the Dublin Trout Anglers' Association, with fishing free and available to all. Currently there's limited access to most of the reservoir with the main fishing area between the M4 Motorway bridge and a picnic area, where there's a wide variety of coarse fish.

See pages 71-74 for details on angling in Ireland, regulations and best times to fish.

More Useful Contacts

- **Dublin Pike Anglers**, Mr Rory McAllorum. ☎ (01) 838-9026.
- **Inchicore & District Angling**, Secretary Brian Devlin. ☎ (01) 455-0745.
- **Dublin Angling Club**, Paul Kelly, 39 Verschoyle Avenue, Saggart Abbey, Saggart, Co. Dublin. ☎ (01) 451 8518.

■ Adventures on Horseback

A number of riding stables are within easy reach of the city, charging about €25 an hour, with or without instruction. Some offer guided trail riding, as well as courses on show jumping and cross-country riding.

Ashdown Riding Stables near Phoenix Park offers trail riding through the park. You can get there easily by bus or car from the center. ☎ (01) 838-3807.

Carrickmines Equestrian Centre, Foxrock, ☎ (01) 295-5990, and **Ballycullen Equestrian Centre**, Knocklyon, Dublin 6, ☎ (01) 494-5415, are both south of the city center.

Others equestrian centers include:

- **Calliaghstown Riding Centre**, Rathcoole, Co. Dublin. ☎ (01) 458-9236.
- **Balcunnin Equestrian Centre** at Skerries offers instruction, trekking and other activities. ☎ (01) 849-0964.
- **Brooke Lodge Riding Centre**, Stepaside, Co. Dublin. ☎ (01) 295-2153.
- **Brackenstown Equestrian Centre**, Knocksadan, Swords, Co. Dublin. ☎ (01) 840-3525.
- **Brittas Lodge Riding Stables**, Blessington Road, Brittas, Co. Dublin. ☎ (01) 458-2726.
- **Thornton Park Equestrian Centre** is at Kilsallaghan, north of the city, off the N2 road to Slane, and has large indoor and all-weather arenas. ☎ (01) 835-1164; fax 835-2725; www.thortonpark.ie.

The Broadmeadow Country House and Equestrian Centre is actually in the next county, Meath, but is only 15 minutes from Dublin Airport on country roads and only 25 minutes from Dublin city center.

It has three arenas, one indoor, and is Dublin's Grand Prix Showjumping venue. You can ride horses and ponies at all skill levels. Broadmeadow is surrounded by lovely gardens and also has a tennis court. You don't have to stay, but it does offer accommodations on a bed-and-breakfast basis. Bullstown, Ashbourne, Co. Meath. ☎ (01) 835-2823; fax 835-2819; info@ irelandequestrian.com; www.irelandequestrian.com.

■ Golf

There are more than 50 courses within an hour of the city, ranging from pay-and-play to championship courses.

Deer Park, Howth, is the largest golf complex in Ireland, with an 18-hole course, two demanding nine-hole courses that can be played as 18 holes, a full-length 12-hole par 3 and an 18-hole pitch-and-putt. ☎ (01) 832-2624; fax 839 2405; sales@deerpark.iol.ie.

The City Golf Club, Ballinascorney, eight miles (13 km) southwest of the city center, must have one of the most scenic locations anywhere. It's a mature 18-hole course maintained to a very high standard, set in the beautiful valley of Glen Na Smól (valley of the thrush), a national heritage area. There's lots of wildlife and you might share the fairways with deer. ☎ (01) 451-6430; info@dublincitygolf.com.

Corballis, which is at Donabate, north of the city, is the only public links course in the country. It's playable year-round and visitors are always welcome. ☎ (01) 843-6583.

The Luttrellstown Golf Club is in the grounds of the magnificent 15th-century castle estate, only 20 minutes from the city center, yet really peaceful, near Castleknock. ☎ (01) 808-9988.

The Royal Dublin Golf Course is a traditional links overlooking Dublin Bay. Visitors welcome; call for hours. It's at North Bull Island, Clontarf, near city center. ☎ (01) 833-6346; fax 833-6504.

The Malahide Golf Club. ☎ (01) 846-1611; malgc@clubi.ie.

■ Shopping

Grafton Street, close to Trinity College, is pedestrians-only and full of shops. Some belong to UK chains, others are specialized, and there are plenty of coffee shops and restaurants, including **Bewleys**, a Dublin tradition. Streets radiating off it are also worth exploring. At the top of Grafton Street is the **Stephen's Green Shopping Center**, with a big selection of shops.

The other main shopping area in the city center is around **Mary Street and Henry Street**, just off O'Connell Street near the GPO.

Dublin, like many cities, is a collection of villages and you'll find plenty of interesting shops in areas such as Rathmines, Dundrum, Howth, Blackrock.

If thinking about gifts, look for linen or woolens, sold in many shops, and don't restrict yourself to those aimed at tourists. Buy where the Irish themselves do. **The Kilkenny Design Center** on Nassau Street, behind Trinity, has a huge range of Irish-made crafts. **DESIGNYard**, 12 East Essex Street, Temple Bar, has a great selection of contemporary jewelry, ceramics, glass and other items. **The Bridge Gallery**, 6 Upper Ormond Quay, has a similar choice, as well as work by Irish artists.

County Dublin

The county is divided into three administrative areas: **Fingal** to the north, parallel to the coast, and south of the city; **Dun Laoghaire/ Rathdown**, which follows the sea; and **South Dublin**, farther inland. It's an interesting county, the landscape generally flat, with the Dublin Mountains forming its natural boundary on the southern side, where it meets Co. Wicklow.

Dublin

TRACING YOUR ANCESTORS

Fingal Genealogy Centre - Swords Historical Society Ltd, Carnegie Library, North Street, Swords. ☎/fax (01) 840-0080; swordsheritage@eircom.net.

Dun Laoghaire Rathdown Heritage Centre, Moran Park House, Dun Laoghaire. ☎ (01) 205-4700, ext 406; enaobrien@ dlrcoco.ie.

■ North County Dublin ~ Fingal

Sightseeing

 The area north of the city has many attractions and facilities. Start exploring close to the center at the **National Botanical Gardens**, where there are about 20,000 different plant species. It's a great place for a walk. The historic curvilinear greenhouses are especially interesting. Open summer, 9 am-6 pm. Sundays, all year from 11 am. Winter, 10 am-4:30 pm. The greenhouse hours vary. ☎ (01) 837-7596/837-4388; fax 836-0080.

There are free two-hour tours of **Glasnevin Cemetery** next door on Wednesdays and Fridays. Meet at the main gate at 2:30. Since 1832 over a million people have been buried here, among them many of those who shaped Irish history – including Daniel O'Connell, Charles Stewart Parnell, Michael Collins, Constance Marcievicz, Eamon De Valera, Maud Gonne MacBride, and Brendan Behan. ☎ (01) 830-1133, 830-1594; www. glasnevin-cemetery.ie.

There's a wonderful panorama of Dublin Bay from **Howth Head**. **Howth Castle Gardens** has an amazing collection of over 2,000 varieties of rhododendron. There's a bird sanctuary on **Lambay Island**, off the seaside resort of Portrane. **Swords**, inland on the N1, is the administrative capital of Fingal and its **medieval castle** is open to the public.

AUTHOR RECOMMENDS

Just as you leave the city, there's one stop you should make. **Marino Casino**, off the Malahide road, is a delight. Built in 1759, it's a tiny neo-classical building, which only 16 people can tour at one time. Open daily, May-end October, 10 am-5 pm, June-September, to 6 pm. Thursday and Sunday only the rest of year; closed December and January. ☎ (01) 833-1618.

Malahide Castle, in 250 acres of parkland, is in the seaside town of the same name, just north of the city. It belonged to the Talbot family from 1185-1973, and is full of period furniture, fittings and portraits from the National Gallery. A highlight is Puck, the castle's ghost. The grounds are also open. Open all year, Monday-Saturday, 10 am-5 pm; Sundays and public holidays, 11 am-6 pm, April to October; 11 am-5 pm, November-March. Note that the castle is closed for tours from 12:45 to 2 pm, but the restaurant is open. ☎ (01) 846-2184; fax 846-2537; malahidecastle@ dublintourism.ie.

Combined tickets are available with **Fry Model Railway** in the Castle grounds, which is delightful. It's a collection of handmade models of Irish trains built up in the 1920s and '30s by Cyril Fry, a railway engineer and draughtsman. Open April-September only, Monday-Saturday, 10 am-5 pm. Closed 1-2 pm; Sundays and public holidays, 2-6 pm. ☎ (01) 846-3779; fax 846-3723; fryrailway@dublintourism.ie.

Skerries

The harbor at Skerries is busy in summer and it's the major landing port for Dublin Bay prawns. A large colony of grey seals lives in and around

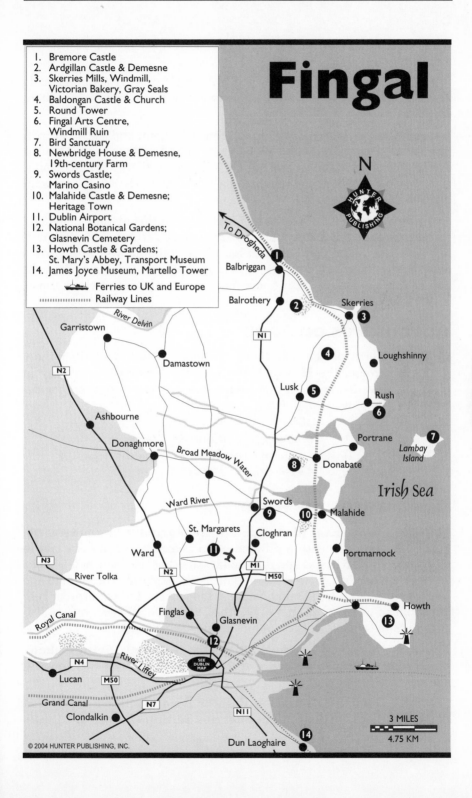

Fingal

1. Bremore Castle
2. Ardgillan Castle & Demesne
3. Skerries Mills, Windmill, Victorian Bakery, Gray Seals
4. Baldongan Castle & Church
5. Round Tower
6. Fingal Arts Centre, Windmill Ruin
7. Bird Sanctuary
8. Newbridge House & Demesne, 19th-century Farm
9. Swords Castle; Marino Casino
10. Malahide Castle & Demesne; Heritage Town
11. Dublin Airport
12. National Botanical Gardens; Glasnevin Cemetery
13. Howth Castle & Gardens; St. Mary's Abbey, Transport Museum
14. James Joyce Museum, Martello Tower

⚓ Ferries to UK and Europe
∙∙∙∙∙∙∙∙∙∙∙∙∙∙∙∙∙ Railway Lines

N

To Drogheda

Balbriggan

Balrothery

Skerries

River Delvin

Garristown

N1

Loughshinny

Damastown

N2

Lusk

Rush

Ashbourne

Portrane

Lambay Island

Donaghmore

Broad Meadow Water

Donabate

Irish Sea

Ward River

Swords

Malahide

St. Margarets

Cloghran

Ward

Portmarnock

N3

River Tolka

N2

M1

M50

Finglas

Glasnevin

Howth

Royal Canal

SEE DUBLIN MAP

N4

River Liffey

Lucan

M50

Grand Canal

N7

Clondalkin

N11

Dun Laoghaire

3 MILES
4.75 KM

Dublin

the harbor, where the sailing club and several of the town's restaurants and pubs are located.

It has a long, safe and sandy beach, with a pleasant grass promenade running along beside it to **Red Island Scenic Park**, from where there are lovely views.

You can visit two restored windmills – one with four, and the other with five sails – dating from 1821-39. Skerries Mills Heritage Centre houses exhibitions of agricultural and milling equipment; there's art on display, a very good craft shop, and relaxing tea rooms. ☎ (01) 849-5208; www.indigo.ie/~skerries.

Ardgillan House (1738) looks like a castle, and this historic home and its grounds are open to the public. There are rose gardens and a fascinating Victorian walled garden which has a free-standing wall with alcoves used to grow delicate fruits. The park is open year-round during daylight hours. There are tours of the house daily in summer; call to check times. ☎ (01) 849-2212.

Adventures on Foot

North of the city there are many walks, including those around the **Hill of Howth**, in the **Ward River Valley** in Swords, or along the **beaches**. Call Fingal Tourism for details, ☎ (01) 840-0077.

*At **Courtlough Shooting Grounds**, near Balbriggan, you can learn clay pigeon shooting, ☎ (01) 841-3096; fax 841-5462.*

Adventures on Water

Head for the **Malahide Village Marina**, a few miles north, for a trip with a difference – a Sea Safari. Trips are run in small RIBs – rigid inflatable boats that take seven-11 people. There's a choice of three safaris, all exploring the wildlife and birds around the North Dublin islands. Lifejackets and waterproof gear are supplied and, except in foul weather, trips run all year. ☎ (01) 806-1626; info@seasafari.ie. Book online at www.seasafari.ie.

Also at the Malahide Village Marina is the **National Diving School**, which runs a variety of courses. ☎ 01 845-2000; natdive@nds.ie; www.nds.ie.

Skerries has a sailing school on Harbour Road. Contact Paul Hick at ☎ (01) 849-0363. Or you can call **Skerries Sailing Club** at ☎ (01) 849-1233.

Sailing trips locally and longer can be organized by contacting P. McNally, **Seabreezes**, Quay Street, Skerries. ☎ (01) 849-1446.

Fishing

Balbriggan, Skerries, Loughshinny and Rush are all boat angling venues where you fish around Lambay Island. The first three are also good shore angling locations. Other shore fishing places include the Rogerstown Estuary, Donabate Strand, the Malahide Estuary and the three-mile-long Velvet Strand at Portmarnock.

There's pier, rock and boat fishing at Howth and Sutton, with ground fishing around the island of Ireland's Eye and on the Kish Bank. There's a scenic cliff walk around Howth to The Baily (or access it via Thormanby Road), though care needs to be taken on the rocks as they become slippery in wet weather. Beach fishing at Dollymount Strand and Poolbeg Lighthouse is particularly popular during mackerel season.

See pages 71-74 for details on angling in Ireland, regulations and best times to fish.

▪ South County Dublin

Sightseeing

Attractions in South County Dublin include the **Corkagh Regional Park**, the **Dodder Valley Linear Park** and the **Dublin Mountains**, all great for walks.

Heading towards Dun Laoghaire along the coast you pass the **salt marsh at Booterstown**, a bird sanctuary. At Sandycove there's the **James Joyce Museum** in a Martello tower. These towers were built as defences during the Napoleonic Wars of the 19th century.

Dun Laoghaire is an interesting town which, though now a city suburb, retains its distinct character and the atmosphere of previous centuries, especially in the houses facing the sea. Take a bracing walk on its pier and gaze at the luxury yachts or watch the ferries arriving and departing from across the Irish Sea. The **National Maritime Museum** is also worth a visit.

Also worth seeing in this part of County Dublin are **Fernhill Gardens** in Sandyford and **Dalkey Castle and Heritage Centre**. Drive or cycle around **Killiney Hill**, passing the homes of the rich and famous, and you get wonderful views over Dublin Bay.

Dublin

*The **Killiney Adventure Company** offers hill-walking, orienteering, rock climbing and abseiling, ☎ (01) 276-2800.*

Adventures on Foot

Take the DART or bus south of the city to **Dalkey** and there's a lovely walk from there. Start on Dalkey Avenue at the Post Office and head south. About half a mile farther there's a road on your left that climbs through fields and is the entrance to Dalkey Hill Park. Steps from the car park take you to the top of the hill, from where you get the most amazing views over the bay, with the Wicklow Hills in the distance.

Nearby is **Killiney Hill** which, like Dalkey Hill, drops steeply into the sea, and is topped by an obelisk. There's a trail from it down to Vico Road, where there's a lovely seaside walk.

You can take the DART to its southern terminus at **Bray**, which is in Co. Wicklow. Follow the promenade south through the town to where it begins to climb to Bray Head. It branches to the left and this cliffside walk will take you the 3½ miles (5.6 km) to **Greystones**, a great way to clear your head and enjoy glorious views back towards Killiney, Dalkey and Bray itself. At Greystones you can get the train back if you're tired.

The beautiful **Dublin Mountains** south of the city can be reached easily by bus.

Adventures on Water

South of the city, **Oceantec Adventures** in Dun Laoghaire runs a PADI diving course and organizes diving vacations on the west coast. ☎ (01) 280-1083, 1800-272-822 in Ireland.

At Seapoint, just north of Dun Laoghaire, and on the DART, is the **Wind and Wave Centre**, offering windsurfing and canoeing lessons and equipment rental. ☎ (01) 284-4177.

Fishing

Sandymount Strand attracts shore fishermen and **Dun Laoghaire** is popular for both boat and shore angling from both the east and west piers and the harbor. Boats head out from here to fish around **Scotsman's Bay** and **Dalkey Island**.

Charters

There are two charter boats operating from Dun Laoghaire Harbor, specialising in general ground, wreck and reef fishing off the Kish and Burford Banks.

Charles Robinson Sea Angling Charters. ☎ (0404) 68751.

Dun Laoghaire Boat Charter. ☎ (01) 282-3426.

Continuing south, at **Bullock and Coliemore Harbor** inshore self-drive boats are available for hire. ☎ (01) 280-6517 (Bullock Harbor) and ☎ (01) 283-4298 Coliemore Harbor.

Killiney Beach is another popular location for shore fishing.

Spectator Sports

 There are lots of opportunities to watch sporting events, including GAA (Gaelic Athletic Association) matches at **Croke Park**, rugby and soccer at **Landsdowne Road**, and on Sundays there are lots of local GAA games. There's a greyhound stadium at **Shelbourne Park**, and three racecourses within easy reach of the city. **Leopardstown Racecourse** is only six miles (10 km) south of the city center, ☎ (01) 289-3607; www.leopardstown.com. **Punchestown Racecourse** is near Naas, in neighbouring Co. Kildare, 30 minutes away by road, ☎ (045) 897-704, racing@punchestown.com, www.punchestown.com, and **Fairyhouse Racecourse**, 12 miles (19 km) northwest of Dublin at Ratoath, Co. Meath, ☎ (01) 825-6167, info@fairyhouseracecourse.ie, www.fairyhouseracecourse.ie.

Don't forget that wherever you are there are also local GAA (Gaelic Athletic Association) matches. For details, check in newspapers, ask at your hotel, guest house, tourist information centers, or check online on the Dublin Tourism website.

AUTHOR'S CHOICE

Watch the best riders from Ireland and overseas at the **Dublin Horse Show**, which takes place in August at the RDS Arena. As well as the excitement of the jumping competitions, especially the Nations Cup held on Friday afternoon, there are lots of other events. You see young riders starting their careers, people who breed horses, others who just love them. It's friendly and entertaining, and could be the highlight of a vacation. See http://www.rds.ie/horseshow/about.htm for details.

Entertainment

 There are many theaters and cinemas in Dublin City and surrounding towns. Check newspapers or *In Dublin* magazine, or enquire at accommodation or tourist information centers. Among them are the famous **Abbey Theatre** and the

Gate Theatre, **Andrew's Lane Theatre** (which also has a small Studio), and **The Olympia**. **The Point** hosts musicals, often from London's West End, and concerts by big name stars. North of the city is **The Helix**, which presents touring productions and concerts, and the **Pavilion Theatre** is south of the city in Dun Laoghaire. The **National Concert Hall** is the venue for all sorts of music. There are concerts in the **National Gallery** at times.

In Dublin magazine is also a good source of information about clubs, pubs and other venues. Check out www.cultureireland.ie, call Callsave at ☎ 1850-202-538 or look for the free map guide to arts events.

Comhaltas Ceoltóirí Éireann organizes evenings of traditional music, song, dance, and storytelling all over Ireland, and publishes a free leaflet. It's based in Monkstown, Co. Dublin, where they host evenings. ☎ (01) 280-0295; www.comhaltas.com.

> **Author Tip:** Check if there are lunchtime shows or recitals – they're often cheaper than in the evenings, and sometimes are free. In the parks there may be free concerts on bandstands. In Dublin you often get the chance to see international acts and shows at a fraction of what you'd pay in London or New York. Avoid entertainment aimed at tourists only and go where the Irish go. *In Dublin* or reviews in the newspapers will help you decide. Book at box offices and save paying booking fees.

Where to Stay

■ Hotels

The Clarence, 6-8 Wellington Quay, is owned by members of rock band U2, and very central. It's decorated with light-oak panelling and brass, in the style of the Arts and Crafts movement. The Octagon Bar is popular with the fashionable set and the Tea Room serves very good Irish cuisine, which is not over-priced. Room/suite rates from $$$ (two sharing). ☎ (01) 407-0800; fax 407-0820; reservations@theclarence.ie; www.theclarence.ie.

HOTEL PRICE CHART	
Price per person, per night, with two sharing, including breakfast.	
$	Under US $50
$$	US $50-$100
$$$	US $101-$175
$$$$	US $176-$200
$$$$$	Over US $200

MY FAVORITE PLACE TO STAY

Lynams Hotel, 63/64 O'Connell Street, used to be the home of the inventor of the Tilly lamp, and retains the intimacy of a private house. You couldn't be more central staying here, a few steps from the historic General Post Office. There's a pleasant sitting room where you can read, and the bedrooms are fine, pleasantly decorated. Breakfast is served in the restaurant on the ground floor, which is open all day. From $$. ☎ (01) 888-0886; fax 888-0890; lynams.hotel@indigo.ie; www.lynams-hotel.com.

☆☆☆☆☆ **The Westin** is almost on O'Connell Bridge, and across the road from Trinity College. It's a wonderful place to stay, hidden behind the listed façade of the former Allied Irish Bank (1863), with some of its features retained and restored. Some of the guestrooms overlook a central atrium, others the Georgian and Victorian landmarks of central Dublin.

The bedrooms are beautifully furnished and spacious. I particularly loved the bathroom and the beds are absolutely wonderful. The staff is charming and unobtrusive. This is a relaxing place to stay, close to all the city's attractions, yet peaceful. Overnight parking for a very small fee can be arranged in advance.

From the elegant **Exchange Restaurant** you can look out on the city without passersby seeing you. It serves excellent Irish and International cuisine.

From 9 am to 11 pm, **The Atrium** is a beautiful place to relax over a coffee, a drink or a light meal, as its glass ceiling means it's always flooded with light. At night you can do a bit of star-gazing. **The Mint Bar** downstairs attracts Dubliners and is pleasantly casual; you can also eat here in daytime. $$$ (for two), ☎ (01) 604-0400; fax 865-6390; www.starwood.com.

☆☆☆☆☆ **Berkeley Court** is on Landsdowne Road, Ballsbridge, just five miles (eight km) from Dublin Airport or Heuston Station and only two miles from the city center. It's in an attractive and quiet part of Dublin, yet only a short taxi ride from all the city's attractions, and very close to bus routes and a DART station.

The bedrooms are spacious and pleasantly furnished. Indeed, that's the impression you get the moment you walk in – spaciousness, as you are immediately in a lounge with comfortable seating, where you can relax, have breakfast, a snack or a drink. There's a bar off the lounge, half of it furnished like a library, with a real fire. There's a choice of dining, with the **Palm Court** serving contemporary cuisine, and the award-winning **Berkeley Room**. Rates from $$$, ☎ (01) 660-1711; fax 661-7238; berkeleycourt@jurysdoyle.com; www.jurysdoyle.com.

Dublin

Clarion Stephens Hall Hotel and Suites. Their 33 suites are ideal for anyone who likes a choice as you can dine in the restaurant, order food in your room, or cook for yourself. Suites are spacious, with a hallway, large bedroom with plenty of closet space, a bathroom, large sitting-room and a dining area/kitchenette.

It really is a home away from home where you can enjoy privacy while using the hotel services, including daily cleaning. There's a lounge bar and the restaurant has a terrace. It is just off St. Stephen's Green, so is very convenient for anyone exploring the city or attending an event at the National Concert Hall, just around the corner. Suites from $$. Earlsfort Centre, Lower Leeson Street, toll-free ☎ 800-CLARION, (01) 638-1111; fax 638-1122; stephens@premgroup.com; www.choicehotelsireland.ie.

Avalon House, 55 Aungier Street, Dublin 2, a member of the Independent Holiday Hostels organization, is centrally located close to St. Stephen's Green and within walking distance of most places of interest. They offer single-, twin-, four- and multi-bedded rooms. It's open on a 24-hour basis, has a café or you can cook for yourself. There is secure bike and luggage storage, money-changing facility and really helpful staff. Online reservations. ☎ (01) 4750-0001; fax 4750-0303; info@avalon-house.ie; www.avalon-house.ie.

☆☆☆☆☆ **Radisson SAS Dublin**, Stillorgan Rd Blackrock, Dublin 1, is three miles south of Dublin city center and overlooks Dublin Bay. Originally built in 1750, this historic mansion blends old world style and luxurious amenities. It's surrounded by woodlands. Two restaurants are on-site, plus a bar, lounge, beauty salon and a fitness center. There are 151 guestrooms, with 24-hour room service. Rates from $$$. ☎ 800-55-7474, toll-free from the USA 888-201-1718; www.radisson.com/home.jsp.

■ Camping & RV Parks

There are two camping and caravanning parks in Co. Dublin.

☆☆☆☆ **The Camac Valley Caravan and Camping Park** is on the N7 Naas Road in Clondalkin in South County Dublin and is open all year. It's a spacious site with top-class facilities set next to a 300-acre park that's ideal for walking. ☎ (01) 464-0644; fax 464-0643; camacmorriscastle@eircom.net; www.irishcamping.com.

☆☆ **The North Beach Caravan and Camping Park** is north of Dublin City at Rush, where most of its sites overlook the Irish Sea. The park is easily accessible from the N1, M1 and Dublin Airport. It's set on the edge of the delightful sandy North Beach, which is safe for swimming and watersports. Open March 1 to October 31. ☎/fax (01) 843-7131; info@northbeach.ie; www.northbeach.ie.

Where to Eat

 There's an enormous choice of places to eat in the center, especially in Temple Bar, and around Grafton Street and Dame Street. The following are just a few suggestions for dining away from the center.

The Abbot Restaurant is on the first floor of the Abbey Tavern in Howth, the attractive fishing village. It's only 200 yards to the harbor so no surprise that it is renowned for its seafood, although those who don't eat fish are equally well cared for. It has a very welcoming atmosphere, with an intimacy that's great for romantics, with its candles. ☎ (01) 839-0307; fax 839-0284; info@abbeytavern.ie; www.abbeytavern.ie.

The King Sitric is also in Howth and also specializes in fish and seafood. It's right on the harbor and is very attractive. You can enjoy a drink in its wine cellar while making your meal selection. King Sitric is a member of The Blue Book (see page 60) and is also a four-star-guesthouse, with rates of $$. ☎ (01) 832-5235; fax 839-2442; info@kingsitric; www.kingsitric.ie.

Beaufield Mews Restaurant is in Stillorgan, south of the center, in an 18th-century coachhouse surrounded by gardens. It claims to be the oldest restaurant in Dublin, and certainly it offers a unique experience. You can have a drink in the gardens or take a look in the antique shop before dining. Its menu includes Irish, French and other European dishes. Open Tuesday-Saturday, 6:30-9:30 pm, Sunday, noon-2:30 pm. ☎ (01) 288-0375; fax 288-6945; beaumews@iol.ie; www.beaufieldmews.com.

The Courtyard Café Restaurant and Piano Bar, at Belmont Avenue, Donnybrook, has an early bird menu that is very good value. At Sunday lunch there's jazz music. ☎ (01) 283-0407.

Dublin

AUTHOR RECOMMENDS

My favorite place to eat in Dublin is the **Trocadero** on St. Andrew Street, very near the Tourism Centre. On its menu are seafood, steaks, traditional Irish cuisine and alternatives for vegetarians. The food is good, but that's not the only reason I love it. It's been there since 1956 and has always been popular with people from the film and theater world, who know they'll be well treated but not fawned on by the marvelous staff, who have worked here for years. The walls are covered with autographed photographs, and you often see famous faces eating here, not just Irish but international too. Booking is strongly advised. ☎ (01) 677-5545; fax 679-2385.

Beshoff's, 14 Westmoreland Street, near O'Connell Bridge, also 5 Upper O'Connell Street. Dublin's most famous fish and chip shops are great value. They're open every day all year from 11am to 11 pm, except December 25 and 26. Open late on Friday and Saturday until 3 am at Westmoreland Street. ☎ (01) 677-8026; info@beshoffsrestaurants.ie; www.beshoffrestaurants.ie.

GAY LIFE IN DUBLIN

Take a look at the publications *Gay Community News* or *In Dublin*, to find out what's on. The most comprehensive websites for gay organizations, events, issues, and information are **Gay Ireland Online** (www.gay-ireland.com), **Outhouse** (www.outhouse.ie) and **Dublin's Queer Guide** (www.dublinqueer.com). There are gay and lesbian bars, clubs, venues and organizations, including the Irish Film Centre, that have special gay events.

Helplines: **Lesbians Organizing Together**, ☎ (01) 872-7770, and **Gay Switchboard Dublin**, ☎ (01) 872-1055.

For More Information

Dublin Tourism, within Ireland, ☎ 1850-230-330, from elsewhere, ☎ 00-353-66-979-2083; www.visitdublin.com. They have information and reservation centers at:

■ Arrivals Hall, Dublin Airport, open seven days all year, 8 am-10 pm.

■ Ferry Terminal, Dun Laoghaire Harbour, open all year, Monday-Saturday, 10 am-1 pm, 2-6 pm.

■ 14 Upper O'Connell Street, Dublin, open Monday-Saturday all year, 9 am-5 pm.

■ Baggot Street Bridge, Baggot Street, Dublin 2. Open all year, Monday-Friday, 9:30 am-5 pm, closed noon-12:30.

■ The Square Towncentre, Tallaght, Dublin 24. Open all year, Monday-Saturday, 9:30 am-5 pm, closed noon-12:30.

Fingal Tourism, ☎ (01) 840-0077, fax 840-4988; info@fingaltourism.ie; www.fingal-dublin.ie.

The **Northern Ireland Tourist Board** office is at 16 Nassau Street, behind Trinity College. ☎ (01) 679-1977, fax (01) 679-1863, infodublin@nitb.com.

East Coast
& Midlands

This region brings together eight of the Republic's 32 counties – Wicklow, Kildare, Laois, Offaly, Westmeath, Meath, Longford, Louth – each unique and with a lot to offer visitors. It stretches from the beaches of the east coast and the mountains of Wicklow, the Cooley Peninsula and the Slieve Blooms, to the Bog of Allen and River Shannon in the Midlands, and is the most varied of the Republic's regions.

It's traversed by both the Grand Canal and the Royal Canal, which link Dublin to the River Shannon, and by the River Barrow, winding its way through wooded valleys to Co. Carlow and eventually joining the Grand Canal with the tidal waters of the Barrow estuary.

There really are activities for everyone, with fine parkland and links golf courses, freshwater and sea angling, wonderful equestrian facilities, great walking terrain, and relaxing cruises on its waterways. There's also a huge choice of accommodations, places to eat, and plenty of entertainment of all kinds. Its visitor attractions include ancient monuments, among them Newgrange, heritage sites such as Glendalough and Clonmacnoise, and historic houses and gardens.

The area has a wide range of excellent game, coarse and sea fishing locations. Salmon, sea-trout and brown trout fishing are available on a number of rivers, and there are also several lakes, especially in Meath, Westmeath, Longford and Offaly. The extensive coastline, from Carlingford Lough to where Co. Wicklow meets Co. Wexford, also offers lots of opportunities for the sea angler.

■ Further Information

 The Midlands East Regional Tourism Organisation is responsible for counties Kildare, Laois, Longford, Louth, Meath, North Offaly, Westmeath and Wicklow and is based in Mullingar. ☎ (044) 48761.

East Coast & Midlands

N

Newry
DOWN
Omeath
Carlingford
Cooley Peninsula
Dundalk
R Fane
Irish Sea

A2
A1
N2
N1

Cavan
ARMAGH

L Gowna
Lough Sheelin
Ardee
LOUTH

L Forbes
Granard
Kells
Drogheda
Balbriggan

Longford **32**
Oldcastle
13
14
Slane
2

LONGFORD
Lough Derravaragh
33
31
MEATH
Athboy
Navan
3

Ballymahon **30**
L Owel

Lough Ree
Glasson
Mullingar
28 **27**
15 Trim
Dunshaughlin
Malahide

Athlone **29**
WEST-MEATH
Lough Ennell
Maynooth
16
Celbridge
Dublin

R Shannon
R Brosne
Edenderry
21
KILDARE
R Liffey
Dun Laoghaire

Tullamore **19**
Naas
Enniskerry **4**
Bray

20
Portarlington
Newbridge
17
Blessington
10 Blessington Lake
9 Greystones

OFFALY
Mountmellick
Kildare
5
7
Wicklow Mountains

Birr **22**
LAOIS
Portlaoise
25
18
6 **8**
Wicklow

Mountrath
23
Athy
12
WICKLOW

Roscrea
24
R Barrow
Rathdrum

R Nore
Abbeyleix
Avoca

TIPPERARY
26
Durrow
Carlow
Arklow

KILKENNY

N4, N5, N3, N6, N4, N7, N9, N8, N11, N2

NOT TO SCALE

1. Carlingford; the Tain Way
2. Mellifont Abbey
3. Hill of Tara; Bective Abbey
4. Glencree
5. Glen of Imaal
6. Glenmalure
7. Glenmacnass
8. Glendalough
9. Sally Gap
10. Blessington House
11. Devil's Glen
12. Vale of Avoca
13. Monastery, St. Columb's Church, St. Columcille's House
14. Slane Castle
15. Trim Castle
16. Maynouth Castle
17. St. Brigid's Cathedral, Kildare
18. White Castle, Athy
19. Allen Bog, Clara Bog
20. Slieve Bloom Mountains
21. Grange Castle
22. Birr Castle Demesne
23. Rock of Dunamase, Maryborough Heath
24. Heywood Gardens, Ballinakill
25. Emo Court House & Gardens
26. Aghmacart Priory, Durrow
27. Belvedere House
28. Uisneach Hill, Catstone
29. Athlone Castle
30. Goldsmith Country Pallas, Co Longford)
31. Tullymully Castle, Fore, Castlepollard

Mid-Ireland is marketed as "Enroute Mid-Ireland," and you see road-signs with the symbol "e" encouraging you to journey on the N52 from Roscrea in neighboring county Tipperary to Kilbeggan in Co. Westmeath, with information points and free brochures available. www.enroutemid-ireland.com.

The Coastal Counties

County Louth

Louth, the smallest county on the island, is on the east coast, on the border halfway between Dublin and Belfast. It's named after Lugh, the great god of the Celts, and its Cooley peninsula was the legendary home of the giant, Finn McCool, and the setting of Ulster's greatest saga, the Táin. That's the epic folk tale of the hero Cúchullain, the Red Branch Knights of Ulster, wicked Queen Maeve of Connaught and the mighty Brown Bull of Cooley. (Read her story on page 10.)

Most of the county's landscape is unspoiled and flat, with a low sandy coastline, except in the north, where the Carlingford Peninsula is hilly, with its highest point Slieve Foy, at 1,933 feet.

Despite its size, Louth offers a great choice of activities – sailing and scuba diving, sea and river fishing, horseback riding, hill walking, rock climbing, golf, exploring historical sites, and great traditional hospitality in its many pubs, restaurants, inns, guesthouses and hotels. Among the many interesting places to visit is the site of the Battle of the Boyne, which changed Irish history and influences events even today.

Dundalk is its largest town and county capital; its other main towns are **Drogheda** and **Ardee**.

■ Getting Here

Main Roads

Dundalk is on the N1 from Dublin (53 miles/85 km) and the N1-A1-M1 from Belfast (52 miles/84 km), the N52-N80-N8 from Cork (202 miles/325 km) and the N52-N6 from Galway (148 miles/238 km).

Drogheda is 35 miles (56 km) north of Dublin on the N1.

Ardee in on the main Dublin-Derry route, the N2, and the Dundalk-Mullingar route, the N52.

East Coast & Midlands

Rail

Dundalk and Drogheda are on the mainline railway between Dublin and Belfast. Rail Station, Dundalk, ☎ (042) 933-5529. Rail Station, Drogheda, ☎ (041) 983-8749.

Bus

The county has a very good bus service, with Dundalk and Drogheda on the express services to and from Dublin and Belfast. Bus Station, Dundalk, ☎ (042) 933-4075.

■ Tourist Information

East Coast and Midlands Tourism, Dundalk Tourist Office, Jocelyn Street, open all year. ☎ (042) 933-5484; fax 933-8070; dundalktouristoffice.tinet.ie.

Drogheda Tourist Office, Bus Éireann, open all year. ☎ (041) 983-7070.

Carlingford Tourism Office, seasonal opening. ☎ (042) 937-3033; carlingfordtourism@hotmail.com.

> ### TRACING YOUR ANCESTORS
>
> If your ancestors came from Louth, you should contact the **Meath-Louth Family Research Centre**, Mill Street, Trim, Co. Meath. ☎ (046) 943-6633; fax 943-7502.

■ Sightseeing

Dundalk

Dundalk is a busy manufacturing town at the head of the bay bearing its name. As Dún Dealga in Celtic times it was a fortress guarding the pass through the mountains into Ulster. Vikings, Anglo-Normans and the English have fought to hang onto it over the centuries, so little is left. Its only significant medieval features are the **bell tower of the Franciscan Friary** (1240) and the **tower of St. Nicholas' Church** (14th century). **The Courthouse** (1818) is modeled on the Temple of Theseus in Athens and the exterior of **St. Patrick's Catholic Cathedral**, also 19th century, on King's College Chapel, Cambridge.

Lord Dungannon introduced the linen trade to Dundalk in 1699. Buildings were erected to house the looms, but the trade only really began to prosper in the 19th century, and you can see some of the flamboyant townhouses with their Italianate facades dating from that time.

Today, Dundalk flourishes as a shopping, business and administrative center, not only for Co. Louth, but also for neighboring counties. Its location half-way between Dublin and Belfast has also led to many cross-border links with Newry.

On Jocelyn Street is **Louth County Museum** housed in a beautifully restored late 18th-century warehouse. As well as permanent displays, it also hosts a number of events, including plays, recitals and temporary exhibitions. ☎ (042) 932-7056; fax 932-7058; dlkmuseum1@eircom.net.

Drogheda

Drogheda, 22 miles (35 km) south of Dundalk, is a busy port and industrial center that developed from a settlement around a ford crossing of the River Boyne. The Vikings arrived in 911 and built the first bridge, which accounts for its name, "Droichead Atha" – Norse for "bridge across the ford."

The huge earthen mound called **Millmount** is the town's most noticeable feature; though never excavated, it's believed to cover prehistoric graves. There's a restored Martello tower on top that offers views of the town. The town's street plan hasn't changed significantly since the 13th century.

Nearby is the **Millmount Museum** in the officers' mess of an 18th-century military barracks. Its exhibits include the only surviving guild banners in the country, and a hand-powered vacuum cleaner dating from 1860. ☎ (041) 983-3097; info@millmount.net.

In the **Millmount Craft Centre** you can buy work by contemporary artists.

St. Laurence's Gate was built in the late 13th century, and is the only one of the town's 10 medieval gates to have survived. It's now one of the best-preserved in the country.

Cromwell's troops massacred about 2,600 of the town's garrison and citizens in 1649; many were burnt to death in **St. Peter's Church**, where they had sought refuge. The present church dates from 1753, and was designed by famous Irish architect Francis Johnston. In a second St. Peter's Church on West Street, erected in his memory, you can see the preserved head of **Oliver Plunkett**, Archbishop of Armagh, who was made a saint in 1975 (the first Irishman in more than 700 years). He was executed in 1681 in London for allegedly taking part in a plot against the Crown.

The ruins of **Mellifont Abbey**, at Collon, six miles (10 km) west of Drogheda, are worth a look. It was built in 1142 as the first Cistercian monastery in Ireland, and for nearly 400 years was one of the most important religious foundations in the country, with 38 other monasteries

East Coast & Midlands

under its rule. In 1539 it was closed by King Henry VIII and handed over to Sir Edward Moore, who turned the church into a fortified mansion. It couldn't withstand Cromwell's soldiers in 1649 and ended up as a pigsty.

High Crosses

High crosses or Celtic crosses as they are also known, are found throughout Ireland on old monastic sites. Some were probably used as meeting points for religious ceremonies and others were used to mark boundaries. The earliest crosses in Ireland were made of wood and metal and probably much smaller than the great stone monuments we see today. It was generally accepted that the Western Ossory group of high crosses were amongst the earliest examples of stone crosses to be found in Ireland, because their design imitates the wood and metal crosses before them, and a recent study suggests they may date to the mid-ninth century.

Not far away is **Monasterboice** and the remains of the monastic settlement founded by St. Buite in the fifth century. One of the best surviving round towers, over 100 feet high and with a base that's over 50 feet across, and two of the most perfect 10th-century high crosses are on the site. ☎ (041) 982-6459.

AN IMPORTANT SITE

The site of the **Battle of the Boyne** is on the south bank of the river, near Drogheda on the Oldbridge Estate, signposted off the N51 road to Slane. Here, King William III and his father-in-law, King James II, fought in 1690, on July 12, according to the modern calendar. At stake were the British throne, French dominance of Europe and Protestant power in Ireland.

Visits are free, and access is by guided tour only. You are advised to wear suitable clothing and footwear, as the terrain is uneven. Open June-Sept daily, 9:30 am-5:30 pm. ☎ (041) 988-4343; fax 988-4323; battleoftheboyne@ealga.ie. There are also self-guided walks in the Oldbridge Estate.

Ardee

Ardee, on the N2, is a pretty little market town on the bank of the River Dee. It takes its name from the Irish, Ard Fhirdia, the ford on the river Dee where the legendary Irish hero Cúchulainn, champion of Ulster, killed his foster brother Ferdia, the champion of the south. The foundation of the town is attributed to the Norman knight Gilbert de Pippard, from whom the Pepper families descend, who obtained a grant of the barony of Ardee from Prince John in 1185 and who was responsible for the construction of the motte-castle on the eastern side of the town known today as **Castleguard**. The town walls date from the late 14th and early 15th centuries, but only fragments now remain.

The town was often the mustering point for the English when they were attacking Ulster, because of its strategic location at a crossroads on the northern boundary of the Pale (see page 13). There are two 13th-century castles in the town. **Ardee Castle** (St. Leger's) is the largest fortified tower house in Ireland, with a museum in its square keep. **Hatch's Castle** on Market Street got its name because it was given to the Hatch family during the Cromwellian Plantation (see page 14).

The Cooley Peninsula

If your time in Co. Louth is limited, don't miss the Cooley Peninsula.

Carlingford is the capital of Cooley, which juts out north of Dundalk, 14 miles (22.5 km) away, facing the Mountains of Mourne in Co. Down to the north across the Lough bearing its name. It is an absolutely delightful place to visit. Although it is so near to both Newry and Dundalk, you feel as if you are in another world, because it has such a peaceful and untouched atmosphere.

Driving from Newry to Carlingford along the R173, you reach the pretty village of **Omeath**, and directly behind it on the slopes of Slieve Foy is the **Long Woman's Grave**, dating from megalithic times. According to the story, Cauthleen, the tall Spanish wife of Lorcan O'Hanlon, "died of disappointment" when she arrived in Ireland and saw the home with a spectacular view (but few amenities) promised by her husband.

Carlingford is one of Ireland's Heritage Towns, and the best preserved from the medieval period, founded by the Anglo-Normans in the 12th century. It retains much of its original layout as a linear settlement, with defensive walls and narrow streets. It's a peaceful and attractive small town, really a village, and is ideal as a base for touring the Cooley Peninsula and the area around Carlingford Lough.

Carlingford is only 10 miles (16 km) from Newry. Its setting is lovely, with great views of the sea and mountains. The name comes from Norse – "the fjord of Carlinn" – but although its sheltered harbor on the Lough may have been used as a base for Viking raiding parties, no signs of them have survived.

Take a walk around Carlingford, which is very rewarding. The **Heritage Centre** is in the tower of the original town wall, now part of the old Holy Trinity Church, and has an exhibition on the area's history. ☎ (042) 937-3454.

Among the fascinating buildings in the village is the 12th-century **King John's Castle**, which guards the harbor entrance from an elevated position. **Taafe's Castle** (15th century) is a good example of a castellated town house with its battlements, murder holes, slits for archers and barrel-vaulted basement. You can also see the ruins of the **Abbey**, a Dominican Friary founded by Richard de Burgo, Earl of Ulster, in 1305; and **The Mint** and **The Tholsel** (medieval toll house), both dating from the 15th century.

■ Adventures on Foot

 At **Ardee**, there's a pleasant walk along the River Dee to the site of the battle between Cúchulainn and Ferdia. Just west of town is the only remaining raised bog on the east coast, where you find flora and fauna not seen elsewhere. It's worth a stroll. The **Cooley Peninsula** provides excellent, moderate hill walking, particularly in the Cooley Mountains and Slieve Foy. You'll come across interesting archaeological sites, including the **Proleek Dolmen**, on the western end of the peninsula, near Ravensdale. It's a 5,000-year-old tomb with three upright stones and a 46-ton capstone which, according to local folklore, was left by a giant. Nearby, a huge gallery grave, roughly outlined by rocks, is said to be the last resting place of the Scottish giant, Ruiscare, who lost a battle with Irish giant, Finn McCool.

Ravensdale Forest offers enjoyable short walks.

The **Táin Trail** is the main long-distance walk in the county. It starts and ends in Carlingford and takes you 16 miles (26 km) through the beautiful surrounding countryside.

■ Adventures on Wheels

 County Louth is ideal for traveling by bike. Among suggested routes are the Cooley Cycle and the East Coast Cycle.

The Cooley Cycle (50 miles/80 km) starts at Dundalk and loops around Dromad before running along beside Ravensdale Forest Park. The next stretch is the most taxing as it climbs steeply until reaching the Long Woman's Grave and then descends towards Omeath, with fantastic views over Carlingford Lough. You then go through Carlingford, Greenore, Gyles Quay, Ballymascanlon, and back to Dundalk.

The East Coast Cycle (34 miles/54 km) also starts at Dundalk. You head south out of Dundalk on the N52 Ardee Road, turn left at the Readypenny Inn, and continue through Castlebellingham, named after the family descended from a captain in Cromwell's army, where there are some pretty cottages. You take the road from the village square to Annagassan on the sea, which was founded by the Vikings. After that, follow the coast, your way marked by blue signs reading "scenic route," and you come upon lovely quiet beaches. Clogherhead is a pretty fishing village with an EU Blue Flag beach (see page 76), where there's a pleasant walk along the rocky cliffs of the headland south of Port Oriel harbor.

After Clogherhead you come to Termonfeckin, another pretty village, which has an early Christian high cross and medieval ruins, as well as an attractive church, designed by Francis Johnston. Next is the seaside resort of Baltray and then, on your right, is Beaulieu House, open to the public for part of the year.

Then the route follows the mouth of the River Boyne, and passes under the big railway bridge into Drogheda's town center.

The Táin Trail Cycling Route is the longest and most historic in Ireland. It runs for 365 miles (588 km) from Co. Roscommon to the Cooley Peninsula, and back again, with 95 miles (153 km) of it in Louth. It's inspired by the ancient Irish saga, *The Táin* or the *Cattle Raid of Cooley*, and follows (as closely as possible) the path of Queen Maeve and her armies in their pursuit of the great Brown Bull of Cooley (see page 10). (Táin is pronounced to rhyme with coin.)

The route is marked by distinctive Brown Bull finger-post signs (they look like a pointing finger), as well as striking pictorial maps in towns along the route, including Ardee, Carlingford and Dundalk, in the Co. Louth section. It passes the battle sites where Cúchulainn and Maeve's armies met in bloody combat and offers the opportunity to visit many of the most important heritage sites and visitor attractions in County Louth.

There's an attractive and useful brochure-map, available from tourist offices. The route can be walked as well, of course. For further information, contact: **Irish Cycle and Cycling Holidays**, Unit 6, Ardee Enterprise Centre. ☎ (041) 685-3772; fax 685-3809; irch@iol.ie; www.irish-insight.com/irish-cycle-hire.

For more information on the epic itself, take a look at www.thetain.com.

■ Adventures on Water

Blackrock, three miles (4.8 km) south of Dundalk, is a small seaside village, which is popular for sail boarding, as the water is shallow.

Carlingford Lough is popular for sailing and windsurfing as it's sheltered and without strong tides, and there are a number of harbors on both shores. In the harbor, **Carlingford Marina** has 200 berths and is an ideal base for visiting yachts; facilities include fuel and a chandlery. ☎ (042) 937-3073; www.carlingfordmarina.com.

Carlingford Adventure Centre, based in an old bonded warehouse encircling the medieval Mint, offers a choice of activities. Among them are sailing, kayaking, canoeing, windsurfing, abseiling, mountain walking, rockclimbing, orienteering, and archery. You can also take courses in sailing, windsurfing and power boating here. They cater for day visitors as well as those staying in their hostel. ☎ (042) 937-3100; fax 937-3651; info@carlingfordadventure.com; www.carlingfordadventure.com.

Fishing

 You'll find the best salmon and sea trout fishing on the **Ballymascanlon River**, northeast of Dundalk, the **River Glyde** at Castlebellingham, the **River Boyne** near Drogheda and the **Cooley River**.

Ask at Tourist Information or in local tackle shops on the Cooley Peninsula about specific stretches of water, permits and licenses. Salmon and sea trout are caught from February to September, and brown trout from March to September. From the pier at Carlingford you can catch dogfish, flatfish, occasional ray and conger.

Sea angling is plentiful along the over 60 miles (100 km) of coast. As well as Carlingford Lough, good fishing areas include Gyles Quay, Annagassan, Clogherhead, Termonfeckin and the Baltray/Drogheda area.

Clogherhead is the most popular sea-angling venue because of visiting shoals of mackerel during July, August and September. The best fishing is from its pier. Other species caught here include mullet, codling, plaice and dabs.

Baltray and **Mornington**, which face each other across Dundalk Bay and the mouth of the Boyne, also attract many anglers, especially for bass during the summer.

Coarse angling is available with pike fishing in **Drumcah** and **Cortail lakes**; and carp fishing at **Stephenstown Pond**, Knockbridge, which has facilities for the disabled.

 See page 71-74 for details on angling in Ireland, regulations and best times to fish.

Boat Rental

Carlingford Lough Sea Angling can be contacted on the Co. Down side of the Lough. ☎ (028) 3026-4906.

For deep sea fishing, call **Deep Sea Fishing North Commons**, Carlingford, ☎ (042) 937-3239 or 932 8061; mobile 087 288 1191.

For daily fishing trips, call Tony Lynch in Clogherhead, ☎ (041) 983-3698.

Local Information

For tackle, bait, state licenses, permits, and local information, contact **The Drogheda Angling Centre**, Stockwell Close. ☎ (041) 984-5442.

To fish particular rivers, you should contact the relevant body: **The Dee and Glyde Development Association**. ☎ (042) 937-2176.

For the Boyne, and Rose Hall, Barnattin and Killineer reservoirs: **Drogheda and District Anglers' Club**. ☎ (041) 983-4078.

For the River Fane and its tributaries: **Dundalk Salmon Anglers' Association**. ☎ (042) 933-5698. **Dundalk Brown Trout Anglers' Association**. ☎ (042) 932-8626.

For Stephenstown Pond, licenses are available from **Brodigans Foodstore** in Knockbridge village.

■ Adventures on Horseback

Ravensdale Lodge Equestrian and Trekking Centre is near Forest Park and the Cooley mountains, and is open all year. You can take lessons here, or go on mountain treks or cross-country. ☎/fax (042) 937-1034; info@ravensdalelodge. com; www.ravensdalelodge.com.

■ Golf

Dundalk Golf Club is north of the seaside resort of Blackrock. ☎ (042) 932-1731. **The Carnbeg Golf Course** is at Kilcurry, near Dundalk. ☎ (042) 933-2518. There's also the course at the **Killin Park Golf and Country Club**, Dundalk. ☎ (042) 933-9303.

County Louth Golf Club, usually called Baltray, is four miles (6.4 km) northeast of Drogheda at the mouth of the River Boyne. It's an excellent links course, considered by experts to be among the top six on the island. ☎ (041) 982-2329; reservations@countylouthgolfclub.com.

Ardee Golf Club. Townparks, .6 mile (one km) north of Ardee, has an 18-hole course, along with practice and catering facilities. ☎ (041) 685-3227.

Greenore Golf Club is on the Cooley Peninsula, and has an 18-hole parkland course along the shore with lovely views across Carlingford Lough to the Mountains of Mourne. ☎ (042) 937-3212.

Seapoint Golf Club is at Termonfeckin. ☎ (041) 982-2333.

Close to Drogheda and on the coast is the **Laytown and Bettystown Golf Club**. ☎ (041) 982-7170.

■ Where to Stay

 ☆☆☆ The **Ballymascanlon House Hotel**, two miles north of Dundalk on the R173, is a Victorian mansion set in 130 acres on the Cooley Peninsula with lovely views. It has its own 18-hole parkland golf course, tennis courts and leisure center with pool, gym, and other facilities. Special golfing and other breaks are available. It's family-run and belongs to the Best Western group. $$. ☎ (042) 937-1124; fax 937-1598; info@ballymascanlon.com; www. ballymascanlon.com.

HOTEL PRICE CHART	
Price per person, per night, with two sharing, including breakfast.	
$	Under US $50
$$	US $50-$100
$$$	US $101-$175
$$$$	US $176-$200
$$$$$	Over US $200

☆☆☆ The **Boyne Valley Hotel and Country Club**, Stameen, Dublin Road, Drogheda, is surrounded by 16 acres of lovely gardens and woodlands. It has a leisure center with pool, and outside there's an 18-hole pitch-and-putt course and two tennis courts, playable all year. Its **Cellar Bistro** has locally caught fish on the menu. $$. ☎ (041) 983-7737; fax 983-9188; reservations@boyne-valley-hotel.ie; www.boyne-valley-hotel. ie.

☆☆ The **Bellingham Castle Hotel**, Castlebellingham, off the M1 midway between Drogheda and Dundalk, is a refurbished early 18th-century castle on the River Dee. The interior combines antique décor with modern facilities. The village of Castlebellingham is also interesting, with a group of Widows' Almshouses and other cottages built by the Bellingham family. $-$$. ☎ (042) 937-2176; fax 937-2766; bellinghamcastle@eircom. net; www.bellinghamcastle.com.

Another castle you can stay in is **Smarmore Castle**, in Smarmore, between Collon and Ardee, a short distance from the N2. It's one of the oldest castles in the country, dating from 1320, and staying there is special, as there are only five spacious bedrooms. These days it's also a leisure club with a gym, pool, steam room and other facilities, including a therapeutic and aromatherapy massage center. $. ☎ (041) 685-7167; fax 685-7650; info@smarmorecastle.com; www.smarmorecastle.com.

☆☆☆☆ **The Táin Holiday Village**, at Omeath on the Cooley Peninsula, has a hostel, a caravan and camping site, cook-for-yourself mobile homes, swimming pool, indoor and outdoor adventure grounds, tennis courts and facilities for kayaking, canoeing, archery. It also has a licensed restaurant and bar with entertainment. ☎ (042) 75385; info@tainvillage.com.

View Point offers motel-style accommodation in Carlingford, with absolutely spectacular views over the lough, the harbor and of the Mountains of Mourne. Take a look at the website and you get some idea. It's excellent value at less than $ per person, including breakfast. ☎ (042) 937-3149; www.carlingford.ie.

The Oystercatcher Lodge and Bistro, Market Square, Carlingford, is an attractive guesthouse offering bed and breakfast. Its seven rooms are more like mini-suites. The Bistro serves food made with the best local ingredients, including oysters farmed in the lough, crab and lobster from Dundalk Bay, and Cooley Mountain lamb. Rates (sharing, breakfast included) from $$, with lots of special break offers. ☎ (042) 937-3922; info@theoystercatcher.com.

Ghan House in Carlingford, built in 1727, is a fine example of a Georgian house. Its first-floor drawing room has a decorative ceiling of rococo plasterwork with flower garlands and medallion busts of the daughters of the original owners. The house is surrounded by castellated walls and a guards' tower. In its basement there are two underground passages, now blocked. For a break with a difference, take one of the courses at its Cookery School. ☎/fax (042) 937-3682; ghanhouse@ eircom.net.

Beaufort House is not only a guesthouse, it's also the **Carlingford Yacht Charter and Sea School Limited**. Here you can charter a yacht, either bare-boat or with skipper, or learn to sail. Courses are run by proprietor Michael Caine, and start at Competent Crew, progressing to Day Skipper, Coastal Skipper and Yachtmaster Offshore. You don't have to have any experience to do the entry level Competent Crew. Beaufort House is on the shore with lovely views and guests can relax in its Chart Room. $. ☎ (042) 937-3879, 937-3878; michaelcaine@ beauforthouse.net; www.beauforthouse.net.

Setanta Bed and Breakfast, 7 Castle Street, Ardee, is a lovely old Georgian townhouse, with high ceilings and wooden floors. $ for two with breakfast. ☎ (041) 685-3319; setanta_ardee@ireland.com.

Hostels

The Green Door Hostel, John Street, Drogheda, is open all year. It belongs to both the Youth Hostels Association (www.irelandyha.org) and

East Coast & Midlands

the Independent Holiday Hostels of Ireland group (www.hostels-ireland.com). ☎ (041) 983-4422; fax 984-5624; greendoorhostel@hotmail.com.

The Adventure Centre and Holiday Hostel, Carlingford, is open from mid-January to mid-December. ☎ (042) 937-3100; fax 937-3651; info@carlingfordadventure.com.

Camping & RV Parks

In addition to camping at Táin Village (see previous page), there is the ☆☆☆☆ **Gyles Quay Caravan and Camping Park**, 10 miles (16 km) from Dundalk off the road to Newry. It overlooks Dundalk Bay on the Cooley Peninsula and has access to a safe beach. There's a leisure center on site, and a licensed clubhouse. It's open May 1-September 21. ☎ (042) 937-6262.

■ Where to Eat

There are lots of places to eat in Co. Louth, among them the following:

PJ O'Hares, Carlingford, is a traditional and welcoming pub that serves sandwiches and lunches at excellent value. ☎ (042) 937-3106.

Monks Expresso Bar, The Quays, Drogheda, is ideal for a relaxed snack or meal. Open every day from 8:30 am to 6 pm. ☎ (041) 984-5630.

The Buttergate Restaurant, Millmount, Drogheda, opens from 11 am to 3 pm for snacks and lunch, and from 6 to 10:30 pm for dinner. It specializes in modern Irish, European and Italian dishes. ☎ (041) 34759.

Rolf's Bistro on Market Street, Ardee, opens only for dinner, from Tuesday-Saturday, 6-10 pm, Sundays from 5-9 pm. It has a special Early Bird menu from 5:30-7 pm, Tuesday-Friday. Its menu includes modern Irish and Swedish specialties.

The Clermont Arms, on Main Street, Blackrock, the seaside village, is open daily from 4 pm, serving dinner from 6-10 pm (9 pm on Sundays). Its menu includes steaks, seafood and traditional Irish dishes. It has a paved outdoor area for use in better weather, and doesn't welcome children under 12, so diners should have a peaceful experience. ☎ (042) 932-2666.

Cube is a modern restaurant at 5 Roden Place, in the center of Dundalk. There's lots of parking space available opposite St. Patrick's Cathedral nearby. The restaurant style is contemporary Irish, using the best local fresh produce, including Black Angus beef and seafood. Dishes include tarte tatin of roasted baby beets with chick pea and garlic purée, ideal for the vegetarian. The menu is changed daily. Cube is open Wednesday-Saturday, lunch 12-3 pm, dinner 6-11 pm. On Sundays brunch is served

11 am-1 pm, and lunch 1-3 pm. Brunch dishes include grilled Clonakilty black pudding with champ and roasted apple, which sounds delicious! ☎ (042) 932-9898; www.cuberestaurants.ie.

■ Useful Websites

- www.carlingford.ie.
- www.louthholidays.com.

County Wicklow

Known as "the Garden of Ireland," Wicklow has wonderful scenery, with mountains, wooded valleys and lakes. It is fringed on the east by golden sandy beaches. Major routes to the east and west go through two of the highest passes in the country – Sally Gap and Wicklow Gap. Among its spectacular valleys are Glenmalure, Glencree, Glenmacnass, the Glen of Immal, and the most famous of all – Glendalough.

The area is very popular with outdoor enthusiasts for the range of activities it offers – walking, cycling, shore, coarse and game angling, golf, riding, watersports. It's also the home of one of the country's most famous early Christian sites, Glendalough, and there are a number of historic gardens and houses to visit.

Because of its wonderful scenery, the county has been used as a location for many films over the years, including *Excalibur, Braveheart, Far and Away* and *Michael Collins*. The very successful Irish television series *Ballykissangel* was made in the pretty village of Avoca. The largest town is Bray, the county capital is Wicklow Town, and its other main towns include Arklow and Greystones.

■ Getting Here

Bray is 13 miles (21 km) south of Dublin City on the N11; from Cork (172 miles/277 km) take the N11-N7-N8; from Galway (151 miles/243 km) take the N11-N4-N6-N18. It's the southern terminus of the DART service.

Wicklow Town is just off the N11 south of Bray and Greystones and north of Arklow.

Bray, Greystones, Wicklow, Rathdrum and Arklow are connected to Dublin by commuter rail services, and there's also an excellent bus service.

East Coast & Midlands

■ Tourist Information

Wicklow Town Tourist Office, Rialto House, Fitzwilliam Square. ☎ (0404) 69117; fax 69118; wicklowtouristoffice@eircom.net; www.ecoast-midlands.travel.ie.

Tourist information is available during the summer only at: Arklow, Bray, Baltinglass, Blessington, Carnew, Glendalough/Laragh, Rathdrum, and Roundwood. Their hours vary. Call the Wicklow office for details.

TRACING YOUR ANCESTORS

The **Heritage Centre** in the historic gaol in Wicklow Town provides a genealogical research service. ☎ (0404) 20126; fax 69980; wfh@eircom.net.

■ Sightseeing

Wicklow Town

Its name comes not from Irish but from Norse – Vykinglo, meaning Viking meadow, which gives you some idea of its early inhabitants.

A **Regatta Festival** is held here in late July/early August. The first regatta was held here in 1878. Since then it has developed into a 10-day festival, which concludes with a fireworks display, just as it did in 1878. Activities include treasure hunts, a raft race and various sporting events,

Wicklow Gaol, at the southern end of the town beside the courthouse, is now a visitor attraction. Inside, you learn its history through displays and tours, with a concentration on the 1798 Rebellion, The Great Famine of 1845-49, life in the gaol, and how prisoners were transported to the Penal Colonies in Australia. It also houses a shop, café and genealogy center. ☎ (0404) 61599; fax 61612; wccgaol@eircom.net; www.wicklow.ie/gaol.

Bray

Bray has been popular for generations with its safe sandy and shingle beach a mile long. It was the first seaside resort town in the Republic from the 19th century on, when the more prosperous Dubliners came here for the summer, and its first esplanade was laid out in 1859.

There's a pleasant walk to **Bray Head**, which rises to almost 800 feet above the sea and offers lovely views. The town retains a charming, rather old-fashioned feeling, with its Georgian and Victorian houses, although today it's the home of many who commute daily to nearby Dublin City. It makes a great base for anyone exploring the county.

The **National Sealife Centre** on Strand Road has over 30 displays, with hundreds of different sea and freshwater creatures to inspect. Open daily from 10 am. ☎ (01) 286-6939; www.sealife.ie.

Greystones

Greystones is five miles (eight km) south of Bray, 18 miles (29 km) from Dublin, and is between the Sugar Loaf Mountains and the sea. It's a quieter resort than its neighbor Bray and, while growing rapidly with the expansion of the commuter belt, retains a charming old-world atmosphere, especially around its fishing harbor. There's both a Sailing Club and a Motor Yacht Club here for cruisers.

Arklow

Arklow is the most southerly of Wicklow's main towns, and is small but lively. Now popular for shopping and as a seaside resort, it was once a busy port. It's on the Avoca River, the N11 main road, and on the Dublin-Rosslare railway line. It was one of the first towns developed by the Vikings, and has sandy beaches on both sides. It hosts a number of annual festivals, including the **Maritime Festival** in August. There's model boat racing in the river, a dog show, stalls, stands, a "Bouncy Castle" for kids, slides and a horizontal bungee, plus a soccer match and a photography exhibition, among other activities.

Its main street is attractive and there's a lovely riverside walk and a **Maritime Museum**. In 1824 the first lifeboat station in the country opened here. Its port still has a sizeable fleet of fishing boats and the town is renowned for boat building, including the Republic's sail training ship, *Asgard II*.

The Vale of Avoca

Home to the country's oldest woollen mill, the Avoca Valley in the south of the county is one of the few places in Ireland where mining was carried out, here for gold and copper. The valley stretches from just west of Arklow, from Woodenbridge to the Meeting of the Waters, north of the picturesque village, where the Avonmore and Avonbeg join to form the River Avoca. It was immortalized by the poet Thomas Moore in the song *Sweet Vale of Avoca*:

> *There is not in this wide world a valley so sweet*
> *As that vale in whose bosom the bright waters meet,*
> *Oh! The last rays of feeling and life must depart*
> *Ere the bloom of that valley shall fade from my heart.*

East Coast & Midlands

At **Avoca Handweavers** you can see the mill, dating from 1723, and watch the weaving process.

Glendalough

Make sure you don't leave Wicklow without visiting Glendalough. The most memorable approach to it is from the west, decending from the Wicklow Gap, 10 miles (16 km) southwest of Enniskerry. The towering peaks of the Wicklow Mountains, covered in forests, are reflected in the two lakes that give the valley its name – "the glen of two lakes." It really is a beautiful and special place.

The **monastic settlement** here was founded in the sixth century by the hermit Saint Kevin, and flourished as a place of pilgrimage until the 16th century, when it was almost destroyed. The surviving buildings, dating from the eighth to 12th centuries, include a round tower, which is in nearly perfect condition, a cathedral, seven stone churches, and some decorated crosses. There's a center for visitors with lots of information and audio-visual shows. Regular guided tours are offered, but you'll also enjoy exploring on your own.

In summer, this is one of the busiest sites in the country. It attracts up to half a million visitors a year, so try and visit early in the morning. The Visitor Centre is open daily all year from 9:30 am to 6 pm, mid-March to mid-October; to 5:30 pm rest of year. ☎ (0404) 45325; fax 45626.

Just two miles (3.2 km) south of Blessington is **Russborough House**, built for the Earl of Milltown in 1740-50, which has beautiful furniture, tapestries, carpets and porcelain to see. The house is in Palladian style, built from local granite, and designed by Richard Castle, or Cassells, considered one of the most important architects of the time.

It's best-known as the home of the Beit Collection of paintings, dominated by Flemish, Dutch and Spanish masterpieces, some of which have unfortunately been stolen a couple of times, but thankfully recovered.

Open May-September, 10:30-5:30 pm; April and October, Sundays and Bank Holidays only. ☎ (045) 865239; fax 865054.

■ Adventures on Foot

The **Slí na Sláinte**, literally "the walk of health," is a signposted coastal and urban walk around Bray for 8.75 miles (14 km). It's one of a network all over the country so named, which have been established to encourage walking.

There's also a scenic cliff walk around **Bray Head to Greystones**, which is four miles (seven km) long.

The **Wicklow Mountains** are so popular with walkers that there are two annual festivals, in spring and autumn, which offer up to four guided walks a day, allowing for all levels of experience. You learn about the county and Ireland's culture, geology and wildlife. Details from Wicklow Town Tourist Office, Rialto House, Fitzwilliam Square, ☎ (0404) 69117; fax 69118, wicklowtouristoffice@eircom.net, www.ecoast-midlands.travel.ie.

Wicklow Mountain National Park, Upper Lake, Glendalough, has steep-sided valleys, mountains shaped by erosion and the Ice Age, oak woods and blanket bog. In addition to walking here, there's a series of organized events, including **bat walks** and **mining walks**, **rut walks** (deer spotting), **woodland**, and **wildflower walks**. Details available from Park Information, ☎ (0404) 45656.

In 1981, **The Wicklow Way** was the first signposted long-distance route to be opened in Ireland. It's 82 miles (132 km) long, running from Marlay Park in Co. Dublin, climbing into the Dublin Mountains and then from glen to glen through the mountains in Wicklow, ending in Clonegal, Co. Carlow. It takes five or six days to walk it all, but you can just do part of it. Some sections are on tracks, others boggy, and a lot of it is at a height of over 1,600 feet (500 m), so you get fantastic views over the Irish Sea to Wales, to the Mourne Mountains in Northern Ireland, and of the beautiful glens below. The Way is clearly marked with wooden posts topped by yellow arrows at each junction. See www.wicklow.ie/sportsleisure/walking/wickloww.html for details.

St. Kevin's Way is another waymarked route. It runs from Hollywood in West Wicklow to Glendalough, following the path taken by pilgrims. A secondary route brings you from Valleymount to join the main Way at Ballinagree Bridge on the R756.

The **Avoca Valley** is another interesting area for walking, both on forest trails and through the old mine workings. The **Mottee Walk** begins at The Meetings pub beside the Meeting of the Waters and is five miles (eight km) long, taking you through mature mixed woodland. Approaching the Mottee Stone you see **Castle Howard**, a fortified house belonging to the mine owners in the 17th century. In the heather are old mine workings and the ruins of walls and cottages, evidence of how densely populated the area was in previous times.

East Coast & Midlands

THE MOTTEE STONE

The **Mottee Stone** may take its name from the French "moitié," meaning half, as it's halfway between Dublin and Wexford. It's a huge granite boulder, different from the surrounding rock, and there's a legend that Fionn MacCool threw it from the top of Lugnaquilla Mountain, Wicklow's highest peak. However, geologists say it's an erratic boulder left behind by retreating ice.

Coillte, the State Forestry Service, has a Forest Park and 15 other sites around the county. Among the latter is the **Devil's Glen**, 2½ miles (four km) west of Ashford. Walks here go through a spectacular gorge to a waterfall.

It's also home to something unique – **Sculpture in Woodland** – a collection of over 16 contemporary sculptures by Irish and international artists. You can walk in the woods, as well as explore the artwork. There are two detailed routes (ranging from 30 minutes to two hours). Take a look at the website for a map and further details: www.sculptureinwoodland. ie or ☎ (01) 201-1111; sculpinfo@coillte.ie.

The Forest Park surrounds **Avondale House** at Rathdrum, which was the birthplace and home of Charles Stewart Parnell (1846-91). He was leader of the Irish Parliamentary Party in the late 19th century. It's now a museum in his memory, with tours and audio-visual presentations.

The estate covers over 500 acres and has miles of signposted forest trails with marvelous views and lots of wildlife, including 90 different species of birds. There's a restaurant/tea room and gift shop. Open daily March 17-October 31, 11 am-6 pm. ☎/fax (0404) 46111; www.coillte.ie.

Walking Vacations

Footfalls Walking Holidays is family-run and offers guided and self-guided walking and hiking vacations in Wicklow and elsewhere. They also rent bikes. They are based at Trooperstown, Roundwood. ☎ (0404) 45152; info@walkinghikingireland.com; www.walkinghikingireland. com.

You can also stay at the family-run ☆☆☆ **Lawless Hotel and Holiday Village**, Aughrim, and go walking nearby. The owners, the O'Tooles, publish a booklet of rambles near their beautiful village, written by expert Tom Phelan. The routes vary in length and difficulty. See *Where to Stay*, page 132.

The Gardens of Ireland

Wicklow has an annual **Gardens Festival** from the beginning of May to the end of July, and it's home to some of the Republic's finest heritage gardens. Among them is **Killruddery**, near Bray, the best example in the country of a garden designed in the French formal style of the 17th century, with terraces, twin canals and sylvan theater. ☎/fax (01) 286-2777. The others are:

The **Powerscourt Estate** at Enniskerry, ☎ (01) 204-6000; fax 204-6900; gardens@powerscourt.ie; www.powerscourt.ie. When visiting Powerscourt, allow time to see the waterfall, the highest in the country, which is a couple of miles from Enniskerry. It's well worth the trip.

Mount Usher Gardens near Ashford, ☎ (0404) 40205; mount_usher_gardens@indigo.ie; www.mount-usher-gardens.com.

Russborough House, already mentioned, and **Avondale House** and **Forest Park**.

■ Adventures on Wheels

Cycling

 With lots of minor roads and varied scenery, Wicklow is suitable for cycling, although there are lots of steep climbs and narrow winding roads. Among the places you can rent bikes or have them repaired are:

Johnny Price's Garage, Main Street, Roundwood. ☎ (01) 281-8128.

Bray Cycle Centre, Main Street, Bray. ☎ (01) 286-3357.

T. McGrath, Rathdrum. ☎ (0404) 46172.

Hillcrest Hire, Blessington. ☎ (045) 865066.

All-Terrain

At Newtownmountkennedy, a village just off the N11, between Bray and Ashford, you can enjoy driving all-terrain vehicles around a cross-country course, at the **Hill Top Quad and Sporting Club**. ☎ (01) 281-8025.

Scenic Drives

Everywhere you go in the county, there are signposted scenic drives, including the **Wicklow Coast Drive**, the **Glencree Drive**, the **Wicklow Gap Drive** and the **Liffey Valley Drive**.

In the western part of the county, inland, there's the **Lake Drive**, which starts in Blessington and takes you around the lakes and the Poulaphuca Reservoir, following its shoreline. The lakes are the result of planned flooding of the Liffey Valley in 1940 in order to provide water to Dublin and surrounding areas. There are some pleasant villages, including Valleymount, Ballyknockan and Lackan.

Tours

You have the option of relaxing and letting someone else do the driving, by taking a guided coach tour of the county. Among those available are:

The Wicklow Tour, run by Irish City Tours, 33-34 Bachelor's Walk, Dublin. ☎ (01) 872-9010; linda@irishcitytours.com or www.irishcitytours.com.

A Taste of Wicklow, ☎ 1-800-609-606 or (01) 834-0941. Book online at www.daytoursunplugged.ie.

Dublin Bus, ☎ (01) 873-4222, www.dublinbus.ie, also offers a choice of tours.

■ Tennis

There are several tennis clubs open to visitors; the larger ones are floodlit so can be played after dark.

Arklow Lawn Tennis Club. ☎ (0402) 33330.

Blessington Adventure Centre. ☎ (045) 865092.

County Wicklow Lawn Tennis Club, Bray. ☎ (01) 287-6505.

Sports & Leisure Centre, Arklow. ☎ (0402) 23328.

Greystones Lawn Tennis Club. ☎ (01) 287-6505.

Wicklow Lawn Tennis Club. ☎ (0404) 41647.

At the **Arklow Sports and Leisure Centre** there are indoor squash and tennis courts. ☎ (0402) 23328.

■ Adventures on Water

Try something different – such as **hovercrafting** at Moneystown Farm, Arklow. ☎ (0402) 32259; mland@eircom.net.

You can swim or take part in other watersports at many locations along the coast.

Brittas Bay, Greystones, Wicklow and Arklow are ideal for **sailing, wind surfing and boating**. From Greystones to Wicklow, the shingle and stone beach extends for 19 miles (31 km), and is popular, not just for swimming, but also for walking and shore angling. From the N11 coast road, you can gain access to beaches at Kilcoole, Newcastle and Killoughter.

South of Wicklow Town there's a choice of **beaches** – Silver Strand, Maghermore, Jack's Hole and Brittas Bay, the latter a three-mile-long beach which has received the EU Blue Flag Award (see page 76) for a number of years. The beach at Bray and the sandy beaches on either side of Arklow are also safe for swimming.

In the western part of the county, the **Blessington Adventure Centre**, just south of the village on the shore of the reservoir, offers a number of land- and water-based activities, including abseiling, archery, clay pigeon shooting, tennis, orienteering, canoeing, sailing and windsurfing. You can also take a lake tour on the *MV Blessington*. There's a restaurant on site as well. ☎ (045) 865092; fax 865024.

Fishing

Wicklow offers a range of rivers, lakes and the sea, so is ideal for anyone interested in fishing.

Bray is a popular boat and shore fishing location. Self-drive or skippered small boats are based in the harbor and can be hired from the Esplanade Hotel. ☎ (01) 286-2056.

At **Greystones**, North Beach is renowned for its shore fishing, and at its harbor there's pier fishing, and small boats head out from there for bottom fishing.

There's a free map-brochure available called A Guide to Angling in Co. Wicklow. The Trout and Salmon Rivers of Ireland: An Angler's Guide by Peter O'Reilly is well worth reading, wherever you are visiting.

Among the other recommended locations are the **River Dargle** for salmon, sea and brown trout; the **River Vartry** for sea and brown trout; the **Avonmore River** for brown trout; the **Aughrim River** for brown trout; the **River Derry** for salmon and brown trout; the **River Slaney** for brown trout and salmon, and the **Upper River Liffey** for trout.

The **Blessington Lakes** are good for brown trout, pike, perch, and roach, and the **Roundwood Lakes** for brown trout.

Angling for All is the National Disabled Angling Facility (NDAF), and is a four-acre lake fully stocked with trout and surrounded by an attractive wildlife area. It's in the lovely village of Aughrim, next to the welcoming Lawless Hotel. It's open 8 am-8 pm in summer, 9 am-5 pm in winter. ☎ (0402) 36552; aughrinit@eircom.net.

Annamoe, between Roundwood and Laragh on the road to Glendalough, has a trout fishery on the banks of the Avonmore River. There's a four-acre lake for fly-fishing, rod hire and bait available. Open daily, 10 am to dusk. ☎/fax (0404) 45470; nally@gofree.indigo.ie; www. annamoetroutfishery.com.

See pages 71-74 for details on angling in Ireland, regulations and best times to fish.

■ Adventures on Horseback

There's a choice of equestrian centers where you can take lessons or go trekking, trail riding, and you can also explore the county by horse-drawn caravan.

Brennanstown Riding School is in the Hollybrook Demesne, Kilmacanogue, near Bray, and caters for all levels of experience. It has both indoor and outdoor facilities. ☎ (01) 286-3778; info@brennanstowrs.ie.

Calliaghstown Riding Centre, Rathcoole, also has all-weather facilities and offers lessons and riding vacations. The **Wicklow Trail Ride** starts at the Centre and explores the mountains and glens, finishing at Glendalough. ☎ (01) 458-9236; calliagh@iol.ie; www.calliaghstownridingcentre.com.

Broomfield Equestrian Centre, Tinahely, can arrange lessons and organizes hacks across 500 acres of beautiful countryside. ☎ (0402) 38117.

Riding Vacations

With **Clissmann Horse Drawn Caravans** you can travel around in a covered wagon that sleeps four. ☎ (0404) 48188; mary@clissmann.com.

The Devil's Glen Holiday and Equestrian Centre, Ashford, has 20 luxury cottages with wood-burning stoves as well as modern facilities at the edge of the forest, a lovely peaceful setting. The riding stables cater to beginners and experienced riders, with trails in unspoiled countryside. ☎ (0404) 40637; info@devilsglen.ie; www.devilsglen.ie.

Macreddin Stables, Aughrim, is attached to the Brooklodge Hotel, between Lugnaquilla and the Cushawn Mountains, and welcomes riders at all levels. ☎ (0402) 36444; brooklodge@macreddin.ie; www.brooklodge.ie.

■ Golf

There are over 20 courses to choose from, including seaside and traditional links, most of them founded in the last 15 years. Many hotels also offer golfing vacations. There's an excellent map-brochure available from tourist offices with details of the courses, as well as a list of pitch-and-putt and driving ranges.

Hi-Tech Golf

You can play a round at a choice of 20 courses on the Golf Simulator at **Moneylands Farm**, signposted on the south side of Arklow. It also has a virtual driving range and a video teaching system. Cook-for-yourself and bed and breakfast accommodation available. ☎ (0402) 32259; fax 32438; mland@eircom.

Golf Courses

Baltinglass Golf Club is just outside the town on the Dublin road, with wonderful mountain views. ☎ (059) 6481350; fax 82842.

The **Djouce Mountain Golf Club** is less than two miles off the N11 at the northern tip of the Vartry Reservoir, north of Roundwood. ☎ (01) 281-8585.

Southwest of there is the **Roundwood Golf Club**, at Ballynhinch, Newtownmountkennedy. ☎ (01) 281-8488; fax 284-3642.

Kilcoole Golf Club is on the other side of the N11, and has a nine-hole course. ☎ (01) 287-2066; fax 287-1803; adminkg@eircom.net; www.kilcoolegolfclub.com.

Nearby is the prestigious **Druid's Glen**, which hosted the Irish Open for four years in succession in the late 1990s, and was voted European Golf Course of the Year in 2000/1. ☎ (01) 287-3600; fax 287-3699; info@druidsglen.ie; www.druidsglen.ie.

Bray Golf Club nestles under Bray Head on Ravenswell Road. It is the oldest course in the county, founded in 1897. ☎ (01) 286-2484.

The **Old Conna Golf Club** is on Ferndale Road, less than two miles from Bray. ☎ (01) 282-6055; info@oldconna.com; www.oldconna.com.

The **Powerscourt Golf Club** is in the grounds of the magnificent estate, close to the picturesque village of Enniskerry, and just off the N11, southwest of Bray. ☎ (01) 204-6033; golfclub@powerscourt.ie; www.powerscourt.ie.

Within walking distance of Greystones is the **Charlesland Golf and Country Club**, which can also be approached from the N11 through Delgany. It's also a hotel with 12 rooms. ☎ (01) 287-4350; fax 287-4360; teetimes@charlesland.com; www.charlesland.com.

One of the older courses, founded in 1908, is the **Delgany Golf Club**. ☎ (01) 282-6055; robbiej@eircom.net

West of Delgany is the **Glen of the Downs Golf Club**. ☎ (01) 287-6240; info@glenofthedowns.com; www.glenofthedowns.com.

Over in the west of the county is the **Boystown Golf Club** at Blessington. ☎ (045) 867146.

The **Woodenbridge Golf Club** is in the south of the county, west of Arklow in the lovely Vale of Avoca. ☎ (0402) 35202; fax 35754; wgc@eircom.net; www.globalgolf.com.

East Coast & Midlands

■ Where to Stay & Eat

☆☆☆☆ **Rathsallagh House Golf and Country Club,** Dunlavin, is a large Grade A country house with its own 18-hole course and a Golf Academy. It is surrounded by over 500 acres of wonderful grounds. Converted from Queen Anne-style stables back in 1798, it is family run and welcoming and offers lots of activities, including tennis in a walled garden, croquet, snooker, clay pigeon shooting and archery. It has an indoor pool and sauna; fishing, horse riding and walking can be arranged. Cuisine is country-house cooking at its best, made with their own vegetables, game in season, and locally caught fish. Member of Small Luxury Hotels of the World and Ireland's Blue Book (see page 60). From $$$, with special breaks available. ☎ (045) 403112; fax 403343; info@rathsallagh.com; www.rathsallagh.com.

HOTEL PRICE CHART	
Price per person, per night, with two sharing, including breakfast.	
$	Under US $50
$$	US $50-$100
$$$	US $101-$175
$$$$	US $176-$200
$$$$$	Over US $200

☆☆☆ **Lawless Hotel**, established in 1787, is on the banks of the River Aughrim in an absolutely lovely setting, surrounded by mountains and forests. You can stay in the hotel or in the recently built vacation village next to it. Guests can fish for brown trout in the man-made angling park next door. They serve delicious food in the bar and restaurant, including the best breakfast porridge I've ever tasted, served with honey and hazelnuts. The bar is full of fishermen and walkers, so you can exchange advice, and the staff are friendly and efficient. It's a member of the Irish Country Hotels group. Special breaks offered. Rates from $$.

The Holiday Village is a group of luxury houses next to the hotel. They are attractive and comfortable, sleep five, have open fireplaces as well as heating, and you can cook for yourself or eat at hotel if you want. Available for weekends or by the week; great value from about €450 per week. Member of Irish Country Hotels and Village Inn Hotel groups. Toll-free from US ☎ 1-800-44-UTELL; (0402) 36146; fax 36384; info@lawlesshotel.com; www.lawlesshotel.com.

☆☆☆ **Hunter's Hotel**, in Rathnew, is in one of the oldest coaching inns in the country, dating from c. 1700. Run by the fifth generation of the Gellettie family, it has a great reputation for its welcome and its good food. There are 16 rooms, furnished with antiques, and it's on the bank of the Vartry River with lovely gardens. The hotel belongs to the Irish Country Houses & Restaurants Association and Ireland's Blue Book (see page 60). Rates from $$. Open to non-residents for lunch, afternoon tea and

dinner. ☎ (0404) 40106; fax 40338; reception@hunters.ie; www.hunters.
ie.

If you need a bit of pampering, then **Powerscourt Springs Health
Farm** is where to go. Treatments include body wraps, body polishes, cili-
ate treatments, body detoxing, Ki massage, reflexology, massages and facials. There's a pool, a Tranquillity Room and, in case you thought you'd
be expected to survive on carrot juice, you're wrong – the food is delicious.
The Health Farm is in lovely quiet rural surroundings, where you can go
for walks, near Enniskerry, and offers short breaks. ☎ (01) 276-1000; fax
276-1626; info@powerscourtsprings.ie; www.powerscourtsprings.ie.

An Unusual Rental

The 18th-century **Wicklow Head Lighthouse** has been restored by the Irish Landmark Trust and can be rented. It includes a kitchen. ☎ (01) 670-4733; info@irishlandmark.com;
www.irish-landmark.com.

Camping & RV Parks

☆☆☆☆ **River Valley Camping and Caravanning Park** is
at Redcross Village, 36 miles (58 km) south of Dublin in one of
the most scenic areas of Co. Wicklow northeast of Avoca on the
R754, which is off the N11. Its facilities include an indoor
sports complex, golf course, bowling green, three tennis courts, and crazy
golf. The park's open from mid-March to end September, serves breakfast
in its coffee bar and runs a take-out service each evening from 6 pm. ☎
(0404) 41647.

☆☆☆☆ **Roundwood Caravan and Camping Park** overlooks Vartry
Lakes and Forest on a six-acre site just off the N11 in the village that
gives it its name. Facilities include campers' kitchen, dining room, TV
room, bikes for hire, car rental and daily bus service from its gates to
Dublin and Glendalough. Open mid-April to mid-September. ☎ (01) 281-
8163; fax 281-8196; roundwoodcaravancamp@yahoo.co.uk.

☆☆☆ **Moat Farm Park** is at Donard, just off the N81 between Blessington and Baltinglass. It's open from March 1 to September 30, and is in the
foothills of the Wicklow Mountains in a quiet rural setting. Facilities include free hot water, laundry, campers' kitchen, TV room. ☎/fax (045)
404-727; moatfarm@ireland.com.

☆☆ **Avonmore Riverside Park** is on the edge of the Wicklow Mountains on the R752, and is a quiet site on the banks of the river, with the
village of Rathdrum just a 10-minute walk away. There are also natural
timber chalets, sleeping four, on the edge of the park's private lake that
are available for rent on a weekly basis. The park is open Easter to the
end of September. ☎ (0404) 46080; info@avonmoreriverside.com.

Hostels

There's a choice of five hostels run by the Youth Hostel Association, at Baltyboys, Ballinclea, Glendaloch, Knockree, and Glenmalure. The latter is basic and gas-lit, and is where Synge wrote his play *The Shadow of the Glen*, and where Iseult Gonne, daughter of Maud (loved by Yeats), lived with her husband, the writer Francis Stuart. Book **Glenmalure** through the head office. ☎ (01) 830-4555; mailbox@anoige.ie; www.irelandyha.org.

There are also two members of the Independent Holiday Hostels of Ireland in Wicklow Town, open January to the end of November. ☎ (0404) 69213; infor@wicklowbayhostel.com.

The **Old Presbytery**, Rathdrum is open all year. ☎ (0404) 46930; theoldpres@eircom.net.

County Meath

County Meath is one of the most fertile areas in the country, lying on a limestone plain watered by the rivers Boyne and Blackwater and their tributaries. A small part of the county is on the coast, with sandy beaches at Laytown and Bettystown.

It's a great destination for anyone interested in fishing and is also a center for horse breeding and racing, with plenty of equestrian facilities for visitors. Despite being close to Dublin, it is a rural and quiet county, with lovely countryside for walking.

Everywhere you go there's evidence of the area's importance historically, with a variety of monuments, castles, wooded demesnes, and historic gardens. It's known as the Royal County because it was here on the Hill of Tara that the High Kings lived in the second century AD.

In the **Loughcrew Hills** near Oldcastle there are **megalithic tombs**. The earliest inhabitants built great stone burial places 5,000 years ago at **Brú na Bóinne** (the palace or mansion of the Boyne), now considered one of the world's most important archaeological landscapes. In the fifth century, St. Patrick lit the Paschal Fire on the summit of the Hill of Slane. In 1690, the Battle of the Boyne took place near Oldbridge, when William's forces defeated the Jacobites, an event that changed Irish history.

Among the many sites worth visiting is the magnificent Anglo-Norman **castle at Trim** and the ruins of the **monastery at Kells**, where the monks created the illuminated manuscript called *The Book of Kells* (which you can see at Trinity College, Dublin).

The county capital and largest town is **Navan**, and other main towns include Ashbourne, Athboy, Dunshaughlin, Kells, Slane and Trim.

■ Getting Here

Navan is served by major routes N1 from Dublin (28 miles/45 km); N51-N2-N52-N1-A1-N1 from Belfast (85 miles/137 km); N52-N6-N18 from Galway (124 miles/200 km).

■ Getting Around

Bus Station, ☎ (041) 983-5023.

■ Tourist Information

Fáilte Ireland Tourist Offices are at:

Ludlow Street, Navan, open March-December, Monday-Friday. ☎ (046) 9073426.

Mill Street, Trim, open May-September, Monday-Saturday. ☎ (046) 9437111.

Brú na Bóinne Centre, Donor, open all year, Monday-Saturday. ☎ (041) 988-0305.

Meath Tourism Ltd markets the county. It's based at Railway Street, Navan, open Mon-Fri. ☎ (046) 9077273; fax 76025; info@meathtourism. ie; www.meathtourism.ie. Meath Tourism is one of the most efficient in the Republic and publishes beautifully illustrated free leaflets that are very useful to visitors.

There are also Tourist Information points at:

- Kells Heritage Centre, Headfort Place, Kells. ☎ (046) 9247840.
- The County Library, Railway Street, Navan.
- Mary McDonnell/Alison Connolly Crafts, Newgrange Mall, Slane.
- Maguires, Hill of Tara.
- Loughcrew Historic Gardens, Loughcrew, Oldcastle. ☎ (49) 854-1922.
- Trim Visitor Centre, at Trim Town Hall, beside Trim Castle.

East Coast & Midlands

TRACING YOUR ANCESTORS

There's a genealogical service at the **Meath Heritage Centre**, Trim. ☎ (046) 9436633; meathhc@iol.ie.

■ Sightseeing

Navan

Navan is right in the middle of the county, where the Rivers Boyne and Blackwater meet, with plenty of shops, restaurants, and pubs. It's a welcoming place for a break when exploring or as a base for a vacation.

The town dates back to Norman times and later was walled to defend the outer boundary of the Pale (see page 13) against frequent attacks, especially during the 15th and 16th centuries, from the O'Neills and other Ulster clans.

It became prosperous with the opening of a canal to Drogheda, and with trades such as milling, distilling and paper-making. Europe's largest zinc mine is nearby and is a major employer today.

There are lots of small shops, including many selling gifts, an exclusive shoe boutique, **Lamont Shoes** on Kennedy Road, with **Bookwise Booksellers** nearby. The shopping center has 60 retail units offering everything from fashion to groceries.

There are plenty of parking spaces, including a well signposted multistory, although they don't tell you that you need to pay in the shopping center before returning to your car.

Slane

If you start exploring the county from Navan, head first for Slane on the N51. It's a good example of an estate village, with some fine Georgian houses, but, unfortunately, heavy traffic passing through has somewhat spoiled its atmosphere.

If travelling from the south you cross a narrow bridge, where the traffic is carefully controlled, and when you turn left on its other side you soon pass **Slane Castle** on the left, which looks like a fairytale castle. It's the home of Lord Henry Mountcharles, and is not open to the public. The castle was badly damaged by a fire in 1991, and to restore it Lord Mountcharles has used its setting in a natural amphitheater to host very successful rock concerts. They take place in August each year – and some of the biggest names in music worldwide have appeared, including Bruce Springsteen and The Rolling Stones. For information about upcoming concerts and to buy tickets, see www.slanecastle.ie/main.htm.

Take the turn on your right opposite the castle for the **Hill of Slane**.

St. Patrick

Ireland's symbol, the shamrock, is associated with St. Patrick, who is reputed to have used it to demonstrate the Trinity – the three persons in one God.

There are different versions of the early life of St. Patrick, but all agree that he brought Christianity to the country in the 5th century. The Hill of Slane is where he is said to have lit the first Paschal, or Easter fire – which coincided with the great festival of the Druids held at Tara. His action caused great consternation, because no fires were allowed to be lit until after the one at the royal residence. He was brought before the High King Laoghaire, but Patrick succeeded in pacifying him, and so the new religion succeeded.

A mile from Slane on the N51 to Drogheda is the birthplace of the poet **Francis Ledwidge**, killed in World War I. The cottage is now a museum dedicated to him and a War Memorial Centre. Open daily. ☎ (041) 982-4544.

At Drogheda turn right then left and follow the mouth of the Boyne. Look out for signs for the site of the **Battle of the Boyne**, admission free, open April-Sept daily, 10 am-6 pm. ☎ (041) 988-4343.

Take in the **beaches** of Mornington, Bettystown, Laytown, and then move inland to Julianstown, Duleek, and Donore, where you visit Newgrange and Knowth.

At Morningtown, look at the **lighthouse beacon**, dating from Elizabethan times, and at the round tower. It was at Bettystown that the Tara Brooch, dating from the eighth century and now in the National Museum in Dublin, was found in 1850. It was discovered near the Hill of Tara (traditionally known as the seat of the High Kings). The brooch was made of silver and covered with precious stones.

Near Laytown is Sonairte, the **National Ecology Centre**, where you can visit an organic garden, learn about alternative sources of energy, or follow a nature trail. There's also a coffee shop.

Between Julianstown and Duleek you pass through wooded countryside, and there's a **ninth-century high cross** (see page 112) in Duleek. From the top of the hill at Donore you get a wonderful view of the Boyne and there's also a **15th-century castle**.

Newgrange

The **Visitor Centre for Newgrange and Knowth** is at Donore. UNESCO has designated the Brú Na Bóinne area a World Heritage Site, one of three in Ireland. Access is through the attractive Visitor Centre, cleverly hidden in the landscape, and housing a very interesting display, a restaurant and tourist office. As it's such a popular site, you are given a timed ticket and you cross by a little bridge to a bus that transports you to the monuments, where you're met by a guide.

Newgrange is the best-known passage tomb in the country, built around 3200 BC, discovered in 1699, and excavated and restored in the 1960s and '70s. It's covered by a mound with a quartz and granite façade and dominates the landscape, yet inside it's very small, so few visitors can enter it at a time. You walk along a narrow passageway to a cross-shaped chamber. Its most interesting feature is the Roof Box, a small opening above its doorway, precisely aligned to catch the rays of the rising sun on the morning of the winter solstice, December 21, the shortest day of the year, when the chamber is lit up for about 20 minutes. People book for years to be present. The second excavated megalithic tomb, **Knowth**, is larger. Newgrange is open daily all year, Knowth from early April to end of October. ☎ (041) 988-0300; fax 982-3072.

As you travel back along the N51 towards Navan, remember to take care and allow extra time when crossing the Boyne at Slane; as you approach the bridge from a steep hill, it's very dangerous and special controls are in place.

The Hill of Tara

The impressive ruins of **Bective Abbey** are just over four miles (6.4 km) south of Navan, just off the main Trim road. A Cistercian monastery, it was founded in 1147 and fortified in the 15th century. Today, the fortress aspect of the abbey prevails, and it has more the feel of a castle than of a monastery. Nearby is the Hill of Tara, famous in myth and legend, and with a special place in Irish history as the country's capital in pre-Christian times. There's a stunning view of the countryside from the summit. The **Visitor Centre**, with an audio-visual show, is in the former church of St. Patrick, and is run by the Heritage Service. Open mid-June to mid-September, 9:30 am-6:30 am; shorter hours in May and October. ☎ (046) 9025903.

Trim

The Heritage Town of Trim, on the R154, south of Athboy and Kells, is one of the prettiest in the country. It has a signposted walking trail you can follow or else go as you will and soak up the atmosphere. It has a friendly **Visitor Centre** with a multi-media exhibition, worth seeing before you explore further, and a small craft shop. Open daily all year, except Thursdays, 10 am-5 pm, Sundays, noon-5:30 pm. ☎ (046) 9437227; trimvisitorcenter@eircom.net.

Trim Castle is the largest Anglo-Norman castle in Ireland, built by Hugh de Lacey in the 13th century, and most impressive. No wonder the makers of the feature film *Braveheart* used it as a location, and that it's a busy site. In medieval times this was the very edge of the Pale (see page 13). Open all year, weekends only in winter, Easter to the end of October, 10 am-6 pm. ☎ (046) 9438619; fax 38618.

The **National Ploughing Championships** take place in late September at Ballinabrackey, eight miles (12 km) from Enfield, 13 miles (21 km) from Trim. They're great fun, with lots to see. Contact Meath Tourism, ☎ (046) 907-7273, for details.

Kells

Kells is on the N3 northwest of Navan. It's another Heritage Town and was a royal residence before St. Columcille founded a monastic settlement here in 550. His monks fled from the Scottish island of Iona to Kells in 806 to avoid Viking raids, and they were the creators of the *Book of Kells*, now in Trinity College, Dublin. The **High Cross of Kells** is outside the **Heritage Centre**, housed in the former courthouse on the Dublin side of town. ☎ (046) 9240723.

PRETEND YOU'RE IRISH

You can pretend you're Irish for a day at the **Causey Farm**, just off the Kells-to-Athboy road. The Murtaghs have been farming here for more than 1,000 years and these days focus on sheep, cattle and Connemara ponies. Visitors try turf-cutting, working with a sheep dog, milking a cow, making brown bread, weaving a rope, Irish dancing, speaking a bit of Irish, playing a bodhrán. It's great fun. Open on Saturdays from 2-8 pm. The fee includes tea and scones at the beginning and a four-course traditional meal before you leave. They'll even pick you up from the Dublin-Kells bus stop. ☎ (046) 9434135; info@causeyexperience.com; www.causeyexperience.com.

A walking trail around Kells takes you to sites including **St. Columcille's House**, an **oratory** dating from the 10th century, **St. Columb's Church and High Crosses**, and to **Kells Round Tower**.

There's an annual **Heritage Festival** here in late June/early July.

THE MEATH GAELTACHT

In 1935-37, 41 families moved from the Irish-speaking area (or *Gaeltacht*) of Connemara to Ráth Cairn, near Athboy, under a State-sponsored scheme. Now Co. Meath has its own *Gaeltacht*, the only one in the country which is inland. There's a program of classes and cultural events there all year, and in July and August you can stay in local homes. ☎ (046) 9432067; fax 32381; rathcairn@eircom.net.

East Coast & Midlands

While in Kells, visit the **Courtyard Craft Centre**, just outside the town. It has a huge variety of items, many the work of local artists, which make ideal gifts. There's an outdoor patio, colorful gardens, a coffee shop with open fire, plus lots of free parking. Open Tuesday-Saturday, 10 am-6 pm, March to end November, Sundays only in December. ☎ (046) 9240346.

The Gardens of Meath

There are wonderful gardens to visit in Co. Meath, and there's a free leaflet with details on them available from Meath Tourism at ☎ (046) 9077273; fax 76025; info@meathtourism.ie; www. meathtourism.ie. They are:

Butterstream Gardens, Trim, ☎ (046) 9436017.

Grove Gardens and Tropical Bird Sanctuary, Kells, ☎ (046) 9434276.

Lakeview Gardens, Mullagh, Kells, ☎ (046) 9242480.

Loughcrew Historic Gardens, Oldcastle, ☎ (049) 854-1922.

Ballinlough Castle Gardens, Clonmellon, ☎ (046) 9433135.

Larchill Arcadian Gardens, Kilcock, ☎ (01) 628-7354.

Hamwood House, Dunboyne, ☎ (01) 825-5210.

■ Adventures on Foot

Meath is a great county for walkers with its quiet roads and attractive landscape. One suggestion is to walk from **Kells to Oldcastle** through Loughcrew and on to **Castlekiernan**. There are forest parks at Lough Sheelin, Lough Bracken, and at Mullameen, five miles (eight km) from Oldcastle.

From Navan to Slane, there's the five-mile **Boyne Valley Towpath**, which follows the banks of the river, parallel with the old canal, passing through beautiful scenery as you go.

Walking Vacations

If you prefer to have someone else look after arrangements, **Kelltic Walking Holidays**, based in Kells, will do that. They organize tailor-made itineraries in the county and farther afield. ☎/fax (046) 9249672; kelltic@eircom.net.

■ Adventures on Water

You can hire boats to cruise the Royal Canal through Meath from **Leisureway Holidays**. ☎/fax (01) 822-5034; info@leisureways.com; www.leisureways.com.

In previous times, the boat called a Boyne currach or coracle was used by fishermen and for transport and was unique to that river. It was almost circular, made with a framework of ash or hazel rods covered with cowhide. There's one on display in the Millmount Museum, Drogheda.

There are indoor **swimming pools** in Navan at Leisure Link, ☎ (046) 9079950, www.e-navan.com/leisurelink; and at Trim, ☎ (046) 9431140; and Kells, ☎ (046) 9240551.

Fishing

The **River Boyne**, which, with its tributaries, drains most of the county, is one of Ireland's main brown trout waters, with good stocks that are well dispersed. It also has a run of sea trout, spring salmon and grilse. Anglers should get advice from local angling clubs or from the Eastern Regional Fisheries Board, which publishes a number of leaflets and guides. Contact David Byrne, the Angling Marketing Co-ordinator at the **Navan Tourist Information Centre**. ☎ (046) 9073375; dbyrne@fishingireland.net; www. fishingireland.net.

Sea angling is popular at the **mouth of the Boyne** around Morningtown, as well as fishing from that beach, and from Bettystown and Laytown.

Among other locations are the 20 lakes around the village of **Drumconrath** in the northern part of the county, which has become a center for coarse angling. The best known include **Moynalty**, **Capragh** and **Ballyhoe**, noted for bream, with rudd, tench and pike also available.

Part of **Lough Sheelin** is in Co. Meath and is famous for its brown trout fishery. Boats can be rented here.

For Licenses, Permits, Information, Tackle & Bait

- **Anglers World**, Angling Centre, Canon Row, Navan. ☎/fax (046) 9071866; anglersworld@hotmail.com.
- **The Flying Sportsman**, Carrick Road, Kells. ☎ (046) 9240205.

■ You can buy permits for the **River Blackwater**, brown trout fishery and spring salmon, looked after by the Navan and District Angling Club, from **Clarke's Sports Den**, Trimgate Street, Navan. ☎ (046) 9021130.

The Royal Canal passes through a short stretch of the county near the village of Enfield in the south, and crosses the Boyne near Longwood, via an aqueduct with three arches, and is a good coarse fishing location.

At Dunshaughlin, the **Rathbeggan Lakes** offer a day-ticket fishery with fly and coarse fishing on five lakes. ☎ (01) 824-0197; fax 824-0196; rathbegganlakes@clubi.ie; www.rathbegganlakes.com.

 See pages 71-74 for details on angling in Ireland, regulations and best times to fish.

■ Adventures on Wheels

 The county is a perfect destination for cyclists, with most of its roads quiet. Meath Tourism publishes a guide called *Cycling Holidays in Louth and Meath*, which includes suggested routes. Among them is one that is just over 100 miles (161 km), divided into four stages. Stage 1 starts in Navan and takes you through Bective, Tara, Batterstown, and on to Dunboyne. Stage 2 goes from there to Maynooth, Kilcock, Summerhill, to Trim. Stage 3 to Rathcairn, Athboy, Crossakeel, to Oldcastle. Stage 4 goes from there to Virginia in neighboring Cavan, back to Kells, ending in Navan.

Organized Cycling Vacations

Easy Riders, based in Clonee, is one company offering vacations by bike in Meath and Cavan. ☎ (01) 825-5484.

■ Adventures on Horseback

 There are equestrian facilities all over the county, with some also offering vacations, among them the following.

Bachelors Lodge Equestrian Centre, Kells Road, Navan, offers lessons, treks and residential riding vacations. ☎ (046) 9021736; lowryfam@eircom.net.

The **Kells Equestrian Centre** has indoor and outdoor arenas. ☎ (046) 9246998; info@meathtourism.ie.

Mackens/Rafeehan Stud, Kells, organizes riding vacations tailored to the individual. Eddie Macken was one of Ireland's best showjumpers ever. ☎ (046) 9240246; susanmacken@hotmail.com; www.eddiemacken.com.

☆☆☆☆ **Broadmeadows Equestrian Centre**, Ashbourne, is a guesthouse on 100 acres with riding facilities. ☎ (01) 835-2823; fax 835-2819; info@equestrianireland.com; www.irelandequestrianireland.com.

Horseracing

There's National Hunt and flat racing at **Fairyhouse**, Ratoath, home of the Grand National, which takes place at Easter. ☎ (01) 825-6167.

Proudstown Park, Navan, with its uphill finish, is where the famous Arkle won his first race. ☎ (046) 9021350.

Meetings have been held at **Bellewstown** for an amazing 300 years. ☎ (041) 984-2111.

Races at **Bettystown** in July take place on the beach, the only ones in Europe. ☎ (041) 23425.

■ Golf

Meath Tourism publishes a free brochure with details of all 11 courses, and lists of pitch 'n putt facilities. They all welcome visitors, but do phone in advance to check hours.

Ashbourne Golf Club. ☎ (01) 835-2005.

The Black Bush Club, Dunshaughlin, is near Fairyhouse Racecourse. ☎ (01) 825-0793; golf@blackbush.iol.ie.

The **County Meath Club** is at Trim. ☎ (046) 9431463.

The **Glebe Club** is a mile from Trim. ☎ (046) 9431926.

The **Headfort Club** is on Navan Road, Kells, and has two 18-hole courses. ☎ (046) 9240146.

The **Kilcock Club** is just two miles (3.2 km) off the M4. ☎ (01) 628-7283.

The Laytown and Bettystown Golf Club has a traditional links course. ☎ (041) 27170.

Moor-Park Golf Course is four miles (6.4 km) from Navan on one of the highest areas in the county at Mooretown. ☎ (046) 9027181.

Navan Golf Club is on the lands of the Racecourse a mile from the town. ☎ (046) 9021350.

The **Royal Tara Golf Club** is right in the middle of the county off the N3 near the Hill of Tara. ☎ (046) 9025508.

East Coast & Midlands

The **South Meath Club** is a mile from Trim and has a nine-hole course. ☎ (046) 9431471.

Famous Meath People

The **Duke of Wellington**, who defeated Napoleon at Waterloo and went on to become Prime Minister of England in 1828, spent most of his youth in Meath. North of Summerhill you can see the remains of Dangan Castle, his family home. Born Arthur Wellesley in 1769 just outside Trim, where he was educated, he later represented the town in Parliament. There's a statue of him in the town.

The father of the Liberator of Chile was born in 1721 nearby. **Ambrose O'Higgins** was sent to his uncle, a member of the Jesuits in Cadiz, and was expected to join the Church. Instead, he decided to head for South America to seek his fortune, where he rose to the rank of Brigadier General in the army and became Viceroy of Peru in 1795. He was involved in the defense of his adopted country when war broke out with England two years later. He died suddenly in 1801, leaving a son Bernardo, who became the Liberator of Chile.

Sir Richard Johnson, who became an Indian trader in what was then the Mohawk Valley and is now New York State, was born in Meath in 1715, and his family emigrated to America in 1737. Because of his fairness and hard work, he was called "the benevolent dictator" by the Indians. He died in 1774 after delivering an address to the Indian Council of the Six Nations.

James Connell, who wrote the words of *The Red Flag*, the Socialist anthem, also came from Meath. He was born in Kilskyre, Crossakeel, in 1850, was a Fenian and a member of the Land League. His career was varied – from laborer to journalist and self-taught lawyer. He died in London in 1929.

■ Where to Stay

☆☆ **The Conyngham Arms House Hotel**, Slane, is small, with only 14 guestrooms, and was built in the 19th century. It has comfortable rooms, traditionally decorated, with four-poster beds. There's a choice of bars – the **Ledwidge Lounge** or **Cannings** – and good food available in the **Gamekeeper's Lodge Bistro**, which is popular with non-residents. It's a friendly place to stay and a good base for touring. Rates from $$. ☎ (041) 988-4444; fax 982-4205; enquiry@conynghamarms.com; www.conynghamarms.com.

☆☆☆ The **Newgrange Hotel** in the center of Navan, is modern, having only opened in 1998. It has 62 bedrooms with good facilities. Guests and non-residents have a choice of where to eat. The **Bridge Brasserie**, which has imaginative Irish and international dishes, belongs to the Meath Good Food Circle. **Buxton's Café** is less formal and serves a carvery lunch every day and has an evening menu. **Rowley's Bar** has a snack menu all day, and live music nightly from Thursday to Mon-

HOTEL PRICE CHART	
Price per person, per night, with two sharing, including breakfast.	
$	Under US $50
$$	US $50-$100
$$$	US $101-$175
$$$$	US $176-$200
$$$$$	Over US $200

day. $$ with special offers and golf breaks available. ☎ (046) 9074100; fax 73977; info@newgrangehotel.ie; www. newgrangehotel.ie.

☆☆ The **Headfort Arms Hotel**, Kells, in the middle of the town, has 18 bedrooms. Its **Vanilla Pod Restaurant** is known for its fine food, available all day from 7:30 am to 10 pm, including a carvery lunch. It belongs to the Meath Good Food Circle. $$. ☎ (046) 9240063; headfortarms@eircom.net; www.headfortarms.com.

Cottage Rentals

There's a delightful group of 300-year-old **thatched cottages** on the beach at Bettystown, furnished and fitted out to a high standard. ☎ (041) 982-8104; info@cottages-ireland.com; www.cottages-ireland.com.

There are 12 lovely mews houses available in a courtyard setting in the Headfort Estate, a mile from Kells. It's a wonderful place, with gardens, open parkland, lots of mature trees, and the Headfort Golf Club with its 18-hole course designed by Christy O'Connor Junior. Toll-free in US ☎ 866-824-9330; (01) 478-2045; fax 478-4327; info@irishluxury.com or info@activeireland.ie; www.activeireland.ie.

Hostels

There are three hostels, open all year, members of the IHHI (Independent Holiday Hostels of Ireland, see page 63).

Slane Farm Hostel. ☎ (041) 982-4390; info@slanefarmhostel.ie.

Kells Hostel. ☎ (046) 9249995; www.kellshostel.com.

Bridge House Hostel, Trim. ☎ (046) 9431848.

■ Where to Eat

Watch for restaurants belonging to the **Meath Good Food Circle**, as they've been independently assessed for their menu, food, service, facilities and wine list.

The Inland Counties

County Kildare

Kildare is home to the **National Stud** and three racecourses, at **Curragh**, **Naas** and **Punchestown**. This inland county has areas of low-lying bogs on its western boundary. To the east, the foothills of the **Wicklow Mountains** meet its unique fertile plain, the **Curragh**, which has 6,000 acres of grassland where, in the early morning, you see beautiful thoroughbred racehorses exercising.

Visitors can walk in the countryside, play golf, fish, ride, or cruise its waterways. As well as the rivers Liffey, Greese, Boyne and Barrow, the county is traversed by both the **Royal Canal** and the **Grand Canal**, and there are historic places, houses and gardens to visit.

Kildare has become part of the commuter belt in recent decades, due to its proximity to Dublin, and huge housing estates have grown up around its towns. People traveling from Dublin south to Cork and other destinations are inclined to stick to the main roads and pass by, missing the attractions of this interesting county. One of the best ways of exploring it is by following the canals, either walking their towpaths or cruising their waters. Away from main roads, it's a peaceful county with plenty of wild fowl, birds and animals in its river valleys, bogs, woodlands and canals.

Its county capital and largest town is **Naas**, and others include **Athy**, **Celbridge**, **Kildare**, **Leixlip**, and the university town of **Maynooth**.

■ Getting Here

By Car

Co. Kildare is linked to other parts of the country by main roads.

The M4/N4/N6 Dublin-Galway/Sligo passes through Leixlip, Maynooth, Kilcock, Enfield.

The M7/N7/N21/N8 Dublin-Cork/Limerick/Killarney route takes you to Naas, Newbridge, Kildare, Monasterevin.

The N78 Dublin-Kilkenny Waterford road passes through Naas, Kilcullen and Athy.

By Rail

Maynooth is on the Dublin-Sligo rail route from Connolly Station.

The county is also served by mainline routes to Mayo, Galway, Limerick, Kerry and Cork, from Heuston Station, with trains stopping at Newbridge and Kildare Town. The Dublin-Carlow/Kilkenny/Waterford train also stops at Athy.

By Bus

The county is on Expressway bus routes between Dublin and Galway, Sligo, Limerick, Cork, Waterford, and its towns and villages are also connected by bus.

■ Tourist Information

i **Fáilte Ireland Tourist Office**, Market Square, Kildare Town, open June-September. ☎ (045) 521-240; www.ecoast-midlands.travel.ie.

Kildare Fáilte, which promotes tourism in the county, is at 38 South Main Street, Naas. ☎ (045) 898-888; kildarefailte@indigo.ie.

TRACING YOUR ANCESTORS

Contact the **Kildare History and Family Research Centre**, Riverbank, Main Street, Newbridge. ☎ (045) 433-602; fax 432-490; capinfo@iol.ie; www.kildare.ie/genealogy.

■ Sightseeing

Naas

Naas takes its name from Nás na Riogh, the assembly place of kings, and was the seat of the Kings of Leinster for almost 700 years, until the death of the last king, Cearbhall, in 904. All that remains of its regal past is a large man-made hill, or motte, in the middle of the town. It's a busy town, full of shops, pubs and restaurants.

Kilcock, Maynooth and Leixlip are in a semi-circle in the northeastern corner of Kildare, close to Dublin and, with nearby Celbridge, have grown an awful lot over the last decade or so with the city's expansion.

Maynooth Castle, built in the 13th century as the main residence of the Kildare Geraldines, is in the middle of the village of Maynooth. It's open from June to September daily and on Sundays in October. ☎ (01) 628-6744.

Leixlip

At the center of Leixlip there's also a **castle**, built about 1172 on a rock where the rivers Liffey and Rye meet. It's owned by the Honourable Desmond Guinness. He founded the Irish Georgian Society, which does excellent work preserving buildings of architectural merit and generally raising awareness of their importance. ☎ (01) 624-4430.

Celbridge

Celbridge is on the River Liffey, south of Leixlip and 12 miles (19 km) northeast of Naas. It's home to **Castletown House**, Ireland's largest Palladian mansion, built in the early 18th century for William Connolly, Speaker of the Irish Parliament, who made his fortune from estates forfeited after the Battle of the Boyne.

It's worth a visit for its magnificent exterior and for its impressive interior, which includes the only surviving intact 18th-century print room, marvelous plasterwork by the Lafranchini brothers in its staircase hall, Irish period furniture and paintings. There are a number of follies in its grounds. ☎ (01) 628-8252; castletown@ealga.ie; www.heritageireland.ie.

Kildare Town

The road through Kildare Town, 12 miles (19 km) southwest of Naas, is always busy. Kildare was founded by Saint Bridget (or Brigid) during the sixth century. The local king promised to give her what land she covered by her handkerchief when she spread it on the ground, and of course there was a miracle and she built a convent here. Today, **St. Brigid's Cathedral** is beside the market square, but little remains of the original 13th-century building, as it was burned down long ago. Its most interesting feature is the window showing the three most important Irish saints, Bridget, Patrick and Columba. There's a 10th-century round tower nearby, open to visitors in summer, with lovely views from its summit.

On the edge of town is the **Irish National Stud**, home to some of Ireland's finest thoroughbreds, where you can enjoy a guided tour and see the racehorses in their paddocks or being exercised or groomed. There's also a museum. Next to it are the **Japanese Gardens**, created by Tassa Eida and his son Minoru in 1906-10, and now considered the finest in Europe. It's a very peaceful place to visit, as you follow the 20 stages that symbolize the journey of a soul from Oblivion to Eternity, passing the Tunnel of Ignorance, the Hill of Ambition and so on. To mark the Millennium, St. Fiachra's garden was created, which visitors enter via an underground passage. Fiachra (590-670) is the patron saint of gardeners. Open February 12-November 12, 9:30 am-6 pm, daily. ☎ (045) 521-617; stud@irish-national-stud.ie; www.irish-national-stud.ie.

SAINT BRIGID

The St. Brigid's cross is believed to protect homes from want and evil, and is made from woven rushes. Generations ago they were worn by Irish girls, but today you'll see them displayed on the walls of many Irish homes. Each year on St. Brigid's Day (February 2) they are blessed by Roman Catholic priests. You can also buy brooches and other jewelry made in the distinctive X shape.

Athy

Athy is a Heritage Town and the largest in South Kildare. It's on the N78/R415, on the Laois border, close to where the Grand Canal meets the River Barrow. It has a fine market square, some Georgian houses and the 16th-century **White's Castle**, which dominates the bridge over the river. There's a modern church, pentagon-shaped, which people either like or loathe.

The **Heritage Centre**, which traces the town's history, also has a Tourist Information point. ☎ (059) 8633075; athyheritage@eircom.net; www. kildare.ie/athyonline.

Ballitore

Ballitore is an interesting little village in the southeastern corner of the county, founded in the late 17th century by Quakers from Yorkshire in England. The restored **Meeting House** (built about 1708) houses the local library and a small museum. **Mary Leadbeater's house** is on the corner of the village square, from where she witnessed the cruelty of the 1798 Rebellion – her account is one of the few independent descriptions.

■ Adventures on Foot

There are two waymarked long-distance walks in the county – the Royal Canal Way in the north, where Kildare meets Co. Meath, and in the south the Barrow Way, near the Laois border.

East Coast & Midlands

It is suggested that you start the **Royal Canal Way** at Maynooth. It is possible to get to Maynooth by bus from Dublin or by train from Connolly station in Dublin. The station and the railway fine follows the route of the Royal Canal Way for much of its distance from Dublin to Mullingar. The trail in fact starts just in front of Maynooth station. Following is the recommended way to walk, or cycle the route.

Day 1: Arrive at Maynooth. Proceed along Way to Enfield. Maynooth and Kilcock are now built-up areas of Dublin City so it is suggested that you set up camp beyond Kilcock.

Day 2/3: Proceed along trail passing through Enfield and Thomastown towards Mullingar.

Day 4/5: Mullingar to Ballynacargy and onwards to Ballymahon

Day 6/7: Ballymahon to Cloonsheerin Junction. From here the canal branches. One branch brings you to Longford town. The other brings you to Clondra and onto the Shannon. The distance to each one is similar so its a matter of choice which one you choose to finish at.

The distances involved are: Maynooth to Enfield 11.5 miles (18.5 km); Enfield to Thomastown 14.4 miles (23 km); Thomastown to Mullingar 10.5 miles (17 km); Mullingar to Ballynacargy 11.5 miles (18.5 km); Ballynacargy to Ballymahon 11.5 miles (18.5 km); Ballymahon to Cloonsheerin 10.5 miles (17km); Cloonsheerin to Longford five miles (8.4 km); Cloonsheerin to Clondra five miles (8 km)

The full length of the **Barrow Way**, from Lowtown to St. Mullins is 70 miles (113 km). You can cover this distance in a single journey in less than a week or explore shorter sections of the walk in a number of easy strolls. Stage 1 of the Barrow Way starts in Lowtown and a distance of 14 miles (23 km) takes you to the town of Monasterevin. The raised banks of the canal offers beautiful views of the surrounding countryside with views of the Hill of Allen and the Wicklow Mountains.

Stage 2 takes you from Monasterevin to Athy – 14 miles (23 km). This stretch offers the visitor much of architectural interest with many old bridges and houses.

Stage 3 runs from Athy to Carlow – 12 miles (19 km). This is the first of four stretches that pass through the county of Carlow.

Stage 4, Carlow to Bagenalstown 10 miles (16km). Milford, approximately seven km south of Carlow is one of the most attractive stretches along the River Barrow.

Stage 5 is Bagenalstown to Graiguenamanagh, a picturesque abbey town – 16 miles (26 km).

The walk ends in Graiguenamanagh, .

Stage 6 covers Graiguenamanagh to St. Mullins – four miles (six km).

There are about 70 miles (113 km) of **canals** – the Grand, Royal and the Barrow line – and they're ideal for short- or long-distance self-guided walks along their towpaths. Do remember to dress for the weather, as there's little shelter on some sections. The paths can be very wet underfoot, so wear appropriate shoes. In places you are far from shops, so carry some refreshments with you.

An example of the towpath walks along the Royal Canal is the one that starts at Cope Bridge on the Confey road out of Leixlip. From there to Kilcock it's an 8½-mile walk (13.5 km). What's enjoyable about this route is that the landscape is surprisingly rural, although you are very near the sprawling Leixlip, and that new housing is hidden from view by hedges.

The Barrow line links the main line of the Grand Canal with the River Barrow at Athy, 29 miles (47 km) south. It cuts through bog and farmland in the southwest, before running into Co. Laois and then back towards the town to join the Barrow.

The waymarked Barrow Way is 68 miles (109 km) long. Starting at Lowtown, it passes through Monasterevin and Athy, then goes south to the Barrow Valley and on to St. Mullins in Co. Carlow, where the river becomes tidal.

There are a number of routes along the Grand Canal, including Hazelhatch to Sallins, eight miles (13 km) and Robertstown to Edenderry, 13 miles (21 km). The latter takes you to Lowtown Junction, where the main Grand Canal continues to the west and its Barrow branch begins, which is 28 miles (45 km) long. Barge horses used to be stabled at Lowtown and these days it's an inland dockyard.

Donadea Forest Park

About eight miles (13 km) north of Naas on the R407 to Kilcock is Donadea Forest Park, run by Coillte, the State Foresty Service. It's a former estate and you can see the ruins of what was first a Norman keep, then from 1624 a house, reconstructed over the centuries with wings added. There's a Nature Trail, a Shrubbery Trail, and other features include a lake, and grove of beech about 150 years old.

■ Adventure on Wheels

 Mondello Park, the only international racing circuit in the country, is near Naas. It hosts events for cars and motorcycles, and kart, rallycross and rallysprint. There's a motorsport museum and a range of performance driving courses. ☎ (045) 860200; info@mondellopark.ie; www.mondellopark.ie.

East Coast & Midlands

■ Adventure in the Air

The Falcons Parateam of **skydivers** is based at Naas. Visitors are welcome. Contact Vernon McCarthy to see if they have an event scheduled. ☎ (045) 897-991; falcons@anything-irish.com.

■ Adventures on Water

Explore the Grand Canal with **Robertstown Barge Tours**, with full bar and buffet on board. Tours last from one to three hours, April-October. ☎ (045) 870-005.

Cruising the Waterways

Lowtown, near Robertstown, is the base for a number of cruise companies operating along the waterways and you'll also see boats of all shapes and sizes moored on both banks.

You can hire a narrow cruiser barge from **Lowtown Cruisers Limited**, based at the marina here, by the week, the day or weekend. On board, explore the Grand Canal, the Barrow and the Shannon. Full instructions are given before you set off. ☎ (045) 860-427; ltmarine@esatclear.ie; www.lowtownmarine.com.

Leisure Afloat, based at Levitstown Lock, Athy, offers cruising vacations and short breaks on barges. ☎ (056) 7764395; info@leisureafloat.com; www.leisureafloat.com.

Canalways Ireland, based at Rathangan on the banks of the Barrow Line branch of the Grand Canal, offers vacations on board traditional steel canal boats. ☎ (045) 524-646; fax 524-019; info@canalways.ie.

Fishing

The county's waterways, its two main rivers the Rye and the Liffey, as well as the Royal and the Grand Canal, attract many interested in fishing. The **Grand Canal** has a big stock of rudd, tench, perch, eels, some pike and roach. The **River Liffey**, with its 82-mile stretch through three counties, including Kildare, has abundant supplies of all fish types. The Leixlip stretch of the Royal Canal is excellent for coarse fishing, all year round for roach, and for other species in summer. Contact **Leixlip Angling Development Society**, ☎ (01) 624-2968.

Athy, Leixlip, Monastervin, Prosperous and Vicarstown are all angling centers. Take a look at **www.irishfishingholidays.com** or contact tourist information.

For local knowledge, advice and gear, contact:

- **The Tackle Shop**, Eyre Street, Newbridge, ☎ (045) 435-853.
- **Noel Conlon and Sons**, Eyre Street, Newbridge, ☎ (045) 433-311.
- **Countryman Angling and Game Supplies**, Pacelli Road, Naas, ☎ (045) 879-341.

See pages 71-74 for details on angling in Ireland, regulations and best times to fish.

■ Adventures on Horseback

It isn't surprising that there are a lot of equestrian facilities here, some aimed at serious and professional riders.

At Punchestown there's the **National Equestrian Centre**, which runs personalized programs and clinics with international instructors. ☎ (045) 876-800; sales@punchestown.com; www.punchestown.com.

The **Coilog Eventing Centre**, Crosspatrick, Naas, has indoor and outdoor arenas, 30 cross-country fences, and organizes treks through bogs, along canals and country lanes. ☎ (045) 860-842; kisbyme@eircom.net; www.kildarehorse.ie.

The **Osberstown Riding Centre**, Naas, offers lessons for all levels, as well as cross-country rides. ☎ (045) 879-074.

The **Kill International Equestrian Centre** runs riding vacations. ☎ (045) 877-208; killinternational@eircom.net

The **Redhills Riding Centre**, Kildare Town, offers scenic treks. ☎ (045) 521-570.

The **Acorn Equestrian Centre**, Maynooth, caters for all levels of rider and has 100 acres of grassland, indoor and outdoor arenas and a cross-country course. ☎ (01) 628-9116; AcornEC@eircom.net; www.acornequestrian.com.

Abbeyfield Farm, Clane, has more than 40 horses and offers expert instruction. ☎ (045) 868-188.

■ Golf

The county has an excellent choice of courses, the most prestigious of them at the K Club, Straffan – see *Where to Stay*, page 155.

East Coast & Midlands

Five miles (eight km) from the K Club is the **Pinetrees Golf Club** at Clane, ☎ (045) 869-525.

Others include:

Killeen, at Kill, ☎ (045) 866-003; admin@killeensc.ie.

Knockanally, Donadea, ☎ (045) 869-322; golf@knockanally.com.

Millicent at Clane, ☎ (045) 893-279; derekkilleen@eircom.net.

The **Athy Club** was founded in 1906 and has a mature parkland course divided in two by a tributary of the Barrow. ☎ (059) 8631729; athygolfclub@ireland.com; www.athygolfclub.com.

Southeast of Athy, the course at the **Kilkea Castle Golf Club**, Castledermot, has been developed around the 12th-century castle, on the riverbank. ☎ (059) 9145556; kilkeagolfclub@eircom.net; www. kilkeacastlehotelgolf.com.

The **Bodenstown Club**, Sallins, has two 18-hole courses. ☎ (045) 897-7096; fax 898-126.

At the **Castlewarden Club**, Straffan, the members have restored the historic house, so visitors can enjoy its grandeur. ☎ (01) 458-9254; castlewarden@clubi.ie.

The **Celbridge Elm Hall Golf Club**'s course has three lakes, making it a challenge. ☎ (01) 628-8208; fax 825-9887.

The **Cill Dara Club** at Little Curragh has a nine-hole course. ☎ (045) 521-433. The **Curragh Golf Club** nearby claims to have the oldest course in the country. ☎ (045) 441-714; fax 442-476; curraghgolf@eircom. net.

There are two clubs near Carbury in the northwest corner of the county:

Highfield. ☎ (0405) 9731021; hgc@indigo.ie; www.highfield-golf.ie.

Edenderry. ☎ (0405) 9731072.

The **Naas Club**, founded in 1896, is the second oldest in the county. ☎ (045) 874-644; naasgolf@eircom.net.

At Prosperous, near Naas, there's the **Woodlands Club**. ☎ (045) 860-777.

There's a choice at Newbridge:

Red Lane Golf and Football Centre. ☎ (045) 435-035 and

Newbridge Golf Club. ☎ (045) 486-110.

In the northeast, the **Kilcock Club** has a parkland course with beautiful mature trees. ☎ (01) 628-4074.

■ Where to Stay

☆☆☆☆☆ The **K Club**, its full name the **Kildare Hotel and Country Club**, is near Straffan and is an absolutely wonderful place to stay.

HOTEL PRICE CHART	
Price per person, per night, with two sharing, including breakfast.	
$	Under US $50
$$	US $50-$100
$$$	US $101-$175
$$$$	US $176-$200
$$$$$	Over US $200

The hotel is in a sensitively restored stately home surrounded by an extensive estate. The excellent staff is so unobtrusive, that you feel you're at home, yet have all the advantages of a five-star hotel. You even get a rubber duck for your bath!

There's a choice of rooms – superior, deluxe and suites – including garden suites with two bedrooms, a lounge and dining room, linked to the hotel.

You can also select where to dine, from the elegance of **The Byerly Turk**, which serves French cuisine with an Irish twist, to the stylish **Legends Restaurant** and its European menu.

Among the excellent facilities is a leisure center with pool, which can be reached directly from your hotel room. The 330 acres of grounds include gardens running alongside the river. More energetic exercise includes indoor tennis and squash, or golf. The K Club course is home to the Smurfit European Open and venue for the Ryder Cup in 2005.

You can also go salmon fishing on the hotel's one-mile stretch of the River Liffey, or coarse fishing with a choice of five stocked lakes. Other leisure activities include clay target shooting, horseback riding, lessons if wanted, and bikes can be hired. Special golf and other packages are available. $$$$. ☎ (01) 627-3333; fax 601-7299; resortsales@kclub.ie; www. kclub.ie.

Non-residents can also enjoy some of the leisure activities at the K Club, so phone and ask.

☆☆☆ **Leixlip House Hotel** overlooks the village and is only eight miles (13 km) from the center of Dublin. It's a Georgian home dating back to 1722 which has been transformed into a luxury hotel with 19 bedrooms, mostly furnished with antiques. The **Bradaun Restaurant** is elegant and its menu is modern Irish, with local and fresh produce a priority, including meat, fish and game. Food is also available in the lounge. Both guests and non-residents are advised to reserve a table in advance here, as it has become popular. $$$ (with special Golfer's Delight and Gourmet

East Coast & Midlands

Weekenders also available). ☎ (01) 624-2268; fax 624-4177; reservations@leixliphouse.com; www.leixliphouse.com.

☆☆☆☆ **Kilkea Castle** in Castledermot is the oldest inhabited castle in Ireland, built in 1180 by Hugh de Lacy, and now transformed into a luxury hotel. There's a huge choice of activities for guests, including fishing on the River Griese, clay-pigeon shooting, horse riding, bird shooting, and golfing on its own course, which encircles the castle. You can wander the lovely gardens or play tennis, and there's an indoor pool, gym and exercise room. The **de Lacy Restaurant** has an imaginative menu. $$$. ☎ (059) 9145156; fax 45187; kilkea@iol.ie; www.kilkeacastle.ie.

Martinstown House, The Curragh, was built in 1832-40 in Gothic cottage orné style in what was originally part of the estate of the Dukes of Leinster. Its grounds are wonderful, including a walled garden and a croquet lawn. It's a very welcoming and attractive place to stay, with just four double bedrooms. Dinner is available, but you must book the day before. The house belongs to the Hidden Ireland group (see page 60), and is not classified under the hotel system. $$$. ☎ (045) 441-269; info@martinstownhouse.com; www.martinstownhouse.com.

Camping & RV Parks

☆☆☆ **Forest Farm Caravan and Camping Park** is three miles (4.8 km) from Athy on the N78 Dublin road, only 13 miles (21 km) from the National Stud, Japanese Gardens and Curragh Racecourse at Kildare Town. The park is on a 140-acre working farm, set back from the road, and is open all year. ☎ (059) 973-1231; forestfarm@eircom.net; www.accommodationathy.com.

Cottage & Apartment Rentals

Rent an apartment at the **Royal Canal Court**, Kilcock, used by students of Maynooth University during term time. You can enjoy the Royal Canal, perhaps go canoeing, stroll along its banks or follow the Royal Canal Way. There are golf courses nearby and you're very close to Dublin. There's a choice of apartments from a two-bedroom penthouse (sleeps three) to a three-bedroom apartment (sleeps five). They offer an amazing value, from about €200-400 per week. Available from late May to early September. ☎ (01) 624-1625; info@royalcanalcourt.com; www.royalcanalcourt.com.

Robertstown Holiday Village has eight cottages, each with its own entrance and garden facing the Grand Canal. They have two bedrooms and are well equipped and furnished. They're available by the week or for short breaks. Very good value at prices from €230-420. ☎ (045) 870-870; fax 870-869; kmbgorey@gofree.indigo.ie.

■ Where to Eat

Some of the best places to eat are in the hotels already listed, and there are plenty of other choices in all of the towns and villages of Kildare.

A favorite is in The Square, Kildare Town, called **Silken Thomas**. It has three bars and a restaurant, and is very popular, especially when there are races at the nearby Curragh course. It serves good meals at great value, including steaks, seafood, poultry, vegetarian options.

SILKEN THOMAS

It's named after a member of the Fitzgerald family, Lords of Kildare, who got his name from the richness of his clothes and the silk banners carried by his standard bearers. In 1536 he was fooled into believing that his father had been executed in the Tower of London and led an uprising against King Henry VIII. It was brutally suppressed and he and his five uncles executed. ☎ (045) 521-695.

Tyrrells Restaurant at Ballindoolin House and Gardens, Carbury, is open for lunch, Wednesday-Sunday, and for dinner, Wednesday-Saturday. In addition to the excellent food, prepared with vegetables grown there, it's a lovely place to be. Ballindoolin is an historic house set in parkland, with woodland walks and walled kitchen gardens, open to the public May-September. ☎ (046) 973-2400; www.ballindoolin.com.

County Offaly

Offaly is a county of contrasting landscapes, from flat boglands to mountains. The longest river in the country, the **Shannon**, forms its western border, and the **Grand Canal** links it to **Edenderry** in the east, passing through **Tullamore**, its main town, on the way.

The **Slieve Bloom Mountains** in the southeast, the largest unbroken area of upland blanket bog and forestry in Ireland, is a National Park, and its deep valleys have lots of streams and rivers meandering through them. The **Clara Bog** is a natural heritage area, preserved for its flora, fauna and soak system, while **Mongan Bog** is protected for its unusual and intricate habitats. The **Lough Boora Parklands** have been developed from former cutaway bogs.

Hills, called "eskers," were formed 10,000 years ago from gravel and sand left behind when the ice melted.

From 1556, when conquered by the English, until 1920, Offaly was known as King's County. Tullamore and Birr are now Heritage Towns. With its streams, lakes, bogs and woodland, Offaly is an ideal destination for anyone interested in fishing, walking, enjoying an unspoiled environment and discovering the natural or built heritage.

AN AMERICAN CONNECTION

Offaly and Westmeath belong to Ely O'Carroll Country – named after the Gaelic lords who ruled here for 600 years. The landscape is dotted with dozens of their castles.

After the O'Carroll lands were confiscated for the Plantations in the 17th century (see page 14), Charles Carroll traveled to America where he settled in Maryland. Among his distinguished descendants is his namesake who was the last to sign the Declaration of Independence and Bishop John Carroll, founder of Georgetown University.

■ Getting Here

Offaly is right in the center of the country and Tullamore is served by main routes N52-N6-N4 from Dublin (66 miles/106 km); N80-N8-N25 from Cork (128 miles/206 km) and N80-N6-N18 from Galway (82 miles/132 km).

Tullamore is on the Dublin-Galway rail line.

■ Tourist Information

Fáilte Ireland Tourist Office is in Tullamore Dew Heritage Centre, **Tullamore**. It's open all year. ☎ (0506) 52617.

There's a **Tourist Office** at **Clonmacnoise**, open from Easter to October, ☎ (090) 9674134; and another on Castle Street, **Birr**, open May to September, ☎ (0509) 20110.

TRACING YOUR ANCESTORS

Irish Midlands Ancestry provides an ancestral research service for counties Offaly and Laois, and is based on Bury Quay, Tullamore, ☎/fax (0506) 21421; ohas@iol.ie; www.irishmidlandsancestry.com.

■ Sightseeing

Tullamore

 Tullamore is a pleasant market town on the river of the same name, which retains some of its historic streetscapes. It's famous for Tullamore Dew whiskey, no longer made here, and is well worth visiting the **Heritage Centre** in the original bonded warehouse, dating from 1897, which stands on the bank of the Grand Canal. The exhibition covers the town's history, as well as focusing on the production of whiskey and of Irish Mist liqueur. There's a charming café/bar there, with a full license, where you can go without paying to visit the Heritage Centre. Open May-September, Monday-Saturday, 9 am-6 pm; October-April, 10 am-5 pm; Sundays, noon to 5 pm all year.

As you wander around Tullamore, there are buildings worth noting, and you can follow a signposted trail. Don't miss **St. Catherine's Church of Ireland**, designed by Francis Johnston in 1815. The **Catholic Church** deserves a look for its impressive timber interiors and its stained glass windows by Irish artist Harry Clark. All that remains of the **jail** is its Gothic façade, and the **Town Hall** dates back to 1790.

Edenderry

Edenderry, northeast of Tullamore, is a market town that takes its name from great oak woods that used to grow on its hill until the last century. It has a signposted town trail and **Grange Castle**, with its wildflower labyrinth, based on an early Christian design, is worth a visit. ☎ (0405) 9733316; www.ils.ie/grange.

Birr

Birr is 22 miles (35 km) southwest of Tullamore on the N52/N62. It's one of Ireland's Heritage Towns, because of its Georgian architecture, and is worth more than a brief visit. There's a signposted trail around the town.

You need to allow at least two or three hours just to visit the **Birr Castle Demesne** and take in its unique collection of rare plants and trees. The wonderful gardens, the biggest in the country, are spread out around where two rivers, the Camcor and Little Brosna, meet and include a Victorian fernery and formal gardens. The Parsons family, the Earls of Rosse, have lived here since 1620, and among them were a number of remarkable scientists, inventors, and photographers. They and other Irish scientists are celebrated and their achievements documented in **Ireland's Historic Science Centre** housed in the former stables of the castle. The largest telescope in the world for 70 years was built here in 1845 by the Third Earl and can be seen in the grounds. The **Little Space**

Café offers snacks and hot meals at reasonable prices. Open daily: March-October, 9 am-6 pm; November-February, 10 am-4 pm. ☎ (0509) 20336; fax 21583; info@birrcastle.com; www.birrcastle.com.

Clonmacnoise

Clonmacnoise is 12 miles (19 km) north of Banagher on the R444, and is one of the largest and most impressive monastic sites in the country. It was founded in 545 by Saint Ciaran. The ruins are on the banks of the Shannon, and include nine churches, two round towers and a castle dating from the 12th century. Rory O'Connor, the last High King of Ireland, is said to be buried in the cathedral, which has an intriguing whispering arch. In the Visitor Centre are three high crosses, early Christian grave slabs and there's an audio-visual show.

Open daily all year, it's very busy in the summer. Open mid-May to early September, 9 am-7 pm; September-October, 10 am-6 pm; November-mid-March until 5:30 pm; mid-March to mid-May until 6 pm. ☎ (090) 9674195. The Tourist Office is open from Easter to October. ☎ (090) 9674134.

■ Adventures on Foot

There are three way-marked long-distance routes in the county: The Slieve Bloom Way, the Offaly Way, and part of the Grand Canal Way.

The **Slieve Bloom Way** (48 miles/77 km) route goes from Glenbarrow through Monicknew, Glendine East, Forelacka to Glenkeen, with memorable scenery, including waterfalls, rocky outcrops and deep glens. Its highest point is the Glendine Gap (1,510 feet/460 m) from where there are wonderful views; and its longest stage is Forelacka to Glenkeen (12 miles/19 km).

The **Offaly Way** (18 miles/29 km) connects the Slieve Bloom Way to the Grand Canal Way and takes in mountains, rivers and bog trails, and a number of historic sites. It goes from Cadamstown to Ballyboy, Kilcormac, reaches the canal at Turraun, and ends in Ferbane. Its longest stage (eight miles) is from Kilcormac to the Grand Canal and the highest point is Knock Hill (458 feet/140 m).

The longest stage of the **Grand Canal Way** (71 miles/114 km) is in Offaly, between Tullamore and Ferbane (16 miles/26 km) and the route, which starts at the Lucan Road Bridge in Co. Dublin and runs through Co. Kildare, also ends here, at Shannon Harbor near Banagher.

There are lots of other walks throughout the county, including those in forests at Garryhinch, Busherstown, Durrow, Goldengrove, Blackwood and in Slieve Bloom Environment Park.

You can also walk along the Grand Canal between Edenderry and Tullamore, passing through the Bog of Allen and Croghan Hill, where St. Brigid is said to have received her veil – in other words, became a nun. There's a lovely view from its summit.

Walking Vacation

Stay at **Ardmore House**, Kinnity, where Christine Byrne arranges walking trips, with a choice that includes the Slieve Blooms Way, shorter and circular walks. Her guesthouse is in the mountains and is a friendly and relaxed Victorian home, with brass beds, turf fire and home cooking. ☎ (0509) 37009.

■ Adventures on Wheels

Bog Train

Between April and early October, you can explore the bog, hear about its history, and see how turf is cut by taking a trip on the **Clonmacnoise and West Offaly Railway**, from Blackwater near Shannonbridge. Tours run on the hour from 10 am and 5 pm. ☎ (090) 9674114; bograil@bnm.ie; www.bnm.ie.

Cycling

The Offaly terrain is ideal for cycling, and you can rent bikes from a number of places, including **Buckley Cycles**, Bury Quay, Tullamore. ☎ (0506) 52240, and from **Eamon and Marie McManus**, Shannonbridge, ☎ (090) 9674189.

■ Adventures on Water

Offaly is the perfect destination for anyone who enjoys cruising or other activities on water. From Banagher and Edenderry you can take a cruise on the River Shannon or the Grand Canal. Leisure traffic has given the canal a new lease of life, and year-round you see colorful boats.

Adventure canoeing vacations are also available from Banagher, which has a sub-aqua club, or you can go rowing at Tullamore. You can rent canoes on a daily or weekly basis from **Shannon Adventure Canoeing** at Banagher Marina, ☎ (0509) 51411.

Celtic Canal Cruisers has been renting out boats for over 25 years, and has a choice of narrowbeam and widebeam, the smallest being two-berth. It offers one-way trips between its Tullamore base on the Grand Canal and Fenniscourt Lock, near Bagenalstown, Co. Carlow, on the River Barrow.

☎ (0506) 21861; fax 51266; celticcanal@eircom.net; www.celticcanalcruisers.com.

From Banagher Marina, **Silver Line Cruisers** operates a fleet of modern diesel cruisers, the smallest being two-berth. ☎ (0509) 51112; fax 51632; silverline@eircom.net; www.silverlinecruisers.com.

Carrick Craft are also based at Banagher. ☎ (01) 278-1666; www.cruise-ireland.com.

Swimming

There are pools at Banagher (outdoor) and Birr (indoor) on the Roscrea Road, ☎ (0509) 20343.

The Shannon Callows is the area next to the river, south of Banagher off the R356. It floods during the winter and, because it has never been drained or ploughed, is unique, unchanged since it was farmed by monks over 1,000 years ago. It boasts a rich diversity of flora and fauna.

Fishing

The environment is so clean here that fish thrive in the county's waters, and many come to enjoy its rivers – the Shannon, Little Brosna and Suck – as well as the Grand Canal.

The Central Fisheries Board and the Shannon Regional Fisheries Board (SRFB) look after this area and have developed access and other facilities. Contact the **Angling Section, SRFB**, ☎ (0509) 21777; info@shannon-fishery-board.ie. Its website links you to others and has lots of information and useful contacts: www.shannon-fishery-board.com.

See pages 71-74 for details on angling in Ireland, regulations and best times to fish.

Banagher is an established angling center, and an ideal base to fish the mid-Shannon, Suck and Brosna rivers, as well as the Grand Canal and the Boora Lakes. It has specialist operators, and anglers are encouraged to hire boats and explore water where access is possible only that way.

There are two **angling festivals** at Banagher, in Spring and Autumn.

Fishing Excursions

Sleepy Hollow Angling Services, Taylor's Cross, Banagher, is also a bed and breakfast. It's 2½ miles (four km) from the Shannon, run by Monica and Paddy Kelleher. He's an expert on fishing, stocks bait and other supplies, and has boats to hire. The guesthouse is comfortable, with good food prepared by Monica. ☎ (0509) 51273.

The Old Forge, West End, Banagher, run by Raymond Duthie, also provides a boat and rod rental service and has a tackle shop, with permits and salmon licenses. It's also a bed and breakfast, with five rooms, each sleeping two. ☎ (0509) 51504; kmduthie2@eircom.net.

Tackle Shops

Other tackle shops in Offaly, where you'll get advice and local knowledge:

Killeens Village Tavern, Shannonbridge, ☎ (090) 9674112; dermot. killeen@mail.esb.ie.

The Tackle Shop, Rahan, Tullamore, ☎ (0506) 55979.

Paul Kelly, Main Street, Birr, ☎ (0509) 21128; kello@indigo.ie.

Alo Moran, Shannonbridge, ☎ (090) 9674124.

Brendan Kenny, Bridge Street, Clara, ☎ (0506) 31866.

Fishing, Walking, Bird-Watching

 Raised bogs covered the landscape here for 10,000 years and have been harvested by Bord na Móna. Now these areas are being developed for other uses, including fishing.

Near Tullamore, the **Lough Boora Parklands**, south of the Grand Canal, provide habitats for a wide range of flora and fauna and has four freshwater fisheries. They are: **Loch an Dochais**, with facilities for the disabled and juniors; **Boora Lake** and **Finnamore Lake** for coarse fishing; and **Loch Clochan** for catch and release fly fishing. Nearby **Kilcormac village** has become a coarse angling center.

You don't have to be interested in fishing to appreciate the Parklands, as there are more than 30 miles (48 km) of paths, ranging in length. From them you can take a look at the flora and fauna and enjoy the peaceful surroundings.

With more than 130 different birds recorded here, it should be a major attraction for anyone interested in our feathered friends. Birdwatchers are catered for with hides, one designed specially for wheelchair access.

Several independent clubs also use the Parklands – including the Midland Rifle Club and the Model Airplane Club. Most Sunday afternoons, when the weather suits, you can watch miniature aircraft in action. ☎ (0506) 45885; loughboora@ eircom.net; www.loughbooraparklands.ie.

East Coast & Midlands

■ Adventures on Horseback

Birr Equestrian Centre offers treks and has indoor and outdoor arenas with showjumping fences. ☎ (0509) 21961.

Kinnity Castle Equestrian Centre offers lessons, trailing and trekking. ☎ (0509) 373-118.

Riding Excursions

Annaharvey Farm, four miles (6.4 km) outside Tullamore on the road to Portarlington, offers accommodations on a bed-and-breakfast or full-board basis in a former grain barn, fitted out to the highest standard. Food is freshly prepared using local produce and there's an open fire.

Equestrian facilities include indoor and outdoor arenas, and it caters for all levels of experience, show jumping, and cross-country. There's also a special walking route and routes for cyclists. ☎ (0506) 43766; info@annaharveyfarm.ie; www.annaharveyfarm.ie.

Croghan Hill Stables, Rhode, has a house available to rent on a weekly basis or for shorter breaks. It's a restored stone farmhouse, 200 years old, with open fire and central heating, sleeps six, and has marvelous views of the countryside. The Stables Equestrian Centre offers cross-country riding, horse hire, and tuition. ☎ (0405) 9737146; info@croghanhill.com.

■ Golf

Tullamore Golf Club is just south of the town on the road to Kinnity, in mature parkland of oak, beech and chestnut. ☎ (0506) 51757.

Esker Hills Golf and Country Club is three miles (4.8 km) northwest of Tullamore off the main road to Clara. Its course has sand-based greens and is renowned for its stunning setting. ☎ (0506) 55999; info@eskerhillsgolg.com; www.eskerhillsgolf.com.

Castle Barna Golf Club is at Daingean, south of Tyrellspass and nine miles (14.5 km) northeast of Tullamore, on the banks of the Grand Canal. It's a mixture of parkland interspersed with challenging water hazards. ☎ (0506) 53384; info@castlebarna.ie; www.castlebarna.ie.

The **Birr Golf Club** is on the Banagher Road. ☎ (0509) 20082.

■ Where to Stay

☆☆☆ **Dooly's Hotel in the Square**, Birr, has welcomed visitors since 1747, when they arrived by horse-drawn coach. The rooms are clean, pleasantly decorated, with big closets, and have spacious bathrooms with large towels. As it's such an old

Above: Kildare Hotel & Country Club, Straffan (see page 155)

Below: Tullynally Castle & Gardens, Castlepollard, Westmeath (see page 180)

Belvedere House, Jealous Wall, Mullingar, Westmeath (see page 177)

Above: Altamont House & Gardens, Carlow (see page 62)

Below: Kilkenny Castle, River Nore (see pages 205-207)

Clashganny Forest, The Barrow Navigation, Carlow (see page 199)

St. Canice's Cathedral, Kilkenny (see page 207)

Above: Jerpoint Abbey, Kilkenny (see page 209)

Below: Waterford Castle, Waterford (see page 225)

building, there are unusual short flights of steps here and there, giving it lots of character. It has a restaurant/coffee bar serving meals and snacks (not very attractive, but the prices are good), and a large bar. With the nightclub on weekend nights, and its location in the center of town on the corner of the main road, if you want silence, this is not the place to stay. Unlike most Irish hotels, it charges the same year-round, and is an excellent value. $. ☎ (0509) 20032; doolyshotel@esatclear.ie; www.doolyshotel.com.

HOTEL PRICE CHART	
Price per person, per night, with two sharing, including breakfast.	
$	Under US $50
$$	US $50-$100
$$$	US $101-$175
$$$$	US $176-$200
$$$$$	Over US $200

☆☆☆☆ **Tullamore Court Hotel** is very unusual. It opened in 1997 and is decorated and furnished in warm and bright colors, with lots of glass, marble and wood. It's popular for conferences and weddings, so can be very busy. There's an excellent leisure center, with pool, sauna, steamroom, and fitness suite. The hotel is built around a courtyard, where it's nice to sit when the weather allows. The **Furlong Bar** is big and has live entertainment regularly. Its staff is efficient and quite friendly and there's a reasonably priced menu available all day. You can also choose to eat in the **Foyer**, which has comfortable seating and is better if you want to talk, especially if there's a band playing in the bar. There's also **The Windmill Restaurant**, serving local produce. $$. ☎ (0506) 46666; fax (0506) 46677; info@tullamorecourthotel.ie; www.tullamorecourthotel.ie.

Stay at a Castle

Kinnity Castle, Birr, has a long and interesting history, dating back to the early 13th century. It's now a lovely country residence with 10 bedrooms retaining their original dimensions in keeping with the period of the castle. It's classified U, which means it meets mandatory requirements but has opted out of the hotel classification system. Enjoy excellent cuisine, fine wines, open log fires and candlelight. Plus there's a huge estate of 10,000 acres to explore, where there's lots of wildlife. Activities include tennis, fishing, shooting and a fully equipped health and leisure center. Equestrian vacations are a specialty, with lessons, trailing and trekking through the estate. $$$. Toll-free from US ☎ 1-888-606-2667; (0509) 37318; kinnittycastle@eircom.net; www.kinnitycastle.com.

East Coast & Midlands

Camping & RV Parks

The **Glebe Touring Caravan and Caravan Park** is in a lovely rural setting near Clonmacnoise, and is open Easter to October 15. It's family-run and friendly. ☎ (090) 6430277.

Hostel

Crank House Hostel, Main Street, Banagher, is open all year. ☎ (090) 6457561; abguinan@eircom.net; www.banagher.net.

■ Where to Eat

At Ferbane on the N62 Birr-Athlone road, there's the delightful **Maidin Gheal**, a home bakery and restaurant, open 9 am-6 pm, Monday-Saturday. It serves delicious snacks and meals, including an all-day breakfast.

The **Riverbank Restaurant** serves fine food in a lovely peaceful setting looking out on the Little Brosna River, a mile from Birr on the N53 road to Borrisokane. It's open for lunch and dinner, Tuesday-Sunday. ☎ (0509) 21528; riverbankrest@msn.com; www.birrnet.com.

County Laois

Laois is an inland county, one of the smallest at 664 square miles (1,726 square km), and is surrounded by Kildare, Offaly, Tipperary and Kilkenny. It's picturesque, especially when you get away from main roads. Its landscape includes the **Slieve Bloom Mountains**, one of the oldest ranges in Ireland, which rise gently from the limestone central plain, with heather and blanket bog on their slopes. **Mount Arderin** is known as the height, or top, of Ireland, from where (weather permitting) the four provinces can be seen. The mountains are a walker's paradise with marvellous features, scenic views, and fascinating flora and fauna.

The countryside is dotted with remains of ring-forts, ruined strongholds and monastic buildings; more than 1,000 of them have been identified. Laois was created out of a number of unrelated Gaelic territories and became Queen's County in 1556, when Mary was on the throne of England. Along with Offaly, this was the first county to be planted in Ireland.

Those early settlers were mainly smallholders, so you won't find as many big estates with grand houses as you do elsewhere, although they did build some attractive towns and villages, and mansions at Abbeyleix and Emo.

The county suffered badly during the Great Famine, its population dropping from over 153,000 in 1841 to just over 73,000 in 1881. Like other counties, it had its workhouses, into which the poor were forced, among them the one at Donaghmore built in 1850.

Laois offers plenty of activities for visitors – riverside walks, charming villages and towns to discover, and lots of historic sites to visit. It's also popular for fishing and playing golf.

Laois is pronounced "leesh" and **Portlaoise**, its county capital and largest town, as "port-leesha." Its other main towns include **Abbeyleix**, **Mountrath**, **Mountmellick** and **Portarlington**.

■ Getting Here

Portlaoise is on main routes N7 from Dublin (52 miles/84 km); N8 from Cork (104 miles/167 km) and N7-N62-N65-N6-N18 from Galway (89 miles/143 km).

Laois is on mainline rail routes, with stations at Portlaoise and Portarlington. There is a regular bus service to Dublin, Cork, Limerick, Athlone and Waterford from Portlaoise, with other routes connecting towns and villages.

■ Tourist Information

Fáilte Ireland Tourist Office, James Finton Lawlor Avenue, Portlaoise, ☎ (0502) 21178; portlaoisetouristoffice@eircom.net; www.ecoast-midlands.travel.ie.

TRACING YOUR ANCESTORS

Irish Midlands Ancestry, based on Bury Quay, Tullamore, does genealogical research for Laois, ☎/fax (0506) 21421; ohas@iol.ie; www.irishmidlandsancestry.com.

■ Sightseeing

Portlaoise

The county's capital was founded by Queen Mary in 1555 as a walled fort to protect the southern end of the Pale, and was named Maryborough after her. The first English court and jail in Ireland were built here, and today there's still a large prison on the edge of town.

There are some interesting old streetscapes in the middle of town, and shops that are full of character, but the town seems rather overwhelmed by more modern developments. You can park just off the ring road and walk through to the center – it's worth the effort in daytime as it's busy with shoppers. But in the evenings it's very quiet and there isn't much choice of places to eat, though there are lots of pubs.

About four miles (6.4 km) east of Portlaoise is the **Rock of Dunamase**, which stands out above the surrounding countryside at a height of 150 feet – it was noticed by Ptolemy, the first-century map-maker. The town was a fort back in 140 AD and since then has had a fascinating history, mirroring Ireland's, including being plundered by the Vikings in 842, and being given to Strongbow by the King of Leinster in 1169 as part of Aoife's dowry. The first castle was built here in the mid-13th century and was the home of William Earl Marshall, then of the O'Moores of Laois. It was given to the Earl of Thomond in 1609, fought over during Cromwell's time and destroyed by his soldiers.

The **Great Heath** at Maryborough below the Rock is one of the most significant archaeological sites in the country, with signs of ring barrows, ring forts and plough ridges.

Touring Route

There's a signposted **Heritage Trail** to follow around Co. Laois, which is a good way of exploring the county and seeing its history, stopping at sites when you're interested. You can start it at various points, and I recommend Durrow on the N8, the main Cork-Dublin road. This estate village was developed by the Viscounts of Ashbrook, and has a group of interesting buildings around a green. Continue from there to Ballinakill, off R432, an example of a 17th-century market town. It's worth stopping here to visit the beautiful **Heywood Gardens**, completed in 1912 by Sir Edward Lutyens, now on the grounds of the Community School. Heywood Gardens has four areas, linked by a terrace which ran in front of the house; sadly, it no longer exists. Open daylight hours all year, and free. Tours every Sunday in July and August at 3 pm. ☎ (056) 51863; heywoodgardens@ealga.ie.

Travel on then to **Abbeyleix**, which is another fine example of an estate town, developed by the Viscounts de Vesci, whose mansion and estate you pass on its outskirts. Although traffic passing through on the Dublin road spoils the enjoyment of its main street, it does have a lot of character. The carpets for the ill-fated *Titanic* were made here.

Go through Ballyroan to the delightful village of **Timahoe**, which has a 12th-century **Round Tower** with an impressive Romanesque doorway. It's all that has survived of the original seventh-century monastic foundation.

Near **Stradbally** is the **Rock of Dunamase**, described on page 168, standing out above the countryside. After that, the trail brings you to the canal village of **Vicarstown**, and on to the gracious Emo Court House and Gardens.

Emo Court was designed in 1790 by Sir James Gandon for the first Earl of Portarlington. Gandon is famous for his Custom House, Four Courts, and other fine buildings in Dublin and elsewhere, including the delightful Coolbanagher Church nearby. Covering 75 acres, its gardens are wonderful, with great sweeps of formal lawns around the house, statuary, and lots of tree-lined walks and wilder areas farther away. They were laid out by two of the most admired garden designers – Capability Brown was responsible for the formal areas, and William Robinson for the others. Winston Churchill used to stay at Emo Court.

It's now in care of the State Heritage Service; the gardens are open all year in daylight hours. Tours run every Sunday at 3 pm in July and August. The house is open mid-June to mid-September, Tuesday-Sunday, 10:30 am-5 pm, last tour 4:30 pm. ☎ (0502) 26573; (056) 21450.

The Heritage Trail next takes you to **Portarlington**, which was settled by French Huguenots, and has many fine buildings, including Georgian houses with gardens stretching down to the river. Next, it's on to **Mountmellick**, which has its own Walking Heritage Trail, with information boards around the town. It's on a bend of the River Owenass, and was founded by Quakers in the 17th century as a center for cotton, linen and woolens.

Out of Mountmellick you follow the signs to **Camross**, a sweet little village at the foot of the Slieve Blooms. Here you can visit **The Poet's Cottage**, which dates from the Great Famine.

Tours

Siúltoirí Cluain na Slí, Clonaslee, runs guided walks and bus tours through the Slieve Blooms. ☎ (0502) 48197.

◾ Adventures on Foot

 There are about 300 miles (483 km) of "off road" walking routes in Laois, in the areas of Sli Dala, Erkina, Cullahill, Abbeyleix, Stradbally, Durrow, Timahoe, Mounthrath, Clonaslee, Spink and Slieve Margy.

The **Slieve Bloom Mountains** have many different walking routes passing ancient geological and other features, with marvelous views.

East Coast & Midlands

The long-distance walking route, **The Slieve Margy Way** (44 miles), is in the southeast of the county. It's a circular network of walking tracks passing through villages, including Graigecullen, Maganey, Arles, Rushes, Wolfhill and the Swan. Running along the banks of the Barrow River, it then takes to the hills, rising over 1,000 feet (305 m) to the top of the Castlecomer Plateau.

In **Cullahill**, between Durrow and Urlingford on the main Cork-Dublin N8 road, you can walk past the castle up onto Cullahill Mountain or take the more leisurely route along the banks of the River Goul and visit the 12th-century ruin of **Aghmacart Priory**.

At **Oughaval Wood**, Stradbally, there's a walk to the **Mass Rock** deep in the forest, where local people gathered to attend Mass during penal times (1691-1727). There's also the **Cobbler's Walk** (about four miles/ 6.5 km), which takes you to a fine example of a folly known as **Cobbler's Castle**. Stradbally is a fine place to begin.

The picturesque village of **Clonaslee** is on **The Munster Way** long distance waymarked route, and tracks follow and cross the Glenlahan, Gorragh and Clodiagh rivers.

Between Rathdowney and Ballacolla, there's some lovely scenery in the **Granstown** area. Once part of the Castletown estate, home of the Fitzpatricks of Upper Ossory, the **Granstown Lake** and surrounding countryside is steeped in history.

Nearby, there's fine walking around **Durrow**, especially the **Leafy Loops**, a 13-mile (21-km) walk through woodlands. Sites of interest include the spectacular **Castle Durrow**, **St. Fintan's Well**, and old and new bridges spanning the River Erkina.

Four waymarked ways begin from the village of **Timahoe**, with its **Round Tower**, where the River Bauteogue wanders through a broad and fertile valley, with Fossy Mountain on one side and Cullenagh Mountain on the other.

From **Mountrath** there are three waymarked routes, and three more start at **Monicknew** in the Slieve Blooms. Tracks go into the mountains and the surrounding areas, passing bogs, forests, rivers and historical sites.

Other signposted walking areas include the **Canal Walk in Portarlington**, the **Nature Trail in Castletown** and **Slí na Sláinte in Ballyroan**.

Part of the **Slieve Bloom Way** runs through Laois. It's a circular trek that can be joined anywhere; the most popular point is the village of **Rosenallis**. The route takes the walker past deep glens, rocky outcrops, waterfalls and lofty summits.

Walking Festival

The **Slieve Bloom Walking Club** hosts an annual three-day walking festival in May with organized walks ranging from three to six hours – details from www.laoistourism.ie/slieve.asp.

■ Adventures on Water

 With the Grand Canal and River Barrow running through it, Laois is a great place to start exploring by water.

Based on the Grand Canal at Vicarstown, the family-owned cruiser rental company, **Barrowline**, offers vacations on board barges. ☎ (0502) 25888; barrowline@eircom.net

Fishing

 The **Barrow** flows past the historic towns of Mountmellick and Portlarlington and offers the game angler the chance of catching large trout and, in late spring, salmon. Downstream of Monasterevin, it holds bream, pike, perch and hybrids of above average size. There are many spots along the river that offer total solitude.

 See pages 71-74 for details on angling in Ireland, regulations and best times to fish.

The **Nore** meanders across Laois before turning south to join up with the Barrow at their common estuary. It is noted for trout, salmon and pike.

Around Durrow and farther downstream, some of the best salmon and trout angling may be found, and tributaries of both the Barrow and the Nore provide very good trout angling, particularly in the early season. Among the better sites are the Owenass, Cushina, Slate and Stradbally Rivers on the Barrow Catchment, and the Erkina, Goul and Whitehorse Rivers along the Nore Valley.

The **Figile River** near Portarlington attracts pike anglers, and close by are also the **Cushina**, **Slate** and the **Black Rivers**. A section of the Erkina near Durrow, known as the **Curragh**, is also renowned for pike.

The Barrow Branch of the **Grand Canal**, including the picturesque Vicarstown, in the east of the county, has good stocks of bream, tench, hybrids, pike and perch.

East Coast & Midlands

Granstown Lake, Ballacolla, which is in a nature reserve, provides stillwater fishing, and is open from April to October. **Rathadaire Lake** offers good coarse fishing in picturesque surroundings, while **Ballyfin Lake**, near Mountrath, has pike, tench and rudd. **Mass Lough** and **Gills Pond** at Ballinakill are two small lakes in a lovely setting. **Templemore Lake** is in the town park, with good pike, tench and rudd angling. **Little Bog Lake** at the Heath, Portlaoise, contains good stocks of rudd and pike.

Bait Stockists

The Tackle Shop, Mountrath. ☎ (0502) 32162.

The Vicarstown Inn. ☎ (0502) 25189.

Angling Permits

For the River Barrow

Victor Cox, The Square, Mountmellick, ☎ (0502) 24107.

Lawlor's, The Square, Durrow, ☎ (0502) 36234.

Finlay's Bar, Bracklone Street, Portarlington, (0502) 23173.

Portarlington Auto Parts, Upper Main Street, ☎ (0502) 23456.

Fisherman's Inn, Ballybrittas, ☎ (0502) 26488.

Harrison's Shop, The Square, Stradbally, (0502) 25359.

For the River Nore

Tom Watkins, 6 Fintans Park, Mountrath, ☎ (0502) 32540.

The Tackle Shop, Mountrath, ☎ (0502) 32162.

Dunne's Hardware Store, Abbeyleix, ☎ (0502) 31440.

Lawlor's, The Square, Durrow, ☎ (0502) 36234.

The Late and Early Shop, Rathdowney, ☎ (0502) 46340.

■ Adventures on Horseback

The Laois landscape is very suitable for trekking and there are a number of equestrian centers in the county.

The Castlewood Equestrian Centre, Durrow, ☎ (0502) 36551.

Kerr Equestrian Activities, Cremorgan, Timahoe, offers treks along mapped routes, plus hourly and daily excursions. ☎ (0502) 27162.

Fossey Mountain Springs, near Timahoe, offers treks through hilly and wooded countryside. ☎ (0502) 36527.

Portlaoise Equestrian Centre has an indoor jumping arena and a cross-country course. ☎ (0502) 60880.

The Equestrian Activity Centre, Mount Briscoe, Daingean, ☎ (0506) 53046.

The Slieve Bloom Trail Equestrian Centre, based at Clononeen, Borris-in-Ossory, takes riders on a trek to the mountains, and also offers lessons. ☎ (0505) 41298.

A Horse-Drawn Excursion

You can take to the roads in one of the **Kilvahan Horse Drawn Caravans**. This is a family-run business. You spend a night at their Georgian farmstead before meeting your horse, learn how to look after him and heading off. ☎ (0502) 27048.

■ Golf

The Abbeyleix Golf Club was founded in 1895 on the Ballyroan road, just outside the town. The course has a lovely backdrop, with the Cullenagh Hills to the north and the Slieve Bloom Mountains to the west. ☎ (0502) 31305.

The Heath Golf Club, near Portlaoise, has one of the few courses in Western Europe over open heath. Golf was played here from the 1880s and the club founded in 1930. The course incorporates three natural lakes and has rough heather and gorse furze features. ☎ (0502) 46533.

The Portlaoise Golf Course, Cork Road, Meelick, has a variety of hazards, including water features, sand bunkers and mature trees. It's also home to wildlife, including mallard ducks and pheasant. ☎ (0502) 61557.

Rathdowney, with the Devil's Bit to the west and the Slieve Blooms to the north, has a beautiful backdrop. Founded in 1930, it was extended to 18 holes in the 1990s. ☎ (0505) 46170.

Portarlington's course was founded in 1909 on part of an old estate, and is bordered by the River Barrow. Players often see pheasant, ducks and other wildlife. ☎ (0502) 23044.

The **Mountrath Club** course, founded in 1929, has the River Nore meandering through it. ☎ (0502) 32558.

■ Where to Stay & Eat

Castledurrow Hotel, in the village of Durrow, has applied for registration as a hotel. Built in the early 18th century, it's a magnificent cut limestone mansion, and each of its bedrooms is individually decorated. Its restaurant serves regional and international dishes, prepared using the best of local produce. Rates from $$, with special midweek and weekend offers. ☎ (0502) 36555; fax 36559; info@castledurrow. com; www.castledurrow.com.

HOTEL PRICE CHART	
Price per person, per night, with two sharing, including breakfast.	
$	Under US $50
$$	US $50-$100
$$$	US $101-$175
$$$$	US $176-$200
$$$$$	Over US $200

☆☆ The **Hibernian Hotel**, Abbeyleix, was built by the Viscount de Vesci in 1840 and now incorporates two other houses from the same period. It has 10 bedrooms, an excellent bar serving food all day, and a very good restaurant open in the evenings. Sunday lunch is particularly popular as it's such an excellent value. $$. ☎ (0502) 31252; fax 31888.

The **Gandon Inn** was designed by the famous architect it's named after, to serve guests visiting nearby Emo Court and claims to be Ireland's oldest family inn, though that's difficult to confirm, offering accommodation as well as food and drink. ☎ (0502) 26622; fax 46781.

Hostel

The **Traditional Farm Hostel**, Ballacolla, Portlaoise, is open all year. ☎ (0502) 34032; www.farmhostel.com.

County Westmeath

While it's an inland county, Westmeath is great for fishing and other water-based activities, as its central area is flat, with bogland and plenty of lakes. The largest lake is **Lough Ree** in the west, which is dotted with little islands, and in the north there's **Lough Sheelin**, which spreads over to Co. Cavan. **Lough Derravaragh** is said to be one of the lakes where the Children of Lír, transformed by an evil spell into swans, lived for hundreds of years. Other lakes include Lough Ennell, Lough Owel, Lough Iron and Lough Lene, Brittas and Bane.

In the northern part of the county, drumlins, small hills with steep sides formed by melting glaciers at the end of the Ice Age, dot the landscape. A line of low hills marks the county's southern boundary.

The seat of the High King of Ireland, 200 years before St. Patrick brought Christianity here in the 5th century, was near Mullingar, and there are also lots of early monastic sites around the county. Signs of the Normans, who arrived here around 1170, can also be seen in numerous mottes-and-baileys.

Mottes & Baileys

A motte is a mound, usually artificial, with a ditch around it, on which early castles were built. A bailey is the external wall surrounding a castle or keep. The most famous of the latter in the world is the Old Bailey, the London Criminal Court.

The county town is **Mullingar**, but the largest is **Athlone**, which straddles the River Shannon and is half in Co. Roscommon.

■ Getting Here

Main routes to Athlone are N6-N4 from Dublin (78 miles/126 km) or from Galway (58 miles/93 km); N55-N3-N54-N12-A3-M1 from Belfast (136 miles/219 km); N6-N62-N8-N25 from Cork (136 miles/219 km).

■ Tourist Information

Fáilte Ireland's main Tourist Office is in the historic Market House, in Market Square, Mullingar. ☎ (044) 48650.

East Coast and Midlands Tourism is based on Dublin Road, Mullingar, and open all year. ☎ (044) 48761; info@ecoast-midlandstourism.ie; www.ecoast-midlands.travel.ie.

Westmeath Tourism Council, Presentation House, Mullingar, ☎ (044) 48571, publishes excellent guides, including *The Fore Trail, The Belvedere Trail, The Glasson Trail: Goldsmith Country*, all routes suitable for bikes as well as cars. Other guides are *Angling in Westmeath, Golf in Westmeath* and *Dining out in Westmeath*.

Tourist Information Offices

Athlone Chamber of Commerce, on Jolly Mariner Marina, open all year. ☎ (090) 6473173.

Athlone Castle, open April-October. ☎ (090) 6494630.

Heritage Centre, Old Schoolhouse, Glasson, open all year. ☎ (090) 6485677.

Fore Abbey Coffee Shop, open June-September, and Sundays all year. ☎ (044) 61780; forecoffeeshop@oceanfree.net.

TRACING YOUR ANCESTORS

The genealogy office for the county is in the **Dún na Sí Heritage Centre**, Knockdomney, Moate. ☎ (090) 6481183; fax 81661; dunnasimoate@eircom.net.

■ Sightseeing

Mullingar

 Mullingar, the county capital, stands on the River Brosna, with the Royal Canal circling it. It's an attractive place to explore, as many of its streets date from the 18th and 19th centuries. You'll find it hard not to notice the **Roman Catholic Cathedral**, built in 1936 in Renaissance style, as its scale is imposing. Nearby is the **Ecclesiastical Museum**, covering the history of Catholicism from Penal days when it was outlawed. ☎ (044) 48338.

Mullingar was a garrison town and there's a **Military Museum** in the old Guard Room at Columb Barracks. In case you think you won't be interested, it also includes exhibits about the IRA, the War of Independence, The Civil War, plus ancient longboats found in nearby lakes that look a bit like canoes.

At the **Market House Museum** you learn about a real eccentric named Adolphus Cooke, who did many strange things. He was so convinced he'd be reincarnated as a bee that he arranged to be buried in a tomb shaped like a beehive, which you can see in the graveyard at Cooksborough Church, eight miles (13 km) east of the town.

If more contemporary activities interest you, the **Mullingar Arts Centre** has a program of exhibitions, concerts, and drama all year. ☎ (044) 47777.

The stadium at Mullingar has **greyhound races** on Tuesday and Saturday nights all year. There's a restaurant and two bars at the stadium. ☎ (044) 48348; www.mullingargreyhoundstadium.com.

Athlone

Athlone, 28 miles (45 km) southwest of Mullingar, is on the N6/R390. It's not just the largest town in Westmeath, it's also the biggest on the River Shannon, and is a very interesting and attractive place to visit. Pause on the bridge and watch all the activity on the Shannon, with colorful cruisers and boats moving up and down.

The town straddles the border between two counties, and is also in two different provinces – Leinster (Westmeath) and Connacht (Roscommon). Because of its strategic location on a major crossing-point of the largest

Irish river, the town has played an important role in the country's history. You can find out about it in the fascinating **Visitor Centre in Athlone Castle**, dating from the 13th century, which dominates the town. Count John McCormack, the famous tenor, came from Athlone, and you can learn about him there too. There is a café and restaurant, and a tourist information office. Open May to September daily, 9:30 am to 6 pm; last audio-visual presentation at 4:30 pm. ☎ (090) 6472107.

Farm machinery, vintage and classic cars and trucks are displayed at **An Dún Transport and Heritage Museum** at Doon, Ballinahown, near Athlone, and there's also a model railway. The coffee bar is quaint and relaxing. ☎ (090) 6430106.

Also near Athlone is the **Derryglad Folk Museum**, run by the Finneran family, where you can see horse-drawn machinery restored to working order, and other interesting items, including butter-making equipment. Open May to September, Monday-Saturday, 10 am-6 pm, Sunday from 2 pm. ☎ (090) 6488192.

Exploring the County

Head out of Mullingar on the N52 road to Tullamore and, after three miles (4.8 km), you come to **Belvedere House**, restored and opened to the public, on 160 acres of parkland along the shore of Lough Ennell. It was built in the early 18th century by Robert Rochfort, Earl of Belvedere, who imprisoned his second wife for 31 years! You can learn about that and much more in its Visitor Centre. The English Poet Laureate Sir John Betjeman wrote about a seduction here, and the grounds include the largest folly in the country, known as the **Jealous Wall**.

Allow enough time to really enjoy the parkland, walled gardens and other features. There's a coffee shop and gift shop. Open all year; January-April/November-December, 10:30 am-4:30 pm; May-August, weekdays 9:30 am-6 pm, weekends 10:30 am-7 pm; September-October, 10:30 am-6 pm; November-December, 10:30 am-4:30 pm. Last admission one hour before closing. ☎ (044) 49060; info@belvedere-house.ie; www.belvedere-house.ie.

Castletown Geoghegan (named after a family dispossessed by Cromwell), is a pretty village southwest of Mullingar near Lough Ennel, which has a Norman moat and a boulder said to mark the inauguration site of the MacGeoghegans.

If you head north from Athlone on the N55, you come to **Ballykeeran** and, from the layby just after the village, there's a wonderful view of Lough Ree. Stop and take a look. Next, you pass through the pretty village of **Glasson**, with pubs and restaurants where you can enjoy a break.

Clonmellon is an attractive little village on the N52 at the Meath border, with a very wide main street. You can enjoy a coffee, a snack or buy crafts in the restored **Old Market Square Centre**, ☎ (046) 9433433. Nearby is the ruined **Killua Castle**, built in 1780, said to be the birthplace of Laurence of Arabia. There's also a monument marking the potato's introduction to Ireland by Sir Walter Raleigh.

Among the other interesting and attractive villages in Westmeath is **Tyrrellspass**, in the southeastern part of the county. It's on the main Dublin-Galway road, the N6, and has won both the National Tidy Towns as well as the European Architectural Heritage awards. A model village, it was laid out in the early 19th century by Jane, Countess of Belvedere. It's named after Sir Richard Tyrrell, who, in 1597, led a small Irish force against the much larger Elizabethan army and won.

Touring Routes

 Travelling by car or bike, you can follow three signposted routes around Westmeath. You can rent bikes from a number of outlets, including **Buckley Cycles**, Garden Vale, Athlone, ☎ (090) 6478989.

Starting in Mullingar, the **Fore Trail** takes in the northern section of the county, passing through pretty villages, with marvelous views over lakes. The **Belvedere Trail** covers the southern part of the county and takes you to **Belvedere House**, already described, **Lilliput** (named after Jonathan Swift), and **Locke's Distillery Museum** at Kilbeggan. The museum, at the junction of the N52/N6, is housed in the building where whiskey was made from 1757 to 1954. You're taken on a guided tour explaining its history and the process involved. There is also a café and restaurant, as well as a money changing counter. Open all year, except Christmas week. April-October, 9 am-6 pm; November-March, 10 am-4 pm. ☎ (0506) 32134.

The N6 route south from Mullingar to Kilbeggan is narrow and windy, but take your time and enjoy the wonderful countryside. En route is **Delvin**, with a motte built by Hugh de Lacy in 1181 and nearby the ruins of the **13th-century castle** of the Nugent family, the Earls of Westmeath.

The **Glasson Trail** is the third route and you could start it at Athlone, then go to Glasson and from there travel around Goldsmith Country.

Goldsmith Country

This is an area of South Westmeath and South Longford named after one of Ireland's leading poets, playwrights and novelists, Oliver Goldsmith (1728-1774). Among his works are the poem, *The Deserted Village*, and the play, *She Stoops to Conquer*. He was born in Pallas, Co. Longford, and moved to Lissoy near Glasson, Co. Westmeath, when he was two. Lissoy became "Sweet Auburn" in his best-known poem.

Sweet Auburn

Sweet Auburn! loveliest village of the plain
Where health and plenty cheered the labouring swain,
Where smiling spring its earliest visit paid,
And parting summer's lingering blooms delayed:
Dear lovely bowers of innocence and ease,
Seats of my youth, when every sport could please,
How often have I loitered o'er thy green,
Where humble happiness endeared each scene!
How often have I paused on every charm,
The sheltered cot, the cultivated farm,
The never-failing brook, the busy mill,
The decent church that topt the neighbouring hill,
The hawthorn bush, with seats beneath the shade,
For talking age and whispering lovers made!

Fore – A Very Special Place

If you visit only one of the county's historic sites, make it Fore, which is absolutely fascinating, yet is not well known even among the Irish. Fore is a tiny village near Castlepollard and Lough Lene in the northeast corner of the county, where there are the ruins of a **monastery** established by St. Fechin in the seventh century. Above them on the hillside is the **Anchorite's Church**, in use by hermits until 300 years ago. There's a stone tablet remembering the last of them, Patrick Beglan, who lived here until 1616.

The place is unique. Science probably gives rational explanations for the following, known as "The Seven Wonders of Fore":

■ Water will not boil

■ Wood will not burn

■ Water flows uphill

■ The monastery is built on a bog

■ The mill has no race

■ The last hermit is encased in a stone

■ The stone was raised by St. Fechin's prayers

There's a restored farmhouse with a coffee shop, information is available, local crafts are for sale, and there's a genealogy service. It's open from 11 am until late every day from June to September and every Sunday year-round. ☎ (044) 61780.

East Coast & Midlands

■ Adventures on Foot

At Mullingar, there's a sign-posted walking route along the towpath of the **Royal Canal**.

About 10 miles (16 km) southwest of Mullingar is **Uisneach Hill**, "the navel of Ireland," the mythological seat of the High Kings before they moved to Tara, Co. Meath. Whether this is true or not is uncertain, as the only evidence were thick ashes, which show it was the site of fire festivals.

At the top of the hill is the ancient boulder, the **Catstone**, known also as the "Stone of Divisions," marking the geographical center of the four ancient provinces of Ireland – Leinster, Munster, Connacht and Ulster. The hill is 250 feet high and worth climbing for the view of 20 of the 32 counties.

In the northwest of the county near Finea is **Mullaghmeen**, the largest planted beech forest in Europe, covering 1,000 acres. Other trees, including sycamore, oak and ash, also flourish. It's a peaceful place for a picnic or walk, with marvelous views, especially from White Hill (894 feet/264 m), the highest point in the whole county. There are walks varying in length here, and there are also walks along the lakeshore at **Donore** near Multyfarnham and at **Portlick** near Glasson.

North of Mullingar, between Loughs Lene and Derravaragh, is **Castlepollard** and **Tullynally Castle**, which has been owned by the Earls of Longford, the Pakenhams, since the 17th century. The gardens are open daily from May to August. They cover nearly 30 acres and are wonderful, with two lakes, a grotto, walled gardens and woodland – a great place to walk. The present owners, Valerie and Thomas Pakenham, added a Chinese garden and a Tibetan garden, with waterfalls and streams. Both of them are authors, and he's had a bestseller with a marvelous book about trees. Gardens, tea room and craft shop are open May-August, 2-6 pm. Tullynally is one of the largest castles in the country that is still a family home, and you can see inside it only July 15-30, when there are guided tours from 2 pm to 6 pm. ☎ (044) 61159; tpakenham@eircom.net.

Near Clonmellon on the N52 are **Ballinlough Castle and Gardens**, where you can take a walk through the walled gardens and lakeside pleasure grounds. It has a coffee shop. Open May 1 to September 30, Tuesday-Saturday, 11 am-6 pm; Sunday, 2 pm-6 pm. ☎ (046) 9433135.

■ Adventures on Water

There are a number of companies based at Athlone or nearby, renting out cruisers and running trips.

Athlone Cruisers is based at the Jolly Mariner Marina in town, and is the longest established cruiser company in the country. They rent luxury self-drive cruisers, which come with dinghies, and they'll pick you up from airports. They can supply extras, including bikes, a TV, and an outboard motor.

The company also runs trips on Lough Ree in the *MV Ross*, which carries 60 and has a bar and coffee shop on board. Cruises last 1½ hours, with commentary from a guide, daily from April to September. ☎ (090) 6472892; fax 74386; acl@wmeathtc.iol.ie; www.iol.ie/wmeathtc/acl.

Waveline Cruisers is based at Killenure Point, Glasson, near Athlone, and rents boats for cruising vacations, the smallest a two-berth. ☎ (090) 6485711; fax 85716; waveline@iol.ie; www.waveline.ie.

Lough Ree Cruisers are based at Mucknagh Point, Glasson, in the middle of the Shannon Erne Waterway. ☎ (090) 6485256; loughreecruisers@eircom.net; www.loughcreecruisers.com.

You can also cruise the Shannon on a replica Viking boat from Athlone to Clonmacnoise, or cruise Lough Ree, where the Vikings plundered and pillaged, with live commentary and refreshments on board. Trips daily, from **Strand Fishing Tackle Shop**. ☎ (090) 6479277.

If sailing interests you, there are two centers near Athlone – the **Lough Ree Yacht Club**, Ballyglass, Coosan, Athlone, info@lryc.ie, www.lryc.ie, and the **Wineport Sailing Centre**, Glasson (090) 6485190, plus another on Lough Owel, north of Mullingar. Ask about them at tourist offices.

Near Castletown Geoghegan is **Lilliput**, named to honor Jonathan Swift, author of *Gulliver's Travels* and frequent visitor to the county. It's an amenity park that holds one of the county's two inland EU Blue Flags (see page 76); the other is The Cut, on Lough Lene, Collinstown. It's a great place to swim; there's also an 18-hole golf course, ☎ (044) 26457, and an outdoor adventure center, ☎ (044) 26789.

Fishing

 With so many rivers, lakes and stretches of canal, the county is a paradise for anyone interested in fishing. For brown trout, head for Loughs Ennell, Lene, Sheelin and Owel, or to Loughs Glore, Bane, Mount Dalton, White Lake or the River Brosna.

Pike and **coarse anglers** will enjoy Loughs Ree and Derravaragh, rivers Inny, Shannon, and the Royal Canal.

Carp fishing is available at Gaulmoylestown and Ballinafid lakes. You can get expert advice and rent equipment and boats.

There's an annual **International Angling Festival** at Athlone in early July.

See pages 71-74 for details on angling in Ireland, regulations and best times to fish.

Learn the Art of Fly Fishing

The **Traditional Lough Style Angling Centre** is five miles (eight km) south of Mullingar on the shores of Lough Ennell and is in an idyllic setting surrounded by woodland. It's the ideal place to learn the art of fly fishing. They also rent boats and organize ghillies (guides). Open Feb 23 to December 31, dawn to dusk, boat or ghillie rental, fully accessible to disabled. ☎ (044) 49086.

Renting Boats & Equipment

Lilliput Boat Hire, Jonathan Swift Park, is also on Lough Ennell, near Tyrellspass, Kilbeggan and the N6. You can rent boats, life jackets, fishing equipment by the hour, day or evening, and get fuel and permits here. ☎ (044) 26167.

At **Lough Derravaragh Boat Hire**, Donore Shore, Multyfarnham, you can rent boats, engines, fishing gear, and get packed lunches if you wish. ☎ (044) 71500; camping@iol.ie.

Angling Trips

At the southern tip of Lough Derravaragh is **Crookedwood**, where you can embark on an angling safari on a fully equipped 16-foot Lund Laker American pike fishing boat. You can also avail yourself of guided fishing trips. Contact Alan Broderick, ☎ (044) 72015; alan@irelandpike.com; www.irelandpike.com.

Incidentally, Crookedwood gets its intriguing name from the Irish Cnoc an Bhodaigh or "the hill of the clown," dating back to the ancient sagas of Fionn and the Fianna. There's an early Christian site nearby, plus the well-preserved 14th-century stone-roofed church of **Taughmon**.

Fionn & The Fianna

Of all the great bodies of ancient Irish legendary lore, none other, with the possible exception of the Red Branch cycle, has had such effect upon the Irish people through the ages as the wonderful body of Fenian tales in both prose and verse, rich in quality and rich in quantity. Fionn MacCumail, leader of the Fian (Fenians), in the time of Cormac MacArt, is the great central figure of these tales. The man Fionn lived and died in the third century of the Christian Era.

It was in the reign of Conn, at the very end of the second century, that was founded the Fian. It was a great standing army of daring warriors, whose duty was to carry out the mandates of the high kin – "To uphold justice and put down injustice, on the part of the kings and lords of Ireland and to guard the harbors from foreign invaders." From this latter we might conjecture that an expected Roman invasion first called the Fian into existence. Fionn, being a chieftain himself in his own right, had a residence on the hill of Allen in Kildare. The Fianna (bodies of the Fian) recruited at Tara, Uisnech and Taillte fairs.

The greatest discrimination was used in choosing the eligible ones from amongst the candidate throng. Many and hard were the tests for him who sought to be one of this noble body. One of the first tests was literary for no candidate was possible who had not mastered the 12 books of poetry. So skilful must he be in wood running, and so agile, that in the flight no single braid of his hair is losed by a hanging branch. His step must be so light that underfoot he breaks no withered branch. In facing the greatest odds the weapon must not shake in his hand. There were three cathas (battalions) of the Fian – 3,000 in each catha. This was in time of peace. In time of war the quota was seven cathas. Although the Fianna were supposed to uphold the power of the Ard Righ, their oath of fealty was not to him, but to their own chief, Fionn.

The best stories of the Fian are preserved to us in the poems of Oisin, the son of Fionn, the chief bard of the fian, in the Agallamh na Seanorach – Colloquy of the Ancients of Olden Time. *(From www.luminarium.org/mythology/ireland.)*

■ Adventures on Horseback

 You can improve your skill at riding and show-jumping, or try trekking or cross-country at the **Mullingar Equestrian Centre** on the Athlone Road. ☎ (044) 48331; info@ mullingarequestrian.com; www.mullingarequestrian.com.

Near Athlone there are riding facilities, including:

Derwins, Auburn, Moate Road, ☎ (090) 6474460.

Kiltoom Stables, ☎ (090) 6489511.

Mannions, Kilkenny West, Glasson, ☎ (090) 6485781.

At **Ladestown Riding Stables**, just outside Mullingar on the Kilbeggan Road, you can go on accompanied rides around Lough Ennell or into the woodlands; or you can take lessons. They have all-weather facilities, show-jumping and cross-country fences. ☎ (044) 48218; fax 48253; ladestown@eircom.net.

Horseracing

Kilbeggan racecourse has evening events between May and August. ☎ (0506) 32176; kilbegganracecourse@eircom. net; www.kilbegganraces.com.

■ Golf

There are a number of courses, all in scenic locations.

The **Athlone Golf Club** is on Hodson Bay, ☎ (090) 6492073.

The **Ballinlough Castle Golf Club**, Clonmellon, is in the grounds of the castle that dates from the early 1600s. The gardens, open to the public, have been restored, and there are lovely lakeside walks and a tea room. ☎ (044) 64544; tonyinballinlough@oceanfree.net.

Delvin Castle Golf Course, Clonyn, is on the N52 Mullingar-to-Dundalk road on the grounds of two castles, in mature parkland that includes 100-year-old cypresses. ☎ (044) 64315.

Moate Golf Course is a mile north of the town of Moate. ☎ (090) 6481271.

Mount Temple Golf Club is four miles (6.4 km) from Moate and five miles (eight km) from Athlone off the N6. ☎ (090) 6481841.

The **Glasson Golf and Country Club** is six miles (10 km) north of Athlone on the N55. See also below. ☎ (090) 6485120; info@glassongolf.ie.

■ Where to Stay & Eat

☆☆☆ **Hodson Bay Hotel** has an absolutely idyllic setting on the shore of Lough Ree next to Athlone Golf Club. It has 133 bedrooms, many with lovely views, little sandy beaches, and there's a marina with cruiser berthing, so you can watch the boats come and go. There are also daily boat trips available in summer from here. The hotel's **L'Escale Restaurant** serves fresh Irish produce and there's a lively **Waterfront Bar and Buttery**. $$ (with special breaks available). ☎ (090) 6480500; fax 80520; info@hodsonbayhotel.com; www.hodsonbayhotel.com.

HOTEL PRICE CHART	
Price per person, per night, with two sharing, including breakfast.	
$	Under US $50
$$	US $50-$100
$$$	US $101-$175
$$$$	US $176-$200
$$$$$	Over US $200

☆☆☆☆ The **Glasson Golf and Country Club**, six miles (10 km) north of Athlone on the N55, not only has a wonderful course with an elegant **Club House Bar**, but also offers accommodation, with 29 tastefully decorated bedrooms, all with fantastic views of Lough Ree. There's a bar menu throughout the day and fine dining in the restaurant in the evening. You can also relax in the lobby or out on the patio, enjoying the fresh air, looking out over the course and the lough. $$. ☎ (090) 6485120; info@ glassongolf.ie.

Wineport Lodge is also in Glasson. It describes itself as "a lakeshore restaurant with rooms" and so is not classified as a hotel with a star rating. It's a member of the prestigious Ireland's Blue Book (see page 60), which means you know that the food will be wonderful, prepared with fresh local ingredients, and that you'll be made to feel really welcome. The Lodge is modern, clad with cedar, and each of the 10 luxurious guest bedrooms has a wine theme, and a spacious bathroom with underfloor heating. Furniture is walnut and all rooms have a view of the lake. Room rates from $$$$. ☎ (090) 6485466; lodge@wineport.ie; www.wineport.ie.

House & Cottage Rentals

Ladestown House stood on a site that has been occupied for at least 2,500 years. Its ruins have been transformed into a terrace garden, and its well-preserved fine stone courtyards into stables (see page 183). There's one cottage available to rent. It sleeps five, has a traditional interior with open fire and central heating. It has wonderful parkland views and overlooks a lake. ☎ (044) 48218; fax 48253; ladestown@eircom.net.

The **Multyfarnham Holiday Village** has a group of 14 modern houses available for rent. Each of them has three bedrooms, and on site there are two tennis courts. The village is quiet, but has two pubs, a restaurant, supermarket and butcher. It's also close to Lough Derravaragh. ☎ (044) 71359; fax 71342; info@irishcottageholidays.com.

Hostel

The **Lough Ree Lodge Hostel** is on Dublin Road, Athlone, and is open from mid-May to mid-September. ☎ (090) 6476738; loughreelodge@ eircom.net.

Camping & RV Parks

☆☆ **Lough Ree East Caravan and Camping Park** is two miles (3.2 km) outside Athlone at Ballykeeran off the N55 road to Cavan. It's on the shore of Lough Ree, with its own jetty and boats for hire, ideal for angling, windsurfing, sailing and canoeing. It's open April 1-September 30. ☎ (090) 6478561; athlonecamping@eircom.net; www.athlonecamping.com.

County Longford

Longford is an inland county lying in the basin of the River Shannon, which, with Lough Ree, forms its western boundary. It's one of the smallest counties on the island, ranking 30th out of 32, and its landscape is flat with rolling bogland, pastures and wetland, dotted with lakes and crossed by rivers.

Co. Longford is one of the most unspoiled areas in Ireland, almost untouched by mass development, so it's of great interest to the eco-tourist for its flora and fauna. Its extensive waterways also mean that there are wonderful angling and watersport locations.

Among its historic monuments are standing stones and a section of the **Black Pig's Dyke**, the ancient boundary formation, near Granard. The route of the Táin passed through the county and is now followed by walkers and cyclists.

The Black Pig's Dyke C. 250 AD

After Agricola abandoned his scheme to invade Ireland in 82 AD, the Roman Emperor Domitian ordered his governor north and, later, after Agricola's recall, the Romans retired behind Hadrian's Wall. It may have been around this time that work began on the construction of a wall to defend Ulster.

Described on maps as the Dane's Cast, the wall begins in the east near Scarva on the Down-Armagh border; the next section, known as the Dorsey, stands at Drummill Bridge in south Armagh; it continues into Monaghan near Muckno Lake, where it is known either as the Worm Ditch or as the Black Pig's Dyke; and further short stretches extend through Cavan and Fermanagh to Donegal Bay.

A tradition survives that it was ploughed up by the tusks of an enchanted black boar; archaeologists, however, have proved this great linear earthwork was a series of massive defences, not continuous, but guarding the routeways into Ulster between the bogs, loughs and drumlins.

The county hosts a number of annual events, including the **ESB Lough Ree Environmental Summer School and Arts Festival** (July), the

Goldsmith Summer School in Ballymahon (June), and **angling competitions** in Arva and Lanesborough every August and September. Contact Longford Tourism, below, for details.

Its county capital and largest town is also called **Longford**, and other main towns are **Ballymahon**, **Lanesborough** and **Granard**.

■ Getting Here

Longford is served by the major routes N4 from Dublin (76 miles/122 km); N4-N55-N54-N2-A3-M1 from Belfast (123 miles/198 km); N6 from Galway (67 miles/108 km).

It's on the railway route from Dublin to Sligo. **Longford Town Station**, ☎ (043) 45208. It is also on bus routes.

■ Tourist Information

Longford Tourism, Dublin Street, Longford, ☎ (043) 42577; info@longfordtourism.com; www.longfordtourism.com. Also check out www.longford.ie.

TRACING YOUR ANCESTORS

For information regarding your ancestry contact: **Longford Roots Research Centre** at 1 Church Street, Longford; ☎ (043) 41235; longroot@iol.ie.

■ Sightseeing

Longford Town

The county capital is on the N4, the east-west route linking Dublin and Sligo, where it meets the N5, the route north-south. Longford's name comes from the Irish for "the fort or stronghold of the O'Farrells," named after the local chieftain who built a fortress here in 1400. The family ruled the area for 600 years, at one stage owning seven castles in the southern part of the county.

The town grew along the south bank of the River Camlin and developed as a gateway to the northwestern part of the country. The British built barracks here in 1700, which led to further expansion. Approaching it from the Sligo direction, you come to a broad tree-lined avenue with houses set back from the road. This is where the British Army officers lived, and you'll see paddocks where their horses grazed.

In the middle of town on Great Water Street there are a number of 18th-century buildings, including **St. John's Church of Ireland** (1760), the **Court House** and the **Longford Arms Hotel** (1807). With the arrival of the Royal Canal in 1830 and the railway in 1855, the eastern side of town developed as the main center of commerce and industry.

Today, dominating the town is the 19th-century gray limestone **Cathedral of St. Mel**, named after a bishop who lived here around 480, and whose crosier can be seen in the museum behind it.

Longford is a busy shopping town, and a pleasant place to visit, with friendly people. You won't see many tourists, apart from those interested in angling or enjoying its quiet countryside.

You can visit the **Longford County Museum**, on Main Street, which is open to the public during the summer months. Among its displays are collections of domestic, historic and agricultural interest, as well as archival and General Sean MacEoin material. Genealogical service is provided. There's a lovely landscaped park, **The Mall**, on the riverbank, which covers 20 acres and is ideal for a walk or picnic. Nearby is a **Sports and Leisure Centre**, where you can enjoy a swim or workout.

Carriglas Manor, close to Longford, has a charming woodland garden nestling between the historic family-owned mansion and the magnificent stableyards. The stableyard was designed by James Gandon (who is responsible for the Custom House in Dublin, Emo Court in Co. Laois, and other beautiful buildings). There's a stream, bordered by water-loving plants, banks of old roses and mixed borders, leading to a lower pond. A visit here includes a guided tour of the splendid interiors, stableyard, woodland/water garden, costume and lace museum and gallery. You pay extra to tour the Manor. Open May-September, Monday, Tuesday, Friday and Saturday only, 11 am-3 pm. ☎ (043) 45165; www.carrigglas.com.

The **Corlea Trackway Centre** is near Kenagh village, off the R397 south of Longford. This is the remains of an ancient bog road (or trackway) built in 148 BC. It's the largest of its kind discovered in Europe, and involved the felling of 200 oaks and laying them across Ringderry bog to reach Derryadd drumlin. In the Visitor Centre you see a section of it, as well as other displays, and it's surrounded by 30 acres of raised bog, which is a nature reserve you can visit on a guided tour. Wear sensible clothing and shoes. There's a restaurant/tea room and picnic area. Open June-September, 9:30 am-6:30 pm, April-May, 10 am-5 pm. ☎ (043) 22386.

At Ardagh, off the N4 Dublin road from Longford Town, you can see the restored **Fetherston Stables**. They're attached to what was a stately home, and are on a grand scale, retaining the original horse feeding and ventilation systems.

Off the R198 is **Ballinamuck** and its **Battlefield Centre**. Housed in a former barracks, it's a lively exhibition that explains "the Year of the French" and the Battle of Ballinamuck in 1798. After that, you can visit the site of the battle. Open all year; call for times. ☎ (043) 24848.

AN UNUSUAL SOUVENIR

If you're looking for an unusual souvenir or gift, or just want to learn about bogwood, then call Michael and Kevin Casey, beside Lough Ree at Barley Harbor, Newtowncashel. Bogwood is found in Irish peatland or bogs, where it's been preserved for 5,000 years, and was once part of the great forest that covered the central plains of the country. The Caseys create beautiful sculptures from this wood, and in their workshop and studio you can learn about the process. Open all year. ☎ (043) 25297; www.bogwood.net.

Granard

Granard is the second-largest town in Longford. It's on the N55 route from the Midlands to the northern counties, surrounded by beautiful forests and lakes, including Lough Gowna.

Its name has many meanings, including "'The Hill of the Sun," "'The Hill of the Grain" or "Ugly Height" – all because of its most memorable feature, the great Norman earthwork or motte, the largest in Ireland, which rises up at the west end of the main street.

This became the site for a castle built in 1199 by Richard Tuite who had been granted the lands by Hugh de Lacy. Neither castle nor any medieval building has survived, and Granard today is a Georgian town, which was laid out during the late 18th and early 19th centuries.

Ballymahon

Ballymahon is in the south of Longford on the N55, along the banks of the River Inny, which enters Lough Ree on the River Shannon, three miles (4.8 km) west of the town. It's attractive, with a wide main street and late Georgian buildings. It's an angling center these days.

The name comes from the Irish "Baile Mathúna," or the town of Mahon, a Gaelic Chieftain who defeated O'Rourke of Leitrim in battle nearby at Shrule, which in Irish means "river of blood."

John Keegan Casey (1846-1870), who was involved with the Fenians and wrote ballads and poems, including the well-known *The Rising of the Moon*, lived in Ballymahon. The poet and playwright Oliver Goldsmith also spent a lot of time here and there's a statue of him in the middle of town.

East Coast & Midlands

Edgeworthstown

Edgeworthstown, eight miles (13 km) east of Longford, is just over the border from Westmeath on the N4. It's named after the family who first settled here in 1583, and Richard Lovell Edgeworth and his daughter Maria were its most interesting members.

Richard (1744-1817) invented an early bicycle, a carriage powered by a sail, and a vehicle that could cross bogs on a primitive form of caterpillar treads, not to mention a central heating system for the Pakenhams at Tullynally Castle, Co. Westmeath. He also built a road on his estate that was ahead of its time, as it had a camber and top blinding layer (camber is the slope and the blinding layer is part of the process of road making still used today).

He founded a school where Catholics and Protestants learned together, again ahead of his time. He believed boys and girls should be educated together and that science and engineering were as important as the classics and arts. He wrote lots of books on education with his daughter Maria, who is best known today as the author of the novel *Castle Rackrent* (1800).

Lanesborough

Lanesborough is at the northern tip of the broad expanse of Lough Ree, and was named after the family of one of the heroes on the English side at the Battle of Kinsale (fought in County Cork in 1601), given lands here as a reward for his loyal services.

The town straddles the River Shannon, and two provinces, spilling over onto the Roscommon side, which is in Connaught, and Leinster. In 1140 Turlough O'Connor, King of Connaught, marched his armies through the fords here and, less than 100 years later, the Norman Lord, Walter de Lacy, fortified the river crossing. You can see the **castle remains**, covered in ivy. Just north of the town is **Cloontuskert Abbey**, founded by Saints Brendan and Faithleach in 520 AD.

■ Adventures on Foot & Wheels

The **Táin Trail**, which originally was a short waymarked way in Co. Louth, has become a much longer cycling and walking route. It crosses into Co. Longford at the Shannon fords at Tarmonbarry. Between there and what's now Longford Town was Trego or "the plain of the spears," where Queen Maeve's army was attacked by the Celtic war-spirit Nemain. After an overnight stay at Granard, they carried on towards Crosskeel in Co. Meath and then on to the Cooley Peninsula.

Near Granard is **Derrycassan Wood** on the shore of Lough Gowna, with a choice of walks, along the river and by the lakeshore, through the lovely native flora and fauna.

Near **Ballymahon** there are six miles (10 km) of landscaped walkways along the Royal Canal, with cut stone bridges, old store house buildings and loughs adding to the pleasure. Also nearby are forest trails in **Newcastle Woods** and on the banks of the Inny River.

■ Adventures on Water

At Ballymahon, the **Inny Kayak Club** is based along the river from Inny Park. The club has qualified instructors who teach seniors and juniors, young and old how to canoe.

Richmond Harbor is on the River Camlin, close to where its meets the River Shannon, and is connected by the 46th lock with the end of the Royal Canal. The **Richmond Inn** used to be a flax mill and the private houses along the harbor were offices. The flax was transported by barge from here to Dublin on the canal. Passengers also embarked here in bad times to begin their long journeys to North America and elsewhere.

The Royal Canal, built between 1790-1817, carried passengers from this area to Dublin until the arrival of the railway led to its decline. It continued to be used to transport goods until 1955. In 1974 enthusiasts got together and formed the Royal Canal Amenity Group. They started developing and, 12 years later, this and the other Irish canals were handed over to the State body, the Office of Public Works. Now the canal is navigable from Dublin all the way to Abbeystrule here in Longford.

Fishing

Ballymahon is popular as an angling center, in the middle of some of the very best game and coarse fishing in the Midlands, among them the River Inny, Lough Drum, Lough Ree, and the Royal Canal. To its north is Lanesborough, and a little farther upstream is the highly acclaimed game fishing at Tarmon Weir. After that is Lough Forbes, an excellent summer and winter venue, known to produce huge pike.

The Camlin Club continuously restocks reaches of the **Shannon** and the **Camlin rivers** with brown trout and the old **Longford reservoir** with both brown and rainbow trout. There's also the stocked trout water at **Mount Dalton Lough** nearby.

Lanesborough is also renowned for its excellent fishing. Near the peat-fueled power station is what's known as the "hot water stretch," which attracts fishermen from Europe and beyond.

There are seven lakes in the **Dromard** area, some straddling the border between Longford and Cavan, which are popular with both locals and visitors.

 See pages 71-74 for details on angling in Ireland, regulations and best times to fish.

Ballymahon has several waterways that have a variety of fish, ranging from bream, trout, roach, and hybrids to perch and pike. Within a mile of Ballinamuck are Lough Sallagh, Fearglass and Cloncoose Lakes, as well as the River Shannon nearby. **Corbeagh Lake** is small and in a secluded setting, about three miles (4.8 km) from Ballinalee.

The **Inny River** near Abbeyshrule is another good source of fish, with roach and pike caught throughout the year. In the Abbeylara area, the Inny and **Derragh Lake** are noted for good fishing.

The regional fishery board is the Shannon, ☎ (0509) 21777; info@shannon-fishery-board.ie.

Tackle Shop

Edward Denniston and Company, Centenary Square, Longford, has been in business for more than 70 years, stocking bait, tackle, and everything else needed. ☎ (043) 46345.

Boat Rental

Mark Shields Boat & Engine Hire, Lanesborough, has 19-foot lake boats with outboards for rent on a daily or weekly basis. They can also arrange a ghillie. ☎ (043) 21008; mjs@eircom.net.

■ Try Something Different

Archery

 Carmel and Brendan Igoe have restored the walled garden at the **Old Bond Estate**, Killoe, to its former glory, and you can try archery in the forested area around it. ☎ (043) 23327.

Adventure in the Air

 There's a tradition of flying in Abbeyshrule, where Abbeyfield Airfield is a popular location for light aircraft enthusiasts. There are two clubs based there offering instruction – the **Inny Aero Club**, O'Dea@tinet.ie, ☎ (044) 55266, and **Aero Club 2000**. The **Abbeyshrule Air Show**, Ireland's longest running airshow, is held annually at the airfield, on the second Sunday of August. The Airshow is an exciting and spectacular occasion and regularly features Aircraft from the Irish Air Corps, US Air Force and some of the best civilian acts in Ireland and the UK.

■ Adventures on Horseback

David Harrison at Mosstown, Kenagh, runs an all-weather equestrian facility so that classes, show-jumping practice and events can be held at any time of year. There's also an outdoor arena. ☎ (043) 22414.

■ Golf

County Longford Golf Club, Dublin Road, was founded over 100 years ago, and its course is in a pleasant parkland setting, playable year-round. ☎ (043) 46310; fax 47082; colonggolf@eircom.net.

■ Where to Stay & Eat

☆☆☆ **Longford Arms Hotel**, built in 1807, has welcomed guests ever since. In recent years it's been expanded, now with a leisure center and a conference center. It has a coffee shop and a good restaurant, and there are 60 bedrooms. It's in the middle of town, so it's ideal as a base. $$ (with special offers). ☎ (043) 46296; fax 46244; longfordarms@eircom.net; www. longfordarms.ie.

HOTEL PRICE CHART	
Price per person, per night, with two sharing, including breakfast.	
$	Under US $50
$$	US $50-$100
$$$	US $101-$175
$$$$	US $176-$200
$$$$$	Over US $200

☆☆ **Park House Hotel**, Edgeworthstown, is right in the middle of the town on the N4 and is popular for weddings, conferences, and other events. It's also well known as an entertainment venue, where many top acts have performed. It has 21 comfortable bedrooms, and food is served in its **Oakwood Bar** and in its **restaurant**. $$. ☎ (043) 71325: parkhousehotel@eircom.net; www.trailblazer.ie/parkhousehotel.

Derryclough Farmhouse, hidden away close to Lough Ree and five miles (eight km) west of Ballymahon, is just one of the welcoming guesthouses in the county. ☎ (043) 22126.

The Rustic Inn, Abbeyshrule, on the village street, has the Royal Canal running behind its garden. It's well known for good food and entertainment. You can choose from the bar menu or eat in the large restaurant. The owners have a brochure available listing all the best locations nearby for fishing. ☎ (044) 57424.

The **Longford Caravan and Camping Park**, at Kilmacannon, Newtownforbes, is run by Dianne and Paul Bailey. ☎ (043) 45503.

The Southeast

The Southeast takes in the two inland counties of Carlow and Kilkenny, and the coastal counties of Waterford and Wexford, joined here by Tipperary. Anyone visiting the area cannot fail to appreciate the wonderful and varied scenery and the many opportunities for outdoor activities. There are plenty of places to visit and lots of indoor entertainment too.

County Carlow

Carlow has an undulating and fertile landscape, with many picturesque towns and villages. The second smallest county (after Leitrim), it is bounded on the east by the granite **Blackstairs Mountains**. It's little known, even among the Irish, as it is off the main routes between cities.

The county's unspoiled environment makes it an ideal destination for walking, cycling, angling, riding or playing golf. There's plenty to keep you busy, from pagan sites and early Christian settlements, to beautiful country homes and gardens. Its central location also makes it an ideal base for exploring.

The county capital is also called **Carlow**, and other main towns include **Tullow**, **Borris** and **Bagenalstown**.

■ Getting Here

Carlow Town is on the N9, northeast of Kilkenny City, and the N80 Portlaoise-Enniscorthy road. It's connected by rail and bus to other parts of the country.

■ Tourist Information

Fáilte Ireland Tourist Office, College Street, Carlow. ☎ (059) 9131554; fax 70776; info@southeasttourism.ie; www. southeastireland.com.

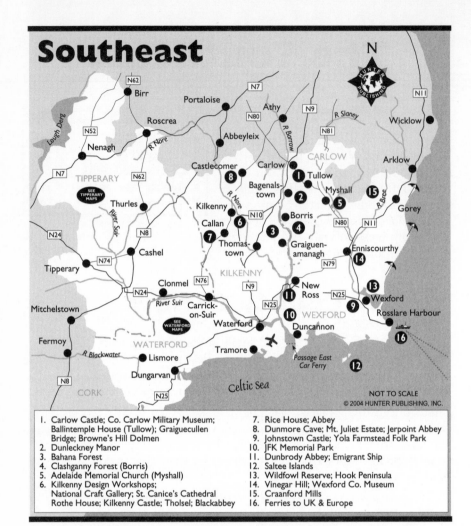

Southeast

N

1. Carlow Castle; Co. Carlow Military Museum; Ballintemple House (Tullow); Graiguecullen Bridge; Browne's Hill Dolmen
2. Dunleckney Manor
3. Bahana Forest
4. Clashganny Forest (Borris)
5. Adelaide Memorial Church (Myshall)
6. Kilkenny Design Workshops; National Craft Gallery; St. Canice's Cathedral; Rothe House; Kilkenny Castle; Tholsel; Blackabbey
7. Rice House; Abbey
8. Dunmore Cave; Mt. Juliet Estate; Jerpoint Abbey
9. Johnstown Castle; Yola Farmstead Folk Park
10. JFK Memorial Park
11. Dunbrody Abbey; Emigrant Ship
12. Saltee Islands
13. Wildfowl Reserve; Hook Peninsula
14. Vinegar Hill; Wexford Co. Museum
15. Craanford Mills
16. Ferries to UK & Europe

TRACING YOUR ANCESTORS

The Carlow Genealogy Project, Old School, College Street. ☎/fax (059) 9130850; carlowgenealogy@iolfree.ie.

■ Carlow Town

Sightseeing

The town grew up around the **castle** built by Hugh de Lacy as a stronghold in about 1180 to defend a strategic point where the rivers Barrow and Burren meet, which also marked the southeastern border of the Pale. The castle survived a number of attacks, including one by rebels, who were slaughtered in 1798. However, it couldn't hold out against a Dr Middleton, who in 1814 decided to knock it down, using explosives, and turn it into an asylum. What survives are the west wall of the keep and two of its former towers. You get the best view of it from across the River Barrow.

Today, Carlow is an attractive and bustling county town, with a rich agricultural hinterland. It is worth at least a brief visit, as there is much to see.

Tullow Street is where you find most of the shops. **The Liberty Tree**, just off it, commemorates the 1798 rebellion and is by leading contemporary sculptor John Behan. On Dublin Street is the **"Cigar Divan,"** with its distinctive Victorian shopfront. **The County Museum**, worth a look, is in the Town Hall, which was built in 1884. It is, however, closed for renovation at the time of writing. **Carlow Courthouse**, designed by William Morrison, looks like a temple on a plinth. It was intended for Cork, but there was a mix-up, which is how a small town got such an impressive building!

St. Patrick's College, opened in 1793, was the first post-penal Catholic seminary in the country, and beside it is the **Cathedral**, completed in 1833. **St. Mary's Church of Ireland** dates from 1727, with its tower and spire added in 1834. The interior is interesting for its galleries and monuments, including some by the neo-classical architect Sir Richard Morrison, son of William.

Take a short walk away from the town along the River Barrow to **Graiguecullen Bridge**, built in 1569 and widened in 1815. Nearby you find the **Croppies' Grave**. After the failure of 1798, the bodies of 640 rebels were thrown here and covered in quicklime. The site was later marked by a monument. They got the name "Croppies" because they cut their hair short as a sign of allegiance to the United Irishmen. Croppy Acre on Ellis Quay in Dublin, in front of the National Museum of Decorative Arts, is their best-known mass grave in the Republic.

A TRADITION REVIVED

Until about 100 years ago this was the malt and hop producing area of Ireland, with a number of breweries. In 1998 the **Carlow Brewing Company** revived the tradition. All of its award-winning products are naturally brewed, based on traditional Celtic beer styles. **The Brewery** is housed in The Goods Store, an old stone building, beautifully restored and converted, with a visitors' bar, beside Carlow Railway Station. Open May-September. ☎ (059) 9134356; fax 40038; ccb@iol.ie; www.carlowbrewing.com.

The Southeast

An American Military Memory

Captain Myles Keogh of the 7th Cavalry, killed with General Custer at the Battle of Little Big Horn, is remembered at the **County Carlow Military Museum**, Old Church, St. Dympna's Hospital, Athy Road, Carlow. Displays also include Ireland's role in UN peacekeeping. Open some Sundays, July-October, 2-5:30 pm. Call to check. ☎ (087) 285-0509; military. museum@ireland.com.

■ Touring the Countryside

Head out into the country to do some more sightseeing. The most impressive prehistoric monument in the county is the **Browne's Hill Dolmen**, east of Carlow Town, believed to be the largest of its kind in Europe, with a capstone weighing 100 tons. Religious rites, perhaps involving human sacrifice, were performed here from 2500 BC.

Around Tullow there are other monuments. The **Haroldstown Dolmen** at Tobinstown, with its two slightly tilted capstones, is a good example of a portal dolmen. **Cloch-a-Foil** at Aghade is a large stone with a hole in it, perhaps part of a megalithic tomb. For more than 2,000 years it was believed that babies would be cured of illness if they were passed through the hole. It's now on private land, so please respect the landowner when visiting. **Rathgall Stone Fort** is a large hillside fortification, with outer walls dating from the 8th century and inner walls built during medieval times.

Near Ardattin, Tullow, is **Ballintemple House**, the birthplace of Pierce Butler, signatory of the American Constitution. Its estate is now a nursery run by the State Forestry Service, Coillte.

Altamont Garden is signposted on the N80 and N81, six miles (10 km) from Tullow. The 100-acre estate has both formal and informal gardens, with rare trees, rhodendrons and shrubs, roses old and modern, and lots of herbaceous plants. There are fascinating walks through the Arboretum, Bog Garden, Ice Age Glen, a River Walk along the Slaney, and a Hill Walk with wonderful views of the Blackstairs and Wicklow Mountains. The 2½-acre lake was dug after the Irish Potato Famine, and took 100 men with horses and carts two years to complete at a cost in 1847-48 of £12,000 – a fortune at the time. Opening times change. ☎ (059) 9159444 in advance.

Bagenalstown, 13 miles (21 km) south of Carlow on the R705/R724 and the River Barrow, is named after founder William Bagenal who planned it to look like Versailles. He didn't get to finish it, but the impressive Courthouse is modelled on the Parthenon in Athens, and other buildings make it a very attractive town with fine streetscapes. You can visit Bagenal's home, **Dunleckney Manor**. ☎ (059) 9721932.

Near the town are the ruins of **Ballyloughan Castle**, built about 1300. Two miles (3.2 km) east of the town are the ruins of **Ballymoon Castle**, probably built at the same time.

Ballon is a pretty village, with great views of the Blackstairs and Wicklow Mountains. There was a Bronze Age settlement on **Ballon Hill**, where these days you can enjoy a two-mile walk.

Borris

Borris is an attractive estate town in the fertile valley of the River Barrow below the Blackstairs Mountains, 16 miles (26 km) south of Carlow on the R702. Handsome stone-cut buildings and traditional shop and pub fronts give the town great appeal and it is worth at least stopping here to take a look. The MacMurrough Kavanagh family, formerly Celtic Kings of Leinster, who built it, still live in the middle of town at Borris House. Arthur MacMurrough Kavanagh was responsible for the graceful 16-arch viaduct at the lower end, which used to carry the Great Southern and Western Railway Line between Bagenalstown and Wexford. There are pleasant walks along the River Barrow at Clashganny Forest, three miles (4.8 km) south of Borris.

The signposted **Mount Leinster Drive** starts in Borris near the railway viaduct and takes a whole day to cover the circular route, taking you to Bunclody, Clonegal, Kildavin, Myshall, Fenagh, Bagenalstown and back to Borris.

The following gives you a taste of what you see en route. **Mount Leinster** (2,600 feet/795 m) is the highest point in the Blackstairs Mountains and is popular for hang-gliding. You see wonderful scenery as you climb and, from its summit or from the Nine Stones viewing point, you get a panorama of the county and its neighbors, Wexford, Kilkenny and Wicklow – even the coast of Wales across the Irish Sea if you're lucky.

Bunclody, on the River Slaney, has a pretty mall lined by trees; **Clonegal** is another picturesque village, and **Huntingdon Castle** nearby is worth a visit. It's the home of the Temple of Isis as well as fascinating items from Egypt, Africa, and prehistoric Ireland. ☎ (054) 77552.

The Durdan or Weavers Cottages in Clonegal date from late 17th century, when weaving was an important local industry. During summer you can watch demonstrations of spinning and weaving in the two cottages that survive of the original six. Driving on, you come to **Kildavin**, where the long-distance walk, the **South Leinster Way**, begins.

Peter Fenelon Collier (1849-1909), who founded Collier's Magazine, was born in Myshall. He arrived penniless in the United States at age 16 and went on to build up a publishing empire worth $12 million.

■ Adventures on Foot

An Unusual Walk

Carlow Bat Walk is a short walk to take at dusk in the town to see bats come out hunting for insects. If that interests you, call Lorcan Scott. ☎ (059) 913620; fax 41503.

The waymarked **South Leinster Way** is 62 miles (100 km) long, stretching from Kildavin to Carrick-on-Suir in neighboring Co. Tipperary, and offers plenty of variety. Its Carlow stretch takes walkers between mountains and along forest tracks over the northern slopes of Mount Leinster, its highest point. It drops down into Borris and follows the towpath along the River Barrow, leading you on into Co. Kilkenny.

The route of the **Barrow Way** from Lowtown, Co. Kildare to St. Mullins in Co. Kilkenny follows the river's towpath for 68 miles (109 km), part of it passing through Co. Carlow. En route you see river life, including swans and mallards, traditional lock gates, pretty lock houses and historic castles and ruins.

Bahana Forest, which probably got its name from "beith," the Irish for birch, is an old wood, sloping down to the Barrow between St. Mullin's and Graignamanagh. You see a great variety of conifers, a diverse range of flora as well as lots of birds, rabbits, squirrels, pheasant and woodcock. You may even see otters on the river bank.

∎ Adventures on Water

Two companies offer cruising trips on the Barrow, the second longest river in the country, after the Shannon. It's navigable from Athy, Co. Kildare, to St. Mullins, Co. Kilkenny.

Barrowline Cruisers is based at Carlow Town, and offers a choice of cruising trips on the River Barrow and Grand Canal. ☎ (059) 9132545; barrowline@tinet.ie; www.barrowline.com.

With **Leisure Afloat** you embark at Levitstown Lock near Athy – see Kildare, page 152. ☎ (056) 7754395; www.leisureafloat.com.

Fishing

If you are interested in salmon or trout angling near Carlow Town, contact the **Anglers Association** at Butlers Bar, 6 Centaur Street, ☎ (059) 9142307.

The River Burren, with a good stock of brown trout, joins the River Barrow at Carlow. The Barrow Angling Club has extensive fishing rights on it. Upstream from Carlow, the River Lerr joins the Barrow, with a small stock of brown trout, and the Barrow Angling Club controls some of the water. Contact **JB Motor & Sport**, Castlehill Centre, Carlow.

See pages 71-74 for details on angling in Ireland, regulations and best times to fish.

The River Greese joins the Barrow north of Carlow Town, and has a good stock of wild brown trout. Fishing is controlled by two angling clubs: the Barrow Angling Club and the **River Greese Anglers' Association** (contact Patrick Leigh). ☎ (059) 8626611.

Fishing in the Southeast

The five great rivers in the Southeast of the Republic, both for game and coarse fishing, are the **Suir**, the **Nore**, the **Barrow**, the **Blackwater** and the **Slaney**. The Suir, especially in its upper reaches, has good trout stocks and the Blackwater is noted for its salmon.

Managed stillwater fishing is also available, including at Ballyshunnock and Knockaderry reservoir, Waterford, Belle

The Southeast

Lake, Dunmore East, and Dromana Lake, Cappoquin, all in Co. Waterford and Oaklands Lake at New Ross, Co. Wexford.

The Southern Regional Fisheries Board looks after the region, one of the largest in the country, with some of the best trout, salmon, coarse and sea angling available.

The sea angler also has lots of locations to choose from, and there are numerous opportunities for fishing from beaches and rocky shorelines.

For more information, check locally at tackle and other outlets, or contact the **Southern Regional Fisheries Board**, Angles Street, Clonmel, Co. Tipperary. ☎ (052) 23624; enquiries@srfb.ie; www.srfb.ie.

■ Adventures on Horseback

Carrigbeg Riding Centre, three miles (4.8 km) off the Bagenalstown-to-Myshall road, is open all year, Monday-Saturday, 10 am-5 pm. It offers instruction to all levels, cross-country rides, and has an indoor arena. ☎ (059) 9721962.

Coole Equestrian Centre is close to the Lisnavagh Estate and Gardens (see *Where to Stay*, page 203) and picturesque Rathvilly. Open daily all year. Caters for all levels, with two all-weather floodlit arenas and offers full- and half-day trail rides and other activities. ☎ (059) 9161000.

■ Golf

The 18-hole **Carlow Golf Club**, Deerpark, Dublin Road, has a parkland course that can be played year-round. ☎ (059) 9131695; www.carlowgolfclub.com. There's also the **Carlow Town Golf Course**, a par 3, 18-hole affair. Quinagh House, Mortarstown. ☎ (059) 9132088. Just outside Carlow Town is **Killerig Castle Golf & Country Club**, playable all year, with some great scenery. ☎ (059) 9163000; fax 63005; www.killerig-golf.ie.

In the northeast of the county is **Clonmore Golf Club**. ☎ (059) 6471244. Situated in the scenic northeast corner of Co. Carlow, in an area noted for its historical interest and photogenic landscape, this golf course is an 18-hole par 3, with additional facilities for skittles and boules. Open all year, with clubs for rent.

Carrigleade Golf Course is on the Barrow Drive between St. Mullins and Graignamanagh, with the Blackstairs and Brandon mountains as a backdrop. ☎ (059) 9724370.

Mount Wolseley Golf & Country Club, Tullow, lies between the Wicklow and Blackstairs Mountains, on a mature estate close to the Slaney. You can also stay there – see below.

Borris Golf Club is a nine-hole parkland course in the south of the county with marvelous views of the Blackstairs to the east and the Barrow valley to the west. ☎ (0503) 73143.

■ Where to Stay

Mount Wolseley Hotel, Golf and Country Club also has houses for rent, and its own golf course. The estate, close to the Slaney, was owned by the Wolseleys, designers of the first British car in 1895, and after that it was owned by a religious order. Now there are 40 bedrooms in the hotel. The houses are actually on the golf course and each sleeps seven, in four bedrooms. ☎ (059) 9151674; fax 52123; www.mountwolseley.ie.

HOTEL PRICE CHART	
Price per person, per night, with two sharing, including breakfast.	
$	Under US $50
$$	US $50-$100
$$$	US $101-$175
$$$$	US $176-$200
$$$$$	Over US $200

☆☆☆ **The Lord Bagenal Inn** is on the River Barrow in the heritage village of Leighlinbridge, just off the main N9 Dublin/Waterford Road, eight miles (13 km) from Carlow and 20 miles (32 km) from Kilkenny. It looks delightful. It has just 12 en suite bedrooms, as well as gardens and a private marina, offering angling and boating. Its restaurant is known for its fine food and wines, and is recommended by Egon Ronay and others. It also offers a carvery lunch from 12:30 to 2:30 pm, with a bar menu until 3 pm. ☎ (059) 9721668; fax 22629; www.lordbagenal.com.

The Old Georgian Step House in the village of Borris has been restored and is furnished in its original style with four-poster beds. It's licensed to sell alcohol and it's gay-friendly. ☎ (0503) 73209; fax 73395.

Cottage Rentals

Near Rathvilly, 12 miles (19 km) from Carlow, is the **Lisnavagh Estate,** a really peaceful place to stay. The two cottages, **The Farm Cottage** and **Blacksmith's Cottage**, are beautifully renovated. Rates are €175 to €295 per week, depending on the season (highest rates are in July and August; lowest are in Novemeber and December). ☎ (059) 916-1104; fax 616-1148; cottages@lisnavagh.com.

The Southeast

Hostel

'The Otterholt Riverside Lodge Hostel is on Kilkenny Road, Carlow, and is open all year. ☎ (059) 9130404; otterholt_riverside_lodge@ hotmail.com.

■ Where to Eat

Reddys is at 67 Tullow Street, Carlow Town, and has been there since 1768. It's both a bar and a restaurant and serves snacks, carvery lunches and full meals. Its menu includes steaks, fish, traditional Irish, Italian, Chinese, and vegetarian dishes. It's open seven days, for lunch from 12:30-2:30 pm and dinner from 5:30 to 10 pm. ☎ (059) 914-2224.

At **Beams Restaurant**, 59 Dublin Street, Carlow Town, you dine in pleasant surroundings. There's both an à la carte and table d'hôte menu of modern Irish dishes, made using home-grown vegetables, which includes a choice of fresh fish and game in season. Open Tuesday-Saturday, from 7:30 pm, with last orders at 9:45. ☎ (059) 9131824.

County Kilkenny

This inland county is called Cill Chainnigh in Irish – meaning Cainneach's or Saint Canice's church, which is the name of the cathedral in its capital. It has a very fertile central plain with higher ground to its northeast, northwest and south, and is bisected by the river Nore, with the Barrow and Suir marking its boundaries in the east and south. Its capital is **Kilkenny City** and the main towns are **Callan**, **Castlecomer**, **Thomastown** and **Graiguenamanagh**.

■ Getting Here

Kilkenny City is served by major roads N77-N78-N9-N7 from Dublin (71 miles/114 km); N76-N24-N8 from Cork (91 miles/ 146 km) and N77-N7-N62-N52-N65-N6-N18 from Galway (107 miles/172 km).

It's also on the mainline rail link from Heuston Station, Dublin, to Waterford, and is well served by Bus Éireann. **MacDonagh Station**, Kilkenny, ☎ (056) 22024.

■ Tourist Information

The **Shee Alms House** in Rose Inn Street is the Tourist Information office, one of the most attractive in the country. It was built by Sir Richard Shee in 1582 to accommodate 12 poor persons. The Shee family was dispossessed by Cromwell, but regained ownership in 1756. The last recorded inmates were in 1830. Upstairs there's the City Scope project – a scale model of the city in the 16th century. During summer, walking tours of the city start here. ☎ (056) 7751500; fax 63955; info@southeasttourism.ie; www.southeastireland.com.

TRACING YOUR ANCESTORS

Kilkenny Archaeological Society, based in Rothe House, Parliament Street, ☎ (056) 22893; fax 51108; rothehouse@eircom.net; www.kilkennyarchaeologicalsociety.ie.

■ Kilkenny City

Known as the Marble City, from the vein of black stone found here, Kilkenny stands on the River Nore and has some beautiful buildings that have been well looked after. Unlike other towns and cities, here the local authorities have taken care of their city's appearance and resisted the proliferation of ugly plastic signs. Visitors have been attracted to Kilkenny for decades, and it's worth at least a daytrip if you are staying in Dublin or elsewhere.

The city was the ecclesiastical and political capital of the ancient kingdom of Ossory, and became the medieval capital of the country under the Normans. In 1172, Richard de Clare, known as Strongbow, built a wooden fortress here, and in 1208 it was granted a charter by William, the Earl Marshall, to attract trade. From the 14th century, Kilkenny Castle was the seat of the Butlers, the Earls and Dukes of Ormonde. King James I granted its charter as a city in 1609, amalgamating its two townships of Hightown and Irishtown.

From 1293 to 1408 and between 1642 and 1648 Anglo-Norman parliaments were held here. In 1642 the Confederation of Kilkenny saw Irish Catholics side with King Charles I. They lost to Cromwell in 1651 and after that most of the families involved were sent to Connaught and the city's trade passed to Protestants.

Kilkenny Today

The town has been a center for brewing since the 17th century, and the tradition continues today. However, if you mention the city to most Irish people, they'll immediately think of design. This is because in 1965 the government established Kilkenny Design Workshops in the 18th-century stables of the castle. It quickly developed an international reputation for the quality of its graphic, industrial and craft design. Since then, designers, artists and craft-workers from all over the world have established studios and workshops throughout the city and county.

The Crafts Council of Ireland has its headquarters here, and runs **The National Craft Gallery**. ☎ (056) 7761804; fax 63754; info@ccoi.ie or ncg@ccoi.ie. It's also behind the Kilkenny E-Commerce Craft Initiative, which lists information and a product catalog on its website, www.ccoi.ie.

Kilkenny Design has retail outlets here. ☎ (056) 22118; fax 65905; in Dublin on Nassau Street, ☎ (01) 677-7066, and in Galway. Check their website at www.kilkennydesign.com.

Kilkenny County Council publishes a guide to *Artists' Studios* and a *Kilkenny Sculpture Guide* – ask for them at the tourist office or you can find them at the Arts Office, 42 Parliament Street, Kilkenny, ☎ (056) 779-4138, www.kilkennycoco.ie/arts.

Entertainment

Kilkenny Arts Festival is one of the oldest in the county, founded in 1974, and brings some of the world's major performers and companies to the city every August; www.kilkennyarts.ie/about_kilkenny.html. The city also hosts **Murphy's Cat Laughs Comedy Festival** in late Spring and music, comedy and theater can be enjoyed year-round, with venues including the Watergate Theatre; www.thecatlaughs.com.

■ Adventures on Foot

Kilkenny City

Tree-lined river walks and meadows make the **Kilkenny Castle Park** a quiet retreat from the city. You see ducks, swans and other waterfowl, as well as bats hunting at night.

Walking along the River Nore near Green's Bridge, you can see some of the old woolen mills.

Less than two miles (3.2 km) northeast of the city, off the Castlecomer Road, is **Newpark Marsh**, ideal for a stroll. Once a lake, it's been colonized by reeds and other vegetation and is home to lots of wild plants, including yellow iris, ragged robin and purple loosestrife.

■ Sightseeing

You can explore the county, with its gentle landscape, by bike or car. Off the main roads you'll discover the attractive countryside. There are signposted routes through the county, taking you to places of historic, cultural or natural interest, which you can ask about at the Tourist Information office, or just go as you please.

Kilkenny City

Kilkenny is compact, so it's easy to explore on foot. **St. Canice's Cathedral**, built in the 13th century on the site of the monastery founded by the saint who gives the county its name, was partly destroyed by Cromwell's troops in 1650, but restored 200 years later. The round tower beside the cathedral is believed to have been built around 849 and is about 100 feet tall. It is missing the usual distinctive conical cap but has a viewing platform for the public to view the city and countryside. During the Arts Festival in August and at various other times, there are recitals in the cathedral. ☎ (056) 7764971; stcanicescathedral@eircom.net.

Kilkenny Castle and its extensive grounds are open to the public. Visits to the castle are by guided tour only. It is one of the most popular sites in the country and can be busy in summer. The 12th-century castle was remodeled in the late 19th century and handed over to the State in the 1960s, having been the home of the Butler family, Earls, Marquesses and Dukes of Ormonde, from 1391-1935. The **Butler Gallery** in its basement shows contemporary art. Tours of Castle Park are on Sundays in July and August at 3 pm. Open daily all year (hours vary); tea room open May-September. ☎ (056) 21450; fax 63488.

The Tholsel (Town Hall) is on High Street and dates from 1761. It has a double five-arch arcade in front that used to be a covered market, and a lantern tower, with a clock that has a beautiful chime. Its name comes from "toll" and "sael" – Old English words meaning "tax" and "hall" (or "the place where the tax was paid"). Today it houses Kilkenny Corporation, so its purpose hasn't changed completely.

The Black Abbey, on Blackmill Street, was founded in 1225 for the Dominicans and has had a chequered history, becoming a courthouse after its repression in 1543. Partly restored in 1778, it wasn't used for worship again until the mid-19th century. It's worth visiting for its stained glass windows, and the statues and relics on display. The Abbey gets its name from the black habits worn by the Dominican friars.

Rothe House is a personal favorite. Although built in 1594 by wealthy merchant John Rothe, in a style influenced by the Italian Renaissance, it's on the scale of a family home. Behind it, around a cobbled courtyard, are slightly newer houses and a well. Open daily, July and August, 9:30 am-6 pm; rest of year, 10:30 am-5 pm. Admission €3. Parliament Street, ☎ (056) 22893, rothehouse@ eircom.net.

Callan

Callan is about 10 miles (16 km) from Kilkenny on the N76. It gets its name from Niall Caille, High King of Ireland, who drowned trying to rescue a servant here in 884, while at war with the Vikings. Cromwell is believed to have stabled his horses in the ruined Abbey, and there's a holy well in the Abbey Meadow.

Edmund Rice (1762-1844), founder of the Christian Brothers, was born here, and there's a monument to him. **Rice House** is open to visitors. ☎ (056) 25141 for times.

THE COCA-COLA CONNECTION

Callan was the home of the Candlers. Asa Griggs Candler bought the Coca-Cola recipe from its inventor Dr John Pemberton in 1888 in Atlanta, and founded the soft drink company, which he sold in 1923 for a fortune. Sadly, the Candler home on West Street has almost disappeared.

Castlecomer

Castlecomer is 10 miles (16 km) north of Kilkenny, where the N77 and R694 meet. A humpback bridge crosses the River Dinan and opens into a pleasant square with Georgian houses surrounded by lime trees. The town was laid out by Sir Christopher Wandesford, whose family started a coal mine here. It lasted for 300 years until its closure in 1969.

Nearby at Ballyfoyle off the N78 is **Dunmore Cave**, which consists of a series of chambers developed over millions of years, with dramatic limestone formations. In the care of the State Heritage Service, there's an interesting exhibition in the Visitors Centre, where refreshments are also available. Open daily from mid-March to the end of October, weekends only in winter; times vary. ☎ (056) 7767726.

Thomastown

Thomastown, 11 miles (17 km) southeast of Kilkenny on the N9/R700, was founded about 1200 on an important river crossing of the Nore by the Norman Thomas FitzAnthony. It has kept the charm of a small medieval walled town, and is still a market town. At one time there were 12 water-powered mills here, but the last one closed in 1963, although some of the buildings survive. Nearby is the magnificent **Mount Juliet estate**, now a hotel with championship golf course, see page 211.

Jerpoint Abbey, southwest of Thomastown on the N9, was founded in the 12th century by the Cistercian order, and its most memorable feature is the sculptured cloister arcade and accompanying carvings. In the care of the State Heritage Service, there's a Visitor Centre with an exhibition. Open daily, March 1-November 31. ☎ (056) 24623; fax 54003; jerpointabbey@ealga.ie.

Urlingford

One of the best-known towns in the county is Urlingford. It's on the main N8 Dublin-Cork road, and is popular as a stop if driving between the two cities, since it's roughly half-way. Its name means "the ford of the big stones" and just north of it are the ruins of a church and castle, with a cutaway bog around it.

■ Adventures on Water

Graiguenamanagh is 22 miles (35 km) southeast of Kilkenny on the R703/R705. It nestles in a valley on the River Barrow, surrounded by hills, with the Blackstair Mountains on one side. The regatta here in August is one of the oldest in the country.

Valley Boats is a small family company, based on the River Barrow at Graiguenamanagh, which offers barge rentals, with a choice of narrow boats, from two- to six-berth. ☎ (059) 9724945; info@valleyboats.ie; www.valleyboats.ie.

Fishing

Kilkenny is a great fishing county and **Thomastown** has been a popular angling center for centuries. Among the county's other attractions is **Ballyhogan Lake**, a three-acre private lake near Graiguenamanagh, which has stocks of bream, rudd, rudd/bream hybrids and tench. Details at ☎ (059) 9724191.

Tackle Shops

Hook Line and Sinker, Rose Inn Street, Kilkenny, ☎ (056) 7771699.

Town and County Sports Shop, High Street, Kilkenny, ☎ (056) 21517.

■ Spectator Sports

County Kilkenny is renowned for GAA (Gaelic Athletic Association – see pages 20, 77), in particular for its hurling team; ask locally about matches.

Gowran Park Racecourse, in a lovely wooded setting, has been the home of horse racing in the county since 1914. ☎ (056) 26225; fax 26173; gowranpk@eircom.net.

■ Adventures on Horseback

The Iris Kellett Equestrian Centre, Mount Juliet, Thomastown. ☎ (056) 7773044; info@mountjuliet.ie; www.mountjuliet.com.

The Top Flight Equestrian Centre, Warrington, Kilkenny. ☎ (056) 7770792; tfwarrington@tinet.ie; www.topflightkilkenny.com.

The Nuenna Farm Equestrian Centre, near Freshford, ☎ (056) 8832614.

■ Golf

Mount Juliet is the most famous course in the county, with its beautiful setting in an historic 1,500-acre estate, and it has hosted international championships (see page 211).

Kilkenny Golf Club is a mile and a half from the city on the N77. ☎ (056) 7765400; enquiries@kilkennygolfclub.com; www.kilkennygolfclub.com.

Mountain View Golf Club, Kiltorcan, Ballyhale, is in South Kilkenny, 12 miles (19 km) from the city and 14 miles (22 km) from Waterford, a mile off the main road. ☎ (056) 7768122; info@mviewgolf.com; www.mviewgolf.com.

Callan Golf Club is a mile from the town. ☎ (0506) 25136; info@callangolfclub.com; www.callangolf club.com.

▪ Where to Stay

☆☆☆☆ **The Mount Juliet Hotel** is in a wonderful setting, a former estate with mature woods and parklands. The 18th-century house is now a luxurious hotel, and accommodation is also available in the Paddocks, Hunters Yard and the Rose Garden. In addition to its own golf course, facilities include a Spa and Leisure Centre, and guests can enjoy river fishing, clay target shooting, archery, or tennis. It has its own Equestrian Centre, and you can ride for 10

HOTEL PRICE CHART	
Price per person, per night, with two sharing, including breakfast.	
$	Under US $50
$$	US $50-$100
$$$	US $101-$175
$$$$	US $176-$200
$$$$$	Over US $200

miles (16 km) without leaving the estate. $$$$. ☎ (056) 7773010; fax 773019; www.mountjuliet.com.

☆☆☆ The **Springhill Court Hotel** is on the Waterford Road, just a few minutes outside Kilkenny City. It's a modern building with 83 spacious and attractive bedrooms, and a Spa and Leisure Center, with pool, sauna, steam room, Jacuzzi and well-equipped gym. The **Claddagh Restaurant** has an excellent reputation, and is popular with locals – always a good sign. It belongs to Kilkenny's Good Food Circle and Bord Bia's (National Food Board) Feile Bia program, which guarantees the use of local Irish suppliers. Its menu features traditional Irish and Mediterranean dishes. Carvery lunch and bar food is served every day in its **Paddock Bar**, and there's also live entertainment twice a week. $, with special weekend break offers. ☎ (056) 77772-1122; fax 77776-1600; springhillcourt@eircom.net; www.springhillcourt.com.

☆☆ **The Club House Hotel** is on Patrick Street, Kilkenny, in the middle of the medieval city. It's in an 18th-century building with modern additions, and has 28 pleasant bedrooms. Guests have free parking. Originally the headquarters of a sporting gentleman's club, the hotel has wonderful Georgian architecture, including detailed plasterwork and brass fittings. Lunch and evening meals are served in the Georgian dining room, and are also available in **Victor's Bar**, which has live music in on Saturday evenings. $, with special midweek and weekend discounts available. ☎ (056) 77772-1994; fax 77777-1920; clubhouse@iol.ie; www.clubhousehotel.com.

☆☆☆ **The Hotel Kilkenny** is on the edge of the city, surrounded by lovely gardens. It has 103 bedrooms and an excellent health and fitness center, with pool, spa area, aerobics room, fully equipped gym, and beauty treatment room. Guests and non-residents can dine in its **Broom's Bistro** or relax in its **Hill Bar**. $$$, with weekend and mid-

The Southeast

week discounts available. ☎ (056) 77776-2000; fax 77776-5984; kilkenny@griffingroup.ie; www.griffingroup.ie.

Guesthouses

Blanchville House is near Kilkenny City in a lovely rural setting, surrounded by farmland. It was built in 1800, has been restored, and belongs to the Hidden Ireland group (see page 60). There's a tennis court, billiards and games room. Open March 1-November 1, six rooms. $$. Dinner available. ☎ (056) 27197; info@blanchville.ie; www.blanchville.ie.

Waterside Guesthouse, The Quay, Graiguenamanagh, is a beautifully converted granite corn store, dating from the 1870s, on the bank of the River Barrow. All of its 10 bedrooms look out over the river and have been refurbished preserving the original beams of the corn store. The guesthouse is popular with walkers, as it's on the long-distance South Leinster Way and near the Blackstairs Mountains. It also attracts those interested in boating, cruising, fishing, or playing golf at nearby courses, including Mount Juliet. Its restaurant, which is also open to non-residents, is listed in top guides and serves excellent local and international cuisine. You can also buy Waterside's unique brown bread made with walnuts and treacle. $. ☎ (059) 9724246; fax 24733; info@waterside.iol.ie; www. watersideguesthouse.com.

Cottage & House Rentals

 Wallslough Village is a wonderful rural retreat, less than three miles (4.8 km) from Kilkenny City. It has an equestrian center, with instruction, trekking and shows year-round. There are six thatched cottages to rent overlooking a fishing lake, and two restored pre-Famine houses. ☎ (056) 23828; fax 23255; info@wallsloughvillage.com; www.wallsloughvillage.com.

Camping & RV Parks

 ☆☆☆ **Nore Valley Caravan & Camping Park**, near Bennetsbridge, is on a family farm, with home-cooked food available from June to August. There's also a river walk through woodland, and bikes for hire. Open March 1-October 31. ☎ (056) 7727229; norevalleypark@eircom.net.

☆☆☆ The **Tree Grove Park** is just outside Kilkenny City, a 20-minute walk or cycle along a tree-lined river path. Bike rental on site. Open March 1-November 15. ☎ (056) 7770302; treecc@iol.ie.

Hostel

Kilkenny Tourist Hostel is on Parliament Street and open all year. ☎ (056) 7763541; kilkennyhostel@eircom.net.

■ Where to Eat

 The Marble City Bar on High Street in Kilkenny is one of the city's oldest and very attractive, so much so that it has been featured on postcards for generations. It's open for breakfast from 10 am, serves food all day, and has won the National Pub Lunch Award. ☎ (056) 7761143.

Bollard's Bar and Restaurant on Kieran Street, in the middle of the city's shopping area, has belonged to the Bollard family since 1904. It's recommended by guides to good food, which it serves all day. During the summer there's traditional music on Tuesdays and Thursdays from 9:30 pm. Open 10:30 am-11:30 pm, Monday to Wednesday, 10:30 am-12:30 pm, Thursday-Saturday, 12:30-11 pm on Sundays. ☎ (056) 772-1352; kieran@bollards.com; www.bollardsbar.com.

Langtons Restaurant and Bar on John Street has won national awards both as a pub and as a restaurant. Food is served all day. There's traditional music on Mondays and Tuesdays and a nightclub on Tuesday, Thursday and Saturday nights. ☎ (056) 776-5133.

The Fléva Restaurant is upstairs beside the historic Tholsel or Town Hall on Kilkenny's High Street. Chef/proprietor Michael Mee brings a hint of the Orient to Kilkenny. A typical dish is baked salmon with a couscous crust on a basil herb mash with roasted Mediterranean vegetables. Open for lunch from 12:30 to 2:30 pm, Tuesday-Saturday, and on Sundays for brunch from noon to 4 pm. Dinner is from 6:30-10 pm. From July-September, dinner is available on Sundays from 5-9:30 pm. ☎ (056) 777-0021.

The Kilkenny Design Centre Restaurant, Castle Yard, is in the coach house and stables for Kilkenny Castle, which it overlooks. It offers a wide selection of traditional home-made foods, from snacks to meals and is open seven days a week, but closed on Sundays and Bank Holidays from January-March. ☎ (056) 772-2118.

At Mount Juliet, Thomastown, there's a choice of where to dine. **The Lady Helen Restaurant** is the most elegant, with a menu of classic cuisine complemented by an extensive wine list. **Kendals**, in the Hunters Yard on the former historic estate, overlooking the golf course, is in contemporary style and more suited to casual dining. ☎ (056) 777-3000.

The Lime Tree Bistro is on Chatsworth Street in Castlecomer, and is a family-run restaurant serving high-quality food, including breakfast and lunch. It's open Monday-Saturday from 8:30 am to 6 pm and for lunch on Sundays from 12:30-3 pm. ☎/fax (056) 444-0966; chubbybrennan@eircom.net.

Josephine's Restaurant on Main Street, Urlingford, is a good place to stop for refreshment when travelling between the Cork and Dublin. It serves traditional Irish food, including seafood and steaks, with vegetarian choices. There's a large free car park. Open Monday-Saturday from 7 am, Sundays from 8 am; it closes at 9 pm Monday-Thursday, and at 10 pm other days. ☎/fax (056) 8831515.

County Waterford

Much of the north and middle of Co. Waterford is mountainous, with the Comeragh, Knockmealdown and Monavullagh ranges. Its coastline is a mixture of rugged cliffs and sandy bays. It really does have some of the most varied and beautiful scenery in Ireland, as well as seaside resorts, historic sites and plenty of activities to keep any visitor busy.

Waterford City is the county's largest town and its administrative capital is **Dungarvan**. Other main towns are **Tramore** and **Lismore**.

■ Getting Here

Waterford City is served by the N24-N9-N7 from Dublin (101 miles/162 km); the N25 from Cork (77 miles/124 km).

It's also on the railway and has a bus station. **Plunkett Rail Station.** ☎ (051) 873-4-1. **Bus Station.** ☎ (051) 879-000.

You can fly from the UK to **Waterford Airport.** ☎ (051) 875-589.

■ Tourist Information

County Waterford Tourism, info@waterfordtourism.com; www.waterfordtourism.org; www.countrywaterford.com.

Fáilte Ireland has offices at:

41, The Quay, Waterford. ☎ (051) 875-823; fax 876-720; info@ southeasttourism.ie; www.southeastireland.com.

Waterford Crystal, Cork Road, Waterford. ☎ (051) 358-397.

The Court House, Dungarvan. ☎ (058) 41741.

TRACING YOUR ANCESTORS

Waterford has a particular affinity with Newfoundland, where there are large numbers of people with roots in the county. **The Genealogical Centre** at Waterford Heritage Survey, Jenkin's Lane, offers a family research service. ☎ (051) 876-123; fax 850-645; mnoc@iol.ie; www.iol.ie/mnoc.

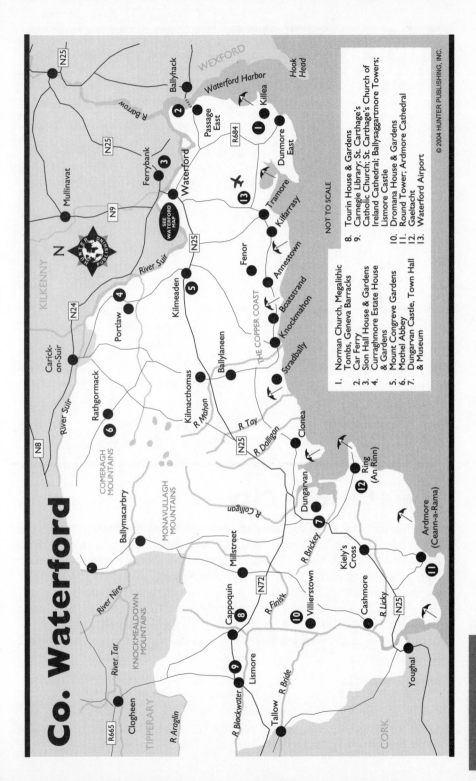

Co. Waterford

NOT TO SCALE

1. Norman Church, Megalithic Tombs, Geneva Barracks
2. Car Ferry
3. Sion Hall House & Gardens
4. Curraghmore Estate House & Gardens
5. Mount Congreve Gardens
6. Mothel Abbey
7. Dungarvan Castle, Town Hall & Museum
8. Tourin House & Gardens
9. Carnegie Library; St. Carthage's Catholic Church; St. Carthage's Church of Ireland Cathedral; Ballysaggartmore Towers; Lismore Castle
10. Dromana House & Gardens
11. Round Tower; Ardmore Cathedral
12. Gaeltacht
13. Waterford Airport

The Southeast

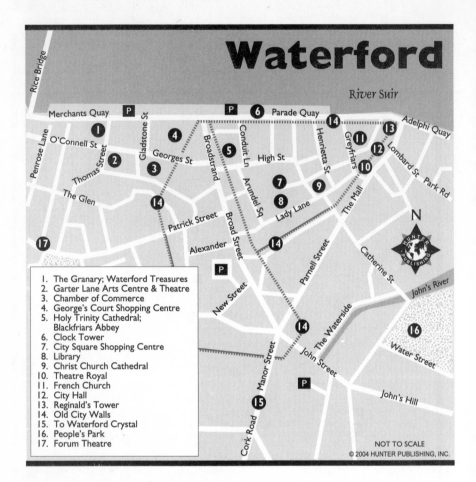

Waterford

River Suir

1. The Granary; Waterford Treasures
2. Garter Lane Arts Centre & Theatre
3. Chamber of Commerce
4. George's Court Shopping Centre
5. Holy Trinity Cathedral;
   Blackfriars Abbey
6. Clock Tower
7. City Square Shopping Centre
8. Library
9. Christ Church Cathedral
10. Theatre Royal
11. French Church
12. City Hall
13. Reginald's Tower
14. Old City Walls
15. To Waterford Crystal
16. People's Park
17. Forum Theatre

NOT TO SCALE
© 2004 HUNTER PUBLISHING, INC.

■ Waterford City

Waterford prides itself on being the oldest tourist destination in Ireland, first visited by the Vikings in 852. They founded the city, the oldest in the country, and it still has an historic atmosphere. Its name comes from the Norse "Vethrafjorthr," meaning "weather haven," due to its sheltered position on the River Suir at the mouth of the harbor that bears its name. It's still an important port, and a lovely place to visit, friendly in scale. Traces of its medieval city walls stand alongside elegant 18th-century buildings, with cobbled back streets, and its waterfront is most attractive.

City Tour

An hour-long walking tour, said to be witty and informative, daily 11:45 am and 1:45 pm, starts outside Waterford Treasures at the Granary, The Quay, Waterford. ☎ (051) 873-711.

Sightseeing in the City

Visit **Reginald's Tower**, which has stood on its Waterford Quay site for more than 1,000 years. Built for defense, it also has been used as a mint, prison and military store. Open Easter to end October, daily, 10 am-5 pm; June-September, 9:30 am-6:30 pm. ☎ (051) 304-220.

As you walk around the city, look out for the elegant **Chamber of Commerce** building, the **City Hall** and the **Bishop's Palace**. The **Granville Hotel** on the Quay was the home of the 18th-century patriot, Thomas Francis Meagher, before passing into the hands of Carlo Bianconi, who ran the first national coach network in the 19th century.

You can learn about the city's history at **Waterford Treasures** at the Granary on the Quay, which has interactive displays and plenty of artifacts on display. Open all year. ☎ (051) 304-500.

The two cathedrals – the **Church of Ireland Christ Church** and the **Catholic Cathedral of the Most Holy Trinity** – were both designed by locally born architect John Roberts (1714-1796), whose sons Thomas and Sautell were both painters.

The city is the home of **Waterford Crystal** and you can visit the factory on the Cork Road and watch the hand-crafted glass being made. It is particularly popular with North Americans. Open all year. ☎ (051) 373-311.

Shopping

The main shopping area is within the old city walls, with some of the shops, including **Shaws department store**, along the Quay. Turn up from the Quay onto **Broadstrand Street** and you find lots of different shops, selling everything from fashion and crafts to books and groceries. There are two shopping centers, **Georges Court** and **City Square**, with plenty of places to have a snack, meal or drink.

PARKING

The easiest place to park is in the linear car park along the Quay; you pay at a machine before returning to your car. If that's full, watch for signs to other car parks in the central area.

Entertainment in Waterford City

There's a long tradition of music and theater in Waterford, and it has a number of venues. The historic **Theatre Royal**, ☎ (051) 874402, hosts the annual **Waterford International Festival of Light Opera** in October (www.waterfordfestival.

The Southeast

com). You can see work by the local professional theater company, Red Kettle, at **Garter Lane Theatre**, 22A O'Connell Street, ☎ (051) 77153, which also presents touring productions. Other venues include **The Large Room** in City Hall and the **Forum Theatre**, ☎ (051) 871111. The **Garter Lane Arts Centre**, ☎ (051) 873501, hosts exhibitions and other events. Many of the pubs have live music. There's also a program of free entertainment during the summer.

*For a really memorable experience, take a trip on **The Galley Cruising Restaurant** from the Quay, between June and August. You gently cruise along the rivers Barrow, Nore and Suir, informed about what you're passing, and you are served delicious food.* ☎ *(051) 421-723. (It operates from New Ross, Co. Wexford, April-November.)*

■ Sightseeing in Co. Waterford

The harbor and coastal routes suit walkers, cyclists, as well as drivers, with lots of places to stop and enjoy, as well as opportunities for adventures on or in water.

Harbor Sightseeing Route

The charming fishing village of **Dunmore East** at the entrance to Waterford Harbor is well worth visiting, with its period houses and thatched cottages. Dunmore East has an EU Blue Flag beach (see page 76), and is popular for watersports and windsurfing, including snorkeling, sailing, and deep-sea fishing.

Traveling towards Passage East on the R685, there's pretty scenery and historic ruins, including part of a **Norman church** in Killea. At Harristown crossroads, before Woodstown and its lovely sandy beach, on the top of the hill there's a **megalithic tomb**. About three miles (4.8 km) from Woodstown you pass the ruins of **Geneva Barracks**, built to house Huguenot silver workers from Switzerland in the 18th century. It became a notorious prison during the 1798 rebellion, and is mentioned in the famous ballad *The Croppy Boy*.

BY HOOK OR BY CROOK

Crooke is the next village – said to be the source of the expression "by hook or by crook" coined by Cromwell, who vowed he'd lay siege to Waterford either from here or across the harbor at Hook Head in Co. Wexford.

Passage East is where Strongbow landed in 1170. There's a car ferry service from here to Ballyhack on the Wexford side of the river, which saves you a long drive. There are more than 130 crossings a day, from 7 am weekdays and 9:30 am on Sundays. Last sailing is 8 pm, October to end of March; 10 pm, April to end of September. ☎ (051) 382-480; fax 382-598; passageferry@eircom.net.

Coastal Sightseeing

Traveling west from Dunmore East along the R685 you come to the best-known resort in the county, **Tramore**, with its long sandy beach backed by sand dunes. It's not my favorite seaside town since it can be busy because of its popularity with Irish families, and there are amusement arcades with gambling machines. Finally, its beach isn't the most attractive in the county. But if you're keen on surfing, it's the place to go.

The Copper Coast Route

The area west of Tramore, known as the Copper Coast, has been awarded European Geopark status for its sites of special geological interest, plus veins of copper, lead and silver. Karen Toebbe of Knockmahon Lodge, which is also a bed & breakfast, has details. ☎ (051) 292-249.

The signposted Copper Coast route passes through five villages, with beautiful views of the sea and of the Comeragh Mountains. At **Fenor** you can walk in the forest, explore the bog or relax at Kilfarrasy Beach. There's a **Mini Farm**, ☎ (051) 396 444, with pets, a museum and coffee shop. **Annestown's beach** is popular with surfers; while **Boatstrand's harbor** attracts divers and swimmers.

Bunmahon has an EU Blue Flag beach (see page 76). Formerly it was a center for copper mining, and you can see the ruins of the workers' cottages. There are hiking trails, a mining trail, and a geological garden. The main feature in the Heritage Centre is a simulated mine. Open weekend afternoons, July to August. ☎ (051) 396-157.

Stradbally is a delightful village with thatched and slated cottages, surrounded by sandy little beaches and woodlands. **Littlewood Gardens** is a traditional cottage garden, open April to September by appointment. ☎ (051) 293-122.

Dungarvan

Dungarvan is the administrative capital of the county and is a busy market town with a lovely setting in a broad bay. It's best approached from the south – on the N25 from Cork – so you can take in the magnificent panorama, but take care driving as the road is windy as you descend into the town.

The Southeast

Dungarvan Castle, in the care of the State Heritage Service, has been undergoing conservation and access may be restricted. Ask locally. There's a **Museum** in the Town Hall, open all year, Monday-Friday, 9 am to 5 pm.

The *Gaeltacht* (Irish-speaking) area of **Ring** is well-signposted off the N25 just south of Dungarvan. **Clonea**, four miles (6.4 km) east of Dungarvan, has an EU Blue Flag beach (see page 76) two miles (3.2 km) long, and is ideal for scenic walks. It's also the starting point for touring routes – the **Gaeltacht and Galltacht Drive**, the **Copper Coast Drive** (mentioned above) and the **Comeragh Mountains and Nire Valley Drive**.

Ardmore - The Earliest Christian Site

Five miles or less to the east of Youghal Harbour, on the coast, a short, rocky and rather elevated promontory juts into the ocean. Maps call it Ram Head, but the real name is Ceann-a-Rama and popularly it is often styled Ardmore Head. Ardmore was where the first Christian settlement was founded in Ireland in 316 by St. Declan, before St. Patrick had arrived. It's one of the most attractive villages in the country, and a personal favorite, with another EU Blue Flag beach, and wonderful views out over the sea, especially from the Round Tower and Cathedral.

At Ardmore, there's a lovely cliff walk and the long-distance walking route, **St. Declan's Way**, starts here, taking you to Cashel in Co. Tipperary (58 miles/94 km). It's also on the signposted **Gaeltacht and Galltacht Scenic Drive**.

Sightseeing Inland

The **Blackwater Valley Drive** takes you from the coast near Youghal inland through the river valley to Lismore. This is one of my favorite areas in the country for a drive. The winding road is skirted by wooded hills and lush greenery. It's always quiet. Along the way there are some delightful villages. Among them is **Villierstown**, built in the 18th century by John Villiers, 1st Earl of Grandison, for workers in his linen weaving industry, which has beautiful stone-cut houses.

Lismore

Lismore is a Heritage Town, in a marvelous setting at the foot of the Knockmealdown Mountains. There's plenty to see, including the 17th-century **St. Carthage's Church of Ireland Cathedral**, and the 19th-century **St. Carthage's Catholic Church** with its Celtic Revival stained glass windows. There's also a **Heritage Centre**. The **Carnegie Library** in the town is one of many in the country funded by Andrew Carnegie, who made his fortune in the US.

In the local cemetery there's a mass grave, a sad reminder of the Great Famine, and nearby what was the workhouse where the starving poor sought refuge.

Lismore Castle, originally built in 1185, was acquired by Sir Walter Raleigh (who brought the potato to the island) and then sold to Richard Boyle, 1st Earl of Cork, in 1602. It now belongs to the Duke of Devonshire, whose family name is Cavendish, and is not open to the public, but you can visit its magnificent gardens. Fred Astaire's sister married one of the Cavendishs so he often visited, and he'd be seen relaxing in Madden's Bar in the town. The walled and woodland gardens are on two levels; one a rare example of an Elizabethan layout. Open April 30-October 15, 1:45-4:45 pm, from 11 am in July and August. ☎ (058) 54424; www.lismorecastle.com.

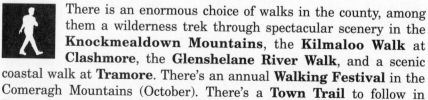

You can rent Lismore Castle, complete with butler and staff, for week-long stays in summer, and for shorter periods at other times of the year. There are 12 bedrooms, so it can sleep up to 23.

Near Lismore is a Gothic gateway called **Ballysaggartmore Towers**. It was part of one Arthur Kiely's grand plan for a house bigger than that of his brother and cost so much that the house itself was never built. **Cappoquin** and **Ballyduff** are other attractive towns in the Blackwater Valley.

On the **Comeragh Mountains** and **Nire Valley Drive** you can see standing stones, fulachta fiadh (cooking pits) and cairns around **Kilbrien** and Ogham stones near **Knockboy**. **Mothel Abbey**, built in the 13th century, is near Rathgormack.

■ Adventures on Foot

There is an enormous choice of walks in the county, among them a wilderness trek through spectacular scenery in the **Knockmealdown Mountains**, the **Kilmaloo Walk** at **Clashmore**, the **Glenshelane River Walk**, and a scenic coastal walk at **Tramore**. There's an annual **Walking Festival** in the Comeragh Mountains (October). There's a **Town Trail** to follow in **Dungarvan** and a number of walks start near the town.

The Southeast

The Brickey River and Kilnafarna Hills walk starts two miles (3.2 km) from Dungarvan on the Clashmore Road. The **Colligan Wood Walk** starts five miles (eight km) from Dungarvan on the road to Clonmel. The **Famine Walk** starts 2½ miles (four km) outside Dungarvan, turning left off the Cork Road and heading towards Ring.

Garden Walks

There are many historic gardens in the county, where you will enjoy a walk, among them the following.

Curraghmore Estate, Portlaw. The home of the Marquis of Waterford since the 12th century. The house isn't open, but there are pleasant walks on the grounds, which include a primeval forest, and there's a shell house and medieval bridge.

Dromana House and Gardens, Villierstown, is a 17th-century house that overlooks a wild and wonderful garden.

Cappoquin House and Gardens, is an 18th-century Georgian mansion with informal gardens overlooking the River Blackwater. Open April to July, Monday-Saturday, 9am-1 pm. Closed Sunday. ☎ (058) 54290.

Mount Congreve Gardens, Kilmeaden. A large garden, in woodlands, with a huge variety of plants. There's a walled garden with an elegant Georgian greenhouse. Open Monday-Friday, 9 am-5 pm. ☎ (051) 384-115.

Sion Hill House and Gardens, Ferry Bank, Waterford. This mature woodland garden overlooking the River Suir has many rare trees and shrubs. It's currently being restored to its 1870 plans. ☎ (051) 851-558.

Tourin House and Gardens, three miles (4.8 km) south of Cappoquin. The gardens on the 17th-century estate are very colorful, with displays of plants, shrubs and trees. Open February to June and September to November. ☎ (058) 54405.

■ Fishing

Cappoquin, **Ballyduff** and **Lismore** are the major angling centers for the River Blackwater, which attracts both game and coarse anglers. The **River Tar** and **River Nire** are both good game angling rivers, close to the villages of Ballymacarbry and Newcastle. If you're interested in fishing the **River Suir** you can stay in Waterford City, Portlaw, as well as in the Co. Tipperary towns of Carrick-on-Suir and Clonmel.

The lakes around Tramore hold stocks of brown trout, as do the rivers Colligan, Finisk and Brickey near Dungarvan.

Shore anglers will find a great variety of species near **Dunmore East**, **Cheekpoint** and **Passage East** in East Waterford, all along the coast-line, and near **Dungarvan** and **Ardmore** in West Waterford.

See pages 71-74 for details on angling in Ireland, regulations and best times to fish.

Useful Contacts

Contact **Rinnashark Sea Angling Club** for details on events. ☎ (051) 843-041.

Charter boats are available from Dungarvan and Dummore East. Contact the **The Sea Angling Centre**, 6 Mary Street, Dungarvan, ☎ (058) 46401; baumann@cablesurf.com.

Dunmore East Angling Charters offer wreck, reef and shark angling, rod hire and tackle sales, with free tuition. Boats are also available for diving and scenic trips.

This part of the Irish Coast saw very heavy U-boat action in the First World War, so around here there's one of the highest concentrations of shipwrecks anywhere off the Irish coast, many within an hour of Dunmore East. ☎ (051) 383-397; workboat@oceanfree.net.

■ Adventures on Horseback

Lake Tour Stables are in the Ballyscanlan Hills overlooking Tramore Bay, and run trail rides, including beach treks off-season. Beginners are welcome. ☎ (051) 381-958.

There are other equestrian options, including the following:

- **Colligan Equestrian Centre**, near Dungarvan.
- **Melody's Riding Stables**, Ballymacarbry.
- **Finisk Valley Riding Centre**, Kilmolash Bridge, near Cappoquin.
- **The Village Stables**, Woodland Heights, Clonea, is near Portlaw.

The **Kilotteran Equitation Centre** is off the N25, four miles (6.4 km) from Waterford City on the road to Dungarvan. It specializes in organizing residential riding vacations and arranging accommodation nearby. Among activities here are cross-country and farm rides. ☎ (051) 384-158.

Horseracing

The **Waterford and Tramore Racecourse**, Graun Hill, Tramore, was redeveloped in the late 90s, has three bars and two restaurants, and hosts a four-day racing festival in August. ☎ (051) 381-425; racing@tramore.ie; www.tramore-racecourse.com.

■ Golf

Visitors are welcome at all courses, but do phone in advance for times.

- **Dungarvan Golf Club**, ☎ (058) 43310.
- **Dunmore East Golf Club**, ☎ (051) 383-151.
- **Faithlegg Golf & Country Club**, ☎ (051) 382-241; golf@faithlegg.com.
- **Gold Coast Golf & Leisure**, Ballinacourt, Dungarvan, ☎ (058) 42416; clonea@indigo.ie.
- **Lismore** (nine-hole), ☎ (058) 54026.
- **Tramore**, ☎ (051) 386-170.
- **Waterford Castle Golf Club**, ☎ (051) 871-633.
- **Waterford Golf Club**, ☎ (05) 876-748.
- **Waterford Municipal Golf Course**, ☎ (051) 853-131.
- **West Waterford Golf & Country Club**, Dungarvan, ☎ (058) 43216.

■ Where to Stay

☆☆☆ **The Granville** in Waterford is run by the Cusack family. It's an historic hotel right on the Quay, with a friendly bar and pleasant restaurant. The hotel is a member of the Best Western group. It has boats available for fishing, and tours of the city can be arranged. $$$. ☎ (051) 305-555; fax 305-566; stay@granville-hotel.ie; www.granville-hotel.ie.

HOTEL PRICE CHART	
Price per person, per night, with two sharing, including breakfast.	
$	Under US $50
$$	US $50-$100
$$$	US $101-$175
$$$$	US $176-$200
$$$$$	Over US $200

☆☆ **The Haven Hotel**, Dunmore East, is owned and run by the Kelly family, and has a genuinely welcoming atmosphere. Its bedrooms all have private facilities, and there's a good choice of food in the bar and restaurant. Locally caught seafood and beef are a speciality. $$. ☎ (051) 383-150; holidays@thehavenhotel.com; www.thehavenhotel.com.

Waterford Castle Hotel and Golf Club is on a little island overlooking the Suir estuary three miles (4.8 km) from Waterford City. You get there by car ferry. The hotel in the 15th-century castle is luxurious, although unclassified under the star system, a combination of gracious living in times past with modern comfort. It has 19 individually decorated bedrooms and four poster suites. Its setting on its own 310 acre island is very attractive, with woodlands, and it has excellent facilities, including its own 18-hole parkland golf course. There are also a choice of activities, including a driving range, tennis, croquet, clay pigeon shooting, archery and scenic walks. $$$$$. Address: The Island, Ballinakill. ☎ (051) 878-203; fax 879-316; info@waterfordcastle.com; www.waterfordcastle.com.

Cottage Rentals

Gold Coast Holiday Cottages are in a lovely location on the edge of Dungarvan Bay, with an on-site leisure centre next to a golf course. There are 16 cottages, all with three bedrooms, open fire and central heating. ☎ (058) 45555; info@clonea.com; www.clonea.com.

Camping & RV Parks

☆☆☆☆ **Casey's Park** has direct access to the beach at Dungarvan, and is open from late April 26 to early September. ☎ (058) 41919.

☆☆☆ **Bayview** overlooks Dungarvan Bay and is open April to October. ☎ (058) 45345; bayview@cablesurf.com.

☆☆☆☆ Newtown Cove is just south of Tramore in a peaceful and sheltered setting, next to the sea. Open May to September. ☎ (051) 381-979; newtown_cove@iol.ie.

Hostels

Dungarvan Holiday Hostel, Youghal Road, is open all year, ☎ (058) 44340; www.dungarvanhostel.com.

Rathgormack Hiking Centre is open from March to the end of October. ☎ (051) 646-969.

■ Where to Eat

Dwyers Restaurant on Mary Street, Waterford, is in a former barracks, and its cuisine is Irish with a French flair. They serve meat, game, and vegetables locally sourced and fish bought at nightly auctions in nearby Dunmore East. Chef and owner Martin Dwyer spent years in France, and when you dine in his restaurant you're surrounded by his fine collection of glass displayed in beech dressers. ☎ (051) 877-478; fax 877-480; info@dwyersrestaurant. com; www.dwyersrestaurant.com.

Orpens Estuary Restaurant, a mile from Waterford City on the road to Dunmore East, just past the Regional Hospital, has lovely views of the estuary and the River Suir. It's popular with families, and caters for a range of tastes, serving traditional Sunday lunch, seafood, steaks, European dishes, vegetarian choices. ☎ (051) 873082; orphens@eircom.net; www.orpens.com.

Eamonn's Place, Main Street, Lismore, is in the middle of the historic West Waterford town. It's a welcoming and cosy pub with a fire to sit by when it's cold. They offer lunchtime specials, and also have a separate restaurant that opens in the evenings. On the menu are vegetable soups, liver and bacon casserole, chicken cordon bleu, sweet braised beef and baked cod, and desserts such as lemon meringue pie and treacle tart. Food served from 12:30-3 pm and 6-9 pm. ☎ (058) 54025.

White Horses Restaurant, in the seaside village of Ardmore, is run by sisters Geraldine and Christine Flavin. As you enter, you see a mouthwatering display of the cakes and desserts available, which can also be bought to take out. Savory dishes show imagination and expertise, with delicious choices such as seared scallops with asparagus, grilled chicken kebab with root ginger and mushrooms, or sirloin steak with brandy and pepper butter. Open May-September, Tuesday to Sunday, 11 am-11 pm; October-April, Friday, Saturday, Sunday, 11 am-11 pm; closed in January. ☎/fax (024) 94040.

McAlpin's Suir Inn is seven miles (11.3 km) from Waterford City in the picturesque village of Cheekpoint, and dates from the 17th century. It's been owned by the McAlpins since 1971 and has won awards for the quality of its food. It's also recommended by good food guides and is best known for its seafood. Lunch and dinner are served. ☎ (051) 382220; suirinn@mcalpins.com; www.mcalpins.com.

County Wexford

The county takes its name from the Norse Weissefiord, meaning "the ford of the flats" and when the Normans invaded Ireland in 1169 they landed here. Like its neighbor Waterford, Wexford has a varied and attractive landscape with mountains and a coastline, lots of pretty villages and historic sites. Its main rivers are the **Slaney** and **Barrow** and it's the home of the busy ferry port of **Rosslare**, serving the UK and Europe.

It's the best area in the country for bird-watching, with a **wildfowl reserve** and off-shore **bird sanctuary**. Its coastline and varied terrain offers plenty of activities, including hill walking, coastal walks, mountain biking and hang-gliding.

Wexford consistently enjoys more hours of sunshine per year than any other part of the country, so is known as "the Sunny South East." The Wexford average is 4.48 hours per day, while the country's average is 3.75 hours.

The area is closely associated with the 1798 Rebellion, including the battle of Vinegar Hill, and there are plaques marking other events associated with the unsuccessful uprising.

Wexford has a special attraction for many Americans, as the late US President John Kennedy's family came from near New Ross, and you can visit their home and the Arboretum dedicated to his memory.

The county capital and largest town is also called **Wexford**, and others include **Enniscorthy**, **Gorey**, **New Ross** and **Rosslare**.

■ Getting Here

Main roads are the N11 from Dublin (88 miles/141 km); N25 from Waterford and Cork (115 miles/185 km).

By rail, you can use **Iarnrod Éireann (Irish Rail) O'Hanrahan Station**, Wexford, ☎ (053) 22522; or **Rosslare Harbour Station**, ☎ (053) 33114.

The **Passage East Car Ferry** saves a long drive, with 130+ sailings daily between Ballyhack (South Wexford) and Passage East (Waterford). ☎ (051) 382 480/488; passageferry@eircom.net.

■ Tourist Information

Fáilte Ireland Tourist Information, Crescent Quay, Wexford. ☎ (053) 23111; fax 41743.

TRACING YOUR ANCESTORS

Yola Farmstead Folk Park, on the N25 to Rosslare Europort, houses the official **Genealogical Centre** for County Wexford.

The Southeast

Yola is also an 18th-century theme park with attractions including a forge, school house, working windmill, and a mini-farm. There's a craft shop and Granny's Kitchen serves good food. Open daily, May-October, 9:30 am-5 pm; March, April and November, Monday-Friday, 9:30 am-4:30 pm. ☎ (053) 32610; fax 32612; yolafst@iol.ie.

■ Wexford Town

This Heritage Town was founded by the Vikings and developed by the Normans. It stands at the mouth of the harbor bearing its name. It's very cosmopolitan, with narrow streets and a long attractive quayside, and is famous all over the world for its annual Opera Festival held in the autumn. For over 50 years the **Wexford International Opera Festival** has attracted top performers and audiences from all over the country and overseas. It presents wonderful productions of rarely performed works, and an art festival has built up around it. The festival takes place in October at the Theatre Royal, High Street, ☎ 053 22400, www. wexfordopera.com.

The town has entertainment year-round, including theater, light opera and exhibitions. It also has lots of craft shops and boutiques, plus plenty of coffee shops where you can take a break. Many of its pubs offer lunches and have traditional Irish music in the evenings. The **Wexford Arts Centre** is right in the center of town. It hosts exhibitions and other events, and has information about what's happening in the area. There's also a café where you can enjoy a snack. ☎ (053) 23764.

Allow time to explore the **Cornmarket**, **Bullring** and **Main Street**. There's an audio-visual presentation (hourly from 10 am to 4 pm) of the town's history at **Westgate**, one of its five medieval entrances.

■ Sightseeing

 The **Irish National Heritage Park** is just outside Wexford Town at Ferrycarrig. In its 35 acres it covers 900 years of history, with replicas of Irish buildings, showing how people lived from the Stone Age to the Norman period. It's a good introduction to the country's history in a pleasant setting. There's a self-guided route and tours available. The **Fulacht Fiadh Restaurant** overlooks the crannóg (a house on a lake) and there's a craft shop. Open all year. ☎ (053) 20733.

Johnstown Castle, Gardens and Irish Agricultural Museum is also near Wexford Town, off the N25 road to Rosslare. The castle isn't open, but you can take some pleasant walks in the gardens, woods and along the lake. You learn about rural life in the museum, which is in old farm buildings. The Environmental Protection Agency has an interactive exhibition here, open Monday to Friday, 9 am to 5 pm. ☎ (053) 60600; g.ruane@epa.ie; www.epa.ie. The Irish Agricultural Museum is open Monday-Friday, 9 am to 5 pm all year, and from April to October, 2-5 pm, Saturday and Sunday. ☎ (053) 42888.

The **Wexford Wildfowl Reserve** is off the R742 to Curracloe, on the opposite shore of the Harbor from Wexford Town and in an area called the Slobs, known all over the world for the wild geese that winter here. About 10,000 Greenland white-fronted geese, a third of the world population, visit. The Reserve is in the care of the State Heritage Service and partly owned by BirdWatch Ireland. There's a Visitor Centre with exhibitions, as well as bird-watching. Open daily all year, from 9 am to 6 pm, Easter to end September; 10 am to 5 pm the rest of the year. Admission free. ☎ (053) 23129.

Our Lady's Island, which can be seen from off the N25 between Rosslare and Kilmore Quay, has been a religious site since before Christianity arrived. Annual pilgrimages are made here, and there are the ruins of an Augustinian priory on the island. The area has been designated of international importance for its wildlife, and attracts bird-watchers. **Carnsore Point** nearby was to be the site of a nuclear plant in the 1970s, but so many people protested that it never went ahead.

New Ross

On the N25 between Wexford and Waterford is New Ross. Its setting is attractive on the joint estuary of the rivers Barrow and Nore, and it's hilly with narrow, medieval streets like those of Wexford. It's a welcoming town and there is so much to see in the surrounding area that you could spend at least a couple of days here. It's a busy port too, so you can watch boats coming and going, and there are two floating attractions on its quayside, the Galley Cruising Restaurant and the Dunbrody Emigrant Ship. **The Galley Cruising Restaurant** operates out of here from April to November (see under *Waterford*, page 218).

The Kennedy Connection

The **Dunbrody Emigrant Ship** is a full-scale reconstruction of the ship that took the late President Kennedy's grandfather to the USA. Your admission ticket is dated March 18, 1845, and you follow in the footsteps of Famine emigrants as they set sail with hope of a new life in North America. There's also a database on board of 2½ million passengers who traveled to the US in the period of 1845-1880 from all ports in Britain and Ireland. Open daily all year, April to September, 9 am-6 pm, October to March, noon to 5 pm. ☎ (051) 425-239; fax 425-240; jfktrust@iol.ie; www.dunbrody.com.

The **Kennedy Homestead**, visited by the late President Kennedy the summer before his assassination, is at Dunganstown, just east of New Ross, off the R733. It's well signposted along a very narrow and winding road (take care). JFK's great-grandfather was born here and its visitor center celebrates five generations of the family. Open May to September; rest of year by appointment. ☎ (051) 388-264.

The **John Fitzgerald Kennedy Arboretum**, run by the State Heritage Service, is seven miles (11 km) south of New Ross off the R733. It's a plant collection displayed on 623 acres (252 hectares) of the southern slopes of Slieve Coillte, with 4,500 different trees and shrubs from temperate areas of the world. There's an interesting visitor center. Open daily all year from 10 am; April and September, to 6:30 pm; May-August, to 8 pm; October-March, to 5 pm. ☎ (051) 88171.

South of New Ross is **Dunbrody Abbey**, Campile, between the R733 and R734, a 12th-century Cistercian monastery. There's a huge maze of 1,500 yews, a craft gallery and tea rooms. Open May, June, September, 10 am-6 pm; July-August, 10 am-7 pm. ☎ (051) 388-603.

Enniscorthy

Enniscorthy is northeast of New Ross on the N50, where it meets the N11 from Dublin. Standing on the River Slaney, it's dominated by a Norman castle, now the **County Museum**, which has displays of agricultural, military and domestic items. The town is very much associated with the 1798 Rebellion, and the home of the **National 1798 Visitor Centre**, which tells its story using the latest technology. Open daily. ☎ (054) 37596; 98com@iol.ie; www.1798centre.com.

Enniscorthy has been associated with the craft of pottery for centuries, and it's worth visiting **Carley's Bridge**, **Badger Hill** or **Kiltrea Pottery**.

Gorey

Gorey is a traditional market town, with many fine buildings. Outside the town is **Craanford Mills**, lovingly restored by the Lyons family, who give you a tour of the 17th-century water mill. It's a pleasant place to stop, with home-made food in the Kiln Loft. Look out for signs to it on the N11 Dublin – Rosslare Road at Camolin, near Gorey. Open Easter to September, 11 am to 6 pm, ☎ (055) 28124.

Courtown Harbour

This is the main town in North Wexford and is only an hour's drive from Dublin. Visitors can enjoy watersports, walks, golf and equestrian activities, as well as plenty of evening entertainment. See www.northwexford. com/courtown.htm for details. There are lots of sandy beaches in the area, including a Blue Flag one at Courtown.

Follow the R742 towards Wexford along the scenic coastline and you come to **Ballinskar**, where Spielberg filmed the opening scenes of *Saving Private Ryan*.

Rosslare

Rosslare, on the opposite side of Wexford Harbor, is not only an important port, it also has a Blue Flag beach and good facilities for watersports, golf courses, an equestrian center, and excellent hotels.

Sightseeing Routes

There are two signposted driving tours southwest of Wexford Town, the Bannow Drive and the Ring of Hook, both suitable for bikes and cars.

The **Bannow Drive** starts at the little market town of Wellington Bridge on the R733, named after the Duke who defeated Napoleon at Waterloo. It covers about 20 miles (32 km), taking in the deserted medieval town of **Clonmines**, the island of **Bannow** where the Normans first landed in 1169, gorgeous views of **Bannow Bay**, and **Cullenstown Strand**.

Nearby is **Kilmore Quay**, a quaint fishing village with a row of thatched cottages and a harbor and marina. You'll see lots of fishing boats tied up and can enjoy seafood in the local pubs. The **Guillemot Maritime Museum** is in the unusual setting of a converted lightship. ☎ (051) 561144.

Ring of Hook & Lighthouse Drive: The low lying Hook Peninsula forms the eastern boundary of Waterford Harbor and has a wonderfully wild landscape. The area is popular for wreck diving. On this coastal route you are surrounded by delightful coves and beaches, and pass many historic sites.

Near Saltmills you come to **Tintern Abbey**, founded about 1200 and named after the one in Wales (of the Wordsworth poem). You can see the remains of its nave, chancel, tower, chapel and cloister. There are lovely walks around it, and it has a tea room. Open mid-June to late September, 9:30 am-6 pm. ☎ (051) 562650.

The Southeast

Fethard is the main village on the Hook Peninsula, its castle is an L-shaped fortified hall house built in the 15th century. The **Hook Tourist Office** is on its main street, ☎ (051) 397-502; hookinfo@iol.ie.

The fishing village of **Duncannon** has a beach, and is popular for deep-sea angling.

Duncannon Military Fort is star-shaped and stands on a strategically important promontory in Waterford Harbour, built in 1588 because an attack by the Spanish Armada was expected. There's a **Maritime Museum** on site, a café and craft shop. Open April to October, the rest of the year by arrangement. ☎/fax (051) 389-454; duncannonfort@ireland.com; www.thehook-wexford.com/heritage.

The **Hook Head Lighthouse**, one of the oldest in the world, is open to visitors, with a café and craft shop. Open daily, March-October, 9:30 am to 5:30 pm. Phone for winter times. ☎ (051) 397-055; thehook@eircom.net; www.thehook-wexford.com.

■ Adventures on Foot

 There's an eight-mile nature walk called the **Three Rocks Trail**, which takes you across the Forth Mountain, west of Wexford Town. You walk through unspoiled countryside, with wonderful views, passing historical sites. It begins at the ruined **Ferrycarrig Castle** on an outcrop overlooking the Slaney and you pass the **Round Tower**, a memorial built in 1858 to Wexford soldiers who died in the Crimean War. Nearby is the **Heritage Park**. Other interesting sights include the ruins of **Carrig Church** and of the Norman castle at **Barntown**, as well as **St. Alphonsus Church**, designed by Pugin. South of Barntown is the ruin of a church used in 1798, and beside it the old one-room school.

The **Three Rocks Camp**, on the eastern end of Forth Mountain, is where the main body of rebels waited before one of the most important battles of the 1798 Rebellion. The rebels won, the troops left Wexford and on May 30 Ireland's first (short-lived) republic was declared.

From **Carrigfoyle Rock** there are panoramic views. Among the other sights you pass on the trail is **Jim Furlong's House**. It's a typical Forth Mountain dwelling, built of stone. He was a well-known fiddle player and people came here up to 50 years ago for music and dancing, so it was called a céilí house.

Céilí literally means "dance gathering" and the word is still used today to mean that – a place where people go to listen to Irish traditional music and dance to it.

There is a **cairn**, or prehistoric burial mound, near the Skeater Rock. This viewing point gives a commanding view of the South Wexford and East Waterford coastline and was used as a lookout in 1798.

SHIELBAGGAN OUTDOOR EDUCATION CENTRE

The Centre caters for individuals as well as groups. It's open from February to the end of November, offering day and over-night activities, such as canoeing, climbing, windsurfing, sailing, orienteering and snorkeling. ☎/fax (051) 389-550; shielbaggan@eircom.net.

■ Adventures on Water

Fishing Charters

Boat trips and charters are available from the pier at **Kilmore Quay**, ideal for angling, diving or sightseeing. Ask locally for tips about fishing and diving locations.

You can cruise around the bird sanctuary on the **Saltee Islands** from Kilmore Quay on board the *Saltee Princess*. Contact Declan Bates, ☎ (053) 29684. June is the best month, but cruises operate from March to October.

There are a number of other places where boats can be chartered, among them the following.

South East Charters, Duncannon, New Ross, for wreck and shark fishing, general sea angling, and relaxing cruises. Fishing rod rental available. ☎ (051) 389-242; hookinfo@iol.ie.

Sea Angling Centre, Kilmore Quay, ☎ (053) 45227.

The Enterprise, for deep-sea angling, reef and shark fishing off the southeast coast, plus scenic trips around Saltee Islands. ☎ (053) 29704.

Mermaid Angling, vessel *Wild Swan*, based at Ballyhack Harbor, available for fishing trips and river cruises, ☎ (051) 389-225; mermaidangling@hotmail.com.

Swimming

If you want to go swimming, but prefer indoor pools to beaches, there's lots of choice, including the following:

Aqua Club at Kelly's Resort Hotel, Rosslare Strand, with two pools. ☎ (053) 32114; kellyhot@iol.ie.

Forest Park Leisure Centre, Courtown Harbor, with a 25-meter pool. ☎ (055) 24849; auracourtown@eircom.net; www.seascapes-holidays.com/mall/seascapes.

Enniscorthy Swimming Pool Leisure Complex, ☎ (054) 34443.

Ferrybank Swimming Pool, Wexford, ☎ (053) 43274.

New Ross Kennedy Memorial Pool, ☎ (051) 421169.

■ Adventures on Horseback

Shelmalier Riding Stables, Forth Mountain, Trinity, Taghmon, is only five miles (eight km) from Wexford Town, in the middle of forests and mountains, and offers lessons and scenic rides. ☎ (053) 39251.

Curracloe House is eight miles (13 km) northeast of Wexford, close to Enniscorthy and to the Raven pine forest and sand dunes. Here you can enjoy a canter on the beach or a trek through the Sloblands. All levels of rider welcome. ☎ (053) 37582.

At the **Glenmoor Riding School**, Ramstown, Fethard-on-Sea, beach rides are very popular, and they cater specially for nervous or first-time riders. ☎ (051) 397-313.

A Riding Vacation

Based in a historic house on a working farm, the **Horetown Equestrian Centre**, Foulksmills, offers riding trips that cater for all, but especially those who have some riding experience. A fine cellar restaurant is part of its charm. ☎ (051) 565-786; iyoung@indigo.ie; www.horetownhouse.com.

■ Golf

Courtown Golf Club, Courtown Harbor, Gorey. ☎ (055) 25166.

Tara Glen Golf & Country Club, Ballymoney, Gorey. ☎ (055) 25413.

New Ross Golf Club. ☎ (051) 421433.

Rosslare Golf Club, Rosslare Strand. ☎ (053) 32113.

St. Helen's Bay Golf Club, Rosslare Harbor. ☎ (053) 33234.

Wexford Golf Club. ☎ (053) 45095.

Enniscorthy Golf Club. ☎ (054) 33191.

■ Spectator Sports

Both **Gaelic football** and **hurling** are popular in Wexford, and matches are held most weekends in villages and towns. There's **greyhound racing** at the **Show Grounds Enniscorthy**, every Monday and Thursday from 8 pm. ☎ (054) 33172.

For horseracing, **Wexford Racecourse** is in Bettyville, overlooking the harbor. ☎ (053) 42307.

■ Where to Stay

☆☆☆☆ **Kellys Resort Hotel**, Rosslare, is popular all year round with the Irish, as it has excellent indoor and outdoor facilities and also runs a program of short courses outside the main tourist season on topics as diverse as art appreciation, gardening, and golf. Since 1895 it has welcomed guests, and today the fourth successive generation of Kellys are in charge. It has a very attractive setting, overlooking a sandy

HOTEL PRICE CHART	
Price per person, per night, with two sharing, including breakfast.	
$	Under US $50
$$	US $50-$100
$$$	US $101-$175
$$$$	US $176-$200
$$$$$	Over US $200

beach. Facilities include: two indoor/outdoor tennis courts, a squash court, indoor golf practice area, table tennis, snooker, badminton, bowls, jogging track, Aqua Club with two pools, sauna, steam room, Jacuzzi, outdoor Canadian hot tub, and a fully equipped gym. You can also rent bikes.

It also has an award-winning restaurant and a more casual bar/bistro called **La Marine**. Both have extensive menus that use the finest local produce – including fresh fish from Kilmore Quay, Wexford beef and the hotel's own lamb. $$. ☎ (053) 32114; fax 32222; kellyhot@iol.ie; www. kellys.ie.

☆☆☆ **The Creacon Lodge Hotel**, Creacon, New Ross, is in a home dating from the 1840s and care has been taken to retain its country house atmosphere. All bedrooms are individually decorated, and guests can relax in the beautiful gardens or beside the log fires. Its restaurant serves interesting food prepared with local produce. $$. ☎ (051) 421-897; fax 422-560; info@creaconlodge.com; www.creaconlodge.com.

☆☆☆ **The Cedar Lodge Hotel and Restaurant**, New Ross, is an elegant family-run hotel close to interesting and historic sites, including the John F. Kennedy Memorial Park, the Irish National Heritage Park,

The Southeast

Dunbrody Abbey, Johnstown Castle Gardens and Wexford Wildfowl Reserve. Its restaurant is noted for freshly prepared local produce, and is recommended by the leading good food guides. $$. ☎ (051) 428-386; fax 428-222; cedarlodge@eircom.ie; www.prideofeirehotels.com.

☆☆☆☆ **The Marlfield House Hotel**, Gorey, preserves all the traditions of the Irish country house, and is owned and run by Mary and Ray Bowe, who bought the house from the Earl of Courtown in 1977. It's an elegant Regency-style mansion full of antiques, paintings and period furniture, always full of flowers from its gardens, with blazing fires when the weather is cold. There's a choice of standard and state bedrooms. Marlfield is surrounded by 35 acres (14 hectares) of gardens and woodlands, has a tennis court, and is only minutes away from sandy beaches. Its restaurant has won many awards for its cuisine, prepared from its own vegetables and local produce. $$$$, with three-, five- and seven-day packages, including dinner. ☎ (055) 21124; fax 21572; info@ marlfieldhouse.ie; www.marlfieldhouse.com.

☆☆☆☆ **The Dunbrody House Hotel and Restaurant** is at Arthurstown, on the R733 at Arthurstown and 15 minutes by car from Waterford City on the Hook Peninsula. It's a lovely Georgian house dating from the 1830s, set in 200 acres (88 hectares) of parkland, and belongs to the prestigious Ireland's Blue Book. There are live-in courses available at the Dunbrody Cookery School. Breakfast is served until noon, and the restaurant, open for dinner to non-residents, has won awards and recommendations. $$$. ☎ (051) 389-600; fax 389-601; dunbrody@indigo.ie; www.dunbrodyhouse.com.

Guesthouses

Ballinkeele House, Ballymurn, Enniscorthy, is surrounded by 350 acres of parkland with a number of lakes and ponds and plenty of mature trees. It was built in 1840 as the home of the Maher family, whose descendants still live here, surrounded by the original furniture. There are only five bedrooms, so staying here is very special. Margaret Maher is a member of Euro Toques, which means she is a very accomplished cook, so dining here is memorable. Fishing, riding, and golf are all available locally, as well as beaches, including Curracloe. $$. ☎ (053) 38105; info@ ballinkeele.com; www.ballinkeele.com.

Richmond House, on the outskirts of Cappoquin, was originally built in 1704, and has now been refurbished as a restaurant with rooms available. Each of the 10 bedrooms has period furniture, and combines Georgian elegance with modern comforts. The food is outstanding, with all the ingredients local. $$, with special weekend rates that include dinner. ☎ (058) 54278; www.amireland.com/richmond.

Cottage Rentals

 The **Self Catering Ireland** organization is based in Rosslare and has a number of properties in the county. ☎ (053) 33999; info@selfcatering-ireland.com; www.selfcatering-ireland.com.

Irish Cottage Holiday Homes has three groups of houses in the county. ☎ (01) 475-7596; info@irishcottageholidays.com; www.irishcottageholidays.com.

Hostels

Macmurrough Farm Hostel, New Ross, open March to the end of November. ☎ (051) 421-383; hostel@macmurrough.com.

Kirwan House, Mary Street, Wexford Town, open February to mid-December. ☎ (053) 21208.

The **Irish Youth Hostel Association** has two hostels, at Rosslare and Arthurstown. See their website at www.irelandyha.org.

Camping & RV Parks

 ☆☆☆ **Ocean Island Park**, Fethard-on-Sea, New Ross, open Easter to the end of September, is in a quiet setting within easy walking distance of sandy beaches. Some facilities only open July and August. ☎ (051) 397-148.

☆☆☆☆ **Morriscastle Strand Park**, Kilmuckbridge, is on the coast, south of Gorey and north of Wexford, with excellent facilities, including tennis courts on site. It does not accept tents. Open May to the end of September. ☎ (053) 30124; camacmorriscastle@eircom.net.

☆☆ **St. Margaret's Beach Park**, Our Lady's Island, Rosslare. It's in a rural area near a safe beach and is open mid-March to mid-October. ☎/fax (053) 31169; stmarg@indigo.ie.

☆☆☆☆ **The Trading Post** is at Ballaghkeen, 10 minutes from Wexford, and open April to end September. Facilities include campers' kitchen, TV room, laundry, plus a delicatessen and shop in its service station. ☎ (053) 27368; thetradingpost@eircom.net.

■ Where to Eat

 The Farmer's Kitchen, on the Rosslare Road a couple of miles outside Wexford, serves good value meals, with a choice of bar menu and à la carte restaurant. ☎ (053) 43295.

A memorable place to dine in the evening is at the **Fulacht Fiádh Restaurant**, which is in the Irish National Heritage Park, just outside Wexford. Full à la carte and early bird menu available. ☎ (053) 20733.

La Marine Bar at Kelly's Resort Hotel, Rosslare, is open for lunch and dinner, serving French and European dishes, and has a relaxing atmosphere. ☎ (053) 32114.

County Tipperary

Tipperary is the largest inland county in the Republic and lies in one of the most fertile parts of the island, its land mainly devoted to dairy farming. Its central limestone plain is called the **Golden Vale**, and is surrounded by mountain ranges, the **Galtees** and the **Knockmealdowns** to the south, the **Silvermines** and **Arra Mountains** on the west, with **Devil's Bit Mountain** in the north and the **Slieveardagh Hills** and Slievenamon in the southeast. Its main rivers include the Shannon, Little Brosna, Nenagh, Nore, Suir and Moyle, with its main lake Lough Derg on the Shannon.

The **Rock of Cashel** is the county's most prominent historical site, dominating the landscape from its rocky outcrop 200 feet above the surrounding countryside. It is best appreciated if first seen by approaching it from the north on the road from Dublin, ideally at sunset, a sight you will not forget. The Rock was the center of religious and secular life in Munster from the end of the 4th century until medieval times, and among its impressive buildings is Cormac's Chapel, with its unique carvings and arches.

The Kings of Munster ruled from here until Brian Boru came to power, and in 1101 it was handed over to the church. When the Normans arrived, the county was given to the Butlers.

The Cromwellian Plantation (see page 14) was disastrous for the natives here, as everywhere else, and led to them supporting movements like the Whiteboys and later the Fenians – so it became known as "Turbulent Tipperary."

It's the only Irish county to be divided into two ridings for administrative purposes (the word "riding" is derived from Old English *thriding*, meaning "third part"), with **Nenagh** the capital of the North Riding and **Clonmel**, also its largest town, the capital of the South Riding. That dates back to the mid-19th century, when the county had one of the biggest populations. Its other main towns include **Cahir**, **Roscrea** and **Tipperary Town**.

Tipperary offers tranquil, unspoiled countryside and fresh clean waters, perfect for walking and fishing, with the mountains and valleys providing spectacular drives and walks. Lough Derg is a lovely location for cruising trips and watersports.

It's an important equestrian area, with racecourses at Thurles, Clonmel and Tipperary Town. There are many racing stables and studs in the county, including the world-famous **Coolmore Stud** in Fethard, and **Ballydoyle Stables** at Rosegreen.

The county is known the world over for the song from World War I that begins "It's a long way to Tipperary...."

■ Getting Here

Clonmel is served by major roads N24-N76-N77-N78-N9-N7 from Dublin (102 miles/164 km); N24-N8-N25 from Cork (60 miles/97 km).

There are **railway stations** at **Carrick-on-Suir, Clonmel, Cahir, Tipperary**, on the Waterford line. Connection can be made at **Limerick Junction**, close to Tipperary Town, to the main Dublin-Cork line. There are stations on that line at **Thurles** and **Templemore**.

It is also well served by **Bus Éireann**, the national bus company.

■ Tourist Information

Two regional tourism organizations market Co. Tipperary – East Coast and Midlands and Shannon Development. Further Information

- www.ecoast-midlands.travel.ie.
- www.shannon-dev.ie/tourism/holidays.
- www.heritageireland.ie.
- www.heritagetowns.com.

There are tourist information offices at:

Cahir, on Castle Street.

Cashel, in the Town Hall, Main Street, with information also available in the Brú Ború Heritage Centre, below the Rock.

Clonmel, at the Community Office, Nelson Street.

Tipperary Town, James Street.

The Southeast

■ Sightseeing

Nenagh

Nenagh is near the shores of Lough Derg, and overlooking its center, almost intact, is the **castle of the de Butlers of Ormond**. By the middle of the 19th century, Nenagh had become a busy market town with a barracks. Today, it prospers due to multinational companies locating around here. As in other rural Irish towns, many of its shopfronts are decorated in a traditional and colorful way.

Clonmel

Clonmel is in the southeastern corner of the county, on the banks of the Suir. Its Irish name, "Cluain Meala," is evocative, meaning "pasture of honey." Vikings may have sailed up the Suir and settled here. It was walled by the Normans in the 14th century and protected by Maurice Fitzgerald, First Earl of Desmond, who brought the Dominicans and Franciscans to the town. In 1650 it was attacked by Cromwell and surrendered.

By the 19th century Clonmel had become a busy market town, milling cereals, with a cotton factory and its own army barracks. A unique development here was Charles Bianconi's national mail coach system, which started from Hearn's Hotel in 1815.

Today, Clonmel is a prosperous and attractive town. Among its sights are the **old town walls**, **Old St. Mary's Church**, the **Abbey of St. Francis**, and the **West Gate** (built in 1831 on the site of the original). It's also well worth visiting the **Tipperary South Riding Museum**, where you can see artifacts associated with local events and characters, including Bianconi.

Thurles

Thurles, in the middle of this huge county, is divided in two by the River Suir. It was founded by the Norman Butlers, and you can still see remains of their **fortresses**, with their 15th-century **tower house** guarding the bridge. On the square is the former home of Lady Thurles, mother of the First Duke of Ormond.

Hayes Hotel is where the GAA (Gaelic Athletic Association) was founded (see page 247, *Where to Stay*) and there's a statue of its first patron, Archbishop Croke (Croke Park in Dublin is named after him). **St. Mary's Church of Ireland** now houses the **Famine Museum**, open on Sundays and Bank Holidays from 2-6 pm or by appointment. Contact George Willoughby. ☎ (0504) 21133.

One of the most picturesque Christian monuments in Ireland, with a charming setting on the bank of the River Suir about 4½ miles south of Thurles, is **Holycross Abbey**. It dates from the early 12th century and took its name from a portion of the true cross, enshrined here. It was restored in the 1970s and is an interesting place to visit, whether you're religious or not. There are a variety of fascinating windows, mural paintings and many fine carvings to see here.

Tipperary Town

Tipperary is one of Ireland's Heritage Towns, an Anglo-Norman settlement that lies in the middle of the Golden Vale, with land the envy of farmers in other parts of the country. It was the scene of many violent incidents during the Land Wars of the 1880s. It has some attractive old buildings and is very much a traditional Irish town. It's close to Co. Limerick in the southwestern corner of the county, and south of it are the Slievenamuck and Galtee Mountains, and the Glen of Aherlow, perfect for hiking and sightseeing.

Cahir

Cahir is by-passed by one of the Republic's busiest roads, the N8, and is a pleasure to visit. **Cahir Castle** dominates it, and is open for visits.

Morrissey's Pub, on the street near the castle, has live music in the evenings. During the season, the **Tourist Office** is open and there's always lots of parking behind it on the bank of the River Suir. Cahir is a lovely base for a vacation. It has a good deal of charm, with some traditional shopfronts and a wide main square on two levels. At one time Protestants and Catholics shared a church with just a curtain between them, very unusual, but a sign of something special about its people.

You can follow a **heritage trail** around the town, and there's also a delightful riverside walk through **Inch Field** beside Cahir Castle. From here, you can walk to **Swiss Cottage**, just over a mile away on the Clonmel Road. It really is one of the most delightful places to visit, a thatched cottage orné, which looks like something from a fairytale. It was

The Southeast

built in the early 1800s as a summerhouse for the Earl of Glengall and has a spiral staircase and dear little rooms. Open from March-November.

Roscrea

Roscrea is close to Tipperary's border with Offaly and Laois. It's one of the country's Heritage Towns, and no wonder. It has some of the finest examples of Irish architecture, spanning 600 years, and all within a small area. There's a **round tower**, **high cross**, **St. Cronan's Church** with its Romanesque façade, the recently restored **Norman Castle**, plus the 18th-century **Damer House**, which is now the heritage center. You can visit the castle, which is furnished and houses exhibitions. So does Damer House. They are open April-October, 10 am to 6 pm; guided tours on request. ☎ (0505) 21850; fax 21904.

The picturesque and interesting **Leap Castle**, which is said to be the most haunted castle in the country, is four miles (6.4 km) north of Roscrea. It can be visited and the Ryan family who live there also host medieval banquets. It was originally the home of the fierce O'Carroll clan. ☎ (0509) 31115.

South of Roscrea on the N62 is **Templemore**. You'll notice its very wide street, attractive in places, but unfortunately some of the buildings are ugly examples of '60s architecture. The national training center for the Republic's police force (An Garda Siochana – literally, "the guardians of the peace") dominates the town. The original barracks was built in 1810 to take 1,000 men, and around it more recent buildings have been added.

Continuing south, turn to the left off the N62 and you come to the delightful little quiet village of **Loughmore**, which is popular for fishing.

County-Wide

There are a number of signposted drives that include the Glen of Aherlow, the Knockmealdown Mountains, the Premier Drive, the Slievenamon, The Bianconi Drive, the Suir, and The Vee, Ballyporeen, Clogheen Drive and Cahir Drive. Look out for the distinctive signs, brown with white lettering.

An easy way of exploring the county is by driving or cycling around, and there's a very useful little guidebook with other suggested routes, written by Donal and Nancy Murphy. It is published by the tourism bodies for the county and is well worth its €3 price. All the routes are circular, so you can start them anywhere. Do remember to check your gas before heading off, if you're driving, and don't almost get stranded as I did. Away from the main roads there aren't a lot of gas stations!

Tour 1 (86 miles/138 km) takes in the western part of the county and includes the signposted Lough Derg Drive. You could start it in Nenagh or Roscrea. It passes through pretty villages, among them Terryglass and its quay, Riverstown, just south of Birr in neighboring Offaly, Kilgarvan Quay, and Borrisokane, where there's a ring fort. You travel through parkland, bog and pasture, with lovely views of the Lough, and come across a variety of historic ruins and monastic remains.

Tour 2 (75 miles/121 km) is south of Nenagh, and journeys along the Lough Derg Drive part of the way. En route is Ballina, the pretty village twinned with Killaloe on the other side of the Lough. You travel up and down hills, on delightful winding roads, which again give panoramic views of the Shannon's largest lake.

Tour 3 (70 miles/113 km) is around Thurles, and includes the memorably named hamlet of Horse and Jockey, a landmark on the Cork-Dublin main road, where there's a pub/restaurant/craft shop of the same name, a good place to stop for refreshments, very moderately priced. The drive takes in part of the wonderful Golden Vale, with an optional diversion to Devil's Bit Mountain.

Tour 4 is in two parts, which, combined, take in two of the best-known and most interesting sites, The Rock of Cashel and Holycross, and the towns of Tipperary, Cashel and Thurles, plus attractive villages like Thomastown and Cappawhite.

Tour 5 (73 miles/118 km) could be started at Cashel or Cahir. Its highlights include the planned estate village of Marlfield, Cahir, Rockwell, the Vee Gap, which climbs into the Knockmealdown Mountains and on into Co. Waterford, where there are amazing views from the summit, if the weather is good.

The Vee is even more spectacular if approached from the Waterford side, where you pass the remote Mount Melleray monastery as you drive or cycle up to it from Cappoquin.

Tour 6 (60 miles/97 km) takes you around Tipperary Town to Bansha, through the Glen of Aherlow, to Galbally. Along the way you can stop at a number of places, including the Mitchelstown Caves, and Ballyporeen, where the grandfather of former US President Ronald Reagan lived, and which he visited.

Tour 7 (82 miles/132 km) goes through Clonmel, Carrick-on-Suir and Fethard, and is dominated by the River Suir, the Comeragh Mountains, the Slieveardagh Hills and their surrounding bogland. You circle Slievenamon ("the women's hill").

The Southeast

■ Adventures on Foot

In addition to the walks in and around Cahir, detailed above, there's a town trail of **Cashel**, which is a pleasant town, once you get away from its main street, which is choked with heavy traffic. At **Dundrum**, there are forest walks and there's another trail to follow nearby at **Marl Lake**.

There are heritage trails to follow in **Clonmel** and in the medieval walled village of **Fethard**; there's a walk through the **Wilderness Gorge** at Clonmel; plus others at **Kilcash**, including one of **Slievenamon**.

Forest Parks

There are a number of forest parks, including **Bansha Wood**, on the Cahir-Tipperary road (N24); **Glengarra Wood**, on the N8, south of Cahir; and **Killballyboy**, on the Clogheen to Lismore R668, which was a famine relief road.

Long-Distance Walks

The **East Munster Waymarked Way** (43 miles/69 km) stretches from Carrick-on-Suir to Clogheen. Its first section from Carrick-on-Suir to Clonmel is on an old towpath by the River Suir, and runs through Kilsheelan Wood, with scenic views. Between Clonmel and Clogheen, it climbs and goes through the picturesque village of Newcastle and along the forested slopes of the Comeragh and Knockmealdown Mountains through the Vee Gap. It links with the Wicklow, South Leinster and Blackwater Ways, to form a waymarked route all the way from Dublin to Killarney.

Part of the **Pilgrim Way**, which starts at Ardmore, Co. Waterford, and goes all the way to Clonmacnoise, passes through the county, and is signposted.

■ Adventures on Water

Shannon Sailing, New Harbor, Dromineer, Nenagh, runs courses in windsurfing, dinghy and big boat sailing. It also operates sailing yachts from Foynes on the Shannon Estuary. ☎ (067) 24295.

Remember to look under Killaloe, Co. Clare, pages 310 and 313, for details of facilities on the other side of the bridge from Ballina, Tipperary.

Fishing

Two of the Regional Fishery organizations look after Tipperary – the Southern Region and the Shannon Region. The **Southern Region** is based in Clonmel, ☎ (052) 80055, srfb@srfb.ie. The **Shannon** is in Limerick, ☎ (061) 300-238, and its website is excellent – www.shannon-fishery-board.com.

Kavanaghs Sports Shop, Upper O'Connell Street, Clonmel has permits for the local area of the River Suir. ☎ (052) 21279.

See pages 71-74 for details on angling in Ireland, regulations and best times to fish.

Dromineer, five miles (eight km) from Nenagh on the eastern shore of Lough Derg, is one of the main angling centers in the county. It's considered a good base both for pike and coarse fish, mainly bream.

For more information, contact the **Angling Section of the Shannon Regional Board**, ☎ (0509) 21777; (Brian McManus at) info@shannon-fishery-board.ie.

Waterside Cottages and Angling Centre on Dromineer Bay, has everything needed for fishing, including boat rental. There are 11 cottages, rustic style, and a tennis court on site. ☎ (067) 24432; info@watersidecottages.ie; www.watersidecottages.com.

☆☆☆☆ **Tomona Lodge**, Ballycommon, Nenagh, sleeps eight, on the harbor, with a day cruiser available for rent. ☎ (067) 24376; valentinecope@eircom.net.

Ashley Park House, near Nenagh, is an 18th-century country house offering B&B accommodations. Set on 76 acres of beech woodland and formal gardens, the historic house is on the shores of Lough Ourna, a private trout fishing lake and bird sanctuary. Guests have private access to the lake, with boats provided. ☎ (067) 38223; margaret@ashleypark.com; www.ashleypark.com.

■ Adventures on Horseback

Ballyporeen Stables is in lovely countryside near the Galtee Mountains, and welcomes riders at all levels. ☎ (052) 67617.

Stay at the **Kilcooley Abbey Country and Equestrian Centre**, Thurles, which has 950 acres of woodland and a 10-acre lake. ☎ (056) 883-4222; kilcooly@indigo.ie.

Homeleigh Farm House in the Glen of Aherlow has horseback riding and pony trekking on the farm and along forest trails. ☎ (062) 56228.

The Hyland Family, owners of the **Cahir Equestrian Centre**, will organize a riding trip for you, where you can trek through Cahir Park and enjoy riding along the banks of the River Suir. They also organize fishing trips on the river, or golf breaks, so if your party has different interests, this could be ideal. The Centre is on the Ardfinnan Road, Cahir, and has a café and a garden. ☎/fax (062) 41426.

Racecourses

Tipperary Racecourse. Limerick Junction, near Tipperary Town. ☎ (062) 51357; peterroe@indigo.ie; www.tipperaryraces.ie.

Thurles Racecourse. ☎ (0504) 22253; thurles@iol.ie.

Clonmel Racecourse. ☎ (052) 22611.

■ Golf

The **Tipperary Golf Club** has the lovely backdrop of the Galtee Mountains, and is just outside the town on the road to the Glen of Aherlow. ☎ (062) 51119.

Ballykisteen Golf and Country Club, Monard. ☎ (052) 51439.

Clonmel Golf Club, Lyreanearla, Mountain Road. ☎ (052) 21138.

County Tipperary Golf & Country Club, Dundrum House Hotel, Dundrum, Cashel. ☎ (062) 71116.

Nenagh Golf Club. ☎ (067) 31476.

Roscrea Golf Club. ☎ (0505) 21130.

Templemore Golf Club. ☎ (0504) 31400.

Thurles Golf Club. ☎ (0504) 21983.

Cahir Park Golf Club. ☎ (052) 41474.

■ Where to Stay

☆☆☆☆ **The Cashel Palace Hotel** is in the center of Cashel, hidden away from the busy main street behind attractive entrance gates. It's set in 28 acres of gardens, which are older than the house itself, including two Mulberry trees planted in 1702 to mark the coronation of Queen Anne in England. There's a private path leading from the hotel directly to the Rock of Cashel, called the Bishop's Walk after Archbishop Bolton, whose palace this was. The hotel has 23 bedrooms, individually furnished, with 10 others in the former

Coach House, called the Mews, and all of them are beautiful. Some have views of the Rock of Cashel.

It's ideal for those interested in fishing, as the hotel owns a five-mile (eight-km) stretch of the River Suir, and in season can arrange hunting and shooting, there are also several golf courses to choose from within driving distance.

Light meals are available in **The Guinness Bar** from noon to 8 pm, Monday to Thursday, and until 6 pm from

HOTEL PRICE CHART	
Price per person, per night, with two sharing, including breakfast.	
$	Under US $50
$$	US $50-$100
$$$	US $101-$175
$$$$	US $176-$200
$$$$$	Over US $200

Friday to Sunday. **The Bishop's Buttery Restaurant** (see below under *Where to Eat*) has vaulted ceilings and a huge open fireplace. $$$$ in main house; $$$ in Mews. ☎ (062) 62707; fax 61521; reception@cashel-palace.ie; www.cashel-palace.ie.

☆☆☆ **Grants Hotel** is on Castle Street in the center of Roscrea and was recently refurbished. It has 25 pleasantly furnished rooms and a choice of where to eat. Its **Kitty's Tavern** serves lunch and evening meals and its **Lemon Tree Restaurant** is open for lunch from 12:30-2:30 and for dinner from 6:30-9:30 pm. $$. ☎ (0505) 23300; fax 23209; grantshotel@eircom.net; www.grantshotel.com.

☆☆☆ **Dundrum House Hotel Golf and Leisure Club** is an elegant manor, built in 1730, which has been transformed into a beautiful and luxurious hotel, with its own 18-hole golf course and award-winning health and leisure club. There are 86 bedrooms, including six luxury family apartments and two penthouse suites. Guests can eat in the dining room or in the **Venue Grillroom**, renowned for its excellent food. It's also known for the peaceful and relaxing atmosphere. $$$. ☎ (062) 71116; www.dundrumhousehotel.com.

☆☆ **The Glen Hotel** is very different – a small family-run hotel in a beautiful location that's comfortable, and very good value. It's in the Glen of Aherlow, just south of Tipperary Town, and between Galbally and Bansha. It has 24 rooms and a bar that's popular with locals. It hosts weddings and other functions, so ask for a room at the back, unless you want to join in the celebrations. The atmosphere is welcoming, with a real fire in the little sitting area near the dining room. Riding, golf, fishing, and bike rental available nearby. $. ☎ (062) 56146.

☆☆ **Hayes Hotel**, Thurles, was founded as The Star & Garter in the 18th century, but is famous as the place where, on November 1, 1884, a group of men met and founded the GAA – the Gaelic Athletic Association. It's right in the middle of Thurles, on Liberty Square. The Hayes is very popular with people today, whether or not they're interested in sport, and

The Southeast

is a good place for a drink, meal, and perhaps a chat. $$. ☎ (0504) 22122; fax 24516; info@hayeshotel.com; www.hayeshotel.com.

Camping & RV Parks

The Glen of Aherlow Caravan and Camping Park is right in the middle of the Glen, between the Galtees and the Slievenamuck Hills. Open all year. This is a new park and is as yet unclassified under the star system. ☎ (062) 56555; rdrew@ eircom.net; www.tipperarycamping.com.

☆☆☆☆ **Ballinacourty House Park**, also in Glen of Aherlow, is open mid-April to the end of September. The park is set in the grounds if an 18th-century stable. Its facilities include a restaurant, but guests must make reservations. ☎ (062) 56000; info@ballinacourtyhse.com; www. ballinacourtyhse.com.

☆☆☆ **The Apple Park**, Moorstown, is beside the N24 close to Cahir. It's open from May to the end of September. The park is on a fruit farm, hence its name, and guests can try some of the fruit or the farm-pressed apple juice. Facilities include a tennis court, with rackets available free. ☎ (052) 41459; traas@theapplefarm.com; www.theapplefarm.com.

☆☆☆ **Carrick-on-Suir Park**, Kilkenny Road, is open from March to the end of October. This is in a lovely rural setting, a five-minute walk from town with views of the mountains. Fishing is available free, and mobile homes are available for rent on site. ☎ (051) 640461; coscamping@ eircom.net; www.coscamping.com.

☆☆☆ **Parsons Green**, Clogheen, stays open all year. There's a farm museum and coffee shop. Guests can walk in its gardens or take a ride in the pony cart or try a boat on the river. ☎ (052) 65290; kathleennoonan@ oceanfree.net; www.clogheen.com.

☆ **Power's the Pot**, Harney's Cross, Clonmel, on the R678 Clonmel-to-Rathgormack road. The park opens from May to the end of September. It's on the side of the Comeragh Mountains, so is ideal for walkers. There's a wine bar on site with a turf fire and facilities include free hot showers. ☎ (052) 23085; powersthepot@eircom.net.

☆☆☆ **Streamstown** is just off the N7 to Nenagh, outside Roscrea. It's on a dairy farm and offers free hot showers, and facilities include a TV room and pool table. It's open from mid-April to the end of October. ☎ (0505) 21519; streamstowncaravanpark@eircom.net.

Hostels

Cashel Holiday Hostel, John Street, is open all year. ☎ (062) 62330; info@cashelhostel.com; www.cashelhostel.com.

O'Briens Holiday Lodge, Dundrum Road, Cashel, is open all year, ☎ (062) 61003.

Lisakyle Hostel, Cahir, is open from March to the end of October. ☎ (052) 41963.

Lough Derg House Hostel, Nenagh, stays open all year. ☎ (067) 24958.

■ Where to Eat

 ☆☆☆☆ **Cashel Palace** (see above under *Where to Stay*) serves the finest of modern Irish cuisine in its Bishop's Buttery Restaurant, using herbs from the hotel's own garden and the best local ingredients. It's open for lunch from 12:30 to 2:30 pm, Monday to Saturday, and for dinner from 6-9:30, Sunday to Friday, and until 10 pm on Saturdays. There's a resident pianist to entertain diners on Friday and Saturday nights. Note that booking is advised for Sunday lunch, served in the Palace Suite. ☎ (062) 62707; reception@ cashel-palace.ie; www.cashel-palace.ie.

The Crock of Gold Café, across the road from Cahir Castle, serves great food at very low prices, and downstairs it also has a gift and card shop. Do try their Irish stew. It's a good place to stop if exploring the area, and there's plenty of parking available.

Knocklofty Restaurant is in the west wing of Knocklofty Country House Hotel, four miles (6.4 km) from Clonmel on the road to Ardfinnan. Its menu includes Irish and French specialties and seasonal dishes such as salmon, trout, lobster and game. The award-winning restaurant looks out over the River Suir and the Comeragh and Knockmealdown Mountains. It's open every day for lunch from 12:30-2:30 and for dinner, Monday-Saturday, 7 to 9:30, Sunday until 8:30. ☎ (052) 38222; fax 38300.

The Derg Room Restaurant is in The Lakeside Hotel, Ballina, and a very pleasant choice for a meal. It has an interesting menu and is open from noon-2 pm for lunch and from 7-9 pm for dinner. ☎ (061) 376122.

Ross Castle, Killarney, Co. Kerry (Cork-Kerry Tourism)

Cork & Kerry

Cork is the largest county in Ireland, covering roughly 3,000 square miles (7,800 square km), and within its borders there is a great variety of landscape, from the inlets and beaches of its western coast to the wooded valleys of the River Blackwater in the northeast.

Kerry, which borders Cork, also has a beautiful coastline. Its scenery is more rugged, especially in the south, around the Dingle Peninsula and the Ring of Kerry. The county is home to Ireland's highest mountain, Carrauntoohill (1,040 feet/317 m). North Kerry is more low-lying, and has its own beauty.

Cork and Kerry are marketed together by Fáilte Ireland, through Cork-Kerry Tourism, and share a lot of characteristics – both have long and indented coastlines and are full of historical sites worth visiting, from ruined castles and abbeys to much earlier signs of human settlement. More than 80 prehistoric stone circles dot the landscape; their original use is unclear, but they were probably used in rituals. Many Ogham stones are also found in this part of the country. Ogham was an early form of writing, dating from about 300 AD, which uses lines and strokes cut into stone. It's worth getting an Ordnance Survey map if travelling around, so you can find these reminders of history, as only some are signposted.

With their coastline of roughly 1,100 miles (1,800 km), counties Cork and Kerry are a paradise for anyone interested in spending time near the sea, whether it's to swim, to enjoy other watersports, to fish, or just to enjoy time in the fresh air.

Part of West Cork and the island of Cape Clear are a *Gaeltacht* (Irish speaking area), and so are the western parts of County Kerry. You'll find lots of places all over both counties where you can hear Irish music and enjoy watching people dance and sing, even joining in yourself.

The region has one city, Cork, and many interesting and lively towns and villages; the largest towns in Kerry are Killarney in the south and Tralee in North Kerry.

Many areas are quiet and remote, particularly the peninsulas, including Beara in Cork and Dingle in Kerry, which jut out into the Atlantic.

This part of Ireland is ideal for activities such as hill walking, golf, horse riding, deep-sea angling, game and coarse angling, cycling, and watersports. It has attracted and inspired writers and artists from all over the world, and many have made their home here, especially along or near the coast. Here is a selection of what these counties offer visitors.

■ Getting to Cork & Kerry

You can fly directly from the US to **Shannon** or **Dublin**, then travel to Cork and Kerry by car, train or bus.

You can also fly to **Cork Airport**, which has scheduled service from the UK, Europe and from Dublin and Belfast.

Kerry Airport is at Farranfore, and is much smaller, with a limited number of flights from the UK.

■ Getting Around Cork & Kerry

While there is reasonably good bus service throughout counties Cork and Kerry, and rail service between some of the main towns in the region, the best way to explore is by renting a car or bike, as there are so many delightful places away from major roads.

By Road

Cork City is served by major routes N8-N7-M7-N7 from Dublin (159 miles/256 km), and N20-N21-N18 from Galway (187 miles/301 km). The N25 links Waterford and Cork, and the N20 links Limerick and Cork.

Within the region, the main routes include the N71, which runs west of Cork City through the costal towns of Bandon, Clonakilty and Skibbereen, then north to Bantry, Glengarifff, Kenmare and Killarney.

The N72 runs from the N8 (main Dublin-to-Cork route) at Fermoy westwards to Mallow and then on through Rathmore to Killarney.

East of Cork City, the N25 bypasses the town of Midleton, passes through Youghal and continues east into County Waterford.

Killarney is connected to Tralee by the N22, which passes Kerry Airport at Farranfore. The N21 connects Tralee and Castlegregory with Abbeyfeale and Adare in neighboring Co. Limerick. Alternatively, from Tralee you can take the N69 to Listowel and on to Tarbert, where a ferry transports vehicles and pedestrians across the River Shannon to Co. Clare.

By Rail

In Co. Cork, there are stations in Cork City, Cobh, Mallow, Charleville, Banteer and Millstreet.

In Kerry, there are stations at Rathmore, Killarney, Farranfore and Tralee.

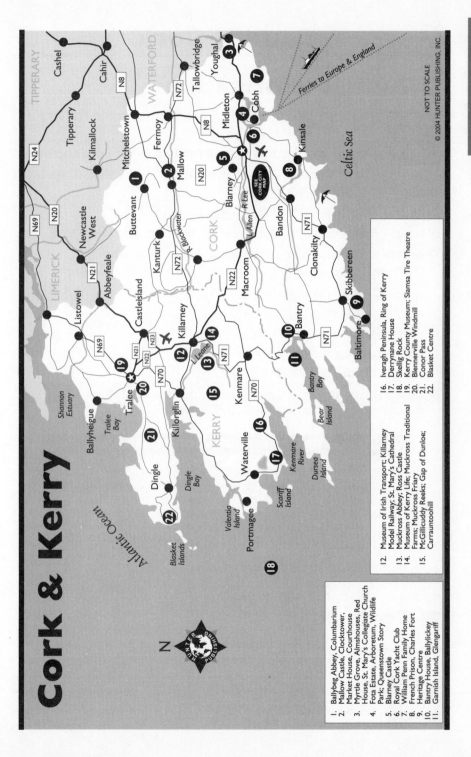

Cork & Kerry

Cork & Kerry

1. Ballybeg Abbey, Columbarium
2. Mallow Castle, Clocktower, Market House, Courthouse
3. Myrtle Grove, Almshouses, Red House, St. Mary's Collegiate Church
4. Fota Estate, Arboretum, Wildlife Park; Queenstown Story
5. Blarney Castle
6. Royal Cork Yacht Club
7. William Penn Family Home
8. French Prison, Charles Fort Heritage Centre
9. Bantry House, Ballylickey
10. Garnish Island, Glengariff

11.
12. Museum of Irish Transport; Killarney Model Railway; St. Mary's Cathedral
13. Muckross Abbey; Ross Castle
14. Museum of Kerry Life; Muckross Traditional Farms; Muckross Friary
15. McGillicuddy Reeks; Gap of Dunloe; Carrauntoohill

16. Iveragh Peninsula, Ring of Kerry
17. Derrynane House
18. Skellig Rock
19. Kerry County Museum; Siamsa Tire Theatre
20. Blennerville Windmill
21. Conor Pass
22. Blasket Centre

County Cork

■ Tourist Information

At Cork Airport, there is a Freefone facility in the terminal and a display of tourist leaflets.

Cork-Kerry Tourism has information offices open all year at:

Grand Parade, Cork City, ☎ (021) 431-554; fax 70776; info@corkkerrytourism.ie; www.corkkerry.ie.

Town Hall, Skibbereen, ☎ (028) 21766.

Blarney, in co-operation with Blarney Tourism, ☎ (021) 4381-624.

There are also offices open in the main tourist season at:

- Bantry, ☎ (027) 50229.
- Clonakilty, ☎ (023) 33226.
- Glengarifff, ☎ (027) 63084.
- Kinsale, ☎ (021) 477-2234.
- Macroom, ☎ (026) 43280.
- Midleton, ☎ (021) 461-3702.

If you're visiting at a quiet time of the year, ask in local shops for information as they often have brochures and maps.

TRACING YOUR ANCESTORS

Cork City Ancestral Project, c/o Cork County Library, Farranlea Road, Cork, ☎ (021) 434-6435; fax 434-3254; corkancestry@ireland.com. The research facility was suspended at time of writing, so check.

In North Cork, there is **Mallow Heritage Centre**, 22-28 Bank Place, Mallow, ☎ (022) 50302; fax 20276; mallowhc@eircom.net; www.irishroots.net.

■ Cork City

Sightseeing

Cork is Ireland's second city and its people (only half-jokingly) refer to it with pride as "the real capital." Founded over 800 years ago as a walled port, some of the medieval town's characteristics have survived in Cork's street patterns, especially in the North and South Main Street area. On North Main Street you'll see brass plates set into the ground marking where the narrow medieval alleys ran.

The city originally developed on what was an island where the River Lee branches before entering the harbor. On South Mall, the city's financial area, you can still see where boats were tied up as recently as 200 years ago when the street was part of the river.

Avoid the city on Sundays, as almost everything, apart from pubs and chain stores, is closed. Anyone interested in learning something of Ireland's history will enjoy a visit to **The Public Museum** in Fitzgerald's Park, on the Mardyke off Western Road. Entrance is free but the opening hours could be improved, as it's closed at lunchtime, all day Saturday and on bank holiday weekends. ☎ (021) 427-0679.

Fitzgerald's Park, within walking distance of the city center, is a pleasant place for a rest or stroll. Close to it is **University College, Cork**, founded in 1845 as Queen's College, the queen being Victoria of England. It has outgrown its original campus, which is also a pleasant place to visit, and where guided tours are organized during the summer.

Cork Harbor is one of the largest natural enclosed harbors in the world and brought much prosperity to the city from the mid-18th century on, when it was at the center of overseas trade. Many of the county's roads developed from the routes used by farmers transporting their goods into the city for export. Pay a visit to the **Butter Museum** in Shandon, next to where the Butter Market stood. You'll learn about the importance of that and other commodities in the city's past. Open daily May-September, 10 am-1:30 pm, 2-5 pm, and the rest of the year by arrangement. ☎ (021) 430-0600; fax 430-9966.

Nearby is **St. Anne's Church**, which has become the symbol of the city. It's known affectionately as "the four-faced liar," because its four clockfaces tell different times. For a tiny fee, you can climb the tower of St. Anne's for a fine view of the city and its waterways, and even play a tune on its bells. Try to resist playing Christmas carols in August! Open Monday-Saturday, May-September, 9:30 am-6:30 pm; January-April, 10:30 am-3:30 pm; October-December, 10:30 am-3 pm. ☎ (021) 450-5906; info@shandonsteeple.com; www.shandonsteeple.com.

Parking in Cork City

A disc parking system is used. Discs can be bought in garages and shops. There are also a number of well signposted public car parks around the city, some at shopping centers.

Shopping in Cork City

 Walk around Cork's shops and you'll see signs of how the city has developed over the centuries. The **English Market**, entered from Grand Parade or from Princes Street, has its own special charm, and if you are looking for food for a picnic this is where to go. It's open Monday-Saturday, 8 am-6 pm. Particularly tempting are the bread stall and another one selling cheeses made by small producers all over the county. There's a whole section of the market devoted to fish, worth a look for the variety. Upstairs, there is a good restaurant called **Farmgate**, open during market hours; it's a branch of the original, which is in the town of Midleton in East Cork.

The **Huguenot Quarter** around Paul Street, just off Patrick Street, the city's most important thoroughfare, is a good place to browse in interesting little shops and where there are plenty of places to eat. Nearby is the **Crawford Gallery**, with its permanent collection of Irish paintings and occasional visiting exhibitions. It has a great café run by Ballymaloe Country House Hotel in East Cork, which is famous for its food and cookery school.

A City of Culture

 Cork is an artistic city. It is the home of the National Sculpture Factory, the Crawford Gallery, Cork Opera House, the Everyman Palace Theatre, Triskel Arts Centre, the Lavit Gallery, and other galleries and performance spaces, including Tig Fili, the Granary Theatre and the Fenton Gallery. Entrance to exhibitions is free, with admission charges for other events such as lectures and readings. It also has an art-house cinema, the Kino, with a year-round program.

It's affectionately known as Ireland's festival city, with annual celebrations of choral music (Spring), folk music (September), film (mid-October) and jazz (last weekend of October), all of which have been running for decades, and all of them featuring international stars. More recently, the Cork Midsummer Festival in June has been added to the calendar.

Nightlife in the City

 The Opera House presents its own shows, as well as histing large-scale visiting by professional Irish companies and by visiting companies from the West End, London, and elsewhere. It has a smaller venue, the **Half Moon**, which doubles as a site for small-scale productions and as a late-night club with live music. ☎ (021) 427-0022.

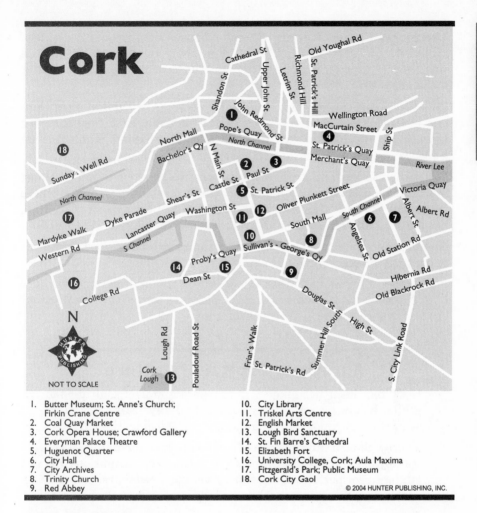

Cork

Cathedral St
Old Youghal Rd
Upper John St
Letrim St
Richmond Hill
St. Patrick's Hill
Shandon St
John Redmond St
Wellington Road
MacCurtain Street
Pope's Quay
North Mall
North Channel
St. Patrick's Quay
Ship St
Bachelor's Qy
N Main St
Merchant's Quay
River Lee
Sunday's Well Rd
Castle St
Paul St
North Channel
Shear's St
St. Patrick St
Victoria Quay
Dyke Parade
Washington St
Oliver Plunkett Street
South Channel
Albert St
Albert Rd
Mardyke Walk
Lancaster Quay
South Mall
Angelsea St
Old Station Rd
Western Rd
S Channel
Proby's Quay
Sullivan's - George's Qy
Dean St
Hibernia Rd
Old Blackrock Rd
College Rd
Douglas St
Summer Hill South
High St
S. City Link Road
Cork Lough
Lough Rd
Pouladouf Road St
Friar's Walk
St. Patrick's Rd

N

HUNTER PUBLISHING

NOT TO SCALE

1. Butter Museum; St. Anne's Church; Firkin Crane Centre	10. City Library
2. Coal Quay Market	11. Triskel Arts Centre
3. Cork Opera House; Crawford Gallery	12. English Market
4. Everyman Palace Theatre	13. Lough Bird Sanctuary
5. Huguenot Quarter	14. St. Fin Barre's Cathedral
6. City Hall	15. Elizabeth Fort
7. City Archives	16. University College, Cork; Aula Maxima
8. Trinity Church	17. Fitzgerald's Park; Public Museum
9. Red Abbey	18. Cork City Gaol

The Everyman Palace is smaller and stages a mixture of professional touring productions by Irish and overseas companies, concerts and local amateur plays – many of them by Irish playwrights John B. Keane and Sean O'Casey. There is a lunchtime series that runs during the summer and occasionally throughout the year. Play readings are also held at times in its Palace Bar. ☎ (021) 450-1673.

The CAT Club (Cork Arts and Theatre Club) is devoted to amateur companies from the city and county, with an intimate auditorium and a bar (open before and after evening shows), where you can meet the actors and others interested in theater. ☎ (021) 450-8398.

The Granary Theatre belongs to UCC, and during the academic year (October to May) most of the productions are by students. It hosts a Fringe Festival (in October) of shows seen at the Dublin and Edinburgh festivals, as well as a summer season with productions by local companies. ☎ (021) 490-4275.

The Firkin Crane Centre in Shandon houses the National Institute of Dance; it runs workshops and hosts dance performances. A "firkin" is a small barrel, used for making butter, and the Centre is next to the Butter Museum. ☎ (021) 450-7487.

Classical music concerts are held in the evenings in **Triskel Arts Centre**, in **Cork City Hall** and in the **Aula Maxima**, UCC, and there's a lunchtime series in the **Crawford Gallery** in the Spring. Summer is not a good time for lovers of classical music, at least not in Cork City.

For authentic Irish music, it's usually best to head for a pub as, apart from headline acts, which appear at the largest venues, that's where you'll hear the best. One of my favorites, **The Lobby**, opposite City Hall, has a varied and interesting program all year round. ☎ (021) 431-1113.

Nightclubs in the city are discos, rather than places for live performance, and are all for the 18-to-30 age group.

For details of shows and other events, check the local newspapers, *The Irish Examiner* and *The Evening Echo*, pick up a copy of the free *Whazon?* or check their website – www.whazon.com.

European Capital of Culture

Cork has been designated European Capital of Culture for 2005, having competed against Galway, Limerick and Waterford to win the prestigious title awarded by the EU.

There will be a full program of events all year, including lots of special sporting events, dramatic performances, exhibitions, recitals, street performances, film screenings, seminars, cultural exchanges, and lots more.

In preparation for the year, improvements have been made to the fabric of the city, including a much-needed revamping of Patrick Street, which will benefit the city long after the celebration has been forgotten.

Details from tourist offices all over the country and overseas or ☎ (021) 455-2005; info@Cork2005.ie; www.Cork2005.ie.

Spectator Sports in Cork City & County

 There are lots of **GAA (Gaelic Athletic Association) matches**; ask locally or check newspapers for details. Also, as you travel around minor roads outside the city, you may come across men enjoying a round of **road bowling**, only seen here and in Co. Armagh.

Curraheen Park Greyhound Stadium, in the Bishopstown suburb of the city, has 10 races every Wednesday, Thursday and Saturday starting at 7:50 pm. ☎ (021) 454-3095, or in Ireland, 1-850-525-525, reservations@ curraheenpark.igb.ie. There's a bar and fine dining there at the **Laurels Restaurant**. ☎ (021) 493-3154.

Tours
Walking Tours

During the summer, there are guided tours of the city; they start from outside the Tourist Office on Grand Parade, where you can ask about them. Walking tours of Kinsale are also available during the summer – ask at the tourist office there.

From mid-May to mid-September, there are **Literary Walking Tours** of Cork City on Tuesdays and Thursdays at 7:30 pm. Meet outside the Imperial Hotel, South Mall. You retrace the footsteps of writers, including Frank O'Connor, James Joyce and Elizabeth Bowen. The tour ends with a pint of locally produced Beamish & Crawford stout in An Spailpin Fanac pub, one of the most traditional in the city. Bookings, ☎ (021) 488-5405.

Bus Tours

Bus Éireann runs open-topped bus tours of the city and nearby Blarney, twice daily (10:30 am and 2.45 pm) from June 1 to mid-September. They depart from the Bus Station. They take about three hours. Pre-booked passengers are also picked up at the City Library, opposite the Tourist Office, on Grand Parade. Don't worry – if the weather is bad, they use an ordinary bus.

The company also runs day tours from Cork City, visiting sites in counties Tipperary, Waterford and Clare, as well as the Ring of Kerry and West Cork, the latter including a cruise to Cape Clear Island. They are a pleasant way of exploring if you don't want to rent a car.

Booking is advised for all bus tours. To book, call the bus station or one of the following:

The Travel Centre, Bus Station, Cork City, ☎ (021) 450-8188.

Tourist Office, Cork City, ☎ (021) 427-3251.

Tourist Office, Blarney, ☎ (021) 438-1624.

O'Driscolls Travel Agency, Macroom, ☎ (026) 41342. info@buseireann. ie; www.buseireann.ie.

Easy Tours runs coach tours to Co. Kerry from Cork City (advance booking essential). ☎ (021) 436-2484.

Road Runners has tours of Kinsale and West Cork by mini-bus, ☎ (021) 477-3423.

The Gift of the Gab

Blarney, six miles (10 km) northwest of Cork City, must be one of the most famous of all towns in Ireland, especially among North Americans, because of the **Blarney Stone**, which is said to give those who kiss it the "gift of the blarney" or "the gab." That means the ability to be as articulate as most of the Irish.

To kiss the stone you have to climb up to the top of the ruined Blarney Castle and be suspended over a hole. It's fun, but not for the unfit or fainthearted, as climbing the narrow and winding stone stairs is difficult if you are large, and can be slippery, especially when descending. Men hold onto you as you are suspended to kiss the stone, and they do wipe it after each person, but if you worry about hygiene you won't like the experience.

Visitors to Ireland, especially from North America, the UK and Australia, have been kissing the stone since the 19th century, when someone thought up Ireland's first tourist attraction. It has never really caught on with visitors from Europe.

You pay an entrance fee to the Castle grounds and receive a certificate stating that you have kissed the Stone. The grounds, including the fascinating Rock Close, are also worth exploring. Open June-August, 9 am-7 pm; May and September, to 6:30 pm, October-April, to sundown or 6 pm. Earlier closing on Sundays. ☎ (021) 438-5252.

■ Exploring West Cork

Kinsale

Kinsale is 16 miles (26 km) west of the city; it's known as "the gourmet capital of Ireland" for the number of great places to dine in the town. The Good Food Circle has been organizing a **Gourmet Festival** here every autumn for over 25 years.

A charming town, its narrow streets are steeped in history and its harbor is always full of boats. Visit the museum housed in the **French Prison** or, just outside the town, the star-shaped **Charles Fort** with its spectacular views, where you will learn about the country's history. Open daily May-October, the rest of the year on weekends. ☎ (021) 477-2263.

As you journey west, you pass through many other pleasant places, including picturesque **Innishannon**, and the bustling market towns of **Bandon** and **Skibbereen**, as well as smaller **Dunmanway**.

At Skibbereen there's a **Heritage Centre** in the beautifully restored Old Gasworks building on the riverside. It houses an exhibition that commemorates the Great Famine. West Cork was one of the areas very badly affected by the mid-19th century famine. Also, the **Lough Hyne Visitor Centre** gives a fascinating insight into Ireland's first Marine Nature Reserve. The lough (lake) itself is nearby. Open March-October, Tuesday to Saturday, 10 am-6 pm; open daily in summer. ☎ (028) 40900.

Clonakilty

Clonakilty is 32 miles (51 km) west of Cork City. It is one of the prettiest towns in West Cork, with colorful buildings and hand-painted signs over its shops and pubs. It has won numerous awards, including the EU Entente Florale. The town calls itself "the gateway to West Cork" and it certainly makes an ideal base for tours of the area. Nearby, there's the wonderful EU Blue Flag beach (see page 76) of **Inchydoney**, as well as lots of little coves to discover. **Courtmacsherry**, a delightful fishing village, proud of having the oldest lifeboat station in Ireland, is 10 minutes away by car.

Bantry

Along the coast is Bantry, which is not the most attractive of towns, especially when you enter it from the east, where there's a huge graveyard reminding all who pass of their eventual fate. What makes it worth visiting is its setting on the beautiful Bantry Bay, and the surrounding area, which has much to offer. There are delightful villages and wonderful views wherever you drive, whether along the coast or inland.

Bantry House looks down on the town – it was the first stately home to open to the public in the Republic and is still occupied by the family that owns it. Every June it hosts the **West Cork Chamber Music Festival**, which brings international stars to perform in its Library.

Just a couple of miles north along the coast road from Bantry is **Ballylickey**, which has a wonderful emporium selling every kind of foodstuff imaginable, most locally produced.

Glengarifff, farther along the coast, is a pretty little traditional village with a small harbor, and a pleasant place to spend at least a few hours.

Cork & Kerry

A TREASURE ISLAND

Garnish Island, off Glengarifff, is unique – the entire island is a garden. Also known as Garinish and Ilnacullin, its 37 acres were transformed by former owner Anna Bryce and Harold Peto, an architect and garden designer, into a magical place. You can spend hours wandering its little paths that climb through the trees to a Martello Tower. Anna Bryce left the island to the Irish nation in her will when she died in 1953.

You usually see seals basking on the rocks as you make the short crossing from Glengarifff, and from the island there are wonderful views of the surrounding area. Even if you have no particular interest in gardens, you'll enjoy a visit. There's a café open in the summer. Garnish Island is open daily, March-end October. Access is by privately operated boats, paid separately. Harbour Queen Ferry Services operates from Glengarifff Harbour to the island.

You could easily spend days or weeks exploring West Cork, wandering up and down its lovely quiet roads. Although popular, it is never crowded, and there are always delightful places to discover. Among personal favorites are **Schull**, **Glandore**, and **Mizen Head**.

■ Exploring East Cork

 East of Cork City lies **Cobh** (pronounced Cove), which has a Mediterranean atmosphere, especially in the sunshine, with its steep streets and curved Georgian terraces looking out over Cork Harbor. You can get there by road or train.

The train to Cobh stops at the **Fota estate**, the home of an arboretum and the only wildlife park in the country. The **Arboretum** at Fota was started by the Smith-Barry family in the 1820s and has a marvelous collection of trees and shrubs from all over the world. **Fota Wildlife Park** opened in 1983 and here animals, many of them endangered in the wild, wander happily. Only the cheetahs are caged; the others are protected from humans by ditches. There's a coffee shop and gift shop on site. Open daily from mid-March to the beginning of November; last admission is at 5 pm and gates close at 6 pm. Weekends only rest of year and gates close at 4 pm. ☎ (021) 481-2678; www.fotawildlife.ie.

Unfortunately, the Fota House itself is more or less empty, and not worth touring. That's a shame, as it won both a national and European award when privately run in the 1980s. Among its contents then was a wonderful collection of Irish paintings and furniture. You can now see some of those paintings in the Foundation Building at the University of Limerick, but the Irish period furniture is sadly in storage. I was Curator and Administrator of Fota House, and lived there for 17 years, which is why I know about it.

Cobh

Cobh was called Queenstown for several years (after Victoria, England's monarch), before reverting in 1922 to its old Irish name. Cobh means the "cove" of Cork and it has a special place in the hearts of many North Americans as one of the places from which their ancestors left to find new lives across the Atlantic.

 Here, in April 1912, the Titanic *picked up the last 123 passengers on her maiden voyage to America.*

If you only visit one heritage site during your vacation, make it the **Queenstown Story**, housed in the old railway station. This is a wonderful exhibition telling the story of those emigrants. Only the truly hard-hearted could fail to be moved, particularly when you relive what it must have been like on one of those coffin ships. Open daily year-round, March-November, 9:30 am to 6 pm, last admission 5 pm; rest of year, closes at 5 pm, with last admission at 4 pm. ☎ (021) 481-3595.

Outside the Queenstown Story on the quayside is a statue of Annie Moore and her little brothers. She was the first Irish person to land at Ellis Island in New York Harbor, and the twin of the Cobh statue can be seen in the Arrivals Hall at the Ellis Island Center.

Midleton

Midleton is a pleasant market town, just off the main road (N25) to Waterford, with interesting shops and plenty of pubs and restaurants, including the original Farmgate (the other is in the city) and a **Craft Gallery** with lots of items that make great souvenirs or gifts.

It's also the home of the **Old Midleton Distillery**, where you can enjoy a tour and a taste of the whiskey. There's a craft shop, restaurant and tourist information point on site. Open year-round, 10 am to 6 pm, with last tour at 4:30 pm. ☎ (021) 461-3594.

Nearby villages include **Ballycotton**, with its fishing harbor, and **Garryvoe**, with its long flat beach, ideal for a walk. The ruins of the **ancestral home of William Penn**, founder of Pennsylvania, can be seen in **Shanagarry**, where Stephen Pearce's pottery is worth a visit.

You also pass through some quite attractive little villages if you stay on the N25 (Waterford road), including **Castlemartyr** and **Killeagh**. Away from the main route there is lovely countryside to enjoy, as well as quiet little beaches.

Youghal

When you enter Youghal from the direction of Cork, the first thing you see is a large pink building, which unfortunately now dominates the skyline. Try to ignore this new development (it houses vacation apartments and a bar), as Youghal is an interesting town in an attractive setting, with a long beach – a delight to stroll along when the tide is out.

There is a clock tower you drive under and there are traces of the town's historic walls. It is worth staying here at least for a few hours.

Myrtle Grove, the home of Sir Walter Raleigh, is an interesting building, but it is not open to the public. Visitors are welcome at the **Almshouses**, the **Red House**, and don't miss **St. Mary's Collegiate Church**, one of the oldest churches on these islands still in use. The town was used as the location for the film *Moby Dick*, starring Gregory Peck, and there's a pub named after it.

On the other side of Youghal, heading into Waterford, you can turn left away from the sea and you're on the **Blackwater Valley Drive** (see under Co. Waterford, page 220).

■ Exploring North Cork

North Cork is dominated by the valley of the **River Blackwater**, and has two of the busiest main roads in the Republic running through it – the N20 to Limerick and the N8 toward Dublin.

The River Blackwater is one of the longest rivers in the Republic at 74 miles (120 km). It rises in Co. Kerry, flows east from North Cork to Cappoquin in neighboring Co. Waterford and then turns south to enter the sea near Youghal.

Mallow

Mallow is 20 miles (32 km) north of Cork City and just off the N20. It grew up around the Blackwater and the ruins of the original 16th-century castle can be seen in the grounds of the present **Mallow Castle**, now privately owned. It was a spa town in the 18th and early 19th centuries, when many people came to take the waters. Interesting buildings here include the neo-Tudor **Clock House**, dating from the early 19th century, and the **Market House** and **Courthouse**, both built of limestone.

Northeast of Mallow is **Doneraile** and its **Forest Park**.

If you stay on the N20, just before you come to Buttevant, you will see the ruins of **Ballybeg Abbey**, which include a "columbarium" – a circular building, almost intact, where doves were kept.

Buttevant

Buttevant, on the N20, got its name from "boutez en avant," the battle-cry of the Barry family who owned much of Co. Cork, including the Fota estate near Cobh. The ruins of the abbey they founded are next to the modern Catholic church in the middle of the town's main street. It was from here that the first steeplechase was run in 1720, literally between the steeples of churches in Buttevant and Doneraile.

After Buttevant you come to **Ballyhoura Country**, already mentioned in the chapter on Limerick, page 331.

Fermoy

Fermoy is also on the Blackwater, along the N8 (Dublin road), and badly needs a by-pass as it gets choked with traffic. It's a busy market town, with some attractive buildings. Before Ireland's independence, it had one of the largest military barracks on these islands, traces of which can still be seen. It's a popular base for those interested in fishing or exploring the Blackwater Valley.

■ Adventures on Water

Cork Harbor offers excellent opportunities for deep-sea anglers, even when weather conditions are not good enough to allow travel past its mouth at Roches Point.

Every August, Cobh hosts a **regatta**, which is hugely enjoyable. A great vantage point for watching the colorful sailboats on the water below is up near the Cathedral. The **Cobh International Deep Sea Angling Festival** has been well established for many years, and every September attracts many visiting anglers from all over the country and overseas.

Boats for Hire

Angling charter boats are available from Cobh, specializing in shark-, bottom- and wreck-fishing. ☎ (087) 225-9869.

Charter boats are also available from Crosshaven for deep-sea angling, with a number of operators involved. The angling specialties are shark, bottom- and wreck-fishing. As well as Cork Harbor, fishing grounds include the area east and west of the harbor mouth at Roches Point.

In West Cork, **Courtmacsherry Sailing and Leisure** specializes in shark-, bottom- and wreck-fishing. ☎ (023) 40607.

A small floating pontoon has been provided by the Courtmacsherry Sea Angling Club to facilitate anglers taking boats out from here.

Take a Harbor Cruise

Those who just want to sit back and enjoy being on the water can take a cruise of Cork Harbor from Cobh. Contact **Marine Transport Services** at ☎ (021) 4811485 for details. They also organize special cruises for groups.

The Oldest Yacht Club

Crosshaven is the home of the **Royal Cork Yacht Club**, the oldest yacht club in the world, founded in 1720. It's an attractive small town on the western side of Cork Harbor, at the head of a long narrow estuary leading to the busy little town of Carrigaline.

The club offers a variety of sailing activities for all ages from young children upwards. It also hosts **Ford Cork Week**, held every two years, regarded as Europe's most competitor-friendly regatta, which attracts contestants from all over the globe. The next one is in 2004. ☎ (021) 483-1023; fax 483-1586; office@royalcork.com; www.royalcork.com.

Watersports

With its many small bays and harbors County Cork is the ideal destination for anyone interested in watersports. Surfing, windsurfing, canoeing, waterskiing, sailing and diving are all available, with classes at a number of centers, among them the following.

Coolmain Sailing, Bandon, offers everything from Taster Sessions, lasting two-three hours – when you can find out if you're interested in learning – to two- and five-day courses in summer, as well as evening courses year-round. Contact Kim or Jean Wood, ☎/fax (023) 44464; enquiries@coolmain-sailing.com; www.coolmain-sailing.com.

Glenans Irish Sailing Club, Baltimore, West Cork, is based in what was the village's railway station, where hostel accommodation is available in the former Stationmaster's House. Classes offered include dinghy and keelboat sailing. Contact them at The Station House, Baltimore, ☎ (028) 20154; fax 20312; info@glenans-ireland.com; www.glenans-ireland.com.

Sovereign Sailing is based in the Kinsale Yacht Club Marina. It has a number of courses available, all designed with a maximum of four participants. So if you can arrange your own group of four the courses can be arranged to suit you. Courses include An Introduction to Crewing, Spinnaker and Sail Trim, or Day Navigation. You can also take a cruise of any length from a half-day to a maximum of six days or four for overnight cruises. ☎/fax (021) 477-4145; james@sovereignsailing.com; www.sovereignsailing.com.

The West Cork Sailing Centre is based at Adrigole on the beautiful Beara Peninsula. It offers dinghy sailing vacations for anyone aged from eight to 80. You can choose from half-day, two-day or five-day sessions. Kayak rental is also available for those who want to take advantage of the sheltered harbor with its seal colony. Classes in powerboats are also offered at the center. There's a lovely Bistro, with a magnificent view of Bantry Bay and the Caha Mountains. Accommodation is available in a nearby hostel, guest houses or in rental cottages or houses. ☎ (27) 60132; fax 60247; info@westcorksailing.com; www.westcorksailing.com.

Other facilities include:

- **Baltimore Sailing School,** ☎ (028) 20141.
- **Bluewater Training**, Inniscarra ☎ (021) 4733-2005.
- **International Sailing and Powerboating**, Cobh, ☎ (021) 481-1237.
- **Kinsale Outdoor Education Center,** ☎ (021) 477-0738.
- **Oysterhaven Windsurfing & Sailing Center**, near Kinsale, ☎ (021) 477-0738, www.oysterhaven.com.

The coastline is known for its outstanding diving conditions, as underwater visibility can be very good when the weather allows. Conditions for surfing and windsurfing are often excellent, and you also have a wide variety of canoeing venues to choose from. Ireland's official national site for disabled waterskiers is on the River Lee near Macroom.

The Baltimore Diving & Watersports Centre runs diving courses for all from the beginner to the experienced, has a restaurant and shop and also offers boat charter. ☎/fax (028) 20300; jkdiving@iol.ie.

Atlantic Sea Kayaking, Skibbereen, offers a variety of courses in kayaking on rivers, lakes and in the sea, including a trip to the Lakes of Killarney. ☎ (028) 21058; atlanticseakayaking@eircom.net; www. atlanticseakayaking.com.

H2O Sea Kayaking, based at Ballinspittle near Kinsale, offers a choice of trips and courses, aimed at everyone from the beginner to the experienced. Its owners also run **H2O Extreme**, the only dedicated whitewater company in Ireland. ☎ (021) 477-8884; whitewater@dol.ie; www. h2oseakayaking.net.

Sea Kayaking West Cork is based at Castletownbere on the beautiful and quiet Beara Penisula on the north shore of Bantry Bay. They have "come and try it" two-hour sessions, as well as a choice of courses, plus half-day and full-day trips. ☎ (027) 70692; info@seakayakingwestcork. com; www.seakayakingwestcork.com.

Beaches

There are numerous beaches, some not even signposted, so get a map, or ask locally, and inquire at Tourist Information Offices for details of EU Blue Flag Beaches (see page 76). Among the most popular and safest strands in Co. Cork are **Garryvoe** and **Youghal** in East Cork, and **Inchydoney** in West Cork.

West Cork Island Ferries

In West Cork there are regular ferries to some of the little islands off the coast – including **Sherkin** and **Cape Clear** – from Baltimore. ☎ (028) 20218.

West Cork Coastal Cruises runs trips to various islands, also from Baltimore. ☎ (028)39153.

Murphy's Ferry Service, from Pontoon, Berehaven, in Bantry Bay, runs frequent trips to Bere Island. ☎ (027) 75014; info@murphysferry. com; www.murphysferry.com.

There's also a daily ferry to Cape Clear and a twice-weekly ferry to the **Fastnet Rock**, from Schull. ☎ (028) 28278.

Cable Car

You cross to little **Dursey Island** off the Beara Peninsula by a cable car – the only one in Europe that transports people over the sea.

■ Adventures on Horseback

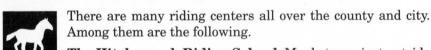

There are many riding centers all over the county and city. Among them are the following.

The Hitchmough Riding School, Monkstown, just outside Cork City. It has both indoor and outdoor arenas and a cross-country course. It offers daily programs suitable for all abilities. Open Monday to Saturday from 9 am to 8 pm, or by appointment. ☎ (021) 437-1267; fax 437-4842; hrs@esatclear.ie.

The Rosscarbery Riding School in West Cork specializes in trekking through forests and on beaches, and it has a special scenic track for beginners. ☎ (023) 48232.

Others include:

Ballymakeigh Equestrian Centre, Killeagh, ☎ (024) 91373.

Follyfoot Riding Farm, Riverstick, Kinsale, ☎ (021) 477-1324.

Ballinader Trekking & Horse Riding Farm, Kinsale, ☎ (021) 477-8152.

Innishannon Horse Centre, ☎ (021) 477-5515.

Bantry Horseriding, ☎ (027) 51412.

Allihies Riding Centre, Castletownbere, ☎ (027) 70340.

Ballinadee Stables, near Bandon, ☎ (021) 477-8152.

Ballincollig Equestrian Center, near Cork City, ☎ (021) 487-3654.

Ballindenisk Equestrian Park, Watergrasshill, ☎ (021) 488-9106.

Dunsfort Riding Centre, Baneshane, Midleton, ☎ (021) 463-1851.

Ford Homestead Riding School, Lisselan, Ballinascarthy, Clonakilty, named after the ancestral home of Henry Ford. ☎ (023) 39117.

Hop Island Equestrian Centre, Rochestown, close to Cork City, ☎ (021) 436-127.

Kingstons Riding School, Kilgarrif, Clonakilty, ☎ (023) 33793.

Limbo Riding School, Creagh, Baltimore, ☎ (028) 21683.

Mallow Equestrian Centre, Newberry, Mallow, ☎ (022) 42245.

Millstreet Horse Village, Green Glens, Millstreet, near Mallow, ☎ (029) 70039; fax 70306.

Monatrea Equestrian Centre, Kinsalebeg near Youghal, ☎ (024) 94550.

Valley View Equestrian Centre, Gooseberry Hill, Newmarket, ☎ (029) 68185.

Other Places of Interest to Horse Lovers

Cork Racecourse is actually 20 miles north of the city and a mile outside Mallow on the N72 road to Killarney. Races are held throughout the year. ☎ (022) 50207; fax 50213; info@corkracecourse.ie; www.corkracecourse.ie.

At Millstreet, west of Mallow, the indoor equestrian center, **Green Glens**, hosts a number of events year-round and is also used as a venue for all kinds of entertainment, including Holiday on Ice, Disney on Ice, Riverdance, and international stars have performed there. ☎ (029) 70707; fax 70306; thomas@millstreet.ie; www.millstreet.ie.

The Cahirmee Horse Fair, originally called "the great fair of Munster," has been held for centuries in Buttevant. These days it's in mid-July, but was probably held at midsummer (June 21) hundreds of years ago. During the Fair, the town is full of people buying and selling horses, and it's well worth a visit.

THE DONKEY SANCTUARY

The Donkey Sanctuary at Liscarroll, reached by turning off the N20 Cork-Limerick road at Buttevant, is a very special place. Donkeys rescued from dreadful circumstances are found new homes from here, and there are always contented animals young and old to see. It's a registered charity and visitors are asked for donations. ☎ (022) 48398; donkey@indigo.ie; www.thedonkeysanctuary.org.uk.

■ Golf in Cork

 Unfortunately, a number of golf courses in both Co. Cork and Kerry have been built on some of the most scenic sites, to which the public previously had access. It's a shame to see some of our land become a private playground, despite objections and protests by the public.

Among the 18-hole golf courses close to Cork City are the following.

The Ted McCarthy Municipal Golf Course is in the suburb of Mahon, and is a parkland course with undulating fairways and many water hazards. It's open daily until dusk. ☎ (021) 429-4280.

Not far away is the **Douglas Golf Club**, ☎ (021) 436-2055; fax 489-5297; admin@douglasgolfclub.ie; www.douglasgolfclub.ie.

Muskerry Golf Club, west of the city at Carrigrohane, has one of the most mature courses in the region, as the club was founded at the beginning of the last century. ☎ (021) 438-5297; fax 451-6860; muskgc@eircom.net.

Blarney Golf Course is six miles from the city and overlooks Blarney Castle. The course is designed in two loops of nine holes. Clubs are available for hire. ☎ (021) 438-2455; fax 438-2416; blarneygolf@esatbiz.com; www.blarneygolfcourse.com.

There are two courses at Little Island, seven miles east of Cork City, just off the N25 road to Rosslare and Waterford.

- ■ **Cork Golf Club**, ☎ (021) 435-3451; fax 435-3410.
- ■ **Harbour Point Golf Club**, ☎ (021) 435-3094; fax 435-4408; hpoint@iol.ie; www.harbourpointgolfclub.com.

Also in East Cork is **Water Rock Golf Club**, close to Midleton. Clubs are available for hire, and there's a pro shop and practice green. The course has lovely views of the countryside. ☎ (021) 461-3499; fax 463-3150; waterrock@eircom.net; www.waterrockgolfcourse.com.

Youghal Golf Club is at Knockaverry, ☎ (024) 92787; fax 92641; youghalgolfclub@eircom.net; www. youghalgolfclub.net.

In North Cork, the **Ballinamona Golf Course** only opened in 2000, and is aimed at the visiting golfer. It's just off the main Cork / Mallow road at Mourne Abbey, and is in an area of undulating landscape. ☎ (022) 29314; www.ballinamona.com.

Charleville Golf Club is in the foothills of the Ballyhoura Mountains, and has both an 18-hole and a nine-hole course. ☎ (063) 81257; fax 81274; charlevillegolf@eircom.net; www.charlevillegolf. com.

Heading west of the city, **Macroom Golf Club** has a lovely setting in the grounds of Macroom Castle on the banks of the River Sullane. ☎ (026) 41072; fax 41391; mcroomgc@iol.ie.

In West Cork there are courses at:

- **Bandon**, ☎ (023) 41111.
- **Bantry Bay**, ☎ (027) 50579.
- **Berehaven**, ☎ (027) 70700.
- **Dunmore**, Clonakilty, ☎ (023) 34644.
- **Glengarifff**, ☎ (027) 63150.
- **Kinsale**, ☎ (021) 774722.
- **Lisselan Estate**, Clonakilty, ☎ (023) 33249.
- **Skibbereen**, ☎ (028) 21227.
- There's also a **Golf Academy** at Ballydehob, ☎ (028) 37700.

■ Where to Stay

Ballymaloe House Hotel, Shanagarry, Midleton, has been run by the Allen family since the 1960s, when they opened their Yeats Room Restaurant – so named because of the Jack Yeats paintings on its walls. This is now the most famous country house hotel in Ireland, and was very influential in developing Ireland's reputation for excellent food.

HOTEL PRICE CHART	
Price per person, per night, with two sharing, including breakfast.	
$	Under US $50
$$	US $50-$100
$$$	US $101-$175
$$$$	US $176-$200
$$$$$	Over US $200

Staying or dining here, you are surrounded by a working farm. In Spring, as you drive into the grounds, you pass lambs in the fields. Its famous cuisine uses home-grown and locally produced ingredients. It's open daily to non-residents for lunch at 1 pm; dinner is served from 7 to 9;30 pm. Sunday lunches here are buffet-style, so you can try dishes and keep going back for more of those you like. You have to book ahead because it's so popular. Overnight rate from $$$ in low season. ☎ (021) 465-2531.

Just down the road is the **Ballymaloe Cookery School** at Shanagarry, which is run by Darina Allen, a TV chef and author of cookbooks. From April to September you can visit the gardens and shop here. Cooking demonstrations are held during the afternoons. ☎ 021 4646785, info@cookingisfun.ie; www.cookingisfun.ie.

☆☆☆☆ **The Bayview Hotel** in the fishing village of Ballycotton is the only four-star hotel in East Cork, and a wonderful place to stay. The hotel has gardens perched on the cliff or when the weather is bad you can enjoy the view from its windows. The **Capricho restaurant** serves such delights as venison accompanied by baby pear and port wine jus. Rates from $$. ☎ (021) 464-6746.

Eccles Hotel, Glengarifff, has a wonderful setting, looking out on the bay and Garnish Island, with a wooded hillside behind it. It's been there since 1745 and literary figures including Yeats and Dickens have enjoyed it as much as I did. Ask for a room at the front; there's nothing like waking up to that view. Rates $-$$, an amazing value. They also have a few rental apartments. ☎ (027) 63003; eccleshotel@iol.ie; www.eccleshotel.com.

Assolas Country House dates back to the 17th century and is in a beautiful and peaceful setting, near Mallow in North Cork, with swans gliding on the lake in its grounds. It's owned by the Bourke family, and all guests are well looked after. It belongs to the Hidden Ireland group and is therefore not classified under the hotel star system. Its dining room is admired for the imaginative use of the garden produce and of ingredients locally sourced. Rates from $$ to $$$. Assolas is also at times available for private rental. It sleeps 12-18 in its nine bedrooms. ☎ (029) 500015; assolas@eircom.net.

Ballyvolane House near Castleyons in East Cork is a member of the Great Fishing Houses of Ireland co-operative marketing group. Surrounded by its own farmland, the house was built in 1728 and now provides excellent accommodation for visitors. Merrie and Jeremy Green make all their guests very welcome, and they are given access to private salmon and trout fishing on the River Blackwater. ☎ (025) 36349; www.ballyvolanehouse.ie.

Guesthouses

You can dine or stay at the welcoming **Barnabrow House** just outside the gates of Ballymaloe, near Midleton, where meals served in its **Trinity Room restaurant** use locally caught and grown ingredients. The restaurant is also open to non-residents; reservations advised. ☎ (021) 465-2534.

In Cobh, I recommend **Elmville**, Lower Road, Rushbrooke, where Olive O'Brien makes guests feel really welcome in her restored Victorian home. It overlooks the harbor, and has lovely gardens. It's only a five-minute walk to the Queenstown Story, the Railway Station, and Cobh itself. Rates $ sharing, including full Irish breakfast. ☎ (021) 4813206; www. dragnet-systems.ie/dira/elmville.

Another lovely guesthouse is **The Lighthouse**, in Kinsale, where Carmel Kelly O'Gorman will make you feel at home in her beautifully furnished and decorated home. It has four-poster and canopy beds, antiques, and a mouth-watering breakfast menu. Rates $$. ☎ (021) 477-2734; info@lighthouse-kinsale.com.

A Rental With a Difference

You can have exclusive use of your own five-star style hotel by renting **Ballinacurra House**, just two minutes drive outside Kinsale. Ballinacurra was built in 1791 and has been lovingly restored. It's set in its own 25 acres of grounds, and among its attractions are its large patio, croquet lawn, playground, helipad, picnic lawn, pond, small boat jetty, forest pagoda, and its woodland walks. There is a massage room and sauna. Cruises of Kinsale Harbor can be arranged as well as deep sea fishing excursions or explorations of the coastline. It has 13 bedrooms, can sleep up to 30. A resident chef is even available at an extra charge.

Daily rate for the house is €4,000, which works out as just over €300 per night per person or €150 sharing a double room. ☎ (021) 477-9040; fax 477-9071; info@ballinacurra.com; www.ballinacurra.com.

Camping & RVing

 ☆☆☆☆ **Barleycove Holiday Park**, Crookhaven, is near Skibbereen in West Cork. It's in a beautiful setting and facilities include tennis courts, pitch and putt and bikes for rent. Mobile homes available for rent. Open Easter and from mid-April to mid-September. ☎ (028) 35302 when open; (0210 434-6466 rest of year; fax (021) 430-7230.

☆☆☆ **Blackwater Valley Park** is at Fermoy on the N72 Rosslare-to-Killarney road and a few yards from the N8 Cork-Dublin road. It's on the bank of the river it's named after, where guests can fish. Open mid-March to end October. ☎ (025) 32147.

☆☆ **Desert House Caravan and Camping Park** is just outside Clonakilty in West Cork. It's a small park on a working dairy farm, where guests can watch activities, and it overlooks Clonakilty Bay. Open Easter and from May 1 to September 30. ☎ (023) 33331; fax 33048.

☆☆☆☆ **Blarney Caravan and Camping Park** is set in sheltered countryside overlooking Blarney Castle. Its facilities include free showers, pitch and putt course, and a large cooking and dining area. Open March 1 to end October. ☎ (021) 451-6519; fax 438-5167; con.quill@camping-ireland.ie; www.blarneycaravanpark/com.

☆☆☆ **Dowlings Caravan and Camping Park** is situated between the mountains and the sea at Glengarifff in West Cork. Guests are welcome to take part in traditional Irish music and dancing in the bar. There's a shop and takeout food store on site which are open during the summer. Park open from Easter to end October. ☎/fax (027) 63154.

☆☆☆☆ **Eagle Point Camping** is in a lovely setting on a peninsula at Ballylickey, just outside Bantry in West Cork. It has excellent facilities and is ideal for touring the area, taking part in watersports or fishing, or just relaxing in scenic surroundings close to restaurants and pubs. Open April 25-end September. ☎ (027) 50630; eagepointcamping@eircom.net; www.eaglepointcamping.com.

☆☆☆☆ **Garrettstown House Holiday Park** is in the grounds of an 18th-century estate, six miles from Kinsale, and is open from May to mid-September. ☎/fax (021) 477-8156.

☆☆ **Sextons Caravan and Camping Park** is at Timoleague, with breakfast available on site. Open mid-March to mid-September. ☎ (023) 46347.

Hungry Hill Camping Site is at Adrigole Harbor on the Beara Peninsula. It's open mid-March to the end of October. It was awaiting classification at time of writing. ☎ (027) 60228.

☆☆ **O'Riordan's Caravan Park** is at Owenahincha near Rosscarbery, and just six miles from Clonakilty. Mobile homes are available for rent on site. Open all year. ☎ (021) 454-1825 or (023) 28216.

☆☆ **Meadow Camping Park** is in a garden setting on the R597 at Glandore. Open mid-March to end September. ☎ (028) 33280; the_meadows@oceanfree.net.

☆☆☆ **Sonas** is at Ballymacoda in unspoiled countryside and its facilities include a shop, laundry, tennis court. Open May to mid-September. ☎ (024) 98960.

☆ **Dunbeacon** is three miles from Bantry overlooking Dunmanus Bay. Open Easter to late October. ☎ (027) 61246; camping@fishpublishing.com.

☆☆☆☆ **The Hideaway** near Skibbereen is a camping and RV park, with excellent facilities. It's only a 10-minute walk into the town. Open end of April to late September. ☎ (028) 22254; the_hideaway@oceanfree.net.

☆☆ **Jasmine Villa Caravan and Camping Park** is at Carrigtwohill on the N25 east of Cork City on the way to Waterford. It's open all year. ☎ (021) 488-3234.

■ Where to Eat

Cork City

 You can find all kinds of restaurants in Cork, varying in price and quality. Among personal favorites are the following.

Fellini's, Patrick Street on the edge of the Huguenot Quarter. Good food at reasonable prices from 9 am to 6 pm. The menu includes delicious scrambled eggs with smoked salmon, enormous open sandwiches. Too busy at lunchtimes to be enjoyed. ☎ (021) 427-6083.

Isaacs, MacCurtain Street, opposite the Everyman Palace Theatre, is great for lunch or dinner. The menu includes homemade burgers and fishcakes, lots of crisp salads, daily specials. Service is efficient and friendly and they are always honest – if they're busy you are given a table for a limited time; when it is slower you can sit and enjoy the atmosphere all evening. ☎ (021) 450-3805.

Ruen Thai Restaurant, Patrick Street, is ideal for lunch from noon to 3 pm or dinner from 5 to 11:30 pm. Allow time and relax; you can stay all evening. ☎ (021) 427-6127.

Café Paradiso, Western Road, on way to the University, is considered one of the best vegetarian restaurants in the whole country. It's so popular that it never advertises and is always busy, so book ahead. ☎ (021) 427-7939.

The Seasons Restaurant in the Ambassadors Hotel, Military Hill, off Wellington Road, is surprising. Unlike many hotel dining rooms, the food here is unforgettable; you choose from a traditional and New World menu. The surroundings are comfortable, though not beautiful, with dreadful paintings on the walls, but you forget all that when you're eating. The foyer also has a welcoming open fire. ☎ (021) 455-1996.

East Cork

Barryscourt Castle, at Carrigtwohill, on N25 to Waterford, is an unusual choice for lunch or a snack. It's in a restored 19th-century farmhouse, next to a medieval castle that is open to visitors. All the food is made upstairs and the cakes are particularly irresistible – forget diets and indulge. Open daily, except Sunday, 11 am-6 pm. ☎ (021) 488-3864.

A couple of miles farther on is Midleton, where you'll find the **Farmgate Restaurant**. This is the original branch; the other is in the English Market in Cork City. It's very popular for snacks, lunch and dinner, and you can also stock up on local produce in the shop. You eat surrounded by flowers, paintings and crafts made by locals. One section is outdoors.

The menu includes traditional Irish as well as European dishes, and there are daily specials. In the evenings, a pianist performs on the baby grand, and you can make requests. Very good value and a unique ambience. Open Monday-Saturday, 9 am-5 pm, and Thursday-Saturday, 7:30-9:45 pm. ☎ (021) 463-2777.

In Youghal, **Ahernes Seafood Bar and Gourmet Restaurant** has delighted palates for decades. Locally landed lobster, oysters, crab, prawns, mussels and salmon share the menu with meat and vegetarian dishes. ☎ (024) 92424.

West Cork

Kinsale Chamber of Tourism produces a great free brochure, *Eating Around*, with details of all the places to eat in the town, which is known as "the gourmet capital" of the Republic. ☎ (021) 477-4026; www.kinsale.ie.

At **The Heron's Cove**, in Goleen, diners can also stay overnight. It specializes in fish, also offering steaks and delicious vegetarian dishes, including Desmond Cheese and Rocket Risotto. ☎ (028) 35422.

The Altar at Toormore Bay, halfway between Schull and Goleen on the road to Mizen Head, uses local, organic and free of genetically modified ingredients. ☎ (028) 35254.

Mary Anne's, the pub halfway down Castletownsend's very steep street, serves the most delicious open-face crab sandwich I've ever tasted. There's a great choice on the menu, and in winter there's a roaring fire, and lots of chat.

County Kerry

■ Tourist Information

Cork-Kerry Tourism has offices at:

Beech Road, Killarney, open all year. ☎ (064) 31633; fax 34506.

Ashe Memorial Hall, Denny Street, Tralee. ☎ (066) 712-1288; fax 60360; touristofficetralee@shannon-dev.ie; www.shannon-dev.ie.

Dingle. ☎ (066) 915-1188.

Kenmare. ☎ (064) 31633.

Waterville. ☎ (066) 74646.

Cahirciveen. ☎ (066) 72589.

TRACING YOUR ANCESTORS

At the **Kerry Genealogical Research Centre**, research was suspended at time of writing, so contact them at info@irishgenealogy.ie for information.

■ Sightseeing

Killarney

 Killarney is Kerry's largest town. Since its foundation in 1750 by Lord Kenmare, Killarney has attracted thousands of tourists every year and continues to do so. No wonder, as few towns anywhere have such a beautiful setting. Killarney is ringed by the famous lakes and mountains that have inspired generations of songwriters, poets and artists. Major efforts have been made to make the town itself more attractive, with the addition of flower beds and brick paving, and by encouraging owners of businesses to use traditional wooden shopfronts and signs.

Among the sites worth visiting in Killarney is the **Museum of Irish Transport** in Scotts Gardens, opposite the Railway Station. It has a spectacular display of veteran, vintage and classic motor cars. There is also a collection of bicycles and motorcycles on display. The museum includes a 1930s garage with all the tools, spare parts and oil cans. There's even a 1930s calendar and an original wooden counter, with telephone, wireless and a ledger account book of that era. The walls are covered with a collection of original early motoring and cycling periodicals and of license plates from all over the world. Even if you are not particularly interested in cars and their history, it is so charming that you should enjoy a visit.

On Beech Road, next to the Tourist Information Office, is the **Killarney Model Railway**. It's one of the largest in the world, with over 50 trains running on a mile of track. It transports you through the landmarks of Europe, with thousands of tiny people depicting all walks of life. There's also a four-lane Scalextric racetrack where you can try out your racing skills, and a shop specializing in model railway items, die-cast rally and F1 models and radio control. Stay as long as you like.

St. Mary's Cathedral in the town is well worth at least a short visit. It was designed by Augustus Pugin and built in the Gothic style; his plan was for a rugged exterior and a smooth light-filled interior. The Cathedral was consecrated in 1855 and extensively renovated in the 1970s (there was some criticism of the renovation).

Killarney 250

From St. Patrick's Day, March 17, 2004, until October 2005, the town celebrates the anniversary of its foundation and its status as the birthplace of Irish tourism, with a comprehensive program of events. It begins with a Homecoming, which should be of particular interest to anyone with Kerry ancestry. Details from ☎ (064) 36622; info@killarney250.com; www. killarney250.com.

The Lakes

If you are in the area, you shouldn't miss taking at least a short trip around the lakes. You can drive yourself or take a jaunting car (a horse-drawn carriage driven by a jarvey, or coachman). Be careful about the charges for your trip on a jaunting car. Make sure you understand and agree on terms before climbing aboard.

The three lakes and the mountains that surround them are all within the **Killarney National Park**, Ireland's largest. Nearest the town is the **Lower Lake** (Lough Leane), which is studded with tiny islands. On its eastern shore are the historic **Muckross Abbey** and **Ross Castle**, which can also be visited by road. At the tip of the Muckross Peninsula is the quaint **Brickeen Bridge**, and **Dinis Island** is farther on, with its sub-tropical vegetation and views of the "Meeting of the Waters," made famous in song.

A narrow strait called the **Long Range** leads to the island-studded **Upper Lake**, surrounded by luxuriant woods of oak, arbutus, holly and mountain ash, with an understory of ferns and other plants.

In addition to the three main lakes, there are many others in the folds of the mountains, with numerous picturesque falls; the best known of them is **Torc Waterfall**. The **Owengarriff River** cascades through the wooded **Friar's Glen** into Muckross Lake. A pretty path takes you up to the top of this 59-foot-high (18 m) waterfall, and as you climb you have fantastic views (unless it is raining).

To the west of the Killarney Valley are the peaks of **MacGillicuddy's Reeks**. These mountains include **Carrauntoohill**, the highest peak in Ireland. Unless there is a mist or it is raining you should be able to see them.

Muckross

Not far from Killarney is **Muckross House**, with its gardens and traditional farms. The imposing neo-Tudor mansion, built in 1843, is on the shores of Muckross Lake, a beautiful location, and its rooms are full of period furnishings – some too full perhaps. Most interesting here is the **Mu-**

seum of Kerry Life, with displays based on the history of southwest Ireland, and the craft center, where you can watch talented people at work.

The beautifully landscaped lakeside gardens make a great setting for a picnic or stroll. The gardens are a joy, as many tender and exotic trees and shrubs flourish in the mild climate and their sheltered location. Particularly attractive features include a fine collection of rhododendrons and azaleas, a garden on a natural rock outcrop, and the tree-fringed lawns.

Muckross Traditional Farms is an outdoor representation of rural life in Kerry in the 1930s. It features three working farms, a laborer's cottage, blacksmith's forge, carpenter's workshop, lime kiln and well, all of which you can visit. The aim of this development is to give you the experience of rural life as it was in the early part of the 20th century. Each season brought its own set of activities in the house, the farmyard and on the land. ☎ (064) 31440; fax 31560; muckros@iol.ie; www.muckross-house.ie.

Before leaving Muckross, take the time to visit the 15th- century monastery dating from the , or go on a boat trip on the lake or a pony and trap ride along the shore. **Muckross Friary** is in a remarkable state of preservation. The tower was added after the church was built and is the only Franciscan tower in Ireland that is as wide as the church. The cloister and its associated buildings are still complete and there's a very old yew tree standing in the center.

Not far away is **Ross Castle**, a tower house that was probably built by the O'Donoghue Ross chieftains in the 16th century, with the barracks next to it dating from the mid-18th century. The castle has been fully restored and furnished and it is well worth taking the guided tour.

The Gap of Dunloe

One of the most famous sites near Killarney is the Gap of Dunloe, a rugged mountain pass on the eastern side of MacGillycuddy's Reeks. It's well worth visiting for the beauty of its rugged scenery, unspoiled landscape and corrie lakes, formed from round hollows in the hillsides. Walking is the best way to see it, but you need nearly a day to really explore it properly, as well as sensible footwear and clothing. If you have the time, leave your car at Kate Kearney's Cottage. Alternatively, if you have neither the time nor the energy to walk, you can hire either a pony or a jaunting car to travel the route, with its marvelous views.

The Ring of Kerry

The Ring of Kerry is the best-known touring route, 110 miles (176 km) long. It circles the **Iveragh Peninsula** through mountain passes, forests, bogs, skirting rivers, lakes and beautiful beaches. The Ring of

Kerry, as its name suggests, is a circular signposted route that passes through Killarney, Killorglin, Glenbeigh, Kells, Caherciveen, Waterville, Caherdaniel, Sneem and Kenmare. To the north of the Iveragh Peninsula is Dingle Bay and to its south is the estuary of the Kenmare River. Off its western edge is **Valentia Island**, which can be reached by road from a bridge at Portmagee and by car ferry from Reenard Point near Caherciveen. The ferry operates all day every day from 8:30 am to 10:30 pm, April 1 to September 30. ☎ (066) 947-6141; fax 947-6377. The harbor at Valentia is Europe's most westerly and it was here that the first transatlantic cable was brought ashore in 1858.

Derrynane

Derrynane House, the ancestral home of Daniel O'Connell, also known as The Liberator, is worth a short detour off the Ring of Kerry near Caherdaniel. It's run by the State Heritage Service and its gardens and the lovely beach nearby are now all part of the **Derrynane Historic National Park**. You can read about O'Connell's role in the history of Ireland in Chapter 1, page 18. Derrynane House, ☎ (066) 947-5113; fax 947-5432; visits@ealga.ie.

The Skelligs

Eight miles off the coast from Ballinskelligs near Waterville are the Skelligs – a group of small and fascinating islands. Monks landed on **Skellig Mhichíl** (pronounced "michael") in the sixth century and built their monastery 600 feet up on a cliff; its ruins stand starkly out from the bare black cliff. They survived there for 600 years by trading with passing ships, before moving to the mainland at Ballinskelligs in the 12th century. **Little Skellig** is home to over 20,000 pairs of breeding gannets, and **Great Skellig** has about 5,000 pairs of puffins, as well as a large number of other birds, including guillemots, stormy petrels and Manx shearwaters.

Next to the road bridge to Valentia Island at Portmagee, you can visit the **Skellig Experience** and learn all about the islands, their history, and their birds. You can also ask about boat trips to tour them. Open from April to mid-November, ☎ (066) 947-6306; fax rest of year, 481-3591; info@skelligexperience.com; www.skelligexperience.com.

Tralee

Tralee is an interesting and attractive town, the commercial capital and largest town in North Kerry. Its setting is lovely, surrounded by mountains, and looking out over a sheltered bay. At any time of year, you could easily spend a few days here and be kept happily occupied.

Every August the town hosts an international festival, **The Rose of Tralee**, which was inspired by the song of the same title. If you haven't heard of it, take a look at **www.roseoftralee.ie**.

Tralee is the home of the **Kerry County Museum**, which mounts fascinating temporary exhibitions as well as having a lively and interactive permanent display on local history and culture. There's a lovely Town Park beside it, and nearby is the attractive modern building housing the **Siamsa Tíre Theatre** and company, which is the National Folk Theatre of Ireland.

If you want to see a show that truly reflects the wealth of Irish culture, then go to one at Siamsa Tíre Theatre. You don't have to speak or understand Irish to appreciate the magic they create on stage. I don't, and I love what they do. Every time I've watched them, at least half the audi-

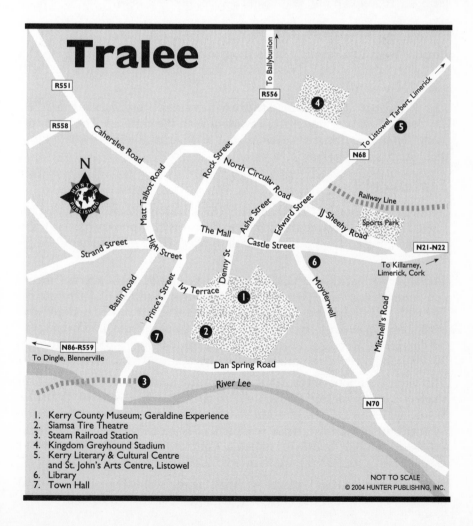

1. Kerry County Museum; Geraldine Experience
2. Siamsa Tíre Theatre
3. Steam Railroad Station
4. Kingdom Greyhound Stadium
5. Kerry Literary & Cultural Centre
   and St. John's Arts Centre, Listowel
6. Library
7. Town Hall

NOT TO SCALE
© 2004 HUNTER PUBLISHING, INC.

ence hasn't been able to speak English either! It really does show that sometimes you don't need words to communicate. Music, dance, mime and movement work just as well. One of their productions is about the Blasket Islands, off the Dingle Peninsula, and how the people living there lost their distinct culture when, in 1953, they left to live on the mainland. Siamsa Tíre Theatre, Town Park, Tralee, ☎ (066) 712-3055; info@siamsatire.com; www.siamsatire.com.

Just two miles outside Tralee is **Blennerville**, which was the main port for emigrants from the county during time of the Great Famine in the 1850s. There's an exhibition about it in the restored **Blennerville Windmill**, built by a local landlord in 1800 and the tallest in Europe. There's a miller on hand to explain the flour-making process, and the complex also includes craft workshops, a gift shop and restaurant. Open daily April-October, 10 am to 6 pm, ☎ (066) 712-1064; fax 712-7444.

Other Activities in Tralee

Manor West is a recently built shopping center outside of town on the N22 with lots of stores, a restaurant, and 1,000 parking spaces. ☎ (066) 719-0755.

The Kingdom Greyhound Stadium has races every Tuesday and Friday evening all year and also on Saturdays in the summer. The first race is at 7:50 pm, and there's a restaurant and bar. ☎ (066) 718-0008; kingdom_stadium@esatclear.ie; www.igb.ie.

Listowel

About 17 miles north of Tralee on the N69 is Listowel, a charming market town, full of traditional shopfronts and interesting pubs, especially the one belonging to the family of the late playwright and author John B. Keane.

The Kerry Literary and Cultural Centre and **St John's Arts Centre** run regular programs of events, including plays, readings and exhibitions. The Cultural Centre has a permanent display, a restaurant and gift and book shop. Open daily April to September, 10 am to 6 pm, and from October to March, Monday to Friday from 10 am to 5 pm. ☎ (068) 22212; fax 22170; info@kerrywritersmuseum.com; www.kerrywritersmuseum.com.

The town is famous throughout Ireland and among those interested in writing for its highly enjoyable annual festival, **Listowel Writers' Week**, which is held in late May/early June. Well known and aspiring writers mix in the town, with readings, book launches, a series of workshops, exhibitions, and lively debates. Contact Listowel Writers' Week at ☎ (068) 21074; fax 22893; writersweek@eircom.net; www.writersweek.ie.

In September Listowel buzzes with life again when thousands descend on the town to watch the horses at the annual **Listowel Races**.

Nearby is the pleasant seaside resort of **Ballybunion**, just five miles from Listowel, which came to international attention when then-President Bill Clinton played a round of golf on its links course.

The Conor Pass

If you leave Tralee and head west, following the coast of Tralee Bay, you're on your way to one of the most spectacularly beautiful areas on the island. Follow the signs for Conor Pass. You'll have difficulty keeping your eyes on the road ahead if you're driving, and you'd better not suffer from vertigo!

As you climb, the road winds round and round, and laid out below is a panorama you won't forget. There's a space to stop at the top and get your breath back.

You descend on the other side into **Dingle**, the main town on the peninsula. Even if there's hardly a tourist to be seen anywhere else in Ireland, there will be visitors here, most of them from Europe.

A major attraction is **Fungie**, who came to live here in 1983. He is a wild bottle-nosed dolphin, and he loves swimming with humans. He got the name from a fisherman, who was trying to grow a beard – and it looked like fungus.

Dingle has brightly painted buildings clustered round its natural harbor, where fishing is carried out as it has been for centuries. No wonder the town is renowned for excellent seafood. It's also the home of **An Café Liteartha**, a great bookshop with café, and lots of interesting craft shops.

Slea Head

Carry on through Dingle, following signs this time for Slea Head. The road winds along, and is very narrow in places, but here at least you are not climbing as well. Eventually, you come to **Dunquin** and the **Blasket Centre**, which faces the Blasket Islands. It is one of the most interesting centers I've ever visited, and its location is wonderful. It traces the history and culture of the people who lived on the islands just off the coast from here, until they were abandoned in the 1950s. ☎ (066) 9156444.

If the weather is clear, you can sit outside and see boats taking visitors out to the Blasket Islands.

Tours

Dero's Tours, based in Killarney, have been running escorted day-tours by coach for decades, and operate daily year-round. They offer a choice of routes: Killarney Highlights, Dingle and Slea Head, the Ring of Kerry, the Gap of Dunloe (which includes a homeward journey by boat). They also arrange jaunting car tours, lake cruises, a 24-hour taxi service, and car rental. ☎ (064) 31251; deroscoachtours@eircom.net; www.derostours. com.

O'Connor Auto Tours, also based in Killarney, runs a choice of three day tours – the Ring of Kerry, Dingle's Slea Head, Gap of Dunloe and Lakes of Killarney. Book the day before by calling ☎ (064) 31052.

Power Tours, Rock Street, Tralee, run day tours of the county, and will pick you up at your accommodation by prior arrangement. ☎ (066) 712-9444.

Finnegan's Tours, based in Kenmare, is a family business which has been taking visitors around Kerry and West Cork for generations. Tours include the Beara Peninsula, the Ring of Kerry and Killarney. Book at ☎ (064) 41491.

■ Adventures on Foot In Cork & Kerry

Long-Distance Routes

 In Cork and Kerry there are a number of long-distance **Waymarked Ways**: The Blackwater Way, part of the Ballyhoura Way, The Sheep's Head Way, The Beara Way, The Kerry Way, The Dingle Way, The North Kerry Way.

The **Blackwater Way** runs from the Knockmealdown Mountains in Co. Tipperary to near Rathmore on the Cork-Kerry border, linking the East Munster Way with the Kerry Way. Its total length is 104 miles (167 km) and its longest section is from Nad to Millstreet (19 miles/30 km).

The **Ballyhoura Way** follows part of the route of the O'Sullivan Beara March in the winter of 1601-2. For 50 miles (80 km) it passes through parts of counties Cork, Limerick and Tipperary, with wonderful views.

There's a linking route connecting the Blackwater Way and the Ballyhoura Way. There are also marked circular walks from Doneraile, Shanballymore, Ballinaboola, Castletownroche, Mitchelstown, Galty Wood (northeast of Mitchelstown), and Kildorrery.

The **Sheep's Head Way** takes in the peninsula of the same name and the Bantry area, and is 55 miles (88 km) long, with its highest point at Gouladoo (1,111 feet/338 m).

The **Kerry Way** is 135 miles (217 km) long and low-level, following old droving paths and coach roads through woodland, valleys and along the coast. If you start near Killarney, you go through the gardens and woodlands of the National Park, where you see the only pure herd of Irish red deer. After that, the route takes walkers through the almost empty valleys of the middle of Kerry and then on to the delightful seaside village of Glenbeigh. You walk alongside Dingle Bay until it reaches the Atlantic.

Information boards are displayed along the routes of all the long distance walks, or inquire locally. You should wear suitable clothing, and get a proper map for the walks.

*For details of the waymarked ways all over the country look at **www.irishwaymarkedways.ie**. This organization produces a free booklet that gives details of all the ways, and includes lists of recommended maps and guides, how to access the ways and route contacts.*

Parks

There are enjoyable walks in forest parks run by Coillte, the State Forestry Service in Co. Cork.

The **Farran Forest Park** is west of Cork City on the N22 to Macroom.

The **Gougane Barra Forest Park** is west of Ballingeary on the R584 to Bantry, at the Pass of Keimaneigh.

The park's name, Gougane Barra, is associated with the patron saint of Cork, Finbar, who, according to tradition, built a monastery on the little island here. Finbar is still a popular first name, and usually shortened to Barry these days.

The forest park has drive-around facilities with a marked trail; it also has a number of signposted walks.

The **Millstreet Country Park** is on the Mallow side of Millstreet, on the northern slopes of Musheramore Mountain. In the Visitor Centre there's a multimedia show on the story of the park, and touchscreens to consult for more information if you wish. There are walks, lakes, moorland, managed wetlands, a deer farm, lots of lovely views. Admission rates are per car. Open daily March-October, 10 am to 7 pm. ☎ (029) 70810; micp@iol. ie; www.micp.foundmark.com.

There are enjoyable walks around **Glengarifff** in West Cork, in the **Caha Mountains National Heritage Area**, and in the **Ancient Oak Forest** and **National Nature Reserve** on the edge of the village. A popular spot is **Barley Lake** high up on the Caha Mountains, which can almost be reached by road (park and walk the last stretch). It's an armchair or corrie lake, left behind after a glacier.

As well as walking in the National Park around Killarney, on the outskirts of the town is the **Coolwood Wildlife Sanctuary**, on a 47-acre complex, seven acres of it a wildlife park and the remaining area a wildlife sanctuary. It's a great place to visit for anyone interested in nature, birds, animals, pets, or just a walk in pleasant surroundings. You'll see lots of red squirrels, there's a well-established rookery, and it is also home to the rare golden eagle.

There are many other walks all over Kerry, including a **cliff walk** at **Ballybunion**, and the more adventurous **Urlee Hill walk** nearby.

The **Shannon Way** follows the route of the river from Ballybunion to Tarbert on the Shannon Estuary.

The **Kenmare Walking Festival** takes place at the end of May and beginning of June. Call for details at ☎ (064) 41034.

Guided Walking Tours

There are many organizations offering guided walks and tours, some including accommodation, among them:

- ■ **Southwest Walks**, Tralee, Co. Kerry. ☎ (066) 712-8733
- ■ **West Cork Discovery Walking Tours**, Rosscarbery, Co. Cork. ☎ (023) 48726
- ■ **Sheep's Head Way Walking Holidays**, all year. ☎/fax (027) 61052; suzannewhitty@hotmail.com
- ■ **Crowley Way Guided Hillwalk**, Clonakilty. ☎ (023) 46107; arigideen@ireland.com; www.reachireland.com

*How about wandering the roads of County Kerry with reins in your hand and no fixed routes. You can set off from the Dingle Peninsula or Killarney. Contact **Slatterys Horse Drawn Caravans**, Russell Street, Tralee. ☎ (066) 718-6240; www. horsecaravanholidays.ireland.ie.*

■ Adventures on Water

There are many facilities for cruises and watersports in Kerry, among them the following.

Lily of Killarney Watercoach has a number of daily sailings from Ross Castle, Killarney, the first at 10:30 am, the last at 5:45 pm. Book at Deros Office, Main Street, Killarney, ☎ (064) 31251.

Dingle Boatmen's Association runs trips to see Fungie, the dolphin, all day, every day; you have to book a separate trip and wear a wet suit to swim with him. ☎ (066) 915-2626.

You can also go on **Eco-Trips from Dingle Marina**. ☎ (086) 285-8802.

Safari runs Eco-Nature cruises from Kenmare Pier, lasting two hours, with free tea, coffee, snacks and use of binoculars, charts and books, with friendly and informative guides. Half- and full-day fishing expeditions, with all gear supplied; and kayaking, sailing, skiing, tube rides and speed boat rides also available. ☎ (064) 83171.

Near Sneem, **Derrynane Seasports** offers classes in wake boarding, surfing, canoeing, sailing, other watersports, with equipment hire, ☎ (087) 908-1208 (mobile); derrynaneseasports@eircom.net; www. derrynaneseasportseircom.net.

Jamie Knox, Castlegregory, Co. Kerry, provides accommodation, lessons, and rents equipment to those interested in windsurfing, surfing, sailing, wake-boarding. ☎ (066) 713-9411; www.jamieknox.com.

Activity Ireland offers a number of water-based and land-based activities, including scuba diving. The center is in the pretty village of Caherdaniel, eight miles west of Waterville, and close to Derrynane National Park in the foothills of the MacGillycuddy Reeks (mountains). Activities include board sailing, waterskiing, swimming, hill walking, abseiling and rock climbing. It also has a dive shop and rents out equipment. ☎/fax (066) 947-5277; info@activity-ireland; www.activity-ireland. com.

Valentia Watersports on Valentia Island, which can be reached by road or by ferry, has a number of different courses for divers, and will also help arrange accommodation for visitors. ☎ (066) 947-6204; fax 947-6367; info@divevalentia.ie; www.divevalentia.ie.

With **Ballinskelligs Watersports**, you can take trips to dive around the Skelligs, beautiful and historic islands, which are very popular with divers from all over the world. The company has two permits to dive there, which is unique. They also run boat trips. ☎ (066) 947-9182; enquiries@ skelligboats.com; www.skelligboats.com.

Fishing in Cork & Kerry

Cork and Kerry have over 100 fishable loughs and miles upon miles of superb salmon, sea trout and brown trout rivers. The environment is fresh, clean and virtually unspoiled, and the gentle warmth of the Gulf Stream ensures a comfortable climate year-round.

See pages 71-74 for details on angling in Ireland, regulations and best times to fish.

The southwest is rich in game, coarse and sea angling and many of its fisheries are world-famous, such as **Lough Currane** in Waterville, Co. Kerry, regarded by many as one of the truly great sea trout fisheries, or **Inniscarra Lake**, Co. Cork, the region's premier coarse angling fishery. Remember that a State license is needed for salmon and sea trout fishing, and that the owner of game fishing waters probably charges a daily fee as well. You'll find lots of information on the **South Western Regional Fisheries Board** website. Contact the SWRFB. ☎ (026) 41221; fax 41225; swrfb@swrfb.ie; www.swrfb.ie.

Fishing Permit Distributors

- **Landers Leisure Lines**, Courthouse Lane, Tralee, ☎ (066) 712-6644.

- **O'Neills Fishing Tackle**, Plunkett Street, Killarney, ☎ (064) 31970; fax 35689.

Deep Sea Angling in Cork

There are many sea angling centers in both counties, where boats and other equipment are available.

Among them are:

South Coast Angling Centre, Ballycotton, for wreck, reef and shark fishing, as well as boat trips. ☎ (021) 464-6002.

Cork Harbour Boats, Glenbrook, Passage West, has a deep sea angling boat. ☎/fax (021) 484-1348; corkharbourboatsltd@eircom.net; www. corkharbourboats.com

Courtmacsherry Sea Angling Center has two sea angling boats and also offers accommodation. ☎/fax (023) 46427; csal@iol.ie.

Gerald O'Neill at Leap, near Skibbereen, runs coastal trips as well as deep sea, wreck and shark-fishing trips. ☎ (028) 33510; fax 33401.

Schull Deep Sea Angling Center offers instruction, plus whale, seal and dolphin trips, as well as coastal cruises. ☎ (028) 37370; fax 37660; shark@angling-ireland.net.

Deep Sea Angling in Kerry

Sean O'Shea, Bunavalla, Caherdaniel, runs deep sea angling trips from Derrynane Harbor, plus boat trips to Skellig Michael. ☎/fax (066) 947-5129; www.sneem.com/seanoshea.

Castlecove Angling runs trips from Westcove Pier. ☎ (066) 947-5305.

An Tiaracht Angling, Ballydavid. ☎ (066) 915-5300.

Activity Ireland, Caherdaniel, runs fishing trips, including wreck and reef fishing, with a choice of day or evening. ☎/fax (066) 947-5277; info@ activity-ireland; www.activity-ireland.com.

Other Useful Contacts in Co. Cork

Maritime Tourism Limited, Castlepark, Kinsale, organizes trout angling at Ballyhass Lakes at Cecilstown near Mallow. They rent all equipment, including boats. ☎ (021) 477-4959; fax 477-4958; maritime@indigo. ie.

The River Ilen Anglers Club, for salmon and trout fishing on the river near Skibbereen, can be contacted at Fallons, North Street, Skibbereen. ☎ (028) 22264.

Good shore and beach angling is available in many parts of both counties, but you should always be aware of the dangers of fishing from ledges, especially in rough or windy weather and never fish alone.

Clontackle and Leisure Limited, Spillers Lane, Clonakilty, supplies fishing and outdoor equipment. They also run shore and boat trips, specializing in bass fishing. ☎/fax (023) 35580.

■ Adventures on Horseback

Killarney Riding Stables is just a mile outside Killarney, and here visitors can enjoy rides lasting from one to three hours. There's also the option of the six-day Killarney Reeks Trail. Open all year. ☎ (064) 31686; fax 34119.

Eagle Rock Equestrian Centre is at Caherdaniel on the shore of Derrynane Bay on the Ring of Kerry. Horses and ponies are available to suit all levels, with instruction if needed. ☎ (066) 947-5145; www. eaglerockcentre.com.

Burkes Horse Trekking Centre, Glenbeigh, on the edge of Rossbeigh beach, offers wonderful coastal treks. ☎ (066) 976-8386.

Coláiste Ide Stables, Dingle, specializes in lessons for all levels and in treks. They are open year-round. ☎ (066) 915-9100.

Dingle Horse Riding has hourly, daily and weekly rates for riding in the beautiful Dingle Peninsula. It also has two luxury apartments available for rent on a weekly basis. ☎ (066) 915-2018; www. dinglehorseriding.com.

Longs Riding Center at Kilcolman, Ventry, near Dingle, has horses to suit all riders, with hourly, daily and three-day trail rides available. ☎ (066) 915-9034; info@longsriding.com; www.longsriding.com.

■ Golf

Among the best-known golf courses in Kerry is Ballybunion, where US President Bill Clinton played, and where that's remembered by a statue of him in the little seaside town. They're also using him in their marketing of a Stay-and-Play program. If you stay in certain hotels or guesthouses, you get guaranteed tee times. Find out about it by looking at www.EasyGolfBallybunion.com. Otherwise, contact them at Ballybunion Golf Course, ☎ (068) 27146; fax 27387; bbgolfc@iol.ie; www.ballybuniongolfclub.ie.

Killarney Golf Club has two 18-hole parkland courses set in beautiful scenery. ☎ (064) 31034; fax 33065; reservations@killarney-golf.com; www.killarney-golf.com.

Five minutes from Killarney is the nine-hole course surrounded by mountains and woodlands of the **Ross Golf Club**. ☎ (064) 31125; fax 31860.

Other courses include:

Beaufort Golf Club. ☎ (064) 44440; fax 44752; beaufortgc@eircom.net.

Dooks Golf Club, Killorglin. ☎ (066) 976-8205; fax 976-8476; office@dooks.com; www.dooks.com.

Kenmare Golf Club, close to town center. ☎ (064) 41291; fax 42061.

Ceann Sibeal Golf Club at Ballyferriter on the western end of the Dingle Peninsula. ☎ (066) 915-6255; fax 915-6409.

Castlegregory Golf and Fishing Club has a nine-hole course and is on the northern side of the Dingle Peninsula. ☎ (066) 713-9444.

■ Where to Stay

☆☆☆ **The Brandon Hotel**, Princes Street, Tralee, is a welcoming and pleasant place to stay. There are 184 rooms, including 22 deluxe rooms and two suites on the fifth floor. It's worth asking for a room at the front on an upper floor, as from there you'll have a wonderful view of Tralee and its surroundings. There's a choice of where to eat, as the bar has a very good menu, and the Galleon Restaurant uses fresh farm produce and locally caught fish. There's lots of parking opposite for a nominal fee. Rates from $$, with special breaks available. ☎ (066) 712-3333; sales@ brandonhotel.ie; www.brandonhotel.ie.

☆☆☆☆☆ **The Hotel Europe** is in one of the most beautiful settings in the country, on the shores of Killarney's lower lake, Lough Leane, just outside the town. It has 205 bedrooms, most with balconies, and 120 of them have a lake view, while the others overlook the golf course. The hotel has a beauty centre, an exercise room, sauna, and indoor heated swimming pool. It also has indoor tennis courts and has Haflinger ponies available for gentle trekking in the hotel grounds.

HOTEL PRICE CHART	
Price per person, per night, with two sharing, including breakfast.	
$	Under US $50
$$	US $50-$100
$$$	US $101-$175
$$$$	US $176-$200
$$$$$	Over US $200

The hotel is beautifully furnished, with some antiques, and the bedrooms are spacious. Its **Panorama Restaurant** is L-shaped and very attractive, with its menu a mixture of Irish and international specialities. From $$. Central Reservations ☎ (064) 71350.

☆☆☆☆☆ **The Park Hotel and Restaurant**, Kenmare, has the most wonderful location, overlooking Kenmare Bay, and surrounded by glorious countryside. All of its 40 bedrooms are spacious and beautifully furnished, with sitting areas, antique furniture (including four-poster beds) and original works of art. The deluxe rooms and nine suites also have views of the sea or a private verandah. In the grounds guests can enjoy walking or playing tennis and croquet; next door is the Kenmare Golf Club.

The Park has won numerous awards and is considered one of the best hotels in the country. It's also admired for the quality of the food served in its restaurant, which is open to non-residents. The Park belongs to Ireland's Blue Book and is open mid-April to end October, and from December 23 to January 2. Rates from $$$$. ☎ (064) 41200; fax 41402; info@ parkkenmare.com; www.parkkenmare.com.

☆☆☆☆☆ **The Sheen Falls Lodge**, Kenmare, is also an award-winner. It has a beautiful setting overlooking the cascading rapids of the River Sheen in its own 300-acre estate, with riverside and forest walks.

All of its 66 spacious bedrooms have beautiful views, either of Kenmare Bay or of the waterfall, and are individually decorated and furnished. Guests have a choice of where to dine, with the elegant restaurant **La Cascade** or **Oscar's Bar and Bistro** on the waterside; food is also available in the Lodge's lounges.

It has excellent facilities, both indoors and out. There's a well-equipped fitness center, as well as an Aqua Suite with indoor heated pool, Jacuzzi, steam room and sauna. Beauty, body and facial treatments are also available.

Guests can explore the estate on horseback, with treks tailor-made. They can also go on guided walks, go clay pigeon shooting (with instruction available) or take a bicycle tour of the surrounding area. As the estate has 15 miles of private river bank, fishing packages are offered, including equipment and the services of a ghillie (guide).

There's a collection of vintage cars on display, which includes a 1978 Rolls Royce Silver Shadow II, a 1936 Buick Roadmaster, a 1975 Bentley, a 1922 Buick and a 1930 Ford Model A. Tailor-made scenic, half-day or full-day trips in the Buick can be arranged, including a champagne picnic lunch.

Rates from $$$$ with special packages available in autumn and winter.

Little Hay Cottage and Garden Cottage, thatched and set in secluded areas of the estate, are also available for a minimum stay of three nights. ☎ (064) 40006 from 9 am to 6 pm GMT Monday to Friday; 41600 at other times; www.sheenfallslodge.ie.

☆☆☆ The **Listowel Arms Hotel** on the Square in Listowel is a welcoming and traditional hotel, which offers good value to the visitor. It has 37 bedrooms, pleasantly furnished, and it serves wholesome Irish food– including huge portions of stew. Its bar is popular with locals, so it's a great place for a chat, and there's often entertainment laid on. Rates from $$. ☎ (068) 21500; fax 22524; listowelarms@ireland.com.

Historic Choices

Coolclogher House, Mill Road, Killarney, belongs to The Hidden Ireland group of historic private houses. It offers a stay with a difference as, with only four bedrooms for guests, it's almost like staying with friends. Coolclogher was built in the early 19th century and is surrounded by 68 acres of grounds, yet is just over a mile from busy Killarney. The bedrooms are spacious. There are lovely views of the grounds and the surrounding countryside with the National Park and mountains in the distance. There's also a conservatory, built around a camelia which is 170 years old, where guests can relax. Open March to November. Rates from $$. ☎ (064) 35996; fax 30933; info@coolclogherhouse.com www.coolclogherhouse.com

☆☆☆☆ The **Caragh Lodge Country House and Restaurant** was originally a fishing lodge and stands on the shore of Caragh Lake, near Killorglin. It is the ideal place to stay for salmon and trout fishing, and in the summer guests can swim or go boating. The Lodge is surrounded by a fine garden, which has won awards. It has 15 bedrooms and is open from April 25 to mid-October. Seafood, wild salmon and locally produced lamb feature on the menu, and non-residents can dine here – reservations recommended. Rates from $$$. ☎ (066) 976-9115; fax 976-9316; caragh@iol. ie; www.caraghlodge.com.

Horse-Drawn Holiday

Wander the roads of County Kerry with reins in your hand, and no fixed routes. You can set off from the Dingle Peninsula or Killarney. Contact **Slatterys Horse-Drawn Caravans**, Russell Street, Tralee. ☎ (066) 718-6240; www. horsecaravanholidays.ireland.ie.

Camping & RV Parks

The most westerly campsite in Europe is **Campaíl Teach An Aragail** or **Oratory House Camping** on the Dingle Peninsula, close to the historic Gallarus Oratory and other interesting archaeological sites and long distance walking routes. It has its own pub restaurant and information center for activities such as bird- and whale-watching. Open Easter to late September. ☎ (066) 915-5143; tp@iol.ie.

☆ **Ballintaggart House Budget Accommodation** is a camping site near Dingle on the grounds of a hunting lodge built in 1703. It's open May to end September. ☎ (066) 915-1454; fax 915-2207; info@ dingleaccommodation.com; www.dingleaccommodation.com.

☆☆☆ **Ring of Kerry Camping and Caravan Park** has beautiful views of Kenmare Bay. Open April to end September. ☎ (064) 41648; fax 41631; info@kerrycamping.com.

☆☆☆ **Glenross** is at Glenbeigh on the Ring of Kerry. Open May to mid-September. ☎ (066) 976-8451 from May to August; (064) 31590 rest of year; glenross@eircom.net; www.killarneycamping.com.

☆☆☆ **Parklands Holiday Park** is at Ballybunion, and its facilities include a tennis court. Mobile homes are available to rent. Park open from May to end of September. ☎ (068) 27275.

☆☆ **Goosey Island Campsite** is in Sneem on the Ring of Kerry, and is open mid-April to mid-October. ☎ (064) 45577; fax 45181; washer@ oceanfree.net; www.gooseyisland.com.

There's a choice of parks near Killarney:

☆☆☆ **Beech Grove** is open mid-April to mid-October. It has mobile homes to rent. ☎ (064) 31727.

☆☆☆ **Flemings White Bridge** is open mid-March to end October, with mobile homes available for rent. ☎ (064) 31590; fax 37474; fwbcamping@eircom.net; www.killarneycamping.com.

☆☆☆☆ **Fossa** also has mobile homes to rent. Open April to end September. ☎ (064) 31497; fax 34459; fossaholidays@eircom.net; www.camping-holidaysireland.com.

☆☆☆☆ **Flesk** is open mid-April to end September. ☎ (064) 31704; fax 35439; killarneylakes@eircom.net.

☆☆ **White Villa Farm** is on the N22 very close to the town of Killarney. Open April to mid-October. ☎ (064) 20671; killarneycamping@eircom.net; www.killarneycaravanpark.com.

Wests Caravan Park is unclassified, and is on the road to Killarney at Killorglin. Mobile homes available to rent. Open April to end October. ☎ (066) 976-1240; fax 976-1833; enquiries@westcaravans.com.

☆☆ **Bayview** is a mobile home and touring RV park at Tralee, where mobile homes are available for rent. Open May to October. ☎ (066) 712-6140; bayviewtralee@eircom.net.

☆☆☆☆ **Woodlands Park** is also at Tralee. It's open from the middle of March to the end of September. ☎ (066) 712-1235; fax 718-1199; wdlands@eircom.net; www.discoverkerry.com/holiday.

☆☆☆ **Sir Roger's Caravan and Camping Park** is at Banna Beach, near Ardfert. Open April to November. ☎ (066) 713-4730; fax 713-4861; sirrogerscaravanpark@hotmail.com.

☆☆ **Creveen Lodge** is on the Healy Pass road, the R574, at Lauragh. Open Easter to end October. ☎ (064) 83131; info@creveenlodge.com; www.creveenlodge.com.

☆☆☆☆ **Wave Crest** is on the Ring of Kerry at Caherdaniel. Open mid-March to mid-October. ☎/fax (066) 947-5188; wavecrest@eircom.net; www.wavecrestcamping.com.

☆☆☆ **Glenbeg** is also on the Ring of Kerry at Caherdaniel. It's next to a sandy beach. Open mid-April to early October. ☎ (066) 947-5182; glenbeg@eircom.net.

☆☆ **Casey's** is in the middle of the village of Ballyheigue and is open from early May to mid-September. ☎ (066) 713-3195; fax 713-3255.

☆☆☆ **Mannix Point** camping and RV park is at Caherciveen surrounded by mountains on three sides and facing out to the Atlantic. It's open from mid-March to October 1. ☎ (066) 947-2806; fax 947-2028; mannixpoint@mail.com; www.campinginkerry.com.

☆☆☆☆ The **Anchor Caravan Park** is at Castlegregory and is open from Easter to end September. ☎ (066) 713-9157; anchorcaravanpark@eircom.net.

Hostels in Cork & Kerry

There are more hostels in counties Cork and Kerry than in any other part of the island, many of them in beautiful locations. Most, but not all, belong to the **Independent Holiday Hostels of Ireland**, ☎ (01) 836-4700; info@hostels-ireland.com; www.hostels-ireland.com.

■ Where to Eat

 Among the many pubs all over the county offering food as well as musical entertainment is **Larkins Pub and Restaurant** on Main Street, Milltown, which is a village surrounded by the McGillycuddy Reeks on one side and the Slieve Mish Mountains on the other. Breakfast, lunch and evening meals are available. ☎ (066) 976-7217; fax 976-7515.

The Danny Mann Pub is part of Eviston House Hotel on New Street, Killarney, and has attracted tourists over many years for its entertainment, as well as for its food. You can enjoy a hearty meal while listening to traditional Irish music and watching Irish dancing. ☎ (064) 31640; fax 33685; evishtl@eircom.net; www.dannymann.ie.

Gaby's Seafood Restaurant, High Street, Killarney, is open Mondays to Saturdays for dinner, from 6 to 10 pm. Seafood, steaks and vegetarian dishes are included on the menu. ☎ (064) 32519.

Keanes of Curraheen is on the N86 main road from Tralee to Dingle, four miles from Tralee. It's a pub with a restaurant and offers good food at reasonable prices. It's open every day from 11:30 am to 11:30 pm. ☎ (066) 712-8054.

Nick's Restaurant in Killorglin is a family-run business that was founded over 25 years ago. It only opens for dinner in the evening and has a good choice of dishes, specialiszing in seafood. A pianist entertains as you examine the menu or enjoy a drink before or after dinner in their lounge. ☎ (066) 976-1219; fax 976-1233.

Mac's Restaurant & Dairy Ice-Cream Parlour in the middle of town on Main Street, Killarney, is where to go for delicious home baking and homemade ice cream sundaes. Mac's ice cream is made using only the best natural wholesome ingredients and is now distributed to shops and other restaurants throughout Kerry and farther afield. ☎ (064) 35213; macsicecream@eircom.net; www.macsicecream.com.

Halfway between Glenbeigh and Cahirciveen on the Ring of Kerry at Kells is **Pat's Craft Shop and Restaurant**. There's also a food store, gas station and post office, so it's a great place to stop. The restaurant also has the advantage of looking out over Dingle Bay. ☎ (066) 947-7601; fax 947-7660; patscraftshop@eircom.net.

The Vestry Restaurant and Bar, Tenplenoe, Greenane, which is on the Ring of Kerry and a 10-minute drive from Kenmare, is a very special place. It's in a beautifully restored 18th-century church, and only opened as a restaurant recently. There's space for 60, some upstairs in the Minstrel Gallery. When the weather is suitable you can also sit outside in the Vestry garden overlooking Kenmare Bay. Choices include venison, sea trout and ostrich; there's a vegetarian menu and there are daily specials. Open from 12:30 daily, with last orders for dinner at 9 pm. Bar snacks available from 12:30 to 5 pm. Early Bird menu from 5-6:30 pm; Sunday lunch 12:30-3:30pm. ☎/fax (064) 41958; davidhillier@oceanfree.net; www.neidin.net/vestry.

The Wild Banks Restaurant is in the middle of Dingle, and is open in the evenings, except Mondays, for dinner from March until January 6. Lunch is available from July to September, and the restaurant has an Early Bird menu from 6 to 8 pm, as well as an à la carte dinner menu. ☎ (066) 915-2888; thewildbanks@eircom.net; www.thewildbanks.com.

■ Further Information On Cork & Kerry

Fáilte Ireland has a website covering both counties: www.corkkerry.ie.

West Cork Tourism does wonderful work, including producing free guides to everything the area offers, all under the "Fuchsia" brand, the shrub found all over this part of the country. If you're heading for this area, get their booklet called *Our Home, Your Holiday*, which is invaluable. UDC (Urban District Council) Offices, North Street, Skibbereen, ☎ (028) 22812; wctc@indigo.ie; www.westcorktourism.ie.

Useful Websites

- A very useful website, listing hotels, guesthouses, activities: **www.cometocork.com**.
- Everything from sport and entertainment to accommodation is on: **www.dodingle.com**; ☎ (066) 915-0898; info@ dodingle.com.

Clare & Limerick

Counties Clare and Limerick are marketed by Fáilte Ireland as the Shannon Region, which also takes in parts of the neighboring counties of Tipperary, Kerry and Offaly. This chapter covers Clare and Limerick only, and the others are described within their respective counties.

Getting Here & Getting Around

You can fly directly to this region from North America to Shannon Airport in Co. Clare, which is exactly halfway between Ennis and Limerick City, 10 miles (16 km) to either destination. There are regular buses from the airport to both Limerick and Ennis. You can also get to this part of the country by car, train or bus, or fly from Dublin.

■ By Rail

Limerick City is connected by rail to mainline services for Dublin, Cork, Waterford and other areas, and there is a limited rail service between the city and Ennis. For information, ☎ 1850-366222 within Ireland or, from outside of Ireland, ☎ 353 18366222. Or check the website at www.irishrail.ie.

■ By Bus

The Expressway bus service operates between Limerick City and Cork to the south and on to Ballina, Co. Mayo, to the north, stopping in Ennis. There are also Expressway services between Limerick and Dublin. Bus services connect most of the main towns and villages around both counties to Ennis and Limerick City.

- Bus Station, Limerick. ☎ (061) 313-333.
- Bus Station, Ennis. ☎ (065) 682-4177.

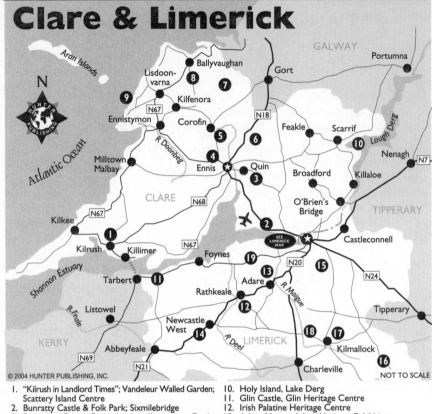

Clare & Limerick

1. "Kilrush in Landlord Times"; Vandeleur Walled Garden; Scattery Island Centre
2. Bunratty Castle & Folk Park; Sixmilebridge
3. Franciscan Friary; Craigaunowen; Knappogue Castle
4. The Friary; County Museum; St. Flannan's College
5. Dysart O'Dea Castle & Clare Archaeology Centre
6. Dromore Wood; O'Brien Castle
7. The Burren; Burren Centre; Cathedral
8. Aillwee Cave
9. Moher Hill Open Farm; St. Brigid's Well; Cliffs of Moher; Doolin Point
10. Holy Island, Lake Derg
11. Glin Castle, Glin Heritage Centre
12. Irish Palatine Heritage Centre
13. Adare Manor; Adare Heritage Exhibition
14. Desmond Banqueting Hall
15. Lough Gur Stone Age Centre
16. Griston Bog
17. Dominican Priory; Collegiate Church; King John's Castle
18. Bruree Heritage Centre & de Valera Museum
19. Curraghchase Forest Park & Celtic Park & Gardens

© 2004 HUNTER PUBLISHING, INC.

County Clare

From the limestone region of the Burren in the northwest to the undulating hills in the east, Clare is a fascinating area to visit, with its contrasting landscapes. The county is almost surrounded by water, with the wide estuary of the River Shannon to the south, the rugged Atlantic coastline along the west and Lough Derg to the east.

The area boasts some of the most wonderful beaches in the country, the majority deserted for much of the year. If you are lucky with clear weather you will also experience unforgettable sunsets, looking west over the Atlantic, when it appears that the sun is setting fire to the sea as it sinks below the horizon.

County Clare was one of the first areas of Ireland to develop tourism, with the idea of catering in particular to North Americans arriving at Shannon Airport. In recent years, there has been a decline in the numbers landing here due to the compulsory stopover being abandoned.

The county town is **Ennis**, and its other main towns are **Kilrush** and **Kilkee** in the west, and **Killaloe** to the east.

■ Getting to Co. Clare

By Road

 The main roads in Co. Clare are the N18 from Ennis north to Galway and south to Limerick; the N85 from Ennis to Ennistymon and on to Ballyvaughan; and the N65 to Kilrush. The N67 links Kilkee with towns and villages near or on the coast, including Milltown Malbay, Lahinch and Ennistymon.

By Car Ferry

If you're traveling to Clare from County Kerry by road, you can avoid Limerick altogether by using the car ferry from Tarbert to Killimer, seven miles (11 km) off the N68 near Kilrush. If you are traveling south from Clare to Kerry, take the N67 coast road. The ferry runs daily, from 7 am to 9 pm, all year except Christmas Day; from Killimer on the Clare side it departs on the hour, and from Tarbert it leaves on the half-hour (last ferry is at 9:30 pm). **Shannon Ferry Ltd**, Killimer. ☎ (065) 905-3124; fax 905-3125; enquiries@shannonferries.com; www.shannonferries.com.

■ Tourist Information

 Fáilte Ireland offices:

Arthur's Row, off O'Connell Street, Ennis, open all year. ☎ (065) 682-8366.

Arrivals Hall, Shannon Airport, open all year. ☎ (061) 471-664.

Open in tourist season:

Cliffs of Moher, near Liscannor. ☎ (065) 708-1171.

The Square, Kilkee. ☎ (065) 905-6111.

Moore Street, Kilrush. ☎ (065) 905-1577.

The Bridge, Killaloe. ☎ (061) 376-866.

TRACING YOUR ANCESTORS

Clare Heritage Centre, Corofin, four miles (6.4 km) from Ennis, is where anyone with roots in the county can trace their ancestors. Housed in an old church, it operates all year round. There's also a museum telling the story of life in the west of Ireland in the 19th century, open daily from April to October, 9:30 am-5:30 pm. ☎ (065) 683-7955; clareheritage@ eircom.net; www.clareroots.com.

■ Ennis

Sightseeing

 Ennis is the county town of Clare and always pleasantly busy. It takes its name from the Irish word "inis" (lake) and stands on the River Fergus. Its streets are narrow and attractive, some of them pedestrianized, and it is worth stopping here for at least a few hours. Many people come here for traditional music, and every May the town hosts **Fleadh Nua**, an international celebration of Irish culture. Ennis looks to the future as well as its past, and is Ireland's first Information Age Town, with the largest community technology project in the country.

The county is closely associated with Daniel O'Connell, who was elected as its Member of Parliament, leading to Catholic Emancipation in 1829 – and later earning Clare the name "Banner County" from the banners carried during rallies and meetings. A monument to O'Connell dominates the narrow main street named after him.

Ennis has been multicultural for decades, more so than most Irish towns, as refugees from Cuba arrived at Shannon, having gotten off flights to the USSR. They've been joined by every nationality in recent years, and that's reflected in the range of shops and restaurants, as well as the faces you see on its streets. Because of its central location, Ennis is the ideal place to stay while you explore counties Clare, Tipperary and Galway.

The Friary, Abbey Street, was founded by the O'Briens in the 13th century. Many of its original features survive and it's well worth visiting. It's in the care of the State Heritage Service, and guided tours are available. Open June to mid-September daily, 10 am-6 pm; April, May, late September, October, open daily except Monday until 5 pm. ☎/fax (065) 682-9100; ennisfriary@ealga.ie.

Just off O'Connell Street is the **County Museum** with its Riches of Clare exhibition. The Tourist Information office is in the same building.

From June to September, the museum is open daily; from October to December, Tuesday to Saturday; from March to May, Monday to Saturday;

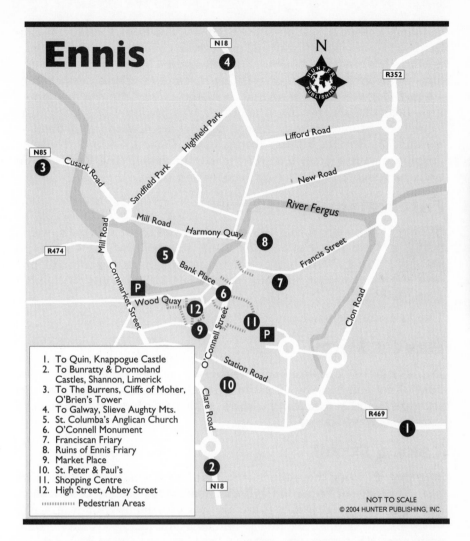

Ennis

1. To Quin, Knappogue Castle
2. To Bunratty & Dromoland Castles, Shannon, Limerick
3. To The Burrens, Cliffs of Moher, O'Brien's Tower
4. To Galway, Slieve Aughty Mts.
5. St. Columba's Anglican Church
6. O'Connell Monument
7. Franciscan Friary
8. Ruins of Ennis Friary
9. Market Place
10. St. Peter & Paul's
11. Shopping Centre
12. High Street, Abbey Street
.... Pedestrian Areas

NOT TO SCALE
© 2004 HUNTER PUBLISHING, INC.

year-round hours are 9:30-5. ☎ (065) 682-3382; fax 684-2119; claremuseum@eircom.net; www.clarelibrary.ie.

Shopping in Ennis

There are lots of fascinating shops in Ennis selling everything from designer fashions to locally produced crafts. My favorite hardware shop in the country is **Rohans** on Parnell Street. Take a peek inside and see the enormous range available – literally everything from needles to saucepans, and a lot more besides. If you're camping or cooking for yourself, you'll find it a useful resource.

In the center of town there's an open-air market. Some stalls are open on weekdays, augmented by many more on Saturdays. There are two secondhand book shops just off Market Square. The **Book Gallery** specializes in books of Irish interest, and also carries general stock. Owner Sean Spellissy is a great source of local knowledge and has written a few books himself, including *Clare, County of Contrast* and *The Ennis Compendium* – a terrific guide to the town and its history, with delightful line drawings. Look out also for the wonderful works produced by CLASP, (the Clare Local Studies Project). Among its titles are *Archaeology of the Burren* and *The Strangers Gaze: Travels in Co. Clare 1534-1950*. The shop upstairs also has great bargains, mostly in fiction. The **Ennis Book Shop** on Abbey Street is where to go for new titles.

Entertainment in Ennis

 There are music sessions in many of the town's pubs; watch for signs or ask locally. **Glór, the Irish Music Centre** on Friar's Walk, has an interesting program all year round, and also hosts exhibitions. ☎ (065) 684-3103; fax 684-5372; info@ glor.ie; www.glor.ie.

There's a multi-screen cinema on Parnell Street.

Have a Swim

Ennis Leisure Complex is open weekdays from 8 am to 10 pm, Saturdays from 10 am and Sundays 10 am to 6 pm. Sessions start on the hour and some are pre-booked, so phone to check. ☎ (065) 682-1604; leisurecomplex@ clarecoco.ie; www.clare.ie.

Take a Stroll

 Skirting the grounds of St. Flannan's College, on the Limerick edge of Ennis, is the Rocky Road, which is perfect for a short and quiet stroll. There are lots of wildflowers and if you're lucky you'll see rabbits and other animals. Look out for wandering cows that graze here between the limestone outcrops.

*Shannon Heritage runs eight sites, in counties Clare, Limerick, and one in Co. Galway, which you can find on www. shannonheritage.com. They include **King John's Castle** in Limerick City, **Bunratty Castle** (shown at left) and **Folk Park** in Co. Clare, and **Dunguaire Castle**, Kinvara, Co. Galway.*

Just north of Ennis at Ruan, off the N18 to Galway, is **Dromore Wood**, a nature reserve covering 1,000 acres. It's a lovely place for a walk.

Because of its different habitats, it has a great variety of flora and fauna, including callows, limestone pavement, reed beds and woodland. There are also a number of historic ruins to be seen, including the 17th-century O'Brien castle by the lake, two ring forts and a lime kiln. The castle is open all year, daylight hours, and admission is free. The Visitor Centre is open mid-June to mid-September, 10 am to 6 pm. ☎ (065) 683-7166.

■ Bunratty

South of Ennis on the N18 to Limerick is **Bunratty Castle and Folk Park**. It's high on the list of top visitor attractions, but don't worry – that doesn't mean it's crowded, as the site is big enough to absorb a lot of people. If you know little about Ireland, go there at the beginning of your vacation as it gives you a good idea of how we lived in earlier times.

Entire houses of various sizes and dates have been taken apart stone-by-stone and reassembled here, along with a school, a pub, a church, a row of shops, and other buildings.

What makes it especially enjoyable is watching activities, including scones and bread being made, as well as work being carried out in the little fields. Chat with the staff; they are very friendly and informative.

Bunratty Castle overlooks the river Shannon. Once the stronghold of the O'Briens, kings and later earls of Thomond, it reflects their style and power. Its Great Hall has a very fine collection of 14th-century furniture, paintings and wall hangings. Open all year, 9:30 am to 5:30 pm; June-August, 9 am to 6:30 pm. Note that last admission to the castle is 4 pm all year, so go there before visiting the Folk Park. There's a tea room and a good gift shop. **Mac's Pub** on the village street serves lunches and snacks. It stays open after the Folk Park closes, with frequent music sessions.

Evening Entertainment

There are Irish Nights in the **Corn Barn** in Bunratty Folk Park from April-October, with dance, music and song, food and wine.

You can also join in the fun at a **medieval banquet** in the three castles run by Shannon Heritage, with plenty of entertainment as well as food and drink. **Bunratty** medieval banquets run year-round. At **Knappogue Castle** they go from April to October, and at **Dunguaire Castle** from May to October, subject to demand. Times for all three are 5:30 pm and 8:45 pm.

For information and to book banquets or the Irish Nights, ☎ (061) 360-788 or ask at tourist offices.

As in most other areas of the country, you'll see much more if you don't keep to the main roads. While you're in the Bunratty area, wander through the little villages, including **Sixmilebridge**, which has a lovely pub, **The Greyhound**, right on the river bank, with waterfowl to watch as you relax over a drink or snack outdoors. Nearby is **Quin**, on the R469, seven miles (11 km) from Ennis, with its well-preserved 15th-century **Franciscan Friary**, founded by the Macnamaras.

■ A Fascinating Re-Creation

Near Quin is **Craggaunowen**, one of my favorite places to visit. It's a re-creation of how we lived in previous centuries, with a crannóg (lake dwelling), ring fort, souterrain or underground dwelling, all around the castle, built in 1550. The castle has wonderful European wood carvings. It all nestles in quiet countryside. The late John Hunt and his wife Gertrude bought the land, restored the castle and generously handed the project over to the State. Their collection is now shown at the Hunt Museum in Limerick (see page 325).

Souterrains

These were underground passages that served as places for safe storage and for refuge, and as secret means of entering or leaving defended places, particularly during the period of Viking raids in the nionth and 10th centuries. Some were simple passages, while others were complex labyrinths.

Even if you're not interested in history, you'd enjoy a stroll here, looking at animals including wild boar and Soya sheep, species bred in prehistoric times. The Celts were great seafarers, and St. Brendan the Navigator may have discovered America before Columbus. Tim Severin, a contemporary adventurer, built a replica of Brendan's leather-hulled boat, which he sailed to Greenland; it's displayed here. There's also a charming tea room. Open May to the end of September, 10 am-6 pm.

■ Knappogue Castle

Also near Quin is Knappogue Castle, built by the Macnamaras in 1467. They owned it until 1815, apart from when Cromwell used it as his headquarters and thus saved it from the destruction he wreaked elsewhere. Much enlarged in the 19th century, it was used in 1921 as a secret meeting place by the Republican Clare County Council. It had become a ruin by 1966, when it was bought and restored by Mr. and Mrs. Andrews of Houston, Texas. It's been open to the public since 1969. Open May to September, Friday to Tuesday, 9:30 am-5:30 pm and for medieval banquets (see above).

■ A Scenic Tour of West Clare

Head southwest out of Ennis on the N68.

The West Clare Railway

On the N67 road between Kilrush and Kilkee, you come to the Moyasta railway junction. Here you can take a short trip in a couple of carriages on a section of the West Clare railway, restored by local enthusiasts, and you also visit the little station. The railway used to carry passengers from Ennis through Corofin, Ennistymon, Lahinch, Miltown Malbay, Quilty, and south to Kilrush until the line closed in the 1960s. I remember the excitement of traveling on it to the sea in childhood. It was immortalized in the song "Are you right there, Michael, are you right?" by Percy French. It's an absolute delight. At Ennis Station one of the original engines is on display. ☎ (065) 905-1284.

Kilrush

Kilrush is one of the country's Heritage Towns. It has a very wide main street with some fine 18th-century buildings. It's a good place to shop, and there are plenty of pubs and restaurants where you can have a snack or meal. In the Town Hall there's an exhibition called **Kilrush in Landlord Times**. ☎ (065) 905-1577; www.westclare.com.

A Garden Walk in Kilrush

The **Vandeleur Walled Garden** is on the river and set among 420 acres of woodland. Many unusual and tender plants thrive here and there are other features, including a maze, and woodland trails to follow, plus a coffee and gift shop. Open daily all year from 10 am; April to October until 5 pm; closes at 4:30 pm other months. ☎ (065) 905-1760; kilrush@clarecoco.ie; www.kilrush.ie.

Scattery Island

The Scattery Island Centre on Merchant's Quay, Kilrush, is where to go for information on the island just off the coast and its **sixth-century monastery**, founded by St. Senan. Admission is free to the Centre, and it's open mid-June to mid-September daily, 10 am to 6 pm. Call to check times off-season. ☎/fax (065) 905-2139; scatteryisland@ealga.ie.

Kilkee

Kilkee, just north of Kilrush, has a beautiful horseshoe-shaped bay, with a beach that is safe for swimmers. It's been a popular resort for years, and there are some fine houses dating from the late 19th and early 20th century overlooking the sea. Many of these were the summer homes of people living elsewhere, or were rented out to visitors by residents.

With the growth in package vacations to sun destinations, resorts like Kilkee lost a lot of their popularity among the Irish, but that's to the visitor's advantage. It's quite peaceful now. It's an attractive and friendly little town, with wonderful walks around the cliffs, and is particularly popular for diving.

■ An Alternative Route to West Clare

Head northwest out of Ennis on the N85 and either continue on to Ennistymon, before turning south along the coast, or turn left at Inagh (where there's a microbrewery) onto the R460, which takes you west to Miltown Malbay and Spanish Point.

There's yet another route to the coast from Ennis; this is the R474, via Inch and Connolly, which climbs to give pleasant views of the countryside, including turf beds on the slopes of Mount Callan.

Miltown Malbay is a market town with plenty of small shops, restaurants and pubs. The town is known for its annual **Willie Clancy Week**, which draws thousands of fans of traditional music, who come to learn as well as listen and enjoy themselves.

Spanish Point has sand dunes and a long beach, but swimming here can be treacherous, although in summer there are lifeguards on duty. It's named after the Spanish Armada, which was wrecked all along Ireland's west coast, and there's a memorial near the beach. It's very popular with surfers and is great for a walk along the dunes, where there's the Spanish Point Golf Club, ☎ (065) 708-4198, www.spanish-point.com. The Crosses of Annagh is just outside the town of Miltown Malbay, near the coast. A welter of small roads, four or five of them, meet at the doorstep of a fine and spacious pub of the **Crosses of Annagh Pub**, which is very popular for its music and traditional dancing sessions.

As you travel, you'll see the patchwork of little fields divided by drystone walls, which have withstood the brisk winds off the Atlantic for centuries.

The N67 coast road from Milltown Malbay takes you north to **Lahinch**, with its lovely safe beach, again popular with surfers. It's an attractive little village and has some good places to eat. If the beach doesn't attract, you can swim in the 82-foot (25 m) pool at Seaworld, which also has an aquarium. ☎ (065) 708-1900; fax 708-1901; enquiries@lahinchseaworld. com; www.iol.ie/~seaworld.

A couple of miles inland is **Ennistymon**, a larger town with lots of traditional shop fronts and pubs.

Turn left at Lahinch and the R478 takes you to **Liscannor**, which used to be a quiet and pretty fishing village, but has changed with the building of an ugly new hotel near the pier as you enter town and lots of new houses dwarfing the more traditional cottages.

After the village, just as the road starts to climb, you come to the **Liscannor Stone Story and Rock Shop**, where you can learn about ancient quarrying around the Cliffs of Moher and buy fossils, minerals and gems from around the world. ☎ (065) 708-1930.

On the way to the Cliffs of Moher, you come to the turning on your right for **Moher Hill Open Farm**, which has a variety of rare breeds, and you can enjoy a quiet walk in lovely surroundings. There's also a teashop. Open Monday-Saturday, 10 am-6 pm, Sunday, noon-6 pm. ☎ (065) 708-1071.

A couple of miles farther on you come to **St. Brigid's Well** on the left. Its entrance has been "improved" recently, but inside it looks as it has for centuries, with tokens and notes begging for the saint's intercession hanging on the wall.

The Cliffs of Moher

The Cliffs of Moher, one of Europe's most spectacular coastal features, rise to a height of 650 feet (200 m) and extend for about five miles (8 km) into the Atlantic. There are well-worn paths along the cliffs, including a short walk to Hag's Head, and you see lots of guillemots and other sea birds. The cliffs are formed of layers of siltstone, shale and sandstone, and look like slices lying on top of each other. Do be careful and don't go near the edge.

There's a Visitor Centre, open all year from 9:30 am to 5:30 pm, and from June-August, 9 am to 7 pm, but I prefer to let this site of outstanding natural beauty speak for itself. Walk up to O'Brien's Tower and look around. There is a fee for parking, even in winter, when there is hardly anyone around.

Continue on from here and you'll come to **Lisdoonvarna**. On the way you come across what must, in my opinion, be one of the most inappropriate buildings to ever have been given planning permission! The Burren Castle Hotel looks like it was designed for Hollywood and dropped into this beautiful landscape by mistake. Try to forget you saw it.

Doolin

You'll see plenty of signs for the village of Doolin, just off the road on the coast, which is famous worldwide for traditional music. It's worth dropping in to the **Doolin Crafts Gallery and Garden** beside the cemetery, which stocks local and Irish knitwear, ceramics, and jewelry. It also has a café, which is ideal for lunch or afternoon tea. ☎ (065) 707-4511.

The **Aran Islands**, visible from the coast in clear weather, are worth visiting for their traditional way of life. There are ferries each morning from Doolin, returning around 5 pm.

Lisdoonvarna

Lisdoonvarna has been a spa town since the 19th century and today the **Spa Wells Centre** features sulfur baths, massage, saunas and other health facilities. Open June-October. ☎ (065) 7074-023.

The town is best known now for its Bachelor Festival in September, founded to find wives for lonely farmers, who came here after the harvest was over and before winter set in. It's an attractive little place, with interesting shops and a choice of places to stay and to eat. You can see how local salmon is smoked and buy some to take home at **The Burren Smokehouse** in the town. ☎ (065) 707-4432.

A Unique Landscape

At Lisdoonvarna you are on the edge of the Burren, one of the most unique landscapes in Europe. Before exploring it take a detour to **Kilfenora** and pay a visit to the **Burren Centre**, where the 20-minute audio-visual presentation is the perfect introduction to the region. ☎ (065) 708-8030; burrencentre@eircom.net; www.theburrencentre.ie.

While in Kilfenora, take a look at the **Cathedral** and **Celtic high crosses** in the churchyard, which date from the year 600 AD (see page 112). For some strange reason, the parish still belongs to the Holy See in the Vatican. In the village, **Vaughan's Pub** has traditional music and dance on Thursday and Sunday evenings in summer.

The Burren takes its name from "boireann" in Irish, meaning rocky place, and resembles a lunar landscape. It covers over 100 square miles (260 square km), part of it a National Park. It's a truly remarkable area, which attracts visitors for many reasons including its unique flora and its archaeological sites. It's a great area for walking and cycling. Its northern shoreline is starkly beautiful, with gray limestone hills stretching to the blue water of the Atlantic, and inland it's like a giant rock garden, with Arctic, Alpine and Mediterranean plants flourishing together in fertile patches between limestone fissures. It's littered with dolmens, burial

Above: Dunbrody Abbey, Wexford (see page 230)

Below: Enniscorthy Town, River Slaney, Wexford (see page 230)

Above: The Healy Pass, Cork

Below: Garnish Island, Glengarriff, Cork (see page 262)

Ross Castle, Killarney, Kerry (see page 279)

Above: Lough Leane, Aghadoe, Killarney, Kerry (see page 278)

Below: Muckross House, Killarney National Park, Kerry (see page 278)

chambers and other fascinating archaeological sites, among them the **Poulnabrone Dolmen**, which is 5,000 years old.

Ballyvaughan

On the coast is the pretty little village of Ballyvaughan, with a choice of places to eat or shop. **Quinn's Craftshop** on the main street stocks local crafts and fashions. ☎ (065) 707-7052. Every Sunday from May to October local craftspeople hold a Fair at the Ballyvaughan Village Hall. www.burrencrafts.com.

Nearby is the **Burren College of Art** at Newtown Castle, internationally recognized for its full-time courses. From May to August it runs workshops. ☎ (065) 707-7200; fax 707-7201; admin@burrencollege.com; www.burrencollege.com.

Something Different

If you would like to try **clay pigeon shooting,** contact the Woodlands Shooting Club near Ballyvaughan. ☎ (065) 707-4038.

Adventure on Water

You can also try **sea kayaking** in the sheltered waters of Ballyvaughan Bay. **River Ocean Kayak**, www.riverocean.com, caters to beginners.

Venture Underground

Just off the R480, south of Ballyvaughan, is the Aillwee Cave, which you can visit, regardless of weather, all year round. You are taken underground by a guide, walking over chasms and under weird formations for a 30-minute stroll that you won't forget. Wear sensible shoes and a warm jacket as it gets cold. The complex also houses craft shops, and you can see cheese and honey being made. There's a restaurant and coffee shop. Open daily, March to October, 10 am to the last tour at 5:30 pm. From November to February, there are six tours daily. ☎ (065) 707-7036; aillwee@eircom.net; www.aillwee.ie.

Perfumery & Organic Garden

Also in the Burren is Ireland's first perfumery and organic herb garden, founded more than 30 years ago. The **Burren Perfumery and Floral Centre** is at Carron, near the Aillwee Cave, open all year (except Christmas), from 9 am. From June to September, it's open until 7 pm; at other times it closes at 5 pm. Admission is free. You can watch the processes involved, explore the garden, and try samples. ☎ (065) 708-9102; burrenperfumery@eircom.net; www.burrenperfumery.com.

■ East Clare

The landscape of East Clare is markedly different from the western part of the county. Here the fields are more fertile and trees fringe the roadsides, and the climate is more gentle, away from the winds of the Atlantic.

Take the R352 from Ennis towards Tuamgraney and Scariff and then follow the Lough Derg Drive, which skirts the lake. Joining it at Tuamgraney, you pass **Raheen Wood** on your left, where you can take a walk, and just after that you get your first wonderful view over the lake.

Killaloe

Killaloe is a delightful little town on the Shannon at the southernmost tip of Lough Derg, with the Bernagh Mountains behind it. It's the perfect destination if you're interested in water-based activities, such as fishing, cruising, boating, sailing, swimming, wind-sailing and water-skiing. Its history is also fascinating, as it was the birthplace of Brian Boru (940-1014), High King of Ireland, who subdued the Vikings and whose O'Brien clan dominated this part of the country as Kings of Thomond.

The town was one of the most powerful religious and political centers in the early medieval period. **St. Flannan's Cathedral**, with its beautiful Romanesque doorway and two oratories, dates from the 13th century. It's the center of a Music Festival each year when leading classical musicians come to perform here from all over the world.

You cross a 13-arch bridge to **Ballina** on the Tipperary side of the river, which is so close that it's hard to distinguish between the two towns.

The **Killaloe Heritage Centre**, run by Shannon Heritage, explores Celtic Ireland, the arrival of Christianity and the monastic tradition, as well as the development of the Shannon River as a transport system.

The Dysert O'Dea Castle & Clare Archaeology Centre

This is one of my favorite sites anywhere. It's seven miles (11 km) from Ennis and three miles (4.8 km) from Corofin, open daily, May to September, 10 am-6 pm. ☎ (065) 683-7401; at other times of the year, call to arrange a visit ☎ (065) 683-7305.

The Castle was built in 1480, and its upper floors and staircase, badly damaged by Cromwell's soldiers in 1651, have been repaired. It houses a fascinating museum and there is an audio-visual presentation. The site also includes a church, mostly dating from the 12th century, and a high cross, one of the finest in the country.

What makes it so delightful is that it is simply done. Elsewhere, it would have beautifully designed panels giving lots of information; here history speaks mostly for itself.

The **Dysert O'Dea Archaeology/History Trail** includes 25 sites all within a radius of a few miles and you can buy a detailed guide to it at the shop, or just follow the signs.

■ Adventures on Foot

There are three waymarked long-distance walks in Clare, the Burren Way, the Mid-Clare Way, and the East Clare Way. Of course, you can walk small sections of them if you want.

The **Burren Way** (28 miles/45 km) takes you to and from Ballyvaughan and Lahinch, with wonderful views along the way. The **Mid-Clare Way** is circular, taking you around Ennis through villages, including Quin, Ruan, Dysert O'Dea, Kilmaley, Clarecastle. It's 86 miles (138 km) long in total, and on the way you'll see castles, abbeys and small farms. The **East Clare Way** is also circular and the longest of the three at 112 miles (180 km). On it you'll discover the Slieve Bernagh and Slieve Aughty mountains, Lough Graney, rivers, woodlands and bogs, and many charming little villages, including Tulla, Feakle, Mountshannon, Ogonnelloe.

Further Information

For the **Burren Way**, contact Ennis Tourist Centre, www.shannon-dev.ie or www.irishwaymarkedways.ie.

For the **Mid-Clare or East Clare Way**, contact Tulla Business Centre. ☎/fax (065) 683-5912; walks.ennis@eircom.net. Or contact Clare County Council. ☎ (065) 682-1616.

There are maps and guides to all the walks available, as well as a book, *The Waymarked Trails of Ireland* by Michael Fewer.

GUIDED WALK

If you are interested in a guided walk, contact **Burren Hill Walks**, Corkscrew Hill, Ballyvaughan. ☎/fax (065) 707-7168; burrenhillwalks@eircom.net.

■ Adventures on Wheels

Co. Clare is ideal for cycling, as the roads are quiet and, away from main roads, almost free of traffic, but watch out for tractors and other agricultural machinery on the move.

The **Burren Cycle Route** is 155 miles long (249 km), stretching from the Shannon River in the east to Loop Head, which juts out into the Atlantic in the south of the county. In the section that gives the route its name, you pass through a landscape dominated by pale gray limestone rock, interspersed with green fields, and lots of wildflowers, especially in spring and early summer. After that, you travel parallel to the Atlantic, with wonderful views.

Bike Rental

One of the places where you can rent (or hire, as the Irish say) a bicycle is at **Ennis Train Station**, part of a network with depots at Dublin, Cork, Killarney, Galway, Westport and Donegal. You can rent them by the day, week or longer, and return them here or, for a small extra charge, at one of the other depots. ☎ (065) 686-8884 or, toll-free in the Republic, 1-800-298-100.

Tierneys of Ennis has been renting Raleigh bikes for over 20 years, and will even arrange accommodation for your first night if you want, plus supply maps and route information. www.ennisrentabike.com.

If you want to start cycling in North Clare, one place to rent from is **Burren Bike**, The Launderette, Ballyvaughan. ☎ (065) 707-7061; info@ burrenbike.com.

■ Adventures on Water

West Clare

Take a trip to Scattery Island, 15-20 minutes away by boat from Kilrush, with **Scattery Island Ferries Ltd**, ☎ (065) 905-1327, which operates from Kilrush Creek Marina. To get the best from it, visit the Scattery Island Centre on Merchant's Quay first. Admission is free to the Centre, and it's open mid-June to mid-September daily, 10 am to 6 pm. Call to check times off-season. ☎/fax (065) 905-2139; scatteryisland@ealga.ie.

The company also run trips to the **Shannon Estuary**, Ireland's first marine Special Area of Conservation, which is home to a group of bottlenose dolphins. There are three or four dolphin-watching trips a day in summer (allow at least two hours). shannondolphins@eircom.net; www.shannondolphins.ie.

Alternatively, you can head to **Carrigaholt**, a quiet and quaint old fishing port on the way to Loop Head, south of Kilrush. The village is overlooked by the ruins of a 15th-century castle and has a beautiful sandy beach.

Dolphinwatch Carrigaholt offers boat trips from here to see the dolphins, and migratory seabirds, by day and in the evenings. They have four or five trips daily from April to the end of October; other months, the schedule depends on weather. You should phone on the day after 8 am. ☎ (065) 905-8156; info@dolphinwatch.ie; www.dolphinwatch.ie.

From June until mid-September, you can also take a trip under sail on the *Anna M*, with **Saoirse Sea Sports**. It's perfect for a memorable scenic excursion, for sea angling or dolphin watching, and carries seven. ☎ (065) 905-8990; killstiffin@eircom.net; www.gannetsway.com.

East Clare

During the summer, you can take a boat trip from Mountshannon, five miles (eight km) north of Scariff, to **Holy Island** and enjoy a guided tour of its monuments, including the Round Tower, Holy Well and the Bargaining Stone, where you can renew your marriage vows. ☎ (061) 921615.

R & B Marine Services, based at the Marina at Killaoe, runs cruises on their river bus *Derg Princess*, passing the Fort of Brian Boru and into Lough Derg. Daily, May-September. ☎ (061) 375-011; fax 376205.

Or you can take a trip on *The Spirit of Killaloe*, which leaves from the Bridge daily, May-September, with a detailed commentary from a guide. It's a luxury 50-seater, with full bar and snacks available, and its upper deck is ideal for enjoying the scenery. ☎ (086) 814-0559; fax (061) 376-691; whelans@killaloe.ie; www.killaloe.ie/thespiritofkillaloe.

Vacations on Water

Williamstown Harbor, in East Clare near Whitegate on the shore of Lough Derg, is the base for the **Shannon Castle Line**. The company's been in business for more than 25 years, and has a fleet of two- to eight-berth cruisers. You pass lots of pubs, restaurants and shops as you cruise along. Don't worry if you've never tried it before – you get expert instruction before you set off. They'll arrange transfers from Shannon Airport an hour away. ☎ (061) 927-042; fax 927-426; sales@shannoncruisers.com; www.shannoncastleline.com.

Based at Killaloe is **Ireland Line Cruisers**, which has been hiring out cruisers on the Shannon and Erne Waterways for 20 years. ☎ (061) 375-011; fax 375-331; www.irelandlinecruisers.com.

If you're part of a small group, you could charter a 28-meter Dutch steel barge with crew of two from the marina at Killaloe, perfect for an angling or golfing vacation for six-12 people. The barges have roomy cabins, even central heating. Each barge has a fishing boat and dinghy; tackle and bikes are available for rent. Contact Michael Bulger, Ogonnelloe, Tuamgraney, East Clare. ☎ (061) 923-044; fax 923-056.

Fishing in Co. Clare

 With the river Shannon, 200 miles (320 km) of coastline on the Atlantic and too many rivers and lakes to count, it's not surprising that this part of Ireland is very popular with anglers.

The Shannon

The majestic Shannon almost divides Ireland in two and is the longest river on the island, with almost 500 miles (750 km) of recreational waters. The river stretches from Belleek in Northern Ireland to Killaloe, here in Co. Clare. On its journey to the sea it is joined by lots of smaller rivers, streams and canals, and has more than a 100 small islands and 12 lakes.

The Shannon is now the backbone of a vast network of inland waterways, joined to the Erne via the restored Shannon-Erne waterway. Pike, trout, salmon, bream, roach, rudd, tench, perch and eels can be found throughout the Shannon system.

Waterways Ireland is one of the North-South Implementation Bodies set up under the Good Friday Agreement. Its HQ is in Enniskillen, Co. Fermanagh, with regional offices in Scarriff, Co. Clare, Carrick-on-Shannon, Co. Leitrim, and Dublin. www. waterwaysireland.org.

There are three main pike-angling fisheries in Co. Clare: the River Shannon and its largest lake, Lough Derg, the river Fergus, and the East Clare lakelands. Remember that you don't need a State licence, but you are only allowed to catch one fish per day per person, maximum 6.63 lbs (3 kgs).

Good bags of bream, tench and other fish are consistently caught on the Shannon and from the lakes dotting East Clare. The Clare coastline and both shores of the Shannon Estuary offer wonderful shore angling, with easily accessible rocks and beaches.

 See pages 71-74 for details on angling in Ireland, regulations and best times to fish.

Inshore Angling

With 50 miles (80 km) of tidal water from Limerick City to Loop Head, the eight-mile-wide (13 km) Shannon Estuary is one of the best places for inshore angling.

There are two main seasons for salmon – the spring run from March to May and, for the grilse, from the end of May until September. The Doonbeg, Fergus and Shannon rivers have good runs of both.

Both the Feale and Doonbeg rivers also have a good run of sea trout from May to July, especially in the upper stretches. Many of the smaller rivers flowing into the sea off the Clare and North Kerry coasts have a small run of sea trout, and, in some, a small run of grilse.

There are wild brown trout in the rivers, including the Shannon and Fergus, and the lakes of the Shannon Region. Most noted for trout are Lough Derg, and Loughs Inchiquin, Dromore and Ballyline on the Fergus.

Licenses & Permits

You must have a State licence for salmon and sea trout angling. There are two types – national and regional – and you can get them for a full season, for 21 days or for one day.

Note that you must have a permit from the ESB (Electricity Supply Board) to fish the Shannon and its tributaries. Also, day tickets may be necessary in some waters controlled by local angling clubs or the ESB, so check with local tackle shops.

Licenses, permits and day tickets are available from local tackle shops and the ESB at Ardnacrusha, Co. Clare. ☎ (061) 345588.

Deep Sea Angling

Off the coasts of counties Clare and North Kerry you can land a huge variety of sea fish. Check locally or at tourist offices, as there are deep-sea charter boats available at several locations. Check out **www.shannon-fishery-board.com**, which is an excellent site with loads of information.

■ Adventures on Horseback

Among the places where you can enjoy a ride is **The Clare Equestrian Centre**, five minutes east of Ennis. Turn left at Clarecastle off the N18 to Limerick, then turn right when you come to Doora Church. It has indoor and outdoor arenas, a cross-country course covering 70 acres. You can also ramble on the surrounding roads. ☎ (065) 684-0136; fax 684-3607; clareequestrian@ esatclear.ie; www.esatclear.ie/~clareequestrian.

At Fanore on the coast, the **Burren Riding Centre** offers beach and hill trekking. ☎ (065) 707-6140.

■ Golf

Among the courses to choose from in Co. Clare are those at Ennis, Kilkee, Kilrush, Doonbeg, Spanish Point and Shannon. The best known is the **Lahinch Old Course**, which has been there since 1892 looking out over the Atlantic. Across the road from it is the newer **Castle Course**. ☎ (065) 708-1003; fax 708-1592.

The **Kilkee Golf and Country Club** was founded in 1896 and has fantastic views over the Ocean and Bay, with some holes right along the cliff edge. ☎ (065) 905-6048.

The **East Clare Parkland Course** is at Coolreagh, roughly equally distant from the villages of Tulla, Scariff, Feakle and Bodyke, and six miles (10 km) from Lough Derg. ☎ (061) 921322; fax 921388.

■ Where to Stay

☆☆☆ **Old Ground Hotel**, Ennis, is a personal favorite. It was an 18th-century manor house, and it combines old-fashioned style with modern facilities. The helpful staff are always cheerful. There's a choice of guestrooms, including suites. The hotel is popular with locals (always a good sign) who meet in the wood-lined **Poets' Corner bar** (it has its own entrance on O'Connell Street), and dine in its restau-

HOTEL PRICE CHART	
Price per person, per night, with two sharing, including breakfast.	
$	Under US $50
$$	US $50-$100
$$$	US $101-$175
$$$$	US $176-$200
$$$$$	Over US $200

rants. In the bar you can relax, surrounded by old theater programs and other memorabilia. Food is served all day and there's traditional music on Wednesday, Thursday and Friday nights. There are two restaurants – the **Town Hall Café** serves Irish and European dishes all day, and has an à la carte evening menu; and the **O'Brien Room** is well-known for its traditional and innovative dishes, using local produce. $$$, with special offers, including golf breaks available. ☎ (065) 682-8127; fax 682-8112; reservations@oldgroundhotel.ie; www.flynnhotels.com.

☆☆☆☆☆ **Dromoland Castle Hotel**, near Newmarket-on-Fergus, is one of the most luxurious and unusual hotels in the country, set in wonderful grounds, covering nearly 400 acres, which includes ancient woodlands. Its golf course is considered one of the best in the country, and guests also have a huge choice of other leisure activities. On the estate you can play tennis, fish, shoot, go boating, or just wander around the beautiful gardens or woods. If you're feeling energetic, you can jog or cycle around the grounds. Guestrooms are beautifully furnished. There's a choice of restaurants, with the **Earl of Thomond** in the Castle, and **The Fig Tree** in the Golf and Country Club. $$$$. ☎ (061) 368-144; fax 363-355; sales@dromoland.ie; www.dromoland.ie.

☆☆☆ What's most enticing about the **Bellbridge House Hotel** at Spanish Point is its location, almost looking down on the beach. It's a modern building, the staff are friendly, and the bedrooms comfortable. There's a pleasant bar serving food all day, and dinner is served at **The Tides Restaurant**, which uses local produce, including fish. It's a pleasant place to stay for a quiet break or to tour the county. They offer packages, including mid-week specials and golf breaks. $$ in summer; $ low season. ☎ (065) 708-4038; fax 708-4830; bellbridge@eircom.net; www. bellbridgehotelclare.com.

☆☆☆ If it's fishing that attracts you to Clare, then the **Magowna House Hotel** at Inch, Kilmaley, couldn't be more ideal. It's equipped with all the facilities to make your trip comfortable and pleasurable, including a tackle shed, drying room, with boat rental and ghillies (guides) available. It's on the River Fergus, just 10 minutes from Ennis on the R474, and is on the Mid-Clare waymarked walking route. The hotel has a comfortable bar looking out on Mount Callan, where you can meet locals, and there's an open fire when it's cold. There's a choice of a table d'hôte or à la carte menu in **Bennett's Restaurant**, using carefully prepared locally sourced fresh ingredients. Rates per room, which sleep three, start at $, with even better value breaks available. ☎ (065) 683-9009; fax 683-9258; info@magowna.com; www.magowna.com.

☆☆☆☆ The most attractive place to stay in the Burren is **Gregans Castle Hotel** on the N67, just over three miles (4.8 km) south of Ballyvaughan and seven miles (11 km) north of Lisdoonvarna. The hotel is at the bottom of a corkscrew hill that gives you amazing views of the landscape. Do take care driving down it, and pull in and stop before taking a look! It's a country house hotel, owned and run by the Haden family for 30 years. Across the road is the original towerhouse dating from the 15th or 16th century, which is privately owned. A member of Ireland's Blue Book (see page 60), it has won numerous awards and recommendations. Each bedroom and suite is individual and beautifully decorated, with four-poster or half-tester beds. They also have lots of suggestions on how to enjoy your stay, including their own booklet of walking trails. Organic Burren lamb and beef are specialties in the restaurant, along with locally caught fish from the Atlantic Ocean. Non-residents can dine here,

Clare & Limerick

but must reserve in advance. $$-$$$$. ☎ (065) 707-7005; fax 707-7111; res@gregans.ie; www.gregans.ie.

☆☆☆☆ For years and years, **Moy House** looked sad and almost derelict. Now it's been sensitively restored and transformed into a four-star guesthouse. It's about a mile south of Lahinch, and overlooks the sea from a height. The River Moy wanders though its 15 acres of grounds – an old estate with mature woodlands. There are only nine very spacious bedrooms, some with freestanding original baths, and the feeling is that of staying in a private home. Dinner is available as well as breakfast. It belongs to Ireland's Blue Book (see page 60). $$-$$$, with special offers November-May. ☎ toll-free from USA 800-323-5463; (065) 708-2800; fax 708-2500; moyhouse@eircom.net; www.moyhouse.com.

The advantage of staying at the **Kincora Hall Hotel** in Killaloe, in East Clare, is that it's actually on Lough Derg and has its own marina. Angling, boating, sailing, watersports, hill walking and bicycle rental are all available at the hotel, with lots of other activities nearby. Its bistro and bar serve wholesome food all day, with dinner nightly in the **Marina Restaurant**, where fresh local fish is one of its specialties. $$. ☎ (061) 376-000; fax 376-665; www.kincorahall.com.

Unusual Places to Stay

☆☆☆ **The Kilkee Thalassotherapy Centre** is a guest house where you can have seaweed baths and body wraps, marine facials, massages and other treatments. ☎ (065) 905-6742; info@kilkeethalasso.com; www. kilkeethalasso.com.

☆☆☆☆ **Nature Quest**, also in Kilkee, is dedicated to raising awareness and understanding of the local environment. Accommodation is in three cottages with kitchens where you can cook for yourself; there's an indoor heated pool and game room, and guests are encouraged to go on self-guided walks, or bird-watching and wildlife tours, led by experts. ☎ (065) 905-6789; www.naturequest.ie.

Hostels

The following hostels are open all year:

Lahinch Hostel. ☎ (065) 708-1040; www.visitlahinch.com.

Flanagan's, in Doolin. ☎ (065) 707-4564.

Rainbow, also in Doolin. ☎ (065) 707-4415; www.rainbowhostel@eircom. net.

Loughnane's, in Feakle. ☎ (061) 924-200; eastclarehostels@eircom.net.

Check out the others, all of them open in summer and some open longer, by contacting the **IHH Independent Holiday Hostels of Ireland**.

☎ (01) 836-4700; fax 836-4710; info@hostels-ireland.com; www.hostels-ireland.com.

Rental Cottages

There's a wonderful view over the Atlantic from ☆☆☆-☆☆☆☆ **Quilty Holiday Cottages** at Caherush, between Quilty and Spanish Point. There's an indoor heated pool, sauna and mini-gym, game room and outdoor tennis court. Run by Geraldine and Danny Mungovan who live on site. There are two types of cottage, three and four star. ☎ (065) 708-7095; fax 708-7388; quilty@iol.ie; www.quiltycottages.com. The owners also have cottages to rent at Spanish Point, called **Westpark Holiday Homes**.

At **Ballyvaughan** there's a group of very attractive thatched cottages in the middle of the village. These are traditionally furnished and have open turf fires, as well as electric storage heaters. They sleep six, and are available for weekends, as well as by the week. ☎ (061) 411-109; info@rentacottage.ie; www.rentacottage.ie.

Rent a Cottage also has groups of houses in other locations around Co. Clare and the country, including one overlooking Lough Inchiquin near Corofin and the other in Corofin itself, which is a traditional angling center.

RV Parks & Camping

There are a number of caravan and camping parks in Co. Clare. Take a look at **www.camping-ireland.ie**. Among them are the following.

☆☆☆ **Nagles** is a caravan park at Doolin, on the edge of the Atlantic only a few yards from the pier. Open April to end September. ☎ (065) 707-4458; fax 707-4936; ken@doolincamping.com.

☆☆☆ Also at Doolin is **O'Connors Riverside Camping and Caravan Park**, which is on the family farm, also a Bed and Breakfast. It's open May to end Sept. ☎ (065) 707-4314; fax 707-4498; joan@oconnorsdoolin.com

☆☆ **The Green Acres Park** is signposted off the N67 road from Kilrush to the seaside resort of Kilkee, just five minutes outside the latter. It's on the shore of the River Shannon in a secluded setting. Breakfast is available on site. Open early April to end September. ☎/fax (065) 905-7011.

☆☆☆ **Corofin Village Park** is on the main street of Corofin, a popular spot with anglers, and is also open April to end September. The owners can provide maps and advice on walking and cycling routes, and about fishing on seven nearby lakes. ☎ (065) 638-7683; fax 683-7239; corohost@ iol.ie; www.claretohere.com/camping.

In East Clare there's a choice of parks – Lough Derg at Killaloe and Lakeside at Mountshannon – both offering plenty of opportunities for watersports, fishing and other activities.

The **Lough Derg Holiday Park** has a shop, restaurant, take-away, games room, and visitors can fish from its well-sheltered setting on the shore of the lake. It also has fully equipped vacation cottages to rent , each of which comes with a boat. At its Activity Center, you can learn windsurfing and sailing, or you can go pony trekking or rent mountain bikes. Open late May to early Sept. ☎ (061) 376777; fax 620700; info@ loughderg.net; www.loughderg.net.

The **Lakeside Holiday Park** is also on the shore of Lough Derg. Watersports facilities include motor and rowing boats and kayaks for rent, as well as swimming and fishing, and there's a tennis court and pitch-and-putt. It has a café/bistro, and bikes are available to rent. Open May 1 to October 1. ☎ (061) 927225; fax 927336; lakesidecamping@ eircom.net; www.lakesideireland.com.

■ Where to Eat

Beyond the hotels already mentioned, where non-residents can eat, there are lots of good restaurants all over the county.

Ennis boasts a huge range of eating places, from fast food to upmarket, as well as lots of pubs, many of them retaining their original features, which serve lunches and snacks. In some you can enjoy traditional music as you eat, especially on weekends and during the summer.

Carvery lunches are also available in many West County hotels, and you can dine in all of them in the evening. An example is **JM's Bistro** in the **Temple Gate Hotel**, The Square, Ennis, ☎ (065) 682-3300, info@ templegatehotel.com, which also has a traditional pub called **Preachers** that serves food. **Auburn Lodge**, Galway Road in Ennis, ☎ (065) 682-1247, is another favorite stop.

Barrtrá Seafood Restaurant, two miles (3.2 km) south of Lahinch, overlooks Liscannor Bay and is open from 5-10 pm (nightly in summer, from Tuesday to Saturday other months; closed November-January). It serves steaks and vegetarian options as well as seafood, and is recommended by various food guides. ☎ (065) 708-1280.

On Lahinch's main street is **Mr Eamonn's Restaurant**, also highly recommended. It's open 5-10 pm daily from April to the end of September, and on weekends from October-December and in March. It serves modern Irish and European cuisine, including game, seafood and vegetarian dishes. ☎ (065) 708-1505.

Byrnes Restaurant and Townhouse, Main Street, Ennistymon, is open all year daily, except Sundays, from 6:30-9:30 pm, with a special Early Bird menu on weekdays from 6:30-7.15 pm. Its style of food is contemporary. ☎ (065) 707-1080.

The Dolmen Restaurant, The Square, Lisdoonvarna, is open all year from early morning to late evening, with a great choice of food at reasonable prices. ☎ (065) 707-4944.

Lantern House at Ogonnnoloe, between Scariff and Killaloe, is open from mid-February to the end of October, 6 pm-9 pm. It serves modern Irish food, including game, seafood and vegetarian choices. ☎ (061) 923-034.

Goosers Bar and Eating House is near the Cathedral in Killaloe. It's open all year from 10:30 am to 11:30 pm, with traditional Irish, vegetarian and seafood dishes on the menu. ☎ (061) 376-791.

Also in Killaloe, on the bridge connecting it with Ballina, is **Molly's Bar and Restaurant**, which has won a number of awards. It's open daily all year from 10:30 am, with last orders at 9:45 pm. Steaks, seafood, vegetarian and traditional Irish meals are served. ☎ (061) 376-632.

County Limerick

County Limerick does not have any spectacular scenery. What it does have is a gentle rural charm, with a variety of landscape from the wide Shannon Estuary on its northwest coast, to the peaks of the Galtee Mountains in the southeast. Co. Kerry is to the west, and Tipperary to the east. Most of Limerick's central area is a fertile limestone plain known as the Golden Vale. The county is a small one, roughly rectangular in shape and about 40 miles (64 km) wide and 30 miles (48 km) from north to south, so it's easy to explore. It's a lovely area for walking, fishing, cycling, playing golf, or just relaxing in attractive surroundings.

Leaving Limerick City on the N18 towards Ennis and Galway, you are immediately in County Clare, as almost all the county lies to the south of the River Shannon on which the city stands.

■ Getting Around Co. Limerick

The main roads radiating out from Limerick City are the N7 to Dublin; the N24 through Pallasgreen to Tipperary; and the N69, which runs parallel to the Shannon Estuary through Askeaton, Foynes, Glin, and on into Tarbert in Co. Kerry. The

N20 links Limerick with Cork, and branching off it after Patrickswell is the N21, which takes you through Adare, Rathkeale, Newcastle West and on into Co. Kerry at Abbeyfeale.

■ Tourist Information

Limerick Tourist Information Centre, Arthur's Quay, is open year-round. ☎ (061) 317-522; fax 317-939; touristofficelimerick @shannon-dev.ie.

Adare Tourist Information Centre is open February-December. ☎ (061) 396-255; fax 396-610; touristofficeadare@shannon-dev.ie.

There are also Tourist Information points at the following:

- **Civic Trust House**, The Square, Askeaton.
- **Kingfisher Angling Club**, Castleconnell. ☎ (061) 377-407.
- **Foynes Flying Boat Museum**.
- **Ballyhoura Failte**, Kilfinane. ☎ (063) 91300.
- **West Limerick Rescources Ltd.**, Newcastle West. ☎ (0690 62808.

TRACING YOUR ANCESTORS

Limerick Archives and Ancestory is in The Granary on Michael Street. ☎ (061) 415-125; fax 312-985; www.irishroots. net.

■ Limerick City

Sightseeing

Founded in 922 by the Danes, who sailed up the Shannon Estuary and built a settlement on an island here, Limerick is the Republic's third-largest city, after Dublin and Cork. It became the seat of the O'Briens, Kings of Thomond and Munster, under Brian Boru. The Normans, arriving in 1194, established two walled towns, Englishtown and Irishtown, and granted Limerick its royal charter as a city – which makes its charter older than London's.

The Earls of Desmond, known as the Geraldines, were at the center of Norman power in the province of Munster, and led a revolt against the English in 1571, which was defeated and cost them their lands. That was only the beginning, as Limerick was the center of rebellions and wars for centuries. Among them was the year-long siege of the city by Cromwell in

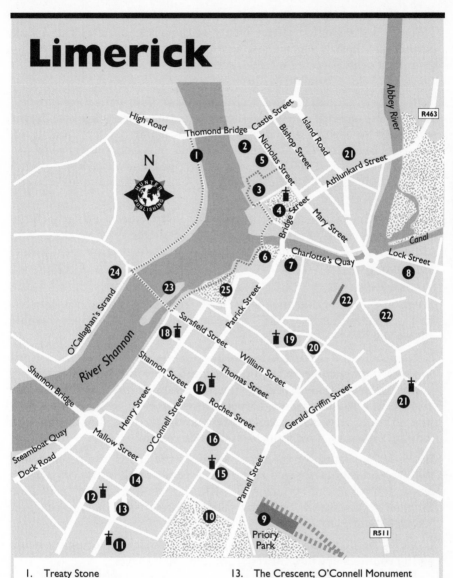

Limerick

1. Treaty Stone
2. King John's Castle
3. City Hall
4. St. Mary's Cathedral
5. Limerick Museum
6. Hunt Museum; Custom House; Footbridge
7. The Granary
8. Kilree Lodge
9. Bus & Railroad Station
10. Art Gallery; People's Park
11. St. Joseph's Church
12. Jesuit Church
13. The Crescent; O'Connell Monument
14. Belltable Arts Centre
15. Glenworth Hotel; Dominican Church
16. Theatre Royal
17. Augustinian Church
18. Franciscan Church
19. St. Michael's Church
20. Milk Market
21. St. John's Cathedral
22. Old City Wall
23. Shannon Rowing Club Museum
24. Jury's Hotel
25. Arthur's Quay & Park

·················· Pedestrian Way

NOT TO SCALE
© 2004 HUNTER PUBLISHING, INC.

Clare & Limerick

1651. The Jacobites, led by Sir Patrick Sarsfield, besieged the city from 1690 until the signing of the Treaty of Limerick in 1691. The **Treaty Stone**, on which it was signed, according to tradition, can be seen on a granite pedestal erected in 1865, across the river from King John's Castle, opposite St. Munchin's church.

As the city expanded in the 18th century most of its walls were removed, though portions still remain. In the 19th century Limerick was an important port for freight and passenger boats departing for Canada and America. Before the Great Famine, Limerick (city and county) had a population of about 300,000. This number dropped sharply to less than half as a result of emigration to the UK and Australia, Canada and the east coast of America.

In the first half of the 20th century it was a city in decline.This is the period documented by Frank McCourt in his Pulitzer-Prize-winning memoir, *Angela's Ashes*. Circumstances began to change dramatically when Shannon Airport was established in the 1950s just 10 miles (16 km) away in Co. Clare.

It was at Shannon that the idea of duty-free purchases by travelers was first introduced to the world – sadly no longer available when traveling within the EU.

Not only did the airport bring large numbers of tourists, from North America in particular, to the Limerick and Clare region; it also brought industrial development, and the town of Shannon developed around the airport. The Shannon Free Airport Development Company (SFADCO) was set up to attract investment and market the area to industries and tourism interests, which has been very successful.

In the 1971 census, for the first time since the 1840s, the population of the city and county showed an increase. Almost half of the city's people are under the age of 30 now and, with a university and an Institute of Technology, thousands of young people live here during the academic year, September to June.

Limerick's central location makes it a great base for exploring the neighboring counties of Clare, Kerry, Cork and Tipperary.

Explore the City on Foot

 The area called King's Island is where the Vikings (or Danes) set up their first colony. Head for this part of the city to explore its past. The following are only a few of the interesting historical sights.

The center of Viking administration, called the **Thingmote**, is believed to have been where **St. Mary's Cathedral** now stands. This was also the site of the **O'Brien Royal Palace**, donated in 1168 for use in building the cathedral. Today, parts of the original palace survive, along with later additions. It's one of the most important buildings in Limerick and, remarkably, it's is still in use, as it has been for over 850 years. There's a guide booklet available and tours can be booked in advance (access may be restricted during services). Open daily year-round, 9 am-1 pm; open to 5 pm from June to September, or by arrangement. ☎ (061) 310-293; fax 315-721.

Next to the Cathedral on Nicholas Street are **columns**, part of the 17th-century **Exchange**, which was the city's administrative center.

King John's Castle was built around 1200 on the orders of the English monarch, and was repaired and rebuilt many times over the years. There's a lot to see today, including underground excavations, the reconstructed courtyard, and a modern center with exhibitions about the castle and city; allow an hour or more. Maps and brochures are available for self-guided tours. A royal mint was established on the site, and today visitors can strike a replica of an original coin as a souvenir, which is fun. There's a café/restaurant and a good crafts shop. Open daily all year; April-October, 10 am to 5:30 pm, November-March, 10:30 to 4:30. ☎ (061) 360-788; fax 361-020; www.shannonheritage.com.I

The **Bishop's Palace** is opposite the castle and was built in the 1660s in Palladian style. It's said to be the oldest domestic building in the city and is now the base for the Limerick Civic Trust, which bought it when it was a ruin and restored it. Open all year, Monday-Friday. Check times. ☎ (061) 313-399; fax 315-513.

Beside the castle is the **Limerick City Museum**, open all year, Tuesday-Saturday, 10 am to 1 pm and 2:15 to 5 pm. ☎ (061) 417-826; www. limerickcity.ie.

A Very Special Collection

The **Hunt Museum** is in the city center, just down the street from the Tourist Information Centre on Arthur's Quay, and should be a priority if you are only stopping for a short time in the city. The museum is in the restored Custom House and has a display on three floors of more than 2,000 artifacts collected by the late Gertrude and John Hunt from the 1920s to 1960s (see also *Craggaunowen* under Co. Clare, page 304).

Visitors can take a tour or walk around on their own. The following will give you just some idea of the quality of this unique collection. It includes a bronze horse by Leonardo da Vinci; paintings by Picasso, Renoir, and Jack Yeats; the personal seal of King Charles I; a cross that belonged to Mary, Queen of Scots; and a coin believed to be one of the 30 pieces of silver received by Judas for betraying Jesus. There's much, much more – all bought by the Hunts because of their craftsmanship, their artistic merit and just because they loved them. They are imaginatively displayed, and it's a joy to spend an hour or two wandering around. There's also a visit-

Clare & Limerick

ing exhibition gallery, a shop, and a lovely restaurant looking out over the river. Open daily all year, 10 am to 5 pm; Sundays, 2-5 pm. ☎ (061) 312-833; fax 312-834; info@huntmuseum.com; www.ul.ie/~hunt.

A Lazy Way to Explore

During the summer, there are tours of the city by horse-drawn carriage, starting at the Tourist Information Centre. ☎ (061) 317-522 for details.

Tours of Limerick City

The **Angela's Ashes Walking Tour** takes in locations from the book by Frank McCourt. Details are available from St. Mary's Action Group. ☎/fax (061) 318-106.

There's also a **Historical Walking Tour** of the city, which you can ask about at the Tourist Information Centre (see page 339).

Shopping

Limerick City is a good place to shop, as its center is compact, and there is a good choice of stores from some of the well-known chains as well as smaller, more specialized shops. Traffic is one-way in the city center (you drive north on Henry Street and south on O'Connell Street), so you would be wise to park and walk.

There's multi-story parking available at **Arthur's Quay Shopping Centre**, at the end of O'Connell Street, which is well sign-posted and means you are right in the center, next to the Tourist Information Centre.

There are other areas where you can park, well signposted. One of them is next to the Railway and Bus Station. Around **Cruise's Street,** off O'Connell Street, there's a pedestrianized shopping area worth exploring.

On Saturday mornings head for the outdoor market at the **Milk Market**, Cornmarket Row off Robert Street, in the northern corner of the city center.

On the Cork side of the city, the **Crescent Shopping Centre** is a good place to stop, with lots of parking spaces, fast food and other restaurants.

Spectator Sports in the City

Ask anyone which sport is associated with Limerick and you'll be told – **rugby**. Teams all around the city compete in local, provincial and national matches, and members of the senior clubs dominate the All Ireland League and the Munster team. It's everyone's game; its supporters come from all backgrounds and travel to support their teams. No one will ever forget October 1978 when at Thomond Park, home of Rugby in the city, Munster defeated the All-Blacks of New Zealand 12-0.

GAA (Gaelic Athletic Association – see page 20) is played at the Gaelic Grounds, Ennis Road, and **soccer** is played on local grounds all over the city. If you can, try to watch a match during your visit.

There's **greyhound racing** at The Markets Field on Mondays and Saturdays, sometimes also on Thursdays. Check locally for details. ☎ (061) 316-788.

Limerick Race Course for **horseracing** is just south of the city at Greenmount, near Patrickswell, off the N20 to Cork. Facilities include bars, restaurants and panoramic views of the track and parade ring. There are day and evening races throughout the year, with four days of racing at Christmas, starting on December 26. ☎ (061) 320-000; fax 355-766; info@limerick-racecourse.com; www.limerick-racecourse.com.

Entertainment in the City

Belltable Arts Centre on O'Connell Street hosts exhibitions, plays, and other artistic events. Call and find out what's on in the Centre and around the city. It has a nice little café too. There's **ten-pin bowling** at **Funworld** on the Ennis Road. ☎ (061) 325-088. Of course, music is played in many of the pubs. There's a multi-screen **cinema** at the Crescent Shopping Centre on the Cork side of the city.

■ Touring in Co. Limerick

There are four signposted routes to help you explore the county, and they're suitable for both cyclists and drivers.

The N69 Drive

This route, west from the City to Tarbert, Co. Kerry, is a meandering drive along the shore of the Shannon, passing through Mungret, Kildimo, Kilcornan, Askeaton, Foynes, Loghill, to Glin. It's 35 miles (57 km) long, and a pleasant way of traveling into Co. Kerry or, via car ferry at Tarbert, to cross the estuary into Co. Clare.

Foynes

Foynes is a busy little port and has a yacht club and outdoor swimming pool. The **Foynes Flying Boat Museum** celebrates the beginning of Transatlantic flights in 1939-45, when seaplanes bringing passengers from North America used the sheltered strait between the town and

Foynes Island. Open daily March 31-October 31. ☎/fax (069) 65416; famm@eircom.net; www.webforge.net.

Foynes is also where Irish or Gaelic coffee was invented by a barman to warm up those weary passengers, and it's celebrated with an annual festival here each July.

Glin

Glin is another pretty village, nine miles (14 km) west of Foynes, which overlooks the Shannon Estuary and is laid out in a large square shape. **Glin Castle** is the home of the current Knight of Glin, Desmond Fitzgerald, whose family has owned land here for 700 years. It's a large white building with lots of windows, built in the 1780s, with Gothic features and battlements added later. Its Gothic gate lodge is a teashop during summer. The castle and gardens are only open to groups of 12 by prior arrangement, or to overnight guests (see page 336). ☎ (068) 34173; fax 34364; knight@iol.ie; www.glincastle.com.

The **Glin Heritage Centre** is in the old Protestant church. Check opening times. ☎ (068) 34001.

West Limerick Drive

The West Limerick Drive, 76 miles (123 km) long, starts at the very picturesque village of Adare on the N21, and then leaves the main road after Rathkeale, taking you on a circular route.

You travel through villages including Ardagh, Athea, Abbeyfeale, Mountcollins, Toornafulla, Broadford, Dromcollogher, and Ballingarry.

Adare

Adare was laid out by Edwin, Third Earl of Dunraven, and has a wide main street lined with thatched cottages, built in 1826, some housing craft shops, others restaurants. One is a gallery. Entering the village from the Limerick direction, you see the entrance to **Adare Manor** on your left, and opposite that is the **Dunraven Arms Hotel**, which opened in 1792. Most of Adare Manor, which was the home of the Dunravens and is now a luxury hotel, dates from 1832.

Adare really is one of the most attractive and tidy villages in the country, so no wonder it attracts tourists. Do make the effort to spend at least an hour or two wandering around.

On Main Street is the **Adare Heritage Exhibition**, open daily from 9 am year-round, closing at 6 pm in summer, 5 pm the rest of year. ☎ (061) 396-666; fax 396-932; adareheritage@eircom.net.

Rathkeale

Rathkeale is where Sir Walter Raleigh planted the first potato in Ireland at Castle Matrix, the tower house built to guard the crossing of the river Deel. The Palatines, refugees from Germany, settled around here in 1709. They were invited to come by Sir Thomas Southwell, who lived in Castle Matrix. The **Irish Palatine Heritage Centre** is in the old railway building. Open June to September, Monday to Saturday, 1 to 5 pm, Sunday, 2 to 6 pm. Other times by appointment. Museum entry: £2. ☎ (069) 63511. www.erin.ie/ipa.

Ardagh is where the famous chalice dating from the eighth century, now in the National Museum in Dublin, was found in a ring fort. Visit the **Heritage Centre**, open May to September, 9 am-2 pm.

Detour from the West Limerick Drive to **Newcastle West**, the largest town in the area, where you'll find the **Desmond Banqueting Hall** in the town square. In the care of the Heritage Service, the two-story building dates from the 15th century. Open daily, mid-June to mid-September, 9:30 am-6:30 pm. ☎ (069) 77408.

The Golden Vale Drive

The Golden Vale Drive, 69 miles (112 km) long, begins just southeast of Limerick City on the N24. After you leave Limerick, you take a right turn toward Ballyneety and Lough Gur, which is just beyond the village. Continue through Bruff, Athlacca, the delightful little town of Kilmallock, Kilfinane, Ballylanders, Galbally, and then through Emly and Pallasgreen to loop back onto the N24.

Lough Gur

Lough Gur is a small lake, surrounded by limestone hills. It's also one of the most important archaeological sites in the country, with the remains of stone circles and standing stones, burial chambers and cairns, dating back 5,000 years to the time of Neolithic or Stone Age settlement.

There's an Interpretative Centre on the lakeshore between Knockdoon and Knockfennell, where you can learn more about the site and see copies of some of the important finds made here. Many of the monuments are on private land; you must respect that and close the gates. The **Lough Gur Stone Age Centre** is open May-September, daily 10 am to 5:30 pm. You should phone to check, as opening times change. ☎ (061) 360-788.

Slí Finn

The Slí Finn route is the shortest at 18 miles (30 km); it's a loop off the Golden Vale Drive. You can join it at Kilfinane or near Ballylanders, and it passes through Ardpatrick, Ballyorgan and Knockanevin.

Ballylanders

The village of Ballylanders, or Baile an Londraigh, "the town of the Londoner," from the Norman surname "de Londres," has an old roofless church dominating its main street. There's a holy well dedicated to Our Lady nearby, where those suffering from sore eyes seek a cure, and where there's an annual ceremony when prayers are said.

To the west of the village is **Griston Bog**, home to a variety of flora and fauna, including waterlife, some in danger of extinction. Brown trout have been put here for anglers, and there's a wooden walkway with interpretative boards. Contact John Crilly for further details, ☎ (062) 46808.

Kilmallock

Kilmallock is now a quiet little town, but was once very important; it guards the passes between the Galtee and Ballyhoura Mountains. It was the chief town of the Earls of Desmond and was very prosperous from 1250 to 1580, but when they lost their rebellion against the English it declined. It's one of only six towns in Ireland that still retains long stretches of its medieval wall. It's worth stopping here to explore.

Drop into **Friars' Gate Theatre and Arts Centre** to see the current exhibition and check out what evening entertainment is available. Then follow the self-guided trail, starting at the little Museum, which is nearby in a 19th-century cottage. If you want more information, ☎ (063) 20002, which is the Ballyhoura regional tourist office in town.

Among the town's historic sites are the **Dominican Priory** beside the Loobagh River, which retains some lovely features, including its window, carvings and cloister; and the **Collegiate Church** across the river. Both sites date from the 13th century.

Others include **King John's Castle** (see page 325), the **old town walls** and **Blossom's Gate** in Emmet Street, which dates from the 16th century and was called Blapat – from the Irish "blath," meaning flower and "porte" or door in French.

Bruree

This village is worth at least a short visit, though it is not on the signposted routes. The name come from Bru Rí – the palace of the kings. It is just off the N20 (the Limerick-Cork road), in the valley of the River Maigue, and there are a number of ancient royal ring forts, or raths, in the area – hence its name.

The village is picturesque, with an old corn mill on a rocky ledge above a waterfall, as well as the remains of a Norman castle, a church built in 1812 and an ancient holy well dedicated to St. Munchin. You are likely to see a variety of wildlife along the river.

Bruree is best known as the place where **Eamon de Valera** (1882-1975), who dominated the political stage for decades, was raised. He was Taoiseach (Prime Minister) for 21 years and President from 1959 to 1973.

The **de Valera Museum and Bruree Heritage Centre** is in the old school that he attended. Open daily all year, Monday to Friday, 9 am to 5 pm; Saturday and Sunday, 2-5 pm. Another site to visit is the cottage that de Valera lived in with his grandmother and uncle after he was brought over from the US at age two. It is now a National Monument. Borrow the key from Mrs O'Gorman in the first house past the cottage on the right.

Bus Tours

 Barratt Scenic Tours runs daytrips by minibus to locations in counties Limerick, Clare, Galway and Cork, with a knowledgeable driver/guide. They leave from the Tourist Information Centre, Limerick City. Book in advance. ☎ (061) 384-800; barrattexec@eircom.net; www.4tours.biz

Bus Éireann also runs daytrips by bus – call the Limerick Bus Station. ☎ (061) 313-333; www.buseireann.ie.

■ Adventures on Foot

 The 16-mile (26-km) **Lough Derg Way** takes you out along the River Shannon from Limerick City to Killaloe, on the Clare and Tipperary border, and then uphill to where you overlook Lough Derg, then on into Dromineer.

There are a number of other interesting walks to follow in the county.

BALLYHOURA COUNTRY

This is part of the region marketed as Ballyhoura Country, which extends into the neighboring areas of North Cork and Tipperary. Among the activities promoted is walking, with over 93 miles (150 km) of waymarked ways through mountains and valleys, varying in length from a short stroll to long distance. Check out their website at www.ballyhouracountry.com.

The **Ballyhoura Way** follows the route taken by the Irish Chieftain O'Sullivan Beare, between December 1602 and January 1603, all the way from Castletownbere in Co. Cork to Co. Leitrim, through the middle of Co. Limerick.

Every kind of walker will find a trail to follow from 22 locations in **Ballyhoura Country**; at each of them there's a map board. You can pick up maps at the Tourist Information Point in Kilfinane, and guided walks are also available. ☎ (063) 91300; info@ballyhoura.org.

The **Slieve Felim Way** in East Limerick is 18 miles (29 km) long and starts a mile and a half east of Murroe, taking walkers to Silvermines in neighboring Co. Tipperary. There are also walking trails in the Clare Glens near Newport.

There's a choice of walks in West Limerick. The **Aughinish Nature Trail** starts at Loop Head Road, Askeaton, on the N69. There are three self-guided routes, taking you through meadows full of flowers, grasses and herbs, through woodland, or through wetlands. Maps are available from the Visitor Centre at Aughinish Alumina. Open daily, year-round. ☎ (061) 604000.

Near Broadford and Ashford on the R515 are the **Mullaghareirk Mountain Trails**, eight routes through hills and farmland, each including a mountain peak. Information and maps from Broadford Post Office. ☎ (063) 84001.

Between Ardagh and Newcastle West, you can follow the **Great Southern Trail** along the disused railway line. Near the middle of Newcastle West is **The Demesne**, where you can take a peaceful stroll. On the outskirts of Abbeyfeale, **Páirc Cois Féile** has walks along the River Feale.

There are lovely views from **Knockfierna Hill** near Ballingarry and its walkways take in the remains of a famine village, a hill fort and a megalithic grave.

Curraghchase Forest Park

On the N69 at Kilcornan in West Limerick is the Curraghchase Forest Park, which covers 600 acres, with a lake, an arboretum, a nature trail and walkways, as well as the ruins of the 18th-century house of the de Vere family. Run by Coillte, the State forestry body. Open daily all year. Admission charges during July and August and on weekends from March-November. It's also a caravan and camping park. ☎ (061) 337-322.

*The **Celtic Theme Park and Gardens** is also at Kilcornan. It has a dolmen, ring fort, and stone circle, along with pleasant gardens. ☎/fax (061) 394-243.*

■ Adventures on Wheels

The **Clare Glens Cycle** is a 30-mile circular bike trail starting and ending at the Tourist Information Centre in Arthur's Quay, Limerick. The trail takes you east of the city and into the Slieve Felim Mountains. It passes through Annacotty,

Castleconnell, Newport, the Clare Glens themselves, Glenstal Abbey, and Murroe.

The Glens form the boundary between Limerick and Tipperary, with a gorge through which the River Clare runs, with waterfalls and rapids, and there are nature trails throughout the area. **Glenstal** is a Benedictine Abbey and second-level school set in attractive gardens with woods and lakes, with lots of rhododendrons in bloom during May and June.

■ Adventures on Water

At Foynes there's a **Yacht Club** with a marina, and there are classes in watersports. ☎ (069) 65543.

Although many of the courses at the **Kilfinane Outdoor Education Centre** are for groups, they do offer canoeing and kayaking for individuals, with introductory sessions at Lough Gur. Contact Keith Bickford. ☎ (063) 91161; fax 91201; kilfinedctr@eircom.net.

Fishing

For full details and a map, contact **Shannon Regional Fisheries Board**. ☎ (061) 300-238; fax 300-308; www.shannon-fisheries-board.ie. Their website is wonderful, with lots of information, including places to stay.

See page 71-74 for details on angling in Ireland, regulations and best times to fish.

You can fish the River Shannon in Limerick City and nearby for trout and coarse varieties, including pike at Annacotty and Plassey.

In the Slieve Felim area of East Limerick there are two major fishing rivers – the Shannon near Castleconnell, six miles (9.6 km) from the city, and its tributary, the Mulcair. The **Castleconnell Salmon Fishery** has eight beats and operates seven days a week. Contact the **ESB Conservation Section**, Ardnacrusha, ☎ (061) 345-589, or Paddy Guerin, **The Kingfisher Angling Centre**, Castleconnell, ☎ (061) 377-407.

The Mulcair is a summer salmon river with some spring salmon. With its tributaries, the Newport and Bilboa, it covers 25 miles (156 km). Contact the **ESB** or Richard and Eleanor Keays, **Millbank House and Angling Centre**, Abington, Murroe. ☎ (061) 386-115; info@millbankhouse.com; www.millbankhouse.com.

In the Ballyhoura area there's fishing for salmon, brown trout and coarse fish (including bream, perch, rudd, pike and eel) in the rivers Maigue, Loobagh, Morning Star and Camogue. Lough Gur also attracts coarse fishing, and Griston Bog near Ballylanders is where to go for rainbow trout. Contact the **Ballyhoura Centre**, Kilfinane, for details. ☎ (063) 91300; info@ballyhoura.org.

The Shannon Estuary in West Limerick is quite sheltered so can be fished in most weathers. Tope, ray, ling and cougar are among the fish caught in-shore. At Foynes, Kilteery and Glin, there's shore angling.

The River Feale rises in West Cork and flows through West Limerick and the town of Abbeyfeale, entering the sea south of Ballybunion in Co. Kerry, and is one of the best for salmon and sea trout. Permits are available from Patsy Ryan, **Abbeyfeale Anglers Association**. ☎ (068) 31411.

For sea trout fishing, best from mid-May to September, both permits and advice, contact the **Brosna/Mountcollins Angling Club**, which controls eight miles (13 km) of fishing. ☎ (068) 44456.

Near Athea, the **Glasha Lake Trout Fishing Centre** has a lake fully stocked with brown trout, open every day from 10 am to dusk, earlier by prior arrangement. ☎ (068) 42295.

■ Adventures on Horseback

 Among riding centers in Co. Limerick is the one at **Adare Manor Hotel**, which includes a cross-country course. ☎ (061) 395-355. Near Adare is the **Clonshire Equestrian Centre**, set in 120 acres of parkland. ☎ (061) 396-770. There's also the **Adare Equestrian Centre** at Kildimo. ☎ (061) 396-373.

Only a 10-minute drive from the city is the **Clarina Riding Centre** on the N69. ☎ (061) 353-087.

Off the N69 between Glin and Tarbert is the **Shannon View Equestrian Centre**, open from May to October, offering trekking and leisure riding. ☎ (068) 36185.

The **Hillcrest Riding Centre**, Glen of Aherlow, Galbally, has trail riding through the scenic area, as well as various courses. ☎ (062) 37915; hillcrest@eircom.net; www.irishabroad.com/travel/horseriding/hillcrest.

Collins Equestrian, Athlacca, Kilmallock, offers lessons from beginner up, as well as polocrosse (a combination of lacrosse and polo played on horseback). ☎ (063) 90679; www.limerickpoloxclub.com.

Woodview, near Newcastle West, gives lessons for all, plus showjumping, cross-country and dressage. ☎ (069) 61554. The **Ballykennry Riding School** is in the same area. ☎ (069) 62529.

Fitzgeralds Equestrian Centre at Abbeyfeale offers trekking along scenic paths. You can stay there too, in its attractive farmhouse. Contact

Kathleen Fitzgerald. ☎ (068) 31217/31558; fitzfarmhouse@eircom.net; www.fitzgeraldfarmhouse.com.

A Riding Vacation

Ash Hill Stud, Kilmallock, stands on the site of Castle Coote. Its ruins can be seen from the avenue leading to the Georgian house, which has Gothic features. Inside, there are friezes and cornices dating from the 1780s. You can take a riding vacation here and also go fishing and walking. ☎ (061) 98035.

■ Golf

There are a number of parkland courses in Co. Limerick, including those at the Adare Manor Hotel and at Killeline, which appear under the Where to Stay section**.

Rathbane Golf Club is about a mile from the city center, signposted off the R512 to Lough Gur. It's open to visitors all year. ☎/fax (061) 313-655; info@rathbane.com; www.rathbanegolf.com.

Limerick County Golf and Country Club, Ballyneety, not only has an 18-hole course, but it also has four-star vacation cottages. It's on the R512 Limerick to Ballybunion road, less than five miles from the city, and is open all year. ☎ (061) 351-881; fax 351-384; lcgolf@iol.ie; www.limerickcounty.com.

The **Newcastle West Golf Club**, Rathgoonan, Ardagh, is set in 160 acres of quiet countryside. It's open all year, but there are restrictions on Sundays and Tuesday is ladies' day, so always phone ahead. ☎ (069) 76500; fax 76511; nswgolf@eircom.net.

Abbeyfeale Golf Club has a nine-hole course, and a driving range. ☎ (068) 32033.

■ Where to Stay

In Limerick City there's a big choice of hotels, many of them belonging to chains, including Jurys and Clarion, so check the contacts listed on pages 59-60.

☆☆☆☆☆ **The Adare Manor Hotel and Golf Club** is an 18th-century castle in its own estate of 840 acres of gardens and parkland, including its own 18-hole golf course. There are 64 bed-

HOTEL PRICE CHART	
Price per person, per night, with two sharing, including breakfast.	
$	Under US $50
$$	US $50-$100
$$$	US $101-$175
$$$$	US $176-$200
$$$$$	Over US $200

rooms in the Manor, with a choice of standard, deluxe and "stateroom." There are also two- and four-bedroom townhouses on the beautiful estate just a few yards away from the Manor across a courtyard from the Clubhouse. You can rent them by the week or less, minimum two nights.

What makes staying here so memorable is not just the attractive historic surroundings, but also that, as at Dromoland Castle in Co. Clare, there's such a choice of activities available to guests. Here they include clay target shooting (great fun, I tried it here), cycling around the estate and the pretty village, an indoor swimming pool, fitness centre, sauna and spa, a garden tour, or taking in the pet cemetery (a feature at many historic homes). Guests can fish on the River Maigue, which runs through the estate, on their own or with a ghillie if required.

Rates from $$$$, but off-season there are special offers, so it's worth checking the website. ☎ (toll-free from USA) 1-800-462-3273; (061) 396-566; fax 396-124; info@adaremanor.ie; www.adaremanor.com.

☆☆☆☆ Also in Adare is the **Dunraven Arms Hotel**, which has welcomed guests since 1792, when they arrived by horse-drawn coach. There's a choice of bedrooms, suites and junior suites, all beautifully furnished with antiques. It's a member of the Manor House Hotels group, and an award-winner.

The Dunraven Arms has a leisure center with a pool, and there are lots of activities available locally, including riding, golf, fishing, archery, shooting and walking, which can be arranged by the hotel. There's a choice for dining. The **Maigue Restaurant** has received awards for its quality; the **Inn Between**, across the road in a thatched cottage, serves traditional Irish dishes. $$$. ☎ (toll-free from US/Canada) 1-800-44-UTELL; (061) 396-633; central reservations (01) 295-8900; dunraven@iol.ie; www. dunravenhotel.com or www.manorhousehotels.com.

Glin Castle, home of the Knight of Glin and his wife, Madam Fitzgerald, is very special, as it's belonged to the family for over 700 years. It's on the banks of the Shannon and is furnished with wonderful paintings and period furniture; there's a tennis court and croquet lawn on the grounds. The castle is a member of Ireland's Blue Book (see page 60**). Meals include fruits and vegetables from its own kitchen garden, along with locally produced meat and poultry or freshly caught fish.

Visitors can stay between March and November; other times by special arrangement. There are 15 double bedrooms, or you can rent the entire castle, fully staffed. Rates from $$$$. Dinner from €47. ☎ (068) 34173; fax 34364; knight@iol.ie.

Castle Oaks House Hotel is in the picturesque village of Castleconnell, 10 minutes northeast of Limerick City. The hotel is in a former Georgian mansion, surrounded by 26 acres, on the banks of the Shannon, and is a relaxing place to stay, yet near all the city's attractions. There's also a self-catering option in its Riverside Holiday Homes.

It is particularly popular with those interested in fishing, as it has its own private salmon fishery, and offers special packages, including trips to fish elsewhere. There are also lovely riverside nature walks in its grounds, and the hotel can arrange other activities for guests, including riding. Rates from €70 per person B&B. ☎ (061) 377-666; fax 377-71; info@castleoaks.ie.

☆☆☆ **The Killeline Park Hotel and Leisure Complex**, in Newcastle West, has an 18-hole golf course and a fully equipped leisure center with pool. Other activities include go-kart racing at the track nearby in Kilcornan, fishing in the Shannon, Maigue and Deel rivers, riding, bike hire and tennis. It also arranges classes with the local **Off-Shore Adventure Centre** in raft building, kayaking and dinghy sailing. $-$$. ☎ (069) 61130; fax 77448; info@killeline.com; www.killeline.com.

Guesthouses

Note that guesthouses often have special rates if you stay for more than one night, so inquire when booking.

Deebert House, Kilmallock, is a Georgian residence, with lovely gardens. It's a member of the Town and Country Homes Association, and is open March 1 to November 30. $ for two, includes breakfast. ☎ (063) 98106; fax 832002; deeberthouse@eircom.net; www.deeberthouse.com.

Knights' Haven B&B is just over a mile from Glin, and belongs to the Irish Farmhouse Holidays Association (www.irishfarmholidays.com). It's another attractive house dating from the Georgian period, overlooking the Shannon Estuary. $ for two, includes breakfast. ☎ (068) 34541; fax 34541; knightshaven@esatclear.ie; www.knightshaven.com.

Rental Cottages

☆☆☆☆ **Ballyhoura Forest Homes**, Ballyorgan, south of Kilmallock, off the Slí Finn driving/cycling route, is a group of 10 timber-clad houses in wooded countryside. ☎/fax (063) 91666.

Hostel

Trainor's Hostel, Ballingarry, is the only one listed as a member of the IHH (Independent Holiday Hostels of Ireland, see pages 63-64). It's open mid-March to the end of September. ☎ (069)/fax 68164; trainorhostel@eircom.net.

Camping & RV Parks

In addition to the **Curragh Chase Caravan and Camping Park** at Kilcornan, ☎ (061) 337-322, already mentioned on page 332, there's ☆☆☆ **Dohertys** just outside Adare. It's open from March 1 to September 30. ☎ (061) 395-376; fax 395-377; dohertycampingadare@eircom.net.

■ Where to Eat

In Limerick City

As in any city, there's a huge choice of places to eat in Limerick, including pubs, hotels, restaurants and coffee shops. Among them are the following.

The Green Onion Café, Old Town Hall, Rutland Street, is open Monday-Saturday, from noon to 11 pm. It serves modern Irish and vegetarian food in a relaxed setting. ☎ (061) 400-710.

Bella Italia, 43 Thomas Street, is family-run and is popular, which is always a recommendation, and especially attracts local rugby players. Its portions are generous and it is a very good value. ☎ (061) 418-822.

In Co. Limerick

Don't forget you can eat in hotels around the county, and that many of the pubs serve lunch, and some serve evening meals. Of special note are:

The Mustard Seed Restaurant, Echo Lodge Country House, Ballingarry. This is a listed Victorian country house on 10 acres of grounds, which include mature trees, shrubbery, a kitchen garden and orchard. It's renowned for its good food and fine wine, offering the best of contemporary Irish cuisine, and is very popular. It's a member of Ireland's Blue Book (see page 60), and you can stay here too. From Adare, you take the N21 Killarney road for half a mile, turn left at the first road junction to the left and follow the signposts to Ballingarry. ☎ (069) 68508; fax 68511; mail@mustardseed.ie; www.mustardseed.ie.

The Wild Geese Restaurant, Rose Cottage, Adare, is another admired restaurant, recommended in guides to fine dining. It's in one of the cottages on the left as you enter the village, and is open from May to September, Tuesday to Saturday, from noon to 3 pm for lunch and 6:30 to 11 pm for dinner. Its cuisine is European and modern Irish, using fresh organic produce and game in season. ☎ (061) 396-451; wildgeese@indigo.ie.

■ Useful Contacts

Limerick Tourist Information Centre. ☎ (061) 317-522; touristofficelimerick@shannondev.ie.

Shannon Development. www.shannon-dev.ie.

Shannon Airport. www.shannonairport.com.

Ballyhoura Country. www.ballyhouracountry.com.

Limerick Visitor Information. www.visitlimerick.com.

Cruise Street, Limerick City

Doorway of Clonfert Cathedral, 1161-1171, East Galway
(Ireland West Tourism – see page 351)

Ireland West

Three counties, Galway, Mayo and Roscommon, make up this region. Both Galway and Mayo have long and indented coastlines, while Roscommon is an inland county, mostly flat and dotted by lakes, with some low hills. The

region is criss-crossed by rivers and streams, and there are three major lakes – loughs Conn, Mask and Corrib. Among the activities you can engage in here are walking, fishing, and riding. There are also plenty of interesting places to visit, from ancient ruins to historic houses.

County Galway

Galway is the second largest county in the country (after Cork) and is almost divided in two by Lough Corrib. Between it and the Atlantic is the wild and beautiful Connemara. To the east is a fertile limestone plain stretching to the border with Roscommon and the River Shannon.

Offshore are the fascinating Aran Islands, where a traditional way of life, with a distinct culture and language, continues.

Galway City is the county capital; other main towns include **Ballinasloe**, **Loughrea**, **Tuam** and **Clifden**.

■ Getting Here

By Air

Galway Airport is at Carnmore, west of the city. ☎ (091) 755-569. You can fly from to and from Dublin with Aer Lingus, and Aer Arann Express (www.skyroad.com) flies from Luton near London to Galway daily.

Main Roads

Galway City is served by N18-N6-N4 from Dublin (136 miles/219 km); N18-N6-N55-N54-N2-A3-M1 from Belfast (190 miles/305 km); N18-N20 from Cork (120 miles/193 km) via Ennis and Limerick; and the N17 from Sligo (86 miles/138 km).

Useful Numbers

- ■ **Galway Bus Station**. ☎ (091) 562-000.
- ■ **Galway Train Station**. ☎ (091) 561-444.

Both are in Eyre Square in the city center.

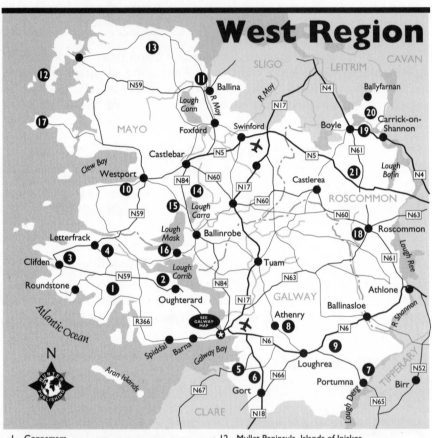

West Region

1. Connemara
2. Aughnanure Castle; Glengowle Silver & Lead Mine; Kylemore Abbey
3. Clifden Station House; Clifden Castle
4. Connemara National Park
5. Dunguaire Castle
6. Coole Park; Thoor Ballylee; Kiltartan Museum
7. Portumna Castle & Forest Park
8. Athenry Castle
9. Pallas Castle, Tynagh
10. Croagh Patrick; Westport House
11. Moyne Abbey; Rosserk Friary

12. Mullet Peninsula, Islands of Iniskea
13. Céide Fields
14. Mayo Abbey; Museum of Country Life
15. Ballintubber Abbey
16. Quiet Man Museum
17. Achill Island
18. Roscommon Castle & Abbey; County Maueum
19. King House; Frybrook House
20. Lough Key & Forest Park; Castle Island
21. Cruathan Aí Visitor Centre

NOT TO SCALE

© 2004 HUNTER PUBLISHING, INC.

■ Tourist Information

 Áras Fáilte, Forster Street, Eyre Square, **Galway**. ☎ (091) 537-700; fax 537-733; info@irelandwest.ie; www.irelandwest.ie. Main Street, **Oughterard**, Co. Galway. ☎ (091) 552-808; fax 552-811; oughterardoffice@eircom.net. Kilronan, Inis Mór, **Aran Islands**. ☎ (099) 61236; 61420.

Connemara Tourism is a voluntary organization, which markets that area of Co. Galway worldwide. Its main office is in **Cleggan**, Galway. ☎ (095) 44955. They have another office in **Letterfrack**. ☎ (095) 41116; info@connemara-tourism.org; www.connemara-tourism.org.

TRACING YOUR ANCESTORS

There are two family-research centers serving the county:

The **West Galway Family History Society**, Unit 3, Liosbaun Estate, Tuam Road, Galway. ☎ (091) 756-737; galwayfshwest@eircom.net.

The **East Galway Family History Society**, Woodford, Loughrea, Co. Galway. ☎ (090) 9749309; fax 49546.

Ireland West

■ Galway City

Sightseeing

 Situated on Galway Bay at the mouth of the River Corrib, this is the fastest growing city in Europe but don't be put off by its sprawling suburbs, as it retains much of its historic charm. Its streets still have their medieval layout, and the center is very compact, and easy to explore.

Galway has been commercially important since the 11th century when it was a center for trade with Spain and Portugal. In 1477 Christopher Columbus paid a visit. Galway earned the title "City of the Tribes" around that time, when it was ruled by 14 wealthy merchant families. Today it's lively, with loads of things to do, and is so popular that it can get very crowded in summer, especially during its annual Racing Festival at **Ballybrit Racecourse**.

The annual **Arts Festival** also attracts thousands, especially for its street parade, organized by the multi-award winning production company, Macnas (www.macnas.com). Its famous **Druid Theatre** produces and stages plays and has toured internationally, winning awards, including Tonys on Broadway.

There's lots of memorabilia associated with **James Joyce** at 8 Bowling Green, former home of Nora Barnacle, his partner. The house has erratic opening times and no phone, so just go there.

A Saturday morning market takes place around **Kirwan's Lane** near the 700-year-old **St. Nicholas' Church**, where for centuries fresh produce has been sold.

The seaside suburb of **Salthill** has sandy beaches, a golf course, and lots of pubs, restaurants, hotels and guest-houses.

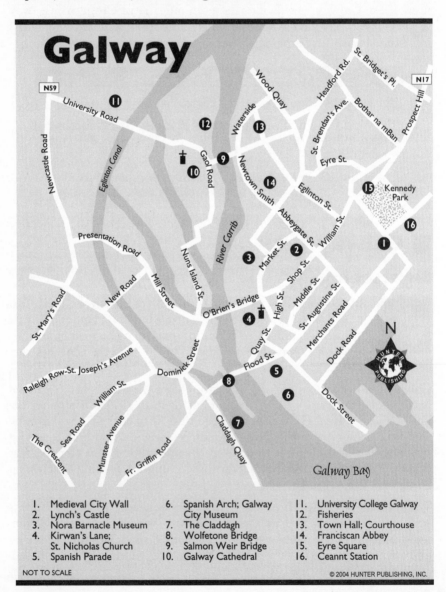

Galway

1. Medieval City Wall	6. Spanish Arch; Galway City Museum	11. University College Galway
2. Lynch's Castle	7. The Claddagh	12. Fisheries
3. Nora Barnacle Museum	8. Wolfetone Bridge	13. Town Hall; Courthouse
4. Kirwan's Lane; St. Nicholas Church	9. Salmon Weir Bridge	14. Franciscan Abbey
5. Spanish Parade	10. Galway Cathedral	15. Eyre Square
		16. Ceannt Station

NOT TO SCALE

© 2004 HUNTER PUBLISHING, INC.

The center of the city doesn't take long to explore. Start at **Eyre Square**, where US President John F. Kennedy spoke in the months before his assassination. There's also a lovely little monument to the writer Padraic O'Conaire. Walk down Williamsgate and into the main thoroughfare, **William Street**, which becomes Shop, High and then Quay streets. Turn left along the promenade to the **Spanish Arches**, where wine, brandy, spices, salt, animal produce and fish were unloaded from ships in centuries past and you'll come to the **Galway City Museum**. Allow enough time to take a look inside. After that, double back until just past William O'Brien Bridge and you can follow the riverside walkway to Salmon Weir Bridge. Cross it and visit **Galway Cathedral**, then continue up University Road and visit the **university** and its **gallery**.

Tours

An easy way to see the city is to take an open-top bus tour from Eyre Square with **O'Neachtain Tours and City Sightseeing**. ☎ (091) 553-188; fax 553-302; naugtour@iol.ie. They also run half- and full-day tours of Connemara and farther afield.

Pubs

Galway's pubs are lively, and many of them have traditional music sessions. There's a belief that **The King's Head** on High Street was given as a reward to the executioner of Charles I. **Tigh Neachtain**, 17 Cross Street, is one of the oldest pubs in the city and **Murphys**, 9 High Street, is great for a quiet drink. Two of the most traditional are **Tig Coili** on Mainguard Street and **Taaffe's**, opposite at 19 Shop Street. The best-known pub is probably **The Quays**, which attracts great musicians, and has a restaurant. ☎ (091) 568-347; fax 567-405; thequays@iol.ie.

THE FIRST LYNCHING

Lynch's Castle, on the corner of Shop Street and Upper Abbeygate Street, is now a bank, but was a 15th-century mansion belonging to one of the powerful families or "Tribes of Galway." In the 1480s, Mayor Lynch hanged his own son for murder, and the people were so shocked that the term "lynch" was born. In the bank lobby there's an account of the trial and sentence.

Shopping

If you want to buy just one thing associated with Galway, then it has to be a **Claddagh ring**. A band of gold or silver with two hands holding a crowned heart, it's a symbol of friendship and love.

The earliest Claddagh ring was made by the goldsmith Richard Joyce around 1700, although the symbol of clasped hands goes back to Roman times. The ring is named after the Claddagh, a fishing village on the outskirts of the city, where it was popular as a wedding ring. It's worn with the heart facing the nail to mean betrothal and towards the heart when married.

Jewelers all over Ireland stock Claddagh rings, but it's special buying one where they originated, and where many of the jewelers make them in their own workshops. Among them are **Woods** on Eglinton Street and **Hartmann** on William Street.

 Kennys Bookshop on High Street is one of the best shops of its kind in the country. It has a huge selection of rare and secondhand, mainly Irish, books, many signed by the authors. It's also an art gallery, so allow plenty of time to browse. They run a mail order service, so if you get carried away and worry about the weight of your luggage you can have your purchases sent home. See their website at www.kennys.ie.

At Mervue, just over a mile from the city center off the N6, is the Royal Tara Visitor Centre, where they now sell fine china. **Tara Hall** was the home of the Joyces, merchant bankers and one of the 14 tribes. Colonel Pierce Joyce was the last owner; he was a friend of Lawrence of Arabia. Today the library and drawing room of Tara Hall are among showrooms where visitors can see examples of fine Royal Tara bone china, and some of the hand-painted pieces are only available here. You can also take a free guided factory tour and watch the craftspeople at work. The Georgian tea rooms serve light snacks – served, of course, on Royal Tara china. Open daily all year. ☎ (091) 705-602; fax 757-574; visitor@royal-tara.com; www.royal-tara.com.

TRY SOME OYSTERS

With some of the cleanest seas in Europe, Co. Galway is famous for its seafood – especially oysters, with annual festivals in the city and in Clarenbridge just outside. The Galway International Oyster Festival was founded in 1954. Over a million oysters are consumed every year at the late September event. ☎ (091) 527-282; oysters@iol.ie.

You really should try oysters at least once with brown bread and a glass of stout, and Galway is the ideal place to do so.

■ Sightseeing in Co. Galway

 Follow the coast west of the city on the R366 via Salthill, and en route, if the weather allows, you'll be able to see the hills of Clare, the Burren and the Aran Islands. Barna is a pretty village with a pier, and next you come to the fishing village of Spiddal, at the edge of the Connemara *Gaeltacht*. There's a good craft center on the way in on your right. Then you come to Inverin and the Connemara airport, from which you can fly to the Aran Islands. Boats to the islands depart from the harbor of Rosaveal, on the coast beyond Inverin.

The Aran Islands

The Aran Islands lie 30 miles (48 km) off the coast of Galway and Clare. There are three island: Inis Mór, Inis Oir and Inis Meain. The largest is **Inis Mór**; and among its attractions is **Dún Aonghasa**, a 2,500-year-old fort clinging to 300-foot-cliffs, in the care of the State Heritage Service. Open year-round daily until 6 pm, March-October; 4 pm the rest of the year. ☎ (099) 61008; fax 61009; dunaonghasa@ealga.ie.

There's a heritage center in Kilronan and lots of pubs, restaurants and guest houses. To get around, you rent a bike, take a jaunting (horse-drawn carriage), car or a mini-bus tour.

Inis Meain is dominated by the massive **Dún Chonchúir**, a fortress dating to the Iron Age. The island is famous for its cliffs, patchwork of fields, its beautifully spoken Irish, and the Aran knitwear known all over the world.

Geologically, **Inis Óirr** is an extension of the Burren in Co. Clare, with the limestone fissures concealing exotic plants and flowers. Other features include a Bronze Age tumulus (mound tomb), **Formna Village**, with its many thatched houses, and a medieval castle – **Caislean Ui Bhrian** – with strange Celtic heads looking out over Galway Bay (see www.westireland. travel.ie/detail.asp?).

With their austere but beautiful landscapes, dry-stone walls, wonderful views of the Atlantic, and historic sites, all three islands are worth visiting. No wonder they have inspired writers and artists, including the playwright John Millington Synge. Their isolation for centuries has meant that they retain much of traditional Irish culture, including the language. They also have safe sandy beaches, sailboarding and boating, as well as facilities for angling. You hear great music, instrumental and vocal, in the islands' pubs.

Getting There

■ By Boat

Innishmór Ferries, owned by the islanders, runs a ferry service to Inis Mór. You travel by boat from Rosaveal in

Ireland West

Connemara. There's a coach to Rosaveal from Galway, which takes an hour; the boat journey is about 20 minutes. There are several trips daily. Tickets are available from the ferry office at 29 Forster Street, or the Galway Tourist Office. ☎ (091) 566-535/534-553/506-925; info@queenofaran2.com; www.queenofaran2.com.

■ By Air

Aer Arann operates four flights daily from Inverin in Connemara to the three islands; the service includes a bus from Galway (see above). Flights take about 10 minutes. ☎ (091) 593-034; www.aerarann.ie.

Connemara

Connemara is one of the most scenic, unspoiled areas in the entire country, with a rugged landscape of bogs and moors. It is dominated by two mountain ranges, called the Twelve Bens and the Maam, and fringed by an indented coastline of wide bays and sheltered harbors.

Although beautiful, the land is poor, so farmers need other incomes to survive. Irish is still spoken here and visitors are made very welcome.

As you travel around you'll see **Connemara ponies**. These lively little animals may be descendants of horses that swam ashore when the Spanish Armada was wrecked off the coast in the 16th century. Donkeys, once popular with farmers in the area because their small feet suited the boggy ground, are not often seen these days.

Connemara National Park, Letterfrack, is open all year, offering walks, talks, an audio-visual show, and displays. The park is on the slopes of the Twelve Bens, and is home to a herd of pure Connemara ponies and red deer, as well as rabbits and foxes, and to the non-native and destructive mink. You see signs of how the area was heavily populated in the past with ruined houses and old sheep pens. The Visitor Centre is open from May to the end of September, ☎ (095) 41054.

As with the entire western seaboard, the weather in Connemara is very changeable – a wet day can end with a wonderful sunset or what began as a warm and sunny day can suddenly feel like winter – so be prepared.

Clifden

Clifden is known as the capital of Connemara, and is set in wonderful scenery. It has a great range of shops, restaurants and pubs. It was one of the last towns to be built in the country when founded by John D'Arcy (1785-1839) as an attempt to create a commercial center in a resource-rich yet very poor area. He received a government grant for relief work to build its quay after the 1822 famine.

The Galway-to-Clifden railway was also constructed as relief work, and opened in 1895, but never made money and closed in 1935. The **Clifden Station House** has been restored and now houses a museum with a focus on the Connemara pony and local events. ☎ (095) 21494. Around it there's a very attractive shopping center.

■ The Sky Road

The Sky Road, as its name suggests, takes you up the hills overlooking Clifden Bay and its islands, and is a circular route suited to cyclists and drivers. Start from Market Square in Clifden and follow the signs. Climb Monument Hill and enjoy spectacular views of the Twelve Bens. There's a memorial to John D'Arcy at its summit, and his former residence, Clifden Castle, is now a romantic ruin.

Roundstone

Roundstone is a picturesque fishing village 14 miles (22.5 km) from Clifden, with beautiful beaches nearby. There are several pubs and cafés in the village. At the **Roundstone Musical Instruments** workshop the traditional Irish goatskin drum, the bodhrán, is made. Contact Malachy Kearns, IDA Craft Centre, Roundstone, ☎ (095) 35808, bodhran@iol.ie, www.bodhran.com.

Around Lough Corrib

Aughnanure Castle, built in 1500 by the O'Flahertys, is off the N59 near Oughterard, close to Lough Corrib. It's a well-preserved example of an Irish tower house. Open daily from mid-June to end September, 9:30 am-6 pm; May and October, weekends only; guided tours. ☎ (091) 552-214; fax 557-244; aughnanurecastle@ealga.ie.

For something different, visit **Glengowla Silver and Lead Mine**, two miles (3.2 km) west of Oughterard. The mine was abandoned in 1865. Open daily, March to November, 9:30 am to 6:30 pm, and most weekends in winter. ☎ (091) 552-360.

Kylemore Abbey is an 18th-century castle, now a boarding school. You can visit its grounds, including a six-acre Victorian walled garden and woodland walk, as well as part of the Abbey. The Abbey exhibition rooms and tea room are open all year, 9 am to 5:30 pm; the Craft Shop is open March to December until 6 pm. Grounds are open Easter to October, 10:30 am to 4:30 pm. ☎ (095) 41146; fax 41145; enquiries@kylemoreabbey.ie; www.kylemoreabbey.com.

Athenry

The medieval walled town of Athenry is a Heritage Town. Its **Castle** dates from about 1250 and is open daily, except Monday, June to mid-September, 10 am to 6 pm; April-October, until 5 pm. ☎ (091) 844-797; fax 845-796;athenrycastle@ealga.ie.

South of Galway City

South of Galway City on the N18 to Ennis road is the Heritage Town of **Gort**. Several attractions nearby make a visit here worthwhile.

Coole Park

The former home of Lady Augusta Gregory, playwright and co-founder with Edward Martyn and W.B. Yeats of the Abbey Theatre in Dublin, this site is just north of the town of Gort. Many Irish literary figures met here in the early 20th century, including George Bernard Shaw, and carved their autographs into a tree in the walled garden. The woods and lake are lovely surroundings for a walk. The estate is now a nature reserve, with a Visitor Centre and tea rooms. Open daily from June to end August, 10 am-6 pm; Tuesday-Sunday from Easter to end September, it closes at 5 pm. ☎ (091) 631-804; fax 631-653; coolepark@ealga.ie.

Nearby is **Thoor Ballylee**, the tower bought by poet W.B. Yeats as a retreat; it has been restored and is open to the public. The **Kiltartan Museum**, housed in a former school in Gort, documents the literary history of Coole Park.

Dunguaire Castle

Dunguaire Castle stands overlooking Galway Bay near Kinvara, south of Galway City. Built in 1520 it was bought by the writer Oliver St. John Gogarty early in the last century and hosted meetings of literary figures including Yeats, his patron Lady Gregory, J.M. Synge, and George Bernard Shaw. Today it's owned by Shannon Development, which runs medieval banquets here. Reserve at Tourist Offices or ☎ (061) 360-788; fax 361-020; reservations@shannon-dev.ie; www.shannonheritage.com.

East Galway

There's plenty of variety in the landscape of the eastern half of the county, with the Sliabh Aughty Mountains, forests, bogland, lakes, and rivers in the valleys, as well as pastures and floodlands stretching along the shores of the River Shannon and Lough Derg.

There are signs of history wherever you go, including **Pallas Castle** near Tynagh, built by the Burkes around 1500, and monastic ruins at Holly Island, Terryglass and Lorrah. Watch out for agricultural machinery on the narrow minor roads.

Numerous monastic settlements from the 5th and 6th century were located in Clonfert. In the heart of the village is **Saint Brendan's Church of Ireland Cathedral**, the oldest living church in Ireland with an unbroken history of public worship. The cathedral itself stands in the grounds of a monastery founded by St. Brendan. The monastery flourished through times of invasion but was burnt down in 1016, 1164, and again in 1179. All that now remains of the settlement is the cathedral, which is famed for its west doorway, one of the finest specimens of Hiberno-Romanesque work in existence. The west front of the cathedral including this doorway is attributed to Peter O'Moore, Bishop of Clonfert from 1161 to 1171.

 Saint Brendan is believed to have sailed up Lough Derg to his monastery at Clonfert before setting off on his voyage to America, 1,000 years before Columbus.

Portumna, 20 miles (32 km) from Ballinasloe, is a fishing center and marina for Lough Derg and the River Shannon, and a pleasant town.

The imposing ruins of **Portumna Castle**, built before 1618 by Richard Burke (or de Burgo), 4th Earl of Clanricarde, are in an attractive setting overlooking Lough Derg and Portumna Forest Park, once part of the demesne. The castle is in the care of the Heritage Service, open daily April 1 to October 31 from 10 am to 6 pm. ☎ (090) 9741658; fax 41889; portumnacastle@ealga.ie.

■ Adventures on Foot

With clean air from the Atlantic and its unspoiled countryside, Co. Galway is ideal for walkers.

The waymarked way called Slí Chonamara or **Connemara Walk** starts in Galway City and goes along the shore of the Bay through Spiddal, Carraroe, Rosmuc, Carna and then turns north towards Oughterard and ends near Recess; it's 150 miles (241 km) long. You can stay overnight in Irish-speaking households along the route and enjoy the culture and landscapes of this wonderful area. Ask at tourist offices for guides and other information.

The **Western Way** was the second waymarked route to be established in the county, after the Wicklow Way. It begins on the shores of Lough Corrib, winds through Connemara's Highlands, with marvelous views of mountains, lakes and coast, including the great fjord of Killary Harbor, and continues on into Mayo.

There are more than 50 mountains in Connemara in four ranges – the Twelve Bens, Maam Turks, Partry and Sheffrey, and they attract experienced hikers. Connaught's highest mountain, **Mweelrea** (2,688 feet/

820 m), is at the mouth of Killary Harbor, one of Ireland's two fjords. The other is at Carlingford, Co. Louth.

Maps are available from Tourist Information offices or from specialist shops, including **The Outdoor Shop** (Faoin Tuath), Market Street, Clifden. ☎ (095) 22838; www.faointuath.com.

Make sure you wear appropriate clothing and footwear, check the weather in advance, and let someone know where you are going, especially if you are mountain climbing.

In East Galway, the **Portumna Forest Park** is open all year, and covers 1,000 acres, with walks through woodland and along the lakeshore. It's home to at least 85 different birds and 16 species of wild mammals, including the elusive pine marten, which was almost extinct.

■ Adventures on Water

Take a cruise from Wood Quay in Galway City on *The Corrib Princess*, which takes you along the River Corrib to Lough Corrib, passing historic monuments and fishing villages on the way. Contact **Corrib Tours**. ☎ (091) 592-447.

Oughterard, on the main Galway-to-Clifden road (N59) is a busy little fishing village. You can take a cruise on Lough Corrib, May to October, from here with **Corrib Cruises**. ☎ (094) 9546029; fax 46568; www.corribcruises.com.

Vacation on Water

Emerald Star has its base at the Marina, Portumna, where you can hire a cruiser for a vacation. With each cruiser comes an 18-foot angling dinghy, so you can enjoy any of the 200 fishing positions along the river. Call the company's headquarters in Co. Leitrim. ☎ (071) 9620234; fax 21433; emeraldstar@clubi.ie; www.emeraldstar.ie.

Adventures Under Water

Scubadive West, in the sheltered Killary fjord in Connemara, runs a variety of courses, suitable for the beginner and the experienced diver. ☎ (095) 43922; scubadivewest@eircom.net; www.scubadivewest.com.

■ Activities on Land & Water

Delphi Mountain Resort and Spa, Leenane, offers 25 different activities, including surfing, rock climbing, pony trekking. ☎ Lo-call in Ireland 1-850-275-275; fax (095) 42303; delphigy@iol.ie; www.delphiadventureholidays.ie.

ORGANIZED TRIPS

Killary Tours, based in Leenane, have a choice of getaways for those who want to have all the organizing done for them. You can go scuba diving, yachting or horseback riding. As an example, you could do a diving course for beginners or go on a diving safari, staying on three different islands. They also have packages for more experienced divers, as well as tours on yachts or on horseback. ☎ (095) 42276; tours@killary.com.

Fishing in Ireland West

 The **Western and North-Western Regional Fisheries Board** looks after this part of Ireland. The Western Board's website is worth a look, and you can link from it to those for other areas. There's a huge amount of information, about game and coarse fishing, sea angling and about the fisheries in the region. They publish a *Sea Angling Guide*, which can be downloaded from their website, ordered online or bought at tourist offices. The Western Regional Fisheries Board, The Weir Lodge, Galway. ☎ (091) 563-118; info@wrfb.ie; www.wrfb.ie.

■ Salmon Fishing Near Galway City

The Corrib River or Galway Fishery starts at Nimmos Pier, near the Claddagh, in Galway Bay, and is made up of the main river, the Galway City canals, the two outlet rivers from Lough Corrib and a portion of Lough Corrib.

For permits and information, contact The Fishery Manager, Galway Fishery, Nun's Island, Galway, ☎ (091) 562-388; fax 562-930; shartgalfish@eircom.net.

 See pages 71-74 for details on angling in Ireland, regulations and best times to fish.

■ Adventures on Horseback

 Visitors to this region can enjoy some of the best scenery and riding trails in the whole country. Here are some of the riding centers:

■ **Feeneys Equestrian**, Bushypark, Galway. ☎ (091) 527579.

- **Aillecross Equestrian Centre**, Loughrea. ☎ (091) 841216.
- **Cleggan Riding Centre**, Cashel, Connemara. ☎ (095) 44746.
- **Clonboo Riding School**, Clonboo Cross, Corrundulla. ☎ (091) 791362.
- **Hilary & Caroline Crosby**, Millbrook, Ballinasloe. ☎ (095) 43683.
- **Errislannan Manor**, Clifden. ☎ (095) 21134.
- **Glencree Riding Stables**, Lackagh, Turloughmore. ☎ (091) 797104.
- **Kinincha Stables Ltd**, Ballinamanton, Galway Road, Gort. ☎ (091) 631297.
- **Milchem Equestrian Centre**, Tynagh, Loughrea. ☎ (095) 76388.
- **Laragan Stable**, Cleggan, Co. Galway, offers beach rides and treks in Connemara. ☎ (095) 44735.

Riding Vacation

Flower Hill Equestrian Holiday Farm, Flower Hill, Killimor, Ballinasloe, Co. Galway. ☎ (095) 76112.

Horseracing

Galway Racecourse, Ballybrit. ☎ (091) 753-870; fax 752-592; galway@iol.ie.

For Horse Lovers

At Kilreekill near Loughrea on the main Dublin road, the N6, is **Dartfield – Ireland's Horse Museum and Park**, which charts the history of the horse, and where you can see horses resting and working. Other attractions include a forge, tack room and art gallery, all on 350 acres of parkland, so it's ideal for a walk. Open all year, 9 am-6 pm. ☎ (091) 843-968; info@dartfieldhorsemuseum.com; www.dartfieldhorsemuseum.com.

The Ballinasloe Horse Fair, held in October, has ancient origins, and horses were bought here during the 18th and 19th centuries for the cavalries of Europe. Horses are led, paraded, admired, examined, bought and sold there still.

■ Golf Courses

Galway Golf Club, Salthill, ☎ (091) 522-033.

Athenry Golf Club, Oranmore, ☎ (091) 794-466.

Ballinasloe Golf Club, ☎ (095) 42126.

Connemara Golf Club, Clifden, ☎ (095) 23502.

Galway Bay Golf Club, Renvyle, ☎ (091) 790-500.

Gort Golf Club, ☎ (091) 632-244.

Loughrea Golf Club, ☎ (091) 4104.

Mountbellew Golf Club, Ballinasloe, ☎ (095) 79259.

Oughterard Golf Club, ☎ (091) 552131.

Portumna Golf Club, ☎ (090) 9741059.

Tuam Golf Club, ☎ (093) 28993.

Golfing Break

Near Portumna is **Green Acres Cottage and Golf Course** at Oldthort. It has a nine-hole golf course, and an 18-hole pitch-and-putt course. Equipment is supplied free of charge (with a refundable fee for balls) and there is a coffee shop. There's also accommodation in the Cottage, and horse-drawn caravans are available for rent. ☎ (090) 9741123; fax 41174; oldthort@gofree.indigo.ie.

■ Where to Stay

☆☆☆ **Shannon Oaks Hotel and Country Club**, Portumna, is an ideal base for exploring Galway and neighboring counties. It's on the edge of the town, a few yards from Portumna Castle and Forest Park, and a short walk to the marina. The staff is charming and helpful, there's a choice of 63 comfortable and well-equipped rooms and suites, and they have a leisure center with gym and pool, health and

HOTEL PRICE CHART	
Price per person, per night, with two sharing, including breakfast.	
$	Under US $50
$$	US $50-$100
$$$	US $101-$175
$$$$	US $176-$200
$$$$$	Over US $200

beauty rooms. There's often music in the **Idle Hour bar**. You can choose to eat in the **Upper Deck** there, which is popular with locals and excellent value, or, for a more extensive menu, in the **Castlegates Restaurant**. The hotel belongs to the Irish Country Hotels marketing group.

Ireland West

Rates from $$. ☎ (090) 9741777; fax 41357; sales@shannonoaks.ie; www. shannonoaks.ie.

☆☆☆☆ **The Abbeyglen Castle Hotel** is a small hotel on the Sky Road overlooking the sea, set in the Alpine-like village of Clifden with the backdrop of the Twelve Bens mountain range. ☎ (095) 21201; fax 21797; info@abbeyglen.ie. It's the hotel used by Connemara Safari as its base for island-hopping and walking vacations. Rates from $$. ☎ (095) 21071 or toll-free in Ireland 1-800-777-200; www.walkingconnemara.com.

If you want to meet other people and experience life in a castle, then **Cregg Castle**, which calls itself neither a guesthouse nor a hotel, is ideal. It's nine miles (14.4 km) north of Galway City near the village of Corandulla, and is surrounded by more than 160 acres of woods and farmland. It dates from 1648, erected by Clement Kirwan, a member of one of the 14 Tribes of Galway, and was the last fortified castle to be built west of the River Shannon.

It feels like staying with friends; the atmosphere is informal, with a huge fire in the Great Hall, plenty of conversation if you want, and impromptu performances of Irish music. Guests are encouraged to bring instruments and join in. Breakfast, with their own eggs and brown bread, is served until lunch time around the huge dining table. There's no bar, but wine is available and guests can bring their own drink, and make tea and coffee (free) at any time.

There's fishing and horseback riding nearby, and walks in the woods and around the working farm. From $ per person sharing, with breakfast and a limited evening menu. ☎ (091) 791434; www.creggcastle.com.

☆☆☆☆ **The Cashel House Country House Hotel and Restaurant**, a member of Ireland's Blue Book (see page 60), has a wonderful secluded location on Cashel Bay, near Recess, surrounded by a 40-acre estate of shrubs and woods. It has its own tiny private beach, a hard tennis court and riding facilities. Salmon and sea trout fishing are available nearby, as is golf. Cashel House has gained an international reputation since it was opened as a hotel by the McEvilly family in 1968, winning lots of awards. From $$$. ☎ (095) 31001; fax 31077; info@cashel-house-hotel. com; www.cashel-house-hotel.com.

For Fishing Vacations

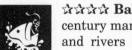
☆☆☆☆ **Ballynahinch Castle Hotel** at Recess, is an 18th-century manor on its own 350-acre unspoiled estate of woods and rivers in the middle of Connemara. It overlooks the Ballynahinch River, famous for its salmon and sea trout, and is surrounded by the Twelve Bens mountain range. It has 40 rooms, with open fireplaces and four-poster beds, along with the modern facilities. There is an elegant restaurant and a more informal **Fisherman's Pub**.

Ballynahinch is associated down the centuries with historical figures, including the O'Flaherty Chieftains, Grace O'Malley, Humanity Dick Martin (founder of the Society for the Prevention of Cruelty to Animals), and HRH the Maharajah Ranjitsinji, also known as "Ranji, Prince of Cricketers." Rates $$$, with special fishing packages, and winter breaks. ☎ (095) 31006/31086; www.ballynahinch-castle.com.

One of my favorite spots in the whole country is around Leenane and a delightful place to stay there is **Delphi Lodge**, a country house surrounded by woods and mountains, overlooking a lake. It belongs to the Hidden Ireland group of historic houses offering high-class accommodation (see page 60). There are only 11 bedrooms; dinner is served at a huge oak table presided over by the person who has caught the day's largest salmon. There's a library and roaring fires, so if you just want to laze and read, you can. Rates from $$. ☎ (095) 42211; fax 42296; delfish@iol.ie; www.mayo-ireland.ie.

Rental Cottages & Apartments

 Irish Cottage Holiday Homes has a choice of houses in the county – at **Renvyle** there are nine traditional thatched cottages; at **Lettermore**, 13 cottages by the sea; at **Carraroe**, 10, also on the coast; and at **Spiddal** there are 23 cottages and four apartments. Central Reservations ☎ (01) 475-7596; info@irishcottageholidays.com; www.irishcottageholidays.com.

If you prefer individual houses, contact one of the tourist offices listed on page 343.

Hostels

There are two hostels in **Galway City**, one at Inishere on the **Aran Islands**, another on **Inishbofin Island**, and seven others around the county. They're all members of the **Independent Holiday Hostels of Ireland**. ☎ (01) 836-4700; info@hostels-ireland.com; www. hostels-ireland.com.

Camping & RV Parks

☆☆ **Ballyloughane Caravan and Camping Park**, Renmore, open mid-April to late September. ☎ (091) 755-338; fax 753-098; galwcamp@iol.ie.

☆☆ **Renvyle Beach Park**, open from March 17 to end September. ☎ (095) 43462; fax 43894; renvylebeach@unison.ie.

☆☆ **Spiddal Park**, open mid-March to mid-October. ☎ (091) 553-372; fax 553-976; paircsaoire@eircom.net.

Ireland West

■ Where to Eat

In Galway City there is a huge choice of places to eat, including in its pubs, and the following are just some suggestions. Take a walk around and check menu boards.

Maxwell McNamaras is on Williamsgate Street, just off Eyre Square as you walk down Shop Street. It's open seven days, from 9 am to 11 pm, and is usually busy, which is a good sign. It serves breakfast, lunch and dinner, and its menu includes steaks, seafood, chicken and pasta dishes. ☎ (091) 565727; fax 564379.

Periwinkles Restaurant, is above the Tigh Neachtain Bar on the corner of Quay Street and Cross Street, and is open from 5:30 to 10:30 pm. It's decorated in traditional style, with an open fire in the winter. It specializes in seafood and steaks, and also serves duck, lamb, pork and vegetarian dishes. ☎ (091) 566858.

Brannagans Restaurant, 36 Upper Abbeygate Street, is at Lynch's Castle Corner just off Shop Street. It's open seven days from 5 to 11:30 pm and its menu is imaginative, with international dishes at reasonable prices. Among them are Oriental, French, Italian, Cajun, all created with fresh local fish and game when available. ☎ (091) 565974; fax 567261; cpbran@indigo.ie; http://indigo.ie/~cpbran/Page1B.html.

Rosleague Manor, Letterfrack, Connemara, is not only a four-star County House Hotel, in a lovely Georgian house overlooking Ballinakill Bay, it's also an excellent restaurant. Its setting in 30 acres of woodland is delightful, with each of its 16 bedrooms individually decorated and furnished with antiques and paintings. It's on the N59, seven miles northwest of Clifden. Rates from $$ in low season, $$$ high season. Open mid-March to November 1. Restaurant open for dinner to non-residents and recommended by the top food guides for the quality of its cuisine. It belongs to the prestigious Ireland's Blue Book and has won the Fáilte Ireland Award of Excellence. All its food is prepared using the finest local ingredients, including fresh seafood and Connemara lamb. ☎ toll-free from US 800-323-5463; (095) 41101; fax 41168; rosleaguemanor@eircom. net; www.rosleague.com.

Mitchell's Restaurant, Market Street, Clifden, is open from the middle of March to the middle of November every day from noon to 11 pm. It serves seafood, steaks, and vegetarian dishes, and its Irish stew is highly recommended. ☎ (095) 21867; fax 21066.

The White Gables Restaurant is at Moycullen, on the shore of Lough Corrib. It's noted for its good cooking in a traditional style and in particular for its excellent fish. Lobster, crab and mussels feature on the menu, as well as daily specials just off the boat. It's in a beautifully restored cottage, with cut stone walls and stone fireplace, tastefully decorated, with original artwork. Open for dinner from Tuesday to Sunday, 7 pm until late, and for Sunday lunch at 12:30 and 2:30 pm, for which booking is advised. ☎ (091) 555744; fax 556004; ann@whitegables.com; www. whitegables.com.

O'Dowds Seafood Restaurant is at Roundstone, eight miles from Clifden, in the middle of the village overlooking the harbor. As well as seafood, traditional Irish dishes are on its menu. It's open every day from noon to 11 pm. ☎ (095) 35809; fax 35907; owdowds@indigo.ie; www. odowdsrestaurant.com.

Paddy Burkes is eight miles south of Galway City at Clarinbridge on the main road to Ennis and Limerick. It's recommended by good food guides, including *Egon Ronay*, and serves modern Irish and vegetarian cuisine. Open Monday-Saturday, 10:30 am to 11:30 pm; Sunday, noon to 9:30 pm. ☎ (091) 796226; fax 796016.

County Mayo

Stretching from Lough Corrib in the south to Killala Bay in the north, and looking out over Clew Bay and the Atlantic Ocean, Mayo has lots of attractions, including beautiful mountain scenery, remote bogs and wonderful beaches. It has excellent fishing waters at Lough Conn, Lough Mask, and the River Moy, great golf courses, lots of walking trails and a host of historic ruins to explore. Achill, Ireland's largest island, is joined to the mainland by a bridge.

County Mayo has a long coastline with many safe beaches and islands, including Clare Island, the home of Pirate Queen Grace O'Malley, who ruled Clew Bay during the second half of the 16th century. Shown at left is Rockfleet Castle, where Grace lived much of her life.

Remains of the area's first settlements dating back 5,000 years can be seen in ancient monuments that include standing stones, fulachta fiadh (Bronze Age cooking sites) and ring forts. A rugged terrain and relative isolation have meant that they are in a better condition than those found in intensively farmed areas. There are ruined abbeys, friaries and churches all over the county, showing the significance of the area in early Christian days. North Mayo and Croagh Patrick in particular have strong associations with St. Patrick.

Ireland West

Inland, Mayo has rolling mountains and hundreds of beautiful lakes, such as Conn, Cullen and Corrib, while parts of the county also feature the endangered bogland habitat, a mecca for wildlife enthusiasts.

In addition to natural beauty, Mayo has fine sports facilities and visitor centres. The three main towns are **Castlebar** (the county capital), **Ballina**, the largest, and **Westport**.

■ Getting Here

By Air

 Knock International Airport is at Charlestown. ☎ (094) 9367222; fax 67232; www.knockinternationalairport.ie. There are flights from Dublin with Aer Arann; from Stansted, near London, with Ryanair; from Manchester with British Airways, and charter flights from Europe.

By Road

 Mayo's capital, Castlebar, is reached from Galway by taking the N17 to Claremorris and then continuing north on the N60. Castlebar is connected to the county's largest town, Ballina, by the N58 to Foxford and then the N26. To get to Ballina from Dublin, take the N26-N5-N4.

■ Tourist Information

 The **Westport Tourist Office**, open all year, except Sundays, is on James Street, ☎ (098) 25711; fax 26709; westport@ irelandwest.ie.

TRACING YOUR ANCESTORS

There are two places in Co. Mayo where you can research your family. The **North Mayo Family Heritage Centre** is at Enniscoe, near Ballina, in woodland on the shores of Lough Conn. It's an agricultural and rural museum with a forge, as well as an ancestry centre. There's a walled garden and tea room. ☎ (096) 31809; fax 31885. The **South Mayo Family Research Centre** is on Main Street, Ballinrobe. ☎/fax (094) 9541214.

■ Sightseeing

Westport

 Westport is a charming and very attractive town, much of it designed by the architect James Wyatt during the Georgian period. **The Mall**, with its lime trees lining both sides of the Carrowbeg River, is very special.

The town is known as a sea-fishing center, and also has many lively traditional pubs with plenty of Irish music. It's at the mouth of Clew Bay, with beaches nearby.

The holy mountain of **Croagh Patrick**, where Saint Patrick is said to have performed his snake-banishing act, is five miles (eight km) from the town. Known locally as the **Reek**, it's climbed regularly by pilgrims, most barefoot, especially on the last Sunday in July when tens of thousands of them attempt the steep ascent. There are wonderful views of Clew Bay and the countryside as you climb. The **Croagh Patrick Information Centre** is in Murrisk on the Pilgrim's Path at the base of the mountain, opposite the National Famine Monument. ☎ (098) 64114; fax 64115; croaghpatrick@ireland.com.

Westport House is a mile from the town. It's the home of the Marquess of Sligo, a fine Georgian mansion designed by Richard Castle with additions by James Wyatt, and open mid-May to mid-September.

Ballina

Ballina, the largest town in the county, is on the River Moy and attracts anglers from all over the world, many of whom fish for salmon from its bridges. **Moyne Abbey** and **Rosserk Friary** are worth a visit, or you can just enjoy the bustle of the town.

North Mayo

The **Mullet Peninsula** in North Mayo is an area of unspoiled natural beauty and a *Gaeltacht* or Irish-speaking region. Its west coast, exposed to the Atlantic, is completely without vegetation, while the east overlooks the inlet of Blacksod Bay.

The uninhabited islands of Duvillaun More, Inishkea North and South, and Inishglora have interesting remains of early ecclesiastical settlements. Inishglora is associated with the Irish myth, *The Children of Lír*. The northern coastline has the remains of a number of promontory forts.

The peninsula is popular for sea angling, and is also renowned for its unique bird life. Termoncarragh Lough, under the protection of the Irish Wildlife Conservancy, is home to the red necked phalarope; admission is by appointment only. The islands of Inishkea are bird sanctuaries, providing habitats for a large colony of barnacle geese (winter visitors to Ireland), and Inishglora is home to a big colony of stormy petrels.

The Largest Stone Age Monument in the World

Near Ballycastle, on the R314, east of the Mullet peninsula but still in North Mayo, are the **Céide Fields**, the biggest Stone Age monument in the world. Preserved under the wild bogland are field systems, dwelling areas and megalithic tombs dating back 5,000 years. It's surrounded by spectacular rock formations and cliffs and the wild flora of the bog are so rare they're of international importance. It's all in the care of the Heritage Service, with guided tours available. Wear sensible shoes and rainwear. There's an exhibition and tea room. Open daily from mid-March to the end of October, until 5 pm; June through September, until 6 pm. ☎ (096) 43325; ceidefields@ealga.ie.

> **AN OUTSTANDING ATHLETE**
>
> **Bohola**, between Swinford and Castlebar, should be of interest to visitors from the US. It was the birthplace of the athlete Martin J. Sheridan (1881-1918), who won a staggering nine Olympic medals for his adopted country in discus, high and long jump, shot-put, and pole-vaulting. There's a memorial to him in the village.

Castlebar

Castlebar, the administrative capital of the county, grew up around a castle built by the de Barra (Barry) family. It became a garrison town and was central in a number of historical events, including the French arriving to support the Irish rebellion of 1798 – known as "the Races of Castlebar."

Today it's a bustling market town, with lively night-time entertainment, including traditional Irish music in hotels and pubs, as well as a choice of good restaurants.

Castlebar is a good place to stay if you are planning outdoor activities as it's surrounded by some of the best fishing lakes in this part of the country, as well as signposted walking routes.

*Nearby is the ruined **Mayo Abbey**, which gave the county its name. It was founded in the 7th century by monks from Lindisfarne, and was called Maigh Eo Sacsan, or "the plain of the Saxon yews."*

The Museum of Country Life, the first branch of the National Museum to be located outside Dublin, is in Turlough Park, off the N5, four miles (6.4 km) from Castlebar on the road to Galway. Open daily except Mondays, admission free. Tours, shop, café. ☎ Lo-call in Ireland 1-890-687-386; www.museum.ie.

A CHURCH FOUNDED BY A KING

About seven miles (11 km) south of Castlebar is the village of Ballintubber. When St. Patrick brought Christianity to Ireland in about 442 he founded a church here. The present Abbey was founded in 1216 by King Cathal O'Conor, and so is the only church in Ireland still in daily use that was founded by an Irish king. **Ballintubber Abbey** is open daily all year, 9 am-midnight; tours May-September, 10 am-6 pm. ☎ (094) 9030934; fax 30050; btubabbey@eircom.net.

Two Unusual Houses

During the late 1870s, bad weather, poor crops and declining cattle prices produced an agrarian crisis in Mayo that left the people heavily in debt and unable to pay their rents. The crop failures revived memories of the Great Famine and resulted in spontaneous mass protest and many evictions. **Eviction Cottage**, Elmhall, Belcarra, is the home of the Walshe family who were evicted by their landlord's agents in October 1886. It has been refurbished as a Heritage Centre by the local community. They also restored the "tigin" or little house – a single room built at the time by the neighbors to house the evicted family. There are life-sized cutouts in the cottage by local artist Bridie Geraghty. Open June to September. ☎ (087) 909-0046 (mobile); marybprendergast@ireland.com. There's a river walk and fishing area nearby.

John Ford's 1951 film *The Quiet Man*, starring John Wayne, Maureen O'Hara and Barry Fitzgerald, was made in Cong on the Galway-Mayo border. You can visit the **Quiet Man Cottage Museum** on Circular Road, Cong. It's a replica of the cottage used, but is full of reminders of the film. Open daily, 10 am to 5pm. ☎ (094) 9546089; fax 46448; quiet.man.cong@iol.ie.

Achill Island

Achill Island is one of my favorite places, so beautiful it's hard to describe. Connected to the mainland by a bridge, it has sea-cliffs, wild moors, mountains, lakes, and valleys. There are several unpolluted sandy beaches, some little villages, excellent deep-sea, shore, and lake angling, and there are traces of famine dwellings on its hillsides. It's also a *Gaeltacht* (Irish-speaking) area.

Achill Sound is at the bridge from the mainland and is the main shopping center for the island. There are facilities for bathing, boating and fishing, and excursions by motor or sailing boat can be made along the coast and to nearby islands. Deep-sea fishing is also available, with Porbeagle shark particularly exciting to catch.

Knock

The village of Knock is on the N17 half way between Galway and Sligo. It was the scene of an apparition by Our Lady, Mother of Jesus, in 1879 and since then the huge shrine and church attracts thousands of pilgrims every year. Pope John Paul II visited it in 1989.

In its grounds is the **Knock Folk Museum**. Open daily in May, June, September and October, 10 am to 6 pm; in July and August, 10 am to 7 pm. ☎ (094) 9388100; fax 88295; knockmuseum@eircom.net.

Foxford

If you're looking for a gift or souvenir, first follow the self-guided tour at the **Foxford Woollen Mills Visitor Centre**, where the shop has a wide range of Irish-made giftware, as well as Foxford rugs, blankets and tweeds, a jewelry workshop, two art galleries and a restaurant. There's also a Tourist Information Office at the gate.

Open yearround, Monday-Saturday, 10 am-6 pm, and on Sunday, 2 to 6 pm; from May to October, Sunday hours are noon-6 pm. ☎ (094) 9256756; foxfordwoollenmills@eircom.net.

■ Adventures on Foot

Mayo offers a great variety of walks, from easygoing to tough mountain climbing. You can buy guides to walks, including The Western Way and The Foxford Way, and ask about guides to shorter walks as they are often produced locally.

Castlebar has the **International Four-Day Walking Festival** in July, designed to encourage people to leave the stress of town life behind for a few days in order to walk and rediscover the bogs, rivers and mountains in the West of Ireland. The walks are non-competitive, and are geared to suit people of varying levels of fitness. On each of the four days there is a 2.5-mile (four-km) and a 15.5-mile (25-km) road walk, and a two-mile (three-km) ramble. If you cannot spare four days, you have the option of joining in for one, two or three days of walking. At night the entertainment ranges from jazz to ceili music at the Walking Club. For further information, ☎ (094) 9024102.

The waymarked **Western Way** (110 miles/177 km) takes the walker from the fjord of Killary Harbor at Leenane on the Galway border to the base of the Ox Mountains on the Sligo border. It is the longest walk in Mayo, passing through some of the most beautiful scenery in the county, including wild and desolate bogs and rugged mountains.

The **Foxford Way** (53 miles/85 km) complements the Western Way, extending it south through the Ox Mountains, from Foxford to Straide and around Lough Cullin.

■ Adventures on Wheels

Although much of the county is suitable for cycling, there's only one signposted trail for bikes, the **Humbert Route**. This runs from Kilcummin, near Ballina in North Mayo, through lovely countryside with lakes and hills, to Charlestown, where it crosses into Co. Sligo. It continues through Sligo and Leitrim, ending in Ballinamuck, Co. Longford.

Mayo Leisure Cycling, Castlebar, is one company offering self-guided tours. ☎ (094) 9025220.

TRY SOMETHING DIFFERENT

There's a school of **falconry** at Ashford Castle Hotel, Cong. ☎ (094) 9546820; falconry@eircom.net; www.falconry.ie.

■ Adventures on Water

Lough Corrib, at 68 square miles (177 square km), is the largest lake in the Republic and is also one of the cleanest and least spoiled in Europe, with some 365 little islands on it. **Corrib Cruises** operates a choice of trips on the Lough from Lisloughrey Pier, including one to **Inchagoil Island**, where you get off and are taken on a guided tour of the 5th- and 12th-century ruins. It also has regular service to and from **Ashford Castle Hotel**. The company is based at Cong, a lovely village near the lake. Check their website at www.corribcruises.com.

There are 10 **Blue Flag beaches** (see page 76) in the county, at Carrowmore Strand, Dooega, Elly Bay, Golden Strand, Mullagharoe,

Mulranny, and Ross Strand, and three of them on Achill Island: Dugort, Keel and Keem.

Watersports, including surfing and diving, are particularly popular in this area, and there are a number of adventure centers (see *Useful Contacts* below).

Fishing

 There's great diversity for anyone interested in fishing in sea, lake and river. Salmon, trout and coarse fishing, shore fishing and deep-sea angling are available, and ghillies (guides), boats and other equipment can be hired. Remember that you must have licenses for trout and salmon fishing and you can get them from tackle and equipment shops in Mayo.

 See pages 71-74 for details on angling in Ireland, regulations and best times to fish.

Trips & Vacations

Tony and Mary Burke, Cashel, Achill Island, offer deep-sea angling vacations and sightseeing trips on a fully insured charter vessel. ☎/fax (098) 47257; tmburke@eircom.net.

Riverside Fishing Holidays, Swinford, offers accommodation with their own tackle shop. ☎/fax (094) 9252729; info@riversidefishing.com.

Peter and Patricia Roberts, Loughbawn, Partry, has B&B accommodations and angling services. ☎ (094) 954-3046; robertspartry@eircom.net.

Useful Contacts:

- ■ **The Killary Adventure Centre**, Leenane. ☎ (095) 43411; adventure@killary.com; www.killary.com.
- ■ **Achill Adventure and Leisure Holidays**, Dugort. ☎ (098) 43148; www.achill-leisure.ie.
- ■ **Achill Outdoor Education Centre**, Cashel. ☎ (098) 47253.
- ■ **Glenans Irish Sailing**, Collanmore Island, runs residential courses. ☎ (01) 661-1481; info@glenans-ireland.com; www.glenans-ireland.com.

■ Adventures on Horseback

There are several equestrian centers offering trekking and trail riding on both the hardy Connemara ponies and Irish hunters. Among them are the following:

Carrowholly Stables and Trekking Centre, Westport, offers guided scenic and coastal treks and trail riding. ☎ (098) 27057; www.carrowhollystables.com.

Ashford Equestrian Centre, in the woods at Ashford Castle, Cong, is now a luxury hotel as well, where US Presidents have been among the guests. ☎ (094) 9546507; timclesham@eircom.net; www.rideatashford.com.

Drummindoo Stud & Equitation Centre, Westport, offers lessons, day trail rides. ☎ (098) 25616; drummindo@anu.ie.

■ Golf

Mayo is a wonderfully scenic area in which to play golf, with a choice of courses.

There is a links course at **Carne**, near Belmullet. **Westport's** 18-hole championship course combines links and parkland; **Ballinrobe**, ☎ (094) 9541118, bgcgolf@iol.ie, **Ballina** and **Castlebar** also have 18-hole courses. There are nine-hole courses on **Achill Island**, and in **Ballyhaunis**, **Claremorris**, and **Swinford**. Contact Westport Tourist Office for details, ☎ (098) 25711, fax 26709, westport@irelandwest.ie.

■ Where to Stay

☆☆☆ **Westport Woods Hotel** is near the harbor in a peaceful wooded area overlooking its own private lake. It's well-equipped for anglers, with a freezer, a tackle room, a drying room, boats for hire, ghillies (guides) available, bait and tackle, and required permits. The hotel will also organize golf at nearby courses. In summer, trekking and trail riding are available. This is a hotel with something for everyone. Rates from $$. ☎ (098) 25811; fax 26212; www.westportwoodshotel.com.

HOTEL PRICE CHART	
Price per person, per night, with two sharing, including breakfast.	
$	Under US $50
$$	US $50-$100
$$$	US $101-$175
$$$$	US $176-$200
$$$$$	Over US $200

✩✩ **Cill Aodain Hotel** is on Main Street, Kiltimagh, a rural village in the middle of County Mayo surrounded by beautiful scenery. It has 15 bedrooms, individually and pleasantly furnished. Its restaurant is open in the evening to non-residents, and serves European and Irish cuisine prepared with good local produce. It's a member of Irish Country Hotels marketing group. Rates from $$. ☎ (094) 9381761; fax 81838; cillaodain@ eircom.net; www. irishcountryhotels.com.

✩✩✩✩✩ **Ashford Castle** at Cong has welcomed many prestigious guests, and is considered one of Ireland's outstanding hotels. It stands in its own 350-acre estate on the shore of Lough Corrib. Each bedroom is individually designed and beautifully furnished. There are also staterooms and suites available, where guests can dine if they wish.

You could spend their entire vacation here as it has such excellent facilities, including its own golf course and health club with gym, sauna, steam room and whirlpool. The estate is so big you can even take guided tours on foot or by bike. Cruising and fishing on Lough Corrib, horseback riding, both indoors and outdoors, archery and falconry, are among the other activities available.

In summer there's a choice of two restaurants, the **George V Dining Room**, with classical Irish cuisine, and the award-winning **Connaught Room**, offering French cuisine. Afternoon tea is served in the elegant **Drawing Room** with panoramic views of Lough Corrib. In the **Dungeon Bar** there's entertainment, with a resident storyteller and Irish music.

Rates from $$$$ in low season, breakfast extra, with golf and tennis included. ☎ from US 1-800-346-7007; (094) 9546003; fax 46260; ashford@ ashford.ie; www.ashford.ie.

Newport Country House is a Georgian house with gardens in the town of Newport, overlooking the river and quay, furnished with antiques and paintings. It belongs to Ireland's Blue Book and is unclassified under the star system. It's famous as an angling center, offering its guests salmon and sea trout fishing on the Newport River and Lough Beltra. Salmon fishing is also available on nearby loughs Feeagh, Furnace, Conn and Mask.

Meals at Newport Country House Restauranr are based on fresh produce from its own fishery, garden and farm, with seafood and home-smoked salmon specialties. The restaurant also has an extensive cellar. Open March 19 to early October. Rates from $$$ in low season. ☎ (098) 41222; fax 41613; info@newporthouse.ie; www.newporthouse.ie.

A Horse-Drawn Vacation

You can really get away from modern life and travel at walking pace on a horse-drawn caravan trip. Each caravan sleeps up to five. Don't worry – you get full instructions about how to handle the horse before setting off, as well as details on overnight stops. **Mayo Horsedrawn Caravan Holidays** are based at Belcarra, Castlebar. ☎ (094) 9032054; fax 32351; post@ mayoholidays.com; www.mayo-ireland.ie and follow links.

Rental Properties

 On Achill Island you can rent a cottage, then explore the island and farther afield. ☆☆☆ to ☆☆☆☆ **Keel Holiday Cottages** are south of Lough Keel under the Slievemore Mountain; you can walk from them to the EU Blue Flag beach at Keel. There's a choice of three-star and four-star houses. ☎ (094) 9032054; fax 32351; post@mayoholidays.com.

There are many other properties to rent all over Mayo, Galway and Roscommon. The tourism organization **Ireland West** has a Self-Catering Department. Contact them at ☎ (091) 537-777; fax 537-780; selfcatering@irelandwest.ie.

Camping & RV Parks

 ☆☆☆ There's a caravan and camping park in the grounds of Westport House, called **Parkland**, open from mid-May to early September. ☎ (098) 27766; camping@westporthouse.ie; www.westporthouse.ie.

☆☆☆ **Seal Caves Caravan and Camping Park** is at Dugort, Achill Island, open from April to the end of September. ☎ (098) 43262.

☆☆☆☆ Also on Achill is **Keel Sandybanks**, open from late May to early September. ☎ (094) 9032054; post@mayoholidays.com; www. mayoholidays.com.

☆☆☆ **The Cong Caravan and Camping Park** is open all year. ☎ (094) 9546089; quiet.man.cong@iol.ie; www.quietman-cong.com.

☆☆☆☆ **The Belleek Park** is just outside Ballina, open from March to the end of October. ☎ (096) 71533; lenahan@indigo.ie.

☆☆ **The Carra Park** at Belcarra, near Castlebar, has a limited number of spaces for tents and touring caravans, as it's the base for horse-drawn caravan trips (see above).

☆☆☆ **Lough Lannagh Caravan Park**, Castlebar, is open from early January until just before Christmas. ☎ (094) 9027111, llv@eircom.net.

☆☆☆ **The Knock Park** is open from March to the end of October. ☎ (094) 9388100; info@knock-shrine.ie; www.knock-shrine.ie.

Hostels

The Wayfarer Hostel, Keel, Achill Island, is open mid-March to the end of October. ☎ (098) 43266; wayfarerhostel@iolfree.ie.

Old Mill Hostel, Westport, is open all year, except Christmas week. ☎ (098) 25657; oldmill@iol.ie.

Cong Hostel is open all year. ☎ (094) 9546089; quiet.man.cong@iol.ie.

Club Atlantic Hostel, Westport, opens from early March to the end of October. ☎ (098) 26644; aran@anu.ie.

Kilcommon Lodge Hostel, Pullathomas, is open all year. ☎ (097) 84621; kilcommonlodge@eircom.net.

■ Where to Eat

The Quay Cottage Restaurant is on the waterfront in Westport, at the gates of Westport House, and looks deceptively small, yet behind its charming red door there's space for up to 100 diners. It has a fully licensed bar and serves dinner nightly from 6 pm. When the weather is good, guests can sit in the courtyard at the back. It's particularly noted for its seafood and shellfish, although it also caters for other tastes. As it's popular, you are advised to reserve ahead. ☎ (098) 26412; fax 28120; reservations@quaycottage.com; www.quaycottage.com.

The Riverside Restaurant is also a guesthouse and is on Church Street, Charlestown, where the N17, N5 and N4 meet, and only four miles from Knock Airport. It's run by the Kelly family and is very welcoming. Food served is prepared as much as possible using local produce. Guesthouse closed November. Overnight rates from $$. Restaurant open May to October, Tuesday-Sunday, from 8:30 am to 9:30 pm. ☎ (094) 9254200; fax 54207; riversiderestaurant@eircom.net; www.riversiderest. com.

Crockets on the Quay is not only a restaurant, it's also a pub with three bars and an eight-bedroom guesthouse. It's on the waterside just outside Ballina on the road to Sligo. There's been a pub here since the 1800s, but that was much smaller; this one opened in 2001 and the following year won a Pub of the Year award, followed a few months later by a Best Newcomer Award. Its restaurant is open daily from noon to 3 pm, and 6 to 10:30 pm. Bar food is also available all day until 8:30 pm. ☎ (096) 75940; fax 70069; info@crocketsonthequay.ie; www.crocketsonthequay.ie.

Gaughran's Pub, on O'Rahilly Street in Ballina, is an authentic 1930s pub where its owner Mary Gaughan offers a different main course daily. It could be meat loaf, chicken fillet in a cream sauce or smoked wild salmon. She also makes delicious brown bread and soup. Desserts include her own ice cream. Food served Monday-Saturday, from 11 am to 6 pm. ☎ (096) 70096.

The Anchor Bar and Restaurant is at Golden Strand, Dugort, on Achill Island, and serves seafood. It looks out over the golden beach and has a real turf fire and traditional music playing. The restaurant is open in the summer from 6:30 to 9 pm. ☎ (098) 47216; martinmasterson@ hotmail.com.

County Roscommon

Roscommon takes its name from two words, "ros," a wooded or pleasant gentle height, and the bishop-saint Coman, who founded an abbey in what is now the county capital.

It's an inland county, mostly flat and dotted with lakes, with some low hills. The River Shannon runs along the eastern edge of the county, and the western part is under bog.

Rathcrogan in its center was the home of the Kings of Connacht and later the High Kings, and there's evidence of ancient human habitation all over the county, with many burial mounds, megalithic tombs and ring forts.

Although the county capital is **Roscommon**, the largest town is **Boyle**; other important towns include **Castlerea** and **Strokestown**.

■ Getting Here

Roscommon Town is served by N61-N6-N4 from Dublin (91 miles/146 km); N61-N6-N62-N8-N25 from Cork (156 miles/251 km); and N61-N6-N18 from Galway (51 miles/82 km). Belfast is 139 miles (223 km) away.

It's on the railway. **Roscommon Station,** ☎ (090) 6626201.

The nearest **airport** is at Knock, Co. Mayo.

■ Tourist Information

Roscommon Tourism, Library Building, Abbey Street, Roscommon. ☎ (090) 6626342; tourism@roscommon.ie; www. visitroscommon.com.

Ireland West

TRACING YOUR ANCESTORS

County Roscommon Heritage and Genealogy Centre, Church Street, Strokestown, ☎ (071) 9633380; fax 33398; info@roscommonroots.com; www.roscommonroots.com.

If you want to do your own research, call the County Library in Roscommon. It's in a building known as the Old Infirmary, which dates from 1783 with later additions, and was used as a hospital until 1941. Open Tuesday and Thursday, 1-8 pm; Wednesday to 5 pm; Friday and Saturday from 10 am to 1 pm and 2-5 pm. Closed Sunday and Monday. ☎ (090) 6637273; roslib@eircom.net.

■ Sightseeing

Roscommon Town

Roscommon Town was founded in early Christian times around the abbey of St. Coman. Later expansion included the Norman castle, built in 1269, and the Dominican priory, built by Felim O'Conor, King of Connacht, in 1253. Before the Cromwellian Plantation in the 17th century, which displaced Irish Catholics to poorer lands (see page 14), much of the surrounding area belonged to the O'Kellys.

An unusual local legend is that the town had a female executioner named Lady Betty, forced to take up that gruesome position to escape the same fate for murder.

Nowadays the town, surrounded by fertile farmland, is lively and prosperous, with some impressive buildings on its wide main street.

The County Museum is open all year, Monday-Friday, 10 am-4 pm. ☎ (090) 6625613.

Nearby is the building that was once the county jail, where Lady Betty carried out her gruesome executions. It was built in the early 1740s by the local landlord, the Earl of Essex. The building was a jail for under 100 years and then a lunatic asylum; later it served as a refuge for smallpox sufferers and eventually became a private house. Only the façade is left; the building now houses an arcade of shops and a restaurant on the ground floor, with apartments above.

Roscommon Castle is on a hill just outside the town and is quite impressive, although it burned down in 1690 and after that fell into ruin. It had an interesting history, surviving sieges and being partly blown up by Cromwell's soldiers in 1652.

In **Roscommon Abbey** there's a late 13th-century effigy of its founder Felim O'Conor on a later tomb with eight mail-clad warriors representing gallowglasses (professional soldiers in medieval times). The Abbey was a seat of learning under Abbot Coman, with close ties to Clonmacnoise.

There's an 18-hole **golf course** near the town, which welcomes visitors, and the **racecourse** has events in summer and autumn.

Visit Craftspeople

There are a number of interesting outlets around the county where craftspeople produce items that would make lovely and original gifts and souvenirs. Don't feel you have to buy, but do take a look. Roscommon Tourism publishes a map-brochure or take a look at www.roscommon.craft.com.

One example is at **Knockroghery**, on the N61 just outside Roscommon Town, where **Ethel Kelly** makes clay-pipes using molds and methods that date back about 300 years. You can use them to smoke, or just to admire. Open Monday-Friday, 9 am-6 pm in season; limited hours off-season, so call ahead. ☎ (090) 6661923; ethelkelly@eircom.net; www.irishclaypipes.com.

Boyle

Boyle is in the north of the county, between Loughs Gara and Key, below the Curlew Mountains, and is a charming small town. The area is popular for fishing.

King House was the 18th-century home of the family that later became Earls of Kingston and Main Street, Boyle, was originally the avenue leading to the house. The Kings abandoned the house in the late 18th century when they moved to Rockingham, now Lough Key Forest Park (see below), and it was used as a barracks for the Connaught Rangers army regiment.

A visit to King House is very worthwhile. The house overlooks the river and its entrance is on Main Street. You explore it at your own pace with a self-guided tour and learn not just about the history of the family and the town of Boyle but also something of the chieftains who ruled the area, including the O'Conors and MacDermotts. Open from April to mid-October, daily 10 am-6 pm (last admission 5 pm); late October, open weekends only. ☎ (071) 9663242; fax 63243; kinghouseboyle@hotmail.com.

At the entrance to King House is the **Una Bhan Tourism Centre**, with a restaurant and craft shop, where you can find out about the area and book accommodation. There's a car park next to it. ☎ (071) 9663033; fax 63077; info@unabhan.com; www.unabhan.com.

Frybrook House, in the center of Boyle, dates from around 1750. The drawing room has some of the finest examples of Georgian decorative plasterwork in the country as well as an Adam fireplace, and you get pleasant views of the River Boyle from the house.

Frybrook was noted for its hospitality and there's a tradition associated with it that a bell was rung at 5 pm every day inviting anyone in who wanted to dine! While you aren't offered the same these days, you can visit. Open from June to September, Wednesday to Sunday, 2 pm to 6 pm. ☎ (071) 9663513.

Beside the Dublin-Sligo road are the restored ruins of **Boyle Abbey**, closely associated with Mellifont Abbey in Co. Louth. Maurice O'Duffy founded the Abbey here in 1161 and it was consecrated in 1220, surviving all sorts of turbulent events for 400 years, due to its location on an important route. It's regarded as one of the finest Cistercian churches to survive, with design elements that bridge the Romanesque and Gothic periods, such as a row of rounded arches on one side of the nave and pointed arches on the other. There's a small interpretative center in its gatehouse. Open April to October daily from 9:30 am-6:30 pm (last tour 5 pm) ☎ (071) 9662604.

Lough Key

Just over a mile east of Boyle on the N4 is the almost circular Lough Key, part of the River Shannon system, with beautiful wooded islands. The area was once part of the Rockingham estate, belonging to the MacDermotts, and was granted to Sir John King in 1617. Rockingham House accidentally burned down in 1957 and on its site is Moylurg Tower from which you get a lovely view of Trinity Island, where poet W.B. Yeats planned to set up a community.

Lough Key Forest Park covers 840 acres and is one of the largest parks in the country. There are several walking trails; one brings you to Trinity Bridge, made of strangely shaped blocks, and then to the Bog Garden. Among other features are an icehouse, underground tunnels and a wishing chair. The entrance to the tunnel is near the lakeside restaurant, built so servants could carry provisions there without being seen.

You can rent boats nearby, go for a trip on the lough on the luxury 50-seater *Trinity*, plus there's a camping and RV site in the park.

CASTLE ISLAND

On the island are the ruins of a 19th-century castle associated with the legend of Una Bhan. She was the daughter of a MacDermott chief, who imprisoned her on the island because her lover was unsuitable. Every winter night he swam to the island to see her until he drowned. She died of a broken heart, and they were buried on the island between two trees, which grew to intertwine above them.

The park is open all year round. ☎ (071) 9662363; RV park 62212; www. coillte.ie/tourism.

Literary Connections

 Woodbrook House is on the N4 between Lough Key and Carrick-on-Shannon. It was the home of the Kirkwood family, made famous in the book, *Woodbrook*, by David Thomson. In 1932, as a young student at Oxford University, he took a summer job as tutor to Phoebe Kirkwood. Published in 1974, the book wonderfully evokes the lifestyle of an Anglo-Irish family and their home in the period before the Second World War, and is well worth reading.

Not far away is **Cootehall**, a beautiful village beside the River Boyle, where the award-winning contemporary novelist John McGahern was brought up.

The Arigna Scenic Drive

The most attractive section of the signposted Arigna Scenic Drive is from Keadue over the Kilronan Mountain and then down to Ballyfarnon. Do take care, as the road is steep and narrow, with tight bends to negotiate, but the drive is worth it for the marvelous views. Arigna used to be Ireland's only coal-mining center, quite a surprise as the landscape around here is very green and beautiful.

 Ballyfarnon is associated with the blind harpist Turlough O'Carolan, known as "the last of the bards," whose harp you can see at Clonalis House, Castlerea. O'Carolan's music reached a new audience in the 20th century through groups like The Chieftains. To commemorate him, the Keadue O'Carolan Harp Festival is held annually in August.

A Holy Well

To the east of Ballyfarnon is Lough Meelagh, and close to it is the Holy Well of St. Lasair. There's a slab opposite the well, said to be a cure for backache. Pilgrims used to climb under it. Stations (traditional devotions) are performed annually here on the first Sunday of September.

The Rock of Doon on the road to Boyle is the best spot for a wonderful view of Lough Key and over the plains. Farther along the same road you see a sign for Doon Shore, where a sandy beach has been created on the bank of the lake and you can swim.

The Dr. Douglas Hyde Interpretative Centre and Garden, Portahard, is on the N5 halfway between Ballaghadereen and French Park. The Centre is dedicated to the first President of Ireland, and is housed in the church where his father was rector. The garden and graveyard are open all year; the house is open May-September, Tuesday-Sunday afternoons only. ☎ (094) 9870016.

Ancient Burial Site

At Tulsk, where the N5 and N61 intersect, between Boyle and Roscommon, is a huge and important ancient site.

Rathcroghan and Cruachan Aí, the burial place of the kings of Connaught, is also the setting for the beginning and end of *The Táin Bo Cuailgne (The Cattle Raid of Cooley)*; see page 10.

The site is spread out over such a huge area that it's difficult to make sense of it. There are 60 National Monuments here; the best thing to do is to visit the **Cruachan Aí (Plain of the Mounds) Visitor Centre** at the entrance to Tulsk village on the banks of the Ogulla River. You'll learn about the archaeology, history and mythology of one of the most important Celtic Royal sites in Europe. Tours are available and there's a café, as well as a craft and gift shop. Open June to September, 10 am-6 pm, shorter hours the rest of the year. ☎ (071) 9639268; fax 39060; cruachanai@esatclear.ie; www.cruachanai.com.

Elphin

Along the N61 towards Elphin you see signs marked "birthplace of Percy French." Ignore them. The songwriter, poet, entertainer and painter was born in 1854 at Cloonyquin. Sadly, the house is gone and all you see is a plaque where its original doorway stood – not worth the detour.

Not sure who he was? Among his most famous words are "Where the mountains of Mourne sweep down to the sea...," and his song about the West Clare Railway, which begins "Are you right there, Michael, are you right, do you think we'll be home before the night..."

The restored **Elphin Windmill**, west of the town, is worth a visit. It dates from the 18th century and is the only working windmill in the west of Ireland. Its unusual features include a thatched and revolving roof; its sails are turned to catch the wind using cartwheels on a circular track.

Open daily all year from 10 am to 6 pm, with guided tours. ☎ (071) 9635181; maud@indigo.ie.

Strokestown

Strokestown, southeast of Elphin, consist mainly of a wide avenue leading to the gates of **Strokestown Park House**, which, along with its Gardens and Famine Museum, is open to the public. Richard Castle (or Cassells) designed both the town and house in the 18th century for the Mahon family. In 1979 a local garage owner bought the house and the last family member packed her case and left – literally. All the family's furniture and other possessions are still there. Books, linen, family photos, toys, even the schoolwork carried out under the watchful eyes of a governess in the nursery, can be seen.

The Famine Museum is housed in the former stables, which is the perfect location. During the Great Famine (1845-50), the Strokestown estate attracted international attention when the landlord, Major Denis Mahon, was shot dead after trying to clear two-thirds of his estate's tenants through eviction and emigration.

The museum uses the extensive collection of estate papers to explain the significance of the Famine nationally and locally, and also draws parallels between contemporary world hunger and the experiences of Ireland in its past. Open daily from Easter to the end of October, 9:30 am to 5:30 pm. There are also guided tours of the house. The **Carvery Restaurant** is open daily. It is in a restored 17th-century building that would once have formed part of the original fortress structure. ☎ (071) 9633013; fax 33712; info@strokestownpark.ie; www.strokestownpark.ie.

Castlerea

In the western part of the county is the busy market town of Castlerea, on the River Suck. It's surrounded by pretty and wooded countryside and was the birthplace, in 1815, of Sir William Wilde, father of Oscar.

THE OLDEST FAMILY IN EUROPE

Clonalis House, the ancestral home of the O'Conor clan, is just west of the town on the N60 to Castlebar. The family dates back to 75 AD and so is the oldest in Europe. Among its ancestors were 11 High Kings and 24 Kings of Connaught. Note that their surname has one letter N, which is fairly unusual.

The current owners, Pyers and Marguerite O'Conor Nash (he inherited it from an uncle) are a lovely couple, who enjoy showing Clonalis to visitors. The house was built in the late 19th century, so is new in comparison to

Ireland West

the antiquity of the family, and the 1,500 years they've owned these lands. Its contents are fascinating, including over 10,000 documents, only a fraction of which are on display, and the O'Carolan harp. The blind harpist and composer of some of the most wonderful music for that instrument used to entertain members of the O'Conor family. Outside the house is the O'Conor Coronation Stone. The surrounding estate is wooded and attractive. For opening times, ☎/fax (094) 9620014; clonalis@iol.ie. You can stay in Clonalis from mid-April to the end of September (see Where to Stay section 381).

Take a Walk

You can walk in the Castlerea Demesne, or along the River Francis, which flows into the River Suck. Also in Castlerea is a most unusual museum "building" – Sean Browne's railway museum is housed in a 1955 A55 diesel locomotive. ☎ (094) 9620181; seanbrowne@eircom.net

■ Adventures on Foot

There's a network of walking routes called The Miner's Way and Historical Trail that wind not only through part of Roscommon, but also through the adjoining counties, Leitrim and Sligo.

The Miner's Way (39 miles/63 km) is named for the men who followed these paths when going to work in the Arigna coal mines. It is circular, starting and ending at Arigna and taking you through Keadue, Ballyfarnon and the Corrie Mountain.

The Historical Trail (35 miles/56 km) leaves the Miner's Way at Keadue and takes you to Lough Key Forest Park, Boyle, Carrowkeel, Castlebaldwin, Highwood and back to the Miner's Way at Ballyfarnon. There's a third walk connecting the Miner's Way to the Leitrim Way, which goes around Lough Allen, passing Drumkeeran, Dowra, Drumshanbo and then back to Arigna.

You would need a week to follow all of the walks, but you can enjoy a section of them in a day or two.

Serious walkers can carry on to follow other walks, such as those linking to the **Cavan Way** at Dowra and then on to the **Ulster Way**, or to the **Sligo Way** and then on to the **Western Way**.

The Suck Valley Way links a 60-mile stretch of countryside in West Roscommon and East Galway. Most of it crosses lowland farms, as well as the boglands and callows of the river Suck, with numerous lakes and drainage channels. The way passes through what are called the Nine Friendly Villages – Ballygar, Creggs, Glinsk, Ballymoe, Ballintubber,

Dunamon, Castlecoote, Athleague and Castlecoote. In each of them there's a Map Board showing the route and historical sites.

Knockvicar Bridge is where the Irish Chieftain O'Sullivan Beare rested on the last night before he and his men reached O'Rourke's castle at Leitrim village. Their journey is remembered in the long-distance waymarked walk, the **Beara Way**. Only 35 survived out of the 1,000 who fled with him from West Cork. There is a pleasant walk along the towpath here. See www.bearatourism.com for details on the walk. Nearby is Riversdale farmhouse, where Hollywood actress Maureen O'Sullivan spent part of her childhood.

The O'Sullivan Beara March

This epic march undertaken by O'Sullivan Beara to Leitrim through the Counties of Cork, Limerick, Tipperary, Galway, Roscommon, Sligo and eventually Leitrim arose as a result of the Irish and the Spanish defeat in the Battle of Kinsale at the hands of the English.

The Battle of Kinsale began on October 17th, 1601, with the 3,400 Spanish soldiers under the command of Aquilla, supported by O'Sullivan Bere, O'Driscoll and the O'Connors of Kerry. Aquilla surrended on January 12th, 1602, and handed over the four Spanish-defended castles along the South West Coast.

Donal Cam, chieftain of the O'Sullivan Bere Clan rushed back to Dunboy and began to fortify the castle against an English attack that started on June 6th and lasted 11 days with the English storming the Castle and bombarding it with cannon-fire.

Harassed by the English and having lost his lands and his herds of cattle and sheep, he left the Beara peninsula and the Bay of Bantry where the French invasion took place in 1796, to begin the long march to Leitrim to meet the O'Rourkes. Accompanying him were 1,000 men, women and children representing the first large-scale exodus of people from Castletownbere region.

In the middle of January 1603 they finally reached their destination with only 35 people remaining, many settling along the route and known since then in these localities as the Bearas.

■ Adventures on Wheels

 Roscommon is a great county for cyclists, as it's so flat and there are so many lovely minor roads to explore. The **Green Heartlands Cycle Route** stretches for 135 miles (217 km) across South Roscommon, between Roscommon Town and Athlone, along a series of quiet country roads. Contact Mrs. Phil O'Connell. ☎ (090) 643-7147.

■ Fishing

 Roscommon is a great destination for fishing, with many different locations and angling centers. The Western, North Western and the Shannon are the regional fishing boards involved.

 See pages 71-74 for details on angling in Ireland, regulations and best times to fish.

Lanesborough is at the head of Lough Ree (in Irish "the looped lake"), which is the second largest, after Lough Derg, of the Shannon lakes. It's 17 miles (27 km) long with 27 islands, many having ruins of monasteries on them. Kilglass Lakes, near Roosky, is a coarse angler's paradise, and all the lakes have an abundance of pike, perch, bream and rudd.

At Athleague, on the N63 southeast of Roscommon Town, a former Protestant church is now an **Angling and Visitors Centre**, where you can get local tourist information, not just about fishing. It's also the booking office for accommodation and tours. The Centre is open all year round, and has a coffee and craft shop. ☎ (090) 6663602; tench@indigo.ie; www.suckvalley.firebird.net.

■ Adventures on Horseback

 Munsboro Equestrian and Leisure Centre, 1½ miles (2.4 km) from Roscommon Town, is on 120 acres surrounded by the Shannon and by bogs, forests and mountains. Lessons available, cross-country course, full hunting course, and it has an indoor riding school. Other facilities include squash courts. ☎ (090) 6626449.

■ Golf

Roscommon Golf Course, Mote Park, is close to the town. ☎ (090) 6626382; rosgolfclub@eircom.net.

There's a nine-hole course at **Boyle Golf Club**, Deerpark. ☎ (071) 9662808.

■ Where to Stay

☆☆☆ **Shannon Key West Hotel** is on the river on the N4 main Dublin-to-Sligo road, with wonderful views of the Shannon from its bedrooms and roof gardens. It has a leisure club and tennis court, and its **Rooskey Inn** and **Kilglass Restaurant** both serve a good choice of food. Rates from $$. ☎ (071) 9638800; fax 38811; shnkywst@ iol.ie; wwwkeywest.firebird.net.

HOTEL PRICE CHART	
Price per person, per night, with two sharing, including breakfast.	
$	Under US $50
$$	US $50-$100
$$$	US $101-$175
$$$$	US $176-$200
$$$$$	Over US $200

☆☆☆ **Abbey Hotel**, on the Galway side of Roscommon Town, is an 18th-century manor house that has been sensitively transformed into a welcoming hotel. It's surrounded by four acres of grounds, with lovely lawns and gardens, and has 51 attractively furnished bedrooms, and a leisure center with swimming pool. Its restaurant is open to non-residents. It's a member of Irish Country Hotels marketing group. Rates from $$, with special breaks available. ☎ (090) 6626240; fax 26021; info@abbeyhotel.ie; www.irishcountryhotels.com.

☆☆ **O'Garas' Royal Hotel** is right in the middle of Roscommon Town, a rather old-fashioned yet welcoming place to stay; perhaps traditional would be a better word to describe it. It's family-run and its bar and restaurant are popular with locals. The bedroom I was given was enormous, but as it's a two-star, had no tea and coffee making facilities, which I missed. I could, however, read in bed – a definite plus. $. ☎ (090) 6626317; fax 26225.

 Why is it that so many hotels, including many of the more expensive places to stay, are designed by those who never read? I always travel with a clip-on light, which you can buy in any electrical supply store.

Clonalis House, near Castlerea, belongs to the Hidden Ireland group (see page 60) so is not classified under the star system. You can stay here from mid-April to the end of September. There are three doubles and one twin room, all with bath, available on a bed-and-breakfast basis. Dinner is available Tuesday through Saturday, but guests must give 24 hours notice. Rates $$. ☎/fax (094) 9620014; clonalis@iol.ie.

Camping & RV Parks

In addition to the Lough Key Park already mentioned, there are other sites.

☆☆☆☆ **Hodson Bay**, open June to September, is on the shores of Lough Ree, on the N61 near Athlone. Boating, fishing and swimming are available locally. The camping area is next to the Hodson Bay Hotel, listed under Co. Westmeath, page 184, which has a marina and an 18-hole golf course. ☎ (090) 6492448.

☆ **Willowbrook** is a family-run park in the Lung Valley, near Ballaghaderreen, and it is open all year. ☎ (094) 9861307; willowbrook@ eircom.net.

☆☆☆ **Gailey Bay** at Knockcroghery is also family-run, and is open from late April to mid-October. It's part of a self-contained vacation park on the shores of Lough Ree, and facilities include a pitch-and-putt course, boat rental and fishing tackle for sale or rent. It also has mobile homes for hire. ☎ (090) 6661058.

■ Where to Eat

Gleesons Townhouse and Restaurant is on the Market Square in Roscommon Town in a tastefully restored 19th-century house of cut limestone. It's next to the Tourist Office and Museum and is a three-star guesthouse with 19 bedrooms, offering standard and superior suites. There's plenty of room to park. Rates from $$, with no single supplement unless a double room is requested. The **Café** is open from 8 am to guests and non-residents, and serves a range of hot and cold dishes, as well as delicious snacks, including home-made cakes, brown bread and scones.

The **Manse Restaurant** has won awards for the quality of its cooking. It's open for lunch and dinner and guests can relax in front of an open fire in its reception area. Its cuisine combines Irish and European influences, and all food is prepared using the freshest ingredients. The Manse Restaurant is open from Sunday to Thursday, 8 am to 9 pm, and on Fridays and Saturdays until 10 pm. ☎ (090) 662-6954; fax 662-7425; info@ gleesontownhouse.com; www.gleesontownhouse.com.

Also in Market Square, Roscommon, is **Regans**, another three-star guesthouse, which is also a bar with a restaurant. It has 14 bedrooms, and two apartments with kitchens. Its restaurant offers good food at rea-

sonable prices. ☎ (090) 662-5339; fax 27833; info@regans.com; www.
regansbar.com.

Donnellan's Pub at Clarendon House, Knockvicar near Boyle, is open
for Sunday lunch and for dinner from Tuesday through Sunday in summer and Thursday through Sunday in winter. Its menu includes steaks
and seafood, and international and vegetarian dishes. It also offers half-
board and cook-for-yourself accommodation. The Donnellans will arrange fishing trips, including boat rental, and they have a tackle and bait
store. ☎ (071) 966-7016; clarendonhouse@ireland.com.

The Chambers Restaurant is beside the Courthouse in The Crescent,
Boyle. It's open for dinner 5-10 pm from Tuesday-Sunday. ☎ (071) 966-
3614.

The Royal Hotel Restaurant, at Bridge Street, Boyle, is open for lunch
every day from 12:30 to 3 pm, and for dinner from 6 to 9 pm (to 9:30 on
Friday and Saturday). Its menu includes traditional Irish dishes, seafood, steaks, game in season and vegetarian options. ☎/fax (071) 966-
2016; royalhotelboyle@tinet.ie.

Ireland West

King House, Boyle, Co. Roscommon
(Ireland West Tourism – see page 373)

Mount Errigal, Co. Donegal

The Northwest

Five counties make up this region, and there's a delightful variety of landscapes, from the rolling hills and lakes of Cavan and Monaghan in the east to the valleys of Leitrim and Sligo and the wild and wonderful Donegal in the west. Donegal and Sligo, and a narrow strip of Leitrim, are on the Atlantic coast, and the Shannon-Erne Waterway connects those two great rivers.

Only about 9% of the population of Ireland lives in these counties, so it's one of the quietest parts of the country, and in some places you can travel for miles without seeing another vehicle. The people are friendly and very welcoming to visitors.

Ireland's Green Box

This is a new initiative, announced in 2003, which designates some of the most unspoiled parts of the Northwest as ecotourism destinations. It takes in most of counties of Leitrim and Fermanagh, west Cavan, north Roscommon, north Sligo and south Donegal. The goal is to encourage visitors to enjoy their time here in harmony with nature, and a network of green tourism providers, including guesthouses, restaurants, outdoor activities and arts centers, is being established. They will be certified under a green star system. For example, a bed and breakfast with one green star will mean that it has reached certain criteria – for instance, using cotton sheets, long-life light bulbs, locally produced food, and recycling waste.

The Green Box, Ireland's first area-based integrated ecotourism plan is being developed by the Western Development Tourism Programme in partnership with the Organic Center, Rossinver, Co. Leitrim.

In September 2003, the first Green Festival was organised to draw attention to the initiative. For more details, contact Alan Hill at the Western Development Tourism Programme, ☎ (071) 91915-5323; alanhill@eircom.net.

Another information source is The Organic Center at Rossinver, ☎ (072) 985-4338; fax 985-4343; organiccentre@eircom.net. You can also visit www.trueireland.com.

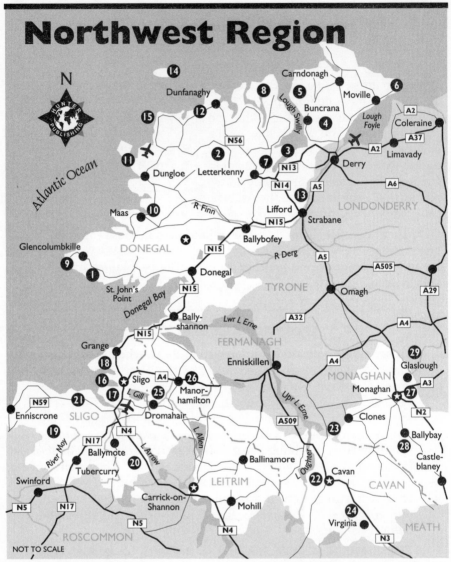

Northwest Region

N

NOT TO SCALE

© 2004 HUNTER PUBLISHING, INC.

1. Sea Cliffs (Slieve League)
2. Glenveagh National Park & Castle
3. Inch Island
4. Inis Eoghan Peninsula
5. Fort Dunree Military Museum
6. Maritime Museum & Planetarium
7. Grianán of Aileach
8. Fanad Peninsula
9. Folk Village Museum
10. Gweebarra Bridge
11. The Rosses; Car Ferry to Aran Island
12. The Workhouse
13. Seat-of-Power Visitor Centre
14. Tory Island
15. Bloody Foreland

16. County Museum; Yeats Memorial Museum;
17. Carrowmore Megalithic Cemetery;
    Tomb of Queen Maeve
18. Benbulben Mountain; Drumcliffe; Lissadel House
19. Ox Mountains
20. Carrowkeel Tombs
21. Culkin's Emigration Museum
22. Clough Oughter; Killykeen Forest Park
23. Black Pig's Dike
24. Cavan County Museum; Ramor Theatre
25. Parke's Castle; Monastery
26. Glens Centre; Leitrim Sculpture Gardens
27. St. Louis Convent Heritage Centre
28. Clones Abbey
29. Castle Leslie

County Donegal

Donegal is the fourth-largest county on the island and one of the most sparsely populated. It's also one of the most beautiful, with a coastline 400 miles (644 km) long, and many lakes and rivers, mountains and moors. Because of its lack of people, it looks much as it must have centuries ago. It also means that it is a very relaxing place to spend time. Everywhere you go there are wonderful views, empty beaches, and charming little villages. Among its many interesting features are the highest sea cliffs in Europe, **Slieve League**, and the **Glenveagh National Park**. The county is famous worldwide for its tweed and for its distinctive Parian china.

The Donegal *Gaeltacht* (Irish-speaking region) is the largest in the country, and stretches from Fanad Head in North Donegal to Kilcar in the Southwest.

*Among some of the county's interesting figures were **Isaac Butt MP**, founder of the Irish Home Rule Movement, born at Glebe House, Cloghan; **James Bustard**, who died alongside General George Custer, came from Drumbar, near Donegal Town; **Enya**, one of Ireland's most successful contemporary singers, is also a native of Donegal.*

There is so much to see and do that you could very easily spend weeks here on vacation. The county capital is **Lifford**, the largest town is **Letterkenny** and other important towns include **Donegal Town**, **Ballybofey**, **Ballyshannon**, **Buncrana**, **Bundoran**, **Dungloe** and **Moville**.

■ Getting Here

Letterkenny is served by major roads N13-N14-A5-N2 from Dublin (148 miles/238 km); and N13-N56-N15-N17 from Galway (160 miles/257 km). The town is very close to Strabane, Co. Tyrone, in Northern Ireland. The nearest railway station is in Derry City, and the closest ferry port is Larne.

There is a small airport at Carrickfin, Kincasslagh, on the coast north of Dungloe, 45 minutes from Letterkenny. Flights from Dublin take 50 minutes. ☎ (074) 91984-8284; donegalairport@eircom.net; www. donegalairport.ie.

The Northwest

■ Tourist Information

 The **Fáilte Ireland** office is on Derry Road, Letterkenny, and is open all year. It's in its own grounds on your left as you enter the town, with plenty of space for parking. ☎ (074) 91912-1160; fax 912-5180; donegaltourism@eircom.net. Other offices are open for part of the year:

- **Buncrana**, May-September. ☎ (071) 91916-2600.
- **Bundoran**, April-October, part-time rest of year. ☎ (072) 984-1350.
- **Donegal Town**, March-October. ☎ (074) 91972-1148.
- **Dungloe**, June-September. ☎ (074) 91952-1297.

TRACING YOUR ANCESTORS

Donegal Ancestry Centre, The Quay, Ramelton. ☎ (074) 91915-1266; fax 915-1702; donances@indigo.ie; www.irishroots.ie.

■ Letterkenny

Sightseeing

 The county's largest town is on the mouth of Lough Swilly, and makes an ideal base for touring both Donegal and Londonderry. Arriving from the direction of Donegal Town, Lifford or Derry, first impressions are good. You pass a replica of the Dry Arch, which used to carry trains, with a sculpture of railway workers by Maurice Harron. The town lives up to your expectations. It's welcoming and attractive, and you will sense an appreciation of the arts and heritage. People here seem relaxed and contented, quick to smile and exchange greetings, their accent soft and reminiscent of Derry not far away.

The town's main street is steep and there's a one-way traffic system, so you'll do better to explore on foot. The streets are full of character, with lots of interesting shops and pubs – some of them little changed for decades or more. **Speer's Drapery** on Lower Main Street is a particularly good example.

About halfway down Main Street there's a small square on the right with a bandstand, and an attractive sculpture remembering Rabble Children. These were children aged 11-16, whose services were sold for periods of six months to wealthy farmers in the Lagan Valley. The Hiring or Rabble days used to be held nearby in May and November at Speer's Lane.

Among the other interesting sights are the two main bank buildings. The **AIB** was built in 1835, and the **Bank of Ireland** was designed in 1874 by Timothy Hevey, a disciple of the great architect Pugin, whose work you see all over the country. The **Library and Arts Centre** is on the corner of Main Street and Oliver Plunkett Road and is in the Old Literary Institute building. The **Courthouse**, still in use, was built in 1829.

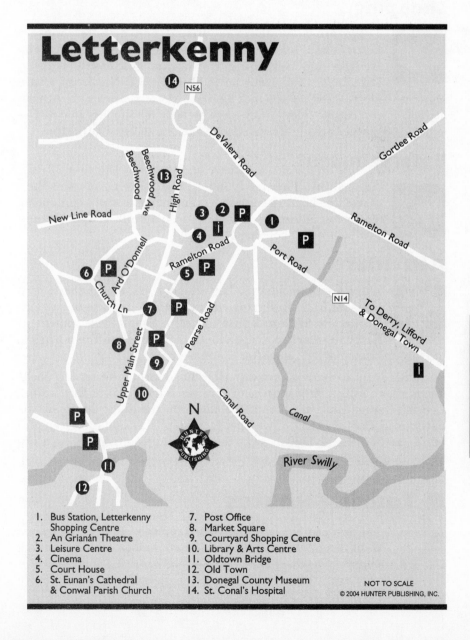

Letterkenny

1. Bus Station, Letterkenny Shopping Centre
2. An Grianán Theatre
3. Leisure Centre
4. Cinema
5. Court House
6. St. Eunan's Cathedral & Conwal Parish Church
7. Post Office
8. Market Square
9. Courtyard Shopping Centre
10. Library & Arts Centre
11. Oldtown Bridge
12. Old Town
13. Donegal County Museum
14. St. Conal's Hospital

NOT TO SCALE
© 2004 HUNTER PUBLISHING, INC.

The Northwest

The County Museum is on the High Road. It occupies part of what was the Warden's House of the Workhouse, which opened in 1843 and was in use until 1922. You can get a good idea of the history of Donegal from the museum's permanent collections; it also runs temporary exhibitions. Admission is free, and opening times are 10 am to 4:30 pm, Monday-Friday; closed from 12:30 to 1 pm for lunch; open 1 pm to 4:30 pm on Saturdays.

Shopping

There are a number of unusual and artistic shops in Letterkenny. Among them are **jewelry designer Marcus Griffin**, and **Geraldine Hannigan, goldsmith**, both on Port Road which leads on to Main Street. Nearby at **Craic Pots**, ☎ (074) 91912-5996, you pick a piece of pottery, draw your own design on it and choose colors (they have stencils for the less talented) – your masterpiece is ready for collection from one to three days later.

Entertainment

An Grianán Theatre is on Port Road which leads onto Main Street and hosts touring shows and plays as well as producing its own excellent work. There's also a multi-screen **cinema** just below the shopping center.

Activities

There are three parks in Letterkenny, so there's a choice for a pleasant walk. **Ballyraine Linear Park** is on the town's outskirts; the **Millennium Park** is a recent development at **Ballyboe Park** in the residential area; and the **Town Park** is at Hospital Roundabout (just after the museum).

Facilities at the **Leisure Centre** on High Road include swimming pools, steam room, sauna, fitness room. There are four courts at the Leisure Centre's Tennis Club. ☎ (074) 91912-5251. On the Ramelton Road, the **Pitch-and-Putt** also has all-weather football pitches and American pool tables. ☎ (074) 91912-1160. Nearby there's a **Karting Centre**, open 1 to 11 pm, Monday-Saturday, all year. ☎ (074) 91912-9077.

▪ Touring Routes

There are a number of signposted routes you can follow, or just wander as you please around the marvelous countryside on a bike or in a car.

The Inishowen 100

This route takes you around the **Inis Eoghan Peninsula**. Take the N13 from Letterkenny. You can pause at the lay-by to take in the view over Lough Swilly. Just after the turn-off from the main Letterkenny-to-Derry road, at the village of Bridge End, you turn left and follow the signs – the route takes you through Buncrana, Clonmany, Cardonagh, Malin Head, and back to Letterkenny via Greencastle, Moville and Muff.

You will see some of the most desolately beautiful scenery as you head toward Malin, the country's most northerly point, passing through the **Gap of Mamore**. There are also lots of other attractions. About seven miles (11 km) north of Buncrana is **Fort Dunree Military Museum**, which has a dramatic view out over Lough Swilly. The fort was built to protect against the French returning, and was enlarged in the late 19th century. The museum covers the fort's fascinating history and its underground bunkers house a collection of artifacts. Open June-September, Monday-Saturday, 10:30 am-6 pm, from 1 pm on Sundays. ☎ (074) 91936-1817; dunree@eircom.net; www.dunree.pro.ie.

Cardonagh is a bustling village, where you could stop for a snack at **The Arch Inn** on The Diamond (see *Where to Eat*, page 406).

At **Greencastle** there's a **Maritime Museum and Planetarium** in the old coastguard station, which looks out on one of the busiest fishing ports in the country, with views over Lough Foyle. ☎ (074) 91938-1363; greencastlemaritime@eircom.net.

> *From Greencastle you can cross in about 10 minutes to Magilligan in Limavady, near the Giant's Causeway. A drive-on ferry operates 363 days a year, with more than 30 crossings a day. This saves you driving 49 miles (79 km).* ☎ *(074) 91938-1901 or info@loughfoyleferry.com.*

Near Burt on the N13, at the top of a hill, there's an ancient round fort, the **Grianán of Aileach** or **"Stone House of the Sun."** From here you can see five counties. Founded by Druids in 1700 BC, the fort was mentioned by the ancient geographer Ptolemy of Alexandria in Egypt. It is associated with the De Dannan and later the O'Neills, who were High Kings of Ireland for 600 years. St. Patrick is said to have preached here in 450 AD, and to have baptized Eoghan O'Neill in the holy well that lies to the rear of the fort.

The Grianán of Aileach Centre, also on the main Burt to Letterkenny road, is a great place to stop for a meal or snack as well as to find out more about the history of the area. It is housed in the old Church of Ireland and tells the history of Grianán from the dawn of history to the present. The

The Northwest

Centre is open all year – in summer from 10 am to 6 pm and in winter until 4 pm. During the tourist season there are Ulster Nights, with music, dance and poetry. ☎ (074) 91936-8000; fullerton@eircom.net; www.griananaligh.ie.

Fanad Scenic Tour

Another signposted route is the Fanad Scenic Tour, just north of Letterkenny, which takes you around the Fanad peninsula. Highlights include Rathmullan, marvelous views over Ballymastocker Bay and its lovely sandy beach, Fanad Head where there is a lighthouse, and Kerrykeel, where there is a dolmen and Knockalla Fort.

Ramelton is a very attractive little town on the bank of the river Leannan (or Lennon) which flows into Lough Swilly. There has been a settlement here since the early Stone Age, about 7000 BC. From the 12th century, it was the seat of the O'Donnells, the area's ruling clan, who built a castle here in 1440.

The Plantation of Ulster (see page 14) led to the arrival of Sir William Stewart, who built the first town, bringing Protestants, most of them from Scotland, to settle here. They built a Reformation church around 1622, which you can see. Around 1680 Scottish Calvinists built the Old Meetinghouse. The local Catholics weren't happy, and there were years of discord. In the 20th century Ramelton came to be called "the Holy City" as it had eight churches, six in use – astonishing for a town its size.

There's also an American connection. In 1682 the Reverend Francis Makemie, who grew up here, was ordained for the American missions and became known as "The Father of American Presbyterianism."

By the 18th century, Ramelton was at its most prosperous – a thriving market town with the biggest linen-bleaching works in the county. Ships from exotic ports unloaded their cargoes here. The Grand Jury Rooms on Castle Street date from this time, as do the elegant houses, the tree-lined Mall, and the warehouses on the Quay.

The Steamboat Store, built in 1683, which now houses **The Ramelton Story** collection and the **Donegal Ancestry Centre**, is a reminder of the connection made to the railway in Derry in the late 19th century. The Ramelton Story/Ancestry Centre is open from 10 am to 5:30 pm, April-September; October-March there is limited opening. ☎ (074) 91915-1266, donances@indigo.ie. The **Town Park** on the riverbank has lovely walks to enjoy.

Rathmullan is a lovely little seaside village on the shore of Lough Swilly, popular with families for generations. It was from here. in 1607, that Ulster Chieftains O'Neill and O'Donnell left Ireland – an event called **The Flight of the Earls**. This is commemorated in the Heritage Centre, housed in an historic battery close to the shore. The display is lively and informative, charting the traumatic period around 1600 and highlighting the main families involved and their descendants, many of whom were influential and famous in Europe. The Flight of the Earls Heritage Centre is open from Easter to September, weekdays 10 am-5 pm; Sundays from noon. ☎ (074) 91915-8178.

Between Ramelton and Rathmullan, on a bend of the Glenalla River, is **Potsmith**, selling pottery and crafts in a very pretty setting on the bank.

The Atlantic Drive

The Atlantic Drive takes in Ramelton, then Milford, a game angling center, Rosapenna on the wonderful Sheephaven Bay, Downings with its sandy beach, and Creeslough and Kilmacrennan, which are also centers for game angling.

■ Donegal Town

Donegal Town is in the southern part of the county, and dates back to the Vikings, who built a fortress here at the mouth of the Eske. It probably takes its name from Dhún na nGall – "the fort of the foreigners" – a reference to those invaders.

The town was the seat of the O'Donnells, who built the **Castle** here. The Castle is furnished throughout and includes Persian rugs and French tapestries. Information panels chronicle the history of the castle owners from the O'Donnell Chieftains to the Brook family. The O'Donnels also brought Franciscan monks and the ruins of their **Old Abbey** dating from 1474, the same year as the Castle, are near the pier. In 1652 Brother Michael O'Cleary and three laymen wrote one of the most significant Irish history texts – *The Annals of the Four Masters*.

The town's center is the **Diamond**, where the roads to Killybegs, Ballyshannon and Ballybofey meet. The Old Station House is now **The Donegal Railway Heritage Centre**, the headquarters of the society restoring some of the county's railways. There's a museum, information center and shop. Railways played a very important role in the lives of Donegal people, including for many the last experience of home as they traveled to the emigrant ships that took them across the Atlantic. The Heritage Centre is open daily, June-September, and on weekdays the rest of the year.

Shopping Around Donegal Town

 Follow the **Donegal Creative Craft Trail**, visiting the studios and outlets of members of the guild called Donegal Creative Crafts, and you'll find plenty of original gifts and souvenirs. There's everything from hand-painted silk scarves

The Northwest

Donegal

N

Ballybofey/Sligo Road

To Lough Eske

Killybegs Road

N56

Tyrconnell St

New Row

N56

3

River Eske

N15

Waterloo Place

New Row

10

Meeting House St.

6

New Row

Castle St

Upper Main Street

P

N15

2

4

Water St

P

5

Bridge St

9

Main Street

Quay Street

8

P

i

P

1

The Bank Walk

River Eske

P

Bay & Harbor Tour Sites

River Eske

12

P

13

15

24

17 **16**

14

Picnic Area

P

Donegal Bay

23

11 P

18

7

Quay Brae

12

20

22

25

19

21

Donegal Bay (see inset for closeup)

Picnic Area

P

1. 1600s Pier, Napoleonic Anchor
2. Donegal (O'Donnell) Castle
3. Donegal Railway Heritage Centre
4. Church of Ireland
5. Methodist Church
6. Presbyterian Church
7. Viewing Point
8. The Diamond, Obelisk to Four Masters
9. St. Patrick's Roman Catholic Church (Church of the Four Masters)
10. Famine Graveyard
11. Donegal Waterbus Office & Pier
12. Old Abbey & Cemetery

13. Donegal Craft Village; Picnic Area
14. Ballyboyle Island
15. Old Ship Booking & Embarking Point
16. Ruins of O'Boyle Castle
17. Old Coast Guard Station
18. The Hassans
19. Donegal Golf Club
20. Belle's Isle
21. Seal Island
22. Rooney's Island
23. St. Ernan's Island
24. Ruins of Magherabeg Abbey
25. Murvagh Beach

NOT TO SCALE

to pottery, lampshades, shawls, jewelry, and much more. Ask at tourist offices for the free brochure.

Just outside Donegal Town, on the road to Ballyshannon and Sligo, is the **Donegal Craft Village**, which showcases the work of a number of talented artists. It's definitely worth stopping to take a look at examples of pottery, sculpture, wrought-iron furniture and jewelry. There's a coffee shop serving homemade produce. Opening times are 10 am to 6 pm, Monday-Saturday; in summer it's open on Sundays from noon. ☎ (074) 91972-2225; donegalcraftvillage@donegal.net.

Lough Eske Drive

From Donegal Town you can follow the Lough Eske Drive along the valley of the Blue Stack Mountains and enjoy terrific lakeside views.

Coast Road

Another option, and an unforgettable way to arrive in the county from the south, is to follow the Coast Road signs from Bundoran, a lovely seaside resort. They take you through Ballyshannon and Rossnowlagh to Donegal Town, and along the way you look out over the Atlantic.

At Donegal Town, you head west through Killybegs, a major fishing port, into Glencolumkille.

The Folk Village Museum at Glencolumbkille was founded in 1967 by the inspirational priest Fr. James McDyer, who wanted to retain the traditional local culture while promoting industry and providing better facilities for the people of the area. Each house in the clachan or village is an exact replica, complete with furnishings and artifacts, of local dwellings from the 1700s, 1800s and 1900s. ☎ (074) 91973-0017; folkmus@indigo.ie.

After Glencolumbkille, you next go through the Glengesh Pass to Ardara and Glenties, crossing the Gweebarra Bridge into the Rosses and Dungloe. Following the Falcomb Coast Road takes you to Burtonport and the *Gaeltacht* and then Bunbeg and Gweedore, passing Bloody Foreland and Gortahork on the way to Dunfanaghy.

At Dunfanaghy you can visit **The Workhouse**. In the 19th century Dunfanaghy Workhouse was the scene of horrific suffering during the Great Famine (An Gorta Mhór) of 1845-1850. Today part of the Workhouse building has been turned into an interpretative center and an art gallery. You now hear "Wee Hannah" tell the true story of her experiences. Open from April 1 to September 30, 10 am to 5 pm, Monday-Saturday; from noon on Sundays; other times by appointment. ☎ (074) 91913-6540; janis@theirishfamine.com; www.theirishfamine.com.

Allow plenty of time to stop, not just to look at the unforgettable views, but also to visit some of the attractions en route, as well as taking in the atmosphere and the friendliness of the inhabitants in the pretty villages and towns.

■ Lifford

Lifford, the county capital, is 15 miles (24 km) southeast of Letterkenny on the N14. It stands on the River Finn, which separates it from the much bigger town of Strabane, which is in Co. Tyrone in Northern Ireland.

It's worth spending a couple of hours here. The town was a stronghold of the O'Donnell clan – the administrative center for the Plantation of Ulster in the 17th century (see page 14) and later the center of the county's legal system.

The 18th-century courthouse now houses the **Seat of Power Visitor Centre**, with a craft shop and restaurant serving homemade food. Open all year, Monday-Friday from 9 am to 5 pm; Saturdays from 10 am and Sundays from 11:30 am. ☎ (074) 91914-1723; seatofpower@eircom.net; www.infowing.ie-seatofpower.

The attractive **Cavancor Historic House and Craft Centre**, just outside Lifford, is also worth visiting. It was the ancestral home of James Knox Polk, 11th President (1845-49) of the US. Visitors can go on a guided tour of the house, built in the early 1600s. King James II is believed to have dined underneath a sycamore here during the Siege of Derry in 1689. ☎ (074) 91914-1143; joannaok7@hotmail.com.

■ Adventures on Foot

Waymarked Ways

There are two waymarked ways in the county: The Blue Stack Way and the Bealach na Gaeltachta - Dhún na nGall (Donegal).

The **Blue Stack Way** starts in Donegal Town and takes you through the mountains of the same name to Glenties and Ardara. www.thebluestackway.com.

Bealach na Gaeltachta is made up of four circular long-distance routes passing through the *Gaeltacht* and the islands. Contact Gaelsaoire, ☎ toll-free within Ireland 1-800-621-600; info@gaelsaoire.ie; www.gaelsaoire.ie.

Glenveagh National Park & Castle

Glenveagh, on the eastern side of the Derryveagh Mountains, takes its name from gleann bheatha, "the glen of the birches," which dissects it.

It includes the county's highest mountains, Errigal and Slieve Sneacht, and in its southwestern end the cliffs called "the Poisoned Glen," which is a corruption of its name in Irish meaning "heavenly glen."

Lough Veagh has natural stocks of salmon, char and brown trout.

The Park is home to the largest herd of red deer in Europe, and there's lots of other wildlife to see, and hear. The golden eagle, which had become extinct here 100 years ago, was reintroduced in 2000.

It's worth recounting something of the estate's history. It was owned by the dreadful landlord John Adair, who in April 1861 evicted 244 tenants and cleared the land so his views of the landscape wouldn't be ruined!

Happily, it passed into the ownership of Henry McIlhenny from Philadelphia, who had made his fortune from Tabasco sauce. He created one of the most celebrated gardens here, around the 19th century castle. In 1975 the Glenveagh estate was bought by the State, and in 1981 he very generously presented the castle and gardens to the Irish people. The estate is open daily, April-September, and in October from Thursday-Saturday. ☎ (074) 91913-7088.

Around Donegal Town

There are organized walking tours of the town and of the nearby hills. ☎ (074) 91973-5967; info@northwestwalkingguides.com.

You can also take an interesting stroll along the **Bank Walk** in the town, which follows the west bank of the River Eske for a mile and a half, with lovely views. You cross Boyce's Bridge on the Killybegs Road and join the walk on the left, just past the stone bridge on the Mountcharles Road.

Six miles (9.7 km) from Donegal Town, on the Ballybofey Road, you can climb either of the two peaks of **Barnesmore** in the Blue Stack Mountains. You can relax afterwards at **Biddy O'Barnes**, a pub that has welcomed travelers for years.

Walking Vacations

Donegal really is a dream come true for anyone who enjoys walking, but you don't have to do all the planning yourself.

☆☆☆ **The Holyrood Hotel**, Bundoran, together with the Homefield Walking Centre, offers a number of walking trips, including a weekend cliff and coastal walk to Mullaghmore. ☎ (072) 984-1232; hrood@indigo. ie; www.holyroodhotel.com.

The Northwest

You can also stay in the **Homefield Hostel** and go on guided or self-guided walks and cycle trips. ☎ (072) 984-12888; homefield@indigo.ie.

Walking is included in the activities at the residential **Gartan Outdoor Education Centre**, Churchill, near Letterkenny. ☎ (074) 91913-7092.

At the **Donegal Adventure Centre**, Bundoran, there are guided and self-guided walking and cycling tours. You can stay at the center or in a nearby hotel or self-catering cottages. ☎ (072) 984-2844; adventures@ donegal-holidays.com; www.donegal-holidays.com.

Time Out Tours, with B&B accommodations, also offers cycling tours following waymarked ways. ☎ (074) 91914-4033; info@timeouttours.com; www.timeouttours.com.

Michael Gibbons organizes walking trips all over Ireland from his base at the **Connemara Walking and Cycling Centre**, Clifden, Galway. ☎ (095) 21379; walkwest@indigo.ie; www.walkingireland.com.

Other operators include:

North West Walking Guides, ☎ (074) 91973-5967; northwestwalkingguides @yahoo.com; www.northwestwalkingguides.com.

Oideas Gael, guided walks as part of cultural courses in the *Gaeltacht*. ☎ (074) 91973-5206.

Walking Festivals

There are three annual walking festivals:

Ardara Walking Festival takes visitors on countryside and coastal walks around Ardara, Narin, Portnoo and Rosbeg. It happens in March. Details from Donal Haughey, ☎ (074) 91954-1518; dhaughey@eircom. net; www.ardara.ie.

Hills of Donegal Walking Festival takes place over a weekend in April in the lovely scenic areas of Fanad, Downings, Ramelton and Gartan, with a choice of moderate and strenuous walks. Contact Kenneth Bradley, ☎ (074) 91915-3682; fax 915-3800; irdmilford@eircom.net; www. hillsofdonegal.com.

The Donegal International Walking Festival in October takes visitors through the same scenic areas of Fanad, Downings, Ramelton and Gartan/Churchill and offers both moderate and strenuous walks. ☎ (074) 91973-5967; info@northwestwalkingguides.com; www. northwestwalkingguides.com.

■ Adventures on Water

 A pleasant and relaxing way of seeing many of the interesting sites around Donegal Town is to take the **Waterbus**. Tours last about 90 minutes and there's a detailed commentary.

Among the places you pass is the **Embarkation Point**, from where emigrants left for Canada and the US during the famine years of 1845-47, and **Seal Island**, which is home to 200 seals. Get details from ☎ (074) 91972-3666.

Discovering the Islands

You can also explore the islands off the Donegal coast. **Arranmore Island** is only 20 minutes by drive-on ferry from Burtonport; during summer it runs every hour. ☎ (074) 91952-1532. Arranmore has spectacular scenery, with memorable walks along the cliffs; there's also a lake with rainbow trout and shore angling. There are traditional music sessions and Irish language courses available on the island. You can stay at **The Glen Hotel**, ☎ (074) 91952-05005.

Tory Island, 11 miles (17.7 km) off the northwest coast, is Europe's most northwesterly point, treeless and only three miles (4.8 km) wide by one mile long. It has been inhabited since Neolithic times, 4,000 years ago. St. Columcille founded a monastery here in the 6th century and you can still see its round tower and its distinctive Tau Cross. The monks fled to the mainland in 1595 when English soldiers destroyed the monastery. The T-shaped Cross still shows the marks of a sword wielded by a Cromwellian attempting to destroy it.

Tory islanders are often cut off from the mainland during storms, and the power of the sea is a recurring theme in their "primitive" paintings, famous worldwide. For details of how to get there and where to stay, call the following: **Tory Ferry Services**, ☎ (074) 91953-1320. **Tory Hotel**, ☎ (074) 91913-5920. **Donegal Coastal Cruises**, ☎ (074) 91953-1991. There's also a **Dive Centre** on Tory Island, ☎ (074) 91913-5282, dive@ toryhotel.com. Snorkeling, boat trips, sea angling and bird-watching are also available; for details, call the Tory Hotel.

Adventures Under Water

The Donegal coastline has lots of beautiful and spectacular sites for deep-sea diving. For local information call (from the Republic) **Marine Sports** in Derry City, ☎ (048) 7134-5444. If a compressor is needed, contact Laurence Strain, Milford, ☎ (074) 91915-3686.

Fishing

The Northern Regional Fisheries Board is the authority responsible for the area. ☎ (072) 985-1435. Salmon and trout fisheries usually belong to the State, an individual club or organization. Permission is needed, except in the case of some State-run lakes, so you should always check locally.

See pages 71-74 for details on angling in Ireland, including regulations and best times to fish.

Coarse angling tends to be organized around centers, usually towns and villages, and coarse fish are returned alive. Pike are also protected and visitors are asked to comply.

There are guides to fishing available from tourist offices and here, as with everywhere else in Ireland, local tackle and bait outlets will also give visitors advice.

Sea angling is so popular in Donegal that there are a number of annual **festivals**, which are open to visitors. In May they are at Downings and Rathmullan, at Culdaff in June, Gweedore in July, at Killybegs and Moville during August and at Malin in September. The simplest way to find out about them, and about boat charters, is to call **North West Tourism**. ☎ (074) 91912-1160.

Rathmullan is a center for sea angling, and **Lough Swilly Sea Anglers** has a boat available for charter for lough and wreck fishing; varieties include pollock, ling, gurnard and tope. The **Lough Swilly International Tope Festival** is held at the beginning of June. Contact Niall Doherty. ☎ (074) 91915-8129.

Charter boats for deep-sea fishing are available from the **Downings Bay Sea Angling Club**. ☎ (074) 91915-5161.

Letterkenny Anglers Association has fishing rights on some of the nearby lakes. ☎ (074) 91912-1160.

Lough Veagh in the Glenveagh National Park has natural stocks of salmon, char and brown trout.

The Northern Regional Fisheries Board

Extending from Mullaghmore Head in Co. Sligo to Malin Head in Co. Donegal, the region takes in some of the most dramatic scenery and productive fisheries in Ireland. It's also home to a significant stretch of the Shannon-Erne Waterway, which links Shannon navigation to Eniskillen in Northern Ireland.

There is great angling available for coarse, game and sea enthusiasts. There's also excellent boat angling for blue shark and other species. For the shore angler there is no shortage of marks.

Coarse angling in the region is superb. Many specimen hybrids, bream and tench have been caught in the many lakes of the northern region, particularly in Leitrim and Monaghan.

Game angling is also first class. There are many wild trout waters for the trout angler. Lough Melvin is justly famous for its gillaroo and sonaghen trout, sporting fish well worth a day's angling. There are many premier salmon fisheries also, so the salmon angler is nearly always guaranteed a fishable river in some part of the region. For details, contact **The Northern Regional Fisheries Board**, Station Road, Ballyshannon, Co. Donegal. ☎ (072) 985-1435; fax 985-1816; hllyoyd@nrfb.ie; www. nrfb.ie.

■ Adventures on Horseback

Homefield Equestrian Centre, Bundoran, welcomes all ages and levels of experience for trekking, trail and beach rides. ☎ (072) 984-1877; homefield@indigo.ie; www. homefieldhouse.com.

Ashtree Stables, Coole, Cranford, overlook Multroy Bay, and offer treks along quiet mountain roads, beginners welcome. ☎ (074) 91915-3312.

Ride on an Open Farm

The Deane Open Farm is 12 miles (19 km) west of Donegal Town on the N56 to Killybegs. The 100-acre farm, looking out over Bruckless Bay, has belonged to the Deane family since 1790. You can feed, nurse and walk animals, large and small, take a tour of the farm or just walk in the forest. It's open for visits from April to September, 10 am to 4 pm. That's not all. The farm also has an equestrian center with an indoor arena and a pitch-and-putt course. You can learn to ride, or go on a cross-country trek. Riding is available all year, and pitch-and-putt from April to October, 9 am to 9 pm. ☎ (074) 91973-7160; deanequestrian@eircom.net.

■ Golf

All the golf courses are in scenic areas, and they do welcome visitors, but phone in advance.

Links Courses on the Atlantic

■ **North West Golf Club**, Lisfannon, near Buncrana. ☎ (074) 91936-1927.

■ **Ballyliffin Golf Club** has two, the Old Links and Glasheady. ☎ (074) 91937-6119.

- **Dunfanaghy.** ☎ (074) 91913-6335.
- **Rosapenna.** ☎ (074) 91915-5301.
- **Portsalon.** ☎ (074) 91915-9459.
- **St. Patrick's Golf Club**. Carrigart, ☎ (074) 91915-5114.
- **Bundoran.** ☎ (072) 984-1302.
- **Donegal Golf Club**, Murvagh. ☎ (074) 91973-4054.
- **Narin Portnoo.** ☎ (074) 91954-5107.

Other Courses

- **Letterkenny**, at Barnhill, on the shores of Lough Swilly. ☎ (074) 91912-1150.
- **Ballybofey** and **Stranorlar**, with views of Finn Valley. ☎ (074) 91913-1093.
- **Cruit Island Golf Club**, nine-hole course on island connected to mainland by bridge, near Dungloe. ☎ (074) 91954-3296.

Irish language and cultural activity tours for adults are available in Co. Donegal, with separate courses in hill-walking, archaeology, painting, pottery, the bodhrán, the flute, dancing, the environment and culture. Contact **Oideas Gael** *in Glencolumbkille.* ☎ *(074) 91973-0248; oideasgael@eircom.net; www. Oideas-Gael.com.*

■ Where to Stay in Co. Donegal

☆☆☆ **The Quality Hotel,** at 29-45 Main Street, Letterkenny, is welcoming and comfortable, with charming and efficient staff. Its 53 bedrooms are spacious – a twin here means not two narrow beds but a double and single – and there's plenty of space in their bathrooms too. Some of the rooms have pleasant views of hills in the distance. The hotel also has 30 luxury suites, with separate living rooms and

HOTEL PRICE CHART	
Price per person, per night, with two sharing, including breakfast.	
$	Under US $50
$$	US $50-$100
$$$	US $101-$175
$$$$	US $176-$200
$$$$$	Over US $200

kitchens. Its **Dillon's Bar** serves coffee, carvery lunch, and bar food until 10 pm and has a delicatessen section, where you can get delicious salads and sandwiches.

Americans should feel at home in **Lannigans Steakhouse**, which also serves dishes from around the world. You can park at a reduced rate in the indoor car park next door.

The hotel belongs to the Choice group, of Quality, Clarion and Comfort brands. International reservations, ☎ 1-800-500-600; (074) 91912-2977; sales@qualitydonegal.com; www.choicehotelsireland.ie.

☆☆☆☆ **The Sand House Hotel**, Rossnowlagh, used to be a fishing lodge and is now a beautiful hotel with marvelous views of Donegal Bay and the Atlantic Ocean from most of its rooms, which are furnished with antiques. There's a choice of standard, superior rooms and suites, some with four poster beds, and many overlooking the sea. The hotel is on the wonderful Rossnowlagh EU Blue Flag beach, two miles long, which is popular with swimmers and surfers. It belongs to the Manor Hotels marketing group.

In the hotel's **Marine Spa**, guests can have a massage or beauty treatment, or enjoy the steam room or Jacuzzi. They can also relax over a drink in the **Cocktail Lounge**, where there's live entertainment on weekends and mid-week during summer.

The Seashell Restaurant has an imaginative menu, complemented by an excellent wine list. Rates from $$$$. ☎ (072) 985-1777; fax 985-2100; info@sandhouse-hotel.ie; www.sandhouse-hotel.ie.

☆☆☆ **Arnolds Hotel** is at the entrance to the picturesque village of Dunfanaghy, on the shore of Sheephaven Bay, and has welcomed guests since 1922. Sheephaven is one of the most beautiful of Donegal's beaches, and a personal favorite. The hotel has a lovely warm atmosphere, something you feel straight away with the open fire in the reception area. Some of its 30 bedrooms have panoramic views of Donegal Bay and Horn Head; others look out on mature gardens.

There's a riding stable on site, which caters to all levels of experience; there's also a putting green and croquet lawn.

Guests can relax in the **Whiskey Fly Bar** or in the **Glenveagh Room**, with its open fire. There's a choice of where to eat. **The Garden Bistro**'s menu includes seafood and vegetarian choices, served with a selection of fine wines. **The Tramore Restaurant** serves good food in elegant surroundings.

Rates from $$. ☎ (074) 91913-6208; fax 913-6352; arnoldshotel@eircom. net; www.arnoldshotel.com.

☆☆☆ **The Mill Park Hotel** is a short walk from the middle of Donegal Town on the Killybegs road, and has a welcoming atmosphere with open fires. Each of its 40 bedrooms and three suites is individually decorated. There's a Leisure Club with pool and gym, and golf can be arranged for guests at courses nearby. Watersports, angling and horseback riding are also available locally.

Local produce is always included on the hotel menu, and with the fishing port of Killybegs so close, it's no surprise that there's a choice of seafood. It belongs to the Irish Country Hotels marketing group. Rates from $$. ☎ (074) 91972-2880; fax 972-2640; millparkhotel@eircom.net; www. millparkhotel.com.

✩✩✩ **The Highland Hotel** is at Glenties, and is known for its welcoming atmosphere and good food. It's family run and has 25 bedrooms, with special golf discount packages offered. Rates from $$. ☎ (074) 91955-1111; fax 955-1564; highlandhotel@eircom.net; www.thehighlandhotel. com.

✩✩ **The Ballyliffin Hotel** is in the pretty village of Ballyliffin at Clonmany on the beautiful Inishowen peninsula, and just a short walk from Pollan Bay and its long beach. It's family-run and friendly, with a choice of where to eat, in its **Rachtan Bar** or **Cruckaughrim Restaurant**. Rates from $$. ☎ (074) 91937-6106; fax 937-6658; info@ballyliffinhotel.com; www.ballyliffinhotel.com.

✩✩✩✩ **The Great Northern Hotel and Leisure Centre** stands on 130 acres on a hillside overlooking the resort of Bundoran and Donegal Bay. It has 110 bedrooms and is a popular entertainment venue all year round, with top Irish and international acts. It's surrounded by its own 18-hole golf course and the Leisure Center has a pool, sauna, Jacuzzi, gym, beauty and hairdressing salon.

The hotel has a choice of bars and restaurants and a conference and banqueting center, so it's a busy and lively place. It belongs to the McEniff Hotels group. Rates from $$, with special weekend rates available. ☎ Locall in Republic 1890-203-203; (071) 91984-1204; fax 984-1114; reservations@greatnorthernhotel.com; www.greatnorthernhotel.com or www. mceniff-hotels.com.

Cottages for Rent

 Donegal Thatched Cottages, Cruit Island, Kincasslagh, are in a fantastic location right on the sea, with a sandy beach, on an island connected to the mainland by a bridge. There are 10 of them, sleeping seven, and they have open turf fires as well as central heating. ☎ (071) 91917-7197; info@donegalthatchedcottages.com; www.donegalthatchedcottages.com.

✩✩✩-✩✩✩✩ **Bunbeg Holiday Homes** are on the coast at Bunbeg, on the R258 west of Gweedore in northwest Donegal and about an hour's drive from Letterkenny. It's a group of eight houses in a peaceful setting, with a choice of two, three or four bedrooms, with central heating and open turf fires. There are miles of sandy beaches a short walk away. A tennis court is on site, and other activities including horse riding are available locally. Contact Helena McGarvey at ☎ (074) 91953-1401; fax 953-2749; info@bunbegholidayhomes.com; www.bunbegholidayhomes. com.

Camping & RV Parks

☆☆☆☆ **Knockalla Park** is near Portsalon, and is open mid-March to mid-September. It overlooks Ballymastocker Bay, with miles of safe golden beaches. There's a shop on site, and mobile homes for rent. ☎ (074) 91915-9108.

☆☆ **Casey's Park** is on the edge of Sheephaven Bay in the fishing village of Downings, beside a mile-long sandy beach. It's open April 1 to September 30. ☎ (074) 91915-5301; rosapenna@eircom.net.

☆☆☆☆ **Lakeside Centre Caravan and Camping Park** is on Belleek Road, five minutes on foot from Ballyshannon, on the shore of Assaroe Lake. Facilities include game and coarse angling on the lake and go-karts for hire. The park is open mid-March to September 30. ☎ (072) 985-2822; erneent@eircom.net; www.donegalbay.com.

Hostels

There are 12 hostels, members of Independent Holiday Hostels of Ireland, ☎ (01) 836-4700; fax 836-4710; info@hostels-ireland.com; www.hostels-ireland.com.

■ Where to Eat

Letterkenny has a good choice of places to eat. Among them I recommend the following.

Galfees Food Emporium is a delicatessen/bistro on Upper Main Street, where you can have anything from a freshly made sandwich to a full meal. It's also a shop with interesting food products. ☎ (074) 91912-8536; www.galfees.com.

On the same street are two branches of **Quiet Moment**, at numbers 1 and 11. Number 1 is also a bed & breakfast. Meals, teas and snacks are available at both in simple, attractive settings. ☎ (074) 91912-8382; www.quietmoment.ie.

Absolutely Thai is next to the Courthouse on Port Road, a continuation of Letterkenny's main street. Here, authentic Thai cuisine is served in an attractive licensed restaurant, entered through a small courtyard. Delicious food at reasonable prices is served by charming and competent staff. Open six days (closed Mondays) for lunch from noon to 2:30 pm; evenings 6:30-10:30 pm. ☎ (074) 91912-4376.

The Forge Restaurant and Guesthouse, in an attractive stone building, is three miles from Rossnowlagh beach and three miles from Ballyshannon. Rates from $ overnight, with special weekend offers. Open for lunch every day from 1:30-3 pm and for dinner from 6-9:30 pm. Menu includes seafood and contemporary cuisine. ☎ (071) 91982-2070; fax 982-2075; theforgeguesthouse@eircom.net; www. theforgeguesthouse.com.

Woodhill House stands in its own grounds a quarter-mile from the village of Ardara. It's both a restaurant and a three-star guesthouse, with nine bedrooms, and it's open from Easter to October. Bar lunches are served from 12:30-2:30 pm and dinner from 6:30 to the last orders at 10 pm. The menu is French-based using fresh Irish produce, especially seafood from the nearby fishing port of Killybegs. ☎ (074) 91954-1112; fax 954-1516; yates@iol.ie; www.woodhillhouse.com.

The Bridge Bar and Restaurant is on the main street of the attractive village of Ramelton. Its restaurant is open seven days in summer from 7-9:30 pm in summer and on weekends only in winter. Bar food is also available all day in summer. Its menu includes seafood, steaks and vegetarian choices. There's also live blues/jazz and traditional Irish music in the bar. ☎ (074) 91915-1833.

McGrory's of Culdaff on the Inishowen Peninsula is a restaurant, bar, guesthouse and music venue that first opened in 1924. It's still a family business, these days run by brothers John and Neil McGrory with their sister Anne. Its three-star guesthouse has 10 bedrooms, and guests get free admission to some entertainment. Rates from $, with special offers for longer stays. Food is available in **The Front Bar**, where Irish traditional music is performed, and **Mac's Backroom Bar** is noted for its range of musical entertainment. The restaurant is decorated in art deco and art nouveau style and its menu reflects local produce, featuring steaks, lamb, seafood and vegetarian dishes. It's open Tuesday-Saturday from 6:30 pm with last orders at 9:30 pm. It also serves the All-Day Sunday Lunch from 1-8 pm. ☎ (074) 91937-9104; fax 937-9235; mcgr@ tinet.ie; www.mcgrorys.ie.

The Arch Inn, Cardonagh, on the Inishowen Peninsula, is a pleasant place where you can relax by an open fire. Despite its attractive traditional setting, the menu is up-to-date and cosmopolitan, including panini, ciabatta, bagels, muffins and croissants, as well as salads, soup and sandwiches, with a variety of sizes and fillings. ☎ (074) 91937-3029

County Sligo

Sligo is one of the Republic's smaller counties, and has a spectacular Atlantic coastline stretching from the seaside village of Mullaghmore in the north to Enniscrone in the west, with beautiful beaches, and dramatic seas, which are popular with surfers.

Inland, it also has wonderful scenery, with unusually shaped hills rising from steep valleys, the most noticeable hill being Benbulben, which can be seen from all over the county. The scenic Ox Mountains are here, and the county's main rivers are the Moy and Owengarve,. The largest lakes are Lough Gill, Lough Arrow, and Lough Gara.

The countryside is perfect for walking or fishing, or for just wandering around and enjoying the pretty villages nestling under the mountains or along lakeshores.

There is much evidence of the past scattered around County Sligo, especially at Carrowmore, close to Sligo Town, where over 30 tombs, spread out across several fields, make up a huge Stone Age cemetery.

Despite its beauty and the range of activities it offers, Sligo remains relatively undiscovered by tourists, so there are plenty of areas where you can enjoy solitude, as you wander its quiet, winding roads.

The surname Yeats is synonymous with Sligo; the poet wrote about it, and his brother Jack used to say he never painted a picture without thinking about the area.

The county capital and largest town is **Sligo Town**, and other main towns include **Ballymote**, **Grange** and **Tubbercurry**.

■ Getting Here

Sligo Town is on main roads N17-N4 from Dublin (135 miles/ 217 km); N15-N16-A4-M1-A3-M1 from Belfast (130 miles/209 km); N17 from Galway (86 miles/138 km).

It has a **rail station**, ☎ (071) 91916-9888, and a **bus station**, ☎ (071) 91916-0066.

Sligo Airport is at Strandhill nearby. ☎ (071) 91916-8280.

■ Tourist Information

North West Tourism, Temple Street, Sligo. ☎ (071) 91916-1201; fax 916-0360; irelandnorthwest@eircom.net; www.ireland-northwest.travel.ie.

The Northwest

TRACING YOUR ANCESTORS

County Sligo Heritage and Genealogy Centre, Áras Reddan, Temple Street, Sligo. ☎ (071) 91914-3728; heritagesligo@eircom.net.

■ Sligo Town

Sightseeing

 Settlement in Sligo started on the southern shore of the Garravogue river where, in the 13th century, the Norman Maurice Fitzgerald built a castle and an abbey; that part of town still has some of its medieval layout. Sligo in Irish means "abounding with shells," which is certainly what you find on the beaches along its coast.

During the 18th century the town began to prosper as a trading port, and Sligo Bay has one of four surviving Metal Men in the world, which point out the safest channel for shipping.

METAL MEN

The Metal Man at Rosses Point at the entrance to Sligo Harbor was one of four identical models made by a Thomas Kirke in England in 1819 and erected on a 15-foot limestone base here two years later. One of the others stands on a headland overlooking Tramore beach in Co. Waterford, and it's believed the other two went to Dalkey, Co. Dublin, and to Australia, but there's no sign of them today. The Man, dressed in the uniform of a Royal Navy Petty Officer, is 12 feet tall and stands with his arm outstretched, pointing to the deep safe channel for shipping. There's a navigational light in front of him for the hours of darkness.

During and after the Great Famine about 50,000 emigrated from here, but the port declined toward the end of the 19th century.

Today the town is attractive, full of life, with lots of traditional shopfronts, pubs, and places to eat. There are modern developments too but, unlike some other towns, modernization has been carried out very well here, with the old and new complementing each other.

Take at least a short walk around. There are, of course, many signs in the town of associations with Yeats, considered Ireland's greatest poet, who spent much of his childhood here and was inspired by his surroundings. There's an eye-catching statue of him by Rowan Gillespie in the center of

the town. Across the river from Sligo Abbey is the Yeats Memorial Building, which houses the **County Museum** and the **Yeats Memorial Museum**, both absolutely crammed with items of interest. Just down the road at Douglas Hyde Bridge is the headquarters of the Yeats Society, venue for the annual **Yeats International Summer School**.

The Model Arts Centre is a short walk away from the town center on the Mall. It's one of the most attractive galleries I've ever seen, with plenty of natural light. Here you can see paintings by Jack, brother of poet William Butler Yeats, as well as temporary exhibitions of work by contemporary artists. ☎ (071) 919141405.

Shopping

If you're cooking for yourself or having picnics, then you're in for a treat here, as the town has some great food shops. On Market Street there's **Kevin Cosgrave's** and **Kate's Kitchen**; **Tír na nÓg** and **Mary McDonnell's** are on Grattan Street, and on John Street there's **The Gourmet Parlour**.

For gifts and souvenirs, try **Sligo Pottery** on Church Street, and for tableware, linens and glassware, **Cross Sections** on Market Street, where the locals do their shopping. You should at least take a look at **Michael Quirke's** hand-carved figures from Irish mythology in his shop on Wine Street.

Entertainment

The **Hawk's Well Theatre**, three minutes walk from the town center, has a year-round program that includes drama, dance, classical and traditional music. ☎ (071) 91916-1526.

If you want to learn a new skill, the **Queen Maeve School of Traditional Music** runs classes daily all year. Contact Carmel Gunning. ☎ (071) 91916-2008.

■ A Coastal Tour North of Town

Head north out of Sligo on the N15 to **Rosses Point**, three miles (4.8 km) away, an absolutely beautiful seaside resort with magnificent beaches. A mile farther and you're at **Drumcliffe**, dominated by the mighty **Benbulben Mountain**, towering above the landscape at 1,730 feet (750 m).

The Northwest

The Church and **Visitor Centre** here are worth a stop. That's not only because Yeats is buried here, but because its history goes back centuries. It's where Columcille founded a monastery in 574, and where one of the most important battles in Irish history took place between the High King and the leaders of the Northern O'Neills. Open daily all year. ☎ (071) 91914-4956; info@drumcliffe.ie; www.drumcliffe.ie.

The Epitaph of William Butler Yeats at Drumcliffe (written by himself)

Under bare Ben Bulben's head
In Drumcliff churchyard Yeats is laid.
An ancestor was rector there
Long years ago, a church stands near,
By the road an ancient cross.
No marble, no conventional phrase;
On limestone quarried near the spot
By his command these words are cut:
Cast a cold eye
On life, on death.
Horseman, pass by!

On a minor road two miles (3.2 km) from here is **Lissadell House**, home of the Gore-Booths, friends of Yeats. Two daughters were involved in the 1916 Rising, and one, Constance Markiewicz, was condemned to death. She survived to become the first female Member of Parliament in England, and later Minister for Labour in the first Dáil (Irish Parliament). The house was open to the public but, sadly, the family announced in 2003 that they would have to sell it. Let's hope it will continue to be open to the public, as it's of such historical and cultural importance. Check at the Tourist Office.

Near Sligo Town

The Carrowmore Megalithic Cemetery is just south of town, so near that you can walk to it. It's open daily from Easter to October, 10 am-6 pm. ☎ (071) 91916-1534.

Nearby is **Strandhill**, where the lovely sandy beach seems to go on forever. The **Knochnarea Mountain** forms a lovely backdrop for the huge waves, and you'll usually see surfers enjoying them. You can take shelter in the sand dunes against any wind. Over 1,000 feet high (231 m), at the top of Knocknarea is the **tomb of Maeve**, Queen of Connacht, and if you have the energy it's worth the climb for the fantastic view of five counties.

Explore Inland

If you arrive in Sligo from the Roscommon direction, the road runs through a pass on the Curlew Mountains and looks down onto Lough Arrow, passing through Ballinafad and winding its way close to the shore. This part of the county is less known than others, and it's worth exploring. You turn onto the minor road marked Ballymote and climb over the Bricklieve Mountains. Take care when you follow the signpost to the **Carrowkeel Passage Tombs**, as it's frighteningly steep and a track rather than a road. There is a place to park, and walk from there. The Stone Age tombs are spread out over the hillside and you can just about stand up in the tallest of them. The view from here is wonderful, taking in Benbulben and Knocknarea in the distance.

After that, you come to **Ballymore**, a sweet little village with an old church on top of a hill. Follow the signs for **Templehouse Lake**, where you could rent a boat or fish.

Next, head for **Tubbercurry**, and on the way you see Knocknashee, another flat-topped mountain like Benbulben. Tubbercurry is on the N17 to Galway, and is a busy market town, nestling at the foot of the Ox Mountains. It's known as the home of an amateur drama festival and also hosts a summer school in traditional music. It has lots of pubs, and a choice of guesthouses.

There's a choice of roads up into the **Ox Mountains**; head for the villages of Clonacool and Carrowneden, four miles (6.4 km) apart. On the way, you'll pass through wonderful scenery, see rushing streams and drive through woods. On the other side of a pass is the valley called Ladies Brae. Driving downhill, you see laid out before you a great sweep of green fields.

At the T-junction, turn left and left again at the main road to go to Dromore West, and continue on until you come to the third crossroads where there's a sign for **Culkin's Emigration Museum**. It's in a little shop that was the Shipping and Emigration Agency years ago, and there's a fascinating collection of memorabilia. From June to September they serve tea and homemade scones.

Return from there to Dromore West and take the coast road to Easkey.

■ A Coastal Route South of Town

Easkey is popular with surfers. If you continue along the coast from there you come to **Enniscrone**, which is on the eastern shore of Killala Bay, facing Mayo, off the N59, 30 miles (48 km) from Sligo. It has a three-mile-long sheltered beach, with fantastic views out into the Atlantic.

It's also the home of **Kilcullen's Bath House**, which has been offering seaweed baths since 1912. The beautiful Edwardian building, considered modern then of course, now has a special charm, reminding you of that time, with its enormous glazed porcelain baths, solid brass taps and paneled wooden shower cisterns. Seaweed baths are recommended for those suffering from ailments like arthritis and rheumatism, but anyone can enjoy the benefit. You lie in a bath full of hot seawater, with seaweed added. They also offer steam health baths. Open daily, May to the end of October, weekends only the rest of the year. ☎ (096) 36238. Also at Enniscrone is **Waterpoint**, an indoor water recreation facility. ☎ (096) 36999.

■ Signposted Sightseeing Routes

 The **Yeats Trail**, marked by the symbol of a quill pen in an inkpot, takes you from Sligo to Dublin, visiting places associated with the two brothers, the poet and playwright William and the painter Jack. You can get a **passport**, entitling you to a discount on entry charges, from **North Western Tourism**. In Sligo it includes the Museum, Memorial Building, Model Arts and, outside the town, Drumcliffe, on the N15, where W.B. Yeats is buried. It also includes Lissadell House (see above).

The **Spanish Armada Trail** is a long-distance drive, following the route taken by Captain Francisco de Cúellar as he escaped from the wrecks of three Spanish Armada ships on Streedagh Strand, September 15, 1588. It's based on a letter he wrote afterwards, and goes all the way from here to the Causeway Coast, Co. Antrim. On the way, there are storyboards with extracts from the letter. For more information: ☎ (071) 91917-3000; www.spanish-armada-ireland.com.

■ Minibus Tours

 Take a narrated minibus tour of the county with **Discover Sligo**. **There's a choice:** *Lakes and Legends* or *Cottages to Castles*, and both last about three hours. ☎ (071) 91914-7919; info@sligo-tours.com.

■ Adventures on Foot

 There's a **walking tour** of Sligo Town with historian and author Paul Gunning, which starts at the Tourist Office, April-September, Wednesday-Friday, 7 pm, Saturday/Sunday at noon. ☎ (071) 91915-0920; sligo.path@ireland.com.

Long-Distance Walk

The **Sligo Way** is a long-distance waymarked walk (46 miles/74 km), which starts at Lough Talt, at the end of another marked route, the Western Way. It follows the northern foothills of the Ox Mountains, passing Lough Easkey, on forest tracks, moorland and quiet country roads. It then climbs gently to cross the Ox Mountains, from where you get lovely views. It continues through the villages of Coolaney and Collooney, until it reaches the shores of Lough Gill, praised by Yeats. Finally, it passes the ruined Creevelea Abbey and crosses the river Bonet to Dromahair, close to the Leitrim Way.

Forest Walks

Union Wood, five miles (eight km) south of Sligo, on the Ballygawley Road, used to be part of an old estate and has three miles (4.8 km) of forest roads, where you are likely to see deer and other wildlife.

At Half Moon Bay, less than two miles (3.2 km) from Sligo, is the **Hazelwood Demesne**, on the shores of Lough Gill. There's a choice of trails, all clearly marked, and as you walk you will pass a unique series of outdoor sculptures by Irish and international artists. Hazelwood House is privately owned and not open to the public.

Organized Walks

Álainn Tours, 12 Stephen Street, Sligo, organizes guided and self-guided walks, with accommodations en route if needed, in counties Donegal, Leitrim and Sligo. ☎ (071) 91914-4536; alainntours@tinet.ie.

Sligo Path Guided Walking Tours, ☎ (071) 91915-0920. Among others, they provide a walking tour of the "Shelley River City," with one of Sligo's leading historical authors and raconteurs, Paul Gunning. You can see Sligo as experienced through the eyes of W.B. Yeats and his brother, the artist Jack Yeats.

∎ Adventures on Water

 Take a **Wild Rose Waterbus** tour of Lough Gill, which includes the Lake Isle of Innisfree, made famous by Yeats in his poem by that title. ☎ (071) 91916-4226.

The Northwest

The Lake Isle of Innisfree

I WILL arise and go now, and go to Innisfree,
And a small cabin build there, of clay and wattles made;
Nine bean rows will I have there, a hive for the honey bee,
And live alone in the bee-loud glade.

And I shall have some peace there, for peace comes dropping slow,
Dropping from the veils of the morning to where the cricket sings;
There midnight's all a glimmer, and noon a purple glow,
And evening full of the linnet's wings.

I will arise and go now, for always night and day
I hear lake water lapping with low sounds by the shore;
While I stand on the roadway, or on the pavements gray,
I hear it in the deep heart's core.

There are EU Blue Flag beaches (see page 76) at **Rosses Point** and **Enniscrone**.

Surfing

The best surfing locations on Sligo's coast are at **Enniscrone**, **Easkey**, **Aughris**, **Mullaghmore** and **Strandhill**.

Surf Schools

- **Seventh Wave**, Easkey/Enniscrone. ☎ (096) 49020.
- **Perfect Day**, Strandhill. ☎ (071) 91916-8464.

Surf Shops

- **Sunset Sails**, Adelaide Street, Sligo. ☎ (071) 91916-2792.
- **Call of the Wild**, Stephens Street, Sligo. ☎ (071) 91914-6905.
- **Malibu Surf Shop**, Strandhill. ☎ (071) 91916-8302.
- **Easkey Surf and Information Centre**. ☎ (096) 49020.
- for surf reports from the Irish Surfing Association, call ☎ (096) 49428.

Adventures Under Water

There's a **dive centre** at Mullaghmore; contact Danny or Attracta Boyle. ☎/fax (071) 91916-6366.

Power Boats

Lough Ree Power Boat School runs lessons at Rosses Point. ☎ 1-890-70-40-90; funcourse@hodsonbay.com; www.hodsonbay.com.

Fishing

Sligo is a great county for fishing, with so many lakes and rivers, as well as its long coastline. The local tourist office will give advice, as will many of the accommodation providers.

 See pages 71-74 for details on angling in Ireland, regulations and best times to fish.

Lough Gill, for instance, has stocks of spring salmon and brown trout, and is also popular for coarse fishing. Boats and a ghillie (guide) service are offered at ☎ (071) 91914-1462.

The western seaboard attracts many species of sea fish, drawing keen shore and sea anglers to Sligo each year. Fully equipped sea-angling boats can be rented at Rosses Point and Mullaghmore.

A Fishing Vacation

Temple House Farmhouse, Ballymote, is a large Georgian mansion overlooking Templehouse Lake on 1,000 acres. It attracts guests interested in coarse angling, with a boat available to hire. ☎ (071) 91918-3329; guests@templehouse.ie; www.templehouse.ie.

■ Adventures on Horseback

Woodlands Equestrian Centre, Loughill, Lavagh, Tubbercurry, has indoor and outdoor facilities, and offers trekking through woods and farmland, with lanes into the Ox Mountains, on home-bred ponies. ☎ (071) 91918-4207.

Other places where you can ride include:

- **Ard Chuan Equestrian Centre**, Corballa. ☎ (096) 45084.
- **Markree Castle Riding Stables**, Collooney. ☎ (071) 91913-0092.
- **Sligo Riding Centre**, Carrowmore. ☎ (071) 91916-1353.

Riding Vacation

Tilman and Colette Anhold of **Horse Holiday Farm**, Grange, have been in operation for more than 25 years. They offer a number of different tours, with trail and beach riding in both Sligo and Donegal. They cater to all abilities, with Irish Hunters and a few Connemara ponies. ☎ (071) 91916-6152; hhf@eircom.net.

Off to the Races

 Sligo Racecourse is in one of the most scenic settings in the country, just outside the town. ☎ (071) 91916-2484.

■ Golf

 There are three classic links courses, all around Sligo Bay, with wonderful views of the sea. **The County Sligo Golf Club**, Rosses Point, was founded in 1894. ☎ (071) 91917-7134. **Enniscrone Golf Club** is at ☎ (096) 36297. **Strandhill Golf Club** has views of the Ox Mountains on one side and Benbulben on the other. ☎ (071) 91916-8188.

■ Where to Stay

 ☆☆☆ **The Sligo Park Hotel** on the edge of the town is a bright and contemporary hotel, set in seven acres of parkland and surrounded by lovely scenery. There are 110 bedrooms and they can arrange activities for guests. There is a leisure center, with pool, sauna, Jacuzzi and gym, plus a bar and restaurant that are popular with locals. The hotel's **Hazelwood Restaurant** offers wholesome food prepared using fine local ingredients. It's open Monday-Friday from 12:30-2:30 for lunch and from 6:30-9:15 for dinner; on Sundays 1-2:15 pm and 7-9 pm. Rates from $$. ☎ (071) 91916-0291; fax 916-9556; sligo@leehotels.com; www.leehotels.com.

HOTEL PRICE CHART	
Price per person, per night, with two sharing, including breakfast.	
$	Under US $50
$$	US $50-$100
$$$	US $101-$175
$$$$	US $176-$200
$$$$$	Over US $200

☆☆ **The Pier Head Hotel** is in the seaside village of Mullaghmore and has a garden for its guests to enjoy. You can eat in its **Harbour Grill** or in the **Olde Quay Bar and Restaurant**. Fishing and a tennis court are available. Rates from $$. ☎ (071) 91916-6171; fax 916-6473; pierhead@ eircom.net; www.pierheadhotel.com.

☆☆☆☆ **The Cromleach Lodge Country House Hotel** is at Castlebaldwin, eight miles west of Boyle, on a hill overlooking Lough Arrow and the Bricklieve Mountains. Its 10 large and comfortable bedrooms/mini-suites have lovely views and the hotel has a pleasant garden. It's a peaceful place to stay while exploring. Cromleach is a member of Ireland's Blue Book and has an award-winning restaurant. It's open from February to November. Rates from $$$. ☎ (071) 91916-5155; fax 916-5455; info@cromleach.com; www.cromleach.com.

☆☆☆ **The Southern Hotel and Leisure Center** is in the center of Sligo Town and retains a historic atmosphere while offering guests modern facilities, including a swimming pool. It has 99 bedrooms, bar and restaurant, and in the summer there's entertainment almost every evening. Rates $$. ☎ (071) 91916-2101; fax 916-0328; reservations@ sligosouthernhotel.com; www.sligosouthernhotel.com.

Markree Castle, not classified under the star system, has belonged to the Cooper family for 350 years. It's one of the few castles in the country whose owners were not rewarded with a title, because they did not support the Act of Union (see page 18). The castle is in beautiful surroundings at the center of its large estate, with gardens leading down to the banks of the River Unsin. It's just outside the village of Collooney, eight miles south of Sligo Town and just off the main N4 road to Dublin.

A fire welcomes guests when you enter the castle. All its bedrooms are unique in style and character, with antique furniture, yet they have modern facilities, including individually controlled heating, and most have wonderful views. There's an equestrian center on the estate. The food in the magnificent gilded dining-room on the first floor has received lots of favorable reviews. It's open to non-residents for dinner every day from 7:30 to 9:30 and for Sunday lunch from 1 to 2:30. Rates from $$$. ☎ (071) 91916-7800; fax 916-7840; markee@iol.ie; www.markeecastle.ie.

Guests at **Coopershill House**, Riverstown, can fish or go boating in its grounds, and they can play tennis or croquet. As a historic house, it's considered a specialist accommodation and is not rated under the star system. It's a beautiful Georgian house that has belonged to seven generations of the O'Hara family since it was built in 1774. It's in the middle of a 500-acre estate, surrounded by farming land and woods, so you can go for lovely walks. Most of its eight bedrooms have four-poster or canopy beds, and all have private bathrooms. Coopershill belongs to Ireland's Blue Book (see page 60), so you know that staying here means a memorable experience and that the food and hospitality will be top-class.

The Northwest

Open April 1-end October. $$, with special three- and six-day rates. ☎ (071) 91916-5108; ohara@coopershill.com; www.coopershill.com.

Cottage & Apartment Rentals

 North West Tourism has a central self-catering and reservation unit, covering counties Donegal, Leitrim, Monaghan and Cavan, as well as Sligo. ☎ (071) 91916-1201; in Ireland 1850-200-555.

Hostels

There are three hostels in Sligo Town, all open year-round:

Eden Hill. ☎ (071) 91914-3204; edenhillhostel@eircom.net.

Harbour House. ☎ (071) 91917-1547; harbourhouse@eircom.net.

White House Hostel. ☎ (071) 91914-5160.

Camping & RV Parks

 ☆☆☆☆ **Greenlands Caravan and Camping Park** is at Rosses Point, west of Sligo Town on the R29. It has direct access to two safe beaches and is beside a golf club. It's surrounded by wonderful views of mountains and sea, and is open mid-April to mid-September. ☎ (071) 91917-7113.

☆☆ **Atlantic Park** is at Enniscrone, with its three-mile golden beach. There are many sports facilities available locally, including river and deep sea fishing, tennis, surfing and cycling. Open March 1-September 30. ☎ (096) 36132.

Lough Arrow Touring Caravan Park awaited registration at time of writing and so is not yet rated. It's on the shore of the lake at Ballynary, Riverstown, close to the Rockview Hotel, with its bar and restaurant and is open April 1-October 31. ☎ (071) 91966-6018; www.rockviewhotel.com/campsite.

☆☆☆ **Strandhill Park** is at Strandhill Beach, which attracts surfers from all over the world, and has miles of sand dunes to walk in. It's open mid-April-end September. ☎ (071) 91916-8111.

■ Where to Eat

 The Embassy Rooms Restaurant is on John F. Kennedy Parade in Sligo Town, and opens at 10:30 am every day. It's on the banks of the river Garavogue, serving lunch daily from 12:30-2:45, with evening meals available from 6-10 pm. There's an Early Bird Menu from 5:30-7:30, Monday to Friday, which is a great value. Lunch can be enjoyed in a choice of two lounges or in The Belfry Bar. ☎ (071) 91916-1250; fax 916-0649; kevo@eircom.net.

Eithna's Seafood Restaurant is on the harbor at Mullaghmore, specializing in seafood and shellfish caught by local fishermen in Donegal Bay. Founded in 1990, it is equally popular with locals and visitors, who enjoy its menu featuring coastal, organic and seasonal ingredients. It's open for dinner from March to October and you should phone for times and to make reservations. ☎ (071) 91916-6407; www.eithnaseafood.com.

Glebe House Restaurant also offers accommodations in individually furnished bedrooms. The Georgian house is in a lovely countryside setting, overlooking Collooney village and surrounded by meadows that run down to the Owenmore River. It's an award-winning restaurant where all meals are carefully prepared using fine local ingredients, including vegetables, fruit and herbs, from its old walled garden. Seafood features on the menu, and there's also an interesting and unusual choice of wines. Open for dinner from 6:30-9:30pm in summer. ☎ (071) 91916-7787; fax 913-0438; glebehouse@esatbiz.com.

County Cavan

The inland county of Cavan is quite small, its area only 730 square miles (1,898 square km). Its name comes from the Irish word cabhán, meaning "a hollow," which is appropriate, as it is set between highlands in the east and the Erne Valley and a mountainous region on the west.

The county is said to have 365 lakes, one for each day of the year, and the largest of them are Lough Gowna, Lough Oughter, Lough Sheelin, and Lough Ramor. Cavan's rivers, streams and tree-lined lakes also provide great opportunities for fishing, cruising and swimming. Its main rivers are the Shannon, Erne, Blackwater and Annalee.

The **Shannon-Erne Waterway** links these two rivers, which spring from the barren Cuilcagh Mountains in the county's northwest. The source of the Shannon, the longest river in Ireland, is known as the "Shannon Pot" and is just a few miles north of Dowra, on the southwest side of Cuilcagh Mountains.

Even if you're not interested in history, you can't fail to notice the number of ancient monuments and ruins wherever you go. The landscape is dotted with **megalithic tombs** – 59 of them. The most interesting are the **double court tomb** dating from 3000-2500 BC at Cohaw and the **Duffcastle Dolmen**.

The Northwest

Crannógs

There are at least 100 crannógs (from crann, meaning timber, tree, wood) in the county as well. They are habitations made of mud, stones and wood and surrounded by palisades, which were erected on small natural or man-made islands. They include defensible corrals so the cattle could be driven over and protected during dangerous times. Crannógs are small and would have been refuges for just one extended family and its cattle. They were used from prehistoric times right up to the late medieval period. In other parts of the country you see replicas of them in folk parks; here they're authentic.

A fortification, dating back to about 500 BC, known as **The Black Pig's Dyke** (see page 186), which divided the ancient province of Ulster from the rest of the island, emerges here near Dowra.

Clogh Oughter dates from a more recent era, and is the best example in Cavan of a medieval stone castle; it was a military fortification and was the seat of the O'Reillys, the ruling family. Other surviving castles were really tower houses, smaller and suitable for refuge during raids, not sieges.

The O'Reillys stayed in power until the 16th century when, early in the reign of King James I of England, the Lord Deputy came to Cavan and held a commission to decide the allocation of lands. Planters from Britain were given land, the boroughs of Cavan and Belturbet were created, and the town of Virginia was founded here in 1610, at the same time as its namesake across the Atlantic – named after the Virgin Queen of England, Elizabeth.

The county capital is also called **Cavan**, and the main towns are **Cootehill**, **Baileboro**, **Kingscourt**, **Belturbet** and **Virginia**.

■ Getting Here

Cavan Town is served by major routes N3 from Dublin (67 miles/108 km); N3-N54-N2-A3-M1 from Belfast (88 miles/142 km); N3-N5-N6-N18 from Galway (103 miles/166 km); and N55-N6-N62-N8-N25 from Cork (187 miles/301 km).

It has a **bus station**, ☎ (049) 433-1353. The nearest **rail station** is in Carrick-on-Shannon, Co. Leitrim, and the closest **airport** and **seaport** are in Dublin.

■ Tourist Information

Fáilte Ireland Tourist Information Office, Farnham Street, Cavan, is open March-October, ☎ (049) 433-1942.

TRACING YOUR ANCESTORS

The County Cavan Heritage and Genealogical Research Centre offers a full genealogical research service for people with Cavan ancestry. Contact Mary Sullivan or Concepta McGovan, Cana House, Farnham Street, Cavan. ☎ (049) 436-1094; 433-1494; canahouse@iol.ie; www. cavangenealogy.com.

■ Cavan Town

Sightseeing

The county town is a pleasant place to visit. Many years ago it was the stronghold of the O'Reillys whose castle, **Clough Oughter**, now in ruins, can be seen standing on an island in Lough Oughter, a mile outside town.

Its name, meaning "hollow," suits the town as much as it does the county, as it is surrounded by hills.

Cavan has the distinction of being the only medieval town in Ireland founded by the Irish themselves, and its narrow streets still follow the same pattern that was set down seven centuries ago.

A local landlord family, the Farnhams, improved Cavan in the early 19th century, by building a new wide street that still bears the family name. This street was lined with comfortable townhouses and public buildings such as churches and the Courthouse, built in 1825. In the late 19th century, Cavan became an important rail junction between the midland and western lines and those of the Northern Railways.

Today it's a busy town. Attractions include **Cavan Crystal**, the second-oldest lead crystal factory (after Waterford) in Ireland, where visitors can watch the process of glass-blowing; and the **Lifeforce Mill**, where part of the visit is spent making a loaf of bread.

Virginia is 19 miles (31 km) southeast of Cavan on the N3, at the edge of Lough Ramor, and is pleasantly laid out, with some pretty cottages on its main street. Writer Jonathan Swift (most famous for his *Gulliver's*

Travels) used to visit his friend, the playwright Richard Brinsley Sheridan here, and some say that the town inspired his novel. On the lakeshore there's a sandy stretch where you can swim, and there are boats to hire. **The Ramor Theatre** hosts touring and local productions, along with other entertainment. ☎ (049) 854-7074.

The Cavan County Museum is at Ballyjamesduff, a few miles from Virginia, in an attractive 19th-century building on lovely grounds. It's worth the trip to see the Pighouse Collection, donated by a Mrs Phyllis Faris, which includes costumes and folk life material from the 18th through the 20th centuries. It also has a craft shop and tea room. Open Tuesday-Saturday, 10 am to 5 pm; Sundays from June to October, 2-6 pm. ☎ (049) 954-4070.

For all you trivia buffs out there, Marcus Daly, who became a mining tycoon in the US, was born in Ballyjamesduff in 1841, and emigrated in 1856. He later founded the city of Anaconda in Montana.

Tours

Maudabawn Cultural Centre, Cootehill, organizes guided heritage tours of both Co. Cavan and Co. Monaghan; you can choose from two-hour, half-day, and full-day tours. The Centre also offers Summer School courses on Ireland's cul;ture and history. ☎ (049) 555-9540.

Sweating It Out

Sweathouses were common in West Cavan and neighboring parts of Leitrim and Fermanagh. They were small structures built of stone without mortar. People suffering a variety of ailments, from rheumatism to skin complaints, used them. A fire was lit in the central chamber and a patient would crawl inside. We don't know how long they were used; certainly many centuries, maybe millennia – but the practice continued until the 1920s. You'll find the Legeelan Sweathouse near Moneygashel.

■ Adventures on Foot

Long-Distance Walk

The Cavan Waymarked Way is a walking route through the pleasant hills and valleys of the county. It's right in the middle of a great inland recreation area stretching from the Erne lakes in Fermanagh to the North Leitrim Glens.

It's 16 miles (26 km) long and stretches from Blacklion to Dowra. The route links up with the Ulster Way at Blacklion, and with the Leitrim Way at Dowra. A map of the route is on display in both Blacklion and Dowra.

At Blacklion it rises, and there are marvelous views back over Lough MacNean. On the western side of the Cuilcagh Mountains, there's the forested Burren area and its ancient tombs, stone megaliths and monuments. The source of the Shannon lies just off the route, and walkers meet the river itself on the descent into Dowra.

Forest Parks

 Killykeen Forest Park surrounds the lake and islands of Lough Oughter, near Cavan. There are a number of marked trails, all of them giving you the opportunity to see lots of animals and hear the many different birds attracted by the mixture of trees and the great expanses of water. Among them are moorhens, cormorants and great crested grebes, mallards and tufted ducks, warblers and herons. Wherever you walk here there are wonderful views.

The park contains sites of historical interest too, including an Iron Age **ring fort** and **Clogh Oughter Castle**, seen from the Derinish Trail. When the site was excavated in 1987, human remains were found from the last Cromwellian siege of 1653. ☎ (049) 433-2541.

The forest park is also ideal for walking and cycling, and bicycles are available for hire, as are boats – see below.

Dun-Na-Ri Forest Park is a mile north of Kingscourt on the R179, in a peaceful glen on the banks of the River Cabra. There are a number of trails, with various interesting features. These include a wishing well, Cromwell's Bridge, Cabra Cottage, the Lady's Lake and an old ice house. All trails are signposted.

■ Adventures on Water

 Boats are available for hire in the Killykeen Forest Park, where canoeing, windsurfing and other watersports can also be enjoyed on Lough Oughter. The complex remains open all year, but some facilities are seasonal, so phone to check. ☎ (049) 433-2541.

With the Shannon-Erne Waterway linking those two great rivers, there are 186 miles (300 km) of navigable waterway, ideal for cruising. **Erne Down Cruisers**, based in Belturbet, organizes daily cruises from April to September. ☎ (049) 952-2219.

Fishing

Lough Oughter is renowned for coarse angling, with bream, roach, perch and pike the main species. A pegged stretch, where international competitions are held, is located within the Killykeen Forest Park.

See pages 71-74 for details on angling in Ireland, regulations and best times to fish.

There are many fine game angling river stretches and wild brown trout lake fisheries; the county also has a great reputation for its coarse and pike fishing. Almost every town seems to be an angling center – just look at a map, and you see that they are in every area. Among them are: Cavan, Cootehill, Baileborough, Kingscourt, Shercock, Virginia, Ballyjamesduff, Mount Nugent, Finea, Gowna, Arva, and Killykeen Forest Park.

A number of different river systems and their associated lakes make up the fisheries. Among them are the River Erne and its main tributaries; the Shannon-Erne Waterway and the Dromore/Annalee system, which dominates the middle of the county. To the east, there's the Upper River Boyne system, and to the south and northwest, parts of the Shannon system.

Local festivals are held annually at Arvagh, Belturbet and Cootehill, with one-day open matches at many centers.

The **Central Regional Fisheries Board** is the authority responsible for Cavan. Contact them at Balnagowan House, Mobhi Boreen, Mobhi Road, Dublin 9, ☎ from Ireland (01) 884 2600, from abroad 353-1-884-2600; info@cfb.ie, www.cfb.ie.

Tackle Shops

MC Sports, Killeshandra. ☎ (049) 433-4438.

Joe Mulligan, Shercock, ☎ (048) 966-9184.

Sports World, Townhall Street, Cavan, ☎ (049) 433-1812.

Sheelin Shamrock Hotel, Mountnugent, Lough Sheelin. ☎ (049) 40113.

Philip Smith, Lavagh, Kilnaleck, Lough Sheelin, ☎ (049) 36156.

Fishing Center

The **International Fishing Center** is French-owned and was established almost two decades ago. It offers accommodation on a full- or half-board basis and has its own restaurant. It specializes in pike and coarse fishing on rivers and lakes from the shore or on its boats, which are equipped with fish finders. Contact Michel Neuville, ☎/fax (049) 952-2616; michelneuville@eircom.net; www.angling-holidays.com.

■ Adventures on Horseback

Cavan Equestrian Centre, Latt. ☎ (049) 433-2017.

Killykeen Equestrian Centre in Forest Park. ☎ (049) 436-1707.

Ashfield Riding Stables, Cootehill. ☎ (049) 555-204.

Redhill Equestrian Centre, Killynure. ☎ (047) 55042.

■ Golf

County Cavan Golf Club, two miles (3.2 km) from the town on the R198 to Killeshandra, was founded in 1894; it is one of the oldest clubs in Ireland. ☎ (049) 433-1541.

Belturbet Golf Club has a nine-hole course. ☎ (049) 22287.

Blacklion Golf Club, has a nine-hole course on the shores of Lough Macnean. ☎ (072) 985-3024.

Cabra Castle, a nine-hole course, with the imposing castle hotel as a backdrop. ☎ (042) 67030.

Virginia Golf Club, a nine-hole course, overlooks Lough Ramor. ☎ (049) 854-8066.

The course at the **Slieve Russell Hotel Golf & Country Club** only opened in 1992, but it has since become one of the top-ranking courses in the country, and is compared to some of the great courses world-wide. ☎ (049) 952-6444.

Pitch-and-Putt

Ballyhaise Pitch-and-Putt, four miles (6.4 km) north of Cavan, is an 18-hole course. ☎ (049) 38430.

■ Where to Stay

☆☆☆☆ **The Slieve Russell Hotel Golf and Country Club**, Ballyconnell, is in a beautiful setting, luxurious and known for its leisure facilities, including two golf courses, one a nine-hole, and a floodlit driving range. The hotel stands in 300 acres of grounds, which includes 50 acres of lakes, so you could easily spend your entire vacation here. Its Country Club has a swimming pool,

The Northwest

incorporating a whirlpool and massage seats, and there's a Jacuzzi, steam room, sauna and gym. They also have a hair and beauty salon, as well as outdoor tennis courts. Other activities can be arranged, including visits to local attractions, and clay pigeon shooting, archery or horseback riding.

There are 159 bedrooms, including 14 suites, many of them looking out over the hotel's gardens and golf course. The **Kells Bar** is decorated with illustra-

HOTEL PRICE CHART	
Price per person, per night, with two sharing, including breakfast.	
$	Under US $50
$$	US $50-$100
$$$	US $101-$175
$$$$	US $176-$200
$$$$$	Over US $200

tions from the historic Book of Kells. The hotel's **Conall Cearnach Restaurant** is considered one of the finest, not just in Cavan, but in the entire area, and has received many awards. The **Brackley Restaurant** is less formal, or guests can enjoy the **Summit Restaurant** and its bar, with their wonderful views over the golf course. Rates from $$$, with special offers sometimes available. ☎ (049) 952-6444; fax 952-6046; slieve-russell@quinn-hotels.com; www.quinnhotels.com.

☆☆☆☆ **The Cabra Castle Hotel** would also be a memorable choice. It's near Baileborough, at Kingscourt. Formerly Cormey Castle, it is said to have welcomed historic figures including King James II and Oliver Cromwell, when its estate covered 1,000 acres. Today it's in the middle of 100 acres of beautiful parkland, including Lady's Lake, and surrounded by the Dún a Rí National Forest Park. There are 20 bedrooms in what's known as the Old House, and 60 Courtyard bedrooms in the converted granary and blacksmith's forge, which dates to 1750. All of its rooms are furnished with antiques and paintings, and guests can enjoy following nature trails through the surrounding forests or walking in the enclosed gardens. It also has a nine-hole golf course. Food in **The Court Room Restaurant** is prepared using fresh local ingredients, and the **Derby Bar** is a pleasant place to relax. Cabra Castle belongs to the Manor House Hotels marketing group. Rates $$-$$$. ☎ (042) 966-7030; fax 966-7039; sales@cabracastle.com; www.cabracastle.com.

☆☆☆ **The Park Hotel** at Virginia is also in an historic building, and in the middle of its own 100-acre estate. It's on the shore of Lough Ramor, and has beautifully landscaped gardens, plus its own nine-hole golf course. There are 25 bedrooms, and there is a very good restaurant that is popular with locals as well as guests. Rates from $$, with special midweek offers. ☎ (049) 854-6100; fax 854-7203; virginiapark@eircom.net; www.bichotels.com.

☆☆☆ **Hotel Kilmore** is on Dublin Road, Cavan, and has 39 pleasantly furnished bedrooms. Its **Annalee Restaurant** offers a good selection of dishes, including locally caught fish and game when in season. Rates $$.

☎ (049) 433-2288; fax 433-2458; kilmore-sales@quinn-hotels.com; www. quinnhotels.com.

Cottages for Rent

 There are a number of self-catering houses available through **www.cavantourism.com** or contact the **Fáilte Ireland Tourist Information Office**, Farnham Street, Cavan, ☎ (049) 433-1942.

Among those listed on the website are a group of three-star modern cottages set in 40 acres and by a lake at Redhills, with lovely views. Each of them has its own private fishing stand, and has an open fire as well as central heating. ☎ (047) 55292; clonandra@hotmail.com.

In the beautiful setting of the Killykeen Forest Park, already described, you can rent a chalet. ☎ (049) 433-2541 (see pages 65 and 423).

Camping & RV Parks

 ☆☆ **Lough Ramor Caravan and Camping Park**, Ryefield, is three miles south of Virginia, off the N3. It's popular for angling and boating on the Lough. Open May 1 to September 30. ☎ (01) 837-1717.

Lakelands Caravan and Camping Park at Shercock is not registered. It's on a three-acre site and opens for Easter and again at the beginning of June until the middle of September. ☎ (042) 69488; fax 27302.

Hostel

The White Star Hostel, Cootehill, is open all year. ☎ (049) 555-2337; whitestar@eircom.net.

County Leitrim

Don't be put off by its Irish name, Liathdroim, which means "the grey hill-ridge," as this county is much more enticing than that sounds. The smallest of the 26 counties that make up the Republic, it lies mostly inland, with only a tiny stretch, two miles (3.2 km) long, touching the Atlantic near Bundoran, Co. Donegal.

There are lots of lakes, streams, rivers, and bogland. In fact, despite being inland, the county is almost surrounded by water. The River Shannon nearly divides it in two and Loughs MacNean and Melvin and the River Erne mark its northern boundary, while part of the expansive Lough Allen shares its eastern border with Co. Cavan.

In ancient times, the western part of the county was ruled by the O'Rourke clan, and the eastern by the O'Reillys. Leitrim as we see it today came into being in 1565, after the confiscation of the territories belonging to the O'Rourkes. In medieval times it was thickly wooded, and that lasted until the 17th century, but the great forests have all disappeared. According to a list of landowners in the late 19th century, by then the O'Rourkes didn't own even one acre of land.

It was part of the Plantation (see page 14) at the beginning of the 17th century, and towns like Carrick-on-Shannon, Manorhamilton and Jamestown were founded and fortified against the native population at that time.

During famine times and even right up to recent decades, many local people left to seek work, the majority emigrating overseas. The population was at its highest at 155,000 in the early 1800s; today it's less than 30,000. That's one of the lowest densities on the island, and there are tax incentives in place to encourage more people to settle here.

The unspoiled landscape and almost-empty countryside are very peaceful, and it's a lovely place to visit. Attractions include cruising on the Shannon, fishing, walking and discovering sites of archaeological, historical and cultural interest. Among them is a section of the Black Pig's Dyke (see page 186) between Lough Melvin and Lough MacNean Upper.

The county capital and largest town is **Carrick-on-Shannon**, and its other main towns are **Ballinamore**, **Drumshanbo** and **Manorhamilton**.

■ Getting Here

Carrick-on-Shannon is on the N4 from Dublin (97 miles/156 km); the N7-N55-N6-N19 from Galway (75 miles/188 km). It is 123 miles (198 km) from Belfast, and 182 miles (293 km) from Cork.

It's on the railway line connecting Dublin and Sligo. The **railway station** is at ☎ (078) 962-0036. The nearest **bus station** is in Sligo Town. The closest **airports** are Knock International and Sligo. The nearest **ferry port** is Dublin.

■ Tourist Information

Fáilte Ireland Tourist Information Office, The Old Barrel Store, Carrick-on-Shannon, is open April to October. ☎ (071) 91972-0170; fax 20089.

■ Sightseeing

Carrick-on-Shannon

 The county town grew up around a river crossing at a strategic location, just a bit south of where the rivers Boyle and Shannon meet. It's 28 miles (45 km) southeast of Sligo, on the N4 Dublin road.

The town prospered with the building of bridges and quays in the area in the middle of the 19th century. Prosperity was helped further by the arrival of the railway in 1862. Today, it makes an ideal base for touring the county and farther afield.

Although small, the town has an inviting and rather cosmopolitan atmosphere, attracting tourists interested in cruising the Shannon or fishing in the area. It has lots of tackle shops and a busy marina, with a huge fleet of cruisers and pleasure craft, a lovely sight.

There's a quaint little building on Main Street, the **Costello Chapel**, built by one Edward Costello in the 19th century in memory of his wife, and you can see their coffins, sunk below the floor, under glass. It claims to be the second-smallest chapel in the world, and I can't help wondering where the smallest one is.

There are plenty of friendly pubs and restaurants, and there's a cinema, ☎ (071) 91966-2678.

Explore the County

Head eastwards out of Carrick-on-Shannon and, after nine miles (14.5 km), you come to **Mohill**, where the R201 and R202 meet. It's a busy little place, and a fishing center. It was the birthplace of the blind harpist O'Carolan (see page 375), and there's a statue of him here.

The village of **Fenagh** is two miles (3.2 km) farther, on the northern shore of Fenagh Lough. There are ruins of two Gothic churches here and an impressive 17th-century mausoleum.

Ballinamore, four miles (6.4 km) past Fenagh, is mainly an angling center these days. It was on coaching routes in former times and has a broad main street. In the former courthouse is the county genealogy center, and a heritage and folk museum.

The Northwest

Manorhamilton

This is the only sizeable town in the northern part of the county. It's 28 miles (45 km) north of Carrick-on-Shannon on the N16, between Sligo and Enniskillen in Co. Fermanagh, Northern Ireland. Before the changes in currency made it more expensive to do so, many people living in Manorhamilton did their weekly shopping across the border, as those towns are closer.

Manorhamilton is in a memorably beautiful location, where four mountain valleys meet, and is surrounded by limestone hills. The scenery really is lovely, with steep hillsides, narrow ravines and fertile valleys.

From Manorhamilton you can head off on any of five different roads to explore the surrounding hills on the **North Leitrim Natural History and Heritage Tour**, and there are information panels and a brochure explaining what you see as you drive or cycle.

One route out of Manorhamilton takes you past Milltown Wood and on to Glencar, and the waterfall that inspired Yeats. Another route takes you to Glenade, where there's a lake and megalithic sites on the mountain slopes. You drive or cycle from there to Kinlough at the head of Lough Melvin, drained by the Drowes River into the Atlantic. Here, a tiny stretch of Leitrim touches the coast, just south of Bundoran.

Another of the routes takes you southeast to Lough Gill, passing between Benbo and Leean Mountain on the way, and along the shore to Dromahair.

The eastern route (N16) takes you to Glenfarne, on the shore of Lough MacNean, where there's a forest area owned by Coillte, with way-marked walks around what was the Tottenham estate. One of its owners, Nicholas Tottenham, unlike his grandfather, was a decent landlord, and provided the workhouse in Manorhamilton with food.

The R282 goes from Manorhamilton to Fowley's Falls and Rossinver, a distance of eight miles (13 km), which makes a pleasant cycle or drive (or even a walk, if you're really fit).

At Rossinver is the **Organic Centre**, where you can visit its demonstration gardens and ask about the courses they run, in everything from designing an edible garden to cheese-making. Most of them last a day, so could easily be done while on vacation. Open daily, 11 am-5 pm. ☎ (072) 985-4338; fax 985-4343; organiccentre@eircom.net.

Manorhamilton is the home of the **Leitrim Sculpture Centre**, ☎ (071) 9620005, founded and run by Robbie McDonald. Its headquarters is on Main Street. The center has brought new life to the town, as sculptors come here to do workshops led by more experienced artists, and stay in the area for months. It has also developed a Sculpture Trail – see below.

Also in Manorhamilton is the **Glens Centre**, which hosts a program of events, including music, drama and exhibitions, and where there are self-catering vacation apartments. ☎ (072) 985-5833; fax 985-6063; nlgdc@eircom.net.

Dromahair

Dromahair is a pretty little village near the shore of Lough Gill, where there are the ruins of the last **monastery** to be founded in Ireland, in 1508, before King Henry VIII suppressed them all.

Nearby, in a really lovely setting, is **Parke's Castle**, built on the site of a much older tower house, the stronghold of the Irish chieftain, Brian O'Rourke. It has a rather fairytale quality about it, perched on the edge of the water, but its history belies that, as it was built on the misfortune of others, literally and metaphorically.

Poor O'Rourke met a sad end; he was executed in England for having sheltered a survivor of the Spanish Armada. A certain Robert Parke was given his lands and he turned the fortress into his new home.

Other than the conventional way of arriving here, on the narrow road, you can also visit Parke's Castle by boat from Sligo, as it's included in trips around Lough Gill to see the "lake isle of Innisfree" that W.B. Yeats wrote about (see page 414). Parke's Castle is under the care of the State Heritage Service. Open daily mid-March to the end of October, 10 am-6 pm. ☎ (071) 91916-4149.

■ Adventures on Foot

Long Distance Walks

Manorhamilton is, with Drumshanbo, the starting point for the waymarked long distance walk, the **Leitrim Way** (30 miles/48 km). This walk takes you through beautiful countryside, along the shore of Lough Allen to the upland wilderness of Barlear. Its highest point is at Doo Lough (1,140 feet/347 m).

At Dowra, walkers can connect with another waymarked route, part of which goes through Leitrim. The **Miners' Way** traces the routes followed by miners to work, north of Lough Allen, through the hills and valleys of Roscommon and Sligo.

Sculpture Trail

Developed by the Leitrim Sculpture Centre, Manorhamilton, this trail takes you around the shores of Upper and Lower Lough MacNean, linking southwest Fermanagh in the North with counties Cavan and Leitrim in the Republic.

Ask at tourist offices, or contact the Manorhamilton Sculpture Centre, for the lovely brochure-guide. ☎ (071) 91917-1905; janie.info@careforfree.net; www.sculpturetrail.net.

Contact the **North Leitrim Glens Tourism Co-operative** in Manorhamilton about the 30 delightful walks in the area. ☎ (072) 985-6217; fax 985-6063; nlwalkingfest@hotmail.com.

■ Adventures on Water

From Carrick-on-Shannon

Emerald Star, the largest inland waterway cruiser rental company in the country, has a base at Carrick-on-Shannon; from here you can head off for a vacation on water. It also has bases in Portumna, Co. Galway, and Belturbet, Co. Cavan. ☎ (071) 91962-0234; fax 962-1433; emeraldstar@clubi.ie; www.emeraldstar.ie.

Other cruiser companies based here are:

Carrick Craft. ☎ (071) 91962-0236.

Crown Blue Line. ☎ (071) 91962-1903.

Tara Cruisers. ☎ (071) 91966-7777.

The waterbus, *Moon River Pleasure Cruiser*, also leaves from here. It seats 110, has a full bar and refreshments are available on board. As it is sometimes rented out to groups, it's a good idea to check ahead for public sailing times. There's an information board on the quay, or ☎ (071) 91962-1777; moonriver@eircom.net; www.moon-river.net.

From Ballinamore

You can take a trip on a **waterbus** from Ballinamore; contact ☎ (071) 91964-4079.

Hire a boat for the day from here by calling ☎ (071) 91964-5135 or (071) 91964-4878.

Riversdale Barge Holidays, Ballinamore, is based at a farm, which is also a guesthouse, with a heated pool, sauna and squash room. From there you can hire one of their luxury barges, centrally heated, and head off for a vacation or break on the Shannon-Erne Waterway. They have boats with from two to eight berths. ☎ (071) 91964-4122; fax 964-5112; riversdalebargehols@eircom.ie; www.riversdalebargeholidays.com.

Locaboat has a fleet of boats based at The Marina, Ballinamore. The company designs and builds its own boats, which look like a cross between a compact barge and a canoe. Most have central heating, and they come in different sizes; the smallest has two berths, the largest sleeps up to 12. They're available by the week, the weekend or for short breaks. ☎ (071) 91964-5300; fax 964-5301; info@locaboat.com; www.locaboat. com.

Fishing

Carrick-on-Shannon is the center for fishing on rivers Shannon and Boyle, loughs Key, Allen, Corry and Drumharlow, and many other smaller streams and lakes.

The River Shannon rises in the Cuilcagh Mountains a short distance north of Drumshanbo. There's free coarse fishing on the Shannon, on Lough Allen and 12 small lakes in the area, including Acres, Derrynahoo, Carrickport and Scur. There's also good trout fishing on the Shannon, especially below Bellantra.

The **Lough Allen Conservation Association** has stocked Lough Allen with over 100,000 trout in the past five years or so. The lough also has a good stock of coarse fish, including specimen pike and some big trout. However, as the lough acts as a reservoir for the power station farther south near Limerick and has sluice gates at its lower end, the waters fluctuate, and at low water there are many hazardous rocks. There can also be sudden strong winds.

The **Lough Allen Angling Club** welcomes visitors. Two trout streams run into the Lough, on which fishing is regarded as free. The Yellow River enters from the east, a spate river, with brown trout in its lower reaches; and the Owennayle, really a mountain stream, enters from the north.

Rooskey is the center for coarse fishing on rivers Shannon, Rinn or Rynn, and many small lakes in the area. There are good catches in Drumdad Lake near Mohill, which is also a good center for Loughs MacHugh and Erril and Lakes Cloonboniagh and Creenagh.

See pages 71-74 for details on angling in Ireland, regulations and best times to fish.

Tackle Shops

- **Rooskey Quay Enterprises**.
- **Lakeland Bait**, Knocknacrory.

- **The Creel**, Main Street, and **Tranquillity Tackle**, both in Kilclare.
- **McGaurtys**, The Square, Drumshanbo.

Information

- **The North Western Regional Fisheries Board.** ☎ (096) 22623.
- **The Northern Regional Fisheries Board.** ☎ (072) 985-1435.

■ Adventures on Horseback

- **Hayden Equestrian Centre**, Carrick-on-Shannon. ☎ (071) 91963-8049.
- **Moorlands Equestrian and Leisure Centre**, Drumshanbo. ☎ (071) 91964-1500.

■ Golf Courses

- **Ballinamore Golf Club**, nine-hole, ☎ (071) 91964-4346.
- **Carrick-on-Shannon Golf Club**, nine-hole, ☎ (071) 91966-7015.

■ Where to Stay

☆☆☆ **The Bush Hotel**, one of Ireland's oldest, was refurbished in recent years and is on Main Street, Carrick-on-Shannon. It has kept its traditional atmosphere and added modern comforts. It has 28 bedrooms, and behind it is a courtyard and pleasant gardens. See under *Where to Eat* below for details of its dining facilities. Rates $$. ☎ (071) 91962-0014; fax 962-1180; info@ bushhotel.com; www.bushhotel.com.

HOTEL PRICE CHART	
Price per person, per night, with two sharing, including breakfast.	
$	Under US $50
$$	US $50-$100
$$$	US $101-$175
$$$$	US $176-$200
$$$$$	Over US $200

The Landmark Hotel, Carrick-on-Shannon, overlooks the River Shannon with its picturesque marinas, and is a short walk outside the town on the N4 main road to Dublin. It's unclassified under the hotel star system, but offers lovely accommodation with four-star luxury. There's a gym if you want to keep fit. **The Boardwalk Café**, **CJ's Restaurant** and **Ferrari's Restaurant** (see under *Where to Eat* below) are all part of the hotel. Rates $$$. ☎ (071) 91962-2222; fax 962-2223; landmarkhotel@ eircom.net; www.thelandmarkhotel.com.

✰✰ **Hartes Hotel** is in Carrigallen, a small, family-run hotel, ideally located for exploring the lakeland counties of Leitrim, Cavan and Fermanagh. It has a garden for guest use, along with a bar and dining facilities. Rates $. ☎ (049) 433-9737; fax 433-9152.

✰ **The Breffni Centre Hotel** is on Dromahair's Main Street and offers guests comfortable accommodation. It has a bar and dining room and a tennis court. Rates $. ☎ (071) 91916-4199; breffnicentre@eircom.net.

Guesthouses

Among the guesthouses in the country are the following:

Hollywell is an historic house with miles of wild river meadows and a garden, it's almost on Carrick Bridge in Carrick-on-Shannon. ☎ (071) 91962-1124.

Gortmor Farmhouse, with angling facilities, is nearby, two miles off the N4. ☎ (071) 91962-0489.

Houses for Rent

 At **Leitrim Quay**, four miles (6.4 km) northeast of Carrick-on-Shannon, on the road to Drumshanbo, each of the houses available to rent comes with a 23-foot (seven-meter) day cruiser, ideal for fishing and exploring the waterways.

The houses sleep six in three bedrooms, have two bathrooms and a large kitchen/diner living area. There's electric heating as well as an open fireplace, and the houses are well-equipped, each with its own garden. ☎ (071) 91962-2989; fax 962-2165; leitrimquay@ireland.com; www. leitrimquay.com.

At **Drumcoura Lake Resort**, three miles (4.8 km) from Ballinamore, guests can ride, fish, go boating, play tennis, walk, or just relax. Accommodation is in self-catering wooden chalets; there's also a bar and restaurant. The chalets sleep from three to seven, and can be rented on a daily basis per person, or on a weekly basis per chalet.

The resort has its own equestrian centre, with American quarter horses and European horses, with jumps, trails, a cross-country course and indoor arena. Lessons are available. ☎ (071) 91964-5708.

Fishing is on the 50-acre lake, where there are boats to hire; or you can fish from the bank. Boating is in a rowboat from the jetty. ☎ (71) 964-5781; info@drumcoura.ie; www.drumcoura.ie.

The Northwest

Camping & RV Parks

Lough Rynn Caravan and Camping Park, Mohill, is on the lakeshore, open Easter to September. It's unclassified. ☎ (071) 91963-1844.

Hostel

Leitrim Lakes Hostel, in Kiltyclogher, has camping facilities as well, open all year. ☎ (071) 91985-4044; llhostel@gofree.indigo.ie.

■ Where to Eat

The Courtyard Restaurant at the Bush Hotel in Carrick-on-Shannon has a very good reputation for its fresh and wholesome food, expertly prepared and imaginatively presented. Most of its dishes use local produce and all are complemented by an extensive wine list. The hotel's Coffee Shop has a carvery and food buffet and is open throughout the day. ☎ (071) 91962-0014; fax 962-1180.

There's a choice of where to eat at the Landmark Hotel (see *Where to Stay* section): **The Boardwalk Café and Bar**, **CJ's Restaurant**, and **Ferrari's Restaurant**. CJ's serves local fresh cuisine. Ferrari's Restaurant has a Ferrari car mounted on its wall and some of its tables have views of the Shannon. It's open every evening from 6-10, with an innovative menu and an informal atmosphere. The award-winning Boardwalk Café has a relaxing atmosphere, and serves carvery lunch and sandwiches from Monday to Friday. noon to 4 pm. It also has entertainment on Thursday, Friday and Saturday nights. ☎ (071) 91962-2222.

The Brandywell Bar and Restaurant is on the N4 in the very attractive village of Dromod. The pub is decorated in a contemporary style, with a welcoming and relaxed atmosphere, and has an excellent reputation for both the quality and variety of the food served. ☎ (071) 91963-8153; fax 965-8937; brandywellpub@hotmail.com; www.brandywellpub.com.

County Monaghan

Monaghan is an inland county and one of the smallest, only covering 500 square miles (1,300 square km). It's often described as "drumlin country" from the small hills dotting the landscape, which were left behind when the glaciers retreated – the word coming from the Irish "droim," meaning back or hump. Patrick Kavanagh, one of Ireland's greatest poets, described his birthplace as having "stony grey soil.'

The county takes its name from the Irish "muineachán," meaning "the place of the shrubs," which is understandable even today, given the areas of woodland and forest parks, which make it so attractive.

Its undulating and fertile landscape, with small sloping hills, is perfect for walking. For the cyclist there is a maze of little roads away from the traffic and off main routes. Because of the gentle terrain, the cyclist will enjoy exploring, stopping in a quiet village to rest. West of Emyvale, in the north of the county, is particularly interesting.

Its streams, rivers and lakes have made the county one of the most popular destinations for anglers in the country for many years. As a result, a number of its towns are well-developed centers. It's also dotted with many interesting and historic sites.

The county capital and largest town is also called **Monaghan** and among its other main towns are **Castleblaney** and **Carrickmacross**.

■ Getting Here

Monaghan Town is on major routes N2 from Dublin (79 miles/ 127 km); and N54-N2-A3-A27-A3-M1 from Belfast (58 miles/ 93 km). It is 132 miles (212 km) from Galway and 216 miles (348 km) from Cork.

The **bus station** in town is at ☎ (047) 82377. The nearest **train station** is in Newry, the nearest **airport** is Belfast City, and the nearest **seaport** is Belfast.

■ Tourist Information

Fáilte Ireland Tourist Office, Market House, Monaghan, open March-October. ☎ (047) 81122.

TRACING YOUR ANCESTORS

Monaghan Ancestry, 6 Tully, Monaghan Town, is the official family research center for the county. ☎ (087) 6310360; theomcmahon@eircom.net.

■ Sightseeing

Monaghan Town

 Monaghan Town is in the north-central area of the county. It was built near a crannóg (lake-dwelling) in early Christian times, but what you see today really began at the time of the Plantations around 1613 (see page 14), when it became a thriving center for the linen industry and also for lace-making. Most of the planters were Calvinists from Scotland, and they built the town around three squares, called the Diamond, Church Square, and Market Square. Around the Diamond some fine Classical and Regency buildings survive, including the Market House, now housing the Tourist Office, and the Courthouse. What you notice first, however, is the Rossmore Memorial, an enormous and flamboyant Victorian drinking fountain. In Church Square, appropriately, there's a Regency Gothic church.

There's a town trail map available from the Tourist Office.

The County Monaghan Museum is on Hill Street, and its collection is a good place to start if you want to learn about the area's past. The museum won a prestigious European award, so is worth at least a brief visit. ☎ (047) 82928; comuseum@monaghancoco.ie.

The St. Louis Convent Heritage Centre links the story of the order with Irish, European and world history and shows its relevance in the immediate area since the time of the Great Famine of 1845. In its grounds is the crannóg where the town began. ☎ (047) 83529.

Today the town is a center for coarse fishing. There are lots of pubs where visitors can enjoy traditional and other styles of music, and there's an annual **Rhythm and Blues Festival** in September. **The Garage Theatre** hosts touring as well as locally produced shows. ☎ (047) 81597; garagetheatre@eircom.net.

Explore the County

Only a little part of the county is north of Monaghan Town, most of it in the flood plain of the River Blackwater with, to the west, the moorland of Slieve Beagh. It's a quiet and unspoiled area of gentle countryside, with ancient forests, and lots of lakes.

Castle Leslie

The picturesque village of Glaslough, six miles (9.7 km) northeast of Monaghan on the N12/R185, is at the gates of Castle Leslie. It is available for special functions. The castle came to international attention when the former Beatle Paul McCartney chose it as the venue for his second wedding in 2002.

The castle has been home to the Leslie family since 1664 and its setting overlooking Glaslough Lake is absolutely beautiful. The 1,000-acre estate has three lakes, rolling parkland and ancient woodland, and is open for the public to enjoy. ☎ (047) 88109; ultan@castle-leslie.ie; www.castleleslie.com.

Castleblaney

Castleblaney is 15 miles (24 km) southeast of Monaghan on the N2, close to the border with Co. Armagh. It's on a narrow strip of land at the head of Lough Muckno, the county's largest stretch of water, covering about 900 acres.

The town was founded on the site of an early Christian church in an area controlled by the Hanratty chieftains. It takes its name from the Blaney family who built it. Its Courthouse, Church and Market House date from the late 18th and early 19th centuries.

These days it's one of the main angling centers in the county, and there are lots of pubs and places to eat, as well as places to stay. If you're looking for an indoor activity, there's a 10-pin bowling complex in town. ☎ (042) 974-9944.

Inniskeen

Take the N53 south from Castleblaney and you come to Inniskeen, birthplace of the late poet and novelist Patrick Kavanagh in 1904. The annual Patrick Kavanagh weekend takes place here in November.

The **Rural and Literary Resource Centre** bearing his name is in the church, and in it you can find out not just about him, but also about the area's history, geology and mythology. Kavanaugh is buried in the churchyard. ☎ (042) 937-8560; infoatpkc@eircom.ie.

There are signposts in town to places in the locality associated with the writer's work, and a round tower and a Norman motte overlook the village. Nearby is the **Fane River Park**, where you can take a stroll, and the river is known for its salmon.

Carrickmacross

South of Inniskeen is Carrickmacross, on the N2. If you've heard of it, that's most likely because of the lace that bears its name. It's an attractive and busy market town that grew up around a castle built by the Earl of Essex in 1630.

The St. Louis nuns, whose convent stands on the site of the castle, were largely responsible for reviving the tradition of lace-making in the area. Nowadays the **Carrickmacross Lace Co-operative** continues to keep the tradition going, and you can buy locally made lace at the **Gallery**

The Northwest

Centre and watch demonstrations by prior arrangement. ☎ (042) 966 2506.

In the **Roman Catholic Church** dating from 1866 there are 10 marvellous stained glass windows designed by Harry Clarke in 1925. The 18th-century **St. Finbarr's Church of Ireland** has a magnificent steeple, and the **Courthouse** is also worth a look.

Ballybay

North of Carrickmacross is Ballybay, beside Lough Major. It used to be involved in the linen industry, and is now an angling center. There are pleasant forest walks in the **Billy Fox Memorial Park** just outside town on the road to Cootehill. John Robert Gregg (1868-1948), who invented the form of shorthand bearing his name when he was 20, was born at Rockcorry nearby.

Clones

If you continue on from here, you pass through Newbliss and reach Clones (pronounced clone-ez), on the N54, 11 miles (18 km) southwest of Monaghan, where there's a **high cross** (see page 112) dating from the ninth or 10th century. This is the birthplace of the award-winning writer Patrick McCabe, whose novel *The Butcher Boy* was filmed here in 1998, directed by Neil Jordan. Film buffs will enjoy recognizing locations.

The town also has historic sites worth seeing. The 12th-century **abbey** has an unusual feature – a Celtic cross sculpted in relief on its northern wall – and the sarcophagus of St. Tiernach, an abbot here in the sixth century, is beside the round tower. Near the town there are the ruins of a **motte and bailey fort**.

Locally made lace is exhibited and sold at the **Ulster Canal Store**. You can also hire bikes, get visitor information or relax over a snack. ☎ (047) 51718.

Just outside Clones is **Scotshouse**, where you can see a portion of the ancient border, the Black Pig's Dyke (see page 186).

■ Adventures on Foot

Signposted Walks

In the Sliabh Beagh area at Knockatallon there are a number of signposted walks, some of them crossing the border into neighboring counties.

Among them is the **Rock Walk**, a circular walk along roadways through the unspoiled countryside and upland blanket bog. The

Eshcloghfin Walk winds through forestry tracks between 600 and 1,000 feet (183-328 m) above sea level, with breathtaking views. Along the **Trá Walk** (on a clear day) you can see 14 counties. The **Stramacilroy Walk** is a short but invigorating circular route, passing through hilly farmland and lovely countryside.

Walking brochures are available both for the local walks, and for the way-marked walks throughout the Sliabh Beagh Region in Ulster. Contact **Sliabh Beagh Rural Tourism Centre**. ☎ (047) 89014; Knockatallon@ eircom.net; www.knockatallon.com.

There's also a waymarked long-distance route being developed, the **Monaghan Way**, from Inniskeen to Glaslough. Check its progress by asking at tourist offices.

Forest Parks

The Rossmore Forest Park, near Monaghan Town, is the former estate of Robert Cunningham, who was a Member of the British Parliament from 1769-96. Walks take in a wedge tomb and a mausoleum, trees include yews and giant redwoods, there are lakes and rivers, and it's a fine habitat for wildlife. ☎ (047) 89915.

The Hollywood Forest Park is less than five miles (eight km) from Monaghan, off the Balloon-to-Scotstown road. There are nature walks, fishing stands, and you can go boating there. ☎ (047) 81968.

∎ Adventures on Wheels

The Kingfisher Cycle Trail covers 229 miles (370 km), taking you through Fermanagh, Leitrim, Cavan, Donegal and Monaghan. It was developed as a cross-border project, which involved local communities, tourism interests and agencies of the State. It has been designed in the shape of a figure eight so you can follow it in sections or as a whole.

The trail is fairly flat and travels through gentle hills, passing rivers, lakes, and places of historic interest. You ride along the Shannon-Erne Waterway and near the source of the River Shannon.

Further information from **Monaghan Tourism** or from the **Tourist Information Centre** in Enniskillen. In the North, ☎ (028) 6632-0121.

Bike Rental

- ∎ **McQuaid Cycle Hire**, Glaslough. ☎ (047) 88108.
- ∎ **Snipe Cycle Hire**, Clones. ☎ (047) 52125.

The Northwest

Rally

At the **Rally School of Ireland** at Scotstown, northwest of Monaghan Town, novice and advanced drivers can enjoy a circuit over mixed terrain. ☎ (047) 89098; info@rallyschoolireland.com.

■ Adventures on Water & Land

Overlooking Lough Muckno is **Hope Castle**, named after Henry Hope, who owned one of the largest uncut diamonds ever and who bought the estate in 1870. Nowadays the estate is the **Lough Muckno Leisure Park**. Activities include pony-trekking, forest walks, orienteering, biking, and watersports. There's a nine-hole golf course, fishing stands, and a bar and restaurant. ☎ (042) 974-6356.

There's a **Water Ski Centre** on Muckno Lake. ☎ (042) 974-0752.

At the **Tanagh Outdoor Recreation Centre**, Dartrey Forest, Rockcorry, south of Monaghan, you can go kayaking, canoeing, abseiling, and pony trekking. ☎ (049) 555-2988; tanagh@eircom.net.

Fishing

 Monaghan has plenty of rivers, lakes and streams, where coarse anglers will be delighted with the stocks of bream, roach, pike, eel, tench, rudd and perch. Game anglers are attracted by salmon and by wild, brown and rainbow trout. There are centers at Carrickmacross, Ballybay, Castleblaney, along the River Blackwater, and around Clones and Monaghan town, where visitors will get all the assistance and equipment needed.

Maps and other advice are also available from tourist offices, and from the **Eastern Regional Fisheries Board**, ☎ (01) 837-9209; www.erfb.ie, and the **Northern Regional Fisheries Board**, ☎ (049) 974-9944.

> *See pages 71-74 for details on angling in Ireland, regulations and best times to fish.*

Horseback Riding

 Day rates are available at the **Greystone Equestrian Centre**, Glaslough, in the Castle Leslie Estate. ☎ (047) 88100; gec@eircom.net.

There's also a **School of Equitation** at Carrickmacross. ☎ (042) 966-1017; jcmxequi@gofree.indigo.ie.

Golf

Outside Monaghan Town is the **Rossmore Club**, close to the Forest Park of the same name. ☎ (047) 81316.

Near Carrickmacross there are two 18-hole courses:

■ **Nuremore Hotel and Country Club**. ☎ (042) 966-1438; nuremore@eircom.net.

■ **The Mannan Castle Club**, off the Carrickmacross-to-Castleblaney road. ☎ (042) 966-3308; mannancastlegc@eircom. net.

There are also **nine-hole courses** at **Clones**, ☎ (047) 56017, and at the very scenic **Castleblaney Golf Course** at Lough Muckno. ☎ (042) 974-9485; rayker@eircom.net.

There are **driving ranges** at Inniskeen, ☎ (042) 937-8425, and in Monaghan Town, ☎ (047) 84909.

If you enjoy **pitch-and-putt** there are a number of courses.

■ **Monaghan Valley Pitch-and-Putt**. ☎ (047) 84928.

■ **Inniskeen**. ☎ (042) 937-8458.

■ **Rowan Springs**, Castleblayney. ☎ (042) 974-0096.

■ **Malones**, Castleblaney. ☎ (042) 974-0613.

■ **Lakeview**, Carrickmacross. ☎ (042) 966 4269.

■ Where to Stay

A very special place is **Hilton Park**, near Clones, which has belonged to the Madden family since 1734. It is part of the Hidden Ireland Group (see page 60), and can be rented from October to March exclusively, or you can stay there overnight or longer during the rest of the year.

There are only six bedrooms, so it's always private. The house is in its own 500-acre wooded estate, with garden

HOTEL PRICE CHART	
Price per person, per night, with two sharing, including breakfast.	
$	Under US $50
$$	US $50-$100
$$$	US $101-$175
$$$$	US $176-$200
$$$$$	Over US $200

and lake. Food is home-grown or local, imaginatively prepared. $$$, with discounts for stays of two nights or longer, as well as special weekend deals. ☎ (047) 56007; jm@hilton.park.ie; www.hiltonpark.ie.

☆☆☆☆ **The Nuremore Hotel and Country Club**, Carrickmacross, has its own 18-hole golf course, tennis courts, and leisure center with pool

The Northwest

and other facilities. There's a choice of rooms and demi-suites. Rates from $$-$$$. ☎ (042) 966-1438; nuremore@eircom.net; www.nuremore-hotel. ie.

☆☆☆ **Glencarn Hotel and Leisure Center** is at Castleblaney on the main road between Dublin and the north-west and beside Lough Muckno Forest Park. It has 27 bedrooms, a restaurant and its **Temple Bar** offers live music and hosts a nightclub at weekends. Rates from $$. ☎ (042) 974-6666; fax 974-6521.

☆☆☆☆ **Hillgrove Hotel** on Old Armagh Road in Monaghan Town is a modern hotel that was refurbished and upgraded in recent years. It makes the ideal base for visitors exploring this part of the country and has 44 bedrooms, which range from twins and doubles to executive suites complete with Jacuzzi baths. Its **Cavendish Restaurant**, which overlooks the bustling town, offers a great choice of food in a relaxed atmosphere, together with an extensive wine list. It's open for breakfast, carvery lunch or a full à la carte selection, and at dinner there's also an excellent choice. You can also enjoy morning coffee and afternoon snacks in the **Dartrey Bar**, where on weekends there is musical entertainment. Alternatively, the **Lathlurcan Lounge** is the place to go for a quiet drink or just to relax. Rates from $$. ☎ (047) 81288; fax 84951; hillgrove-sales@quinn-hotels.com; www.quinnhotels.com.

A Riding Vacation

On the Castle Leslie estate, but separately run, is the **Greystones Equestrian Centre**, which has a great variety of programs, catering for all levels of rider. They all include staying in the Hunting Lodge, a large Victorian house on the estate.

Accommodation is comfortable country-house style, with all bedrooms centrally heated. Guests dine in the **Hunting Lodge Restaurant**, also open to non-residents, where the menu lists fresh local produce, home-made soups, fresh salmon, steaks, lamb, and home-made desserts and ice creams. Vegetarian and special diets can be accommodated. ☎ (047) 88100; fax 88330; gec@eircom.net; www.greystones-ireland.com.

Rental Properties

☆☆☆ **Sliabh Beagh Mountain Lodges**, Scotstown, are on the outskirts of the village of Knockatallon, just over nine miles from Monaghan Town and close to the border with Co. Fermanagh. It's a lovely rural area, surrounded by the Sliabh Mountains and their waymarked trails. The lodges are made up of four apartments that sleep four or five, and have been tastefully designed using lots of wood and stone. They have a courtyard and landscaped garden with a barbecue. ☎ (047) 89997; fax 89926; mullen@eircom.net. Guests can enjoy the amenities at the **Sliabh Beagh Tourism Centre** in the village as well. ☎ (047) 89014; knockatallon@eircom.net; www. knockatallon.com.

☆☆☆ Overlooking its own private lake is **Lisanisk House**, within walking distance of Carrickmacross. It has two apartments, which sleep eight, and guests are offered the use of boats free. ☎ (042) 966-1035; rosaleenmcmahon@eircom.net.

■ Where to Eat

 Castle Leslie at Glaslough is open for dinner on weekends. Its award-winning chef prepares wonderful food, and it has an à la carte menu, as well as a full vegetarian menu, plus a good wine list. Diners can relax over a drink in the elegant and historic drawing room afterwards. Booking is advised. ☎ (047) 88109.

Tommies Restaurant on Glaslough Street, Monaghan, is a good place to stop any time, as it's open from 9 am to 8 pm every day of the week. It's on the town's main street, and is popular with travelers as well as locals. It serves breakfast, traditional dishes, and caters well for vegetarians. ☎ (047) 81772.

McNello's Bar and Lounge is in the village of Inniskeen, the birthplace of poet Patrick Kavanagh, who used to spend some of his time in the pub, and it's decorated in keeping with the atmosphere of the area. It won an award as one of Ireland's Pubs of Distinction in 2000. McNello's serves good bar food. ☎ (042) 937-8355.

The Squealing Pig Bar and its **Mullan Mills Restaurant** is in The Diamong in the center of Monaghan Town. Bar food is available from noon to 3 pm, Monday to Friday. The restaurant is open from 5-10:30 p,m Monday to Saturday, and on Sundays from 4 pm. Its menu includes steaks and traditional Irish food. ☎ (047) 84562; fax 71976.

■ Further Information

■ www.irelandnorthwest.ie.

The Northwest

Carrick-a-Rede Rope Bridge (see page 476)

Northern Ireland

Although covering only 5,500 square miles (14,300 square km), Northern Ireland has a fascinating variety of landscapes. It's divided into areas by the Tourist Board that correspond roughly to the Six Counties that make up the North: the drama of the Causeway Coast and its inland Glens; Derry City and County Londonderry; the Sperrins mountains and surrounding moors, taking in County Tyrone and parts of

Londonderry; the Kingdoms of Down; the city of Armagh and its county; and the Fermanagh-Lakeland region. The capital, Belfast, is on the border between County Antrim and County Down.

While essentially rural, there are lots of towns and villages dotted around Northern Ireland's lakes and hills, as well as five cities to explore. Queen Elizabeth of England marked her Golden Jubilee in 2002 by conferring city status on **Lisburn** and **Newry**, so they have joined the ancient cathedral cities of **Belfast**, **Derry** and **Armagh**.

CURRENCY

The Republic of Ireland was one of the EU Member States that adopted the single currency of the European Economic and Monetary Union (EMU) in 1999. The United Kingdom did not, so Northern Ireland, which is part of the UK, remains a Sterling area. Don't forget to change some of your money if crossing the border. See page 39 for details.

Belfast

Belfast, the capital of Northern Ireland, is on the River Lagan in the southeastern corner of County Antrim, with a small portion of the city edging into County Down. About a third of the population of Northern Ireland – about half a million people – live here.

Its setting is very attractive, nestling in a semicircle of hills, where the River Lagan enters Belfast Lough. The city got its name from Beile Feirst – "the mouth of the sandy ford" – and was founded in 1177 when the Anglo-Normans built a castle here. It began to really expand in the 17th century with the development of the local linen industry.

The Industrial Revolution of the early 19th century heralded the city's boom time, with industries including rope making and shipbuilding, as well as linen, leading to its doubling in size each decade. The great industrialists and entrepreneurs have left their mark, with the magnificent buildings of red brick and sandstone you see today. It's worth taking a look inside the beautifully carved stone and ironwork of the Victorian **St. George's Market** near the waterfront, which has been restored.

Civil unrest from 1969 on meant stagnation until the end of the 20th century, but an enormous amount of building has been going on since the Peace Process began, so that when you visit these days the city's skyline seems dominated by cranes.

If all you know about Belfast are the images in newspapers and television during the 30 years of The Troubles, then you will be as surprised and delighted as I was when you visit. It's a lively and friendly city, with historic buildings standing side-by-side with modern creations, among them the circular Waterfront Hall, close to the 19th century Harbor Office and Custom House.

■ Getting Here & Getting Around

From the Airports

There are two airports: **Belfast City Airport**, three miles (4.8 km) east of the city, ☎ (028) 9093-9093, www.belfastcityairport. com, and **Belfast International**, ☎ (028) 9442-2888, www. belfastairport.com, 19 miles (30 km) west of the city.

By Rail

A shuttle bus service operates between the City Airport Terminal and the adjacent rail stop at Sydenham, which has a twice-hourly rail service (6 am-6 pm) Monday-Friday to Central and Victoria Street Stations. (Service is hourly after 6 pm and on Saturdays and Sundays.)

Approximate fare from City Airport to Central Station is £1.05. You can connect at Central Station with the rail network in Northern Ireland and on to the Irish Republic.

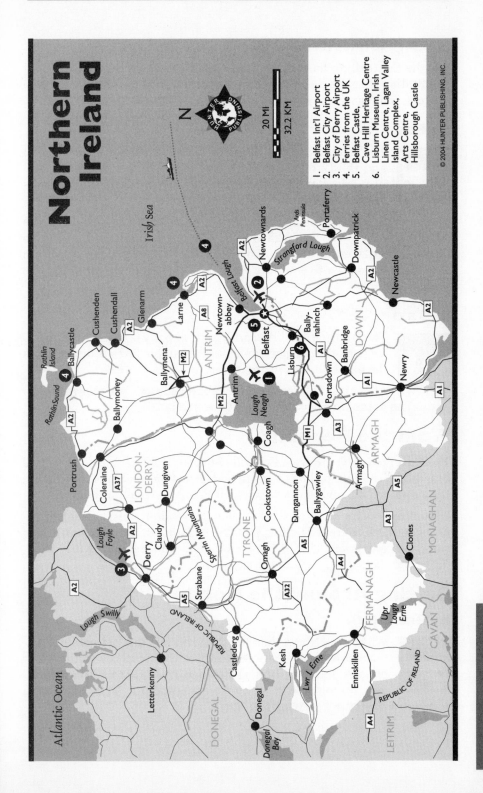

Northern Ireland

1. Belfast Int'l Airport
2. Belfast City Airport
3. City of Derry Airport
4. Ferries from the UK
5. Belfast Castle,
   Cave Hill Heritage Centre
6. Lisburn Museum, Irish
   Linen Centre, Lagan Valley
   Island Complex,
   Arts Centre,
   Hillsborough Castle

© 2004 HUNTER PUBLISHING, INC.

20 MI

32.2 KM

N

HUNTER PUBLISHING

Irish Sea

Atlantic Ocean

Rathlin Island
Rathlin Sound
Ballycastle
Cushenden
Cushendall
Glenarm
Larne
Newtown-abbey
Newtownards
Ards Peninsula
Portaferry
Strangford Lough
Downpatrick
Newcastle

Ballymoney
Ballymena
Antrim
Belfast
Ballynahinch
Banbridge
Newry

Portrush
Coleraine
Dungiven
Lough Neagh
Coagh
Cookstown
Lisburn
Portadown
Armagh
Clones

Derry
Claudy
Sperrin Mountains
Strabane
Omagh
Dungannon
Ballygawley

Lough Foyle
Lough Swilly
Letterkenny

Castlederg
Kesh
Enniskillen
Lwr L. Erne
Upr Lough Erne

Donegal
Donegal Bay

Belfast Lough

ANTRIM
LONDON-DERRY
TYRONE
DOWN
ARMAGH
FERMANAGH
MONAGHAN
CAVAN
LEITRIM
DONEGAL

REPUBLIC OF IRELAND

A2, A21, A8, M2, A37, A2, A5, A32, A4, A5, A3, A1, A2

Northern Ireland

Making Connections

Use the CentraLink bus to travel between the Europa Bus Centre, Central Station, Laganside and the city center. It's free to rail and bus passengers, Monday-Friday.

By Bus

 The **Airbus** service operates between Belfast International and the Europa Bus Centre, Glengall Street, every 30 minutes, Monday to Saturday, and at 30- or 60-minute intervals on Sunday, from 5:45 am to 11:20 pm.

There is a direct **citybus** link from the City Airport to the Europa Centre every 40 minutes between 6:25 am and 9:50 pm. In addition, Citybus No 21 runs every 20 minutes from Sydenham, the **rail stop** at the airport, to City Hall. It's only a five-minute walk from the air terminal to the bus stop.

By Taxi

 The International Airport Taxi Company is the official operator from that airport, and a list of sample fares is displayed in the exit hall. Approximate fare to Belfast is £23.

At Belfast City Airport only approved taxis are allowed to operate. The approximate cost to the city center is £6.

From the Republic

The **Enterprise Train** from Connolly Station, Dublin, costs around €40 round-trip, runs eight times a day in both directions and takes two hours. It's a comfortable and fast way to reach Belfast – ideal for a daytrip.

Ulsterbus covers all of Northern Ireland outside Belfast, including express services to/from Dublin. ☎ (028) 9033-3000. **Bus Éireann** also runs an Expressway service between Dublin and Belfast. ☎ (01) 8366-6111 from the North. www.buseireann.ie.

Getting Around the North

By Bus & Rail

 Within the North there's a good rail and bus network, including express buses between towns without rail connections. For all bus and rail timetable inquiries, contact **Translink**, ☎ (028) 9066-6630 or www.translink.co.uk. They also run a number of daytours exploring the North.

By Road

 Main roads radiating from Belfast are the M1, which runs southwest to Lisburn and then westwards to just south of Dungannon; and the M2, which goes through Templepatrick northwest of the city and on to Antrim.

North of the city, the A2 brings you along by the coast from Derry, passing the port of Larne. East of the city the A2 takes you along Belfast Lough to Bangor and then follows the coast southwards to Portaferry and Strangford.

To travel to Dublin you take the M1 to Lisburn, then the A1 to Newry and on to the border with the Republic, where the A1 continues to Dublin.

Getting Around Belfast

By Bus

 Citybus (red) serves most areas – get tickets from the kiosk in Donegall Square West, Monday-Friday, 8 am to 5:30 pm, and from some newsagents. **Ulsterbus** (blue) serves some suburbs. And **Citystopper buses** (either red or blue) run along the Falls and Lisburn roads.

By Taxi

 Call ☎ 1-800-TAXI-CAB to connect with local taxi companies at no extra charge. A system of shared black taxis developed in West Belfast during the Troubles when official bus services withdrew during riots. Known as the **People's Taxis**, they operate along fixed routes for a pound a trip. They leave the city center from a depot on the corner of Castle and King streets. You can hail them en route just as you would any other taxi and, if there's room for you, they will stop.

 Remember, all over Northern Ireland, check www. translink.com with all public transport inquiries.

■ Tourist Information

 Before exploring, call the **Belfast Welcome Centre** at 47 Donegall Place, opposite City Hall, and pick up a free map of the city and lots of other free brochures covering Northern Ireland. The friendly staff will help with any queries and you can also change money and book accommodations here. ☎ (028) 9024-6609; fax 9031-2424; belfastwelcomecentre@nitic.net; www.gotobelfast.com or www.discovernorthernireland.com.

Northern Ireland

■ Sightseeing

City Center

Head first for **Belfast City Hall**. The building, of Portland stone in Classical Renaissance style, dominates the city center. It has a cool marble interior, and you can take a free 45-minute tour and hear about the city's history. Tours: June-September, Monday-Friday, 11 am, 2 pm, 3 pm; Saturday, 2:30 pm; October-May, Monday-Friday, 11 am and 2:30 pm; Saturday, 2:30 pm. ☎ (028) 9027-0456; civicbuildings@belfastcity.gov.uk; www.belfastcity.gov.uk.

One of my favorite places in the entire country is **The Linen Hall Library**, 17 Donegall Square North, with its main entrance around the corner on Fountain Street.

The library was founded in 1788, and has survived even a bombing. It's an absolute delight, a cultural center with exhibitions and other events, as well as a library. Of special interest is its Political Collection, which is unique, comprising some 80,000-plus publications documenting political life here since 1966. Other items in the collection include baby bibs and tiny letters smuggled out of Long Kesh prison in body orifices.

The Linen Hall also has a huge number of early printed books, a Theatre and Performing Arts Archive, and a Genealogy and Heraldry collection. There's a coffee shop on its second floor and a gift shop.

Admission is free, but The Linen Hall needs money, so if you can give them a donation, please do, or become a member and so contribute to its invaluable ongoing work. Open Monday-Friday, 9:30-5:30, Saturday until 4 pm. Free tours (one hour) June-August, Mondays and Fridays at

Above: Gap of Dunloe, Kerry (see page 279)

Below: Blasket Islands, from Mount Eagle, Dingle Peninsula, Kerry (see page 283)

Above: Dromoland Castle Hotel, Newmarket on Fergus, Clare (see pages 316-17)

Below: Ennis Town, Clare (see page 300)

Above: Bunratty Castle, Durty Nelly's Pub, Clare (see page 303)

Below: Adare Manor Hotel, Limerick (see page 334)

Above: Kylemore Abbey, Galway (Ireland West Tourism - see page 349)

Below: Atlantic Drive, Achill Island (Mayo Tourism - see pages 363-64)

Above: Ashford Castle, Cong, now a hotel (Mayo Tourism - see pages 365, 368)

Below: Lacken Bay, near Kilcummin, North Mayo (Mayo Tourism)

Above: Frybrook House, Roscommon (Ireland West Tourism - see page 374)

Below: Rhaes Wood, Antrim, Loughshore Trail, National Cycle Route 94
(Steven Patterson, SUSTRANS - see page 511)

Antrim Coast, County Antrim (see page 467)

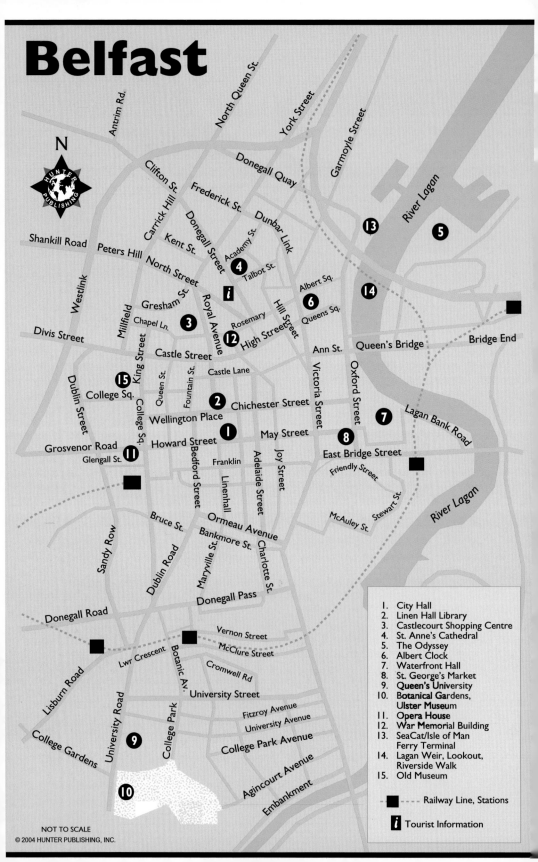

Belfast

N

Antrim Rd.

North Queen St.

York Street

Garmoyle Street

River Lagan

Donegall Quay

Clifton St.

Frederick St.

Dunbar Link

Academy St.

Talbot St.

Shankill Road

Peters Hill

North Street

Carrick Hill

Kent St.

Donegall Street

Westlink

Gresham St.

Royal Avenue

Rosemary

Albert Sq.

Hill Street

High Street

Queens Sq.

Chapel Ln.

Millfield

Divis Street

Castle Street

Ann St.

Queen's Bridge

Bridge End

Queen St.

Fountain St.

Castle Lane

Victoria Street

Oxford Street

Lagan Bank Road

College Sq.

King Street

Wellington Place

Chichester Street

Dublin Street

College Sq.

Howard Street

May Street

East Bridge Street

River Lagan

Grosvenor Road

Glengall St.

Franklin

Joy Street

Friendly Street

Bedford Street

Adelaide Street

McAuley St.

Stewart St.

Sandy Row

Bruce St.

Linenhall

Ormeau Avenue

Bankmore St.

Maryville St.

Dublin Road

Charlotte St.

Donegall Pass

Donegall Road

Vernon Street

McClure Street

Lwr Crescent

Botanic Av.

Cromwell Rd

Lisburn Road

University Street

University Road

Fitzroy Avenue

University Avenue

College Park

College Park Avenue

College Gardens

Agincourt Avenue

Embankment

1. City Hall
2. Linen Hall Library
3. Castlecourt Shopping Centre
4. St. Anne's Cathedral
5. The Odyssey
6. Albert Clock
7. Waterfront Hall
8. St. George's Market
9. Queen's University
10. Botanical Gardens,
    Ulster Museum
11. Opera House
12. War Memorial Building
13. SeaCat/Isle of Man
    Ferry Terminal
14. Lagan Weir, Lookout,
    Riverside Walk
15. Old Museum

■ - - - Railway Line, Stations

i Tourist Information

NOT TO SCALE
© 2004 HUNTER PUBLISHING, INC.

2:30 pm. You must pre-book in person or by phone. ☎ (028) 9032-1707; fax 9043-8586; info@linenhall.com; www.linenhall.com.

Another fascinating place to visit is the permanent exhibition, **Northern Ireland in the Second World War**, housed on the ground floor of the War Memorial Building, at 9 Waring Street, off Royal Avenue, on one of the sites devastated by the Blitz. More than 300,000 American and other Allied servicemen were based in towns and villages around the North during the war, so visitors from overseas will find it of particular interest. What's especially charming is the simplicity of the displays, and the custodian who loves talking to visitors. Open Monday-Friday, 9 am to 5 pm, admission free. ☎ (028) 9032-0392.

From Waring Street head to the **Lagan Weir and Lookout**. There are a number of exhibits that explain how the Weir, or dam, works, and that also cover the city's history. There are great views from the walkways. Open daily. ☎ (028) 9031-5444; lookout@laganside.com; www.laganside. com.

The **riverside walk** along the River Lagan is very pleasant. A port since the 12th century, Belfast's waterside is a vital part of the city's personality. Pay a visit to the attractive **Waterfront Hall**, which has a bar/restaurant, and you can find out about entertainment during your stay.

Away from City Center

Ulster Museum & Botanic Gardens

The **Ulster Museum** in the Botanic Gardens, near Queen's University, has miles of galleries and exhibitions. Learn about the city's industrial past in Made in Belfast; other permanent exhibitions are equally interesting and give you some background on the North's political unrest, and how people lived in past times. The museum's collection of Irish art and its display of treasures from the Spanish Armada shouldn't be missed either, so allow a couple of hours for a visit. There are also temporary exhibitions, and a series of events and lectures. To get to the museum and gardens, take a taxi or a 69, 70 or 71 bus from outside City Hall. Or you can walk from the City Center/City Hall area. Admission free. Open Monday-Friday, 10 am to 5 pm, Saturday, 1-5 pm, Sunday, 2-5 pm. ☎ (028) 9038-3000; www.ulstermuseum.org.uk.

The surrounding **Botanic Gardens** are absolutely wonderful, with herbaceous borders, a rose garden and **Palm House**, and lots of space where you can relax. If your time is limited, make sure you visit the **Tropical Ravine**, with its lily pond and amazing collection of bamboos, palms, all sorts of climbers and tree ferns. Gardens always open. The Palm House and Ravine are open April-September, Monday-Friday from 10 am to 5 pm, Saturday, Sunday, Public Holidays, 2-5 pm; October-March, they

close at 4 pm. Note that they're also closed at lunchtime. Admission free.
☎ (028) 9032-4902.

Political Murals

Most of the world-famous icons of the Troubles, a series of political murals, can be seen in West Belfast, both in the Shankill and around the Falls Road. If you don't take an organized tour, the best thing to do first is to head to where you can get some information about the two areas. At 216 Falls Road is **Cultúrlann**, where you can find out about tours of the nationalist area, including its historic cemeteries. There is an informative brochure available listing all the tours, and the arts center has a program of events too. ☎ (028) 9096-4188; failte@culturlann.org.

Before exploring the Shankill area, head for **Fernhill House** in Glencairn Park, which belonged to the Cunninghams, a merchant family prominent in the Orange Order and against Home Rule. At Fernhill is the **People's Museum**, which explores the history of the Greater Shankill since the 19th century, and has the largest collection of Orange memorabilia in the world. Open Monday-Saturday, 10 am-4 pm, Sundays, 1-4 pm. ☎ (028) 9071-5599. Ask for the map-leaflet, which gives a history of the Shankill. James Buchanan, 15th US President (1857-61), is featured on a mural, which is part of the Ulster-Scots tour.

You'll also see the famous Peace Walls, huge 16- to 18-foot-tall barriers, erected to keep neighbors apart. They run down the interfaces where Catholic areas meet Protestant areas.

FOR MUSIC FANS

Fans of **Van Morrison** may like to gaze at his birthplace. Take the Newtownards Road (A20) east of the city and, after a mile, turn right onto Beersbridge Road. The ninth turn on the left is Hyndford Street, and on number 125 there's a plaque.

Belfast Castle & Cave Hill

Three miles north of the city, Belfast Castle overlooks the city from Cave Hill Country Park; you can get there by Citybus 45-51. Cave Hill is the highest point on the hills surrounding the city. The Castle was built in Scottish baronial style in 1870 for the 3rd Marquis of Donegall and, with its gardens, was given to the city in 1934. The house was refurbished in the 1980s. Open daily, admission free. There are free guided tours in summer; call to check times ☎ (028) 9077-6925. There's an **Antique Shop** in the cellars with a fascinating selection of items that would make great souvenirs or gifts. Open Monday-Saturday, noon to 10 pm, Sunday until 5 pm.

Guided Tours

One of the easiest ways of getting to know the city, especially if your stay is short, is to take a bus tour.

Citybus Tours leave from Castle Place on the corner of Castle Street beside the main Post Office. They are operated by Translink, the main transport company, and there's a choice of tours from May to September. ☎ (028) 9066-6630 or www.translink.co.uk.

The Belfast City Tour (1½ hours) runs Monday-Saturday at 11 am. It takes in many of the main sites, including Stormont, Belfast City Hall, the Albert Clock, Queen's University, the Grand Opera House, and the Botanic Gardens. You can also take a *Titanic* **Tour**, on Wednesdays at 11 am and Sundays at 2:30 pm (1½ hours), which shows you where the ill-fated liner was built. ☎ (028) 9066-6630; www.translink.co.uk.

The Belfast Living History Tour (1½ hours) is run by Belfast City Sightseeing on open-top buses. Sites include those associated with the city's industrial achievements, such as the shipyard where the *Titanic* was built, and its turbulent political past. It gives you a chance to see the many wall murals, including those on the Falls and Shankill roads. Monday-Saturday, 2:30 pm. ☎/fax (028) 9062-6888; www.city-sightseeing.com.

Alternatively, go for a more intimate tour in a black taxi with **All Ireland Historical Tours**. They also offer tours farther afield, including the **North Antrim Coast**, and run a service to and from both airports. ☎ (028) 9030-1832; taxitour@netscapeonline.com; www.allirelandtours.com; www.belfastcityblacktaxitours.com.

Take a Tour by Bike

 A novel way to discover Belfast is to take a guided tour by bike. **Life Cycles**, 36-7 Smithfield Market, runs self-guided and guided tours of Belfast and Antrim. ☎ (028) 9043-9959; info@lifecycles.co.uk; www.lifecycles.co.uk.

Irish Cycle Tours, 27 Belvoir View Park, runs city tours in the evenings and on weekends, as well as tours of Antrim and Fermanagh. ☎ (028) 9064-2222; fax 9064-0405; bgt@btinternet.com; www.irishcycletours.com.

Lisburn Area

Lisburn, recently designated a city, is 10 miles (16 km) southwest of Belfast, off the M1 motorway. Sadly, in 1707 a fire destroyed most of the older buildings and its castle. It was, however, a very important linen town from the late 17th century on, and the history of that industry is well told in the **Irish Linen Centre** and **Lisburn Museum** which are housed in the 18th-century Assembly Rooms in the Market Square. You can even try a bit of scutching or spinning yourself. Open Monday-Saturday,

9:30 am-5 pm. ☎ (028) 9266-3377; www.lisburn.gov.uk. There's also a shop and café, so it's a good place for a stop before further exploration. On Saturdays from 10 am-4 pm there's a food market in the square.

There's been a lot of urban regeneration in recent years and the city has facilities for plenty of activities, including the oldest cricket club in the North in Wallace Park. ☎ (028) 662407; info@lisburncricketclub.com.

On an island in the river is the new **Lagan Valley Island Complex**, from where you get lovely views of the Regional Park, which is very popular with walkers. The Island Complex is arranged around a central rotunda, and includes a restaurant and **Arts Centre**, which hosts all sorts of events and performances. Check out its program. ☎ (028) 9250-9509; arts.information@iac.lisburn.gov.uk. There's lots of parking on Queen's Road and Gregg Street, and the Island Complex is within easy walking distance of the city center.

In the village of **Hilden**, a mile outside Lisburn, is a **real-ale brewery**, in the courtyard of what was the home of the Barbours, one of the linen manufacturers. Visitors can watch and smell the process and sample the ale, or eat in the **Tap Room Restaurant**. Open Tuesday-Saturday, 10:30 am-4 pm. ☎ (028) 9266-3863; www.hilden.brewery@ukgateway. net.

Just south of Lisburn is **Long Kesh Prison**, notorious for its H-block cells, where in 1981 Bobby Sands MP and nine other Republican prisoners died on hunger strike and where, in 1998, Billy Wright, leader of the Loyalist Volunteer Force, was shot dead, setting off a series of murders in retaliation. You can see the prison from the M1.

Hillsborough, off the A1, south of Lisburn, and 10 miles (16 km) from Belfast, is one of the most English-looking villages in Northern Ireland. **Hillsborough Castle** (c.1797), which you can see through its magnificent wrought-iron gates, is where US Presidents and British and Irish Prime Ministers have met to discuss the political situation over the years. The very attractive village has a Gothic church, fine Georgian architecture, and many of the terraced buildings along its steep main street house antique and craft shops. There's an International Oyster Festival here in September.

■ Shopping in Belfast

Donegall Place, opposite City Hall, is the center of the shopping area, and parts of it are pedestrian-only, so it's a real pleasure to explore. You'll find chain stores and specialty shops, with lots of pubs, cafés, and restaurants on the streets radiating out from here. **Castle Court** on Royal Avenue is an indoor center with more than 70 shops on two levels. **The Spires Centre** on

Wellington Street is a restored 1905 building with stained glass windows, housing designer fashion and giftware shops. It also has a café on the ground floor.

If you're looking for gifts to take home check out the following:

Halls Linen and Celtic Crafts, Queen's Arcade, Donegall Place, opened in 1850, and stocks a huge range of Irish linen, wool rugs, traditional Aran knitwear, tweed caps, and items like blackthorn sticks and leprechauns, which are only bought by tourists. It's the first left after the Belfast Welcome Centre. ☎ (028) 9032-0446.

Smithfield Market, at the junction of West Street and Winetavern Street opposite Castle Court Shopping Centre, has 28 units selling everything from model soldiers to camping equipment, so is worth a visit.

Smyth's Irish Linens, 65 Royal Avenue, has a wide selection and will also take commissions and send them home for you. ☎ (028) 9024-2232.

The National Trust Gift Shop is on Fountain Street and has a great selection, including Irish knitwear, jewelry, glassware, and stationery. You can also join the Trust in the shop and then visit its sites all over the North free. ☎ (028) 9032-0645.

Away from the city center, **Conway Mill** on Conway Street, just off Falls Road in West Belfast, has locally produced crafts and artistic items for sale, including linen, cards, ceramics, and woodwork, made by artists who have studios in the listed building (it was formerly a flax spinning mill). While you're there, take a guided tour. Open Monday-Friday, 10 am to 4 pm. ☎ (028) 9024-7276; www.conwaymill.org.

Don't forget that many outlets operate acoording to the VAT-free export scheme, so take your passport with you when shopping and ask.

■ Adventures on Foot

 The **Cave Hill Heritage Centre** is in Belfast Castle, and is well worth visiting. Admission free, open Monday-Saturday, 9 am to 10 pm; Sunday, 9 am to 6 pm. Go there before setting off to explore at least part of the 750-acre **Cave Hill Country Park**, which includes Belfast Zoo, the Castle estate, Hazelwood and Bellevue estates to the north, Carr's Glen Linear Park to the west and the former Wallace Estate to the east.

As Cave Hill is 1,182 feet (360 m) above sea level, you get great views of the city, with the Mourne Mountains, Strangford Lough and the Antrim Hills visible in good weather. There are many signs of early settlements, including raths or ringforts, a stone cashel and a crannóg or lake dwelling. Only the lowest of the five caves, which date from the Stone Age, are accessible and there are signs of industry and mining to the south of the

Northern Ireland

Hill. Each type of habitat, from upland meadow to rocky outcrop, woodland and moor, has its own flora and fauna. It's a wonderful area for walking and relaxing.

There are also a number of waymarked walking routes close to the city, including along the **Lagan Valley Regional Park towpath**, also used by cyclists. South of the city, the **Barnett Trail** is very picturesque. Details from Belfast City Council Parks and Amenities section. ☎ (028) 9032-0202.

Colin Glen Forest Park is a mile northwest of Dunmurry, near the M1, and is easy to reach from the city in 15 minutes. It's a wooded river glen, covering 200 acres (80 hectares), with ponds, waterfalls, and grassland, plus a network of paths. There are self-guided waymarked routes – over 3½ miles (4½ km) of paths with differing lengths and difficulties. The main starting point is at the Forest Park Centre, where you can learn more about the park.

The Upper Colin Glen is owned by the National Trust. It is more suited to experienced walkers, and it seems the views make the climb worthwhile. Suitable footwear is advised. ☎ (028) 9061-4115; www.colinglentrust.org.

The **Sir Thomas and Lady Dickson Park**, Upper Malone Road, is on the southern outskirts of the city, and is a pleasant place to relax or walk. It covers 128 acres (50 hectares), with rolling lawns and meadows, mature trees, and roses in season. There's also a Japanese garden and a walled garden.

At **Lisburn**, there's a **river walkway** along the Lagan, with public gardens and the reinstated historic canal. If you're staying for a bit, contact Bill Ervine of the **Lagan Valley Rambling Club** and see can you join in their activities. ☎ (028) 9267-2294.

At **Hillsborough**, 10 miles (16 km) from Belfast, there's a **circular walk**, which takes about an hour, around the lake. It begins near the ruins of the fort built by Colonel Arthur Hill in 1650. There are also **walking tours** – both guided and self-guided; details from the Tourist Information Centre in Hillsborough. ☎ (028) 9268-9773.

■ Adventures on Wheels

There's a network of traffic-free routes for cyclists around the city. The **Lagan Towpath** is one of the most scenic, so is the **Shore Path** to Hazelbank Park and Upper Malone Road and the Shaw's Bridge area. **The Millennium National Cycling Route** is developing about 20 miles (32 km) of cycling pathways from the Whiteabbey area through Belfast to Lisburn. Inquire at Tourist Information, or call the Cycling Officer, Department of Environment Roads Service. ☎ (028) 9025-3000. Bikes can be rented from **Life Cycles**, 35 Smithfield Market. ☎ (028) 9043-9959.

■ Adventure on Water

At the Lagan Weir and Lookout, you can take a trip with the **Lagan Boat Company**, which runs a regular daily service. ☎ (028) 9033-0844; info@laganboatcompany.com; www. laganboatcompany.com.

Fishing

The stretch of the River Lagan from Stranmillis Weir to Shaw's Bridge in Belfast is over five miles (eight km) long, and offers decent coarse fishing, especially in summer. The cities of Belfast and Lisburn are very near Strangford Lough in Co. Down to the east, and Lough Neagh to the west, where there's shore and boat fishing. See chapters on Down, page 534, and the Sperrins, page 512, where there is more information. You can also contact Paddy Prunty at the **Kinnego Marina**, Oxford Island, Craigavon, about Lough Neagh. ☎ (028) 3832-7573.

Regional angling guides are available from the Belfast Welcome Centre and other Tourist Information Centres, or info@nitb.com; www. discovernorthernireland.com/angling.

See pages 71-74 for details on angling in Ireland, regulations and best times to fish.

Permits & Licenses

Game and coarse anglers need a license for each rod plus a permit for game waters from the Department of Culture, Arts and Leisure (DCAL), or from the club or private owners involved. What's ideal for tourists is the Combination Licence/Permit available from DCAL for fishing its waters. ☎ (028) 9025-8861.

For further information about permits and licenses, check at tackle shops where you'll get local knowledge and advice. Outlets in Belfast include:

Shankill Fishing Tackle, 366 Shankill Road. ☎ (028) 9033-0949.

The Village Tackle Shop, 55a Newtownbreda Road. ☎ (028) 9049-1916.

Professional Guides

You might want to engage a professional angling guide, such as:

Flatfield Flyfishing. ☎/fax (028) 6638-8184.

Gillaroo Anglers. ☎/fax (028) 9086-2419.

■ Adventures on Horseback

 The Lagan Valley Equestrian Centre, Upper Malone Road, Dunmurry, Belfast, has indoor facilities and riders can enjoy the local woodland. ☎ (028) 9061-4265.

The Birr House Riding Centre, Craigantlet, Belfast. ☎ (028) 9042-5858.

The Burn Equestrian Club, six miles (10 km) south of Belfast on the A24, offers lessons at all levels, and basic instruction in cross-country and dressage. ☎/fax (028) 9046-2384; www.newrider.com.

The Ballyknock Riding School is at Hillsborough. ☎ (028) 9269-2144.

Riding Vacation

Lime Park Equestrian Centre is seven miles (11 km) west of Lisburn, and easily accessible from Belfast. It runs residential and day camps during summer for all ages, which include trips to beaches and forest parks. Among its facilities are an all-weather ring and three show-jumping arenas. ☎/fax (028) 9262-1139; info@limeparkequestrian.com; www.limeparkequestrian.com.

Horseracing

Down Royal Racecourse, Maze, Lisburn, is just 10 miles (16 km) from Belfast, and hosts 11 race meetings a year. Check local newspapers or ☎ (028) 9262-1256.

■ Golf

There are a number of golf courses in the city suburbs and nearby that welcome visitors, and some will rent clubs, but do phone in advance to check times and details.

Fortwilliam Golf Club is on Cave Hill overlooking Belfast Lough. ☎ (028) 9037-9770.

Malone Golf Club is in the suburbs south of the center, and has two 18-hole courses. ☎ (028) 9061-2758.

Belvoir Park Golf Club is also south of the city in mature parkland. ☎ (028) 9064-1159.

Balmoral Golf Club is on Lisburn Road, and has an 18-hole parkland course. ☎ (028) 9066-7747.

Knock Golf Club at Dundonald has large tree-lined fairways with lots of water hazards. ☎ (028) 9048-3251.

Dunmurry Golf Club has a very attractive setting, beside the Sir Thomas and Lady Dixon Park. ☎ (028) 9061-0834.

Mount Ober Golf Club is an 18-hole course. ☎ (028) 9079-2108.

Rockmount Golf Club, Carryduff, is on 120 acres (48 hectares), incorporating a lake and streams, and has panoramic views. ☎ (028) 9081-2279.

Shandon Park Golf Club also has spectacular views. ☎ (028) 9040-1856.

Colin Valley Golf Course is a nine-hole, open to non-members daily, but doesn't rent clubs. ☎ (028) 9061-4871.

Gilnahirk Golf Club is another nine-hole, a hilltop course with great views of Belfast Lough and the North Down Peninsula. Club rental available. ☎ (028) 9044-8477.

Ormeau Golf Club, a nine-hole parkland course, open to the public, except Tuesdays and Saturdays. ☎ (028) 9064-1069.

Royal Belfast Golf Club is 15 minutes by car from the city at Holywood, on the sloping shores of the North Down Course; it was founded in 1881. ☎ (028) 9042-8165.

The Lisburn Golf Club is on Eglantine Road. ☎ (028) 9267-7216; lisburngolfclub@aol.com.

Golf Tours

Celtic Golf organizes tailor-made programs for golfers from North America, taking in the finest courses, sightseeing, dining and nightlife. ☎ (028) 9024-2433.

■ Other Sports Activities

You may have access to a leisure complex in your hotel, but if not you can use one of the 13 leisure centers run by Belfast City Council, where you can swim, enjoy a workout in a fitness suite, or relax in a steam room. Some have other facilities, but phone first to check details and to ask about public hours.

- **Avoniel Leisure Centre** also has squash courts. ☎ (028) 9045-1564.
- **Andersonstown Leisure Centre**, West Belfast, has squash courts. ☎ (028) 9062 5211.
- **Ballysillan Leisure Centre** has squash courts. ☎ (028) 9039-1040.
- **Grove Leisure Centre**. ☎ (028) 9035-1599.
- **Maysfield Leisure Centre**. ☎ (028) 9024-1633.

- **Shankhill Leisure Centre** also has indoor five-a-side courts (this is a variant of soccer/football played with smaller than normal teams), squash courts and snooker rooms. ☎ (028) 9024-1434.
- **Olympia Leisure Centre**. ☎ (028) 9023-3369.
- **Whiterock Leisure Centre** is attached to the Falls Park recreation grounds, which have fields for soccer, Gaelic football and camogie (similar to field hockey). ☎ (028) 9023-3239.
- **Beechmount Leisure Centre**, Falls Road, has tennis courts, a handball court, and a squash court. ☎ (028) 9032-8631.
- There's an indoor tennis arena with four courts, an indoor climbing wall, and a fitness suite at the **Ormeau Embankment**. ☎ (028) 9045-8024.
- In Lisburn, the **Lagan Valley LeisurePlex** has a pool, diving pool, and fitness suite. ☎ (028) 9267-2121; leisureplex@lisburn.gov.uk.

■ Spectator Sports

You can watch cricket, athletics(Means what? Track & Field?) and hurling in Belfast during the summer, and rugby, Gaelic football, soccer and hockey in winter. International and All-Ulster provincial Rugby Union matches take place at **Ravenhill Stadium**. ☎ (028) 9064-9141. International soccer is played at **Windsor Park**, Donegall Avenue, which is also the home venue of Belfast clubs. ☎ (028) 9024-4198.

The most popular city venue for GAA (Gaelic Athletic Association) games is **Casement Park** in Andersonstown, West Belfast, and matches are usually on Sundays.

The Mary Peters Track on the Upper Malone Road is named after Belfast's 1972 Olympic pentathlon gold medalist. Nearby is the Queen's University Club Pavilion where other sports, including soccer, hockey, rugby and Gaelic games, are played. Check local press or call The Sports Council of Northern Ireland. ☎ (028) 9038-1222.

■ Entertainment

Belfast is a lively city, with lots to do all day and in the evenings. **The Odyssey Arena**, on Queen's Quay, is the largest all-seater (with no standing areas) venue in Ireland, and hosts concerts and shows as well as being the home of the

Belfast Giants ice hockey team. It also has multi-screen and IMAX cinemas, restaurants, bars and shops in its Odyssey Pavilion. ☎ (028) 9045-1055 for general information, or check local press. www.odysseyarena. com.

Dundonald International Icebowl caters to all abilities and is also the home of the Castlereagh Knights ice hockey team. It also has 10-pin bowling and interactive laser games. ☎ (028) 9048-2611.

The historic and beautiful **Grand Opera House** hosts a varied program that includes touring productions from London's West End. The ticket shop is across the road from the Opera House itself at 2-4 Great Victoria Street. ☎ (028) 9024-1919; info@goh.co.uk; www.goh.co.uk.

The Lyric Theatre on Ridgeway Street, near the Ulster Museum, looks out over the Lagan. It's an intimate repertory theater where some of the finest plays written in recent decades were first performed – among them the Broadway and West End hit *Stones in his Pockets* by Marie Jones. It also hosts music, dance and comedy. ☎ (028) 9038-1081; info@ lyrictheatre.co.uk; www.lyrictheatre.co.uk.

The Old Museum Arts Centre, 7 College Square North, near the city center, hosts theater, dance and exhibitions. ☎ (028) 9023-5053; www. oldmuseumartscentre.org.

Ormeau Baths Gallery, Ormeau Avenue, partly incorporates the old swimming baths built during Queen Victoria's time. It's the city's main space for showing contemporary art, and always worth a visit. Open Tuesday-Saturday, 10 am-6 pm. Admission free. ☎ (028) 9032-1402.

In general, for information on what's happening in the arts, check local press, tourist offices or the arts directory online at www.belfastcity.gov. uk/arts.

■ Where to Stay

☆☆☆☆ **The Europa Hotel** is very central, next to the Grand Opera House and across the road from the Crown Liquor Saloon (see page 465). It used to be known as the most bombed hotel in Europe, but that's happily in the past now. It's part of the Hastings Group, and has a cosmopolitan atmosphere, with stylish bedrooms and lots of space in its public areas. It's actually the largest hotel in the North, with 240 bedrooms, but you wouldn't know that by the level of service you receive

HOTEL PRICE CHART	
Price per person, per night, with two sharing, including breakfast.	
$	Under US $50
$$	US $50-$100
$$$	US $101-$175
$$$$	US $176-$200
$$$$$	Over US $200

Northern Ireland

from the friendly staff. It has two bars, a nightclub and two restaurants. **The Brasserie** has a bistro menu and is open from 6 am to midnight, while **The Gallery Restaurant** offers fine dining and à la carte. Rates from $$ per person, sharing, room only. ☎ (028) 9032-7000; fax 9032-7800; res@eur.hastingshotels.com; www.hastingshotels.com.

☆☆☆ All rooms at **Jurys Inn** accommodate up to three adults or two adults and two children. It's an excellent value and is very close to all the attractions of the city, near the Grand Opera House and about a two-minute walk to City Hall and Donegall Place, the main shopping district. The rooms are well-furnished and equipped. **The Arches Restaurant** is open for breakfast and dinner, table d'hôte and à la carte, and **The Inn Pub** is ideal for a light meal or drink. There's a public car park nearby. Fisherwick Place, Great Victoria Street. Room rates $ per person, sharing. ☎ (028) 9053-3500; fax 9053-3511; jurysinnbelfast@jurysdoyle.com; www.jurysdoyle.com.

☆☆☆☆ **The McCausland Hotel**, 34/38 Victoria Street, is a member of the Small Luxury Hotels of the World and is elegant and peaceful. It's in a listed building, a warehouse on Laganside in classic Italianate style that was derelict for many years, and has been given a beautiful contemporary interior. It's a very convenient place to stay, in the regenerated riverside area, and is easy to get to by road or rail. Rates per room from $$, two sharing, breakfast extra. ☎ (028) 9022-0200; fax 9022-0220; mccausland@slh.com; www.slh.com/mccausland

Coffee, lunch and afternoon tea are served here in its **Café Marco Polo**, and dinner is available in the **Merchants Brasserie**, which offers Irish dishes made with the best local produce. Main courses from £6-£20 up.

Wellington Park Hotel is on Malone Road in South Belfast near the Ulster Museum and Botanic Gardens. It offers a choice of suites or family-sized bedrooms, and is in a quiet area where there are lots of restaurants and entertainment options. Its own **Piper Bistro** has a reasonably priced menu. The hotel often has special weekend and other rates available, so take a look at its website. Room rates from $$.Central Reservations ☎ (028) 9038-5050; hotel (028) 9038-1111; fax 9066-5410; mooneyhotelgroup@talk21.com or mail@bestwestern.ie; www.mooneyhotelgroup.com or www.bestwestern.com.

Hostels

The Linen House Hostel on Kent Street, ☎ (028) 9058-6400, and **Arnie's Backpackers** on Fitzwilliam Street, ☎ (028) 9024-2867, both belong to the IHH (Independent Holiday Hostels of Ireland). There's also the **Belfast International Hostel** at 22 Donegall Road. ☎ (028) 9032-4733; info@hini.org.uk.

RV Parks & Camping

 ☆☆☆ **Dundonald Touring Caravan Park**, 111 Old Dundonald Road, is part of the Dundonald Leisure Park, and is open from Easter to October 31. ☎ (028) 9080-9100; www. castlereagh.gov.uk.

☆ **Jordanstown Lough Shore Park** is five miles north of Belfast on the A2 at Newtownabbey and is open all year, with booking essential from October to March. Note that it does not have tent spaces. ☎ (028) 9034-0000; info@newtownabbey.gov.uk; www.newtownabbey.gov.uk.

Useful Contacts for Northern Ireland

■ **Bed & Breakfast Association Northern Ireland.** ☎ (028) 9077-1529; bernarddevenny@aol.com; www.countrysiderecreation.com.

■ **Northern Ireland Farm and Country Holidays.** ☎ (028) 8284-1325; www.nifcha.

■ **Northern Ireland Self-Catering Association.** ☎ (028) 9077-6174; info@nischa.com; www.nischa.com.

■ **Rural Cottage Holidays.** ☎ (028) 9024-1100; www. cottagesinireland.com.

■ Where to Eat

Note that non-residents can dine in all of the hotels listed above.

Kelly's Cellars is one of the most historic pubs in the city – it's where the United Irishmen met in the 18th century – and has a wonderful atmosphere. Serving great food, and with music, it's on Bank Street off Royal Avenue.

The Crown Liquor Saloon has to be the most famous hostelry in Belfast. It's on Great Victoria Street, right in the center of town and across the road from the Grand Opera House and Hotel Europa. It's owned by the National Trust and dates back to the time of Queen Victoria, with an unforgettable interior lit by gaslamps, and with cozy little paneled private rooms. Try a traditional Ulster dish here like champ (delicious mashed potatoes) and sausages. Or just have a drink, of course. Open Monday-Saturday, 11:30 am-12:30 am; Sunday, 12:30-10 pm. ☎ (028) 9027-9901.

The Cellar Restaurant in Belfast Castle, overlooking the city, is open every day serving snacks, lunch and dinner. The food is very good and prices are reasonable, and it's in a memorable setting, with a Victorian atmosphere of narrow paved streets, shop fronts and gas lights. Menu includes smoked trout, baked ham, spinach and mushroom pita bread, and lots more. Dinner main courses are from £10-£15. ☎ (028) 9077-6925; www.belfastcastle.co.uk.

Skandia, 50 Howard Street, west of Donegall Square, is a good place to eat almost any time of day, as it's open from 11 am to 11 pm. The menu includes steaks, salads, pastas, burgers, salmon, scampi, omelets, vegetarian dishes, and the atmosphere is relaxed – which is why it's popular with families. You should probably reserve for dinner, but you could take a chance. Main courses are from £5-£13. ☎ (028) 9024-0239.

Harry Ramsden's, in the Yorkgate Complex on York Street, offers traditional fish and chips (and other dishes). It's a franchise, with branches in Dublin, Cork and other cities and towns. Full license, open Monday-Thursday, 11:30 am-10:30 pm, Friday and Saturday, 11:30 am-11 pm, and Sunday, 12:30-10:30 pm. ☎ (028) 9074-9222.

■ Further Information

Belfast Welcome Centre at 47 Donegall Place. ☎ (028) 9024 6609; fax 9031 2424; belfastwelcomecentre@nitic.net; www.gotobelfast.com or www.discovernorthernireland.com.

The Cultúrlann, 216 Falls Road. ☎ (028) 9096-4188; fax 9096-4189;failte@culturlann.org.

Fáilte Feirste Thiar, 202 Andersonstown Road. ☎ (028) 9050-0470; fax 9080-9200; info@wbpb.org; www.westbelfast-failte.com.

Lisburn Tourist Information Centre, The Square. ☎ (028) 9266-0038.

Hillsborough Tourist Information Centre, The Courthouse, The Square. ☎ (028) 9268-9717.

Robinson's Pub, Belfast

Causeway Coast & Glens

County Antrim is absolutely beautiful. Its coast, from the busy port of Larne to the resorts of Portrush and Portstewart, is dotted with beaches and rocky inlets. Inland, between Glenarm and Ballycastle, there are nine steep-sided glens, which descend from the inland plateau to the sea.

In addition to wonderful scenery, with forests, rivers and waterfalls, the landscape is dominated by spectacular ruins of fortresses built by Gaelic chieftains and Norman invaders. Ireland's first inhabitants, nomadic boatmen from Scotland, are believed to have landed in this area around 7000 BC.

The region called Causeway Coast and Glens takes in not just Co. Antrim but also part of the neighboring Londonderry. Among the sites of interest are the famous **Giant's Causeway** and the world's oldest licensed whiskey distillery at nearby Bushmills. The activities you can enjoy here include fishing, sailing, diving, horse riding, cycling and walking, or just exploring.

■ Getting Here & Getting Around

By Bus & Rail

 Ulsterbus Ltd. runs services throughout the area; for information on buses or trains. **The Causeway Rambler** (Ulsterbus 376) runs between Bushmills and Carrick-a-Rede in the summer. ☎ (028) 2827-2345; www.ulsterbus.co.uk; www.translink.co.uk.

The Antrim Coaster Bus, Bus 252, takes you along the coast from Larne to Coleraine, Monday-Saturday twice daily in both directions year-round. www.citybus.co.uk.

Northern Ireland Railways operates suburban services from Belfast's Great Victoria and Central stations to Larne, and to Coleraine and Derry in neighboring Co. Londonderry. ☎ (028) 9089-9411.

AN ADVENTURE ON WHEELS
From early May to the end of September, you can travel the two miles (3.2 km) between Bushmills and the Giant's Causeway by a delightful **narrow gauge steam railway**. ☎ (028) 2073-2594.

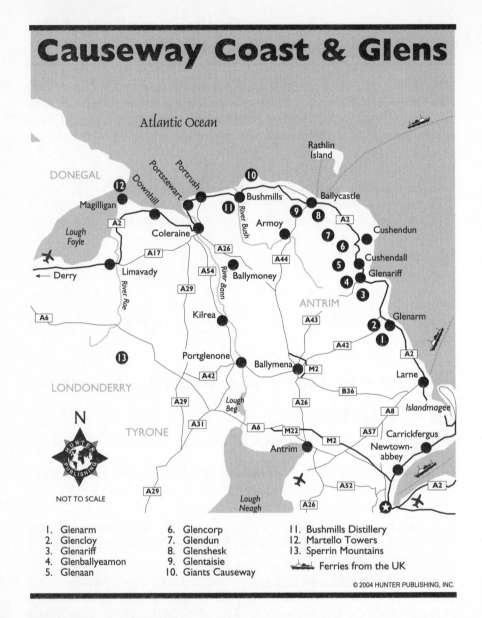

Causeway Coast & Glens

Atlantic Ocean

Rathlin Island

DONEGAL

Portstewart
Portrush
Downhill

Magilligan

Bushmills
Ballycastle

River Bush
Armoy

Lough Foyle

Coleraine

Cushendun

Cushendall

Glenariff

Derry

Limavady

Ballymoney

River Bann

ANTRIM

River Roe

Kilrea

Glenarm

Portglenone

Ballymena

Larne

LONDONDERRY

Lough Beg

Islandmagee

N

TYRONE

Antrim

Carrickfergus

Newtown-abbey

HUNTER PUBLISHING

NOT TO SCALE

Lough Neagh

1. Glenarm
2. Glencloy
3. Glenariff
4. Glenballyeamon
5. Glenaan
6. Glencorp
7. Glendun
8. Glenshesk
9. Glentaisie
10. Giants Causeway
11. Bushmills Distillery
12. Martello Towers
13. Sperrin Mountains
⛴ Ferries from the UK

© 2004 HUNTER PUBLISHING, INC.

■ Main Roads

The A2 runs along the coast from Newtownabbey, northeast of Belfast, to Carrickfergus, Larne, through the seaside villages of Glenarm, Carnlough, Waterfoot, Cushendall, to Ballycastle, and then on through Portrush to Coleraine in Co. Londonderry.

Inland, the M2 and then the M22 take you from near Newtownabbey to Antrim Town and Randalstown. From there, you take the A26 to Ballymena, where a second section of the M2 bypasses the town. Return to the A26 for Ballymoney and on to Coleraine.

To explore the central plateau, take the A42 up from Carnlough to Ballymena, or the A44 from Ballycastle , which brings you through Armoy and then on to the A26.

■ Tourist Information

Larne Tourist Information Centre is just off Main Street on Narrow Gauge Road. ☎/fax (028) 2826-0088; mcwilliama@ larne.gov.uk; www.larne.gov.uk.

In **Ballycastle**, the **Tourist Information Centre** is in Sheakburn House, Mary Street. ☎ (028) 2076-2024; fax 2076-2515; ballycastle@nitic.net.

Portrush Tourist Information Office (seasonal opening) is in Dunluce Center. ☎ (028) 7082-3333

■ Sightseeing

Carrickfergus

The area is perfect for a drive or cycle, stopping to explore as you go. The walled garrison town of **Carrickfergus** is eight miles (13 km) north of Belfast on the A2. The last witch trial in Ireland took place here in 1710 in what is now the Town Hall. **Carrickfergus Castle** is on the seafront, the largest and the best-preserved castle in the North. Built to guard Belfast Lough by the Norman John de Courcy in 1180, it was here William of Orange landed on his way to the Battle of the Boyne in 1690. The castle is worth a visit, and also has a program of interesting events. Open Monday-Saturday, 10 am-6 pm, Sunday, 2-6 pm. October-March it closes at 4 pm. ☎ (028) 9335-1273.

US President **Andrew Jackson's** parents emigrated from Carrickfergus in 1765. In a reconstructed cottage in nearby Boneybefore, there's a museum. An exhibition on the US Rangers, whose first battalion was raised here, is in its grounds. Open April-September, Monday-Friday, 10 am-1 pm, 2-6 pm, and weekend afternoons. ☎ (028) 9336-6455.

Islandmagee, north of Carrickfergus, is a narrow peninsula protecting Larne Lough. At 91 Ballylumford Road you'll find something extraordinary – a prehistoric monument in the front garden of a private house!

The dolmen (stone tomb), known to locals as the **Druids' Altar**, is at least 4,000 years old.

Larne

Larne is 18 miles (29 km) north of Belfast and is both a busy port, with ferries arriving from Scotland and England, and a thriving market town. Overlooking the harbor is a round tower built in 1888 as a memorial to James Chaine, a Member of Parliament, who was responsible for establishing sea routes from here. It's actually an unusual grave as he's buried upright in it, as he'd ordered. You can see the coast of Scotland from here on a clear day.

The town has a simple layout dominated by Main Street, with its mix of chain stores, independent shops, bars and restaurants. In Curran Park there's a statue of a family on their way to an emigrant ship. *Friends Goodwill* was the name of the first ship to sail for Boston from Larne in 1717, full of Ulster-Scots, mostly Presbyterians. Thousands followed, bound for New York, Philadelphia and other American cities.

Larne is developing an **Ulster-American Heritage Trail** – ask at the Larne Tourist Information Centre (see above) for details.

SOMETHING DELICIOUS

Watch award-winning Pooh Bear ice cream being made in **Maud's Dairy** in pretty Gleno village near Larne. Open 8:30 am-4 pm; phone to check times of production. ☎ (028) 2827-2387; fax 2826-0375; roberta@mauds.co.uk. There's a coffee shop serving ice cream and snacks, and a glen with a waterfall behind the dairy where you can take a walk. Admission is free.

The Nine Glens of Antrim

The glens are all beautiful and enthralling, but do take great care when exploring as the roads winding through them are narrow and steep in places and can be affected by mist as you climb. They are usually pleasantly free of traffic.

Going south to north, they start with **Glenarm** – "the glen of the army" – nine miles (14 km) north of Larne on the A2 coast road at the picturesque village of the same name. There's a tradition that King John (1199-1216) granted Glenarm a municipal charter, making it one of the oldest towns in Ireland.

Two miles (3.2 km) farther north is **Glencloy** – "the glen of the hedges" – with the charming little fishing port of Carnlough at its foot.

The best known of the glens comes next, **Glenariff** – "arable or fertile" – which meets the sea at Waterfoot. At the foot of **Glenballyemon** – "Edwardstown" – and the Sea of Moyle is delightful Cushendall, known as the Capital of the Glens. This has been designated an Area of Outstanding Natural Beauty. Only 16 miles (26 km) away is Scotland and its Kintyre Peninsula, made famous by the song called *The Mull of Kintyre*, written and performed by former Beatle Paul McCartney. Many families here are of Scottish origin.

This area is closely associated with the Irish legend, The Children of Lír, who were turned into swans by their evil stepmother Aoife (Eve) and banished to the Sea of Moyle for 300 years.

The warrior poet Ossian, a legendary figure, is said to be buried in the next glen, **Glenaan**, which means "rush lights" or "colt's foot."

Nearby is **Glencorp**, running parallel to the coast road from Cushendall to Cushendun – "the glen of the slaughtered." Both of these villages are on the sea and very pretty. The next green glen is **Glendun** – "of the brown river" – where the road from Cushendun crosses the River Glendun by a red stone viaduct and travels over a high plateau to Ballycastle.

East of that town is the **Glenshesk** – "glen of sedge" – which sweeps towards the ruined Bonamargy Friary. On the other side of Ballycastle is the last of the nine glens – **Glentaisie** – "Taisie of the bright sides.

The Glen of Taisie was named after Princess Taise, the daughter of a Rathlin chieftain who married Congal, the son of the King of Ulster. Congal received the glen and other lands along the coast, including Dunseverick, as a wedding gift from Taise's father. Congal later succeeded his father to become King of Ulster. Small hills and drumlins cover its length as its sweeps down the western flank of Knocklayde to Ballycastle Its many interesting features include the remains of two motte forts and several standing stones.

Ballycastle

Ballycastle has a very attractive seafront, with tennis courts, and a Blue Flag beach (see page 76) a short walk across the River Maigey. Ireland's oldest fair, **Ould Lammas**, has been held here since 1606, these days on the last Monday and Tuesday of August. It's a lively resort town, with attractive houses built in the mid-1700s.

Ballypatrick Forest, five miles (eight km) southeast of Ballycastle on the A2, is a five-mile drive through peatland forest with great views of Rathlin Island and Ballycastle. Open daily 10 am to dusk. You pay a small fee per car. ☎ (028) 2955-6000.

Rathlin Island

Do take at least a day-trip from Ballycastle to Rathlin Island, which is just over six miles (10 km) off the coast. It's L-shaped, four miles (6.4 km) on one side, three on the other, and almost treeless, with cliffs over 200 feet high. Nowhere is it more than a mile across and, with fewer than 100 inhabitants and even fewer cars, the island is ideal for walking and cycling. Home to 175 species of birds, it's also popular with botanists, divers and sea-anglers, and there's lots to see, including seals sleeping on the rocks along the shore from Harbor to Mill Bay.

You take a 45-minute boat trip from Ballycastle to get there. The service runs four times a day, June to September, twice daily from October to May, advance booking advised. ☎ (028) 2076-9299. www.calmac.co.uk. You can take your bike for a small fee, tour the island by **Irene's Minibus**, ☎ (028) 2076-3949, or hire a bike, ☎ (028) 2076-3954. See page 480 for where to stay and to eat on Rathlin Island

The Giant's Causeway

Continue along the A2 from Ballycastle, passing Whitepark Bay, and you come to the Giant's Causeway, a World Heritage Site in the care of the National Trust. The picture shows the cliffs at the site.

The Causeway is a cluster of black basalt pillars formed 60 million years ago by volcanic activity. It is in a National Nature Reserve and has also been designated an Area of Special Scientific Interest. It's been attracting visitors since 1693 when it was declared one of the great natural wonders of the world by the Royal Geographical Society. The site is associated with the mythological giant Finn MacCool; it is open all year and is so popular with visitors that it's busy even during winter. You can walk from the Visitor Centre or take the little bus for a small fee (free if you're a member of the National Trust). Perhaps because of all the images I'd seen I was disappointed when I visited, as it doesn't seem as majestic or awe-inspiring as I had expected. But maybe you won't agree.

You pay to park and the fee goes towards maintaining and developing visitor facilities all along the coast. There's also a Visitor Centre with audio-visual show (for which you pay an extra charge), a shop and café. ☎ (028) 2073-1159/2073 1855; causeway@nitic.net; www.nationaltrust.org.uk.

Next to the Visitor Centre is the Causeway School Museum, with a 1920s-era classroom, open daily July and August only, 11 am-5 pm. ☎ (028) 2073-1777.

Bushmills

The village of Bushmills, connected to the Giant's Causeway by a charming little steam train from May to the end of September, is a good place to stop and take a walk or even stay. It's been designated a "conservation village," one of several that are considered dedicated to conserving their natural ecology. The village stands on the River Bush, where several mills used to process everything from spades to flax, timber to corn.

Bushmills is famous as the home of the world's oldest licensed whiskey distillery, founded in 1608. You can take a one-hour guided tour, which includes a tasting. Open April-October, Monday-Saturday, 9:30 am-5:30 pm, Sunday from noon; rest of the year, phone for hours. ☎ (028) 2073-1521; www.whiskeytours.ie.

As you travel between the Giant's Causeway towards Portrush, you come upon what must be some of the most romantic ruins, three miles (4.8 km) from the town. They're standing on an absolutely breathtaking cliff with waves crashing below. These are the ruins of **Dunluce Castle**, which was the stronghold of the MacDonnells, Lords of the Isles, in the 16th century. Part of its kitchens and the poor cooks were killed during a banquet in 1639.

Open year-round, 10 am to 6 pm. Closed Mondays from October to March; shorter hours in winter and on Sundays, longer hours from June through October. ☎ (028) 2073-1938.

Portrush

With a very attractive location on the peninsula of Ramore Head, Portrush has long been a popular family resort and has lots of guesthouses, hotels, restaurants and pubs. It has two sandy beaches and a harbor and, despite modern amusements, retains an atmosphere of times past, with some lovely houses overlooking the sea.

*Be lazy and take the **Portrush Puffer**, a road passenger train, around the resort; it only operates from April to September.*

Northern Ireland

The Portrush Countryside Centre, once the bathhouse for a local hotel, now houses an exhibition on the natural history of the coast. Open June through August, admission free. ☎ (028) 7082-3600. Next to it is the **Nature Reserve**, where the rocks on the seashore have thousands of fossil impressions. Offshore you can see **The Skerries**, a line of little islands about two miles (3.2 km) away; in summer you can take a boat trip around the islands from the harbor.

Just up the street from the Countryside Centre there's a **charity shop** on the corner where you'll pick up great bargains, including books.

The Portrush **Tourist Information** office (seasonal opening) is in the Dunluce Centre, where one of the attractions is a multi-media show on the myths and legends associated with the area. ☎ (028) 7082-4444.

Antrim Town

Exploring inland is equally rewarding. Antrim Town stands on the northeastern corner of Lough Neagh, just a few miles from Belfast International Airport. It's a prosperous town, and it has expanded dramatically in recent years, so little of its historic core survives. What does remain includes the remarkably intact **Round Tower** (free access all year). The tower was probably built around 900 and is all that remains of an important sixth-century monastery, abandoned in 1147. There is also part of a tower of **Antrim Castle**. It's worth visiting Antrim just to see the **Castle Gardens**, now restored to their original form. The gardens were designed by André Le Notre (1613-70) – famous for his formal gardens at Versailles, outside Paris. Features here include ponds, as well as riverside and woodland walks. The **Clothworthy Arts Centre**, which always has something of interest going on, is in the former coach house, and also houses displays about the gardens. Free admission, open daily. ☎ (028) 9442-8000.

The childhood home of Alexander Irvine (1863-1941), who became a missionary on the Bowery in New York, is called **Pogue's Entry** and is on Church Street, Antrim. It's open during the main tourist season; phone for hours. ☎ (028) 9442-8000.

Ballymena

Follow the A26 north from Antrim Town and you come to Ballymena, which in the 17th century was settled by people from southwest Scotland. The town's prosperity was based on the linen industry, which continues here in a small way, but nowadays this inland area, including Ballymoney farther north along the A26, is mainly agricultural.

East of Ballymena on the A42 to Carnlough there's the picturesque village of **Broughshane**, and just west of it (also on the A42) is **Gracehill**, settled by a group of Moravians in the 18th century. It's built around a green, with separate houses for the brothers and sisters. Even in the graveyard, a path divides them. The church, built in 1765, has stained glass windows and a pulpit in the middle.

On the B96 from Ballymena to Portglenone, you come to **Cullybackey** and the ancestral home of the 21st US President, Chester Alan Arthur (1881-85). His father, a Baptist clergyman, emigrated from here in 1816. The restored farmhouse is up a lane through potato fields; watch out for the sharp turn on the road. Open Easter-September, Monday-Friday, 10:30 am-5 pm, Saturday to 4 pm. ☎ (028) 2563-8494.

■ Adventures on Foot

 Allow plenty of time to explore at least portions of the Causeway Coast and Glens on foot. A great place for a walk is the **Carnfunnock Country Park**, three miles (4.8 km) north of Larne on the A2 coast road. It covers 473 acres (189 hectares), with mixed woodland and gardens, dotted with ponds. There are also interesting signs of the original estate, which belonged to Lord and Lady Dixon, with a walled garden, icehouse, home farm and private church. There's also a nine-hole public golf course where you can rent clubs. ☎ (028) 2827-0541, (summer) 2826-0088; mcwilliams@larne.gov.uk.

Among the charming little villages along the coast is **Glenarm**. You can pick up a descriptive brochure (called *The Layde Walk and History Trail*) at the Glenarm Information Centre or at the Larne Tourist Office. The "layde" was a waterway built to bring water down from the glen, and is now a walkway. There are also footpaths leading into the **forest park** from the village. The **castle** has a walled garden and there's a small museum in the old gatehouse, open all year; phone for times. ☎ (028) 2884-1305. Highland Games are held here each July.

Carnlough is a friendly little fishing port with a beach. In the early 19th century a railway was developed to transport limestone from the Cregar and Gortin quarries above the village to the harbor, for shipment to Scotland. The railway bridge dominates Carnlough. The old railway itself is now a walkway leading to the **Cranny Falls**, and part of the Ulster Way long-distance walking route. The area around the Falls is a **nature reserve** with grassland and wetland habitats.

On the A43 to Ballymena, signposted off the coast road at Waterfoot, is the **Glenariff Forest Park Visitor Centre**. It's a good place to start exploring the park, with waterfalls, wooden walkways, and great views. Open daily from 10 am, with a small fee. ☎ (028) 2955-6000.

There are waymarked paths around the village of **Cushendun**, with its distinctive white cottages, and into the surrounding woods.

At **Ballintoy**, west of Ballycastle, you walk a mile along a coastal path, then – if you dare – cross the precarious **Carrick-a-Rede rope bridge** over an 80-foot chasm to a what's described as a peaceful little island with lovely sea views. It's run by the National Trust, and is very popular with those more daring than myself. The bridge is open from April to September, depending on weather. You pay a small fee to park. Tea room and exhibition open May, Saturday-Sunday 1-5 pm; June-August daily, 12 to 6 pm.

The North Antrim Coastal Path runs for 14 miles (22.4 km) from the Giant's Causeway to Carrick-a-Rede, passing the ruins of Dunseverick Castle, Portradden, the open sands of Whitepark Bay and Ballintoy.

The two miles (3.2 km) of golden beach at Portstewart are protected by dunes; these are a haven for wildflowers and butterflies, and are in the care of the National Trust. There's a waymarked **nature trail** to follow, which is accessible all year. Take the **cliff path**, part of the Ulster Way, from Portrush to Portstewart to get there.

■ Adventures on Water

Sailing, Surfing & Rowing

Watersports are particularly well-provided-for on the Causeway Coast. Portrush is a mecca for surfers, windsurfers, and bodyboarders. **Troggs Surf Shop** at 88 Main Street is where you'll get detailed information and can rent equipment. You can also inquire there about the Causeway Coast Surfing Association, which provides a daily surf report. ☎ (028) 7082-5476; www.troggs.com.

Other useful contacts are **Woodies** at 102 Main Street, ☎ (028) 7082-3273, and the **Portrush Yacht Club,** ☎ (028) 7082-3932.

Sailing is also popular from the numerous small ports dotted around the coast or from the Carrickfergus and Ballycastle Marina: ☎ (028) 2076-8525; www.moyle-council.org. Berths are available from the **East Antrim Boat Club** in Larne Lough, Glenarm Harbor, Carnlough Harbor and Ballylumford Harbor.

Four-oared gig rowing, once seen in every village along the coast, has retained its popularity in Carnlough, where crews can be seen training in the bay every summer, and the village has an annual regatta in May.

Inland, there are marinas on the River Bann, including **Drumaheglis** near Ballymoney, which has excellent fishing, camping, caravanning and cruising facilities. ☎ (028) 7032 0666, enquiries@edgewatersports.co.uk.

Fishing

 The entire area is blessed with a huge choice for anyone interested in coarse or game fishing, including the eastern shores of Lough Neagh, the Causeway Coast, the nine glens, the coast road, and many rivers and lakes. Coarse anglers can enjoy sea angling or beach casting. The River Bann, which drains Lough Neagh into the Atlantic, is a major attraction, its lower stretch popular for rod fishing.

 See pages 71-74 for details on angling in Ireland, regulations and best times to fish.

Boats can be rented for sea angling in many of the villages, including Carnlough, where fishing rights for the lakes are owned by the Carnlough Angling Club; day tickets can be bought at the Londonderry Arms Hotel.

Ask at your accommodation or at tackle and bait outlets about licenses, permits, boat rental, and ghillies (guides). Tourist Information Centres, such as the one at Portrush, ☎ (028) 7082-4444, will also advise you.

More details about the fisheries appear on page 512.

■ Adventures on Horseback

 There are many riding centers; these are just a few of them.

Watertop Farm Trekking Centre, six miles (10 km) east of Ballycastle in one of the most beautiful parts of the area, offers one-hour treks through glen and moors. It's also an open farm with a museum, shearing demonstrations, scenic walks, and is a camp site. Open daily July-August. ☎ (028) 2076-2576; fax 2076-2175; watertopfarm@aol.com.

Maddybenny Riding Centre and Stud is on a hill with great views of the coast, two miles (3.2 km) from Portrush, three miles (4.8 km) from Coleraine. All levels of rider are welcome, and it also offers accommodation. ☎ (028) 7082-3394 daytime.

Castlehill Equestrian Centre, off the A26 and two miles (3.2 km) from Ballymena, has riding and jumping classes for all ages, as well as cross-country riding, all year. ☎ (028) 2588-1222; fax 2586-2006.

The Islandmagee Equestrian Centre is on Brown's Bay Road. ☎ (028) 9338-2108; www.islandmagee.co.uk/irs.

■ Golf

There are more than 30 golf courses in the area, some open to visitors every day, others on certain days or times, so it is advisable to phone in advance. The following is a selection.

Royal Portrush Golf Club has two 18-hole links courses at Dunluce and Valley, a mile east of Portrush. ☎ (028) 7082-2311; fax 7082-3139; info@royalportrushgolfclub.com; www.royalportrushgolfclub.com.

Ballycastle Golf Club is a links/parkland course a half-mile southeast of the town. ☎ (028) 2076-2536.

The Cairndhu Golf Club, four miles (6.4 km) north of Larne, has an undulating parkland course, with views over North Channel. ☎/fax (028) 2858-3324.

Carrickfergus Golf Club has a mainly flat parkland course with tree-lined fairways, looking out over Belfast Lough. ☎ (028) 9336-3713.

There's also the nine-hole **Bentra Municipal Golf Course** at Carrickfergus. ☎ (028) 9337-8996.

Among nine-hole seaside courses in the area are: **Cushendall Golf Club**, ☎ (029) 2177-1318; **Bushfoot Golf Club**, a mile north of Bushmills, ☎ (028) 2073-1317; and the **Larne Golf Club** on the Islandmagee Peninsula, ☎ (028) 9338-2228; fax 9338-2088.

■ Entertainment

With the many festivals in the area, and welcoming pubs in every village and town, there is much to keep visitors happily entertained. In Larne there is a **Leisure Centre**, which includes a theater, pools and spa, squash courts, and fitness equipment. ☎ (028) 2826-0478. In Portrush during the summer there are shows in the **Town Hall**, and the two screen **Playhouse Cinema** is open all year. **Barry's Amusement Park** has been at Portrush for 50 years, with outdoor rides and indoor entertainment, and **Waterworld** has pools and water slides. ☎ (028) 7082-2001.

■ Where to Stay

☆☆☆ **The Londonderry Arms Hotel**, Carnlough, is on the A2 coast road. Rarely have I been made as welcome as I was here. The hotel has spacious old-fashioned bedrooms, charming and helpful staff, and an open fire in the sitting room, where you can have a drink or read. Staying here is like being with friends, rather than in a hotel. It's run by the O'Neill family, who obviously love making visitors welcome. They are very knowledgeable about Antrim, and you can hire bikes from them or buy permits for fishing, get special golf rates, and find out about other activities in the area.

The food is outstanding too, with mouth-watering brown bread, soups, locally caught fish, and delicious meat and vegetarian choices. Desserts include traditional favorites like apple crumble. Dinner is about £20 for three

HOTEL PRICE CHART	
Price per person, per night, with two sharing, including breakfast.	
$	Under US $50
$$	US $50-$100
$$$	US $101-$175
$$$$	US $176-$200
$$$$$	Over US $200

courses. The bar is popular with locals, so you can meet them too if you wish. You have to, at least once, enjoy an Ulster Fry (made from eggs, sausages, tomatoes and mushrooms) for breakfast during your vacation and this would be a great place to do so.

The hotel is named after Marchioness Londonderry who developed the limestone industry here, and was once owned by Winston Churchill. It belongs to the Irish Country Hotels marketing group. There's plenty of parking on the street outside or in the car park across the road. B & B £50 sharing, $$. ☎ (028) 2888-5255; fax 2888-5263; Lda@glensofantrim.com; www.glensofantrim.com; www.irishcountryhotels.com.

☆☆☆ **The Counties Hotel** in Portrush is centrally located at 73 Main Street, where it overlooks the sea and the Countryside Centre. It belongs to the Comfort chain and offers very good value. Rooms are big enough for up to two adults and two children, are pleasantly decorated and well equipped. It has a **Café Bar and Restaurant**, ideal for a snack or more substantial meal. Rates from $$. International reservations ☎ 1-800-500-600; (028) 7082-6100; fax 7082-6160; info@comforthotelportrush.com; www.comforthotelportrush.com.

☆☆☆ **The Bushmills Inn**, in the historic village of the same name, has been tastefully restored and retains the atmosphere of its days as a coaching inn, with oil lamps, and nooks and crannies. It's a member of Ireland's Blue Book (see page 60). The bar is still lit by gaslight, and you can try Bushmills malt from the Inn's private cask. Its restaurant has won awards for the quality of its food – made from the best of local produce. Of course, you can eat here while staying elsewhere. The restaurant is open all day; dinner is served from 7 to 9:30 pm, and costs about £28. There's a choice of accommodation in the Inn itself or in the Mill House, where the rooms are bigger and have a sitting area. B & B in the Inn from $$, and from $$$ in the Mill House. ☎ 028 2073-2339; fax 2073-2048; mail@bushmillsinn.com; www.bushmillsinn.com.

☆☆ **The Causeway Hotel**, owned by the National Trust, must have one of the best locations anywhere, looking out over the sea and a few steps

Northern Ireland

from the Giant's Causeway. It's been there since 1826 and has retained an atmosphere of old grandeur while offering contemporary comfort. There are mini-weekend and week-long breaks available, which are very reasonable. B & B rates from $ sharing. ☎ (028) 2073-1210; fax 2073-2552; reception@giants-causeway-hotel.com; www.causeway-hotel.com.

On Rathlin Island

The Manor House, overlooking Church Bay, is owned by the National Trust, and offers B&B accommodation all year, with evening meals and packed lunches if prearranged. $ sharing. ☎ (028) 2076-3964.

Alternatively, on Rathlin, you can stay at the **Guest House**, ☎ (028) 2076-3917; at **Soerneog View Hostel**, ☎ (028) 2076-3954; or in the **Camping Barn**, ☎ (028) 2076-3948.

Cottages for Rent

 ☆☆☆-☆☆☆☆ **North Irish Lodge and Diving Centre** at Islandmagee has luxurious self-catering cottages set on a Victorian farm on the coast overlooking Larne Lough. They won the Northern Ireland Tourism Award in 2003 for the Self-Catering Premises of the Year. You can laze or take advantage of the activities available – horseback riding at the Rainbow Equestrian Centre, learning to scuba dive or maybe taking a scenic high-speed boat trip. Each cottage sleeps four to six and you can cook for yourself or have breakfast and dinner delivered. ☎ (028)

If you stay in one of the **Antrim Glens Cottages**, not only will you have a comfortable and attractive setting for your vacation, you'll also be helping the locals; the North Antrim Community Network leased nine derelict properties and renovated them as vacation homes. You can rent them for weekends at certain times of year, or by the week.

Among them is **Rock Cottage**, right beside the sea with glorious views, a mile from Ballycastle near the Golf Club. It's a restored farm outbuilding, now a luxurious whitewashed cottage that sleeps four. There's an open turf (peat) fire as well as central heating, and everything is laid on, including linen and towels. The cottage even has a walled garden. Rates are from £210-400 per week, with discounts for stays of two or three days also available. Take a look at the choice of properties. ☎ (028) 2177-2990; fax 2177-2129; cottages@antrim.net; www.antrim.net/cottages.

Hostels

Castle Hostel on Quay Road, Ballycastle. ☎ (028) 2076-2337; info@castlehostel.com.

Sheep Island Hostel, Main Street, Ballintoy, Ballycastle. ☎ (028) 2076-9393; sheepsisland@hotmail.com.

Both are members of the IHH and are open all year.

RV Parks & Camping

There are a number of caravan parks, some with spaces for tents, but always phone in advance as space can be limited, especially in the summer.

☆☆☆ **The Curran Court** is on the road to Larne Harbor, open April to September. ☎ (028) 2827-3797.

☆☆☆ **Sixmilewater Marina and Caravan Park**, Lough Road, is a mile from Antrim town center. Open Easter to end September. ☎ (028) 9446-4131; abs@antrim.gov.uk.

☆☆☆ **Silvercliffs Holiday Village** overlooks the sea at Ballycastle, with an indoor pool and bar, open all year. ☎ (028) 2076-2550.

Watertop Farm is six miles (10 km) east of Ballycastle on a working farm, open April to end October. ☎ (028) 2076-2576; watertopfarm@aol.com.

☆☆☆ **ECOS Millennium Environmental Centre** is just off the M2 at Ballymena, open April to September. ☎ (028) 2566-4400; www.ecoscentre.com.

☆☆☆☆☆ **The Drumaheglis Marina and Caravan Park** is on the Lower Bann near Ballymoney and has an on-site water ski school, as well as other watersports and fishing. ☎ (028) 2766-6466; info@ballymoney.gov.uk; www.ballymoney.gov.uk.

At **Glenariff Forest Park**, the caravan and camping park is open all year. ☎ (028) 2175-8232.

Moyle District Council runs parks at **Cushendall**, ☎ (028) 2177-1699, and **Cushendun**, ☎ (028) 2176-1254. Both are within a third of a mile of beaches, shops and other facilities.

Close to Bushmills there are three parks. The ☆☆☆☆☆ **Ballyness** is open from March 17 to the end of October. ☎ (028) 2073-2393; info@ballynesscaravanpark.com; www.ballynesscaravanpark.com. The ☆☆☆☆ **Bush Caravan Park** is also open March to October. ☎ (028) 2073-1678. ☆☆☆☆ **Portballintrae** is open March to November. ☎ (028) 2073-1478.

At Portrush there are three to choose from. ☆☆☆☆☆ **Bellemont** is open March to September. ☎ (0280) 7082-3872. ☆☆☆☆ **Ballymacrea** is open all year. ☎ (028) 7082-4507. ☆☆☆ **Carrick Dhu** opens from April to early October. ☎ (028) 7082-3712.

■ Where to Eat

 The Harbour Bar, 36 Harbour Road, Portrush, won the Northern Ireland Tourism Award in 2003 as the Hostelry of the Year. It's not just one of the town's oldest pubs but among the oldest in the North, and is very popular with locals and visitors. It's on the quay overlooking the harbor, and has won other awards, including the Best Seafood Restaurant, for the quality of its food and its welcoming atmosphere. Lunch and dinner are available and the menu is varied. ☎ (028) 7082-2430.

Glass Island Restaurant, Marine Hotel, North Street, Ballycastle. On the seafront, open daily 12:30-10 pm with carvery and à la carte. All dishes feature local produce. You can have morning coffee, tea with scones, pastries in the roomy foyer, or snacks all days from 12:30-9 pm in the **Fairhead Lounge** or **Quay Bar**. Main courses from £5-£25. ☎ (028) 2076-2222; mail@marinehotel.net; www.marinehotel.net.

The Meetinghouse, 120 Brustin Brae Road, Cairncastle, Larne, is on the B148 a mile inland from the coast, and is one of the oldest pubs in Antrim, with bar food available every day, as well as evening dining. There are traditional music sessions on Wednesdays and Saturdays; on Fridays and Saturdays it has a late license and there's a varied music program. Book ahead to dine in the evenings. ☎ (028) 2858-3252.

Morelli's/Nino's is on the Promenade at Portstewart and is bright and cheerful. As you're relaxing here you can look out over the sea. Morelli's has been going for years as an ice cream parlor, and the café has a good choice of hot dishes. It's open every day (except Christmas Day) from 9:30 am, in summer staying open to 11:30 pm, the rest of year until 5:30 weekdays and 11 pm on weekends. It doesn't accept credit cards, but that shouldn't be a problem, as main dishes cost only around £5. ☎ (028) 7083-2150.

On Rathlin Island

- ■ **McCuaig's Bar and Restaurant**. ☎ (028) 2076-3974.
- ■ **Brockley Tea Room** at The Manor House. ☎ (028) 2076-3964.

■ Further Information

 Causeway Coast and Antrim Glens. ☎ (028) 7032-4570; fax 7032-7719; mail@causewaycoastandglens.com; www.causewaycoastandglens.com.

Tourist Information Centres

Generally open Monday-Friday, 9 am-5 pm, all year; Easter to September, also on Saturdays, 10 am-4 pm; and in July and August on Sundays, 1-4 pm.

- 16 High Street, Antrim. ☎ (028) 9442-8331; fax 9448-7844; abs@antrim.gov.uk; www.antrim.gov.uk.
- 7 Mary Street, Ballycastle. ☎ (028) 2076-2034.
- 76 Church Street, Ballymena. ☎ (028) 2563-8494.
- Knight Ride, Antrim Street, Carrickfergus. ☎ (028) 9336-6455.
- 44 Causeway Road, Bushmills. ☎ (028) 2073-1855.
- Narrow Gauge Road, Lisburn. ☎ (028) 2826-0088.
- Dunluce Centre, Portrush. ☎ (028) 7082-3333. Open in season.

Dunluce Castle, 13th centery,
Causeway Coast (see page 473)

Northern Ireland

St. Columb's Cathedral, Derry City (see page 489)

Derry City &
County Londonderry

■ Derry City

Named after the Irish "doire" meaning "oak grove," Derry is the second largest city in Northern Ireland, and is delightful, standing on a hill on the estuary of the river Foyle, which divides it in two. The area called Cityside includes at its core the only intact medieval walled city in Ireland or the British Isles. Facing it across the river is the Waterside area.

The city's origins go back to 546 when St. Columba founded a monastery on the hill, before heading off in 563 to Iona to convert Scotland and Northumbria to Christianity. The English first arrived in 1566 after the revolt by Shane O'Neill. They installed a garrison, which was wiped out the following year after the arsenal accidentally exploded. In 1613, Derry's charter gave it a mayor and corporation and added London to its name – a bone of contention with nationalists who are the majority in the area.

 Those of us living in the Republic know immediately which part of the community a person comes from in Northern Ireland by how they refer to this city or county. In an effort to be fair, I am calling the city Derry and the county Londonderry.

After a couple of rebellions, King James I cajoled the City of London into taking on the responsibility of sorting out not just Derry but its surrounding region. It did so by creating a new county called Londonderry and setting up The Honourable The Irish Society, a cumbersome title for the body that controlled Derry, Coleraine and Limavady, and divided the rest of the county between the 12 ancient London livery companies. It was the Society that built the walls in 1613-18 to defend the city. The Siege of Derry (1688-89) was one of the most important events in Ireland's history and still has influences today (see page 15).

Derry is a port city and throughout the 18th and 19th centuries many emigrants left from here for new lives in America, founding the colonies of Derry and Londonderry in New Hampshire. Other destinations included Philadelphia, Charlestown, Liverpool in England and Hobart in Australia. With the Great Famine (1845-49), emigration expanded to Canada.

Northern Ireland

During World War II Derry was a naval base and airbase, with 20,000 sailors of different nationalities stationed here, and was chosen as the site for the surrender of the German U-boat fleet.

Today, there's an atmosphere of optimism in Derry and the city buzzes with life. The peace process has brought investment, and many new buildings, which fit in remarkably well with the Georgian townhouses and grand public buildings, including the Guildhall, and the smaller houses and shops cramming its narrow side streets. It's an artistic city, with theaters, galleries and other cultural centers and a number of annual festivals. Its people, with their gentle accent, are very welcoming.

■ County Londonderry

A flat plain extends eastwards from the city, skirting Lough Foyle, to Limavady on the River Roe and the university city of Coleraine on the River Bann. To the north is the Atlantic coast with marvelous beaches, including the longest on the whole island, Magilligan, and popular resorts like Castlerock and Portstewart.

Inland, there are hills, glens and river valleys, backed by the Sperrin Mountains, with well-wooded areas that are a legacy of the Plantation (see page 14). Across Lough Foyle is County Donegal in the Republic and that county's land border is just outside Derry City.

■ Getting Here & Getting Around

By Air

City of Derry Airport is at Eglinton, four miles (6.4 km) east of the city on the A2, and has direct flights from Scotland, England and Dublin. ☎ (028) 7181-0784; fax 7181-1426; info@ cityofderryairport.com; www.cityofderryairport.com.

Rail & Bus

The city has good rail service operated by **Northern Ireland Railways**, connecting it to Belfast and the main towns throughout Northern Ireland, and from there to the Republic. **Waterside Railway Station** is across the river close to Craigavon Bridge; the ticket office is open Monday-Saturday, 7:30 am-5 pm, Sunday 4:15-7 pm; the station is open longer hours. ☎ (028) 7134-2228; fax 7131-1221.

Ulsterbus has service throughout the city and beyond. Bus 143 goes to the airport, and the Maiden City Flyer 212 links Derry and Belfast. The Ulsterbus depot is on Foyle Street close to the Tourist Information Centre. Open Monday-Friday, 6 am-6 pm, Saturday until 5:30 pm; limited hours on Sunday. ☎ (028) 7126-2261; fax 7137-4442.

 Remember, all over Northern Ireland, check www. translink.com with all public transport inquiries.

Main Roads

 Derry City is reached by the M2/A6 from Belfast via Antrim and Dungiven; the A2/A37 from Coleraine and Limavady; the N13 from Letterkenny, Co. Donegal in the Republic; the N15 from counties Sligo and Galway in the Republic; and the A5 from Dublin via Omagh and Strabane.

■ Tourist Information

You can't miss the **Derry Visitor and Convention Bureau** as it's large and in a very prominent position as you enter the city with the river on your right. It's well signposted from whatever direction you arrive. The bureau stocks information leaflets and brochures covering the whole island, most free, and you can also book accommodations, change money and buy gifts here.

Open Monday-Friday, 9 am-5 pm, year-round, with additional hours of 10 am-5 pm from mid-March through October, and later weekday hours from July through September. ☎ (028) 7126-7284; info@derryvisitor.com; www.derryvisitor.com.

TRACING YOUR ANCESTORS

The Heritage Library, 14 Bishop Street, Derry, is actually not a library but a genealogy center that undertakes research for a fee. ☎ (028) 7126-9792; fax 7136-0921; niancestors@btclick.com.

■ Derry City

Sightseeing

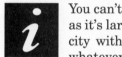 Before doing anything else, take a walk along the **walls** of the medieval city. The circuit is a mile long, and you get a good look at the layout of the city below you, including Free Derry corner at the entrance to the Bogside, where in January 1972 one of the most controversial events of the Troubles took place – known as

Northern Ireland

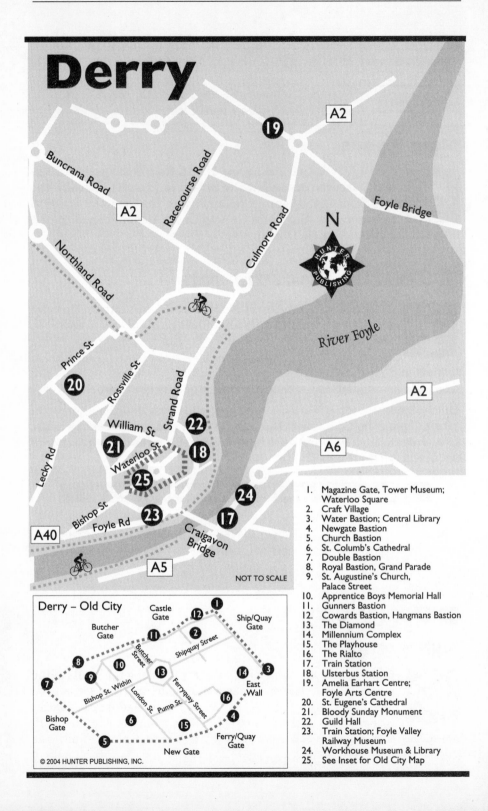

Derry

Buncrana Road

A2

Racecourse Road

A2

Culmore Road

Foyle Bridge

N

Northland Road

River Foyle

A2

Prince St

Rossville St

Strand Road

A6

William St

Waterloo St

Lecky Rd

Bishop St

Foyle Rd

A40

Craigavon Bridge

A5

NOT TO SCALE

1. Magazine Gate, Tower Museum; Waterloo Square
2. Craft Village
3. Water Bastion; Central Library
4. Newgate Bastion
5. Church Bastion
6. St. Columb's Cathedral
7. Double Bastion
8. Royal Bastion, Grand Parade
9. St. Augustine's Church, Palace Street
10. Apprentice Boys Memorial Hall
11. Gunners Bastion
12. Cowards Bastion, Hangmans Bastion
13. The Diamond
14. Millennium Complex
15. The Playhouse
16. The Rialto
17. Train Station
18. Ulsterbus Station
19. Amelia Earhart Centre; Foyle Arts Centre
20. St. Eugene's Cathedral
21. Bloody Sunday Monument
22. Guild Hall
23. Train Station; Foyle Valley Railway Museum
24. Workhouse Museum & Library
25. See Inset for Old City Map

Derry – Old City

Castle Gate

Butcher Gate

Ship/Quay Gate

Shipquay Street

Butcher Street

Bishop St. Within

London St.

Pump St.

Ferryquay Street

East Wall

Bishop Gate

New Gate

Ferry/Quay Gate

© 2004 HUNTER PUBLISHING, INC.

Bloody Sunday – when 14 people on a civil rights march were shot dead by the British Army.

Among the best-preserved city fortifications in Europe, the walls rise to a height of 26 feet in places and are 30 feet at their widest. They were built in 1618 to defend the Plantation city (see page 14) and have never been breached, despite three major sieges. The most famous one lasted 105 days in 1689, when a shocking 7,000 of the 30,000 inside died of starvation.

The Apprentice Boys

On December 7th, 1688, 13 young apprentice boys closed the gates of Londonderry against the advancing Catholic army of King James II. The city was the last refuge for many thousands of Protestants from all over Ulster who feared that they would be mercilessly slaughtered, as had happened in the previous Irish Rebellion in the year 1641. The siege that followed was to last for 105 days until the brave defenders were relieved on 31st July 1689.

The original gates are Shipquay, Butcher, Bishop and Ferryquay, the latter closed by the apprentice boys against the army of King James II. Three other gates were added later – Magazine, Castle and New Gate. The scale of the city within them will surprise you – it's tiny, with all roads converging on the central square called the Diamond, and you can explore it easily.

St. Columb's Anglican Cathedral, built in 1633, is within the walls, and worth a stop. Note the date-stone in the porch, which proclaims:

> *If stones could speake then London's prayse should sound*
> *Who built this church and cittie from the grounde*

The cathedral is open April-September, Monday-Saturday, 9 am-5 pm, and October-March, 9 am-1 pm, 2-4 pm. ☎ (028) 7126-7313; www.stcolumbscathedral.org.

Don't miss **The Tower Museum**, inside the city walls at the Magazine Gate, one of the most interesting anywhere, and you'll see why it has won awards. It covers the whole history of Derry and does so in an accessible way, managing to tell both sides of the story, right up to recent political divisions, with admirable balance. Open daily, July-August, Monday-Saturday, 10 am-5 pm, Sunday, 2-5 pm; rest of year, Tuesday-Saturday only. ☎ (028) 7137-2411; fax 7137-7633; tower.museum@derrycity.gov.uk.

The Guildhall, the civic center for the city, is just outside the walls near Shipquay Gate. It's open Monday-Friday, 9 am-5 pm. For the last few years it has been hosting the Bloody Sunday Enquiry set up by the British government. Hearings are suspended during summer, but if you're in Derry when it is running take the opportunity to attend. I found it very moving, watching witnesses give evidence. The information technology system used enhances the experience and has won awards.

Cross the river by the Craigavon Bridge and at 23 Glendermott Road in Waterside you find the **Workhouse Museum**, which is a slight misnomer, as it also covers the city's role in World War II. Admission free. Open July and August, Monday-Saturday, 10 am-4:30 pm; rest of year, Monday-Thursday and Saturday only. ☎ (028) 7131-8328.

Guided Tour

You can take a guided tour of the walled city, starting from the Tourist Information Centre. In July and August, tours are Monday-Friday, at 11:15 am and 3:15 pm; September-June, they start at 2:30 pm. Tours last an hour and a half.

Shopping in Derry City

Foyleside Shopping Centre proudly announces that it has "the biggest selection of shops in the North West." It's close to the Tourist Information Centre and the Bus Station, surrounded by multi-story carparks. On its four floors you'll find many Irish and UK chainstores, as well as smaller shops. There are also public toilets, ATMs and a bureau de change, and Kylemore Café is a good place for a reasonably priced snack or meal.

Exit at Orchard Street level and enter the walled inner city, where there are lots of little shops. **Austin's Department Store** on the corner of the Diamond is worth a look, as it's the oldest such store in the country and retains some interesting features.

Go down steep Shipquay Street and on your left is the entrance to the **Craft Village**, full of fascinating little shops, including the excellent **Foyle Books**, with a huge stock of second-hand books at very low prices. For new books head for **Bookworm** on Bishop Street, which also has a coffee shop.

If you're thinking about gifts to take home, **Colmcille Stone Crafts**, at 22 Glasgow Terrace, The Glen, is a local craft business making unusual mirrors. **Faller the Jeweller**, at 12 Strand Road, has an exclusive range of "handmade in Derry" items. There are many outlets selling **Irish linen**, **tweeds** and **woolens**.

Parking

The easiest place to park is in one of the multi-storeys next to the Tourist Information Centre or across the road next to the Foyleside Shopping Centre. There are other car parks, but those two spots are well sign-posted so try them first.

Entertainment

 Visitors enjoy Derry's creative and cultural atmosphere. The city has lots of pubs, many historic, and others built in recent years, some offering music and other entertainment. Remember, you don't have to drink alcohol to enjoy the pub experience. Among the most interesting are **The Anchor** on Ferryquay Street in the old city, ☎ (028) 7136-8601, www.anchorbar.co.uk, the **Monico Lounge** beside the Guildhall, ☎ (028) 7126-3121, and the art deco café bar and nightclub called the **Carraig** on Strand Road, ☎ (028) 7126-7529.

Many of the city's writers and artists have become well-known internationally, including Phil Coulter, The Undertones, and Dana, now a Member of the European Parliament, who won the Eurovision Song Contest as a teenager. Although playwright Brian Friel is from Omagh, he is very much associated with Derry, where the Field Day Theatre Company produced his work.

It's a city of festivals including the **St. Patrick's Day Celebrations**, **Guth an Earraigh/Irish Language Festival**, the **City of Derry Drama Festival**, the **Jazz Festival**, the **Derry Cycling Festival**, the **Maiden City Festival**, the **Foyle Film Festival** and the biggest **Hallowe'en Carnival** in Ireland.

Derr's newest venue is the 960-seater **Millennium Forum** on New Market Street, which hosts touring productions, including musicals from the West End, dance performances, and classical, rock and pop concerts. ☎ (028) 7126-4455; info@millenniumforum.co.uk; www. millenniumforum.co.uk.

On Artillery Street is **The Playhouse**, home to a number of theater companies. It has a dance studio, art gallery, and presents new plays by local, national and international companies. ☎ (028) 7126-8027; info@ derryplayhouse.co.uk.

The Verbal Arts Centre, Bishop Street Within, promotes the written and spoken word through a variety of events. Open Monday-Thursday, 9 am-5 pm, Friday until 4 pm, weekends for events. ☎ (028) 7126-6946; info@verbalartscentre.co.uk.

The Nerve Centre at 7-8 Magazine Street is a hive of activity, home to film production companies, with editing and recording facilities. There's also a bar, coffee shop, cinema, and two venues that host international acts. ☎ (028) 7126-0562; info@nerve-centre.org.uk; www.nerve-centre. org.uk.

During July and August, there's a **Cultural Trail**, with walking tours that explore the city's history. Check www.derrycity.gov.uk/ walledcityculturaltrail. Or see the Visitor Centref at 50 High Street, Draperstown, Derry, ☎ (028) 7962-7800, for a brochure.

■ Explore the County

Head east out of the city by Shore Road, passing the Magee University campus, cross the Foyle Bridge taking the A2, and a mile and half later off the B194, north of the city, you come to **Ballyarnett Country Park** and the **Amelia Earhart Centre**. Watch for signs. It recalls the first woman to fly solo across the Atlantic, who landed here in 1932. Cottage open Monday-Friday, 10 am-4 pm, free. **The Wildlife Sanctuary** is open Monday-Friday, 9 am-dusk, Saturday and Sunday from 10 am, and you're asked for a donation. ☎ (028) 7135-4040; ameliaearhart@compuserve.com.

As you drive towards Limavady on the A2, the landscape on your left is unusual. That's because it was reclaimed from the sea in the 19th century to be used in flax growing for the linen industry. These fertile areas are called "levels" by locals, and are below sea level so have to be drained by pumping stations. Grain and vegetables, especially potatoes, are grown here these days.

Limavady, 13 miles (21 km) farther on, is a bustling market town founded in the early 1600s by an enterprising Welshman, Thomas Phillips. Some historic features survive, including an elegant bridge (1700) and Georgian buildings on Main Street.

At number 51 Main Street, Limavady, lived Jane Ross, who wrote down the tune of the Londonderry Air, *which she'd heard played by a passing fiddler. The song is now best-known globally as* Danny Boy.

The town is in an attractive location on the river Roe, surrounded by mountains to the north and southeast. This area is part of the Sperrins region (see next chapter).

North of Limavady is the six-mile-long beach of **Magilligan**, with a Martello Tower, built during the Napoleonic Wars of the 19th century, overlooking a **National Nature Reserve**, which is always accessible. The Tower's walls are over nine feet thick and it's only open for group tours, but you could check. ☎ (028) 7776-3982.

Martello Towers: The British Navy in 1794, following the French Revolution, needed to capture a fortified tower at Point Mortella on Corsica. The tower was round, with thick walls and a flat top with a gun emplacement that could fire in all directions. The troops in the tower held the attacking forces at bay for two days. When Napolean began to cause trouble in Europe not long afterward, Britain remembered the design of that formidable Corsican tower, now known as a Martello Tower, and built dozens of them along the coast.

One of the best-known images of Northern Ireland is the **Mussenden Temple** at Castlerock, overlooking Magilligan Strand. This elegant building with a domed roof is clinging to the eroding cliffs. It was a "summer library" for the eccentric Anglican Bishop of Derry, Frederick August Hervey, who was also Earl of Bristol. It was built in 1783, and now belongs to the National Trust. He sounds rather fun and ahead of his time – he let the local Catholics use the Temple for their weekly Mass, traveled widely and collected art. His residence, **Downhill Castle** nearby, is now in ruins and was last used by US troops during WWII. Its grounds, with gardens and a glen walk, are open dawn to dusk all year.

Mussenden Temple is open June-August, daily, 11 am-6 pm; September open weekends; 17 March-May, open weekends and public holidays only. You pay a charge per car. ☎ (028) 7084-8728.

*Opposite the Mussenden Temple in Downhill Forest is the **Pretty Crafty Design Studio**, where you can buy imaginative handcrafted gifts. Phone to check opening times. ☎/fax (028) 7084-8146.*

Coleraine, about three miles inland from Magilligan on the River Bann, is the third largest town in the North and, unless you want to go shopping or eat, it's not worth stopping here, as there's nothing particularly interesting about it. The most attractive area is as you leave it and cross the River Bann.

A mile south of the town on the A54 is **Mountsandel Fort**, a big oval-shaped mound 200 feet (60 m) high, overlooking the river, which is said to be the oldest inhabited place in Ireland, about 9,000 years old.

Follow the A54 and the River Bann south and you come to **Bellaghy**, where Nobel Prize-winning poet Seamus Heaney was born. This Plantation town (see page 14) was built around 1618 by Baptist Jones for the Vintners' Company and so, like the others, had to have a "Bawn" or fortified enclosure. The **Bellaghy Bawn** is the largest to survive; it originally included two big houses and two round corner towers. One of the houses has been restored, with exhibits about local history, the Ulster Plantation, and on contemporary poetry, including Seamus Heaney. Guided tours available, and there's a café. Open daily Easter-September, 10 am-6 pm; rest of year Tuesday-Saturday, 9 am-5 pm. ☎ (028) 7938-6812.

 Bellaghy Bawn is linked with other centers that tell the story of the Flight of the Earls and Ulster's history. They are: **Manor Lodge** at Moneymore nearby, ☎ (028) 8674-8910; **The Ulster Plantation Centre** at Draperstown on the B41 a few miles farther north, ☎ (028) 7962-7800; the **Tower Museum**, Derry; and heritage centers in Co. Donegal. See page 13, or ask at the Bawn or info@theflightoftheearls.com.

Continue south on the A54/A31 to **Magherafelt**, another of the Plantation towns in the area, built by the Salters' Company of London, with an orderly and spacious layout.

Near the next village, Moneymore, is **Springhill**, a 17th-century manor house in the care of the National Trust, with a Costume Collection displayed in its Laundry. It's a simple and pretty Plantation house, and touring it is very enjoyable. It has a tea room, and lovely woodland walks and gardens. To reach Springhill, take the B18 (Moneymore-Coagh road) 1.6 km from town. The house is open July-August, daily, noon-6 pm, and open weekends only from June to September. ☎ (028) 8674-8210; www.nationaltrust.org.uk and www.gardensireland.com/springhill.

■ Adventures on Foot

 The **Roe Valley Country Park**, one mile south of Limavady off the B192, is popular for canoeing, rock climbing, game fishing and camping. It's also a delightful place to walk. The first domestic hydroelectric power station in the North opened here in 1896 and a lot of the original equipment has been preserved. You also see the ruins of water mills used in linen production. There are riverside walks and a history trail to follow. Visitor Centre is open daily, Easter-Auguist, 10 am-6 pm; September-Easter, Monday-Friday, 10 am-5 pm. The car park is open at all times. ☎ (028) 7772-2074.

Also near Limavady is **Banagher Glen**, where there are panoramic views as you walk in the county's largest forest to the Altnaheglish Reservoir, on the west bank of the Owenrigh River, about three miles (5.5 km) south-southwest of Dungiven. Open to pedestrians all year, and to vehicles daily during July and August and weekends Easter-September.

Admission free, phone for times. ☎ (028) 7776-0304; fax 7776-8107; rich-ard.gillen@limavady.gov.uk.

■ Adventure on Wheels

The **Foyle Valley Cycle Route** takes you along the banks of the Foyle for a scenic and relaxing cycle. The route is 21 miles (34 km) long, following traffic-free paths and quiet country roads. and connects Derry City with the border towns of Lifford in Co. Donegal and Strabane in Co. Tyrone.

■ Adventures on Water

In Derry you can take a trip on the river with **Foyle Cruises**, departing daily at 2 and 4 pm from City Cruise Berth, with a full bar and refreshments on board. Other cruises include eve-ning trips to Greencastle in Co. Donegal. ☎ (028) 7136-2857; fax 7136-2854.

Swimming

There's a choice of indoor and outdoor activities in Derry and surround-ing area. There are centers with pools, fitness suites, and some with other facilities. Always phone in advance to check public access.

- **City Swimming Baths**, William Street. ☎ (028) 7126-4459.
- **Lisnagelvin Leisure Centre**, Richill Park. ☎ (028) 7134-7695.

Fishing

The Foyle is known for its salmon and, to a lesser extent, sea trout and brown trout. It has four main tributaries – the Mourne, Derg, Strule and Finn – and has an unusually long season, stretching from March to October. It's one of the rich-est fishing waters in Europe and one of the best for salmon in the world. In Derry, the Creggan Country Park, Westway, is a peaceful fishing loca-tion. Inquire about fees. ☎ (028) 7137-1544; info@foylefishing.net; www.foylefishing.net. Contact Gerry Quinn there, who can advise you about fishing throughout the Foyle system and you can hire local ghillies (guides) who know every nook and cranny.

See pages 71-74 for details on angling in Ireland, regulations and best times to fish.

There's further information in the next chapter. page 512.

■ Other Activities

- **Brandywell Sports Centre**, Lane Moor Road, is next to the soccer stadium and has a handball/racquetball court. ☎ (028) 7126-3902.

- **Brooke Park Leisure Centre**, Rosemount Avenue, has two squash courts, tennis courts and a fitness suite. ☎ (028) 7126-2637.

- **Brunswick Superbowl** has 10-pin bowling, restaurant, bar, café, and pool tables. It's open every day from 9 am to late. It's on Brunswick Lane, Pennyburn Industrial Estate. ☎ (028) 7137-1999; fun@brunswicksuperbowl.com; www.brunswicksuperbowl.com.

■ Adventures on Horseback

Ardmore Stables, 8 Rushall Road, Ardmore, offers lessons for beginners and hillside trekking for more experienced riders. ☎ (028) 7134-5187.

Faughanvale Pony Trekking Centre in Greysteel is on a 70-acre working farm, four miles from Eglinton, eight miles from Derry and 10 miles (16 km) from Limavady. Off-road treks are tailored to the abilities of the riders and range over different terrain, including hills and glens. Book in advance. ☎ (028) 7181-1843; daltonpatricia@hotmail.com.

The Island Equestrian Centre is two miles from Coleraine, off the B67. It caters to everyone from beginner to more experienced, and is set in 160 acres of farmland.

Other riding facilities include the **Banagher Equestrian Centre**, Feeny, Derry, ☎ (028) 7778-1117, and **Streeve Hill House**, Limavady, ☎ (028) 7776-6563.

■ Golf

The **Foyle Golf Centre**, less than two miles (3.2 km) north of Derry at 12 Alder Road, has both an 18-hole and nine-hole course, and an indoor floodlit driving range. Open Monday-Friday, 9 am-dark, Saturday and Sunday, 8 am-dark. It also has the **Pitchers Wine Bar and Restaurant**, where there's entertainment on Thursday-Saturday nights. ☎ (028) 7135-2222;mail@foylegolfclub24.co.uk; www.foylegolfcentre.co.uk.

The City of Derry Golf Club, three miles (4.8 km) west of the city on the Strabane Road, has both an 18-hole and nine-hole course with picturesque views over the Foyle. ☎ (028) 7134-6369; cityofderrygolfclub@aol.com; www.cityofderrygolfclub.com.

The Radisson Roe Hotel and Golf Resort is on the A2, 16 miles (26 km) from Derry and one mile (1.6 km) west of Limavady, and welcomes visitors any day. It has an 18-hole parkland course, and also has excellent facilities, including a driving range, pool, and gym. ☎ (028) 7776-0105; drgolf@radissonroepark.com; www.radissonroepark.com.

■ Where to Stay

Derry City

Hotels

City Hotel on Queen's Quay has a marvelous location, close to the Guildhall, walled city and the Foyle. When I stayed it had just opened, so was awaiting classification, but it should be a four-star. The foyer's décor is bright and welcoming and the staff are helpful and charming. There's a choice of rooms and suites.

I stayed in a Junior Suite, which has a separate spacious living room, with

HOTEL PRICE CHART	
Price per person, per night, with two sharing, including breakfast.	
$	Under US $50
$$	US $50-$100
$$$	US $101-$175
$$$$	US $176-$200
$$$$$	Over US $200

desk, comfortable seats, a large bedroom with plenty of hanging space for clothes, enormous bathroom with bath and shower, and all with wonderful views of the River Foyle and the city. The beds are really comfortable too, and the décor is contemporary – browns and beiges, very relaxing. It has a leisure centre with pool, gym, and other facilities, and free parking underground for guests.

At the City Hotel is **Thompson's on the River restaurant**, overlooking the Foyle. It offers a varied menu, and is popular with locals for dinner and at lunch-time. The food is delicious and not over-priced, with a three-course dinner, including a miniature bottle of wine, less than £30.

It's a really convenient and comfortable place to stay, a few steps from the medieval city, shops, other attractions, and on one of the main roads, so if you're exploring farther afield, it's ideal. Room rates from $ per person sharing. ☎ (028) 7136-5800; res@derry-gsh.com; www.gshotels.com.

☆☆☆☆ **The Tower Hotel** is on Butcher Street just off the Diamond, and the only hotel inside the walled medieval city. It blends in really well with its historic surroundings. The rooms are pleasantly decorated and well-equipped. There's a mini-gym and sauna, and it is gay-friendly. It has a **Bistro restaurant** with a Mediterranean menu, which overlooks the city walls, and a café-style bar with buffet lunch, snacks and bar menu all day.

Rooms from $ sharing. Tower Hotels also have a choice of special deals for two, three and four nights, including dinner, which are excellent value. ☎ (028) 7137-1000; fax 7137-1234; info@thd.ie; www.towerhotelderry.ie.

City of Derry Travelodge, Strand Road, is within easy walking distance of the walled city and other attractions. Rooms are comfortable. Like all Travelodges, it's great value for two traveling together, as rates are by room. Breakfast available. $. ☎ (028) 7127-1277; www.travelodge. co.uk.

Rental Cottage

 ☆☆☆ **Cathedral Cottage**, 16 London Street, is inside the walled city, and dates from 1767 when the lease was acquired from The Honourable The Irish Society. It's a tastefully restored three-story terraced house that retains its former character and elegance and even has some fine old furniture. There's a lovely view from it of St. Columb's Cathedral and its grounds. It sleeps four in two bedrooms, one double, the other twin and en suite.

It's centrally heated and is very well equipped with washing machine, tumble dryer, clothes drying facilities, fridge/freezer, dishwasher, microwave, TV, VCR, and telephone. Bed linens and towels are supplied.

The owners will arrange bike rental, and other activities including hill walking, pony-trekking, tennis, theater booking and walking tours. It's an excellent value too, from £300 per week, or £50 per night, minimum two nights. ☎ (028) 7126-9691; fax 7126-6913; saddlershouse@btinternet.com; www.thesaddlershouse.com.

> **Author Note:** The owners of Cathedral Cottage are members of NISCHA – the Northern Ireland Self-Catering Association. The Association publishes a guide to member properties, available free from the Northern Ireland Tourist Board, or contact NISCHA at ☎ (028) 9077-6174; info@nischa.com; www.nischa.com.

Hostels

- **Derry City Hostel**, 4-6 Magazine Street. ☎ (028) 7128-0280; fax 7128-0281; www.derrycitytours.com.
- **Steve's Backpackers**, Asylum Road, Derry. ☎ (028) 7137-7989; derryhostel@hotmail.com

Outside the City

Hotels

✰✰ **Best Western White Horse Hotel, 68 Clooney Road,** is minutes from the Derry airport and close to the city center. The hotel overlooks Lough Foyle and the Donegal Hills. It's comfortable and welcoming, an ideal base for anyone touring the area. It has a swimming pool, gym, spa and other facilities, and its rooms are pleasantly furnished. The restaurant has a mixture of international and traditional dishes, using local produce. Rates from $ sharing. ☎ (028) 7186-0606; fax 7186-0371; info@white-horse.demon.co.uk; www.whitehorse-hotel.com.

✰✰✰✰ **The Beech Hill Country House Hotel** is only two miles (3.2 km) from the city on the A6 main road to Dublin and Belfast and yet it retains the atmosphere of country living. It's privately owned and beautifully furnished and part of the charm is its setting in wooded grounds. You can enjoy curling up by the fire in the Gallery Lounge if it's cold, and take traditional afternoon tea, which includes a selection of homemade bread. Dining here is particularly memorable, and the extensive menu includes lamb, beef, fish. Rates from $$ sharing. ☎ (028) 7134-9279; fax 7134-5366; info@beech-hill.com; www.beech-hill.com.

Guesthouse

Brae Head House, 22 Brae Head Road, is less than two miles (3.2 km) from Derry, and has a panoramic view of the Foyle and Dunhugh golf course. It's a Georgian farmhouse on a mixed farm, and is in a great location for exploring the city and the surrounding region. The rooms have tea- and coffee-making facilities and televisions, and there's a garden. ☎/fax (028) 7126-3195. Rates (£20 per person) $ including breakfast.

Camping & RV Parks in the County

 There's a choice of parks in the area. Phone in advance, particularly if camping, as some have very limited spaces.

✰✰✰ **Benone Tourist Complex** on A2 coast road, 12 miles (19 km) north of Limavady, has heated splash pools, and a golf practice range among its facilities. Open all year. ☎ (028) 7775-0555.

✰✰✰ **Golden Sands**, off A2 between Limavady and Coleraine, is close to a beach, and open March to end October. ☎ (028) 7775-0324.

✰✰✰✰ **Castlerock Holiday Park**, six miles (10 km) northwest of Coleraine on A2, is open March to end November. ☎ (028) 7084-8381.

✰✰✰✰ **Tullans Farm Caravan Park** is on a working farm, a mile (1.6 km) from Coleraine, and is open from March to end October. ☎ 9028) 7034-2309; tullansfarm@netscapeonline.co.uk.

☆☆☆ **Juniper Hill Caravan Park** is a mile (1.6 km) east of Portstewart on the A2, open April to October 2. ☎ (028) 7083-2023. Also at Portstewart is the ☆☆☆ **Millfield Holiday Village**, open from March to end October. ☎ (028) 7083-3308.

■ Where to Eat

Derry City

 The Sandwich Company has two branches in Derry – at 62 Strand Road and at 25 The Diamond in the medieval center. They offer a great selection of hot and cold sandwiches, home-made cakes and excellent coffee. The Strand Road branch has live folk and bluegrass music most Saturdays, 12:30-2:30 pm. Both branches open at 8:30 am and close at 5 pm. ☎ (028) 7126-6771.

Rafters Restaurant, 122 Northland Road, has a reputation for using local produce and specializes in chicken, steaks, fish and pizzas cooked in a traditional Italian wood-burning oven. Main courses £8-£12. ☎ (028) 7126-6080.

Outside the City

The Lime Tree Restaurant is on the main street in Limavady. It has a warm and welcoming atmosphere and uses fresh seasonal produce in the preparation of its dishes. It specializes in modern Irish cuisine and is open for lunch from Wednesday to Sunday, noon to 2 pm, and for dinner from 6 to 9 pm. ☎ (028) 7776-4300; info@limetreerest.com; www. limetreerest.com.

Dittys Coffee Shop is on Rainey Street, Magherafelt, which is halfway between Belfast and Derry – so it's a good place to stop for a snack when traveling. The shop is small, and you're surrounded by delicious smells as it's inside a home bakery selling lots of breads and confectionery. Breakfast and a choice of three or four hot dishes are served daily, as well as snacks. Open Monday to Saturday from 8:30 am to 5:30 pm. ☎ (028) 7963-3944.

The Cromore Halt Inn in Portstewart is a restaurant and guest house, with 12 bedrooms – the overnight rates is from less than $ per person. It is popular for Sunday lunches and its menu includes steaks, chicken, pork, fish and vegetarian choices. ☎ (028) 7083-6888; fax 7083-1910; info@cromore.com; www.cromore.com.

■ Further Information

Tourist Information Centres

Foyle Street, Derry. ☎ (028) 7126-7284; fax 7137-7992; info@ derryvisitor.com; www.derryvisitor.com.

Railway Road, Coleraine. ☎ (028) 7034-4723.

Council Offices, Connell Street, Limavady. ☎ (028) 7776-7284.

Useful Websites

■ **Rural Tourism Ireland**. www.ruraltourismireland.com.

Guldhall in Derry City

Ulster-American Folk Park, Mellon Homestead

The Sperrins

The Sperrins region is right in the center of Northern Ireland, stretching from the western shores of Lough Neagh to the border with Donegal, taking in most of Co. Tyrone and the southern portion of Co. Londonderry. Its main towns are **Omagh**, **Strabane**, **Cookstown** and **Dungannon**, as well as Limavady and Magherafelt, which were covered in the last chapter.

Criss-crossed by mountains, moorland and inland waters, the Sperrins has been designated an Area of Outstanding Natural Beauty. What makes it such a wonderful region to visit is that it is so peaceful. Tyrone is the largest county in the North yet has the smallest population, so its roads are very quiet once you get away from the towns. Whitewashed stone farmhouses with brightly colored doors are a distinctive feature in the countryside.

From the 18th to the last century, a huge number of its people left to seek new lives in North America, Canada, Australia and Britain, and there are many places to visit closely associated with some of them, including the family homes of US Presidents. There are also nature trails and forest parks to explore, and you can just take it easy and discover the area's beauty for yourself.

The region is steeped in heritage and its hills littered with prehistoric remains. It was here that the Earls of Tyrone and Tyrconnell, O'Neill and O'Donnell, held out against the British in the late 16th century. Some local Irish Catholic landowners managed to hold onto their land after the Flight of the Earls in 1607, but lost it after the 1641 rebellion. You'll hear about the area's rich past, including legends of giants in Gortin and Shane the Highwayman, from those fortunate to live here. If you don't – ask!

The Sperrin Mountains are the main focus of the area, named from the Irish "na speirini" meaning "spurs of rock," with their highest point Sawel at 2,240 feet (941 m). The region offers a huge choice of activities in unforgettable surroundings. It's a paradise for anyone interested in being outdoors – cycling, walking, angling, golf, watersports – even parachuting.

■ Getting Here

The nearest **airport** is Derry City, and Belfast International Airport is just across Lough Neagh.

You can reach the region on the following **roads**: the M1/A29 from Belfast; the A29 from Armagh through Dungannon to

Cookstown; the A28/A4/M1/A29 from Dublin; the N14 from Letterkenny through Lifford, Co. Donegal, to Strabane; the A2 from the Inishowen peninsula to Derry and on to Limavady; and the B52/B46/A32 from Enniskillen, Co. Fermanagh, to Omagh.

■ Getting Around

 Ulsterbus runs services between its towns and villages. You can explore much of the region on the **Ulsterbus Sperrin Rambler,** which runs between Castledawson and Omagh, passing through Magherafelt, Draperstown, Plumbridge, Gortin. Details ☎ (028) 9066-6630 or www.translink.com.

■ Tourist Information

The **Omagh Tourist Information Office** is on Market Street. ☎ (028) 8224-7831; fax 8224-0774; omagh.tic@btconnect.com.

The **Cookstown Tourist Information Centre** is on Burn Road, Open July and August, Monday-Saturday, 9 am-5 pm, Sunday, 2-4 pm; June-September, Monday-Saturday, 9 am-5 pm; October-May, Monday-Friday, 9 am-5 pm, Saturday 10 am-4 pm. There is a 24-hour information kiosk outside. The building also houses The Burnavon Arts and Cultural Centre, and the tourist information office opens two hours before performances. ☎ (028) 8676-7727; tic@cookstown.gov.uk; www.cookstown.gov.uk.

■ Sightseeing

Omagh

 Omagh stands where the rivers Camowen and Drumragh join to become the wide and shallow Strule. It's had an interesting history, founded as a monastic settlement in the 8th century; centuries later the O'Neills had a fortress where the courthouse stands today. Sadly, most people remember its bombing in August 1998, the worst single atrocity of the Troubles, carried out by a breakaway Republican group who don't support the Good Friday Agreement.

Omagh has character and is a busy market town serving its agricultural hinterland. Among its famous sons are songwriter Jimmy Kennedy (*Red Sails in the Sunset, Teddy Bears' Picnic*) and playwright Brian Friel (*Translations, Dancing at Lughnasa, Philadelphia, Here I Come!*).

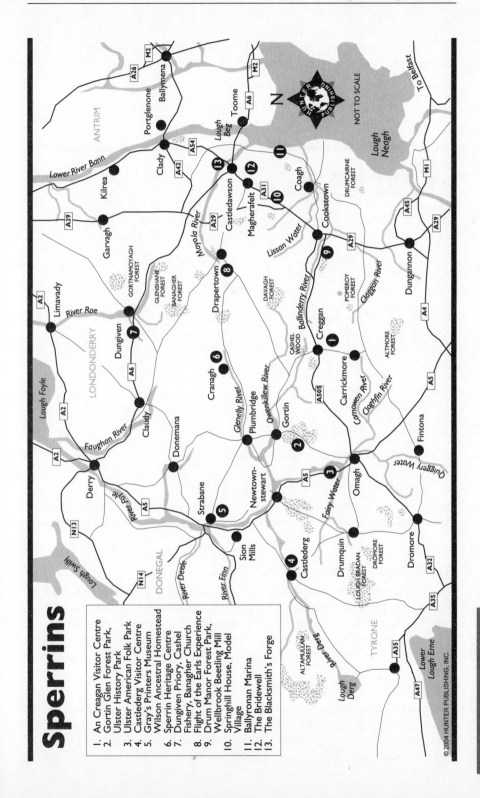

Sperrins

1. An Creagan Visitor Centre
2. Gortin Glen Forest Park, Ulster History Park
3. Ulster American Folk Park
4. Castlederg Visitor Centre
5. Gray's Printers Museum Wilson Ancestral Homestead
6. Sperrin Heritage Centre
7. Dungiven Priory, Cashel Fishery, Banagher Church
8. Flight of the Earls Experience
9. Drum Manor Forest Park, Wellbrook Beetling Mill
10. Springhill House, Model Village
11. Ballyronan Marina
12. The Bridewell
13. The Blacksmith's Forge

Leading contemporary Irish poet John Montague was born in New York but grew up near here at Garvaghey, Fintona.

There are lots of shops, cafés, restaurants and pubs in the town, and it would be a good place to use as your base while exploring the region.

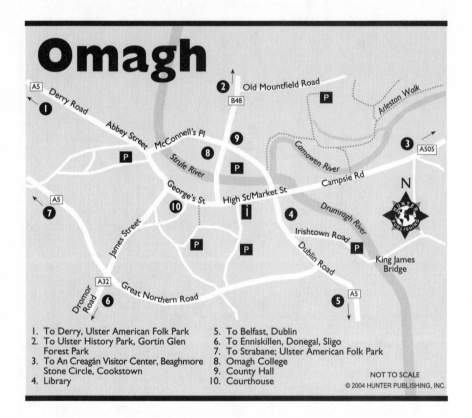

1. To Derry, Ulster American Folk Park
2. To Ulster History Park, Gortin Glen Forest Park
3. To An Creagán Visitor Center, Beaghmore Stone Circle, Cookstown
4. Library
5. To Belfast, Dublin
6. To Enniskillen, Donegal, Sligo
7. To Strabane; Ulster American Folk Park
8. Omagh College
9. County Hall
10. Courthouse

NOT TO SCALE
© 2004 HUNTER PUBLISHING, INC.

The Ulster American Folk Park

Three miles (4.8 km) north of Omagh on the A5 is The Ulster American Folk Park. It's one of my favorite places, an outdoor museum that isn't a bit like one – you feel as if you are in a real place as you wander round. That has something to do with the activities going on, the animals and the smells. The Park is divided into the Old and New World and you cross between them by ship – a full-scale replica of part of one that carried emigrants to North America during the 18th and 19th centuries.

The park contains reassembled houses and other buildingss. Staff in costume and in character tells you about life in these simple surroundings. Among them is the ancestral home of Thomas Mellon (born 1813), who left here for Pennsylvania and became a judge, leading banker and millionaire. His son Andrew built Pittsburgh. Another is the boyhood home of John Joseph Hughes who became Archbishop of New York and built St. Patrick's Cathedral.

Indoors, there are displays from which you learn a lot of facts. What I find most interesting is the influence of the Irish, in particular the Ulster-Scots, on life in North America – including the number who signed the Declaration of Independence, and that the families of so many American Presidents emigrated from this part of the island of Ireland. It was an eye-opener for me, as I'm sure it would be for many. The park is also the **Centre for Migration Studies** and has an extensive database, useful for researching family history. ☎ (028) 8225-6315; fax 8224-2241; uafp@iol.ie; www.qub.ac.uk/cms.

There's also an annual program of special events – including an Appalachian and Bluegrass Music Festival. It has a Restaurant, a craft and gift shop, bureau de change, and plenty of free leaflets about the area.

The Ulster American Folk Park is open Easter through September, Monday-Saturday, 11 am-6:30 pm, Sunday and public holidays to 7 pm; October-Easter, Monday-Friday, 10:30 am-5 pm. ☎ (028) 8224-3292; fax 8224-2241; uafp@iol.ie; www.folkpark.com.

Strabane

Strabane is 20 miles (32 km) north of Omagh on the A5 to Derry, beside the River Mourne and across the River Foyle from Lifford in Co. Donegal. It's another busy market town, which in the 18th century was an important center for printing. On Main Street is an important reminder of that – **Gray's Printing Shop**, now a museum run by the National Trust. This was where John Dunlap, who printed the American Declaration of Independence, and James Wilson, grandfather of US President Woodrow Wilson, learned their trade. You get a guided tour, and a visit is particularly worthwhile when there's a compositor at work so, if you can, phone in advance. Open April-September, Tuesday-Saturday, 2-5 pm. ☎ (028) 7188-4094.

John Dunlap's old home is on Meetinghouse Street, marked with a plaque. He published the Declaration of Independence on the front page of his *Pennsylvania Packet*, which became America's first daily newspaper. The Wilson ancestral home (above left) is two miles (3.2 km) outside Strabane at Dergalt on the B536 road to Plumbridge. It's a thatched farmhouse, almost unchanged since **James Wilson** left for America in 1807. Wilsons still live next door and continue to work the farm. Guided tours July-August, Tuesday-Sunday, 2-5 pm. ☎ (028) 7138-2204.

The restored corn-, flax- and sawmills on Brook Road, Donemana, Strabane, known as **Silverbrook Mills**, are a good place to see something of the area's industrial past. There's also a tea room and gift shop. Open Easter-September; Monday-Saturday, 11 am-6:30 pm, Sunday until 7 pm; October-Easter, Monday-Friday, 10:30 am-5 pm. ☎ (028) 7139-7097.

Cookstown

Cookstown, close to Lough Neagh, is the perfect base for exploring the eastern section of the Sperrins. The town's most notable feature is its main street, which must be the longest and widest anywhere – it's 1¼ mile long (two km), with a hump in the middle, and is 130 feet (40 m) wide. It was part of an ambitious toown-improvement plan of local landlord William Stewart of Killymoon in the 18th century, but neither he nor his descendants ever did anything about expanding it. Still, there is lots of space to park, and there's a tour you can take called the Long Hungry Cookstown Town Trail along one of Ireland's longest and widest main streets, featuring castles, railway stations and churches in this original market town. ☎ (028) 8676-2382.

Just four miles (6.4 km) north of the town off the A505 is the **Wellbrook Beetling Mill** (National Trust), which has nothing to do with insects – beetling is part of linen-making, when the fabric is hammered to give it a sheen. The Mill is in an idyllic setting in a valley surrounded by woods. Open March through September, weekends and holidays, noon to 6 pm. In July and August, open daily, same hours. ☎ (028) 8674-8210; www.nationaltrust.org.uk.

Dungannon

Dungannon looks like a typical Planter town, with its planned main street, some attractive Georgian terraces, and a Royal School founded by King James I.

Its police station looks like a castle – and so it should, as it was designed to guard the Khyber Pass and there was a mix-up, so presumably the one meant for here ended up in Southern Afghanistan!

Shopping

While in Dungannon, visit **The Linen Green**, Moygashel, where you can learn about linen-making in its Visitor Centre. There's a marvelous collection of shops to browse in, including Irish designer outlets, and the **Ulster Weavers Gift Store**, where you'll find pure linen goods and unique gifts. ☎ (028) 8772-4004. You can also eat at the **Loft Restaurant** or **Village Pantry**. The Linen Green has free parking and is open Monday-Saturday, 10 am-5 pm. ☎ (028) 8775-3761; enquiries@thelinengreen. com; www.thelinengreen.com.

Just outside Dungannon is the **Tyrone Crystal factory**, where you can take a guided tour, buy gifts and eat in its restaurant. Open all year, Monday-Saturday, 9 am-6 pm; Sunday, 1-5 pm. ☎ (028) 8772-5335; tyrcrystal@aol.com; www.tyronecrystal.com.

Sightseeing Routes Around The Sperrins

 Follow any of the river valleys in the region and you have a natural touring route taking you through sweet little villages and introducing you to the glorious countryside, along with other activities you can enjoy along the way. Here are a few suggestions for scenic routes.

Close to the border with Donegal in the southwest is the **Derg Valley**. Start your tour at **Castlederg**, on the B72, where there's a visitor center on the banks of the river, a good introduction to the area.

 Davy Crockett's family came from this remote little village and exhibits include a model of the Alamo where he made his last stand. Open April-October, Tuesday-Friday, 11 am-4 pm; Saturday, 11:30-4; Sunday, 2-5 pm. ☎ (028) 8167-0795.

You can follow the valley of the Foyle along the A5 road between Strabane and Derry City, although you get closer to the river along the National Cycle Route, which runs along its bank (see page 511).

The Glenelly River runs through the scenic mountainous area just south of the Sperrins around Plumbridge and Cranagh, and you can explore its valley along the B47. At **Cranagh**, nine miles (14.4 km) east of Plumbridge, there's the **Sperrin Heritage Centre**, where you'll find out about the area and can even try panning for gold. It also has a café and shop. Open April-October, 11:30-5:30 pm; Saturday, to 6 pm; Sunday, 2-6 pm. ☎ (028) 8164-8142.

You can circle the eastern slopes of the Sperrin Mountains by continuing east on the B47 toward Draperstown, then take the B40 to the northwest towards **Claudy** on the Faughan River, another scenic area.

Parallel to the B40 on the A6 is the **Glenshane Pass** between Castledawson and Dungiven. At Dungiven, the River Roe is joined by the smaller Owenbeg and Owenrigh rivers, before making its way to Lough Foyle via Limavady. In this area are the **Glenshane Forest**, the **Gortnamoyagh Forest** and the **Roe Valley Country Park** (see chapter on Derry, page 494).

Northern Ireland

On the eastern side of the region, the A54 follows River Bann between Portglenone and Coleraine.

■ Adventures on Foot

If you're a walker you have plenty of options here, with everything from town trails to forest walks to hill walking. Following are some suggestions.

An Creagán Visitor Centre off the A505 at Creggan, between Omagh and Cookstown, is the starting point for a number of walks, ranging from two to nine miles (14.4 km). These explore the archaeological sites in the area, including the Creggandeveskey and Cregganconroe court tombs and the Aghascrebagh standing stone. The Centre is open daily, April-September, 11 am-6:30 pm; October-March, it closes at 4:30 pm. There is a charge to see its displays about the area. It also has a licensed restaurant and a shop selling crafts. ☎ (028) 8076 1112; www.an-creagan.com.

Ballyronan Wood on the shore of Lough Neagh, east of Magherafelt on the B160, has a number of circular routes to follow around Traad Ponds. **Cairndaisy Wood**, an evocative name, is north of Moneymore off the A29, and **Davagh Forest**, 10 miles (16 km) northwest of Cookstown in the foothills of the Sperrins, is populated by Sika deer. On the B4 between Cookstown and Omagh is the upland village of **Pomeroy** and its forest has a series of nature trails to follow.

Around the picturesque village of **Gortin**, north of Omagh on the River Owenkillew, you have a choice. **The Burn Walk** (two miles/3.2 km) is part of the Ulster Way long-distance route and follows a burn (or stream) through Gortin Gap into the **Gortin Glen Forest Park**. Among other walks is the **Nature Trail** (under two miles/3.2 km), and longest of all is the **Loop Walk** (14 miles/22.5 km), which wanders through and beyond the Forest Park to the "Robbers' Table." The Robbers' Table got its name from robbers who used to waylay travellers in times past by spying on them from here. From there you can enjoy fantastic views out over North Donegal before returning.

If you're not exhausted after exploring the Ulster American Folk Park, near Omagh (see page 506), take the circular **Carrigans Walk**. It's 13 miles (21 km) long, crosses the historical McCormack's Bridge, and then follows the old railway line into Omagh. It joins the National Cycle Network route there and loops back along the River Strule on your return.

Walking Festivals

A number of special events and festivals take place annually. The walks are non-competitive, and are geared to suit varying levels of fitness. You have the option of joining in for one, two or three days of walking. Festivals include:

- **Golden Sperrins Walking Weekend** (June), Strabane. Contact District Council. ☎ (028) 7138-2204.

- **Cookstown District Walking Festival** (June-July). Tourist Office. ☎ (028) 8876-6727.

- **Carntogher Festival** (July), Garvagh/Dungiven. Contact Tourist Office, Magherafelt. ☎ (028) 7963-4570.

- **Cairn Sunday** (July), Gortin/Omagh. Contact Gortin Accommodation Suite. ☎ (028) 8164-8346.

- **The Sperrins Walking Festival** (August), Magherafelt. Contact Tourist Office. (see page 504).

- **Feeny Folk and Hill Walking Festival** (October), Feeny/Dungiven.Contact Feeny Community Association. ☎ (028) 7778-1876.

> *The Wild Geese Parachute Centre at Garvagh is open all year. It has static line courses and also offers tandem sky diving, and is considered one of the best-equipped centers belonging to the British Parachuting Association. Restaurant and game room on site. ☎ (028) 2955-8609; fax 2955-7050.*

■ Adventures on Wheels

Because its roads are so quiet, the region is ideal for cycling. Here are some suggestions.

From just north of Cookstown, Route 95 of the recently established **Sustrans National Cycling Route** (Sustrans is the UK charity dedicated to sustainable transport), part of the Belfast-to-Ballyshannon route, takes you west, following the Ballinderry River and passing close to the mysterious Beaghmore Stone Circle from the Bronze Age. It then follows the Owenkillew River to Gortin.

Another route is the **Loughshore Trail**, fully signposted, which follows the banks of Lough Neagh (it's also Route 94 of the National Cycle Network). Start at Toome on the B160 and go south towards Coagh (pronounced coke) and along the shore.

There's a choice of routes at **Portadown**. Either turn northwards and continue the circuitous route back to Toome, clinging to the eastern bank of the Lough as you pass Antrim town, or travel on southwards to Armagh.

Author Tip: There are free brochures available and you can buy cycling route maps at Tourist Information Centres or online at www.nationalcyclenetwork.org.uk. www.loughshoretrail.com is also worth a look.

Mountain Biking

Opportunities for mountain biking are available at **Gortin Glen Forest Park** outside Omagh, and at **Davagh Forest** near Cookstown, which have tracks designed for both amateurs and the more experienced.

Bike Rental & Repair

- **Allen's of Omagh**, Market Arcade, Market Street. ☎ (028) 8225-1991.
- **An Creagán Visitor Centre**, Creggan. ☎ (028) 8076-1112.
- **Conway Cycles**, 157 Loughmacrory Road, Carrickmore. ☎ (028) 8076-1258.
- **Glenelly and Sperrin Cottages**, 11b Main Street, Plumbridge. ☎ (028) 8164-8000.
- **Sperrins Cycle Breaks**, 1 Lisnaharney Road, Lislap, Omagh. ☎ (028) 8164-7998.

■ Adventures on Water

There's a **Marina at Portglenone** on the River Bann.

Ballyronan Marina Centre on the shore of Lough Neagh, within the village of Ballyronan, on 94 approximately 12 miles northeast of Cookstown, offers a variety of watersports – including sailing, windsurfing, water-skiing and jet-skiing, with lessons if you want. Boats can also be rented from here, and the Centre also has a coffee shop serving snacks. It's in a scenic area, and you can take a walk and see the wildlife. There is a campground here, which is open year-round. ☎ (028) 7941-8399.

Fishing

The Sperrins region is ideal for anyone interested in game or coarse fishing, with so many loughs and rivers. Among its attractions are the following.

The Foyle System

The Foyle system is one of the most prolific salmon and sea trout fisheries not just in Ireland but in all of Europe. The River Foyle's main tributaries in the North, the Mourne, Derg and Strule, all fast-flowing and rocky, have large stocks of salmon, sea trout and brown trout from mid-June to October, and lots of grilse can be caught from March to April. The Owenkillew and Glenelly rivers provide spate river fishing through summer and autumn, while the Camowen and Owenreagh rivers can be fished throughout September and October.

■ Useful Contacts

The Foyle Carlingford and Irish Lights Commission Loughs Agency is the joint fisheries authority for both sides of the border. ☎ (028) 8165-8027.

In the Omagh area, permits and local information are available from:

C.A. Anderson, 64 Market Street. ☎ (028) 8224-2311.

Kenny Alcorn, Lough Muck, Omagh. ☎ (028) 8224-2618.

G. Trainor, Butcher's Shop, Gortin. ☎ (028) 8164-8543.

The Lough Neagh System

Lough Neagh is the largest freshwater lake in the UK, with tributaries including the Ballinderry and the Moyola, which is good for trout. The dollaghan is unique to the Lough; it's a migratory brown trout and can be caught from mid-July to the end of the season (October 31). Other main species include river brown trout, salmon and eel. For more about Lough Neagh, see the chapter on Armagh, pages 550-55.

The Lower Bann System

This is one of Europe's finest coarse fisheries, particularly the 14-mile stretch from the Eel Weir at Toomebridge, which includes Lough Beg, Newferry and Portglenone. Lough Beg has abundant bream, roach, hybrids and pike. Magherafelt District Council runs a facility at Portglenone, with 89 platform fishing points, open all year and free. ☎ (028) 7939-7979 during office hours.

> **Important Note:** To fish the Bann you need a Coarse Fishing Permit from the owner, Bann System Limited, and also a Rod Licence issued by the Fisheries Conservancy Board. Each system and individual rivers throughout the Sperrins, as in other areas of Ireland, have what seem like bewildering rules about permits and licenses – the easiest way of checking is to contact Tourist Information, permit outlets or tackle shops. Permit Outlet for Bann System: Richard Mulholland, Lough Beg Coach Houses, Bellaghy, Magherafelt. ☎ (028) 7938-6235.

Northern Ireland

Further Information

Victor Refausse, Secretary of the Ulster Coarse Fishing Federation, Omagh. ☎ (028) 8224-5363 (evening) or 8224-5433 (daytime).

The Foyle Fisheries Commission. ☎ (028) 7134-2100.

Fisheries Conservancy Board. ☎ (028) 3833-4666.

Department of Culture, Arts and Leisure. ☎ (028) 9025-8861.

Bann System Limited. ☎ (028) 7034-4796.

Tackle Shops

C.A. Anderson, 64 Market Street, Omagh. ☎ (028) 8224-2311.

Smith & Co, 63 Market Street, Omagh. ☎ (028) 8224-2534.

Divers, 5 Castle Place, Strabane. ☎ (028) 7188-3021.

Derek Hamilton & Co, Cycle & Leisure Sports, Cookstown. ☎ (028) 8676-3682.

Bannvalley Gun & Tackle, 18 Main Street, Portglenone. ☎ (028) 2582-1383.

David Campbell, Tackle Shop, Newtownstewart. ☎ (028) 8166-1543.

Huestons, 55 Main Street, Castledawson. ☎ (028) 7946-8282.

N.M. Tackle, 9 Alexandra Place, Sion Mills. ☎ (028) 8165-9501.

R.A. Crawfords, Sports Shop, 34 Main Street, Maghera. ☎ (028) 7964-2672.

Bert Atkins, 67 Coleraine Road, Garvagh. ☎ (028) 2955-8555.

See pages 71-74 for details on angling, regulations and best times to fish.

■ Adventures on Horseback

There are a number of equestrian establishments in the Sperrins area.

The Clanabogan Riding Stables, Omagh. ☎ (028) 8225-2050.

The Ecclesville Equestrian Centre, Fintona, about seven miles (11.2 km) from Omagh, on 280 acres (112 hectares), which hosts international, national and regional horse shows and has an indoor and outdoor arena. ☎ (028) 8284-0591; fax 8284-0726.

The Ashlee Riding Centre, Strabane. ☎ (028) 7188-2708.

Tullywhisker Riding School, Sion Mills, Strabane. ☎ (028) 8165-8015.

■ Golf

There's a choice of 18-hole courses throughout the Sperrins, among them the following.

Omagh Golf Club, half a mile south of the town on the A5 road. ☎ (028) 8224-3160; fax 8224-3160.

Strabane Golf Club is a mile (1.6 km) south of the town. ☎ (028) 7138-2271; fax 7138-2007.

Dungannon GC is an undulating parkland course, a mile (1.6 km) west of town. ☎ (028) 8772-7338.

Newtownstewart has an undulating parkland course, two miles (3.2 km) south-west of the town. ☎ (028) 8166-1466; fax 8166-2506; newtown.stewart@lineone.net.

Killymoon Golf Club is south of Cookstown. ☎/fax (028) 8676-3762.

Among the nine-hole courses in the area is **Traad Ponds Golf Club**, on the edge of Lough Neagh, near Magherafelt, surrounded by a conservation area. ☎/fax (028) 7941-8511.

■ Entertainment

Omagh

In Omagh, there's a **leisure center**, which includes a pool and fitness equipment. ☎ (028) 8224-6711. There's also a six-screen **cinema** on the Drumquin road. ☎ (028) 8224-2034. Dún Úladh is the headquarters of **Comhaltas Ceoltori Eireann** (an organization that promotes traditional music and dance). It presents sessions of Irish music, song and dance on Saturday nights. ☎ (028) 8224-2777. **McCanns** and **Sally O'Brien's**, both on John Street, Omagh, are just two of the traditional music pubs in the town. Ask at your hotel or at tourist centers about others.

Cookstown

There is a **leisure center** with pool, fitness suite, 10 pin bowling, and squash courts. ☎ (028) 8676-3853. **The Burnavon Arts and Cultural Centre** at the Cookstown Tourist Information Centre hosts a variety of events. ☎ (028) 8876-7727 or www.cookstown.gov.uk .

■ Where to Stay

☆☆☆ and ☆☆☆☆☆ **The Brown Trout Golf and Country Inn** has been owned and run by the O'Hara family for four generations. In addition to three-star hotel rooms in the courtyard, it has self-catering suites that were the first to receive five-star status from the NITB. They have real turf fires, and their kitchens and lounges overlook the golf course. Bar food varies from homemade crab chowder to home-baked pies, and the restaurant has an extensive menu, with the focus on excellent home cooking.

HOTEL PRICE CHART	
Price per person, per night, with two sharing, including breakfast.	
$	Under US $50
$$	US $50-$100
$$$	US $101-$175
$$$$	US $176-$200
$$$$$	Over US $200

Guests can enjoy a choice of activities, including golf on the inn's nine-hole course, or at the nearby **Royal Portrush Golf Club**. Pony-trekking can be organized with **Timbertops Riding School**. ☎ (028) 7086-8209. **Bert Atkins** will organize rod, license permit and tackle rental for game fishing. ☎ (028) 2955-8555.

It's only half an hour to Derry, to Limavady, or to the beaches at Portrush, Portstewart or Ballycastle, and is very near the River Bann, on the A54 between Coleraine and Kilrea. The Brown Trout is a member of the Irish Country Hotels group – www.irishcountryhotels.com. Rates $ per person sharing, including breakfast, with cottage suites for an additional charge. ☎ (028) 7086-8209; fax 7086-8878; bill@browntroutinn.com; www.browntroutinn.com.

☆☆ **The Silverbirch Hotel** on the outskirts of Omagh is family-run and friendly, near shops, pubs, restaurants and other attractions. It's on the B48, which is on the Ulster Way and leads to the Sperrin Mountains, Gortin Glens and Ulster American Folk Park. The hotel is in spacious and mature grounds and has undergone extensive renovations recently. Rates $ per person sharing. ☎ (028) 8224-2520; info@silverbirchhotel.com; www. silverbirchhotel.com.

Guest House

Grange Lodge, Dungannon, is a Georgian house, dating back to 1698; it stands in 20 acres of well-kept grounds in the Holywood Hills. Guests can enjoy award-winning cooking, including home-baked afternoon teas. It's close to Dungannon and to a variety of attractions and activities available locally, including golf, boating, horseback riding and angling.

In 2003 the lodge won the Northern Ireland Tourist Board's B&B/Guest-house of the Year Award. It was chosen by the judges for its "true family hospitality and gracious appetizing dining," where the Browns "make the visitor feel at home in this delightfully furnished residence with its many collections of old Irish pewter and china." B&B $. Dinner about £25 must be booked each morning. ☎ (028) 8778-4212; fax 8778-4313; grangelodge@nireland.com.

Budget with a Difference

Why not stay in a castle set in 22 acres of parkland? You can do so for about £15 per person! The town of Dungiven is on the main Derry-Belfast road, the A6, south of Limavady in the Roe Valley, an absolutely beautiful area. **Dungiven Castle** is just off its Main Street, and all its rooms have fantastic views of the valley and the Sperrins. The Castle has had an interesting history since the 1600s. The existing building dates from the 1830s, and has been put to different uses, including housing American troops during World War II, and as a dance hall. It was falling down when the local community renovated it and turned it into budget accommodation. There are dormitories, family and private rooms. You cook for yourself, and there's a large lounge and dining area.

On the grounds are a walled garden, ponds, butterfly garden, a one-mile (1.6-km) loop walk, and a path leading to Dungiven Priory. It also has the advantage of being on the bus route between Derry (17 miles/27 km) and Belfast (52 miles/84 km). ☎ (028) 7774-2428; enquiries@dungivencastle.com; www.dungivencastle.com.

Hostels

- **Omagh Independent Hostel.** ☎ (028) 8224-1973; marella@omaghhostel.co.uk.
- **The Flax Mill Hostel**, Derrylane, Dungiven. ☎ (028) 7774-2655.
- **Downhill Hostel and Pottery**, 12 Mussenden Road, Downhill, Coleraine. ☎ (028) 7084-9077; downhillhostel@hotmail.com.
- **Rick's Causeway Coast Hostel**, Victoria Terrace, Portstewart. ☎ (028) 7083-3789; rick@causewaycoasthostel.fsnet.co.uk.

Rental Cottages

 ☆☆☆☆☆ **Magheramore Courtyard**, Dungiven, has three cottages available – The Dairy and the Shepherd's Nook, both sleeping four, and the Stable, which sleeps six. They have open log fires, are very well equipped, and linen and towels are provided. There are enjoyable walks in the area, and bike hire can be arranged, as well as pony-trekking (they have two ponies) or something different – a scenic tour by horse drawn gig. You can also take a golfing break here, playing a different course each day. Rates are about £350 for four nights, with two-night breaks from £100. ☎ (028) 7774-1942.

An Clachan Self-Catering Cottages are in the grounds of An Creagán Visitor Centre, described above on page 510, on the A505 road between Omagh and Cookstown. There are only eight cottages, with a choice of one, two or three bedrooms, and they're built in the style of traditional homes in the area. Each has a cultighe (pronounced cultytee) in the kitchen – a seat in daytime, a bed by night. They have all the modern facilities, including central heating, TV, phone, and there's a laundry on site. Rates start at £180 for a week in July or August, in a cottage sleeping two, with weekend and mid-week breaks also available. ☎/fax (028) 8076-1112; info@an-creagan.com; www.an-creagan.com.

Camping & RV Parks

 There's a choice of caravan and camping parks, which are open all year, unless otherwise stated.

☆ **Clogher Valley Country Caravan Park**, open March-October, just off the A4 on the way to Fivemiletown. ☎ (028) 8554-8932.

☆☆☆☆ **Drum Manor Forest Park**, on the A505 three miles (4.8 km) west of Cookstown, has two lakes, nature trails and a walled butterfly garden. ☎ (028) 8676-2774.

☆☆☆☆ **Dungannon Park**, a mile (1.6 km) south of town on the A29 to Moy, is in a 70-acre woodland park with paths and view of lake. ☎ (028) 8772-7327.

☆☆☆☆ **Ballyronan Marina's Caravan & Camping Park** is open April-end September, it is ideal for anyone interested in watersports or walking. ☎ (028) 8676-2205.

☆☆ There is a park At **Kilmaddy Tourist Information Centre**, six miles (10 km) west of Dungannon on the A4. ☎ (028) 8776-7259; kilmaddy@nitic.net.

☆☆ **Round Lake**, Murley Road, Fivemiletown, in the center, is open April-end September. ☎ (028) 8776-7259; kilmaddy@nitic.net.

☆☆☆☆ **Gortin Glen**, Lislap, seven miles (11 km) from Omagh, is opposite the Forest Park. ☎ (028) 8164-8108; gortinholidays@omagh.gov.uk.

■ Where to Eat

You can enjoy wonderful views over Lough Neagh from **The Quay Wall Restaurant** at the Marine Centre in Ballyronan, while dining on good food. It's fully licensed and serves lunch and dinner. ☎/fax (028) 794-8399.

The Mellon Country Inn is on the A5 north of Omagh, and just a mile (1.6 km) from the Ulster American Folk Park. It's a great place to stop for a snack or meal, and is a member of the Healthy Eating Circle as well as Taste of Ulster. **The Granary Grill Bar** has a hot and cold buffet service at lunchtime and in the evenings table service and a choice of grills. **The Mary Gray Restaurant** offers fine dining; reservations are required. It's open every day from 7:30 am-9:30 pm, and until 10 pm on Friday and Saturday. Main courses start at £6. ☎ (028) 8166-1224; fax 8166-1891.

Whistlers Inn, Main Street, Sixmilecross, seven miles (11 km) south-east of Omagh on the B46, has a great bar menu all week. Their à la carte menu on Friday, Saturday and Sunday evenings includes unusual dishes like wild boar and ostrich, all using the best of local ingredients. From March to October they host **Bluegrass Music weekends**. It's open for breakfast from 10:30-noon, for lunch until 2:30 pm and dinner from 5:30-10 pm. Lunches are from £5 and dinner starts at £15. ☎ (028) 8075-8349.

At Augher, where the A4 and A28 meet, **Rosamund's Coffee Shop** is in what was the Clogher Valley Railway Station before the line closed in 1941. It's open Monday-Saturday, 9 am-5 pm, serving hot and cold snacks and lunch, under £5. There's also a shop selling local crafts and Irish linen. ☎ (028) 8554-8601.

■ Further Information

Sperrins Tourism Limited. ☎ (028) 8674-7700; fax 8674-7754; info@SperrinsTourism.com; www.SperrinsTourism.com.

Tourist Information Centres

- 1 Market Street, Omagh. ☎ (028) 8224-7831.
- Ballygawley Road, Kilmaddy, Dungannon, off A4. ☎ (028) 8776-7259.
- Bridewell Centre, Church Street, Magherafelt. ☎ (028) 7963-1510.
- The Burnavon, Burn Road, Cookstown. ☎ (028) 8676-6727.

Northern Ireland

■ Abercorn Square, Strabane. ☎ (028) 7188-3735 – open in
season only.

Useful Contacts

■ **Cycling the Lough Neagh Region**. www.loughshoretrail.
com.

■ **Sustrans** (from "sustainable transport" and a UK charity)
for cycling routes. ☎ (028) 9043-4569; www.sustrans.co.uk.

The Grant Ancestral Home is where John Simpson,
the great-grandfather of Ulysses Simpson Grant, 18th
President of the USA, was born in 1738 and emigrated to
America in 1760. Ulysses Simpson commanded the Union
Army during the American Civil War and was twice
elected President. The ancestral home has been fully restored, and the nearby visitor center has information as
well as displays on US Grant, the American Civil War and
rural life of the time. Location: Dergina, Ballygawley,
near Dungannon

The Kingdoms of Down

County Down is surrounded on three sides by water, with more than 200 miles (320 km) of coastline, and is also the home of the Mountains of Mourne, made famous in song. Not only is its land more fertile than many other parts of the island, it's also favored with a climate that is drier and sunnier than most of the country.

On its east coast is the Ards Peninsula, a long, thin stretch of land, shaped like a hook, which almost encloses Strangford Lough, with just a narrow channel near Portaferry open to the Irish Sea. There are long stretches of sandy beaches and lovely views as you travel around this part of the county. The area south of here, between Strangford Lough and Dundrum Bay, is known as the Lecale region, and has many associations with Ireland's patron saint, so is often called St. Patrick's Country. He landed for the first time in Ireland on the shore of Strangford Lough in 442 AD and is believed to be buried at Downpatrick. Still farther south is the fjord of Carlingford Lough, facing County Louth in the Republic.

The region is dotted with prehistoric monuments, including standing stones, cairns, and dolmens dating from around 3000 BC. There are also fascinating stately homes and their wonderful gardens, forest parks and other beautiful sights to enjoy.

County Down is a great destination for anyone interested in outdoor activities, such as walking, golfing, riding, or watersports. Not only does it have the sea, it also has the sheltered waters of Strangford Lough and Carlingford Lough, so it is particularly popular with sailing enthusiasts and sea anglers.

Among the county's main towns are **Banbridge**, **Downpatrick**, **Newry** which was given city status in 2002, and **Bangor**, which is the largest.

■ Getting Here

Belfast City Airport is just off the A2 on the road to Bangor.

Bangor is 13 miles (21 km) from Belfast on the A2; Dublin is 118 miles (189 km) via the A2-M1-A1-M1-N1-M1, and Bangor is also connected to Belfast by rail and bus.

Newry is served by major roads A27 north to Portadown, and then A3 east to Lurgan and the M1 to Belfast; the A25 west to Co. Monaghan and east to Castlewellan and Downpatrick; the A2 south to Warrenpoint and then around the coast all the way to Belfast; and the A1 north to the M1 to Belfast or south toward Dublin.

Kingdoms of Down

COUNTY ANTRIM

A6
A26
Antrim ⑱
M2
A57
A8

Belfast Lough

Bangor
⑤
A2

⑮

A48
⑯

Lough
Neagh

Glenavy
⑦
A52
BELFAST ★

A20
④ Newtownards
A2

A30 Dunmurry
⑥

Comber
A21
⑰
⑬ Greyabbey
②

Strangford Lough

Lisburn
A26

A7

Moira
Lurgan
River Lagan
M1
A49
Saintfield
⑨
R. Quoile
A22

M1
A1

⑧ Hillsborough

A27
Portadown
A26

Killyleagh
⑫

① Portaferry
Strangford

A3
A51

Ballynahinch

Tandragee
A1
Banbridge
River Bann
A50
Clough
A25
Downpatrick

Rathfriland
A25
⑩ Castlewellan
A50
⑭
Ardglass

Hilltown
B27
⑪ Newcastle
B180

B8
Irish Sea

⑬
Newry
A2
Mountains of Mourne
A2

N

Warrenpoint
Rostrevor

COUNTY ARMAGH
Carlingford Lough
Kilkeel

A1

NOT TO SCALE

1. Castle Ward	10. Castlewellan Forest Park
2. Grey Abbey	11. Tollymore Forest Park
3. Mount Stewart	12. Delamont Country Park
4. Scrabo Country Park	13. Slieve Gullion
5. Crawfordsburn Country Park	14. St. Patrick's Country
6. Colin Glen Forest Park	15. Ulster Folk & Transport Museum
7. The Ballance House	16. Ballycopeland Windmill
8. Hillsborough Village	17. Giants Ring
9. Rowallene Garden	18. Round Tower

■ Tourist Information

Tower House, Quay Street, Bangor. ☎ (028) 9127-0069.

Gateway Tourist Information Centre, Newry Road, Banbridge. ☎ (028) 4062-3322.

The St. Patrick Centre, Market Street, Downpatrick. ☎ (028) 4461-2233.

The Courthouse, The Square, Hillsborough. ☎ (028) 9268-9717.

Bridge Street, Kilkeel. ☎ (028) 4176-2525.

Newcastle Centre, Central Promenade. ☎ (028) 4372-2222.

Regent Street, Newtownards. ☎ (028) 9182-6846.

The Stables, Castle Street, Portaferry, open in season only. ☎ (028) 4272-9882.

Cranfield Beach, off A2 Rostrevor-Kilkeel road, open in season only. ☎ (028) 4176-2525; info@newryandmourne.gov.uk; www.seenewryandmourne.gov.uk.

TRACING YOUR ANCESTORS

If your family roots are in Co. Down or Co. Antrim, contact the **Ulster Historical Foundation** in Belfast – see page 452.

■ Sightseeing

Bangor

Bangor is on the northern coast of the Ards Peninsula, at the mouth of Helen's Bay on Belfast Lough. It was founded by James Hamilton from Scotland, who was granted this part of the county by King James VI in 1605, and who became Lord Clandeboye in 1622. He brought men from Ayrshire to build the town on the site of St. Comgall's abbey of 558 AD.

It's been a popular seaside resort for many years and more recently has become a commuter town, as it's linked so well to Belfast by road, rail and bus.

Most of the town's buildings date from the time when Queen Victoria was on the British throne, including **Bangor Castle**, now the Town Hall, which houses the **North Down Heritage Centre**. Open July and August, Monday-Saturday, 10:30 am-5:30 pm, Sunday 2-5:30 pm. Rest of year closed Monday; phone to check hours. ☎ (028) 9127-1200.

There are a number of public parks in Bangor, the most interesting being **Ward Park**, which has two large ponds with wildfowl, including a resident flock of barnacle geese.

The Ulster Folk & Transport Museum

This museum has been developed over the last 40 years or so. It is on the lovely estate of Cultra Manor, on the A2 near Holywood, between Belfast and Bangor. Some trains stop here, and it's also on a bus route.

As at the Ulster American Folk Park near Omagh, Co. Tyrone, and the Bunratty Folk Park in Co. Clare in the Republic, buildings have been transported stone-by-stone from other areas and re-erected here.

In the Folk section at Cultra there's a village, which has grown into a town, and a variety of buildings, including a forge, a flax mill, and a watchtower. There's a museum and photographic archive, and there are demonstrations of traditional farming, including threshing and harrowing.

You cross a bridge over the main Belfast-Bangor road to the Transport section, which includes the Irish Railway collection, a lifeboat, and other exhibits, including a full-scale model of the monoplane that was flown by Harry Ferguson in 1909. He's much better known for his tractors, but Ferguson was the first man to fly in Ireland.

What's enjoyable about visiting the Folk & Transport Museum is not just all the interesting buildings and other exhibits, but also the amount of space – and you can picnic anywhere. There's also a tea room in Cultra Manor. Open all year from 10 am, Monday-Saturday, 11 am on Sundays. Closes at 6 pm daily from July to September, and on weekends from March to June; closes earlier rest of year. You can buy a combined ticket, or pay separately for Folk and Transport. ☎ (028) 9042-8428; fax 9042-8728.

■ Along the Coast

Continue on the A2 along the coast from Bangor, and you come to interesting villages. At Groomsport, three miles (4.8 km) from Bangor, there's a harbor with a sandy beach on both sides. **Cockle Row Cottages**, two 18th-century fishermen's cottages, one with a thatched roof, are open in summer for craft demonstrations. Boat trips to the three **Copeland Islands** run from here in summer. They are a favorite destination for kayakers, since they make a good stopover point between Lund and Desolation Sound. The islands also provide opportunities for scuba diving, wildlife viewing, wilderness camping, swimming and fishing.

The town of **Donaghdee** has a large harbor and a lighthouse, and for centuries offered refuge to ships from the dangers of the reefs along the coast. It's also the nearest port in Ireland to Britain – it's only 21 miles (34 km) across to Portpatrick.

> *You see edible seaweed, called dulse, being gathered here at low tide. It is dried and sold in little bags – it's not to everyone's taste but is worth trying and it's believed to be very good for you.*

There used to be over 100 windmills in Co. Down, and you can see remnants of them – just the stumps. At **Ballycopeland**, a mile (1.6 km) west of Millisle, you have the chance to see a working windmill that was built about 1790 and was still in use until 1915. In the miller's house there's a model and you can follow the process of turning corn into flour. Open July-August, Wednesday-Thursday, 10 am to 1 pm, Tuesday, Friday-Sunday, 2-6 pm. ☎ (028) 9054-3033.

Millisle is a seaside resort popular with families. **Ballywalter** has a busy harbor, and just south of it is **Long Strand**, a wide and safe beach with good facilities for watersports.

At **Portavogie** there's a modern harbor, boat-building yards and a lively fish auction on the quay most evenings, as one of the North's main fishing fleets is based here.

Kearney, just off the A2, on the tip of the peninsula, is owned by the National Trust. It's a dear little fishing village on a low rocky coast. Some of its traditional houses have been restored, and it is worth the detour. Walk along the coast southwards to the lovely sandy beach at **Knockinelder**. You'll probably see seals basking on the rocks.

Strangford Lough

Portaferry is on the eastern entrance to Strangford Lough and is very attractive, with a long and low waterfront. Until the famines of the 1840s, it was a thriving industrial town, and nowadays it's a center for yachting and for sea angling, both in the Lough and sea.

Castle Ward nearby is a curiosity, as inside and out it was built in two distinctive architectural styles in the 18th century. The entrance façade is in the Classical style, while the garden side is Gothic and looks down on the Lough. It's surrounded by a beautiful 750-acre (300-hectare) walled estate, with paths through the woodland leading to features including a sunken garden, a Classical-style summer house, and a bird hide on the shore of one lough.

There's a converted barn in its courtyard, which is a venue for opera and concerts. It has a tea room and a large shop selling National Trust items which are always great value, often unusual and make lovely gifts – plus you can feel good, knowing you're helping a great cause!

Northern Ireland

Grounds open daily all year from 10 am; to 4 pm, October-April; to 8 pm May-September. House and wildlife center open every day from 12 to 6 pm, April 18-27, July 1-August 31. Open only certain days during the rest of the year. Call for details. You can get a combined ticket or pay separately for grounds only. ☎ (028) 4488-1204; fax 4488-1729; castleward@ ntrust.org.uk.

South of Bangor

South of Bangor on the A21 is the busy manufacturing town of **Newtownards**. Just before you come to it is the **Somme Heritage Centre**. It recalls the part played by the 10th and Ulster Divisions in the ghastly battle in 1916 during World War I. Staff wear battledress and tell what happened. There are reconstructed frontline trenches, which capture some of the horror. Open July-August, Monday-Friday, 10 am-5 pm and Saturday-Sunday from noon. Closed January, open daily rest of year; phone for times. ☎ (028) 9182-3202.

South of Newtownards, on the A20, is **Mount Stewart** on the eastern shore of Strangford Lough, which is most famous for its wonderful gardens created by Edith, Lady Londonderry, from 1921 on.

This was the home of Robert Stewart, Lord Castlereagh (1769-1822), who was Foreign Secretary of England during the Napoleonic Wars. Unlike many others, he was a good landlord and funded schools, built a chapel and homes for tenants, and a pier for local fishermen in front of the house. However, as he helped destroy the Irish Parliament and bring about the Act of Union (1801), he became a disliked, even hated, figure among many Irish nationalists. He committed suicide 18 months after succeeding his father as Marquis.

Mount Stewart is a National Trust property. The Bay Restaurant and lakeside gardens and walks are open all year, daily from 10 am; closing hour varies with the season. The mansion is surrounded by an intricate series of colorful formal gardens, each in its own style, with paths taking visitors into the surrounding woodland. There are lovely views from the Temple of the Winds.

House tours are given March through October. Ulsterbus 10 from Belfast to Portaferry stops at garden gate. ☎ (028) 4278-8387; fax 4278-8569; mountstewart@ntrust.org.uk.

Across the Lough from Mount Stewart, through Newtownards on the A22, is **Comber** and, five minutes away, **Castle Espie**, run by the Wildfowl and Wetlands Trust. It has the largest collection of swans, ducks and geese in Ireland, with hides, gardens and woodland walks. There's an art gallery, nature center, gift shop and coffee shop. Open all year, July-August, Monday-Saturday, 10:30 am-5:30 pm; from 11:30 am on Sunday.

Hours vary in off-season. ☎ (028) 9187-4146; castleespie@wwt.org.uk; www.wwt.org.uk.

Downpatrick

The town is charming. It is set on two low hills, and has lots of late Georgian and early Victorian buildings. It was the main county town in medieval times.

The present **Cathedral** was built in 1826 and incorporates parts of a 12th-century building. Although no one knows for certain if St. Patrick was really buried here (Armagh also claims his final resting-place), the country's patron saint is commemorated by a granite boulder in the churchyard marked with his name and by a huge statue on the top of Slieve Patrick, the hill across the valley. There are great celebrations here on March 17, St. Patrick's Day.

Ego Patricius - The Saint Patrick Centre is next to the Cathedral and the Down County Museum, and tells the story of the saint and his legacy, using interactive techniques. It also houses temporary exhibitions and the town's **Tourist Information Centre**. Here you can learn more about sites associated with the saint all over the country, as well as a variety of other information. The Saint Patrick Centre is open daily all year, from June-August on weekdays from 9:30 am-7 pm, and from 10 am to 6 pm on Sundays; different hours in off-season. ☎ (028) 4461-9000; fax 4461-9111.

The Down County Museum is in the former 18th-century jail and among its exhibits are restored cells with life-size figures. It has temporary exhibitions, a teashop and gift shop. Admission free. Open Monday-Friday, 10 am-5 pm; Saturday-Sunday from 1 pm. ☎ (028) 4461-5218.

Historic Holy Sites

Three of the four Cistercian monasteries in the county were built around **Strangford Lough** – a stone in the parish church is all that's left of **Comber**, while there are substantial remains of Inch Abbey (1180) and Grey Abbey (1193). They had close connections with abbeys across the sea in Cumbria and Lancashire, and for almost 400 years took wheat, salt, fish and flour to them on 60-oar galleys, bringing back stone and iron ore.

The ruins of **Inch Abbey** are a mile (1.6 km) northwest of Downpatrick, on an island in the River Quoile, reached by a causeway, with free access always. There's a Visitor Centre next to the ruined **Grey Abbey**, which is in lovely parkland with a medieval-style "physick" garden with various medicinal plants. Open daily except Mondays from April-September; weekends rest of year. ☎ (028) 9054-3037.

Northern Ireland

Banbridge

In the western part of Co. Down is Banbridge, 10 miles (16 km) north of Newry where the A1 and A26 meet. It used to be a prosperous linen town, and nowadays is still the industrial center of this area. Its only unusual feature is its main street, which in the days of coach travel presented a problem because it climbs a very steep hill. To avoid being bypassed, the town leaders had a deep underpass cut into the middle of the hill in 1834, crossed by a bridge. In Church Square there's a statue of Captain Francis Crozier RN, who discovered the Northwest Passage; he is shown surrounded by polar bears.

Newry

Newry is named after a yew tree, said to have been planted by St. Patrick. It straddles the River Bann and the border with the neighboring county, so its Town Hall is actually half in Co. Down and half in Co. Armagh.

It's also at the head of "the Gap of the North," a pass between two hills where in ancient times the men of Ulster swept through to attack the tribes of Leinster in the days of the Fianna (see pages 182-83). Its location has had disadvantages, as over the centuries the town was destroyed many times.

In 1578 the first Protestant church in Ireland was built on top of the steep hill close to the Town Hall by Sir Nicholas Bagenal, and his coat of arms can be seen in its porch.

In the 18th century, a canal was built between Lough Neagh and Newry, the first inland canal in Ireland. Built primarily for transportation of coal from the mines at Brackaville, soon to be known as Coalisland, the canal brought prosperity; its single swing-bridge has been carefully preserved and can be seen at the bottom of Monaghan Street.

Buried in the cemetery on High Street is John Mitchel (1815-75), author of the famous *Jail Journal*, an Irish revolutionary classic. He was transported to Australia in 1848 for treason-felony. He escaped to the United States in 1853, where he led a turbulent and contentious career as a journalist during the Civil War. Returning to Ireland and was elected (1875) to Parliament shortly before his death. There's also a statue of him in the shopping center.

Newry is an interesting place to explore. Don't miss River Street, where there's a row of tiny houses with eagles over their doors; and Trevor Hill, where No. 1 is the oldest in the row of fine Georgian houses.

South of Newry

Head out of Newry on the A2, southwards toward Warrenpoint, and after four miles (6.4 km) you come to **Narrow Water Castle**, standing on a rock jutting out into the estuary. It was built in 1560 to defend the Clanrye River, which flows into Carlingford Lough, a mile (1.6 km) farther south.

Warrenpoint and **Rostrevor** are three miles (4.8 km) apart, both small resorts looking out over the Lough. When the port at Newry closed in the 1970s, the harbor at Warrenpoint was enlarged to handle container and other shipping traffic.

AN AMERICAN CONNECTION

On your way into Rostrevor, still on the A2, you pass an obelisk in memory of Major General Robert Ross (1766-1814), who captured Washington in 1814 after defeating the Americans at Bladensburg during the War of 1812. He burned the White House after eating in President Madison's dining room – and was killed soon afterwards in a skirmish at Baltimore.

Rostrevor

Rostrevor has a long seafront and a mild climate, so palm trees and mimosa flourish here. It has an air of gentility, with oak trees in its square and some fine old houses. There's an annual folk festival here in August.

On the slopes of Slievemartin, which looks down on Rostrevor, there's a geological curiosity called the **Cloghmore**, which means "great stone" – it's a huge block left behind by a glacier and weighs 40 tons.

The Mountains of Mourne

The Mountains of Mourne are probably the most famous in Ireland because of the Percy French song, *Where the mountains of Mourne sweep down to the sea.*

It's a compact range of mountains, 15 miles long (24 km) and eight miles (15 km) wide, with only about 12 of the 60 or more individual summits rising above 2,000 feet (610 m). Slieve Donard at 2,796 feet (852 m) is the highest peak in the North. Whether approached from Newry on the A25 or B8, from Belfast on the A50 via Banbridge, or from the direction of the Ards Peninsula, they are equally beautiful.

Cranfield Beach is in an absolutely beautiful setting at the mouth of Carlingford Lough, with the Mountains of Mourne forming the perfect backdrop. It's off the main A2 Rostrevor-Kilkeel road, and worth the detour.

Northern Ireland

■ Kilkeel

Kilkeel is a busy country town, home to the largest fishing fleet in the North, with landings and auctions on the quay that are fascinating to watch. Around the port are fish-processing factories, and the piers are popular with anglers. The town has attractive winding streets with interesting terraces of shops and houses. Outside of town there are ancient monuments, including an eight-foot-high (2½-m) dolmen called the **Crawtree Stone** and the megalithic tomb of **Dunnaman**, a court grave with a long gallery. A court grave is a Neolithic tomb consisting of a chamber tomb adjoined by an open space marked off by large standing stones. The remains of this one are quite impressive, although only the gallery itself remains, consisting of four chambers. The tomb has huge side-stones making up the walls of the gallery.

On the A2 north of Kilkeel is **Annalong**, a pretty fishing village with a marine park and harbor, set against the lovely backdrop of Slieve Binnian and its craggy slopes. Unfortunately, on the outskirts of the village are rather uninteresting modern houses. People do have to live somewhere, so perhaps that's unfair, but it is sad how some lovely places are being overwhelmed.

Overlooking the harbor is the **Annalong Corn Mill**, built around 1830 and powered by a waterwheel. There's a Visitor Centre and behind it a pleasant herb garden. Guided tours April-October, daily except Tuesdays, 2-6 pm. ☎ (028) 4376-8736.

Newcastle

Newcastle is one of the North's most popular resorts, with a long sandy beach on the edge of Dundrum Bay. This is the place songwriter Percy French celebrated in *Where the Mountains of Mourne sweep down to the sea*, famous in Ireland, and there's a memorial fountain to him in the gardens on the promenade.

There's an inscribed stone to Harry Ferguson in the promenade wall at Newcastle – the first man to fly in Ireland. He flew along the beach in 1910. There's a model of his monoplane in the Folk & Transport Museum (see page 524). He also invented the four-wheel-drive system in the 1920s and in 1947 sued the Ford Motor Company for $340,000,000, accusing them of infringing patents for his best-known invention, the tractor. He finally settled out of court in 1952.

■ Adventures on Foot

 The area around Strangford Lough is perfect for walking and for cycling. The Lough is a bird sanctuary and is dotted with drowned drumlins (low ridges), which are great breeding grounds for wildlife, including seals. The National Trust (NT) manages almost 15,000 acres of foreshore, the seabed, including 50 islands, woodland, wetlands, saltmarsh and agricultural fields. Head to the **Strangford Lough Wildlife Information Centre** before exploring the area on foot; it's on the shore at Castle Ward, a National Trust property. Walks, including those at low-tide over to South, Horse and Ballyhenny islands, are organized from there, plus guided boat trips. ☎ (028) 4488-1668 for details.

The Centre is open daily June-August, noon-6 pm; shorter hours in off-season; closed from the end of October to mid-March. ☎/fax (028) 4488-1411;uslwcw@smtp.btrust.org.uk.

In the Steps of Saint Patrick

The waymarked **Lecale Way** follows in the steps of St. Patrick, but don't worry – you don't have to be religious to enjoy it. Highlights include wonderful views of Strangford Lough, the Mourne Mountains, the pretty village of Strangford and Murlough Bay National Nature Reserve.

The route is 40 miles (64 km) long and, of course, can be undertaken in stages.

It starts on the shore of the lough near Raholp, where the saint is believed to have landed, and then follows the coastline to Newcastle inside the Lecale Area of Outstanding Natural Beauty, where it ends.

There's an illustrated guide available at tourist offices – try first at the St. Patrick Centre, Market Street, Downpatrick, ☎ (028) 4461-2233, or Newcastle Centre, Central Promenade, ☎ (028) 4372-2222). Or take a look at www.countrysiderecreation.com.

Self-Guided Trails

There's a self-guided trail in Newry, and a guided historical tour of nearby Bessbrook. For details, ☎ (028) 3026-8877.

There are also self-guided trails around Castlewellan, Kilkeel, Dundrum, Newcastle and Rostrevor. For details, contact tourist information or call the Mournes Heritage Trust. ☎ (028) 4372-4059.

The Mountains of Mourne

The Mountains of Mourne provide numerous opportunities for walkers and climbers. Following are suggested routes.

North of Kilkeel, on the A2, is the **Blue Lough Walk**, five miles (eight km), a lovely introduction to the Mountains of Mourne. It starts in the car park at Carrick Little and crosses the Mourne Wall, where it descends from Slieve Binnian and then follows old quarry tracks across open heath beside Annalong Wood.

En route, there's a great view of Slieve Donard to the northeast. From above the Blue Lough there's a bird's eye view of the Ben Crom Dam and Mountain.

Among other walks is a 12-mile (19-km) circular route from the Donard car park on the A2 at Newcastle, farther along the coast from Kilkeel.

The **Mourne Mountain Walk** follows the Glen River through woodland, crosses the Mourne Wall under Slieve Donard, and then joins the Brandy Pad, an old smugglers' trail. Passing under The Castles (rock towers) close to the 400-foot-high (120-m) Diamond Rocks, it then follows the Trassey River. On the way you see sheep pens where strays were probably kept. Next the route joins a short section of the Ulster Way, and then leaves it to follow the Shimna River, passing through Tollymore Forest, with gorse banks, hazel coppices, young fir plantations and a mature wood of Douglas firs, then Curraghard viewpoint, before returning to the car park.

The National Trust maintains coastal and mountain paths to **Slieve Donard** and neighboring **Slieve Commedagh**. Park in Newcastle or at Bloody Bridge on the A2, two miles (3.2 km) south of Slieve Donard.

From Bloody Bridge, you can follow the **Brandy Pad** to Slieve Donard or enjoy the **Mourne Coastal Path**. Details from the National Trust's South Down office at ☎/fax (028) 4375-1467.

Forest Parks, Nature Reserves & Gardens

 A mile (1.6 km) south of Dundrum is **The Murlough National Nature Reserve**, with its network of self-guided paths and boardwalks through dunes, woodland and heath. It's looked after by the National Trust, and is accessible all year, with an admission charge from May through the middle of September, when facilities are open. ☎/fax (028) 4375-1467; umnnrw@ntrust. org.uk.

Castlewellan Forest Park is at the junction of the A50 and A25, northwest of Newcastle. Among its features is the national arboretum, started in 1740, a hedge maze and a three-mile (4.8-km) trail around the lake with sculptures made from natural materials. There's a Visitor Centre and café. Open daily, 10 am-dusk. ☎ (028) 4377-8664; customer. forestservice@dardni.gov.uk; www.forestserviceni.gov.uk.

Tollymore Forest Park is in the foothills of the Mournes on the B180 west of Newcastle, and is noted for its fascinating follies, bridges and gateways, as much as for its magnificent trees. Among the follies is a barn that looks like a Gothic church. It houses the Information Centre and café. Take a walk along the Shimna River and you pass curiosities, natural and man-made, including bridges, grottos and caves. It's also a good starting point for exploring the Mournes, with marked paths to follow. Open daily, 9 am-dusk. ☎ (028) 4372-2428; e-mail and website same as Castlewellan, above.

The **Silent Valley** and **Ben Crom reservoirs** supply 30 million gallons of water a day to Belfast and Co. Down, and around them is the **Mourne Wall**, which took over 18 years to complete between 1904 and 1922. Many skilled people were employed seasonally to build the wall, which stands up to eight feet high and three feet wide. It is 22 miles long and connects the summits of no fewer than 15 mountains, including Slieve Donard.

To get to Silent Valley, take the B27 from Kilkeel, turning right after four miles (6.4 km). There's an Information Centre, craft shop and café, open daily April-September, 10:30 am-6:30 pm; phone for hours other times of year. ☎ (028) 9074-1166.

Rowallane Garden, another National Trust property, is a mile south of Saintfield and 11 miles southeast of Belfast just west of the A7 to Downpatrick. Planting and collecting started in the 1860s and continues today, and there's a huge variety of trees, shrubs, and plants from all over the world. At every time of the year it is enchanting. Open daily; May-September, 10 am-8 pm; to 4 pm the rest of the year. ☎ (028) 9751-0131; fax 9751-1241; rowallane@ntrust.org.uk.

Walking Festivals

The **Down District Walking Festival** takes place in early August, and the **Wee Binnian Walking Festival** in the middle of September. Each festival provides two-three days of walking that can be as challenging or as tranquil as you wish. Walks are graded to suit all levels of fitness and experience, with routes varying from four to 12 miles (seven to 19 km).

Details from Mourne Activity Breaks, 28 Bridge Street, Kilkeel. ☎ (028) 4176-9965; festival@mournewalking.com; www.mournewalking.com.

■ Adventures on Water

The marina at Bangor is the largest in Ireland, and there are four yacht clubs. Boating and sea angling are very popular.

Note the plaque on the old pier, which records how a convoy assembled off here in 1944 before taking part in the Normandy landings, which helped bring World War II to an end.

The MV *Salutay*, based in Bangor, is available for charter for wreck, scenic and drift diving. ☎ (028) 9181-2081; fax 9182-0635; salutay@btinternet.com; www.salutay.com.

A useful source of information for divers is the website www.planadive.co.uk.

You can cross to Strangford on the other shore of the lough by car ferry from Portaferry; the trip only takes about five minutes, but grab the chance to see the views of the lough and of Portaferry from it.

Boats are available to rent for sea fishing at Portaferry from **Des Rogers**, ☎ (028) 4272-8297, or **John Murray**, ☎ (028) 4272-8414.

Fishing

The South East fishery region stretches from Belfast Lough to Carlingford Lough and westwards to Craigavon and Armagh in the neighboring county. There are lots of wonderful opportunities for game fishing, for catches including brown trout, rainbow trout, salmon, and sea trout in its many lakes and rivers.

Near Newcastle you can fish Castlewellan Lake, and other lakes include McCourts, Writes Lough, Ballykeel, Cowey, Money and Loughbrickland.

There are also the rivers descending from the Mournes to the sea, including Moneycarragh, Shimna and Whitewater. Salmon are caught on the Shimna; the Whitewater is great for sea trout and the Moneycarragh for both, while saltwater sea trout are caught on Strangford Lough.

WWW *Take a look at the website www.fjiordlands.org, which has lots of advice about angling and coarse fishing in the Strangford Lough area.*

Coarse fishing is popular, with roach, bream, perch, rudd, eels and pike, caught at various locations, from the busy town of Newry to the sea locks on the Omeath road.

Near Downpatrick is the Quoile Basin and its mixed coarse and wild brown trout fishery. Rudd, perch, eels and pike are also available in the National Nature Reserve, where there are lots of birds. Also nearby is the mixed coarse and game fishery of Lough Money.

See pages 71-74 for details on angling in Ireland, regulations and best times to fish.

Banbridge is a good center for fishing the lakes, including Lough Shark, Drummiller, Drumaran, Drumnavaddy and Skillycoban, an old mill dam with eels, as well as roach/bream hybrids, rudd, pike and perch.

Remember to check with local tackle shops, or with tourist information centers, about licenses and permits.

 The regional guide, Angling in Armagh and Down, *is very useful. The Tourist Information Centre, 40 English Street, Armagh,* ☎ *(028) 37521800, may be able to help you get it.*

■ Adventures on Horseback

Co. Down has lots of beautiful countryside, wonderful beaches and forest parks, and most of its roads are quiet, so it's an ideal setting for riding.

The **Ardminnan Equestrian Centre** is 1½ miles (2.4 km) from Cloughy near Portaferry on the Ards Peninsula. The scenery is pretty, with beaches nearby, and the quiet roads are ideal for hacking. ☎/fax (028) 4277-1321; info@ardminnan.com.

The **Newcastle Riding Centre** is two miles (3.2 km) from the village, near the beach and forest tracks, and offers lessons and excellent hacking. ☎ (028) 4372-2694.

The **Mourne Trail Riding Centre**, two miles (3.2 km) from Newcastle, caters for experienced riders, with treks of one-four hours, mostly through Tollymore Forest Park. ☎/fax (028) 4372-4351; mgtnewsam@aol.com; www.mournetrailridingcentre.com.

Other riding facilities include:

- **Ballynahinch Riding School.** ☎ (028) 9756-2883.
- **Cherry Tree Riding Centre**, Newtownards. ☎ (028) 4272-9639.
- **Gransha Equestrian Centre**, Bangor. ☎ (028) 9181-3313.
- **Millbrook Equestrian Centre**, Bessbrook, Newry. ☎ (028) 3083-8336.
- **Oakwood Riding Establishment**, Mayobridge, Newry. ☎ (028) 3085-1484.
- **Tullymurray Equestrian Centre**, Aghadowey. ☎ (028) 4481-1880.
- **Western Riding Company**, Kilcoo, Newry. ☎ (028) 4065-0320; mail@westernridingcompany.com; www.westernridingcompany.com.
- The **Mount Pleasant Riding and Trekking Centre** is a mile (1.6 km) from Castlewellan, not far from the beach at Newcastle, and on the edge of Castlewellan Forest Park, with

both Donard Park and Tullymore Forest Park nearby. Holidays and weekend breaks here are organized with local hotels. ☎ (028) 4377-8651; fax 4377-0030; equestrianmountpleasant@ virgin.net; www.mountpleasantcentre.com.

■ Golf

 There is a great choice of 18-hole golf courses in the county, with some nine-hole courses as well. Always check in advance if clubs are available for rent, and at which times visitors are welcome. The following are some of the 18-hole courses.

The most famous is the **Royal County Down Golf Club** at Newcastle. Its course was first laid out in 1889 and stretches out along the shore of Dundrum Bay under the Mourne Mountains. It claims to be the most beautiful course in the world and it seems that few visitors disagree. Alongside the Championship links course, consistently rated among the top 10 in the world, is a second and less challenging course, the Annesley Links. ☎ (028) 4372-3314; fax 4372-6281; golf@royalcountydown.org.

The seaside course of **Ardglass Golf Club** is in the town. ☎ (028) 4484-1219; fax 4484-1841; golfclub@ardglass.force9.co.uk; www.ardglass. force9.co.uk.

Kirkinstown Golf Club has a links course, and is 15 miles (24 km) southeast of Newtownards. ☎ (028) 4277-1233; fax 4277-1699; kirkinstown@aol.com; wwwkcgc.org.

The Royal Belfast Club is seven miles (11 km) northeast of the city at Holywood; note that visitors here need a letter of introduction. ☎ (028) 9042-8165; royalbelfastgc@btclick.com.

The Down Royal Park Golf Club is inside the popular racecourse. ☎/ fax (028) 9262-1339.

Bangor Golf Club has an undulating parkland course. ☎ (028) 9127-0922. A mile (1.6 km) west of Bangor is the seaside meadowland course of the **Carnalea Club**. ☎ (028) 9127-0368; fax 9127-3989. A mile (1.6 km) farther west is the **Blackwood Golf Centre**. ☎ (028) 9185-2706; fax 9185-3785.

South of Bangor on the way to Newtownards, the **Clandeboye Club** has two courses. ☎ (028) 9127-1767; fax 9147-3711.

The Downpatrick Golf Club is a mile (1.6 km) from the town. ☎ (028) 4461-5947; fax 4461-7502; info@downpatrickgolfclub.com; www. downpatrickgolfclub.com.

The Bright Castle Golf Club is four miles (6.4 km) south of Downpatrick. ☎ (028) 4484-1319.

Ringdufferin has a drumlin course (one with little hills) and is two miles (3.2 km) north of Killyleagh, close to Strangford Lough. ☎/fax (028) 4482-8812.

The Scrabo Golf Club is a mile (1.6 km) southwest of Newtownards. The Scrabo Tower on the course was built as a memorial to the third Marquis of Londonderry in the 1850s. It has 122 steps up to a good view of Strangford Lough and is open in summer. ☎ (028) 9181-2355; fax 9182-2919.

The Warrenpoint Club is close to Carlingford Lough, a mile (1.6 km) from the town. ☎ (028) 4175-3695; fax 4175-2918; warrenpointgolfclub@bttalk21.com.

The Banbridge Golf Club is just over a mile (1.6 km) northwest of the town. ☎ (028) 4066-2211; fax 4066-9400; info@banbridge-golf.freeserve.co.uk

■ Where to Stay

☆☆☆☆ **The Canal Court Hotel**, Merchants Quay, Newry, is a comfortable and pleasant base from which to tour counties Down and Armagh. It has 51 nicely decorated bedrooms, a leisure center with pools and other excellent facilities. Guests can choose between **The Old Mill Restaurant** or the **Carvery** and snacks are available in the **Granary Bar** all day – all open to non-residents too. $$. ☎ (028) 3025-1234; fax 3025-1177; manager@canalcourthotel.com; www.canalcourthotel.com.

HOTEL PRICE CHART	
Price per person, per night, with two sharing, including breakfast.	
$	Under US $50
$$	US $50-$100
$$$	US $101-$175
$$$$	US $176-$200
$$$$$	Over US $200

☆☆☆ **The Old Inn**, Main Street, Crawfordsburn, is one of the oldest hostelries in Ireland, dating back to 1614. It's only six miles (10 km) to Belfast City Airport and is on the way to Bangor. Partly thatched, it attracts admirers of C.S. Lewis, creator of the *Narnia* books, who brought his American bride here for their honeymoon in 1958. The feature film, *Shadowlands*, starring Anthony Hopkins, is their love story.

Other famous guests have included Peter the Great, Tsar of Russia, and former US President George Bush. The restaurant is much admired for its delicious food, made from local produce, and its extensive wine list.

All of its 32 bedrooms are individually and tastefully furnished with antiques, and have wood-panelled walls, some with carved four-poster beds. There's also the Cottage, tucked away in the grounds, with a cosy log fire

Northern Ireland

in its living room. Guests staying in the Cottage can cook for themselves, have meals served to them there or join guests in the Inn's restaurant.

There's a sandy beach nearby and another at Helen's Bay. Both are part of the Crawfordsburn Country Park, with a lovely walk in a glen under the railway viaduct, so it's a fine place to stay or to eat. Rates from $$ with special breaks and weekend offers available. ☎ (028) 9185-3255; info@theoldinn.com; www.theoldinn.com.

Tyrella House, Downpatrick, is hidden away under the Mourne Mountains, sheltered by tall beech trees. Tyrella was the first member of the Hidden Ireland group in the North, and therefore is not classified under the hotel star system. It has its own private sandy beach, which stretches for miles, and there are cross-country courses and a polo ground, with lessons available. Fishing can be arranged, as can golf at Newcastle. It's like staying with friends, as there are only three bedrooms. and guests can enjoy delicious dinners, including home-produced lamb and vegetables, as well as breakfast. $$. Open March 1-November 30. ☎/fax (028) 4485-1422; tyrella.corbett@virgin.net; www.hidden-ireland.com/tyrella.

☆☆☆☆ **The Glassdrumman Lodge Country House and Restaurant** is on the coast just off the A2 at Annalong, close to the forests at Tollymore and Castlewellan, the Mountains of Mourne and many beaches. In its grounds is a one-acre fishing lake, well stocked with rainbow trout. There are eight bedrooms and two suites, with 24-hour room service available, overnight laundry, and other facilities. Open all year. Rates from $$.

It's not just its peaceful and attractive setting that makes a stay here so enjoyable; it's also the quality of the food. Glassdrumman is a member of Ireland's Blue Book (see page 60). Oysters are a specialty, as are locally caught fish and shellfish, served with home-produced vegetables. Many good food guides have recommended its family-run restaurant, open to non-residents (you must book in advance). ☎ (028) 4376-8451; fax 4376-7041;glassdrumman@yahoo.com.

☆☆☆ **The Narrows** is a guesthouse in Portaferry which, since opening in the late 90s, has won many awards. Its waterfront setting is part of what makes it so special; it also has a walled garden and a sauna, so is very relaxing. There are just 13 bedrooms, all with great views of Strangford Lough, and its restaurant is open to non-residents. Rates from $. ☎ (028) 4272-8148; fax 4272-8105; reservations@narrows.co.uk; www.narrows.co.uk.

Stay & Ride

Drumgooland House is more than 100 years old and is set in 100 acres of mountain scenery in the Mournes, with three rooms available on a B&B and evening meal basis. Here you can enjoy quiet lanes and tracks for an hour or two, or go on a three- or six-day trail ride. It's seven miles (11 km) north of the seaside resort of Newcastle and caters for all ages and abilities. ☎ (028) 4481-1956; fax 4481-1265; frank@horsetrek-ireland.com; www.horsetrek-ireland.com.

The Mount Pleasant Riding and Trekking Centre (see under *Adventures on Horseback* above) organizes tours and weekend breaks, with guests staying in local hotels. ☎ (028) 4377-8651; fax 4377-0030; equestrianmountpleasant@virgin.net; www.mountpleasantcentre.com.

Rental Cottages

 At **Castle Ward** on the shore of Strangford Lough, you can rent the **Potter's Cottage** in the old farmyard, which sleeps four. Near Dundrum Inner Bay and in walking distance of the National Nature Reserve and beach is **Murlough Cottage**, which also sleeps four. Both are owned by the National Trust. ☎ (44) 870-458-4422; cottages@ntrust.org.uk; www.nationaltrustcottages.co.uk.

Hostels

All the hostels listed are approved by the tourist board.

The Greenhill YMCA National Centre, Donard Park, Newcastle, is close to the Ulster Way walking route. Mountain walking, canoeing and rock climbing can be organized. ☎ (028) 4372-3172.

Newcastle Youth Hostel is in a townhouse on the seafront, and meals are available if booked in advance. ☎ (028) 4372-2133; fax 4372-2133.

Ballinran Mourne Centre Hostel, Kilkeel, is at the foot of the Mourne Mountains in an area of outstanding natural beauty, three miles from Kilkeel and 12 miles from Newcastle. ☎ (028) 4176-5727; fax 7137-1030.

The Barholm Hostel, Portaferry, overlooks Strangford Lough. ☎ (028) 4272-9598; fax 4272-9784; barholm.portaferry@virgin.net; www.barholmportaferry.co.uk.

Northern Ireland

Camping & RV Parks

Remember to phone in advance, as arrangements vary, and some sites may not welcome campers or have very few spaces for them.

There's a good choice of parks, among them ☆☆☆☆☆ **Cranfield Caravan Park**, which is family-run, in a peaceful and picturesque setting south of Kilkeel, by the sea, with wonderful views of the Mountains of Mourne. It's open March 1-October 31, signposted off the A2. ☎/fax (028) 4176-2572.

☆☆☆☆☆ **The Camping and Caravanning Club** is in the Down District Council Country Park, a mile (1.6 km) south of Killyleagh on the A22, four miles (6.4 km) north of Downpatrick, on the shores of Strangford Lough, also open March 1-October 31. ☎ (028) 4482-1833; www.campingandcaravanningclub.co.uk

☆☆☆ **Sandilands Caravan Park** is three miles (4.8 km) south of Kilkeel, and four miles (6.5 km) from Cranfield East, signposted off the A2 Newry-Kilkeel road. It's near a private beach, and is open from St. Patrick's Day to the end of October. ☎ (028) 4176-3634; www. chestnuttcaravans.co.uk.

Also near Kilkeel is the ☆☆☆☆ **Chestnutt Caravan Park**, four miles (6.5 km) south, open March through October. ☎ (028) 4176-2653.

Close to Rostrevor is the **Kilbroney Park**, overlooking Carlingford Lough, where visitors can also enjoy forest walks. Open April through October. ☎ (028) 4173-8134.

If you stay at the **Annalong Caravan Park**, you have a private beach to enjoy. The park is on the Millisle-to-Ballywalter road, open mid-March to mid-November. ☎ (028) 4275-8062; info@sandycove.co.uk; www. sandycove.co.uk.

There are two parks at Millisle – the ☆ **Rathlin Caravan Park**, ☎ (028) 9186-1386, and ☆ **Walker's Caravan Park**, ☎ (028) 9186-1181.

☆☆☆ **Tollymore Forest Park**, with its 2,000 acres (800 hectares) of woodland at the foot of the Mournes, is a beautiful setting for camping or caravanning. There's also a choice of activities available, including pony trekking, hill climbing and game fishing (permit needed). The site is on the B180, three miles (4.8 km) from Newcastle; open all year. ☎ (028) 4372-2428.

At Newcastle there's the ☆☆ **Windsor Caravan Park**. ☎ (028) 4372-3367.

Staying at the ☆☆☆ **Castlewellan Forest Park** means you can explore the arboretum, established around 1740, with shrubs, trees and exotic plants from all over the world. There's much to see and do, including trout fishing (permit required), an orienteering course, a sculpture trail, or exploring the 18th-century farmstead, and it's open year round. There's a Visitor Centre with café. ☎ (028) 4377-8664.

☆☆☆ **Exploris Touring Caravan Park** is at Portaferry, open Easter to end September. ☎ (028) 4272-8610.

At Hillsborough there's the ☆☆☆ **Lakeside-View Park**, signposted off the B177 road, open April to the end of October. ☎ (028) 9268-2098; bookings@lakeside-view.8m.com; www.lakeside-view.8m.com.

On the A1 Belfast-Newry road, the ☆☆☆ **Banbridge Gateway Tourist Information Centre** has a caravan and camping site, which is open all year. ☎ (028) 4062-3322; Banbridge@nitic.net; www.banbridge.com.

■ Where to Eat

 The Old Schoolhouse Inn is near Strangford Lough, three miles south-east of Comber. It won the Northern Ireland Tourist Board's Best Restaurant Award and specializes in steaks, seafood and delicious desserts. It also offers accommodation in 12 bedrooms, each named after an American President of Ulster ancestry. ☎ (028) 9754-1182; fax 9754-2583; www.oldschoolhouseinn.com.

The Lobster Pot in The Square, Strangford, has a delightful old-fashioned charm. It's renowned for seafood, in particular lobster, and offers bar food all day. ☎/fax (028) 4488-1288.

The Jolly Judge on Regent Street, Newtownards, serves a wide range of bar food every day of the week, and booking is not necessary. ☎ (028) 9181-9895.

Knotts Cake and Coffee Shop on High Street, Newtownards, is a great place to stop for a snack or meal during the day, Monday to Saturday. In addition to a range of delicious cakes and breads, it serves pies, casseroles and stews. It's located in a large and airy Victorian building and is smoke-free. ☎ (028) 9181-9098.

An unusual place to stop is the **Cairnmore Antiques Tea Shop**, Lambeg Road in Lisburn, where you can enjoy a snack and browse among the antiques on sale. Open 2-5 pm from Monday to Friday and on Saturdays from 11 am to 5 pm, it serves tea, scones and pastries. ☎ (028) 9267-3115.

The Wildflower Inn, Main Street, Greyabbey, is a former coaching inn with a cozy atmosphere and a log fire. It caters for all tastes, its menu including salads, fish and roast beef. ☎ (028) 4278-8260.

■ Further Information

The Kingdoms of Down. ☎ (028) 9151-6150; info@
kingdomsofdown.com; www.kingdomsofdown.com.

**Ards Peninsula-Newtownards Tourist Information
Centre.** ☎ (028) 9183-6846; fax 9182-6681; tourism@ards-
council.gov.uk; www.ards-council.gov.uk.

Newry and Mourne District Council. ☎ (028) 3031-3031; fax 3031-
3077. www.newryandmourne.gov.uk.

 *A fascinating site, with lots of background on the
area is www.strangfordlough.org.*

County Armagh

Armagh is the smallest county in the North, yet within its 484 square miles (1,258 square km) there is a great variety of scenery. In the southeast are mountains and rocky glens, including the Ring of Gullion, to the south is a rolling terrain dotted with drumlins (low hills formed by glaciers), while its central area is wild and open moorland. South of Portadown, the county boundary follows the line of the Upper Bann River and the Newry Canal.

For 3,000 years, apples have been grown in the county, mostly in the gentle landscape of the northeast around Loughgall, which is surrounded by 5,000 acres (2,000 hectares) of orchards – a lovely sight in May when all the trees are covered in blossoms.

Parts of Armagh are reminiscent of some of the western counties of the Republic, as fields resemble a patchwork, divided by dry-stone walls. This is a legacy of Gaelic times when land was shared equally between family members.

As you travel around the countryside, look out for games of road bowling, also known as "bullet," which is unique to Armagh and Co. Cork.

The county capital is **Armagh City** and other main towns are **Craigavon**, **Lurgan** and **Portadown**.

■ Getting Here & Around

The nearest **air** and **seaports** are in Belfast. **Ulsterbus** service connects the county's towns and villages. ☎ (028) 9033-3000.

Main Roads

For the fastest journey to Armagh City from Belfast take the M1 and then A29; alternatively, head for Portadown on the M1 and then the A3; or take the A1 towards Banbridge and then the A51, passing through Tandragee.

Lurgan, Craigavon and Portadown are close to the M1 from Belfast on the A27.

From Derry City, take the A5 through Strabane and Omagh to Aughnacloy, then the A28.

From Dublin take the N1 through Dundalk, the A1 from Newry, and then the A28.

From Monaghan Town in the Republic, take the A3.

Armagh

N

COUNTY ANTRIM

Crumlin

A52

Lough Neagh

COUNTY TYRONE

To Coleraine & Derry

River Blackwater

A4

Aughnacloy

Moy

Lisburn

Lurgan

Craigavon

M1

Portadown

River Lagan

M1

A1

A29

Loughgall

A3

Tandragee

A26

River Bann

Killylea

A28

Armagh

A51

A3

A28

Newry Canal

Monaghan

Keady

COUNTY MONAGHAN

A29

Newtown-hamilton

A27

A50

A25

Newry

COUNTY DOWN

A25

Castleblayney

Omeath

Carlingford Lough

Crossmaglen

A2

10 MILES

16 KM

No.	Site	No.	Site
1.	Killevy Churches	9.	Tí Chulainn Centre
2.	Slieve Gullion	10.	Creggan Graveyard
3.	Fort Navan (Emain Macha)	11.	Derrymore Cottage
4.	The Argory	12.	Brackagh Moss Nature Reserve
5.	Ardress House; Charlemont Fort	13.	Palace Demesne; Franciscan Friary Ruins;
6.	Oxford Island		St. Patrick's Cathedral; Armagh Observatory
7.	Belfast International Airport		& Planetarium; Cardinal O'Fiaich Memorial
8.	Keady Heritage Centre		Library & Archive

■ Tourist Information

i **Armagh Tourist Information Centre** is at 40 English Street. ☎ (028) 3752-1800; fax 3752-8329; armagh@nitic.net; www.armagh-visit.com.

South Armagh Tourism Initiative is based in O'Fiaich House, O'Fiaich Square, Crossmaglen. ☎ (028) 3086-8900; fax 3086-0001; sati@newryandmourne.gov.uk; www.south-armagh.com.

Cascades Leisure Centre, Thomas Street, Portadown. ☎ (028) 3883-2802.

Slieve Gullion Courtyard Centre. ☎ (028) 3084-8084.

TRACING YOUR ANCESTORS

Armagh Ancestry, 38A English Street, Armagh. Genealogical research library for public consultation, open Monday-Friday, 11 am-4 pm. Locally produced crafts, family crested shields, surname history scrolls, local history and maps on sale and available through mail order. ☎ (028) 3752-1802; fax 3751-0033; ancestry@acdc.btinternet.com; www.armagh.gov.uk.

■ Armagh City

Sightseeing

The city of Armagh is one of the most historic on the island. It was the seat of the ancient Kings of Ulster, who were crowned at nearby Emain Macha (Navan Fort).

There's a graciousness about the city, with its steep streets following the curves of the ditches that surrounded the ringfort or rath where Saint Patrick built his stone church in 445.

In the **Palace Demesne** are the ruins of a Franciscan friary, founded in 1263. Few medieval buildings have survived, but there are many fine examples of Georgian architecture, especially around the tree-lined **Mall**, which used to be the city's racecourse. Richard Robinson, who became Archbishop of Armagh in 1765, was responsible for most of them, including the Palace, Public Library, Infirmary and Observatory. He spent about £40,000 (a fortune in those days) improving Armagh to encourage the foundation of a university, which didn't happen – although today the Armagh campus of Queen's University, Belfast, is housed in his Infirmary. He was the patron of Armagh-born architect Francis Johnston (1761-1829), who later left his mark on Georgian Dublin and elsewhere. Today, the Palace Demesne even includes a golf club.

Armagh City is small, with a population of under 20,000, but there is a lot to see and do.

Visit **St. Patrick's Church of Ireland Cathedral**, built on the site of the saint's church, which is mostly a 19th-century restoration around a 13th-century shell. Brian Boru, who drove the Norsemen out of Ireland in 1014, is said to be buried in its churchyard, and among other interesting monuments is an 11th-century high cross (see page 112). ☎ (028) 3752-3142. www.stpatrickscathedral-armagh.org.

The grounds of the **Armagh Observatory**, a modern research facility, include the Robinson dome with 10-inch telescope, and other interesting features, with free access always. There's a self-guided **Observatory Grounds Trail**. Call for details. ☎ (028) 3752-2928; fax 3752-7174; www. arm.ac.uk. The **Armagh Planetarium** is nearby, with daily audio-visual presentations. ☎ (028) 3752-4725; www.armagh-planetarium.co. uk.

St. Patrick's Trian derives its name from the ancient division of Armagh City into three distinct districts, or "Trians." They were known as Trian Mor (to the south and west), Trian Masain (to the east) and Trian Sassenach or Saxon (to the north). The city today has an English Street, Irish Street and Scotch Street, which roughly mark the boundaries of these Trians. The visitor complex now is in three 18th- and 19th-century buildings on English Street. There are three major exhibitions: The Armagh Story, Saint Patrick's Testament and The Land of Lilliput, inspired by *Gulliver's Travels*, whose author, Jonathan Swift, spent a lot of time in Armagh. ☎ (028) 3752-1801; fax 3751-0180; info@ saintpatrickstrian.com; www.visitarmagh.co.uk.

The **Cardinal Tomas O'Fiaich Memorial Library and Archive** is at 15 Moy Road, and admission is free. Material is from the late Cardinal's collection, and includes Irish history, the Irish language, Church history, the Irish diaspora and Irish sport. There's also an annual program of events and lectures. Library and Archive open Monday-Friday, 9:30 am-1 pm and 2-5 pm. ☎ (028) 3752-2981; fax 3752-2944; eolas@ofiaich.ie; www. ofiaich.ie.

Tours

The Pilgrim's Trail is a self-guided walking tour you can take around the city. Allow an hour, longer if you want to visit any of the attractions en route.

Guided tours are also available, from June through September on Saturdays at 11 am and 2 pm, and on Sundays at 2 pm only, with booking essential. Tours last an hour and a half, and start at the Tourist Information Centre. Bookings and queries: ☎ (028) 3752-1800; waiferguson@aol.com.

Shopping

The street layout of Armagh City is much as it was in the 19th century, with Scotch Street, English Street, and Thomas Street its principal shopping areas. The old tradition of street trading continues on **Market Street**, with open-air stalls. The **Mall Shopping Centre** is right in the center of town, with lots of different shops under one roof. As its name suggests, it's on the historic Mall, with easy access on foot from Scotch Street and Market Square.

PARKING

There are car parks, signposted, all around the central area. Try the one at the Mall Shopping Centre first.

Entertainment

 There's a four-screen cinema, **Armagh City Film House**, and **The Market Place Theatre and Arts Complex** hosts plays, exhibitions and other events. ☎ (028) 3752-1820; admin@ marketplacearmagh.com; www.themarketplacearmagh.com.

Spectator Sports

 The Armagh Road Bowls Association is based at 23 Ennislare Road, if you want to find out more about this almost unique sport or to watch it being played. The only other place where you'll see it played is Cork in the Republic. The All-Ireland Road Bowls Finals are held annually in early August. ☎ (028) 3752-2437.

The County Cricket Club is on The Mall West, and there's a second club, **Laurelvale**. **The Armagh Rugby Club** is in the Palace Demesne, and the **City Football Club** (soccer) is on Ballynahonemore Road.

The **Armagh Harps Gaelic Football Club** is on Loughall Road, and you can check out the County GAA (Gaelic Athletic Association) team and other Gaelic sports locally or on www.armagh-gaa.com.

■ Navan Fort

On the A28, 2½ miles (four km) west of Armagh, is Navan Fort, or Emain Macha, capital of the Kings of Ulster from 600 BC. Access is free and it's open all the time. ☎ (028) 3752-1800.

The name Emain Macha means "twins of Macha" and it's associated with the Ulster saga, *The Táin*. The story is that Macha was forced to race against the King's horses when pregnant; she gave birth to twins and died after the race, but cursed the Ulstermen, saying that they would become weak with labor pains in Ulster's hour of need.

When Queen Maeve of Connaught marched her armies to Ulster to steal the famous brown bull of Cooley, sure enough the Knights were struck down with labor pains and only Cúchulainn was able to guard the pass at Glendhu, near Slieve Gullion.

Northern Ireland

■ South Armagh

Head out of Armagh on the A29 south and you come to **Keady**, where the Heritage Centre in an old mill tells the story of local linen production. It's open only by arrangement, so phone in advance. ☎ (028) 3753-9928.

Continue from there through Newtownhamilton and look for a sign for Crossmaglen. Near Crossmaglen, off the B30 at Mullaghbawn, is the **Tí Chulainn Centre**, dedicated to the culture of South Armagh. There's a tea room and shop and you can ask about courses and performances. Open Monday-Friday, 10 am-4 pm; Saturday, 10 am-1 pm. ☎ (028) 3088-8828; www.tichullain.ie. There's also a folk museum nearby, only open by appointment. ☎ (028) 3088-8278.

Slieve Gullion

Slieve Gullion, "the mountain of the steep slope," is the highest in Armagh. The Slieve Gullion Forest Park is on the B113, five miles (eight km) southwest of Newry, and it's an eight-mile (11-km) drive up and around it. There's a mountain-top trail to walk (at 1,880 feet/573 m), which takes you to megalithic cairns and a lake with fantastic views. There's also a walled garden, and a Visitor Centre with craft shop and a café. Open daily, Easter through the end of summer, 10 am to dusk. ☎ (028) 3755-1277.

It's not only the striking landscape that makes South Armagh interesting, but also its people. The area has been inhabited for more than 6,000 years, as you can see from burial chambers, megalithic tombs and cairns. It's also associated with the saga from the Ulster Cycle, *The Táin Bo Cuailgne* (or The Cattle Raid of Cooley), as it's here that Cúchulainn defended Ulster against the marauder, Queen Maeve of Connaught. See page 10 for the story..

THE HAG OF BEARA

It's here as well that another mythic figure, Fionn MacCumhaill (Finn McCool) was tricked. He saw a lady sitting by the lake near the summit of Slieve Gullion, looking sad. She told him she'd lost her ring and he leapt into the lake to retrieve it; when he got out he was turned into an old man. Although he recovered later, his hair stayed white. The lady was really the Cailliagh Berra (the Hag of Beara) and the lake is named after her. The superstition lives on that if you bathe in the Lough your hair will turn white.

The Cailliagh Berra, the hag or witch of Beara, which is an area of West Cork, makes many appearances in Irish folklore, and is often associated with passage tombs. For example, at Loughcrew in Co. Meath there's The Hag's Chair and a low mountain named after her.

The Slieve Gullion area retains its culture and identity through music, poetry, folklore and art. It was known as "the District of Songs" and was home to all the most important Ulster poets of the 18th century, the last great age of literature in the Irish language. In **Creggan Graveyard**, northeast of Crossmaglen, there's a beautifully kept Poets' Glen. The graveyard is also where the Ulster chieftains, the O'Neills, were buried.

On the southern slope of Slieve Gullion is a large stone cairn covering a Neolithic (New Stone Age) passage tomb, known locally as Caillaigh Berra's House. Its layout is similar to the one at Newgrange, and is probably the highest so far discovered on the island, with wonderful views from it. It's also a notable feature in the landscape, as it sticks out from the mountain slope.

Killevy Churches, Graveyard **& Holy Well** on the eastern side of the mountain is well worth a visit. One of the earliest convents in the whole country was founded here by Saint Moninna, who died around 518. Her feast day is July 6, still celebrated with visits to the well higher up, reached by a path. The saint's name survives locally as "Bline." Water from this holy well, like many others all over the 32 counties, is said to cure a specific ailment – in this case eye problems. Many of the wells are signposted and are worth a look.

■ Moy

The village of Moy is just inside neighboring County Tyrone, north of Armagh on the A29 to Dungannon. At the junction of that road with the B28 outside Moy are the ruins of **Charlemont Fort**, built in 1602 by Lord Mountjoy to control the activities of Hugh O'Neill. The star-shaped fort faced across the Blackwater into O'Neill's territory and was crucial in the English defeat of the Irish Chieftain.

Moy itself has a pretty square lined with trees, and its eight pubs and two restaurants make it a good place to stop. The **Blackwater River Park** nearby is popular for fishing, canoeing, and diving.

There are two National Trust properties nearby worth visiting. **Ardress House** is a lovely 17th-century manor (with later additions) on the B28, five miles (eight km) from Moy. It has elegant plasterwork by Michael Stapleton in the drawing room, good furniture and a picture gallery. Outside, there's a magnificent 18th-century pink-cobbled working farmyard with a piggery, blacksmith's, chicken houses, and a well. For an adventure on foot, you can take woodland and riverside walks among its orchards. Open June-August, daily, 2-6 pm; mid-March to end April and September, on weekends only. ☎/fax (028) 3885-1236; ardress@ntrust. org.uk.

The Argory is on a hill set in 200 acres (80 hectares) of wooded countryside overlooking the River Blackwater, four miles (6.4 km) northeast of Moy on the Derrycaw Road. This 1820 Neoclassical house still contains its original furniture and is lit by its own acetylene gas plant, one of the very few surviving examples in the British Isles. Grounds open daily, October-April, 10 am-4 pm; May-September, to 8 pm. House open June-August, noon-6 pm; mid-March-end April and September, weekends only. ☎ (028) 8778-4753; fax 8778-9598; argory@ntrust.org.uk; www. nationaltrust.org.uk.

■ Craigavon

Named after the first Prime Minister of Northern Ireland, James Craig, Lord Craigavon, this New Town was established to relieve pressure on Belfast, 30 miles (48 km) away, and to rejuvenate the area. It brought together the existing towns of Lurgan and Portadown with nearby small villages that had one thing in common – the linen industry. Craigavon has officially existed since 1973, and is not particularly attractive, surrounded by industrial buildings, business parks and busy roads, including the M1 from Belfast to Dungannon.

However, it's close to **Lough Neagh**, the largest fresh-water lake in the UK, and the area attracts visitors interested in watersports, fishing, and bird watching or in walking or cycling around it.

There's a map and guide available to **The Loughshore Trail**, the 128-mile (206-km) route around Lough Neagh and Lough Beg; check out www.loughshoretrail.com.

■ Lurgan

The town was granted to the Brownlows after 1607. They came from Nottingham in the English Midlands. But Lurgan didn't prosper until around 1700, when Samuel Waring introduced linen-damask weaving to Ulster. You can see cottages built for the weavers around Bownes Lane. Textiles and clothing are still important industries here. **Brownlow House** is now the HQ of the Imperial Grand Black Chapter of the British Commonwealth, a close relation of the Orange Order, and its grounds are a public park with landscaped gardens, a lake and golf course.

The Book of Armagh, *oldest of the great illuminated manuscripts and now in Trinity College Library, Dublin, somehow found its way into the collection of Arthur Brownlow, after being pawned for £5 in 1680!*

James Logan (1674-1751), a scientist and scholar, who helped found Pennsylvania, is remembered at the Quaker Meeting House on High Street (the first in Ireland in 1653) with a plaque on a gate pillar.

Another American connection is Field Marshall Sir John Dill, buried in Arlington Cemetery, who liaised between the US and British governments in World War II. He was born here.

■ Portadown

The town has seen sectarian strife even in recent years, due to the Orange Order marching down the nationalist Garvaghy Road from nearby Drumcree Church. Even when passing through on the train you can't help noticing the number of Union Jacks, the UK flag, on display.

In the 1730s the building of a canal from Newry to Lough Neagh, which passes through the town, brought prosperity. Building started in 1730 and took 12 years, and it was extended down to Carlingford Lough as a ship canal in 1761, bringing prosperity to Portadown, Scarva, Poyntzpass, and other places along its route. By the 1840s it had declined and was last used in the 1930s. Portadown was also a major junction in the heyday of rail, with large marshaling yards.

It has a wide and sloping main street and the center seems full of churches and chapels; there are more than a dozen of them within a small area.

There are lots of bands in the town, including flute, pipe and accordion, and there is also a very good male choir.

Six miles (10 km) west of Portadown is **Loughall**, where the Battle of the Diamond in 1795 led to the foundation of the Orange Order, three miles (4.8 km) away in Dan Winter's House. His traditional thatched cottage is now a museum, which can be visited (key at farmhouse). Open Monday-Saturday, 10:30 am-8:30 pm, Sunday from 2:30 pm. Donation voluntary. ☎ (028) 3885-1344; www.orangenet.org/winter.

■ Near Newry

Derrymore is a delightful late-18th-century thatched cottage built by the politician Isaac Corry, where it's believed the Act of Union was drafted. It's on the A25, two miles (3.2 km) from Newry on the Camlough Road. The cottage is surrounded by a lovely park with terrific views and is the perfect place to stop if you're traveling – either by bike or by car – from Belfast or Dublin. The grounds are open all year, to 4 pm from October-April, and until 8 pm from May-September. The house is open between May and August, Thursday to Saturday afternoons only, 2-5:30 pm. ☎ (028) 3083-8361. The Slieve Gullion Waymarked Way ends here (see below).

■ Adventures on Foot & by Cycle

The Newry Canal Way

 This route is 20 miles (32 km) long and follows the towpath of the disused canal between Bann Bridge, Portadown, and the Town Hall in Newry. Parts of the walk are in neighboring County Down.

Walkers and cyclists share the Way, as it is part of Route 9 of the National Cycle Network. There is much to see, including lots of wildlife and art pieces – some commissioned to mark the Millennium, others that reflect the former life of the canal. You can continue from the towpath on Route 9 from Newry to Camlough and the Slieve Gullion Courtyard Centre, via the National Trust property, Derrymore.

Highlights En Route

Along the Newry Canal Way there are a number of interesting stopping places. **Moneypenny's Lock** is the last lock before the Newry Canal joins the Upper Bann river. The lock-keeper's house has been restored and contains exhibits that tell the story of the life and times of the lightermen who worked on the canal. Admission free. Open April-September, Saturday-Sunday only, 2-5 pm. ☎ (028) 3832-2205.

Point of Whitecoat is at the end of the canal where the rivers Bann and Cusher meet, and is crossed by a distinctive bridge.

Scarva Visitors' Centre is actually in Co. Down, beside the only port on the canal where barges passed each other or delivered and collected cargoes. Here you learn about the history of canals in Ireland, and of Scarva, as well as the building of the Newry Canal. There's also a coffee shop, so it's a good place for a rest. Open April-October, Tuesday-Friday, 12-5 pm; Saturday-Sunday, 2-5 pm. Admission is free. ☎ (028) 3883-2163.

Acton Interpretative Centre is on the site of a former sluice-keeper's cottage beside Lough Shark, a small lake used to top up the water level if there was a drought.

Gamble's Bridge, south of Poyntzpass, was also known as Crack Bridge – either because it had a crack in it or because it was where people met for fun (craic in Irish, from Ulster-Scots). Farther south is **Steenson's Bridge**, which is a very picturesque three-arched structure.

There's an illustrated guide, *The Newry Canal Way*, which is well worth getting, and a map-leaflet, available from tourist offices, or check out www.countrysiderecreation.com.

The Brackagh Moss Nature Reserve

 Just off the A27, two miles (3.2 km) southeast of Portadown, is the Brackagh Moss Nature Reserve. This was originally a raised bog, but after more than 300 years of turf cutting what's left is a maze of pools, drainage channels and peat ramparts. Because of its different soils, it has an extremely varied flora, from dense woodlands to fens and shallow pools. There are rare butterflies, dragonflies, and other insects; you see flocks of ducks, and even mink or otter. Look out for the two pull-offs along the road, which have information panels with details of the path system north of the road. You can't visit the south side without special permission from the warden, as it's dangerous.

Waymarked Way

The waymarked **Ring of Gullion Way** starts in Newry. It follows the natural geological formation known as a ring-dyke through this Area of Outstanding Natural Beauty (AONB), ending at Derrymore House near Bessbrook. It's 33 miles (53 km) long but you can tackle it in stages. The terrain includes forestry tracks, rugged open hillside, grassy tracks, parts that are boggy and in places it is steep. Walkers are rewarded with wonderful views of Slieve Gullion, of the ring-dyke, and of Carlingford Lough and the Mountains of Mourne. You'll also see plenty of historic monuments and standing stones.

Forest Parks

Other walking areas include Carnagh Forest, Gosford Forest Park, and Slieve Gullion Forest Park, managed by the Forestry Service. It's worth looking at the website **www.forestserviceni.gov.uk** for details of other forests and their amenities.

Carnagh Forest is natural woodland, with mixed conifers and broadleaf trees, off the Keady-to-Castleblaney road. It has fishing lakes and an anglers' inn, where you can have a snack.

Gosford Forest Park at Markethill is the former estate of Gosford Castle, a mock-Norman battlemented extravaganza. There's an arboretum, which was established in the 1820s, with some magnificent specimens.

Northern Ireland

There's also a walled garden, two raths or prehistoric forts, a nature trail, and a camping and caravan site. The park is associated with writer Jonathan Swift (author of *Gulliver's Travels*) who mentions it in some of his poems. He's remembered with Dean Swift's Well and Chair in a secluded spot. ☎ (028) 3755-1277.

Close to Lough Neagh

The Wetlands Way is a series of waymarked trails on quiet roads and paths through the South Lough Neagh wetlands, an area rich in natural and human heritage.

Maghery Country Park, on the shores of Lough Neagh, offers woodland walks. **Portadown People's Park** is also ideal for walking. The City Park has a network of walking and cycling paths in 250 acres (100 hectares) of parkland around Craigavon Lakes. **Lurgan Public Park** covers 200 acres (80 hectares) with wooded areas, a lake, and open grassland.

The Lagan Canal Towpath

This walk near Craigavon is a mile and a half long (2.4 km). It's easy to walk (or cycle) as the towpath, which opened in 1794, is flat and smooth. Half of the walk follows the National Cycling Network Route 9 and the Lough Neagh Cycleway: the Loughshore Trail.

Starting points are Goudy Bridge, Cranagh Bridge or Annadroghal Bridge, which are all very attractive. There are marks in the stone made by the ropes from the horse-drawn barges used to transport goods between Belfast and Lough Neagh ports.

Nearby is the **Montiaghs Moss** area, a peat habitat, where the traditional activities of fishing the Lough and willow basket-making continue.

Cycle Repair & Sales

In the Craigavon area, south of Lough Neagh, there are a number of outlets:

Central Cycles, 4 Church Lane, Portadown, ☎ (028) 3833-7910.

Raymond Ross , 65 Bridge Street, Portadown.

The Cyclery, Giant House, 56 Edward Street, Lurgan, ☎ (028) 3834-8627.

T.W. Dynes, 23 William Street, Lurgan, ☎ (028) 3832-6863.

T.J. McCabrey, 70 William Street, Lurgan, ☎ (028) 3832-5720.

TRY SOMETHING NEW

There's a **Clay Pigeon Shooting Range** at Newtownhamilton, open in the evenings and on weekends. It's on the Old Coach Road, signposted on the A29 to Dundalk. ☎ (028) 3087-8126.

■ Adventures on Water

Oxford Island is north of Craigavon; take Junction 10 off the M1 if arriving from Belfast or Dungannon. It's a National Nature Reserve offering a huge choice of activities, some on Lough Neagh, others close to the lake.

Kinnego Marina is the largest on Lough Neagh, and you can get expert instruction in sailing or power-boating here. You can also stay in a converted farmhouse now a hostel, or in the caravan park. Open April 1-October 31, 8 am-9 pm; November-March, 8:30 am-5:30 pm. ☎ (028) 3832 7573; kinnego.marina@craigavon.gov.uk; www.craigavon.co.uk.

The *Master McGra*, a cruiser named after a famous greyhound, runs tours on the lough to Coney Island, Maghery and The Lough Neagh Discovery Centre, also in the Nature Reserve.

There are lots of different displays in the Discovery Centre, including interactive games about the culture, history and wildlife of the area. It also has a craft shop and a café with a panoramic view of the Lough. Among its outdoor facilities are bird-watching hides, guided walks, and lots of special events. Open April-September, 10 am-7 pm daily; October-March, Wednesday-Sunday, 10 am-5 pm only. ☎ (028) 3832 2205.

Fans of singer Van Morrison (from Belfast) will recognize *Coney Island* as the title of one of his most successful songs. **Coney Island** is tiny, only seven acres, and has lots of unusual trees and birds, so makes a pleasant place to visit. It's in the care of the National Trust and you can ask about it at the Discovery Centre.

Fishing

There's a guide, *Angling in Armagh and Down*, available from tourist offices. **Angling Fisheries Limited**, which incorporates Armagh District Angling Club, is the body responsible for fishing and angling. You can get advice and daily permits from **GI Stores**, 5 Dobbin Street, Armagh. ☎ (028) 3752-2335.

There are six lakes around Armagh City recommended for fishing. Only fly-fishing is allowed at the following:

Seaghan Lake, off the A29 between Armagh and Newtownhamilton; **Lowry Lake**, off the A51 Armagh-Hamiltonsbawn road; **Shaw's Lake**, outside Glenanne on the B134; and **Tullinawood Lake**, on the A29 between Keady and Newtownhamilton, which has an island reached by a footbridge.

All legal methods of fishing are allowed at **Darkley Lake**, between Keady and Newtownhamilton, and the **Aughnagurgan Lake**, on the A29 nearby.

The Blackwater River Park near Moy has one of the best fishing rivers in Ireland, famous for its big bream. The river park extends for three miles (4.8 km), opposite Benburb, which has an ancient castle and priory.

Craigavon City Park Lakes cover an area of 168 acres (67 hectares) and are stocked with rainbow trout. Anglers may bring along their own boats or rent boats from Craigavon Borough Council Recreational Department.

South Armagh has some of the best waters for game and coarse angling, which suit all levels of experience. **Carlingford Lough** nearby also offers sea angling.

There are many small lakes in the area, including Carrigan, Aughnagurgan, Upper and Lower Cashel, Glassdrumman, Mullaghbane, all recommended for trout. Eels, rudd, perch, pike, as well as trout can be caught from the Newry Canal, at the Omeath Road. Ask locally for advice and about licenses and permits.

See pages 71-74 for details on angling in Ireland, regulations and best times to fish.

■ Adventures on Horseback

Armagh's wonderful rural countryside is ideal for riding, and there are a number of facilities to choose from.

The Moy Riding School offers classes with a qualified instructor and also has showjumping on Friday evenings, which is open to the public. ☎ (028) 8778-4440.

The Millbrook Equestrian Centre, Newtownhamilton, has two indoor arenas and one outdoor. Among its activities are beach riding, and hacks through the forest and Mourne Mountains. ☎ (028) 3083-8336.

The Newtownhamilton Equestrian Cross-Country Course is signposted off the A29 road to Dundalk. It's built over 15 acres (six hectares) of rolling hills and has 27 fences, some unsuited to the novice rider. Open weekends and evenings; phone for details. ☎ (028) 3087-8126.

The Ring of Gullion Trekking Centre at Mullaghbane, below Slieve Brack, has a number of natural habitats, with themed trail rides for adults and classes for beginners. It also has a coffee shop, and offers accommodation. ☎ (028) 3088-9311.

The Greenvale Trekking Centre is at Forkhill at the foot of Slieve Gullion. It offers pony trekking, activity weekends and half-day treks, with instruction available. Accommodation is also available. ☎ (028) 3088-8314; greenvale@yahoo.com.

Equestrian Events

- There's a **Two-Day Event** at Richill every August. ☎ (028) 4482-8734; www.eventingireland.com.

- **The Irish Draught Horse Society** is based at Moy. Contact them for details of events. ☎ (028) 8778-4440; armagh@ nitic.net.

■ Golf

There are eight 18-hole courses in the county.

The Armagh County Golf Club is on Newry Road, in the Palace Demesne, and has a practice fairway. ☎ (028) 3752-5864; fax 3752-5861.

At the **Loughall Country Park** you can rent clubs, and there's a practice area and putting green. It also has facilities for fishing and walks. ☎ (028) 3889-2900; fax 3889-2902; loughgallcountrypark@ukgateway. net.

The **Craigavon** course, two miles (3.2 km) north of Lurgan, is part of the **Golf/Ski Centre**, which also has an artificial ski slope, as well as a driving range. ☎ (028) 3832-6606; fax 3834-7272.

Ashfield Golf Club is four miles (6.4 km) north of Crossmaglen, off the B30. ☎ (028) 3086-8180; fax 3086-8611; ashfield.golfing@virgin.net.

Cloverhill is 10 miles (16 km) southwest of Newry. ☎ (028) 3088-9374; fax 3088-9199; info@cloverhillgc.com; www.cloverhillgc.com.

Lurgan's Golf Club is in the town park, the former demesne of Brownlow House. ☎ (028) 3832-2087; fax 3831-6166.

The **Portadown** course is three miles (4.8 km) southeast of the town. ☎ (028) 3835-5356.

Just half a mile south of **Tandragee** is its **Golf Club**. ☎ (028) 3884-1272; fax 3884-0664; office@tandragee.co.uk; www.tandragree.co.uk.

■ Other Leisure Activities

If you want to swim or use a gym, there's a **leisure center** in Craigavon, a facility called **Waves** in Lurgan and another called **Cascades** in Portadown. The **Orchard Leisure Centre** is on Folly Lane, Armagh. ☎ (028) 371-5920. In City Park, Craigavon, there's a **Watersports Centre**.

There are public **tennis courts** in parks in Lurgan, Brownstown and Portadown.

■ Where to Stay

☆☆☆☆ **The Armagh City Hotel** is on Friary Road, next to the Palace Stables and overlooking the County Armagh Golf Club. It has 82 spacious bedrooms and guests can enjoy a choice of dining from the contemporary menu at **The Friary Restaurant**. Its leisure center has a pool and fitness suite and other facilities. Rates from $$ with special offers available online. ☎ (028) 9038-5050; fax 9038-5055; reservations@mooneyhotelgroup.com; www.mooneyhotelgroup.com.

HOTEL PRICE CHART	
Price per person, per night, with two sharing, including breakfast.	
$	Under US $50
$$	US $50-$100
$$$	US $101-$175
$$$$	US $176-$200
$$$$$	Over US $200

☆☆ **The Charlemont Arms Hotel** on English Street, Armagh, has looked after travelers since the early 19th century. It's been run by the Forster family since 1934, and in recent years has been refurbished. There are 31 bedrooms, a restaurant serving traditional dishes and a bar. In its basement is a café/winebar called **downstairs@turners**, where fish is prominent on the menu. In 2003 chef Bob McDonald, who looks after both Turners and the hotel dining room, won Chef of the Year in a competition organized by the Hotel and Catering Management Association. $$. ☎ (028) 3752-2028; fax 3752-6979; info@charlemontarmshotel.com; www.charlemontarmshotel.com.

Guesthouses/B&B

De Averell Guest House on Upper English Street, Armagh, is named after John Averell, Dean of Emly and Bishop of Limerick, who in the late 18th century built seven houses for his sisters – because, it's said, he didn't want them to own their own! The guesthouse is No 3 Seven Houses, and is a marvelous Georgian retreat, with five bedrooms. $. It also has a restaurant – **The Basement** – which is open to non-residents, serving local and international dishes, using the best of local produce. ☎ (028) 3751-1213; fax 3751-1221; tony@deaverellhouse.com; www. deaverellhouse.com.

Ballinahinch House is surrounded by green fields and offers guests the pleasure of staying in an historic home with modern facilities. It was built around 1835 and has been carefully restored, decorated and furnished in keeping with that period. It's between Armagh and Portadown on the B131 to Richhill. Breakfasts are delicious, featuring home-grown tomatoes (nothing like the commercial variety), potato bread, and eggs from free-range chickens. It also offers packages with the Tandragee Golf Club. $ for two sharing. ☎/fax (028) 3887-0081; info@ballinahinchhouse. com; www.ballinahinchhouse.com.

Rental Cottages

 ☆☆☆☆ **TK's Cottage** is in a small development of houses near Crossmaglen and has three bedrooms, sleeping six. It can be rented by the night, weekend or by the week, and is excellent value, with an overnight mid-week costing only about £60 from May-October – that's for the house, not per person. It's near lots of activities, including four golf courses, fishing, horseback riding, as well as the lively pub culture of Crossmaglen and Dundalk. ☎ (028) 3086-8780; kierantony@hotmail.com; www.irishcottages.biz.

☆☆☆ **Woodside Cottage** is at Meigh in the Ring of Gullion, four miles (6.4 km) from Newry and eight miles (12.8 km) from Dundalk, with a view of the Mournes and Carlingford mountains. It sleeps from six to seven and costs from about £175-225 per night. ☎ (028) 3083-8172.

The Slieve Gullion Courtyard is in an Area of Outstanding Natural Beauty (AONB) and is a quadrangle of buildings dating from the 1820s. There are seven apartments to rent, some suitable for two, others for up to eight. It's excellent value, with rates starting at about £50 a night mid-week in low season, up to about £200 a week for the smaller ones at the busiest time of year. There's a licensed restaurant and shop, with regular entertainment, plus all the activities available in this scenic area, so you could spend your entire vacation here. ☎ (028) 3084-8084; fax 3084-8028; info@ slievegullioncourtyard.com; www.slievegullioncourtyard.com.

Camping & RV Parks

 ☆☆ **The Kinnego Marina Caravan Park**, Lurgan, is signposted off the M1 at Junction 10 for Oxford Island, and is on the shores of Lough Neagh in the National Nature Reserve. Open April 1-October 31. ☎ (028) 3832-7573; kinnego.marina@craigavon.gov.uk; www.craigavon.co.uk.

☆☆☆ The **Caravan and Camping Park in Gosford Forest Park**, Markethill, is in wonderful surroundings, including a nature trail, walled gardens, and a red deer park. It's off the A28, seven miles (11 km) from Armagh, 12 miles (19 km) from Newry. There's a barbecue site and café, and it's open all year. ☎ (028) 3755-1277/3755-2154.

☆☆☆ **The Clare Glen Caravan Park** is a mile (1.6 km) from Tandragee on the Markethill Road, and is open all year. ☎ (028) 3884-1110; www.armagh-visit.com.

Hostel

Armagh City Hostel at 39 Abbey Street and belongs to Hostelling International Northern Ireland. Constructed as a hostel, it provides a range of comfortable accommodations. Open year-round, but note that, unlike the majority of hostels today, it retains the traditional custom of closing during the day so you have to be out from 11 am to 5 pm. ☎ (028) 3751-1800; fax 3751-180; info@hini.org.uk www.hini.org.uk.

■ Where to Eat

The Yellow Door Deli, Woodhouse Street, Portadown, is a coffee shop using the best of the North's produce, including specialty breads, pastries and a daily choice of dishes. ☎ (028) 3835-3528.

The Planters Tavern, Banbridge Road, Warringstown, is a listed 17th-century coaching inn, which is open every day for breakfast, lunch and bar lunch, with an à la carte menu and snacks. Local beef and poultry are specialties in its medieval-themed dining room, **Cloisters Brasserie**. Main courses from about £5-15. Warringstown is a picturesque village on the A26 south of Lurgan; note that you can also stay at the Planters Tavern. $ sharing. ☎ (028) 3888-1510; fax 3888-2371.

The Four Trees Bar on Main Street, Moira, in an attractive historic building, has a separate dining area called the **Loft Bistro**. Food is available in the bar from 11:30 am to 8 pm, Monday to Saturday, and from noon to 8 pm on Sundays. The Bistro is open from Thursday to Sunday, 6 to 10 pm, and for lunch on Sundays from noon to 3 pm. ☎ (028) 9261-1437; fax 9261-3939; thefourtrees@aol.com; www.wheretotonight.com.

The Avanti Restaurant and the **Junction Bar** in the Seagoe Hotel on Upper Church Lane, Portadown, belong to A Taste of Ulster – the eating-out initiative supported by the Northern Ireland Tourist Board. Its members use fresh local produce in dishes that suit every taste and budget. There's a free brochure available from tourist offices. The Avanti is open every day for lunch and dinner, and there's a snack menu in the Junction Bar. ☎ (028) 3833-3076; fax 3835-0210.

The Coffee Shop in The Navan Centre on Killylea Road, Armagh, is open to the public for snacks and meals year-round (except Christmas week). It also belongs to A Taste of Ulster. Open Monday to Friday from 10 am to 5 pm; Saturdays, 11 am-5 pm; Sundays, noon-5 pm. Its menu includes a variety of hot and cold dishes. ☎ (028) 3752-5550; fax 3752-2323; navan@enterprise.net; www.navan.com.

■ Further Information

■ **Armagh Marketing Initiative** – www.armagh-visit.com.

Castle Coole, Enniskillen,
chromolithograph c. 1880 (see page 568)

Fermanagh-Lakeland

Fermanagh is dominated by Lough Erne, which is 50 miles (80 km) long from one end to the other and is divided in two. Lough Erne is actually two lakes – Lower and Upper – joined by the meandering River Erne. The county capital, Enniskillen, stands on the bank of the river between the two lakes.

There are many little wooded islands on the loughs, with evidence of ancient cultures and ruins from the Early Christian era.

The county's landscape is a patchwork of gentle rolling hills and fertile fields dotted with woods and forests. Yet what you're most aware of as you walk, cycle or drive around, are its lakes and rivers.

In addition to Lough Erne, on the county's western boundary are Upper and Lower Lough Macnean, with Belcoo between them, and Lough Melvin in its northwestern corner. More than a third of the county lies under water.

There's a lot to see and do, with historic sites, stately homes, museums and other attractions to visit, plus activities such as cycling, walking and playing golf. The county's ancient heritage is revealed on the islands in its lakes and particularly in the Burren area near Belcoo, which has lots of archaeological monuments, including portal and wedge tombs and a court tomb. On Boa Island, there are two Celtic Janus (two-faced) statues, probably from the first century AD.

The Erne River and Lake System has been joined in recent years to the River Shannon by the Shannon-Erne Waterway, and is the perfect destination for anglers and those who enjoy cruising, canoeing or windsurfing. Looking at a map, it seems strange that Lower Lough Erne is above Upper, but they're named in relation to the sea.

Fermanagh's main towns are **Irvinestown**, **Lisnaskea** and **Roslea**, and the largest is **Enniskillen**, the county capital.

■ Getting Here

Enniskillen is served by major roads: A4-M1-A3-M1 from Belfast (86 miles/138 km); A509-N3 from Dublin (109 miles/174 km); A4-N16-N15-N17 from Galway (114 miles/182 km).

Enniskillen Airport (St. Angelo) is at Trory, three miles (4.8 km) from the town, with flights to Jersey (in the Channel Islands) and Zurich, from May to September only. ☎ (028) 6632-8282; airport@ fermanagh.co.uk. The closest airports with regular services are Derry City, Belfast International and Dublin.

The nearest **train station** is in Sligo.

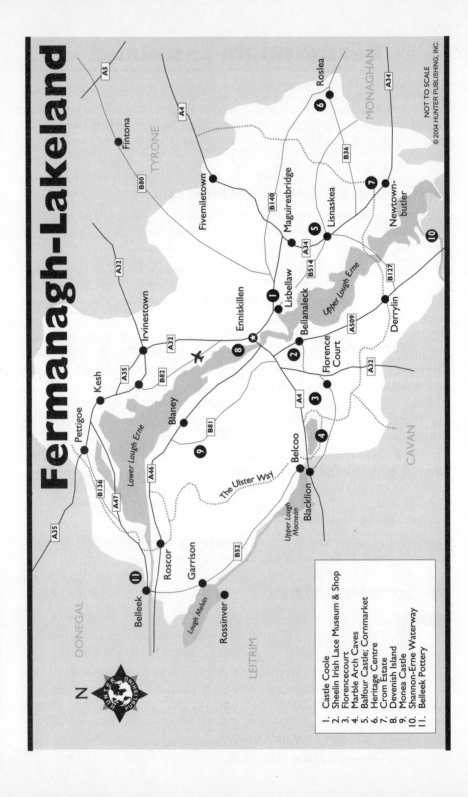

Fermanagh-Lakeland

NOT TO SCALE

© 2004 HUNTER PUBLISHING, INC.

MONAGHAN

TYRONE

CAVAN

DONEGAL

LEITRIM

Roslea

Fintona

Fivemiletown

Maguiresbridge

Lisnaskea

Newtown-butler

Lisbellaw

Enniskillen

Bellanaleck

Florence Court

Derrylin

Irvinestown

Kesh

Pettigoe

Blaney

Belcoo

Blacklion

Belleek

Roscor

Garrison

Rossinver

Upper Lough Erne

Lower Lough Erne

Upper Lough Macnean

Lough Melvin

The Ulster Way

A5

A4

B80

A32

A35

B82

A4

A32

B81

A46

A47

B136

A35

B52

B140

A34

B514

A509

A32

B127

B36

A34

N

1. Castle Coole
2. Sheelin Irish Lace Museum & Shop
3. Florencecourt
4. Marble Arch Caves
5. Balfour Castle; Cornmarket
6. Heritage Centre
7. Crom Estate
8. Devenish Island
9. Monea Castle
10. Shannon-Erne Waterway
11. Belleek Pottery

■ Getting Around

 Ulsterbus has a terminal in Enniskillen and operates a full range of services throughout the county, Ireland and the UK. Contact Ulsterbus at ☎ (028) 9033-3000; www.ulsterbus.co.uk.

Contact **Bus Éireann** for services to the Republic. ☎ (01) 8366-111.

■ Tourist Information

 The **Tourist Information Centre**, Wellington Road, Enniskillen, is open all year. ☎ (028) 6632-3110; fax 6632-5511; tic@fermanagh.gov.uk; www.fermanagh-online.com.

There's also a tourist office in **Belleek**, open in season, where the Belleek Pottery Visitor Centre has a museum, guided tours and a shop.

TRACING YOUR ANCESTORS

The Genealogy Centre for those with ancestors from Co. Fermanagh is shared with the one for the neighboring county: **Irish World Family History Services**, 51 Dungannon Road, Coalisland, Co. Tyrone. ☎ (028) 8774-6065; info@irish-world.com; www.irish-world.com.

There's also a genealogical searching service in the **Roslea Heritage Centre**. ☎ (028) 6775-1750.

■ Enniskillen

Sightseeing

Enniskillen is in the middle of the county, on an island in the River Erne, between Upper and Lower Lough Erne. The town developed around the castle, which dates back to the 15th century. This was once the stronghold of the Maguire chieftains, whose navy of 1,500 boats, stationed at Enniskillen Castle and on Hare Island, patrolled the lakes.

Enniskillen became a garrison town when granted to Sir William Cole, who enlarged the castle and built the lovely **Water Gate**, which looks best seen from the Lough. It was the most important of a ring of castles built by the planters around the Lough to control the waterway; the others included **Portora** – its ruins are in the grounds of the Portora Royal

Northern Ireland

Enniskillen

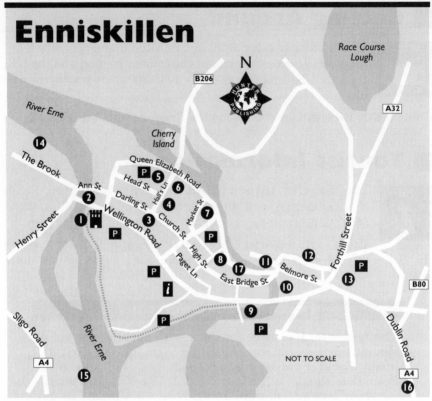

Race Course
Lough

N

B206

A32

River Erne

Cherry
Island

The Brook

Queen Elizabeth Road

Ann St

Head St

Hall's Ln

Darling St

Church St

Market St

Henry Street

Wellington Road

Paget Ln

High St

East Bridge St

Belmore St

Forthill Street

Sligo Road

River Erne

NOT TO SCALE

Dublin Road

A4

A4

B80

1. Enniskillen Castle; Fermanagh County Museum
2. West Bridge; Castle Bridge
3. St. Michael's RC Church; Methodist Church
4. St. Macartin's Church of Ireland Cathedral
5. Library
6. Crown Buildings
7. Boston Quay Craft Shop; Buttermarket
8. Town Hall
9. Footbridge (Inish Walk)
10. Inis Cethlenn Bridge & Park
11. East Bridge
12. Forthill; Coles Monument
13. Fairgreen
14. Brook Park; *Kestrel* Waterbus
15. Lochside Cruises
16. To Ardhowen Theatre; Castle Coole
17. Court House; Presbyterian Church

School, founded by James I in 1608. Famous students include writers Oscar Wilde (1854-1900) and Samuel Beckett (1905-1989).

The town has a long and winding main street that keeps changing its name and off it there are fascinating medieval lanes. The tower of **St. MacCartan's Church of Ireland Cathedral**, all that survives from a 17th-century church, has a bell cast from cannon used in the Battle of the Boyne. Facing it is the tall and narrow **St. Michael's Catholic Church**.

In the lobby of the town hall there's a brass plate memorial to Captain Oates of the 6th Inniskilling Dragoons, an icon of self-sacrifice because, ill and unable to move at the pace of the rest of the party, he walked out into a blizzard and perished during Scott's return from reaching the South Pole in 1912, rather than slow their progress.

The town bustles with life and commerce, and attracts visitors interested in fishing, boating and other activities. There are lots of bait and tackle shops and gift shops selling the distinctive cream-colored pottery made nearby at **Belleek**.

Dominating the skyline is **Enniskillen Castle**, with its picturesque location on the water. It was a Maguire fort, Plantation castle and, from the late 18th century, artillery barracks. Its 15th-century keep houses the **Fermanagh County Museum** and the museum of two regiments, the Royal Inniskilling Fusiliers and the Dragoons. There are also other displays and a shop. Open daily, May-September; weekdays only the rest of the year. ☎ (028) 6632-5000.

Tours

The self-guided Enniskillen History Trail features over 20 landmarks in the town. Ask about it at the tourist office.

Guided Tours

Lakeland Tours runs a program of day tours by luxury coach. ☎ (028) 8954-1646; fax 8954-1424; ian@lakelandtours.co.uk.

There's a choice with **Heritage Tours**, led by qualified guide and broadcaster Breege McCusker, including a walking tour of Enniskillen, Plantation Castles and Stately Homes, Lough MacNean and Marlbank. ☎ (028) 6862-1430; bmccusker@talk21.com.

Erne Heritage Tours has general, customized and specialized trips led by qualified guides, on foot, by car and coach. ☎ (028) 6865-8327; adam4eves@aol.com; www.erneheritagetours.com.

Shopping

 The Buttermarket, built in 1835 in the Boston Quarter as a marketplace for the county's dairy produce, had been derelict for years but is now restored and houses the **Enniskillen Craft and Design Centre**. You can watch craftspeople at work or buy original items.

It's a lovely place to wander around. There is the **Boston Quay Craft Shop**, named after the quay below it, as well as a number of small shops, and you can relax over traditional food in **Rebecca's Coffee Shop**, or in the courtyard outside. Boston Quay, ☎ (028) 6632-3837; Rebecca's, ☎ (028) 6632-9376; www.thebuttermarket.com.

Northern Ireland

It was from Boston Quay that people once boarded the ferry from the island to the workhouse. As you stroll through the courtyard you can still hear the ghosts of the past, not least Oscar Wilde and Samuel Beckett, both of whom were schooled in Enniskillen at the Portora Royal School. Boston Quay Craft Shop stocks a range of Wilde memorabilia.

Erneside Shopping, The Point, Derrychara, is a modern center with many outlets and places to eat. Open daily, to 9 pm on Thursdays and Fridays, Sunday afternoons. ☎ (028) 6632-5705.

Entertainment

The Ardhowen Theatre has a 290-seat auditorium and a smaller studio, as well as an exhibition area, and has a varied program – everything from touring productions of plays to classical music to pop.

It also has two bars and a restaurant, which is open for coffee and lunch, Monday-Saturday. Visitors should call in and find out what's on; the staff will know about other events around the town and farther afield. ☎ (028) 6632-3233; ardhowen.theatre@fermanagh.gov.uk.

The best known of Enniskillen's many pubs is probably **Blake's of the Hollow** at 6 Church Street. It has a distinctive Victorian shopfront and inside are wood-paneled private rooms. It's been welcoming customers and entertaining them with music since the late 19th century. ☎ (028) 6632-2143; blakep@btconnect.com.

There are lots of other pubs with traditional and other styles of music, as well as nightclubs, and many restaurants. Inquire at the Tourist Office, or just walk around.

■ Explore the County

Castle Coole, on the A4 just outside Enniskillen, is a lovely place for a walk at any time of the year, and there's no charge in winter. As you walk up the drive you pass golfers on the Enniskillen Club course (see below).

It's a National Trust property, and the house is magnificent, standing above its landscaped parkland. James Wyatt designed it in the 18th century, and it has a beautiful Regency interior, including a bedroom prepared for a visit by the King in 1821. You can walk though the tunnel used by the servants, and see the memorable stable-yard and coaches.

House open mid-March to end September; times vary. ☎ (028) 6632-2690; castlecoole@ntrust.org.uk.

South of Enniskillen

South from Enniskillen on the A4, turn left onto the A509 Cavan Road and after four miles (6.4 km) you're in the village of **Bellanaleck**, where you can stop and enjoy the **Sheelin Irish Lace Museum and Shop**. Exhibits all date from 1850-1900. Open Monday-Saturday, 10 am-6 pm. ☎ (028) 6634-8052; rosemary.cathcart@virgin.net; www.irishlacemuseum.com.

After your visit to Bellanaleck, return to the A4 (signposted Sligo) and turn left. Just over a mile farther on, you reach the A32 junction (marked Swanlibar) and turn left. Look for signs on your right for the road to Marble Arch Caves and **Florence Court**. It's a National Trust property and the grounds are open all year. It's the home of the Irish yew, now found all over the world. The original tree, discovered about 1760, can be seen on the edge of Cottage Wood to the southeast of the house. The magnificent Georgian mansion is open for visits from March to end September. ☎ (028) 6634-8249; florencecourt@ntrust.org.uk.

After that, follow signs for the nearby **Marble Arch Caves**, where the fascinating guided tour includes an underground boat journey through stalagmites and stalactites. Open March-September, daily. ☎ (028) 6634-8855;mac@fermanagh.gov.uk

Irvinestown

Irvinestown is in the north of the county, where the A32 and A35 meet.

It was founded in 1618 by Sir Gerald Lowther and named after him, but changed its name when it passed to the Irvines of Dumfries in Scotland.

Like most Plantation towns (see page 14), it's built around a very wide main street where a market is held all year round and where there's a 10-day festival and carnival in summer. It's called **The Lady of the Lake Festival** and it begins on the Friday after July 12. This is the largest cross-community festival to take place in the North. Its name comes from the mythical figure said to appear gliding over Lower Lough Erne, wearing a flowing blue dress and carrying flowers – she's believed to be a sign of good fortune to come.

Lisnaskea

Lisnaskea is south of Enniskillen, at the B514/A34 junction. It's the county's second town, but small, with a population of under 3,000. It's built around a long main street, which bends at almost a right angle at one point.

Northern Ireland

It was once the seat of the Maguire clan, where their kings were crowned and from where they ruled Fermanagh. Sir Michael Balfour was in charge through the years of the Plantation, and in 1821 the town came under the control of the Earls of Erne.

Generally they were good landlords; they built the Cornmarket (1841), which has a high cross from an historic monastery. Sandstone and limestone were produced in the area, and used in the town's buildings.

Just off Main Street are the ruins of **Balfour Castle**, built about 1618 by Sir James Balfour, a Scottish planter. The castle was occupied until the early 19th century. It's being restored, and can be visited at any time, free.

Today Lisnaskea continues to thrive as the market town for the surrounding agricultural area.

Roslea

Roslea seems tucked away in the easternmost corner of the county, nine miles (14.4 km) west of Monaghan in the Republic. The Slieve Beagh mountain range stretches for miles to its north and west, and is lovely walking country.

There's a **Heritage Centre** housed in an old school (1874), which still has its desks, and displayed are old farming implements, crochet pieces and other crafts. It also runs a genealogical service. Open Monday-Friday, 10 am-4 pm, weekends by appointment. ☎ (028) 6775-1750.

Scenic Drives

Take the scenic drive to **Lough Navar**, where there's a point with an unforgettable view across Lough Erne to the mountains of Donegal in the distance.

The **Cuilcagh Scenic Drive** takes you around the mountains of that name through counties Fermanagh and Cavan. The 50-mile (80-km) drive starts in the little car park at Cladagh Bridge, on the road between Florence Court and Blacklion, and takes in the underground world of the **Marble Arch Caves**, and the house and gardens at **Florence Court**.

In Cavan it explores the limestone pavements of the Marlbank and Burren, the old spa wells at Swanlibar, and the Shannon Pot, the source of Ireland's longest river.

▪ Adventures on Foot

There's a guide called 25 Walks in Fermanagh, which covers everything from Enniskillen Town to mountains. Each walk is described with details of terrain and nearby attractions. It's available from the Tourist Information Office in Enniskillen and other outlets.

There are many forest parks, including Necarne, Cuilcagh Mountain Park, Lough Navar, Castle Archdale, Castle Caldwell, Florence Court, Ely Lodge, Claddagh Glen, Crom Estate.

Crom Estate, Newtownbutler, is on the shores of Upper Lough Erne, three miles (4.8 km) off the A34, south of Enniskillen. There are lovely woodland and lakeside walks in this 1,900-acre estate, which includes the largest oak woodland in the North and an important freshwater habitat. The property is owned by the National Trust. There's a Visitor Centre, open March-September. ☎/fax (028) 6773-8118.

You can climb **Cuilcagh Mountain** (2,188 feet/667 m) from near Florence Court, but you'll need boots and suitable clothing. Details of the climb are included in the free booklet called *Walking*, published by the Northern Ireland Tourist Board, which I recommend.

▪ Adventures on Wheels

Two of the **National Cycle Network** routes pass through Fermanagh. There are maps available from tourist offices, or check out **www.sustrans.co.uk** (the UK charity dedicated to sustainable transport).

The **Kingfisher Cycle Trail**, the first long-distance route marked out in Ireland, follows minor country roads through the border counties of Fermanagh, Leitrim, Cavan, Donegal and Monaghan. It starts at the Enniskillen Visitor Centre, and is 230 miles (450 km) long, with shorter loops possible.

The **Belfast-to-Ballyshannon Route** passes through Enniskillen and on towards the Atlantic Ocean, along quiet roads.

▪ Adventures on Water

Lough Erne is wonderful for both cruising and fishing, and is one of the least congested lakes in Europe. In addition to its 154 islands, there are coves and inlets to explore.

Northern Ireland

Ferries to **Devinish Island**, one of the islands on Lough Erne, leave from Trory Point, down a lane at the junction of the B52 to Kesh and the A32 to Ballinamallard, a mile and a half (2.4 km) north of Enniskillen. They run from Good Friday to mid-September.

Devenish has the ruins of an important monastery, founded in the 6th century by St. Molaise. The remains include a Romanesque church, crosses, and the Priory Church. Visitors can climb the round tower. Open April 1-September 30, 10 am-6 pm.

Since the re-opening of the historic **canal** between the Erne and the Shannon, the system is the longest navigable, inland waterway in Europe. There are well-equipped cruisers to hire and lots of public jetties and small marinas, many with shops, in Fermanagh.

Cruising Vacations

Belleek Charter Cruising is based at the Erne Gateway Marina, Belleek, ☎ (028) 6865-8027; beelleektrust@ btinternet.com.

Shannon Erne Waterway Holidays have bases on both the Shannon and Erne, and offer one-way as well as round-trip cruises. Their boats are fully equipped with everything you need, including dinghies. You can even rent mountain bikes from them to explore the area. www.sew-holidays.com.

Fishing

Lough Erne has claimed many coarse angling match records, and the county's rivers and lakes are renowned among the angling community. The Lough is known for its brown trout, and other waters are fished for roach, bream, perch and eels.

No fishing licence is required on the **Shannon**, but you do need a permit for the Erne, available at tackle outlets and tourist offices.

The shores of Lough Erne and of **Upper Lough Macnean** and **Lower Lough Macnean** are particularly noted for their stocks of pike. **Lough Melvin** has a good run of spring salmon and unusual kinds of trout peculiar to remote lakes.

Wherever you are in Fermanagh, there are clearly marked access points, excellent parking facilities, fishing centers and well-stocked tackle shops.

See pages 71-74 for details on angling in Ireland, regulations and best times to fish.

Useful Contacts

- **Belleek Angling Centre**. ☎ (028) 6865-8181.
- **Cloughbally Mill Angling Centre**, near Enniskillen. ☎ (028) 6632-2008.
- **Coolyermer Lough Fishery**. ☎ (028) 6634-1676; robhenshall@lineone.net www.flyfishery.com.
- **Flatfield Flyfishing**. ☎ (028) 6638-8184; michael@ flatfieldflyfish.fsnet.co.uk.
- **Knockbracken Trout Lakes**. ☎ (028) 6638-9990; TSK58@ aol.com.
- **Manor House Marine Day Boats**. ☎ (028) 6862-8100; info@manormarine.com; www.manormarine.com.

Fishing Vacation

Erincurrach Cruising is run by locals Charles and Helen Parke, from the marina on Tully Bay, Lower Lough Erne. They offer coarse fishing all year, and game fishing in season, with licenses and permits available. They also organize sea fishing in Killybegs or Mullaghmore. A local ghillie (guide) can be booked in advance. ☎ (028) 6864-1737.

■ Adventures on Horseback

The Forest Stables, based in Fivemiletown in neighboring Co. Tyrone, offers treks through the forests and foothills of both counties, and is open all year. ☎ (028) 8952-1991.

■ Golf

The parkland course of **Enniskillen Golf Club** is inside the Castle Coole estate, half a mile east of the town. ☎ (028) 6632-5250.

The **Castle Hume Golf Club** is 3½ miles (5.6 km) north of Enniskillen. ☎ (028) 6632-7077; fax 6632-7076.

The **Lisnarick Golf Club** has a nine-hole meadowland course, and is in Lisnarick village on the A32/B82. ☎ (028) 6862-8091; fax 6862-8648.

■ Where to Stay

☆☆☆☆ **The Killyhevlin Hotel** is just outside Enniskillen, on the A4, very close to Castle Coole. It offers a choice of rooms, suites, as well as cottages/lodges on the waterside. Many of the rooms have wonderful views over the lake and surrounding countryside. It's a very modern hotel, and belongs to the Irish Country Hotels marketing group. It has comfortable accommodations with a choice of dining, a bar menu or a more extensive choice in its restaurant. Rates from $$. ☎ (028) 6632-3481; fax 6632-4726; info@killyhevlin.com; www.killyhevlin.com.

Belle Isle Castle Country House is on an island on Upper Lough Erne, connected to the mainland by a bridge. The castle was built in 1680 and extended in 1850, and is owned by the Duke of Abercorn. It's furnished with antiques and Victorian paintings, with a color scheme by international interior designer, David Hicks.

On the 470-acre (188-hectare) estate there's a dairy herd, a tennis court, croquet lawn, a wooden cruiser to tour the Lough, and boats for hire. Dinner is available to guests, and Belle Isle has a reputation for good food. They're a member of Ireland's Blue Book (see page 60). Note that there's a minimum stay of two bedrooms for two nights. $$. ☎ (028) 6638-7231; fax 6638-7261; accommodation@belleisle-estate.com; www.belleislecastle.com.

Rental Cottages

There are seven cottages available to rent around two sides of an open courtyard on the shores of Upper Lough Erne on the Crom Estate. They vary in size. The largest is Erne View (sleeps six) and the smallest, Alder Cottage, has a double bedroom. You can also rent the Head Gardener's Cottage at Florence Court by the week. They all belong to the National Trust. ☎ (0044) 870-458-4422; cottages@ntrust.org.uk; www.nationaltrustcottages.co.uk.

Hostels

The hostel in **Enniskillen** is part of the William Jefferson Clinton International Peace Centre, named after the US President who was closely involved with the Good Friday Agreement. The hostel was the first public building in Ireland to use both photovoltaic cells and solar panels as part of its energy efficiency system. It's called **The Bridges**, and is on Belmore Street, close to the Bus Station, open all year, except December 23-Jan 2. Note that from April-September it's open all day (unlike some hostels) but from October-March it closes from 11 am-5 pm. ☎ (028) 6634-0110; fax 6634-6873.

North of Enniskillen on the B82, three miles (4.8 km) south of Kesh, is the **Castle Archdale Hostel** in the heart of the Country Park. This traditional hostel is a converted 1773 house set in the heart of Castle Archdale Country Park. The hostel is on the banks on Lough Erne, and is ideal for those who want to get away from it all. It's open March 1-October 31. ☎/fax (028) 6862-8118.

It belongs to Hostelling International Northern Ireland (HINI) and has a choice of rooms, from en suite twin to dormitories. Reach HINI at ☎ (028) 9032-4733; fax 9043-9699; info@hini.org.uk; www.hini.org.uk.

Camping & RV Parks

 ☆☆☆☆ **Lakeland Caravan Park** is two miles (3.2 km) outside Kesh on the Belleek/Boa Island Road, and is open all year. It has marina berths, waterside walks, facilities for watersports, sauna, and a fully licensed bar and restaurant. ☎ (028) 6863-1578; mail@drumrush.co.uk; www.drumrush.co.uk.

☆☆☆ **The Share Holiday Village** is at Smith's Strand, three miles (4.8 km) south of Lisnaskea on the B127 Derrylin Road. It has a marina for cruises and watersports on Lough Erne, indoor swimming pool, fitness suite, sauna, steam room, and coffee shop. It's open Easter to October 31. ☎ (028) 6772-2122; share@dnet.co.uk; www.sharevillage.org.

Erincurrach Cruising, based at the marina on Tully Bay, Lower Lough Erne, also has accommodations at ☆☆☆☆☆ **Tully Bay Holiday Homes**, near the A46 Enniskillen-to-Donegal road. On site there's an all-weather tennis court, and they'll organize riding if you wish, as well as fishing. ☎ (028) 6864-1737.

■ Where to Eat

 The Crow's Nest, 12 High Street, Enniskillen, in the middle of the shopping area, claims to be the oldest licensed inn on the island (whether that means Enniskillen or Ireland is uncertain). On its Bistro menu is a big all-day breakfast and Guinness and oysters (which everyone should try at least once). It also caters to vegetarians and for healthy eating, and is open every day for meals and snacks. When the weather suits, you can sit outdoors on its balcony. It's the only pub in town with live bands every night in the back bar from 10:30 pm, and The Crow's Nest is also home to **The Thatch Niteclub**, open every Friday, Saturday and Sunday, from 11 pm, with free admission on Wednesdays. www.crows-nest.net.

The Sheelin is a lovely thatched restaurant in the village of Bellanaleck. It's open all year for dinner from 5 pm and for Sunday lunch from 12:30-3 pm. ☎ (028) 6634-8232; www.thesheelin.com.

Recommended Books

All the books I recommend would make excellent souvenirs of a visit as well as being useful while you are here.

Travellers' Trails by Hugh Oram, (Appletree Press, 2001)

This attractive little book covers 24 different themed tours, including battle sites, film locations, James Joyce, The Easter Rising, and has lovely photographs. You can dip in and out, gaining information on the area you are in, if you don't want to follow a tour.

Footloose in the West of Ireland by Mike Harding, (Michael Joseph, 1996)

Walks in the western counties of the Republic, with sketch maps and suggested routes (you'll need detailed maps to actually walk). What makes this book so worthwhile is that it's much more – it covers the music, history and folklore of the areas, and is written with love and humour by a man who grew up in England in a family of Irish descent.

The Dingle Peninsula by Steve MacDongah, (Brandon, 2000)

Illustrated with marvellous color photograublishing companyphs, this is the best book about this beautiful area of Co Kerry. It includes detailed maps of the Dingle Way long-distance walking route. The author has lived in the area for more than 25 years, running a p. Among his authors is Gerry Adams of the IRA.

Literary Tour of Ireland by Elizaabout all of the island's 32 counties. It is lavishly illustrated with color andbeth Healy (Wolfhound Press, 2001)

Even if you aren't interested in writers, you will find this book valuable, as it is packed with information black and white photographs and sketch maps.

The Visitor's Guide to Northern Ireland by Rosemary Evans, (Blackstaff Press, 1998)

Regularly updated, this is a useful guide, very readable and it has lots of photographs and some maps.

For Historical Background

Atlas of Irish History, general editor Dr Seán Duffy, (Gill & Macmillan, 2000)

An enjoyable way of learning about Irish history, using maps as well as many other illustrations.

Oliver Cromwell: An Illustrated History by Helen Litton (Wolfhound Press, 2000)

One of a series on historical figures, an excellent overview of the period and the impact of the man on the country. It has lots of illustrations in both color and black and white.

The Easter Rising: A Guide to Dublin in 1916 by Conor Kostick and Lorcan Collins, (O'Brien Press, 2000)

This little book takes you through the streets during the six days that changed Ireland forever, with lots of historic photographs to help bring that time to life.

A Walk through Rebel Dublin 1916 by Mick O'Farrell (Mercier Press, 1999)

This covers the same events in a different way, by focusing on locations such as St Stephen's Green, Dublin Castle, and so on, and is again illustrated with maps and contemporary photographs.

Index

Adventure Guides
from Hunter Publishing

"These useful guides are highly recommended." *Library Journal*

ALASKA HIGHWAY

3rd Edition, Ed & Lynn Readicker-Henderson

"A comprehensive guide.... Plenty of background history and extensive bibliography." (*Travel Reference Library on-line*)

Travels the fascinating highway that passes settlements of the Tlingit and the Haida Indians, with stops at Anchorage, Tok, Skagway, Valdez, Denali National Park and more. Sidetrips and attractions en route, plus details on all other approaches – the Alaska Marine Hwy, Klondike Hwy, Top-of-the-World Hwy.

Color photos. 420 pp, $17.95, 1-58843-117-7

BELIZE

5th Edition, Vivien Lougheed

Extensive coverage of the country's political, social and economic history, along with the plant and animal life. Encouraging you to mingle with the locals, the author entices you with descriptions of local dishes and festivals. Maps, color photos.

480 pp, $18.95, 1-58843-289-0

CANADA'S ATLANTIC PROVINCES

2nd Edition, Barbara & Stillman Rogers

Pristine waters, rugged slopes, breathtaking seascapes, remote wilderness, sophisticated cities, and quaint, historic towns. Year-round adventures on the Fundy Coast, Acadian Peninsula, fjords of Gros Morne, Viking Trail & Vineland, Saint John River, Lord Baltimore's lost colony. Color photos.

632 pp, $21.95, 1-58843-264-5

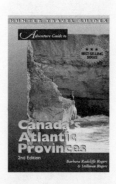

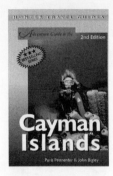

THE CAYMAN ISLANDS

2nd Edition, Paris Permenter & John Bigley

The only comprehensive guidebook to Grand Cayman, Cayman Brac and Little Cayman. Encyclopedic listings of dive/snorkel operators, along with the best dive sites. Enjoy nighttime pony rides on a glorious beach, visit the turtle farms, prepare to get wet at staggering blowholes or just laze on a white sand beach. Color photos.

256 pp, $16.95, 1-55650-915-4

THE INSIDE PASSAGE & COASTAL ALASKA

4th Edition, Lynn & Ed Readicker-Henderson

"A highly useful book." (*Travel Books Review*)

Using the Alaska Marine Highway to visit Ketchikan, Bellingham, the Aleutians, Kodiak, Seldovia, Valdez, Seward, Homer, Cordova, Prince of Wales Island, Juneau, Gustavas, Sitka, Haines, Skagway. Glacier Bay, Tenakee. US and Canadian gateway cities profiled.

460 pp, $17.95, 1-58843-288-2

COSTA RICA

4th Edition, Bruce & June Conord

Incredible detail on culture, history, plant life, animals, where to stay & eat, as well as the practicalities of travel here. Firsthand advice on travel in the country's various environments – the mountains, jungle, beach and cities.

360 pp, $17.95, 1-58843-290-4

PUERTO RICO

4th Edition, Kurt Pitzer & Tara Stevens

Visit the land of sizzling salsa music, Spanish ruins and tropical rainforest. Explore archaeological sites and preserves. Old San Juan, El Yunque, the Caribbean National Forest, Mona Island – these are but a few of the attractions.

432 pp, $18.95, 1-58843-116-9

THE VIRGIN ISLANDS

5th Edition, Lynne Sullivan

A guide to all the settlements, nature preserves, wilderness areas and sandy beaches that grace these islands: St. Thomas, St. John, St. Croix, Tortola, Virgin Gorda and Jost Van Dyke. Town walks, museums, great places to eat, charming guesthouses and resorts – it's all in this guide. Color photos.

320 pp, $17.95, 1-55650-907-3

THE YUCATAN including Cancún & Cozumel

3rd Edition, Bruce & June Conord

"... Honest evaluations. This book is the one not to leave home without."
(*Time Off Magazine*)

"... opens the doors to our enchanted Yucatán." (Mexico Ministry of Tourism)

Maya ruins, Spanish splendor. Deserted beaches, festivals, culinary delights. Filled with maps & color photos.

448 pp, $18.99, 1-58843-370-6

Other Adventure Guides include: *Anguilla, Antigua, St. Barts, St. Kitts & St. Martin; Aruba, Bonaire & Curacao; The Bahamas; Bermuda; Jamaica; Guatemala; Grenada, St. Vincent & the Grenadines, Barbados,* and many more. Send for our complete catalog. All Hunter titles are available at bookstores nationwide. or direct from the publisher. Check our website at **www.hunterpublishing.com**.

We Love to Get Mail

This book has been carefully researched to bring you current, accurate information. But no place is unchanging. We welcome your comments for future editions. Please write us at: Hunter Publishing, 130 Campus Drive, Edison NJ 08818, or e-mail your suggestions to comments@ hunterpublishing.com.